Table of Contents

Index to Maps .... Inside Front Cover
Table of Contents 1
Key to Abbreviations 1
How To Use Guide 2,3
Map Legend 3
Downtown Indianapolis 4,5
Maps (322-327,356-361,388-395,422-429) 6-33
Notes 34
Maps (455-463) 35-43
Notes 44
Maps (489-497) 45-53
Notes 54
Maps (523-531) 55-63
Notes 64
Maps (527-565,592-599) 65-81
ZIP Code Index 82
Marion County Street Addressing & Directional System 83
Territory Codes 83
Index To Map Features:
  STREETS 83-106
    • includes Named Interstates, Federal, State, County, City,
     and Private Roads, Alleys, and Trails
  NUMBERED STREETS 106-107
  ROUTE NUMBERS 107
    • includes Interstate, Federal, State, and County
  PLACE NAMES 107-111
    • includes Incorporated Towns & Cities, Townships, Area Names,
     Subdivisions, Apartments, and Trailer Parks
  AIRPORTS 111
  BRIDGES 111
    • includes Dams, Ferries, Fords, Tunnels, and Locks
  BUSINESS PARKS 111
    • includes Commercial, Corporate, Industrial, Office,
     and Technical Parks
  CAMPSITES 111
  CEMETERIES 111
  COLLEGES & UNIVERSITIES 111,112
    • includes Private & Public Schools above 12th Grade
  COMMUNITY & RECREATION CENTERS 112
    • includes Centers for Community Gatherings

Index To Map Features, Continued:
  FIRE COMPANIES 112
    • includes Rescue Squads, Ambulance, and
     Emergency Medical Services
  GOLF COURSES 112
    • includes Country Clubs
  HOSPITALS 112
    • includes 24 hour Emergency Care Facilities
  INFORMATION CENTERS 112
    • includes Chambers of Commerce and State, County, or
     Municipal Centers that distribute visitor information
  LAKES & STREAMS 112,113
    • includes Creeks, Rivers, Reservoirs, Bays, and other water features
  LIBRARIES 113
  MARINAS & RAMPS 113
    • includes Piers, Docks, Yacht Clubs, and other launching
     facilities or areas
  MILITARY & FEDERAL FEATURES 113
    • includes Federal Government Buildings, Military
     Installations, National Guard & Reserve Armories
  PARK & RIDE 113
  PARKS & RECREATION 113
    • includes Forest, WMA, Race Tracks, Stadiums, Recreational
     Areas, and other related features
  PLACES OF WORSHIP 113-115
  POINTS OF INTEREST 115
    • features without a specific category
  POLICE STATIONS 115
  POST OFFICES 115
  RAILROAD STATIONS (AMTRAK) 115
  SCHOOLS 115,116
    • includes Private & Public Schools
     12th Grade and under
  SHOPPING CENTERS 116,117
    • includes Malls, Plazas, and Shopping Areas
  STATE, COUNTY &
  MUNICIPAL FEATURES 117
    • State, County, Townships & Municipal Features without
     a specific category
Notes 118-120

Key to Abbreviations

Admin ..... Administration	Dr ..... Drive	Lp ..... Loop	Ref ..... Refuge
Al ..... Alley	Driver Ed ..... Driver Education School	Luth ..... Lutheran	Reg ..... Regional
Alt ..... Alternate	E ..... East	Med Ctr ..... Medical Center	Res ..... Reservoir
AME ..... African Methodist Episcopal	EMS ..... Emergency Medical Services	Mem ..... Memorial	Res Sqd ..... Rescue Squad
Apts ..... Apartments	Epis ..... Episcopal	Meth ..... Methodist	Resv ..... Reservation
Ave ..... Avenue	ES ..... Elementary School	Mgmt ..... Management	RR ..... Railroad
Bapt ..... Baptist	Est ..... Estate	MHP ..... Mobile Home Park	Rte ..... Route
Batl ..... Battlefield	Ests ..... Estates	MI ..... Michigan	S ..... South
Bd of Ed ..... Board of Education	Expwy ..... Expressway	Mil ..... Military	Sch ..... School
Bk ..... Brook	Ext ..... Extension	MO ..... Missouri	Sec ..... Secondary
Bldg ..... Building	Fed ..... Federal	Mon ..... Monument	SHA ..... State Highway Administration
Bltwy ..... Beltway	Frwy ..... Freeway	MS ..... Middle School	Shop Ctr ..... Shopping Center
Blvd ..... Boulevard	GC ..... Golf Course/Club	Mt ..... Mount	SHS ..... Senior High School
Boro ..... Borough	Gdns ..... Gardens	MTA ..... Mass Transit Administration	Soc ..... Society
Br ..... Branch/Bridge	Gen ..... General	Mtn ..... Mountain	Spec ..... Special
Bus ..... Business	Govt ..... Government	Mun ..... Municipal	Spec Ed ..... Special Education
By-P ..... By-Pass	Hdq ..... Headquarters	Mus ..... Museum	Sq ..... Square
Cath ..... Catholic	Hgts ..... Heights	MVA ..... Motor Vehicle Administration	St ..... Saint/State/Street
CC ..... Country Club	Hist ..... Historic/Historical	N ..... North	Sta ..... Station
Cem ..... Cemetery	Hlth Ctr ..... Health Center	Nat ..... Natural	Tech ..... Technical
Ch ..... Church	Hosp ..... Hospital	Natl ..... National	Terr ..... Terrace
Chr ..... Christian	HOV ..... High Occupancy Vehicle	Nat Res ..... Natural Resource	Tpk ..... Turnpike
Cir ..... Circle	HS ..... High School	Nbhd ..... Neighborhood	Tr ..... Trail
Co ..... Company/County	Hwy ..... Highway	No ..... Number	Tr Ct ..... Trailer Court
Coll ..... College	I ..... Interstate	NRMA ..... Natural Resource Management Area	Tr Pk ..... Trailer Park
Comm ..... Community	IA ..... Iowa	OH ..... Ohio	Trans ..... Transportation
Condos ..... Condominiums	IL ..... Illinois	Orth ..... Orthodox	Trk ..... Truck
Cong ..... Congregational	IN ..... Indiana	PA/ Penn ..... Pennsylvania	Twnhse ..... Townhouse
Conn ..... Connector	Ind ..... Industrial	Pent ..... Pentecostal	Twp ..... Township
Corp ..... Corporate	Inst ..... Institute/Institution	Pk ..... Park	Unitn ..... Unitarian
Cr ..... Creek	Intl ..... International	Pkwy ..... Parkway	Univ ..... University
Cres ..... Crescent	IS ..... Intermediate School	Pl ..... Place	US ..... Federal Route/United States
Cswy ..... Causeway	Is ..... Island	PO ..... Post Office	UT ..... Uptown Map
Ct ..... Court	Jct ..... Junction	Prep ..... Preparatory	Vet ..... Veterans
Ctr ..... Center	JHS ..... Junior High School	Presb ..... Presbyterian	Vill ..... Village
Dept ..... Department	Jr Coll ..... Junior College	Prim ..... Primary	Vis ..... Visitors
Dev ..... Development	JS ..... Junior School	Prof ..... Professional	Vly ..... Valley
Dist ..... District	KY ..... Kentucky	Prot ..... Protestant	Voc ..... Vocational
DMV ..... Department of Motor Vehicles	La ..... Lane	Pt ..... Point	VoTech ..... Vocational/Technical
DN ..... Downtown Map	Ldg ..... Landing	Rd ..... Road	W ..... West
DOT ..... Department of Transportation	LDS .... Church of Jesus Christ of Latter Day Saints	Rec ..... Recreation	WI ..... Wisconsin
			WMA ..... Wildlife Management Area

1

A Step-By-Step Guide To Using Your Street Atlas

Thank You For Using The AMC Street Atlas

After you use the Street Atlas once or twice, you won't need any help at all. And you may not need it now. But just in case, we've included this helpful guide for your convenience.

1. It all starts with the Street Index.

Let's say you want to go to the 10,000 block of 21st Street, which is in Warren Township, Marion County (Indianapolis). First, you would turn to the Street Index for numbered streets on page 106 of your book and find 21st Street in the numerical listing. Note the numbers you see listed after the street name.

Street Index Page 106

Xenia Cir 562-C7 PeT	2nd St SE 391-K4 Ca	WrT	38th St 459
Xenia Dr 562-D7 PeT	2nd St SW 391-J4 Ca	19th Ave 528-D4 BG	462-B8, F
	2nd Way 392-D3 Ca	19th Pl 494-H3 WrT	458-A9 P
Y	3rd Ave 528-G5 BG; 391-J3 Ca	19th St 492-K4; 493-E4, F4, G4;	H8; 460-A
	3rd Ave NE 392-A4 Ca	494-B4, E4 CTM; 359-K3, K4 N;	458-A9 W
Yacht Harbor Cir 424-J10 WTM	3rd Ave NW 391-J4 Ca	492-G4 WnT; 494-J4; 495-B3,	462-B8, F
Yale Dr 425-H3 WTM	3rd Ave SW 391-J4, J6 Ca	D4 WrT	38th St Dr
Yandes St DN-F1; 493-H3, H5	3rd St 429-C8 McC; 359-G5 N;	20th Ave 528-D4 BG	460-A8, B
CTM	389-H8 Z	20th Pl 494-H3 WrT	39th Pl 461
Yardley Ct 424-G4 PTM	3rd St NE 391-K4; 392-A3 Ca	20th St 493-A3, B3, D4, F3, J3;	39th St 460
Yarmouth Pl 393-C10 F	3rd St NW 391-K4 Ca	494-B3, F3 CTM; 491-K3;	K8; 462-A
Yates La 490-E6 WaT	3rd St SE 391-K4 Ca	492-A4 S; 492-E4, G4 WnT;	459-C8, D
Yazoo Dr 528-F9 BG	3rd St SW 391-K4 Ca	494-G3, J3; 495-B3, F3 WrT	C8, D8, E
Yeager Ct 562-K1 FT	4th Ave 528-F7, G6 BG	21st Ave 528-C4 BG	40 & 8 Ave
Yeager Dr 528-H9 FT	4th Ave E 526-E6 DTM	21st Pl 496-C3 WrT	40th Pl 461
Yeager La 528-K10 FT	4th Ave NE 392-A4 Ca	21st St 492-K3; 493-C3, D3, F3,	40th St 460
Yeagy Ct N 560-J10 WTJ	4th Ave SE 392-A4 Ca	J3; 494-C3 CTM; 496-F3 Cu;	40th St Dr
Yeagy Ct S 594-J1 WTJ	4th Ave SW 391-J4 Ca	491-G3; 492-A3 S; 489-J4;	WTM
Yeagy Rd 594-J1 WTJ	4th Ct E 392-D3 Ca	490-A4 WaT; 490-K3; 491-G3;	40th St Dr
Yearling Run 423-G9 PTM	4th Ct W 392-D3 Ca	492-E3, F3, G3 WnT; 494-K3;	40th St Dr S
Yellow Birch Ct 523-D4 WaT	4th St 359-G5 N; 389-H8, H9 Z	495-H3; 496-A3, F3 WrT	41st Pl 461
Yellow Birch Way 457-D5 PTM	4th St NE 391-K3 Ca	21st St Annex 493-E3 CTM	PTM
Yellow Pine Ct 561-B6 PeT	4th St NW 391-K3 Ca	22nd St 492-K3; 493-E3, J3;	41st St 460
Yellow Poplar Ct 492-E3 WnT	4th St SE 391-K4; 392-A4 Ca	494-C3, F3 CTM; 491-J3;	LTM; 458
Yellowstone Pkwy 561-B4 PeT	5th Ave 528-F5 BG	492-A3 S; 492-F3, H3 WnT;	460-D7, F
Yellowwood Cir 325-A8 N	5th Ave E 526-E6 DTM	494-G2, J2 WrT	42nd Pl 461
Yellowwood Ct 424-K4 WTM	5th Ave NE 391-K3; 392-A3 Ca	23rd Ave 528-C4 BG	42nd St 461
Yellowwood Dr 595-A4 WTJ	5th Ave NW 391-K3 Ca	23rd St 492-K3; 493-C3, F3, H3,	461-A7, B
Yoke St 527-E4, G4 CTM	5th St SE 391-K5 Ca	K2; 494-B3 CTM; 492-F3 WnT;	LTM; 456
Yolanda Ct 428-J9 L	5th St SW 391-K5 Ca	494-G2, J2 WrT	PTM; 458
York Cir 325-A8 N	6th Ave 528-F5 BG	24th Ave 528-C4 BG	G7, J7; 46
York Dr 391-J4 Ca; 389-F6 Z	6th Ave E 526-E5, F5 DTM	24th St 493-C2, E2, F2, J2;	43rd Ct 460
York Pl 393-E7 F	6th St 359-H5 N; 389-H9 Z	494-A2 CTM; 492-A2 S; 494-H2,	43rd Pl 461
York Rd 455-G8 B	6th St NW 391-K3 Ca	J2; 495-A2; 496-A2 WrT	43rd St 461
York St 527-B1 CTM; 596-C5, D2	6th St SE 391-K5 Ca	25th Ave 528-C4, C5 BG; 528-C4	461-K7 L
G	7th Ave 528-F5 BG	CTM; 528-C5 PeT	459-B7, B
York Town Rd 595-H3 G	7th Ave NE 391-K3; 392-A3 Ca	25th S 489-G9 A	43rd Terr 4
Yorkshire Blvd 496-J6, K6 Cu	8th Ave 528-F5 BG	25th St 492-K2; 493-C2, F2, G2;	44th St 460
Yorkshire Cir 359-J7, J8 N	8th St 359-H3, H5 N; 389-G8, G9 Z	494-B2 CTM; 492-A2 S; 494-H2,	44th Terr 4
Yorkshire Ct 495-K3 WrT	9th Ave 528-F5, F6, F9 BG	K2; 495-A2, B2, H2, K2; 496-A2,	45th St 461
Yorkshire La 392-E4 Ca	9th St DN-C1, D1, E1, F1; 493-C6,	D2 WrT	45th St 461
Yorktown Crossing 390-D8 CTH	F6, G6, H6; 494-A6, D6, G6	26th St 492-K2; 493-B2, C2;	45th Terr 45
Yorktown Dr 461-K5 LTM	CTM; 496-G5 Cu; 359-H3, H5 N;	494-C2, D2 CTM; 491-K2 S	46th St 461
Yorktown La 490-F7 WaT	492-H6 WnT; 494-G6, J6, K6;	26th St E 495-A2 WrT	460-J6; 4
Yorkville Ct 457-F4 PTM	G9 Z	27th St 492-K2; 493-A2, C2, E2,	459-E6, F
Yosemite Ct 561-D4 PeT	10th Ave 528-E4, F5 BG	G2, J2, K2; 494-A2, B2 CTM;	45th Terr 45
Yosemite Dr 561-B4 PeT	10th St DN-B1, D1, E1, F1;	494-H1, J1 WrT	46th St 461
Young Ave 494-F8 CTM	492-J6; 493-A6, F6, G6; 494-A5	28th St 492-K1; 493-A1, D1, G1,	46th St 461
Young Lake Dr 496-D8 WrT	CTM; 496-E5 Cu; 359-H9, J4 N;	K1; 494-A1, D1 CTM; 492-B2	460-J6; 4
Youngwood La 394-B2 F	359-H9 NT; 492-A6 S; 490-K6;	WnT; 494-G6, J6;	457-D6,
Yount Blvd 491-K7 WnT	491-A6, H6; 492-A6, J6 WnT;	29th Pl 491-H1, J1 S	458-F6,
Yucatan Ct 526-B6 DTM	494-H5; 495-B5, H5; 496-A5, E5	29th St 492-K1; 493-C1, H1, K1;	WTM
Yuma Ct 526-B6 DTM		494-A1, E1 CTM; 492-F1, G1	458-F6,
Yuma Dr 526-B6 DTM		WnT	47th St 461
Yvette Dr 490-C5 WaT		30th St 493-C1, H1; 494-A1, F1,	458-B6,
		G1 CTM; 491-G1, K1; 492-A1 S;	G6, J6;
			48th St 461

2. Finding your page and using the grid coordinates.

As you can see, there are fourteen sets of numbers for 21st Street, with the sets separated by semi-colons. The first number in each set is the map number, which you'll find on the upper corner of each page.

21st St 492-K3; 493-C3, D3, F3, J3; 494-C3 CTM; 496-F3 Cu; 491-G3; 492-A3 S; 489-J4; 490-A4 WaT; 490-K3; 491-G3; 492-E3, F3, G3 WnT; 494-K3; 495-H3; 496-A3, F3 WrT

Together, the letter/number combinations are grid coordinates. You'll see that the letters run across the top and bottom of each map, while the numbers are on one side. The letters following the coordinates are territory codes, which are referred to on page 83 and tell which city, town or township and county the item is in. Following the example, first look on map 495, grid coordinate H3 for 21st Street. But, as you'll notice, 21st Street reaches the edge of map 495 in about the 9000 block. But right where it ends, there's a notation that says "Joins Map 496."

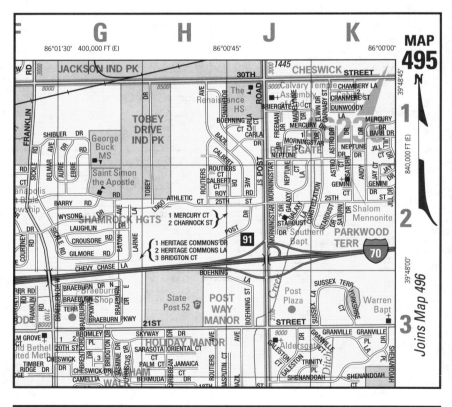

3. So now you've got two choices.

If you want, you can just turn to map 496, and, taking a visual cue from map 491, find 21st Street. Or you could go back to the Index where you'll see that 21st Street is in grid coordinate A3 on map 496. When you look in that coordinate, you'll see the 10,000 block of 21st Street. But what's the best way to get there from where you are?

4. Now for the big picture.

You know that the 10,000 block of 21st Street is on map 496. Now look at the Index to Maps, shown here. Assuming you're in Carmel you'll see that your current location is in square 392 (square numbers correspond to those of full size maps) and your destination is in square 496. Use the Index to Maps to plot your route from Carmel to 21st Street.

The Index also includes Place Names, Shopping Centers, Schools, Places of Worship and more, all broken down by category. So if you have a name, but not a precise address, these listings will help you find your destination. It's also a good idea to study the Map Legend so you'll be acquainted with the various symbols used on the maps. Knowing them will help you find things more quickly.

Finally, let us hear from you. We like getting ideas for improving the AMC Street Atlases. Write to: American Map Corporation, 780 W. Belden Ave., Suite A, Addison, IL 60101-4939, or fax your comments to 630-458-1511 (Toll-free 1-800-458-1226). Your suggestions are always welcome.

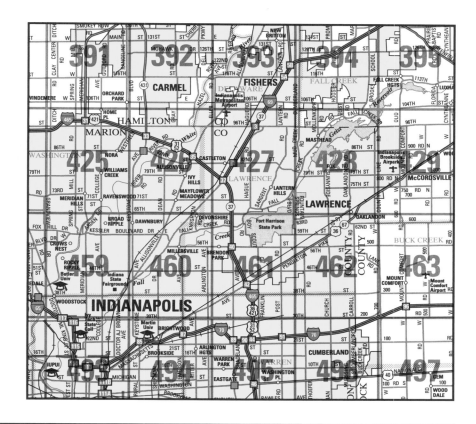

Indianapolis & Vicinity Map Legend

ROADS AND ROUTE SHIELDS

Interstate.................................... 65

Other Controlled Access Highway.....................

Interchange/Exit Number............................ 66

U.S.; State............................ 40 37

U.S. or Primary State Highway.......................

Through Route; Traffic Direction Flow...............

Highway Proposed or Under Construction........

Street; Block Number............................ HALL RD / 7000

Proposed Street..

Trail..

PLACE NAMES

Area Name.. AUGUSTA

Subdivision....................................... COBBLESTONE SPRINGS

Business Park..................................... SCHMOLL IND PK

BOUNDARIES

State.. INDIANA / ILLINOIS

County.. HAMILTON CO / MARION CO

Incorporated.................................... CARMEL

Township.. GUILFORD

Boundary Definition.............................

Postal Zone/ZIP Code........................... 46143

ZIP Code for Post Office Boxes................. 46253

OUTDOOR FEATURES

Park, Forest, Recreation or Wildlife Area..........

Community/Recreation Center; Playground....... PG

Campsite; Picnic Area............................

Golf Course or Country Club......................

Beach; Ski Area.................................

Marina; Boat Ramp/Launch......................

Swamp...

MASS TRANSIT

Railroad; Station............................... S

Park & Ride/Commuter Parking.................. P

GOVERNMENT & PUBLIC FACILITIES

Military, Federal, State or County Property........

Airport..

Hospital....................................... Kendrick Mem Hosp

Special Property Limits.........................

School; College or University....................

Places of Worship............................. + C

Cemetery......................................

Municipal Building............................. City Hall

Library; Post Office............................ L P

Fire Station/EMS; Police Station................. F P

Information Center; Parking...................... ? P

Point of Interest; Gate/Barrier..................

Scale 1"= 2000'

1	½	0	1 Mile
2000	1000	0	2000	4000	6000	8000 Feet
1	½	0	1 Kilometer

BLACK NUMBERS AND BLUE GRID LINES INDICATE LATITUDE AND LONGITUDE.
BLACK NUMBERS AND BLACK TICKS INSIDE THE NEATLINE INDICATE THE 10,000 FOOT GRID BASED ON THE EAST AND WEST ZONES OF THE INDIANA COORDINATE SYSTEM.
THE FOLLOWING COUNTIES IN OUR STREET ATLAS CONSTITUTE THE EAST ZONE (INDICATED BY "E"): HAMILTON, HANCOCK, JOHNSON, MARION AND SHELBY.
THE FOLLOWING COUNTIES IN OUR STREET ATLAS CONSTITUTE THE WEST ZONE (INDICATED BY "W"); BOONE, HENDRICKS AND MORGAN.
THE HORIZONTAL DATUM REFERENCED IN THIS STREET MAP BOOK IS BASED ON THE NORTH AMERICAN DATUM OF 1983 (NAD 83).

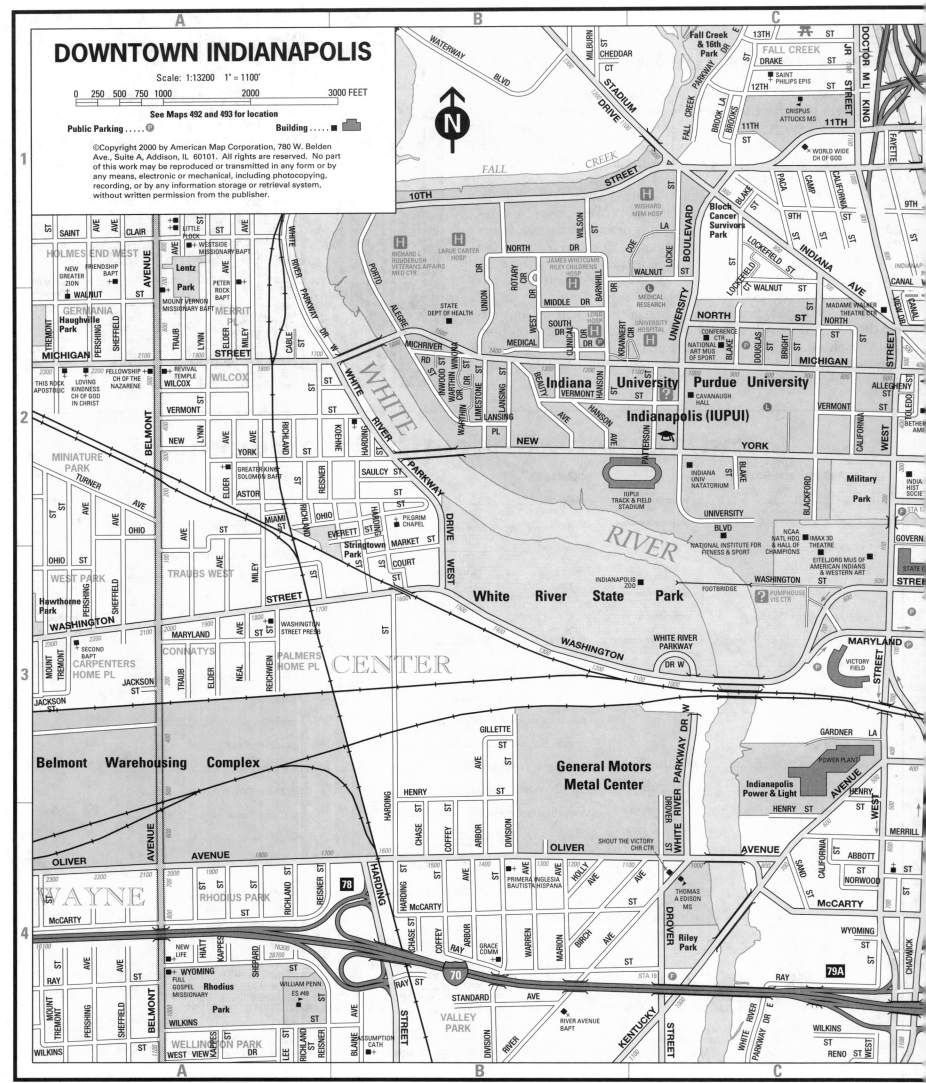

DOWNTOWN INDIANAPOLIS

Scale: 1:13200 1" = 1100'

0 250 500 750 1000   2000   3000 FEET

See Maps 492 and 493 for location

Public Parking . . . . . Ⓟ   Building . . . . . ■

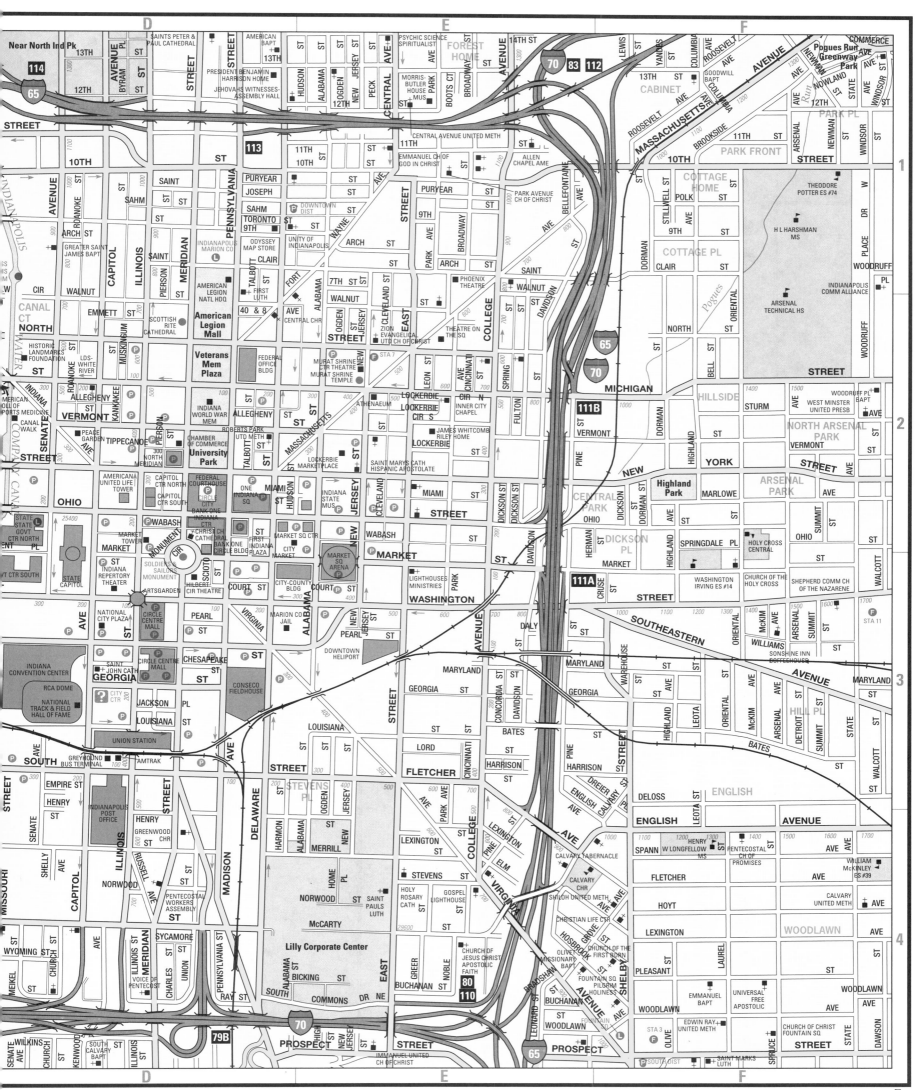

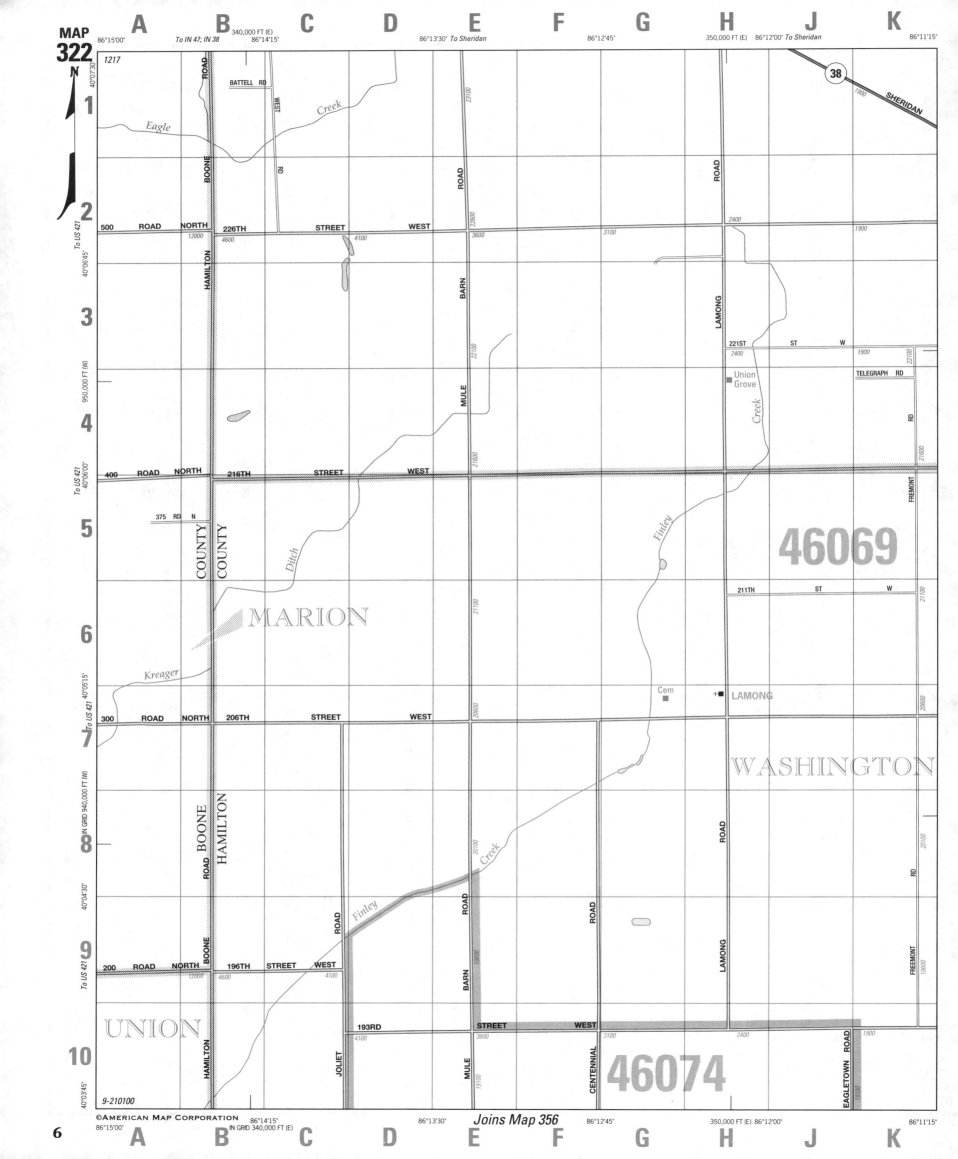

MAP
322

N

A B C D E F G H J K

1217

40°07'30"

1

Eagle   Creek

BATTELL RD

38

SHERIDAN

WEST

BOONE

RD

ROAD

ROAD

1900

2

86°06'45"

500   ROAD   NORTH   226TH   STREET   WEST

12000   4600   4100   3600   3100   2400   1900

HAMILTON

22600

BARN

3

950,000 FT (W)

LAMONG

221ST   ST   W

2400   1900   22100

Union
Grove

TELEGRAPH   RD

MULE

22100

RD

Creek

4

40°06'00"

400   ROAD   NORTH   216TH   STREET   WEST

21600

FREMONT

5

375   RD   N

COUNTY

COUNTY

Ditch

Finley

46069

21600

211TH   ST   W

21100   21100

6

MARION

20600

Kreager

Cem   Lamong

7

40°05'15"

300   ROAD   NORTH   206TH   STREET   WEST

20600

WASHINGTON

20600

8

IN GRID 940,000 FT (W)

BOONE

HAMILTON

Creek

20100

ROAD

LAMONG

RD

20100

9

40°04'30"

BOONE

Finley

BARN   ROAD

ROAD

FREMONT

200   ROAD   NORTH   196TH   STREET   WEST   19100

12000   4600   4100   19900   19600

UNION

193RD   STREET   WEST

JOLIET   MULE   CENTENNIAL   EAGLETOWN ROAD

4100   3600   3100   2400   1900

10

40°03'45"

46074

9-210100

19100   19100

86°14'15"
IN GRID 340,000 FT (E)   86°13'30"   *Joins Map 356*   86°12'45"   350,000 FT (E) 86°12'00"   86°11'15"

86°15'00"

A B C D E F G H J K

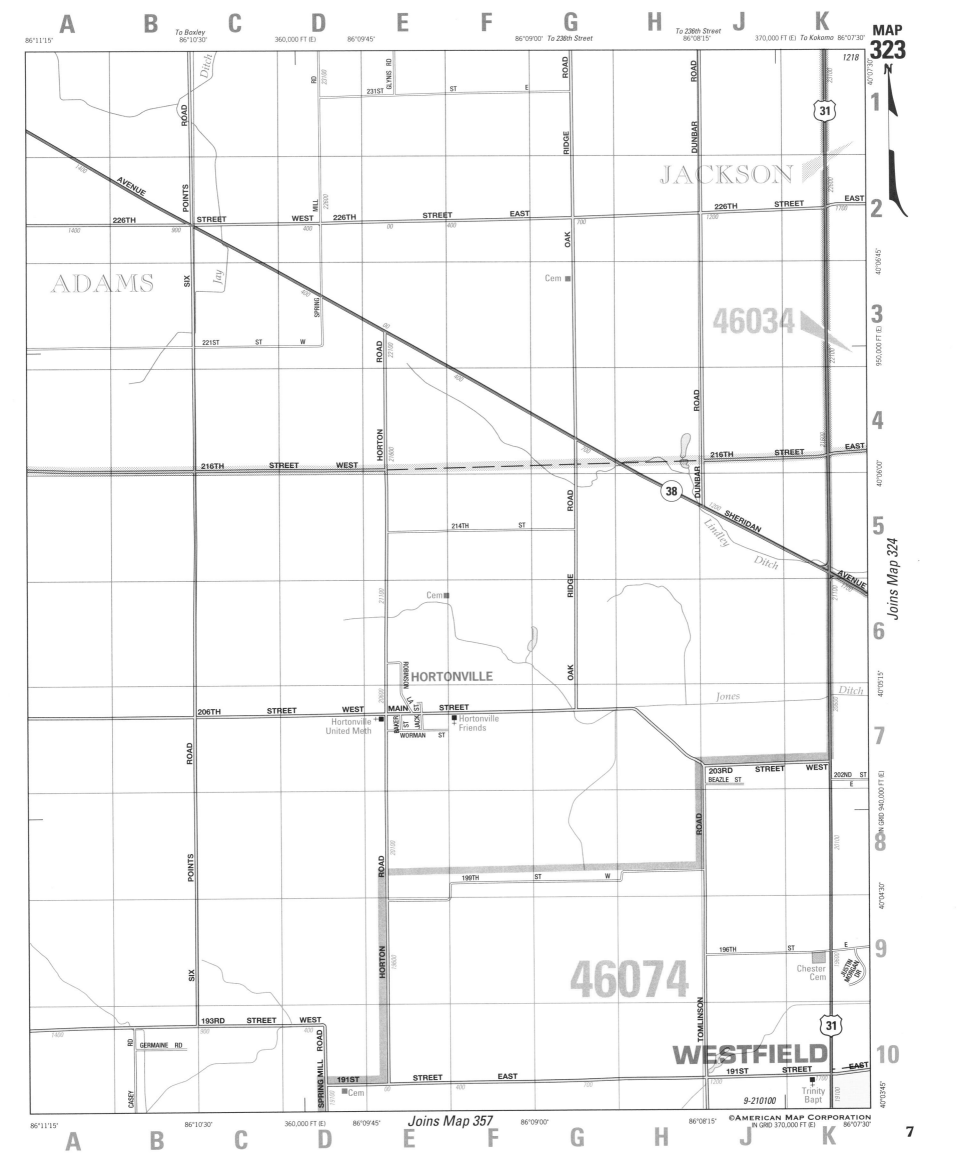

MAP
323

ADAMS

JACKSON

46034

HORTONVILLE

46074

WESTFIELD

To Boxley
To 236th Street
To 236th Street
To Kokomo

Joins Map 324

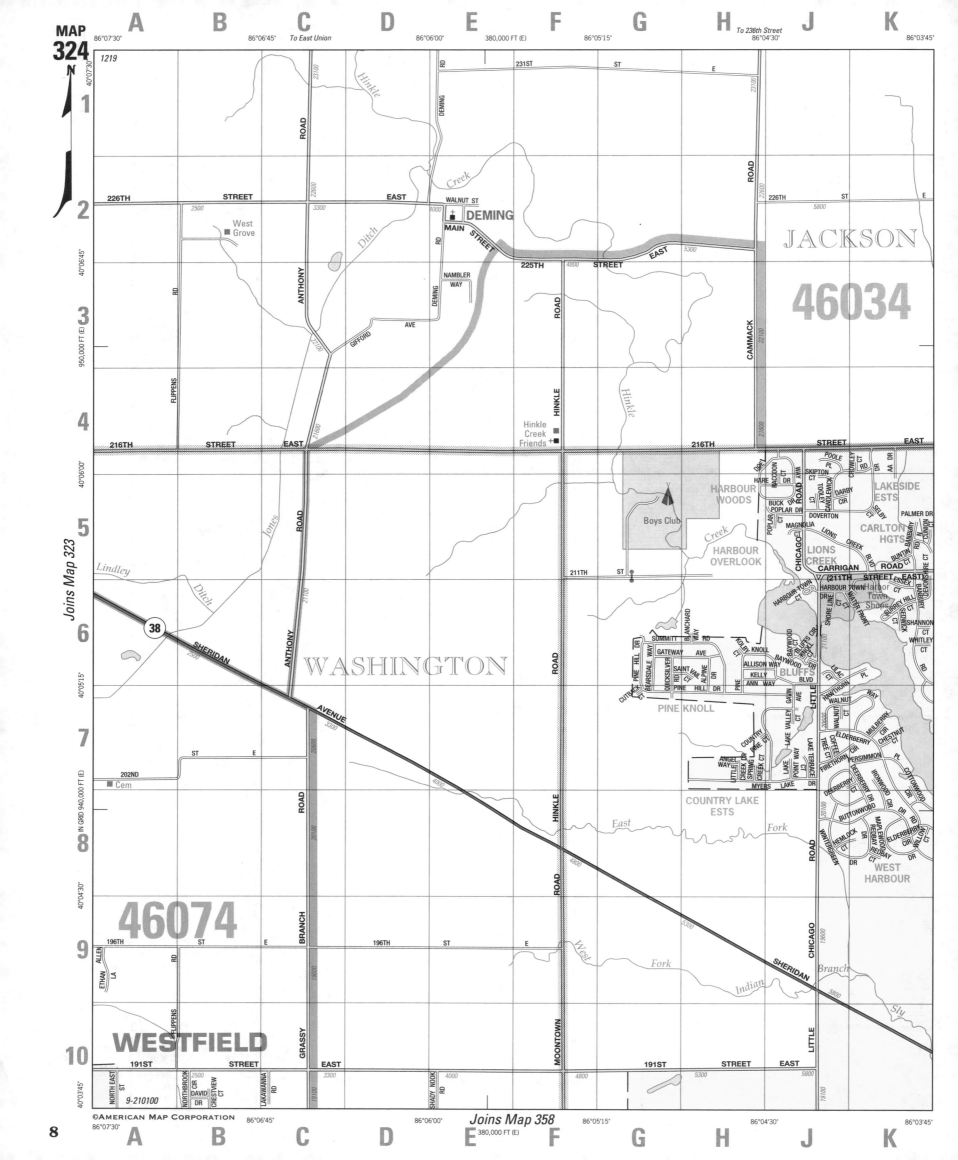

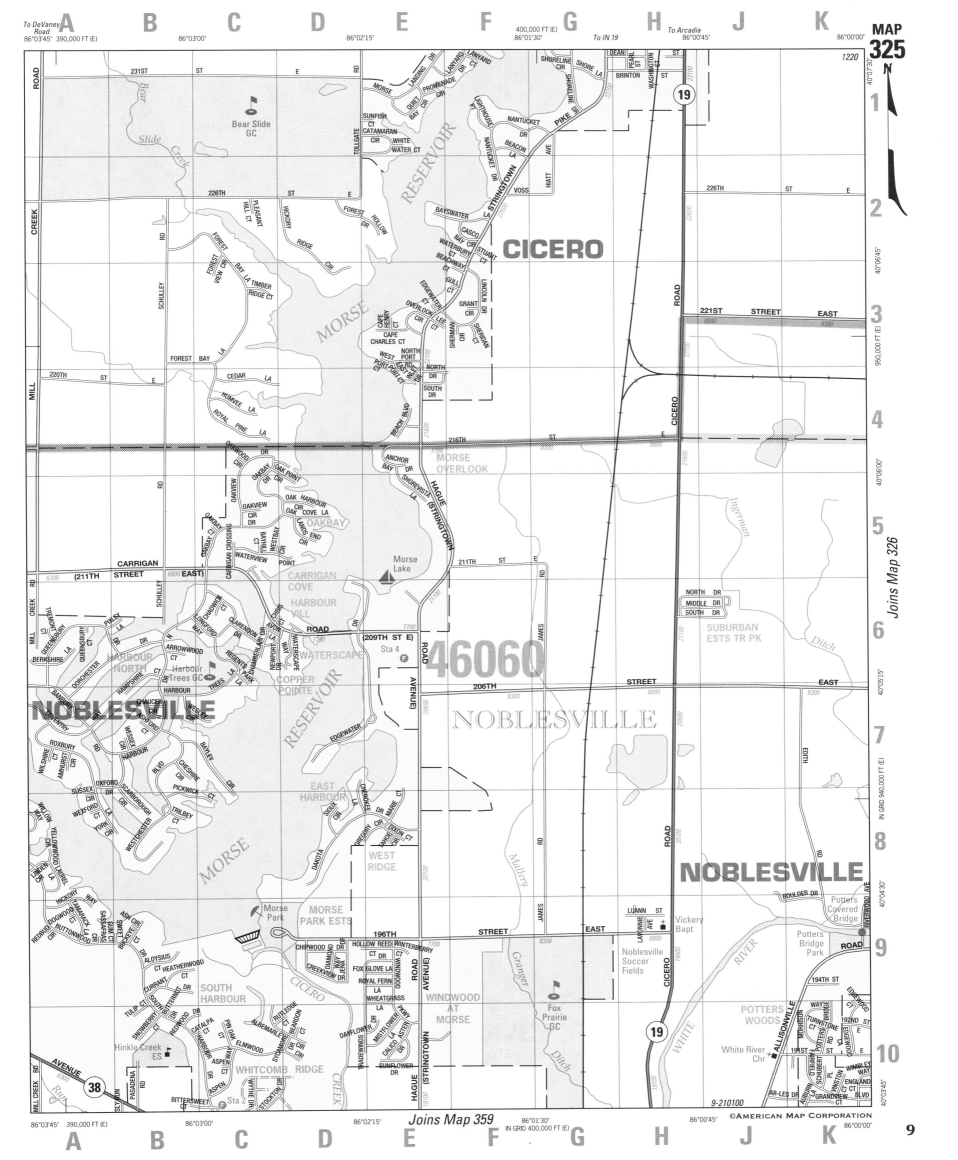

MAP
325
N

CICERO

46060

NOBLESVILLE

NOBLESVILLE

Joins Map 326

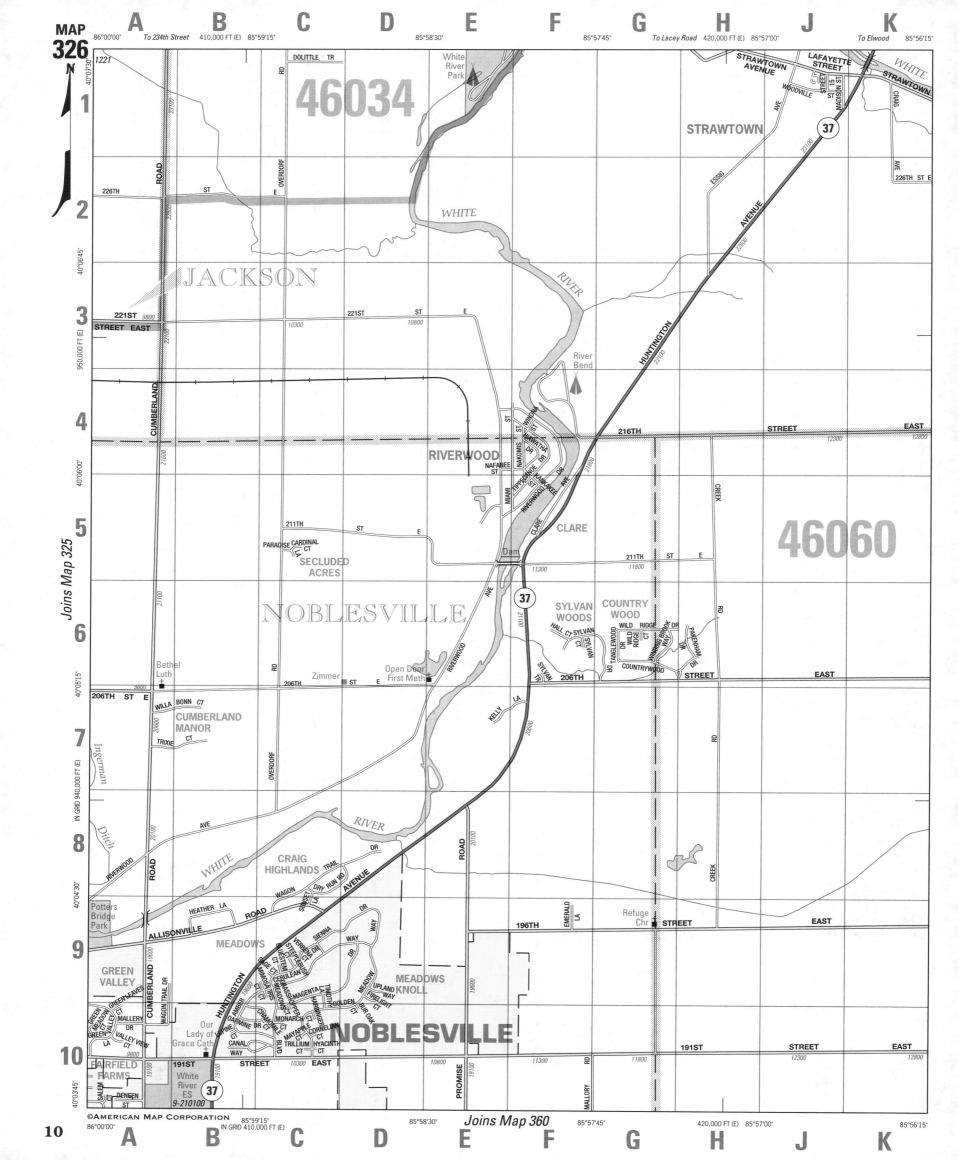

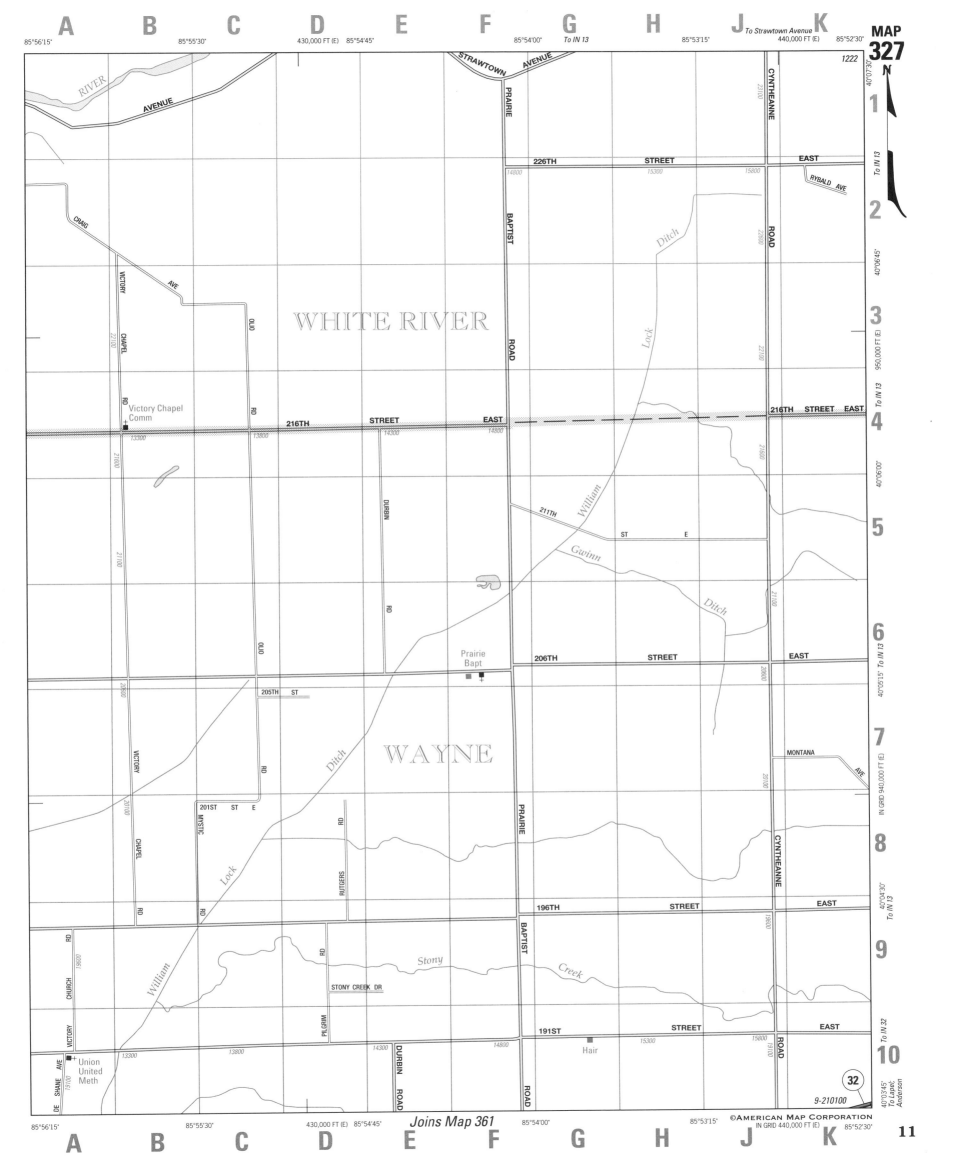

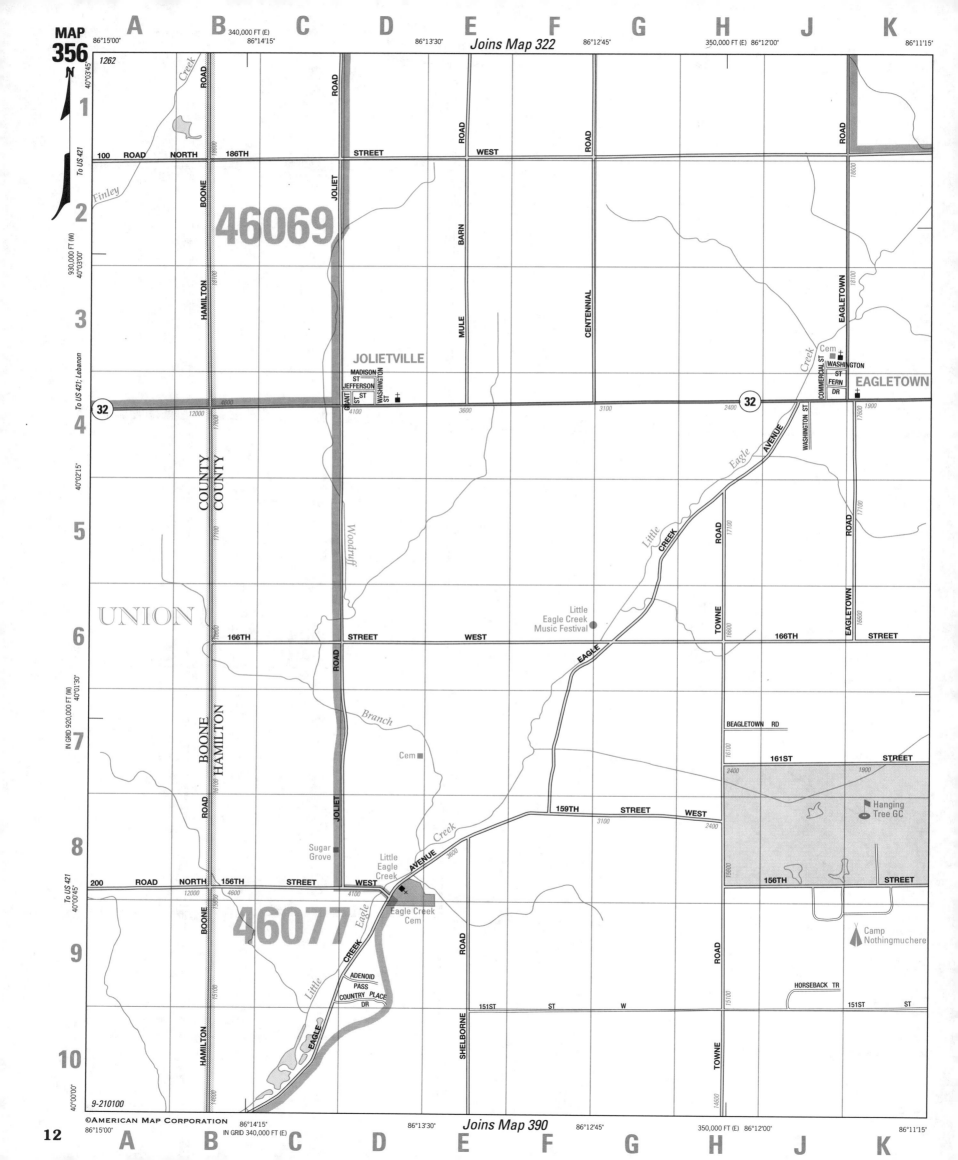

MAP 356

46069

JOLIETVILLE

MADISON ST
JEFFERSON ST
GRANT ST
WASHINGTON ST

EAGLETOWN

Cem
WASHINGTON ST
FERN DR
COMMERCIAL ST

UNION

BOONE COUNTY
HAMILTON COUNTY

Woodruff

Branch

Cem

Little Eagle Creek
Music Festival

EAGLE

Little Creek

TOWNE ROAD

EAGLETOWN ROAD

BEAGLETOWN RD

161ST STREET

159TH STREET WEST

Hanging Tree GC

156TH STREET

Camp Nothingmuchere

HORSEBACK TR

151ST ST

Sugar Grove

Little Eagle Creek

Eagle Creek Cem

46077

ADENOID PASS
COUNTRY PLACE DR

Little Eagle Creek

EAGLE

200 ROAD NORTH   156TH STREET WEST

100 ROAD NORTH   186TH STREET WEST

SHELBORNE ROAD

166TH STREET WEST   166TH STREET

Joins Map 322

Joins Map 390

To US 421
To US 421; Lebanon
To US 421

HAMILTON ROAD
BOONE ROAD
JOLIET ROAD
BARN ROAD
MULE ROAD
CENTENNIAL ST
WASHINGTON ST

9-210100

1262

340,000 FT (E)
86°15'00"   86°14'15"   86°13'30"   86°12'45"   350,000 FT (E) 86°12'00"   86°11'15"

930,000 FT (W)
40°03'00"
40°02'15"
40°01'30"
IN GRID 920,000 FT (W)
40°00'45"
40°00'00"

IN GRID 340,000 FT (E)

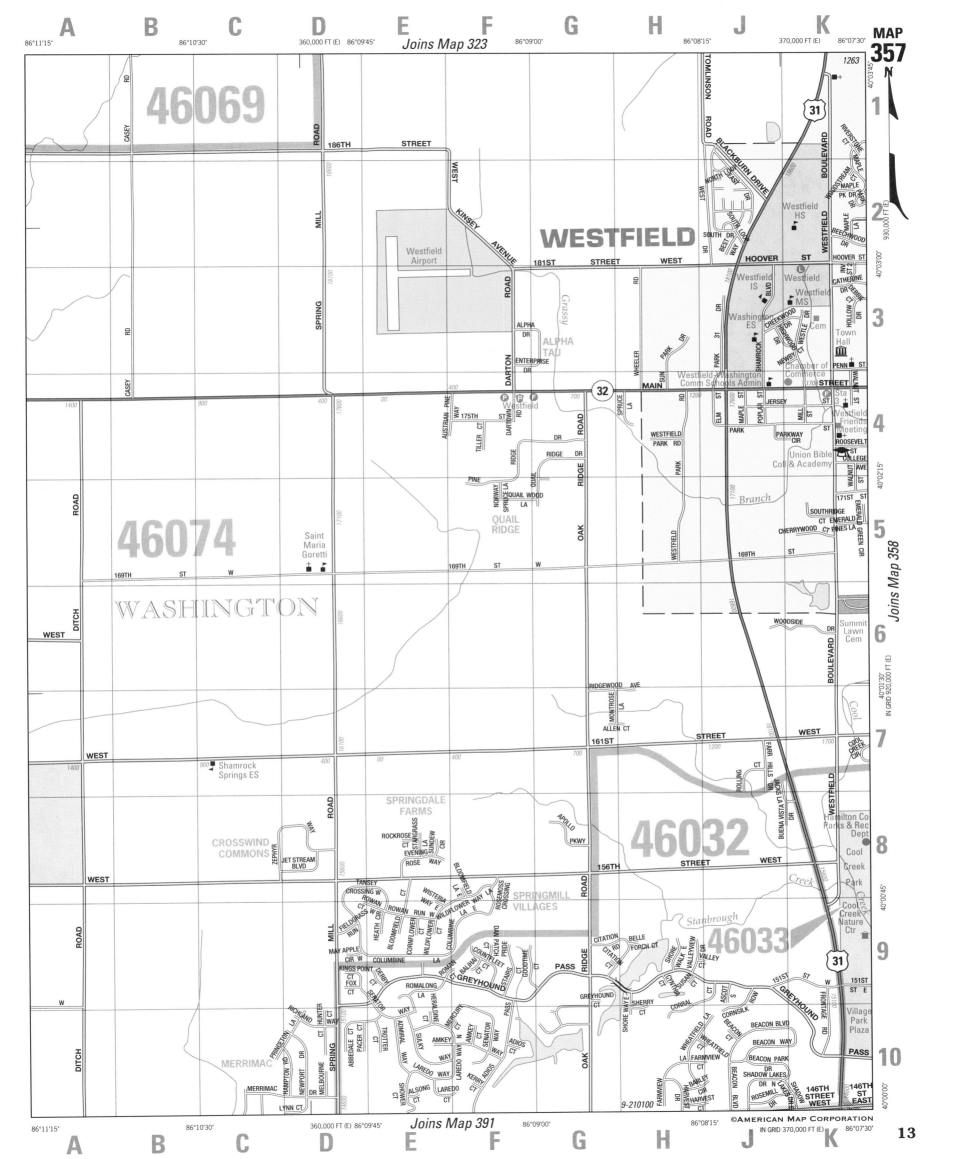

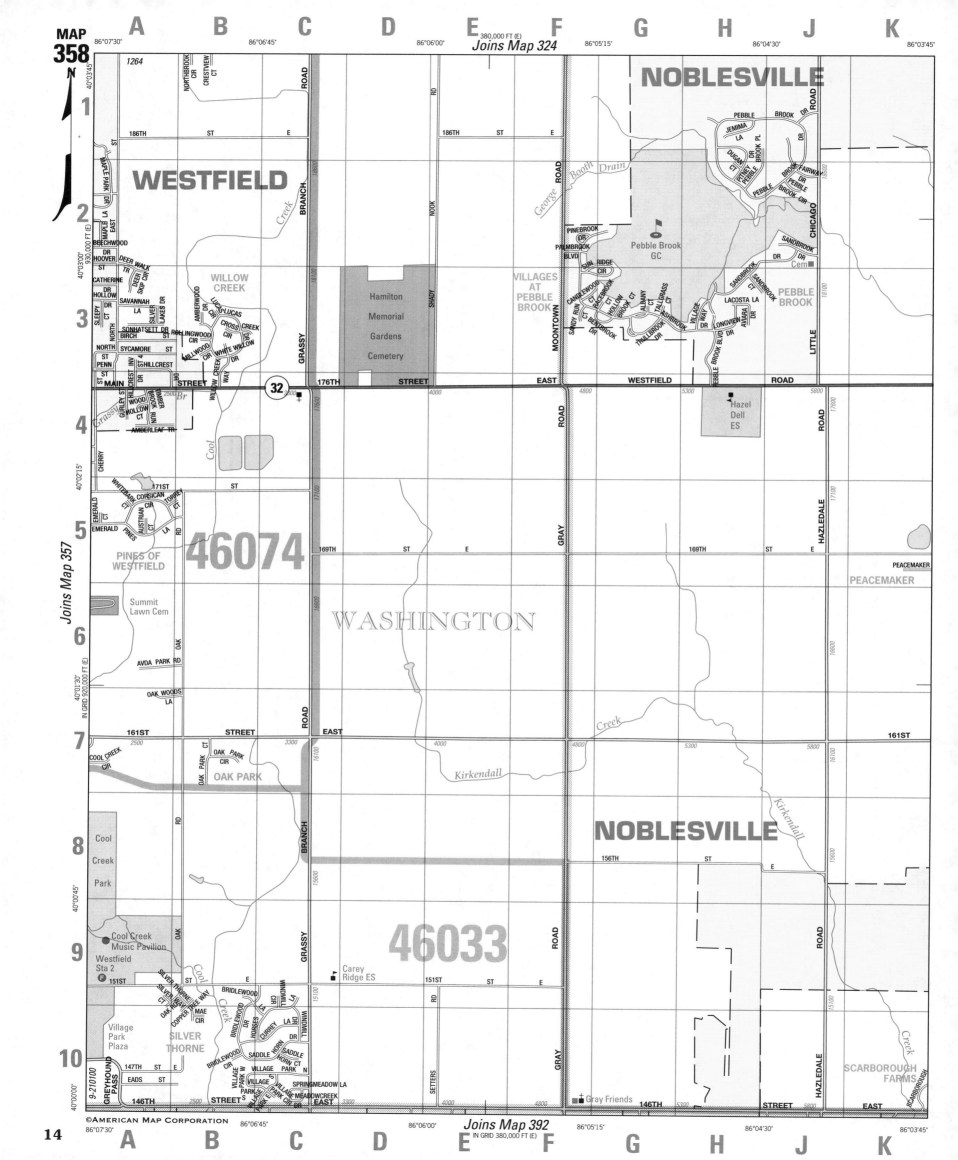

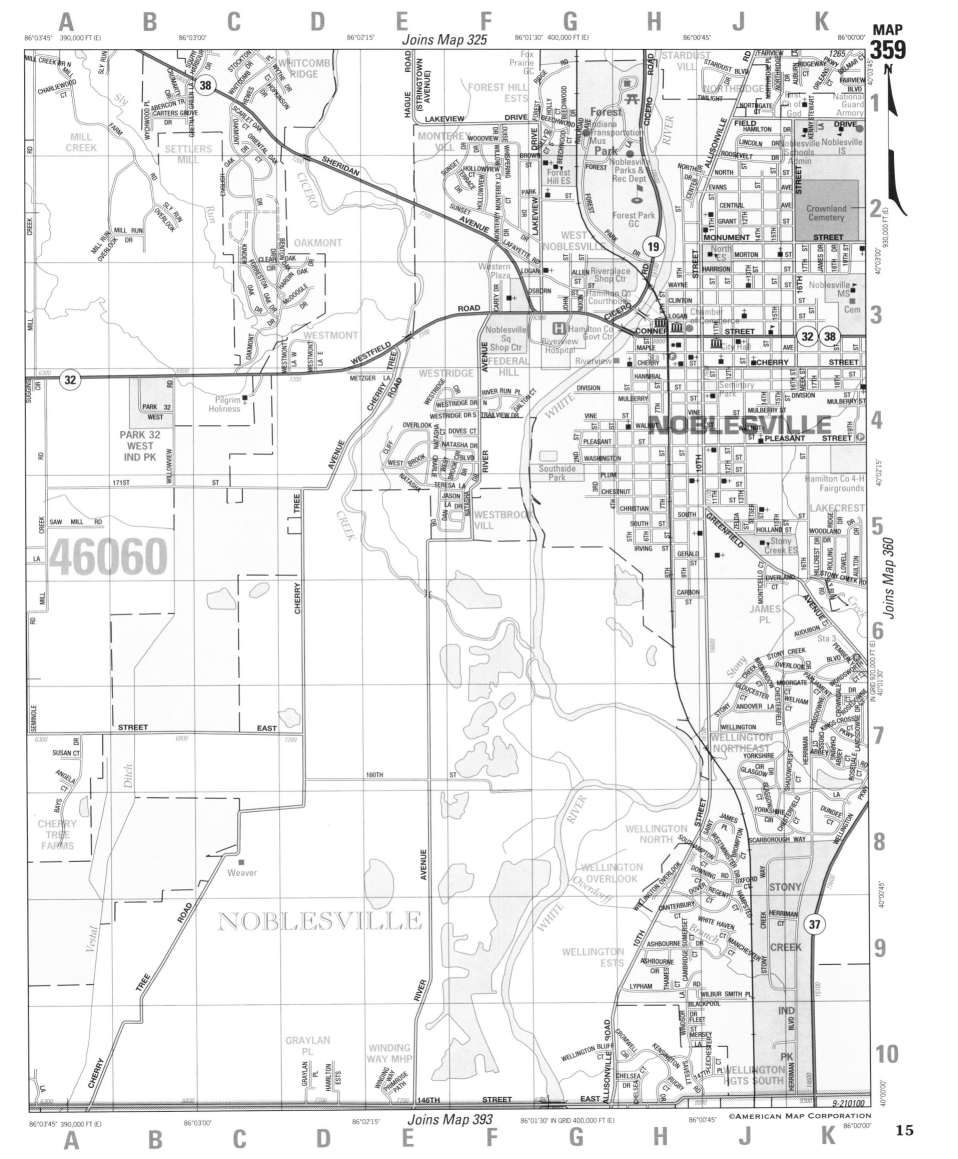

MAP
359
N
1
2
3
4
5
6
7
8
9
10
15

Joins Map 325

Joins Map 393

Joins Map 360

NOBLESVILLE

46060

©AMERICAN MAP CORPORATION
9-210100

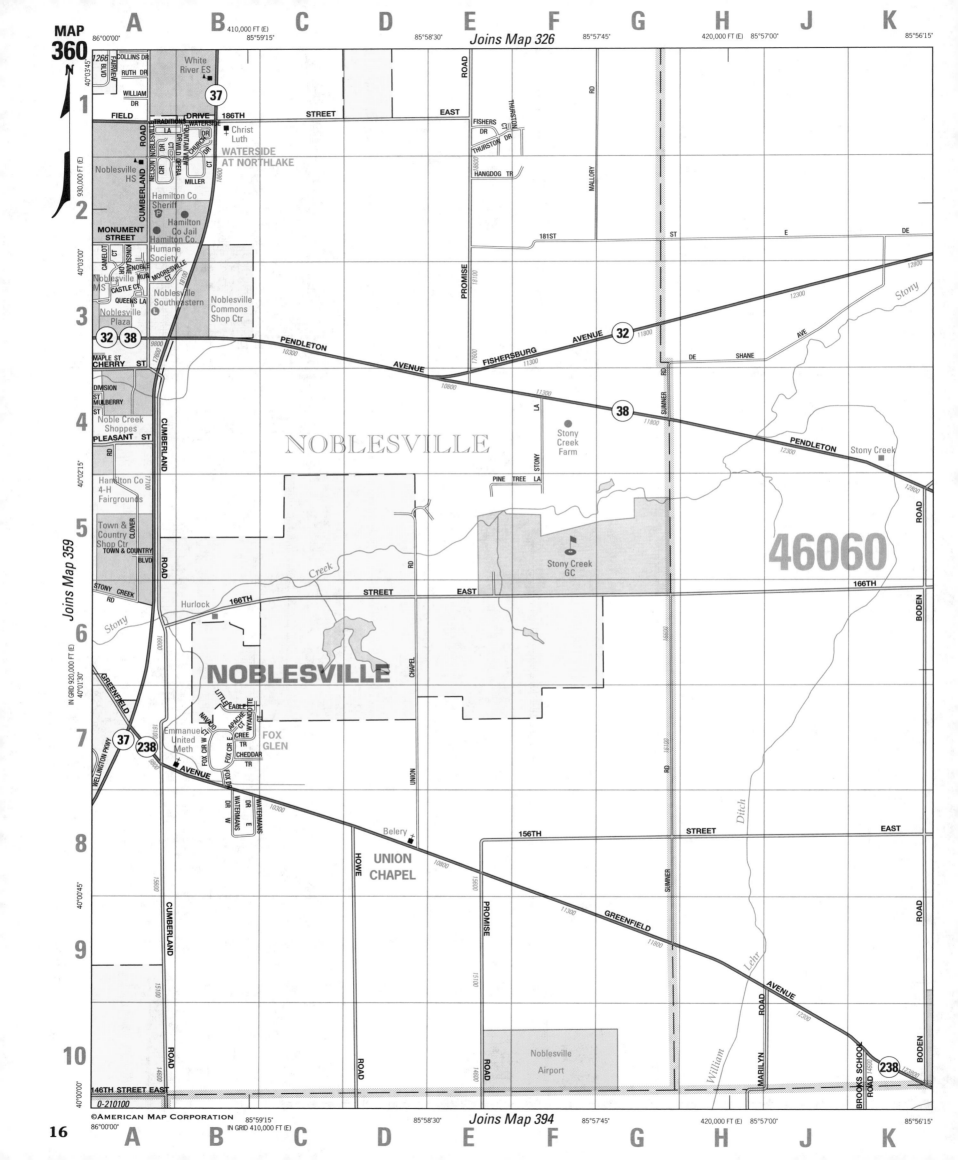

MAP
360
N

Joins Map 326

WATERSIDE
AT NORTHLAKE

White
River ES

Christ
Luth

Noblesville
HS

Hamilton Co
Sheriff

Hamilton
Co Jail

Hamilton Co.
Humane
Society

Noblesville
MS

Noblesville
Southeastern

Noblesville
Commons
Shop Ctr

Noblesville
Plaza

Noble Creek
Shoppes

Hamilton Co
4-H
Fairgrounds

Town &
Country
Shop Ctr

NOBLESVILLE

Stony
Creek
Farm

Stony Creek
GC

46060

NOBLESVILLE

Hurlock

Emmanuel
United
Meth

FOX
GLEN

Belery

UNION
CHAPEL

Noblesville
Airport

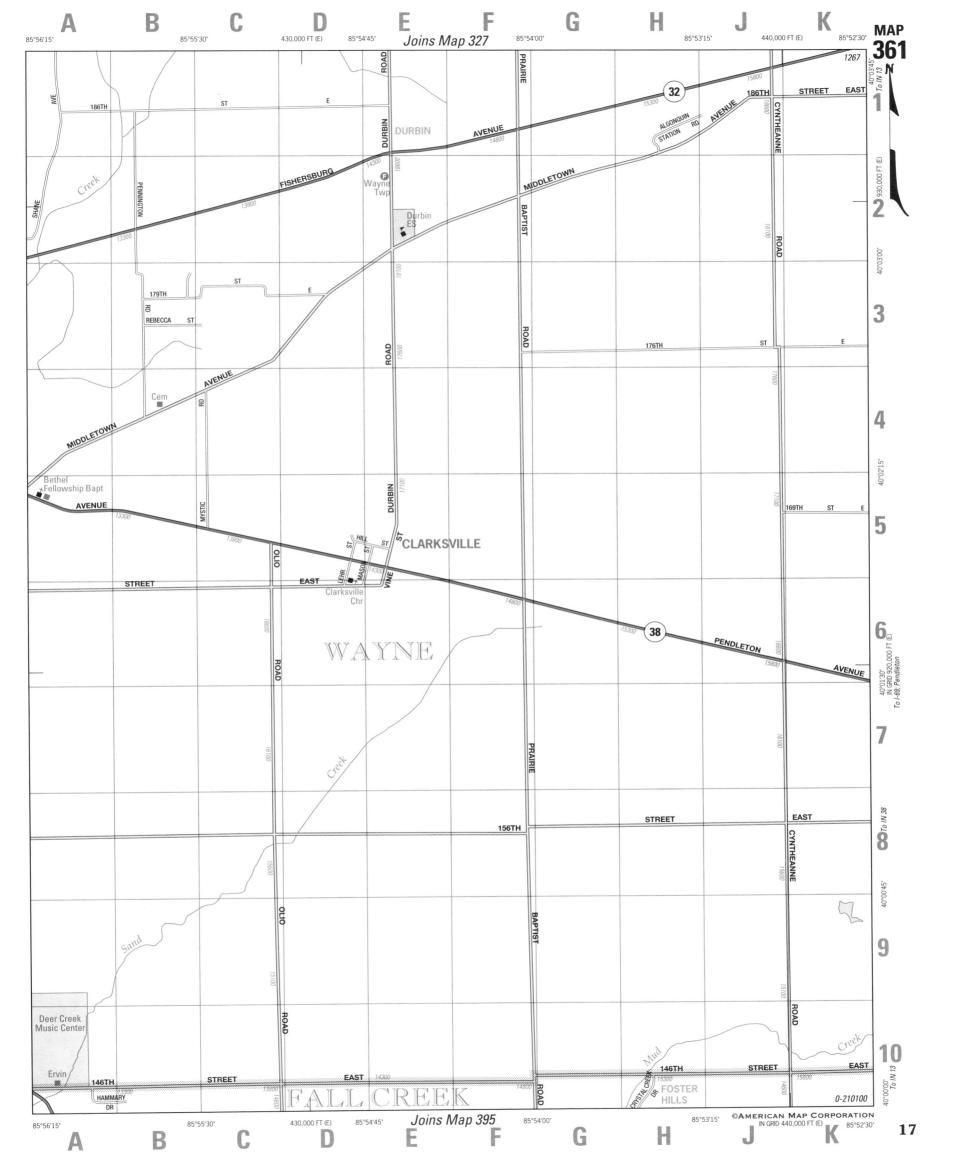

MAP **361**

Joins Map 327

Joins Map 395

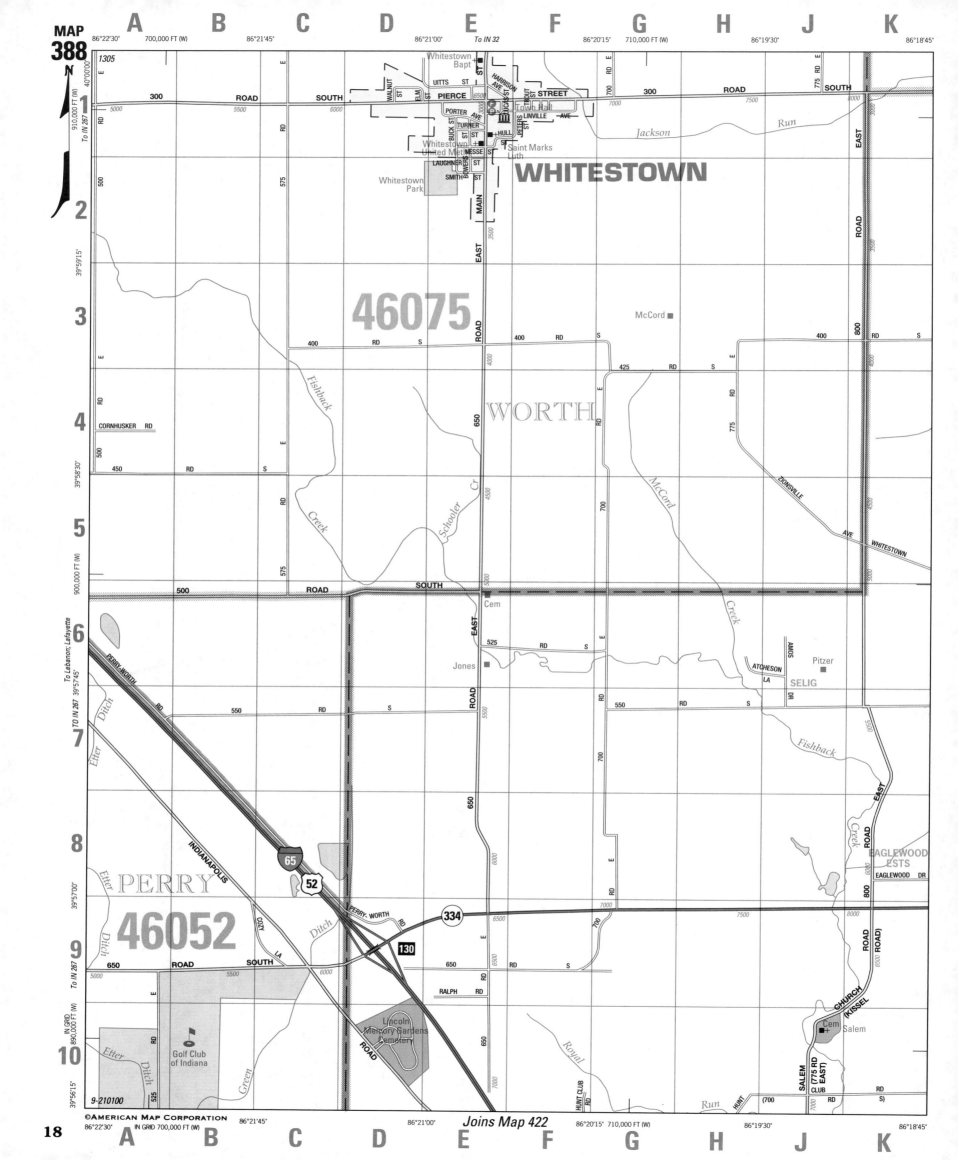

MAP
388

WHITESTOWN

46075

WORTH

PERRY

46052

©AMERICAN MAP CORPORATION

Joins Map 422

To IN 32

To Lebanon; Lafayette

To IN 267

To IN 267

Golf Club
of Indiana

Lincoln
Memory Gardens
Cemetery

EAGLEWOOD
ESTS

SELIG

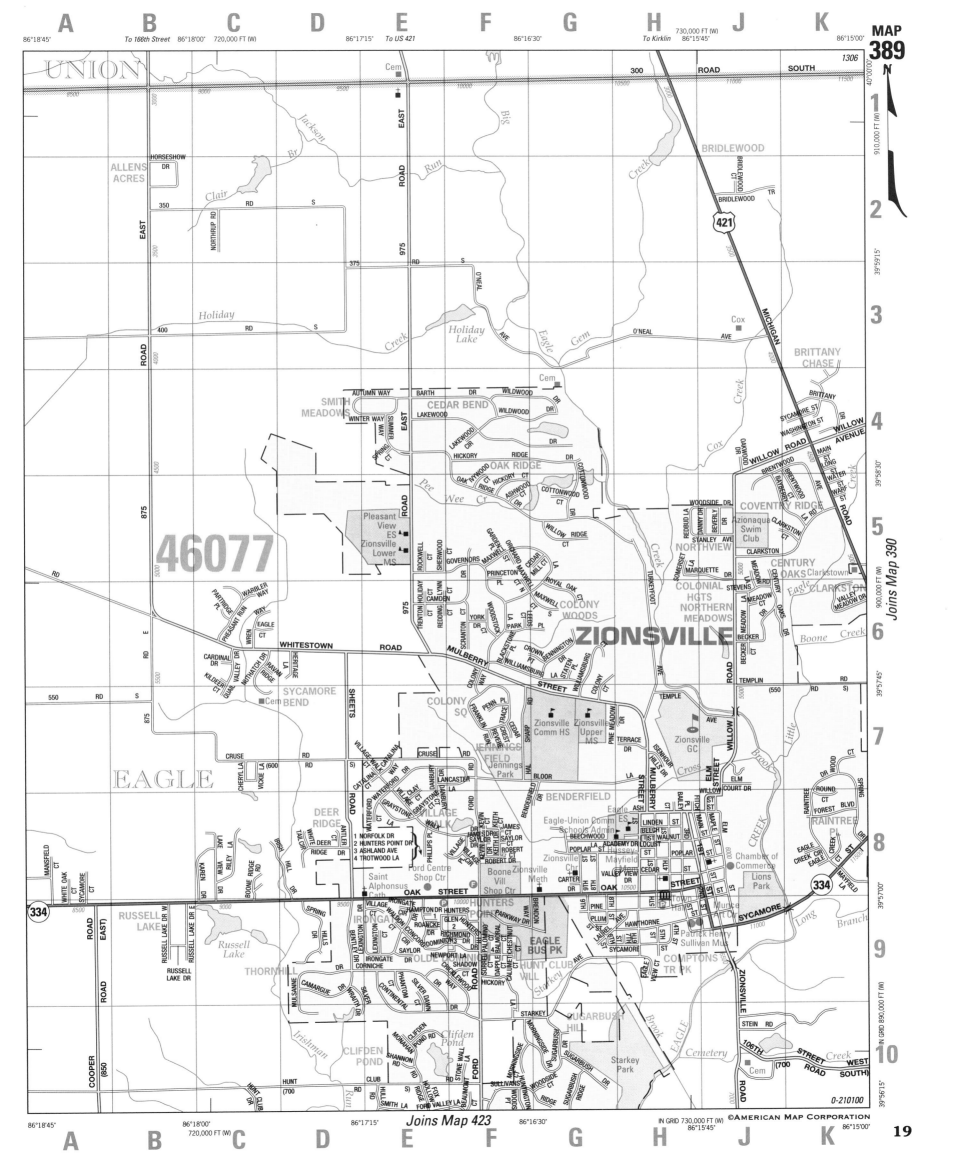

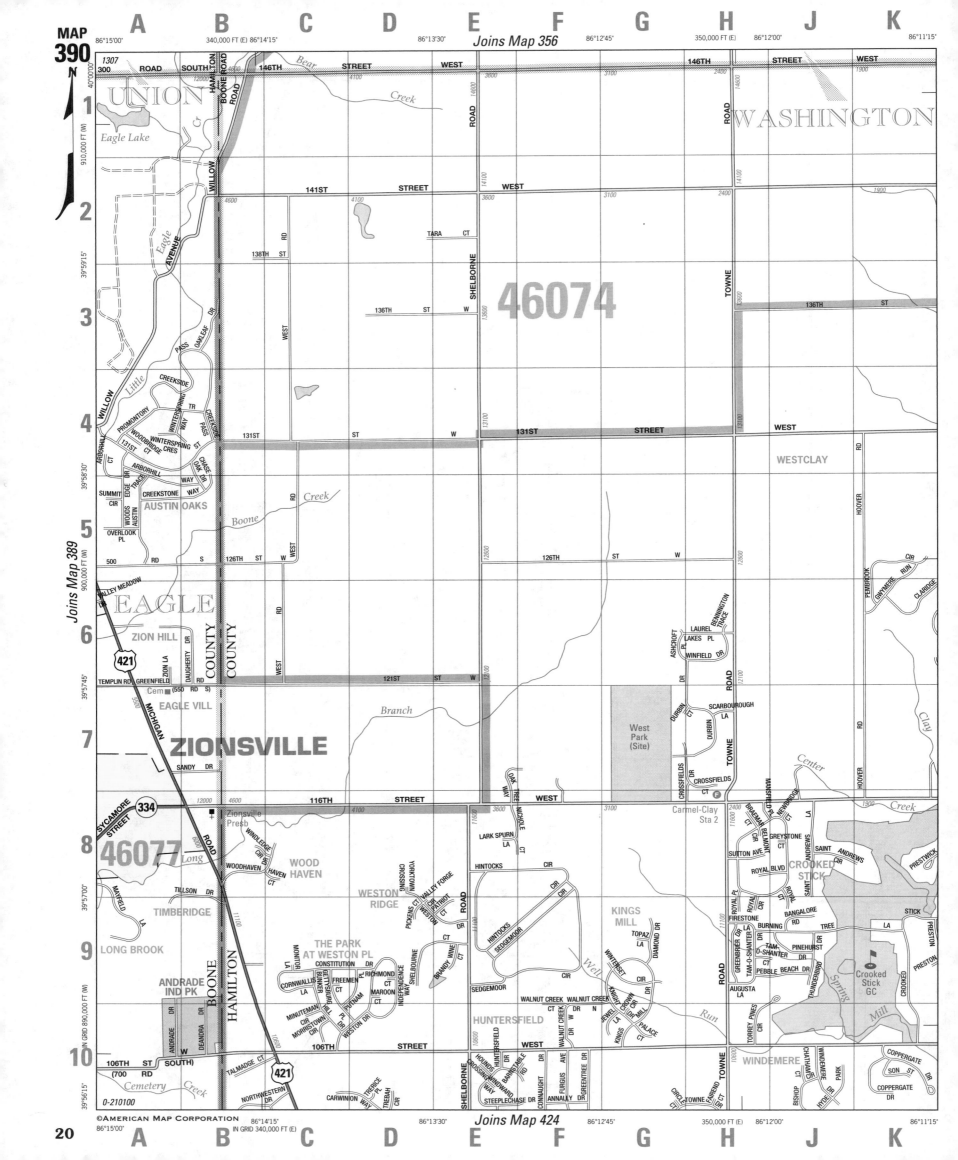

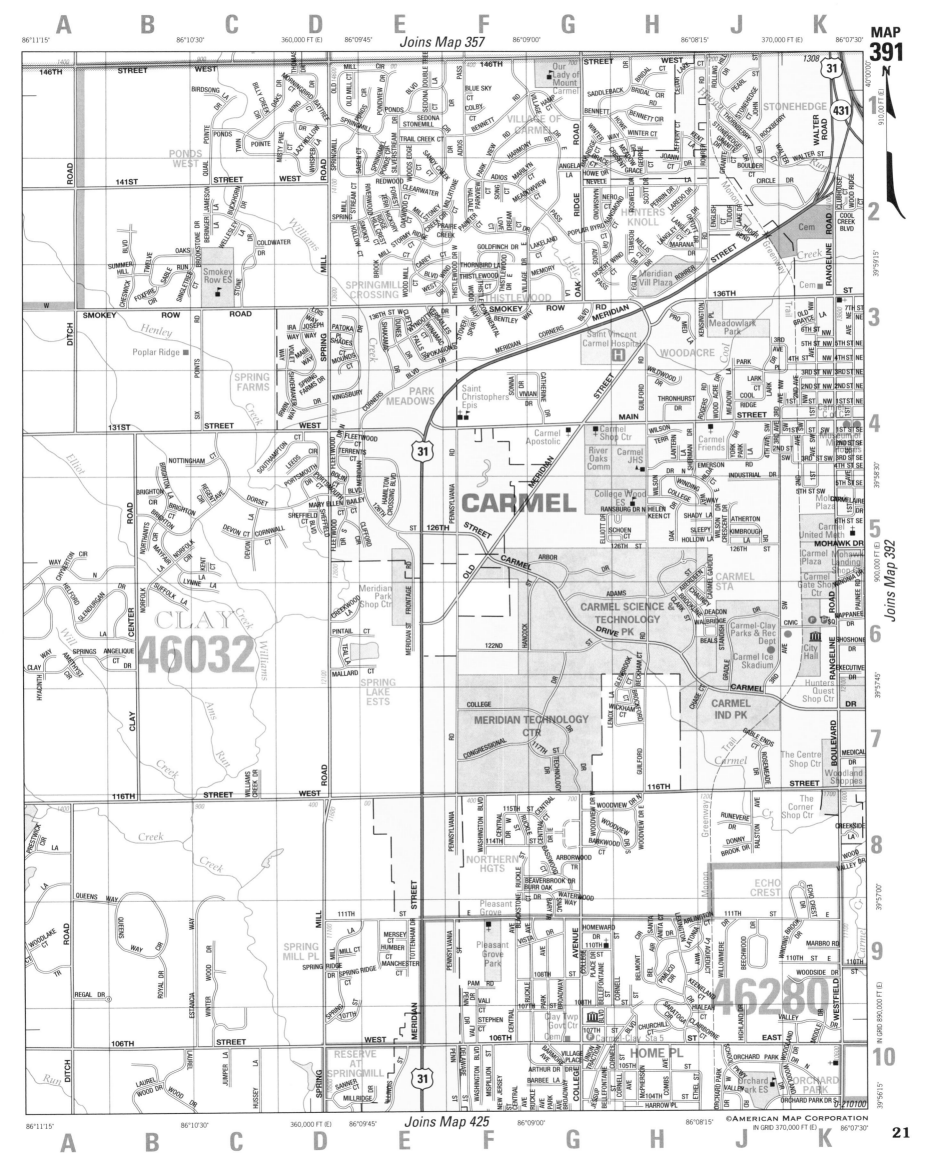

MAP
391
21

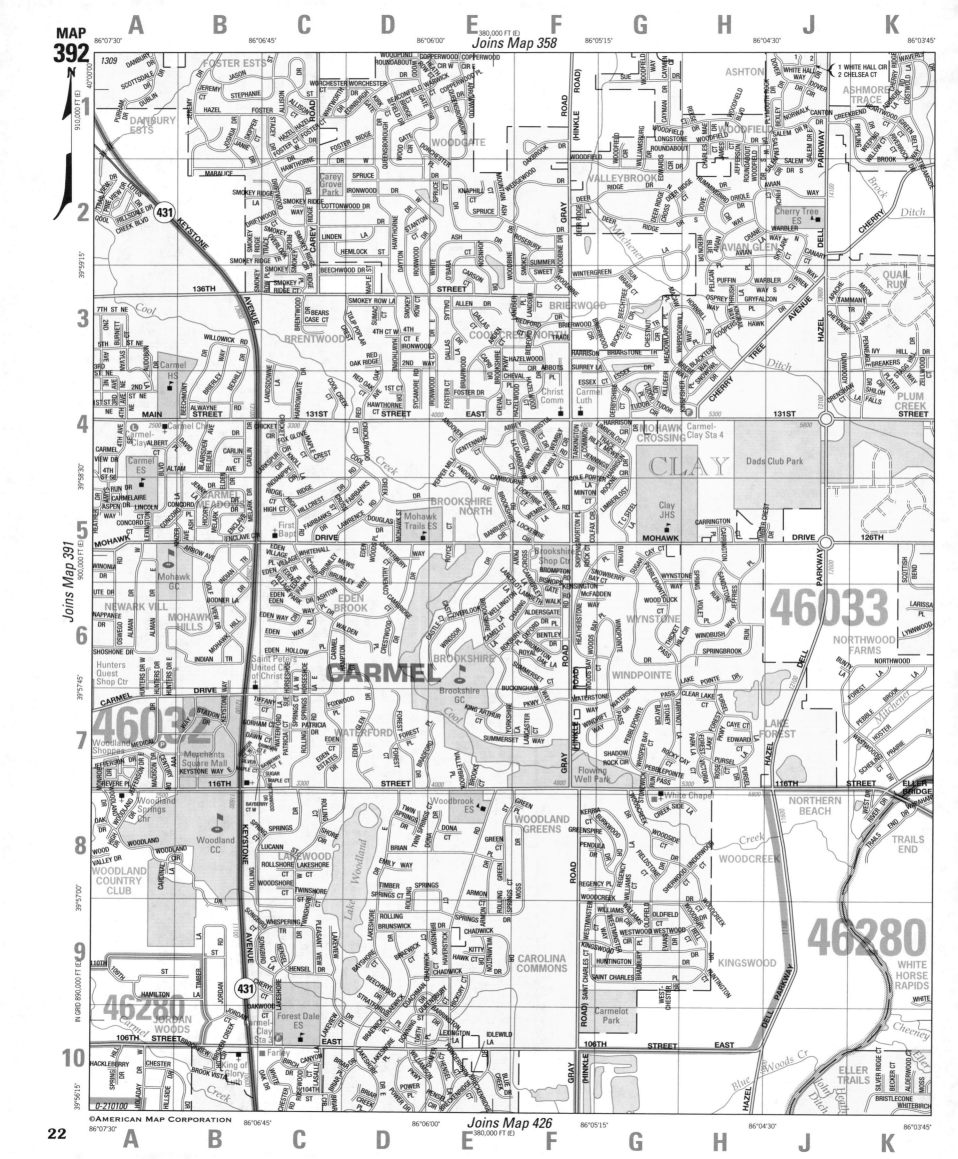

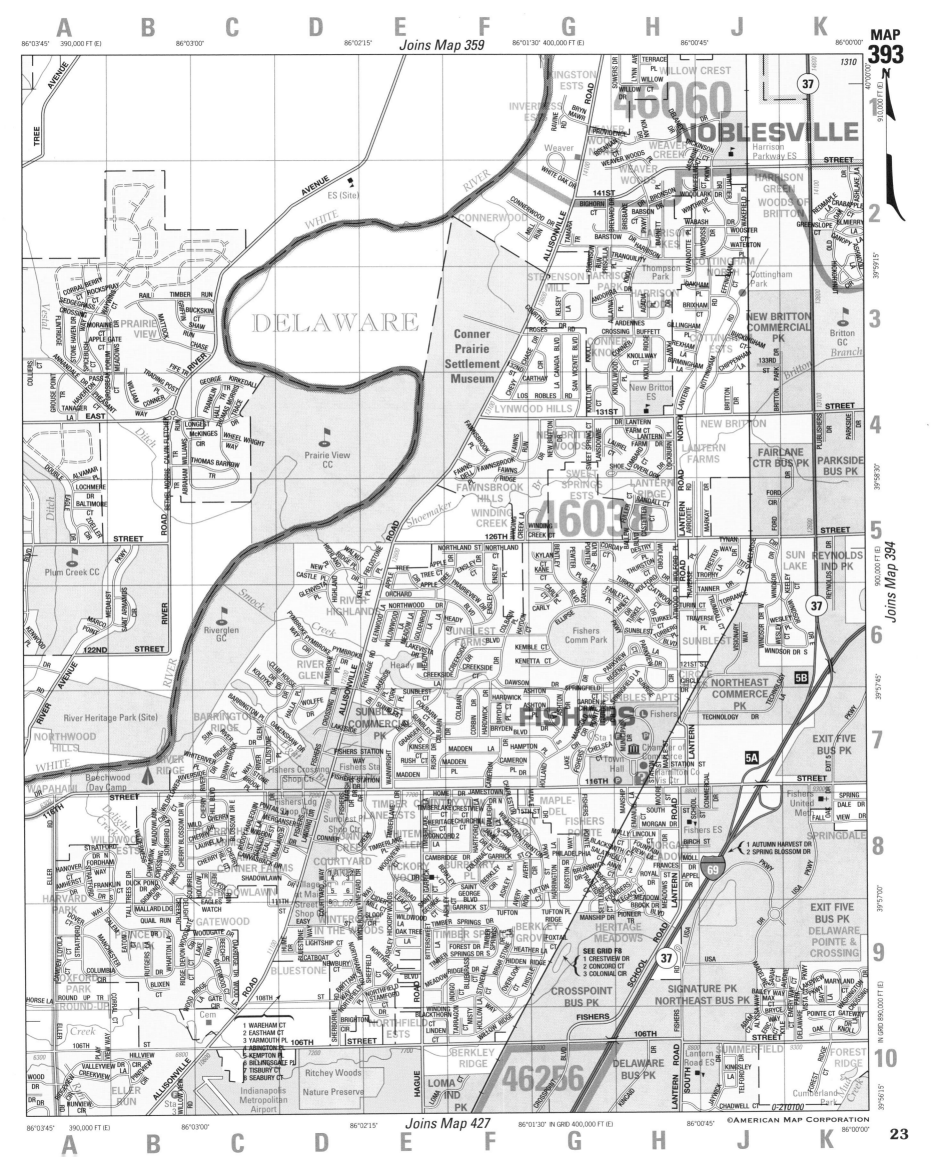

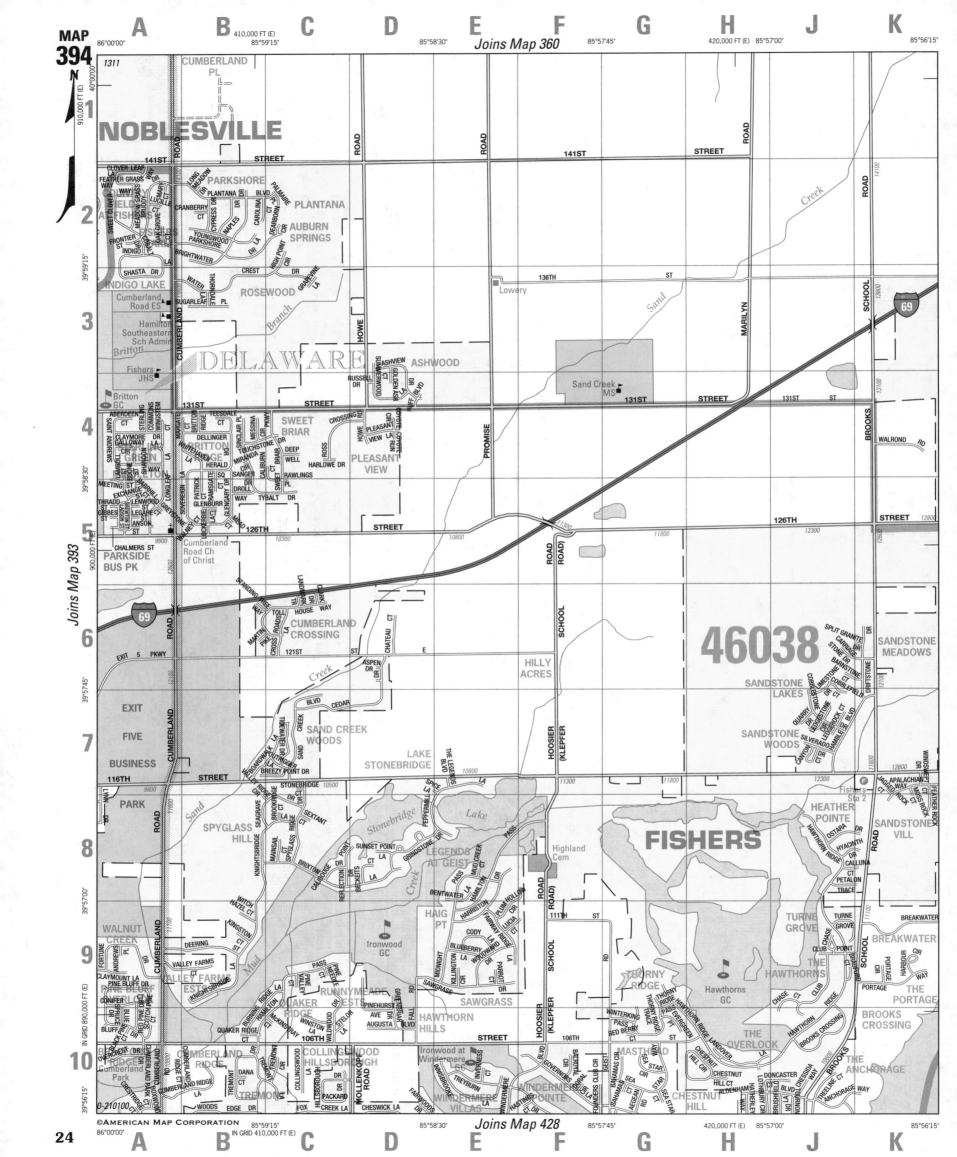

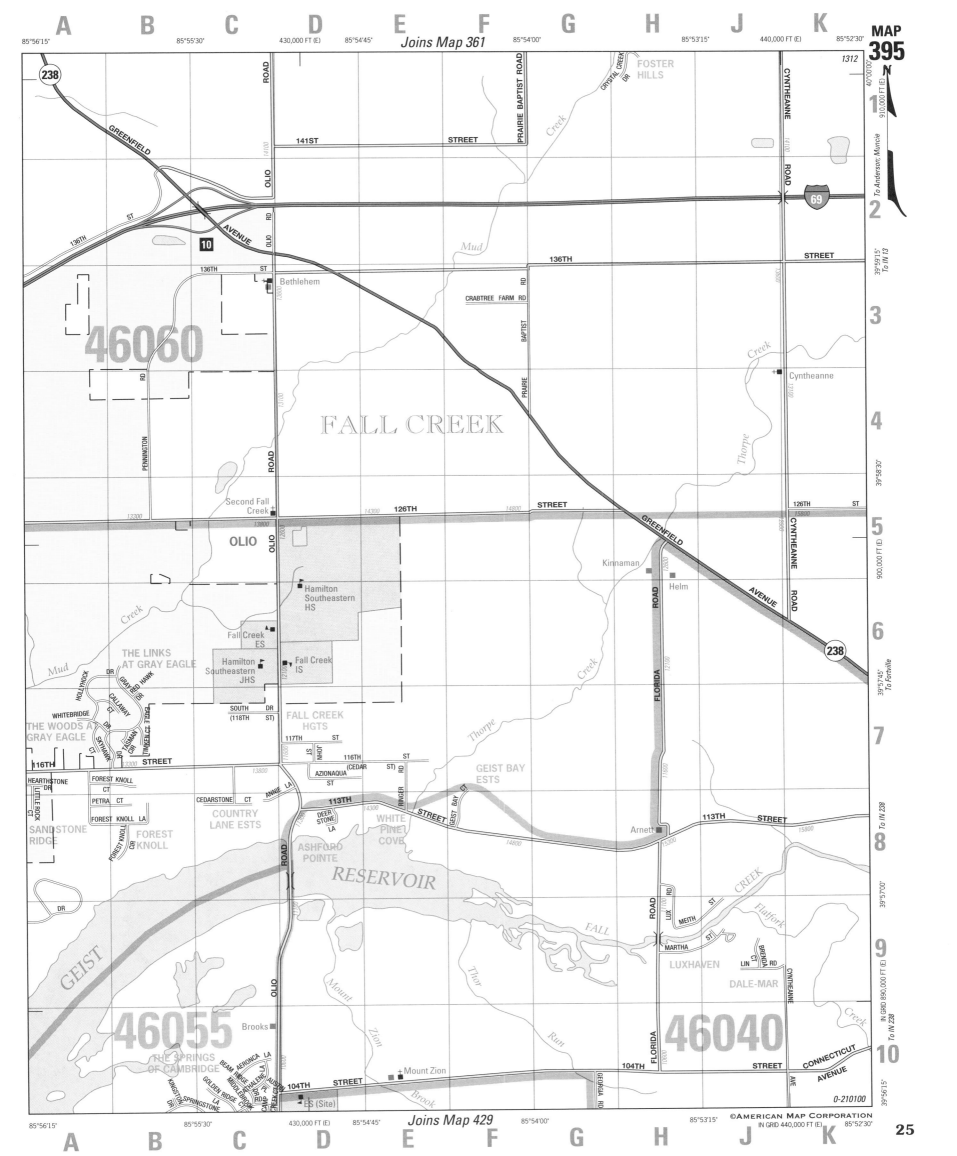

MAP
395
Joins Map 361

46060

FALL CREEK

46055

46040

GEIST

RESERVOIR

THE LINKS AT GRAY EAGLE

THE WOODS AT GRAY EAGLE

SANDSTONE RIDGE

FOREST KNOLL

COUNTRY LANE ESTS

ASHFORD POINTE

WHITE PINE COVE

GEIST BAY ESTS

FALL CREEK HGTS

Hamilton Southeastern HS

Fall Creek ES

Hamilton Southeastern JHS

Fall Creek IS

Bethlehem

Second Fall Creek

OLIO

Kinnaman

Helm

Arnett

Luxhaven

DALE-MAR

Brooks

THE SPRINGS OF CAMBRIDGE

Mount Zion

FOSTER HILLS

Cyntheanne

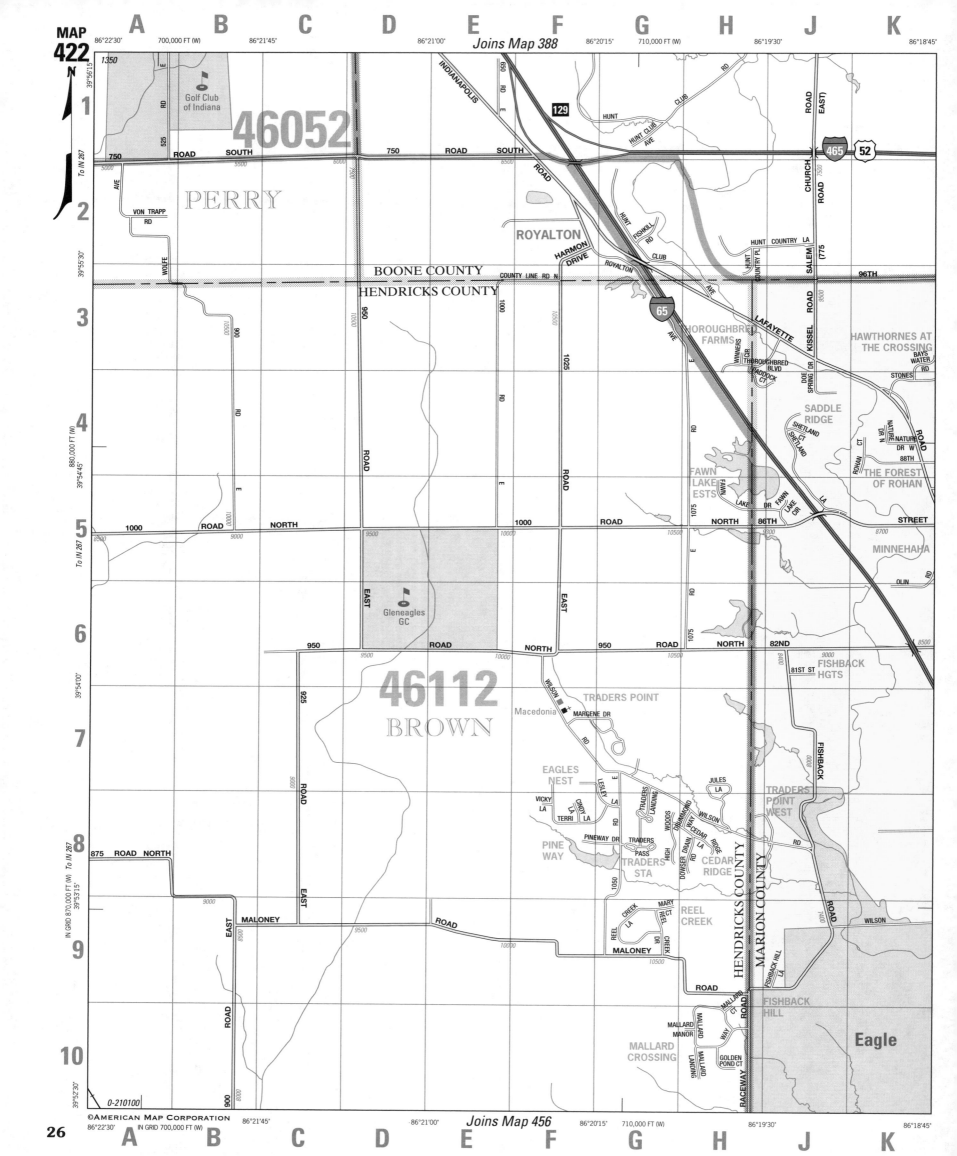

MAP
422

46052

PERRY

VON TRAPP RD

Golf Club of Indiana

WOLFE

ROAD SOUTH

750 ROAD SOUTH

1000 ROAD NORTH

BOONE COUNTY

HENDRICKS COUNTY

COUNTY LINE RD N

ROYALTON

HARMON DRIVE

THOROUGHBRED FARMS

SADDLE RIDGE

HAWTHORNES AT THE CROSSING

THE FOREST OF ROHAN

FAWN LAKE ESTS

MINNEHAHA

46112

BROWN

Gleneagles GC

950 ROAD NORTH

950 ROAD NORTH

TRADERS POINT

Macedonia

FISHBACK HGTS

EAGLES NEST

PINE WAY

TRADERS POINT WEST

FISHBACK

875 ROAD NORTH

MALONEY

MALONEY

TRADERS STA

CEDAR RIDGE

REEL CREEK

HENDRICKS COUNTY

MARION COUNTY

FISHBACK HILL

MALLARD CROSSING

Eagle

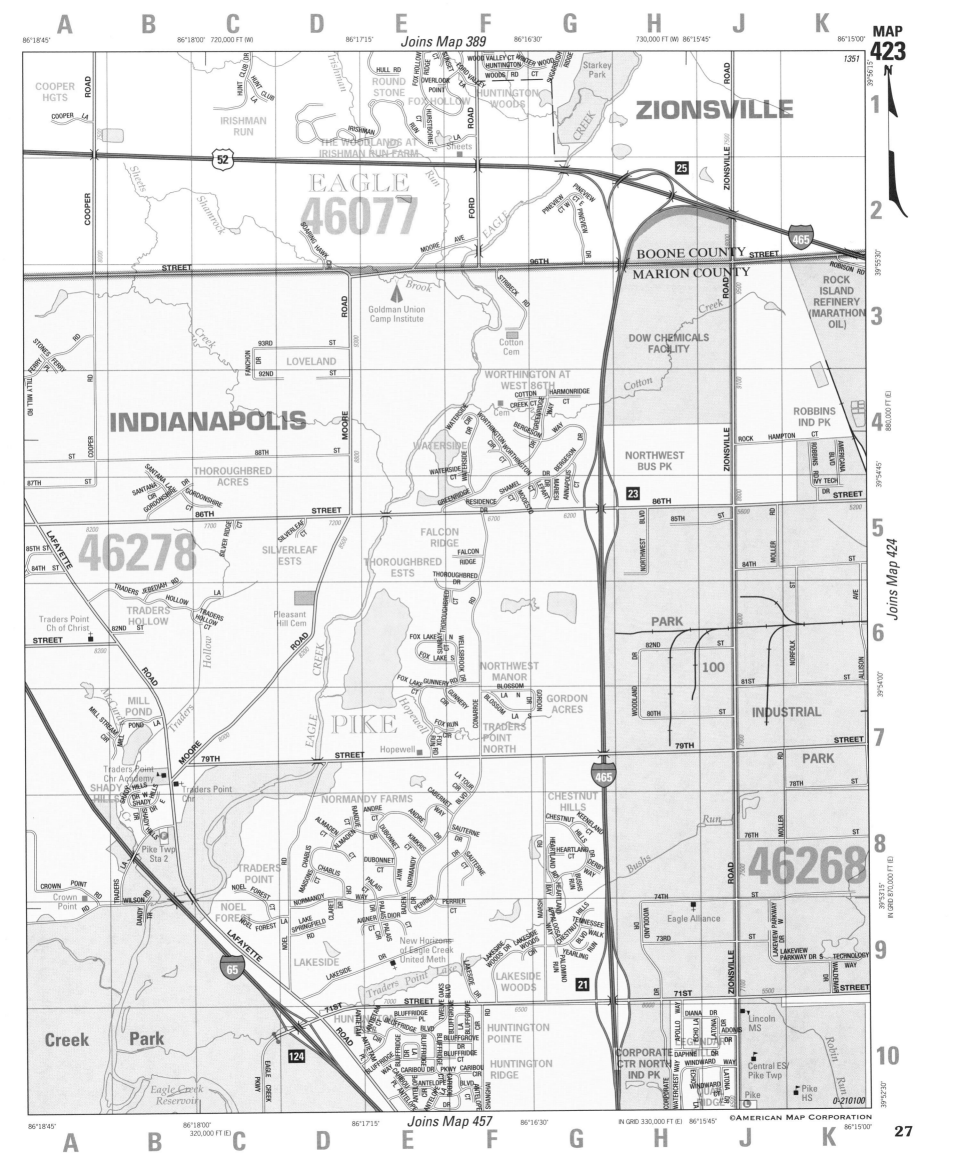

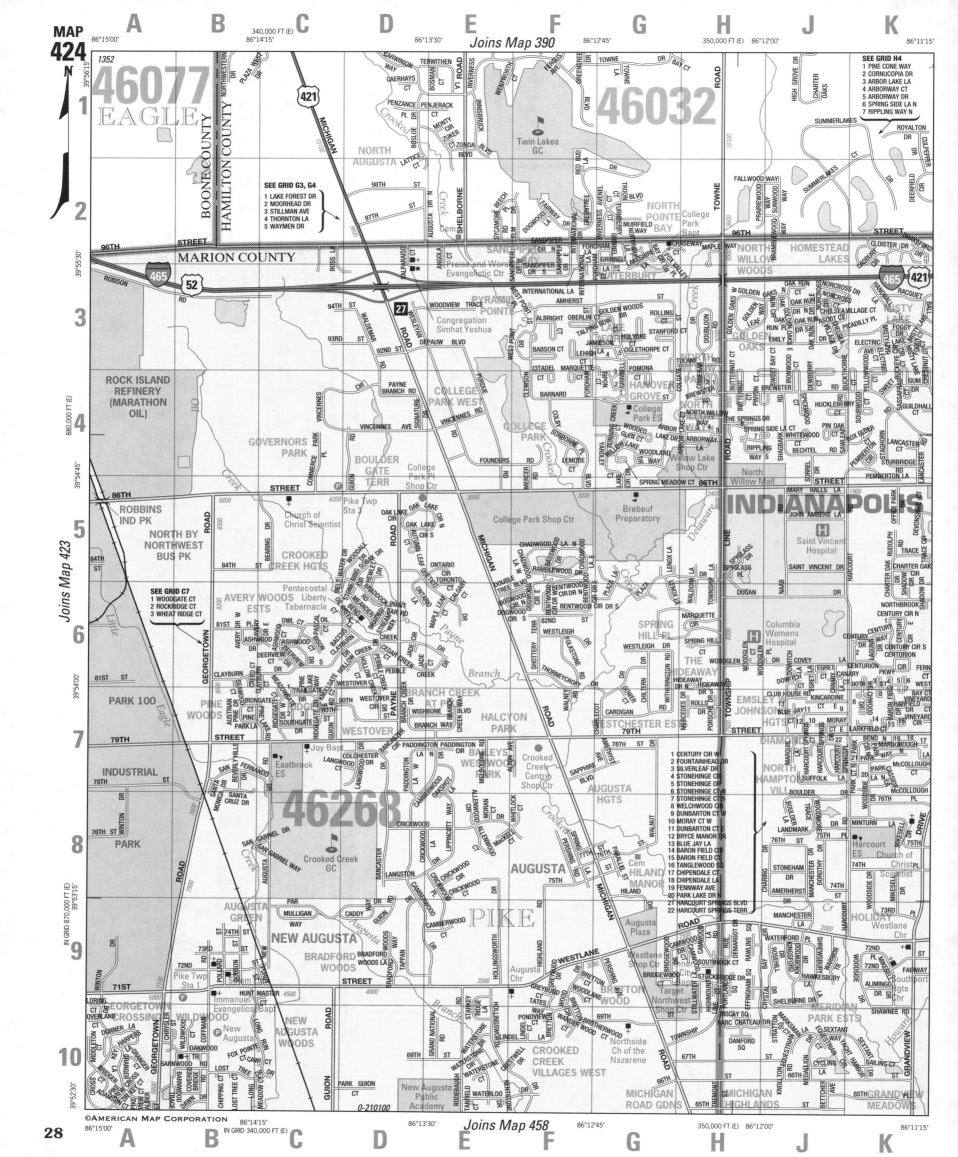

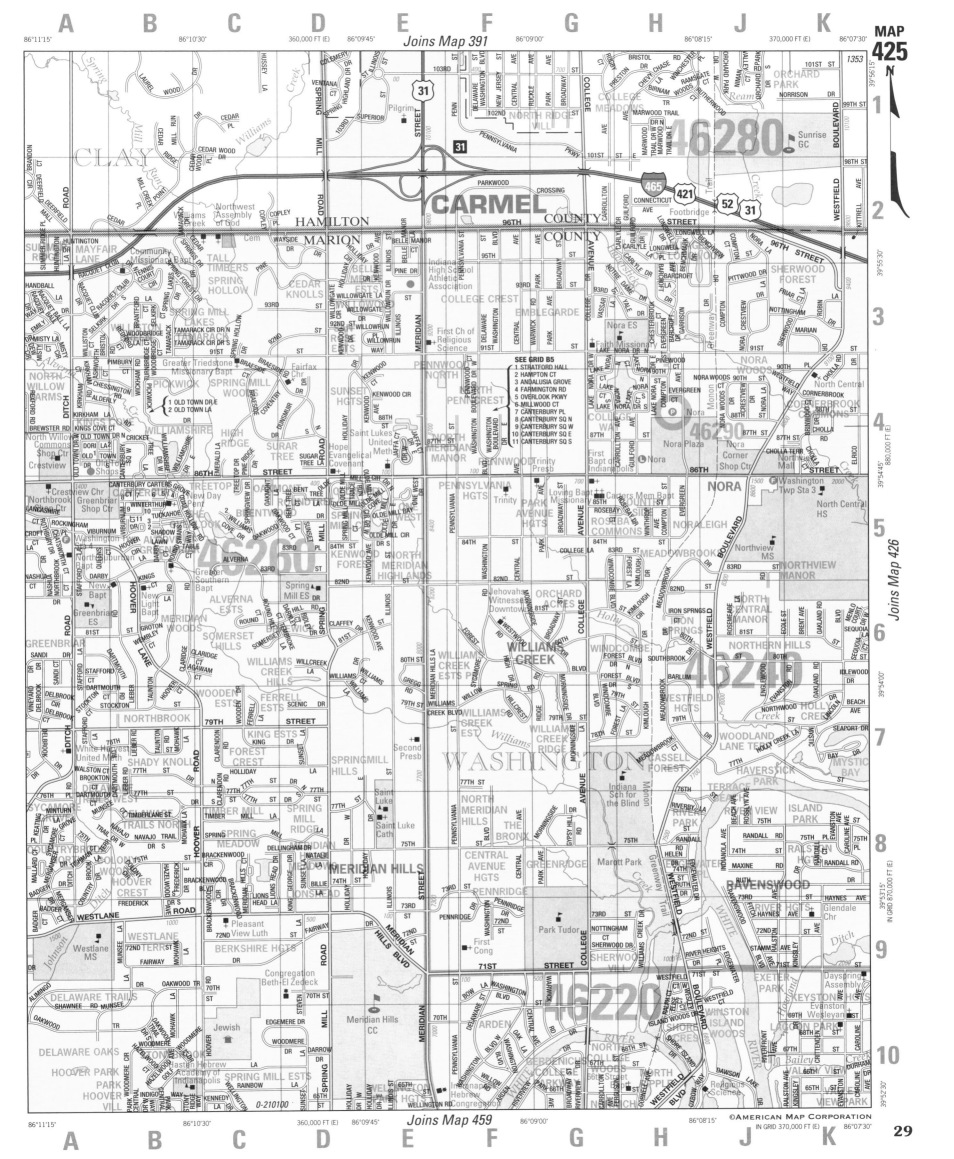

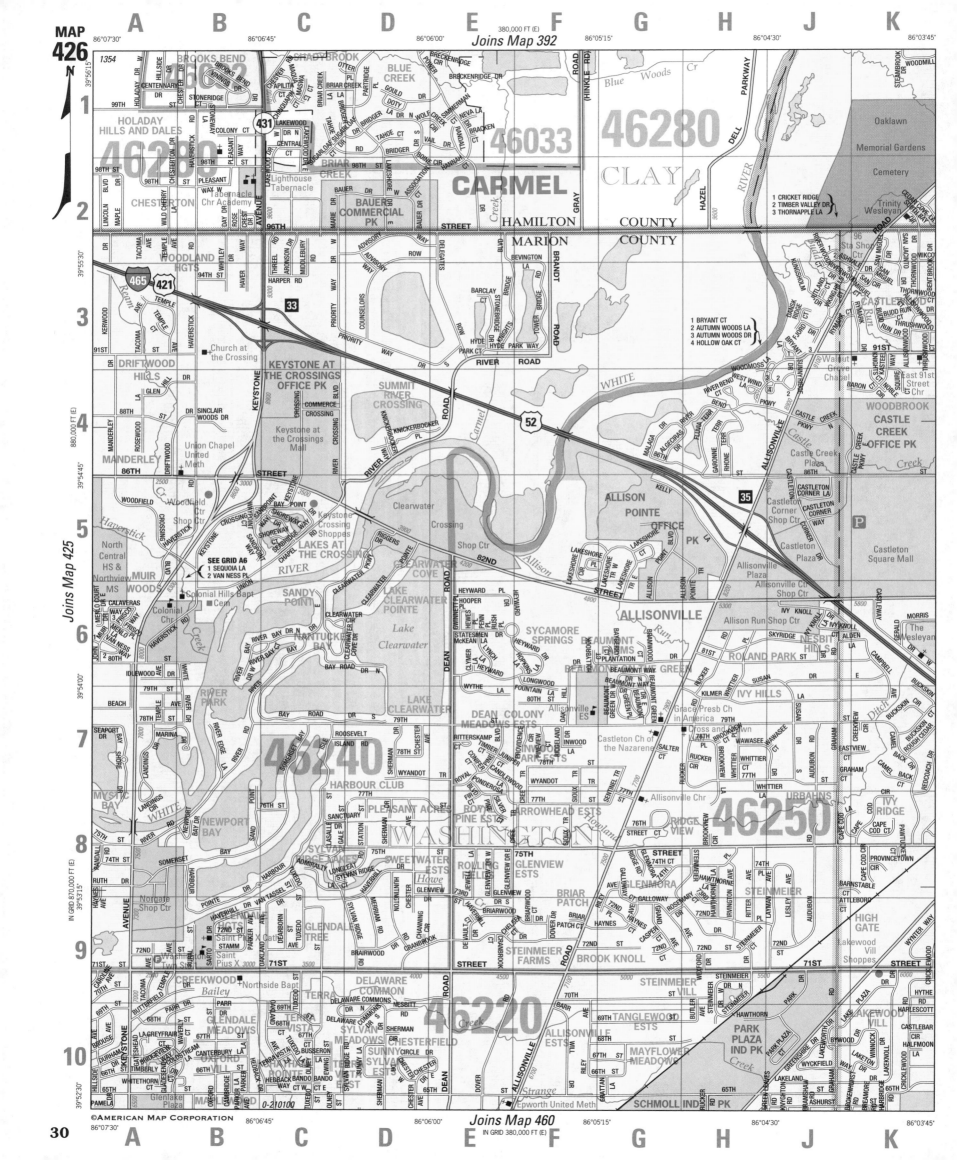

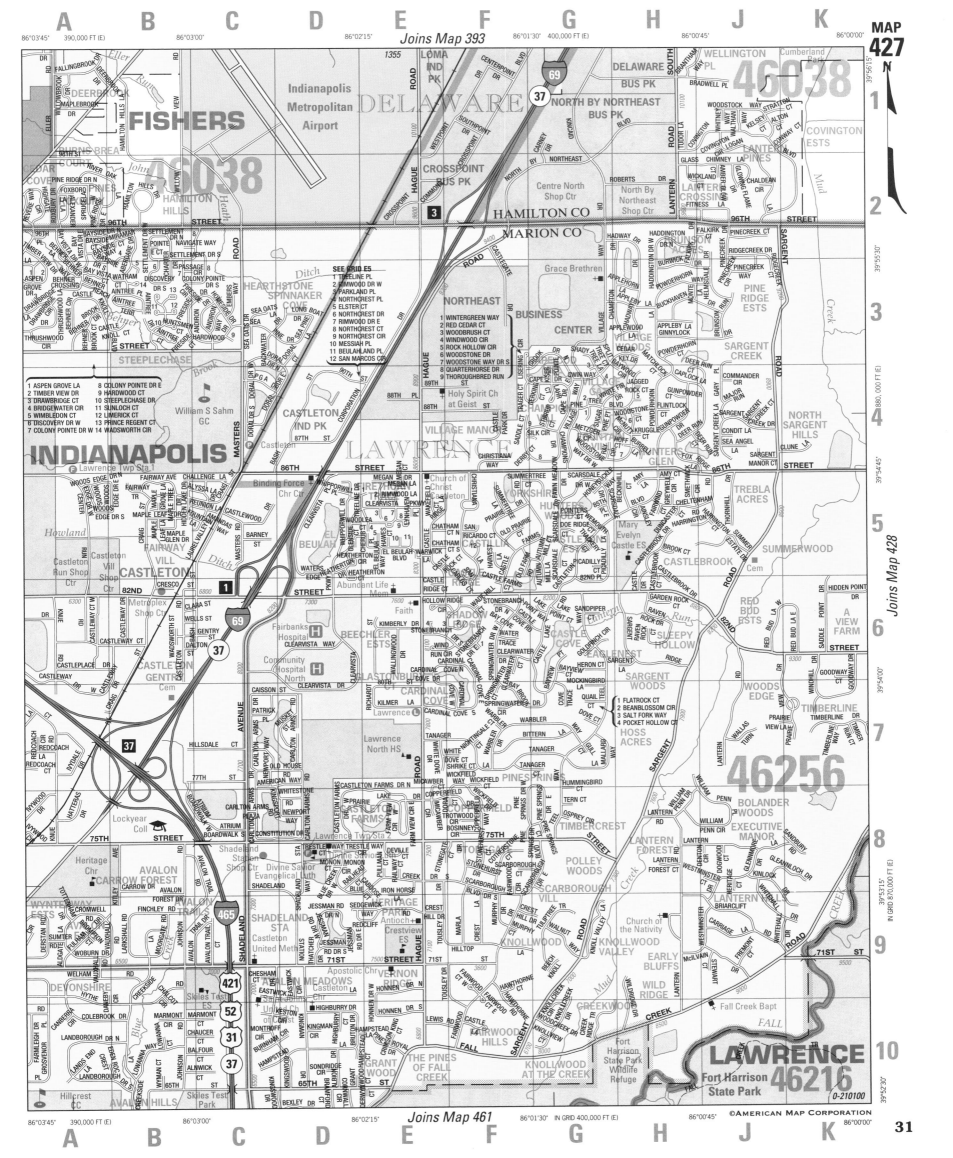

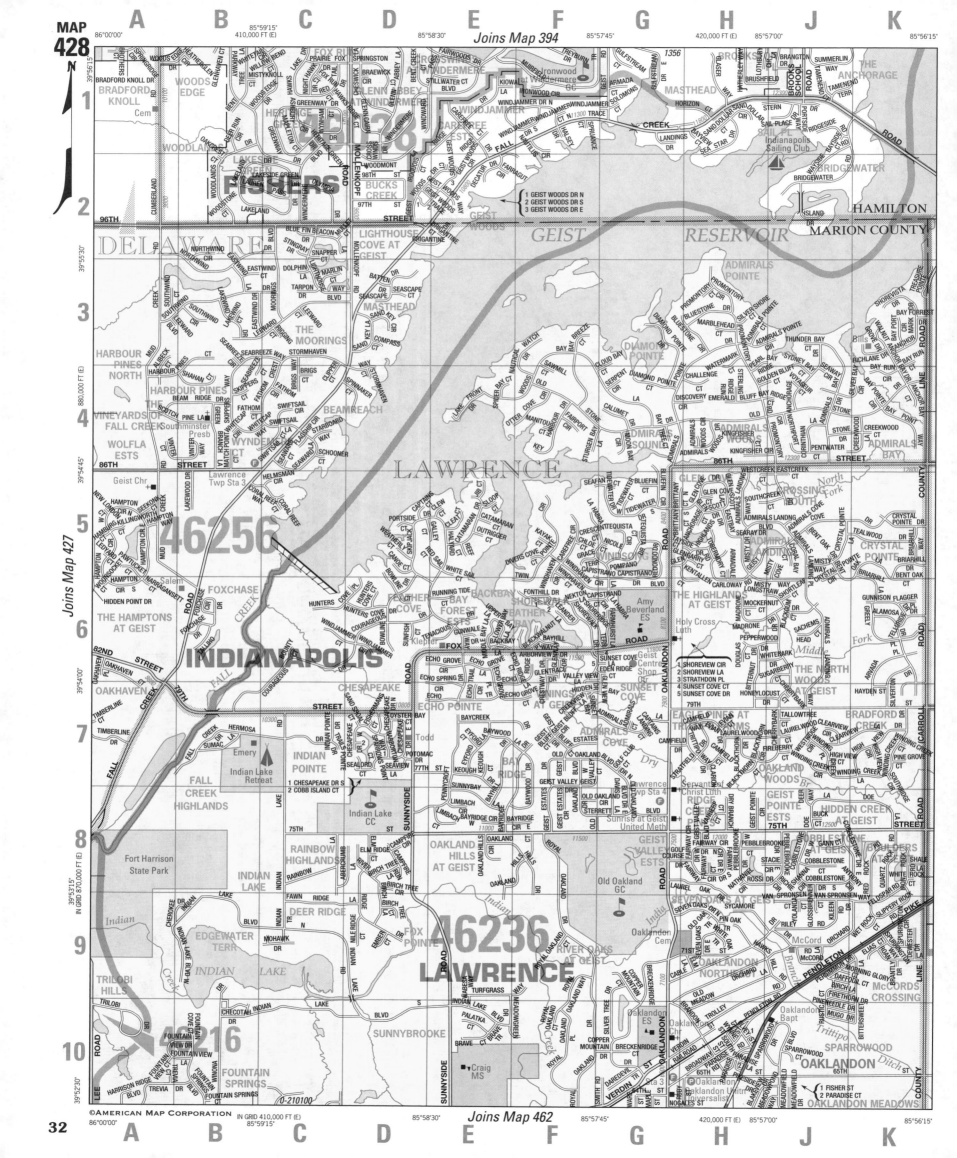

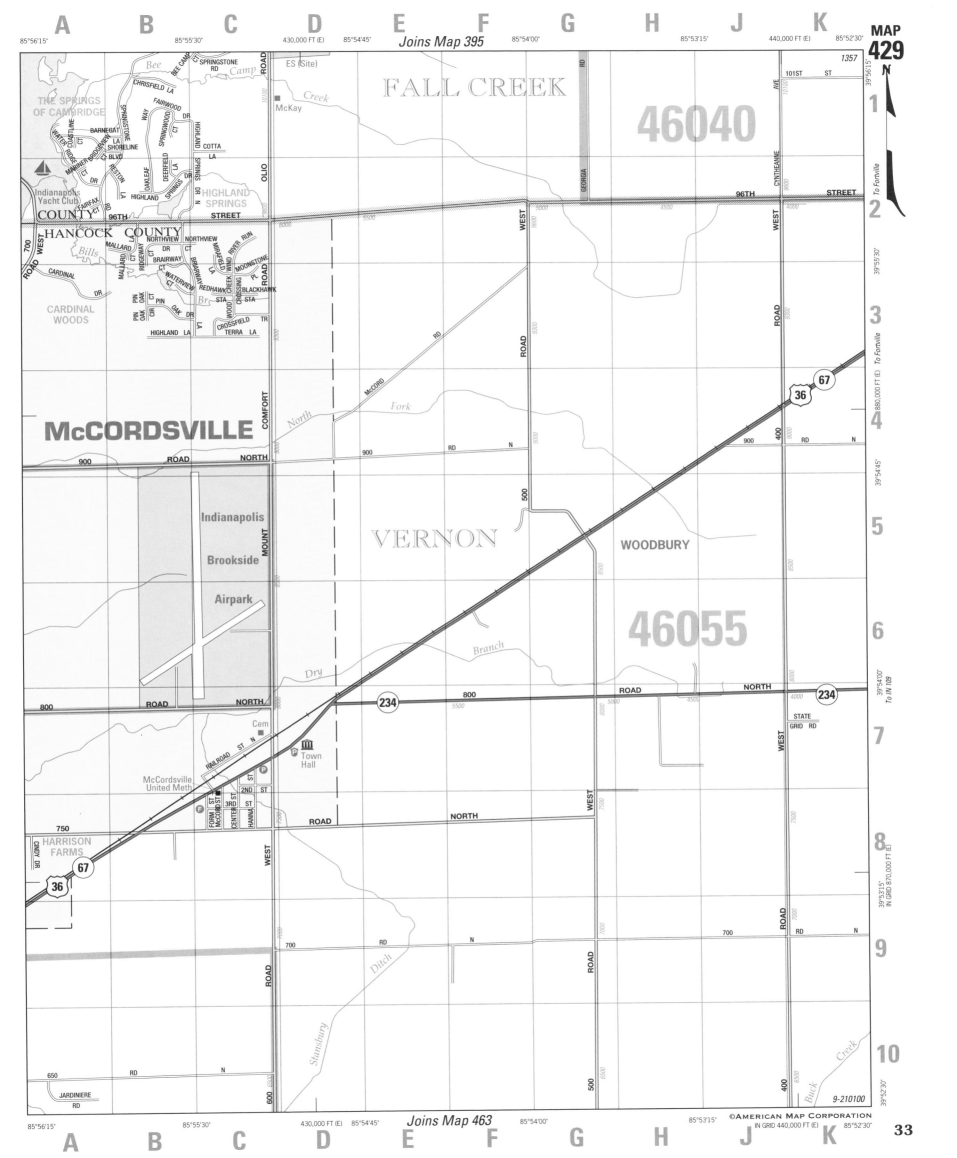

MAP
429
N

Joins Map 395

FALL CREEK

46040

1357
101ST ST

THE SPRINGS
OF CAMBRIDGE

Indianapolis
Yacht Club

COUNTY

HANCOCK COUNTY

CARDINAL
WOODS

96TH STREET

96TH STREET

McCORDSVILLE

VERNON

WOODBURY

Indianapolis

Brookside

Airpark

46055

900 ROAD NORTH

800 ROAD NORTH

234

800 ROAD NORTH

234

Cem

Town Hall

McCordsville
United Meth.

McCordsville

HARRISON
FARMS

ROAD NORTH

750

36
67

700 RD N

234

STATE
GRID RD

650 RD N

700 RD N

500

400

JARDINIERE
RD

Buck Creek

9-210100

NOTES

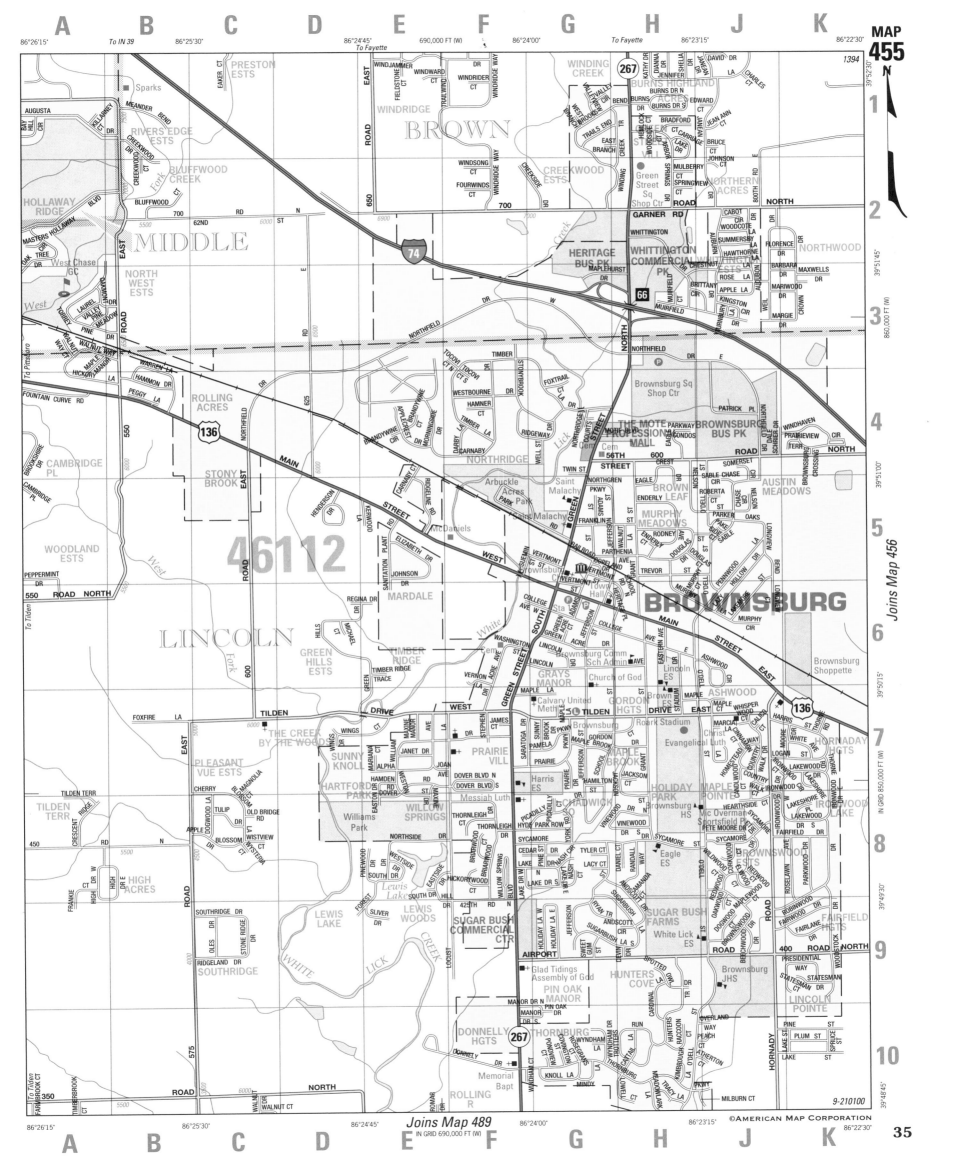

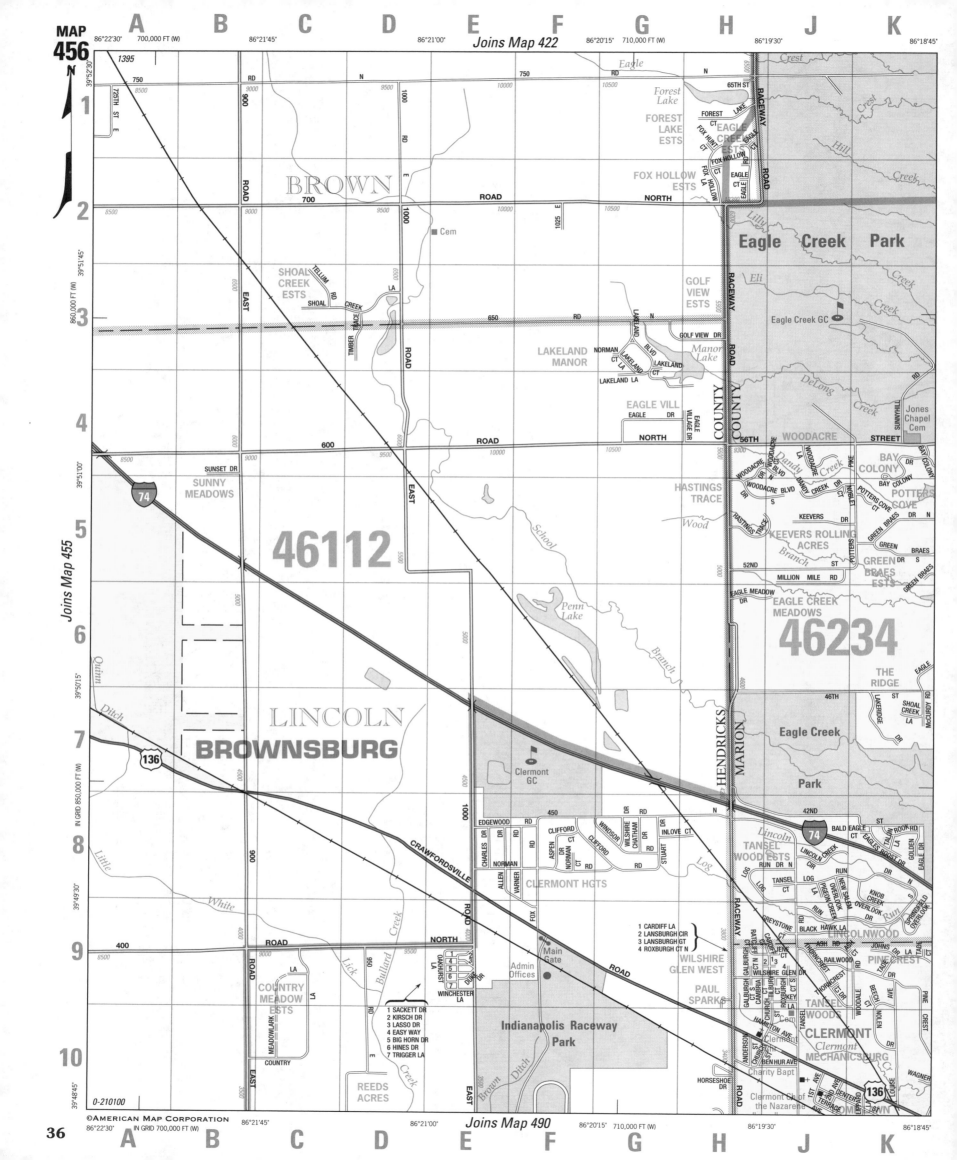

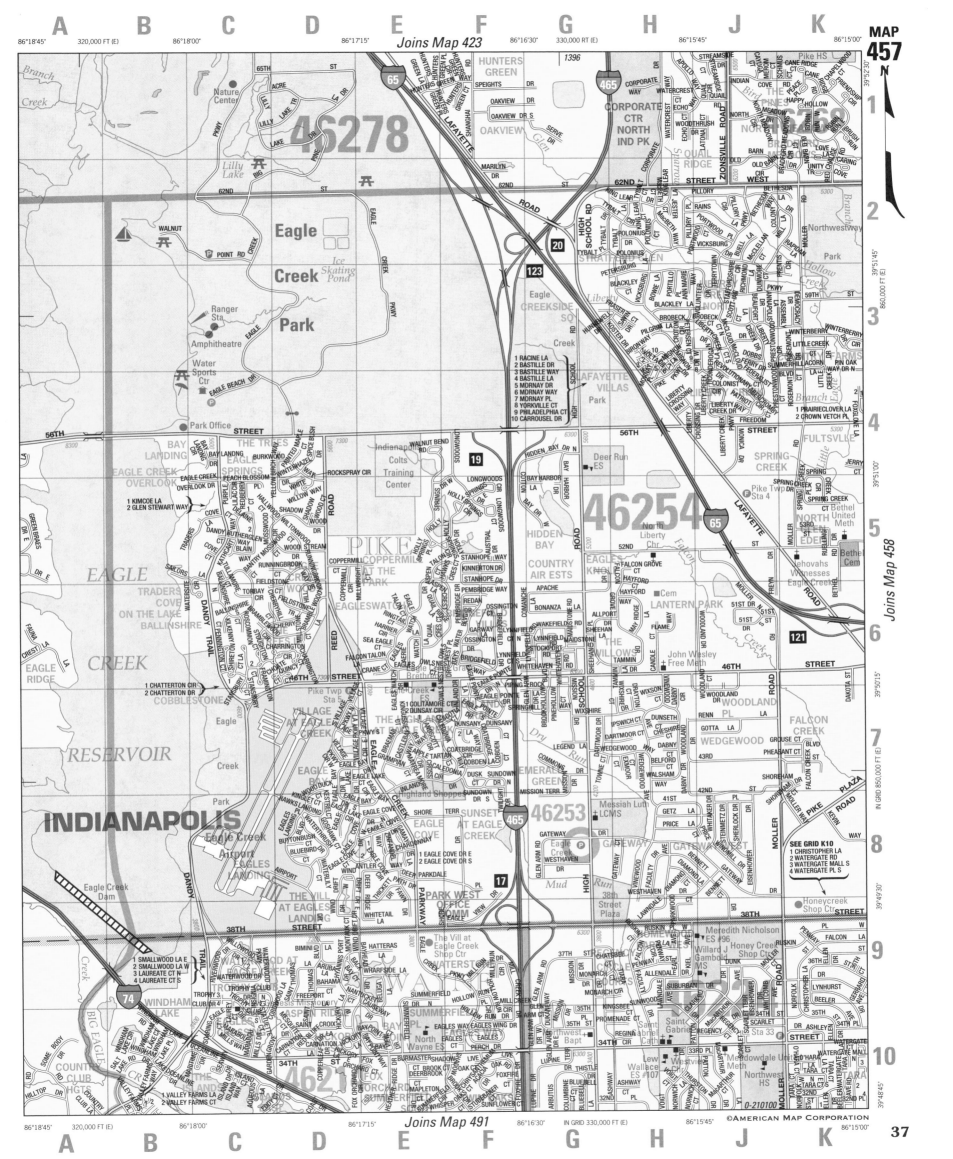

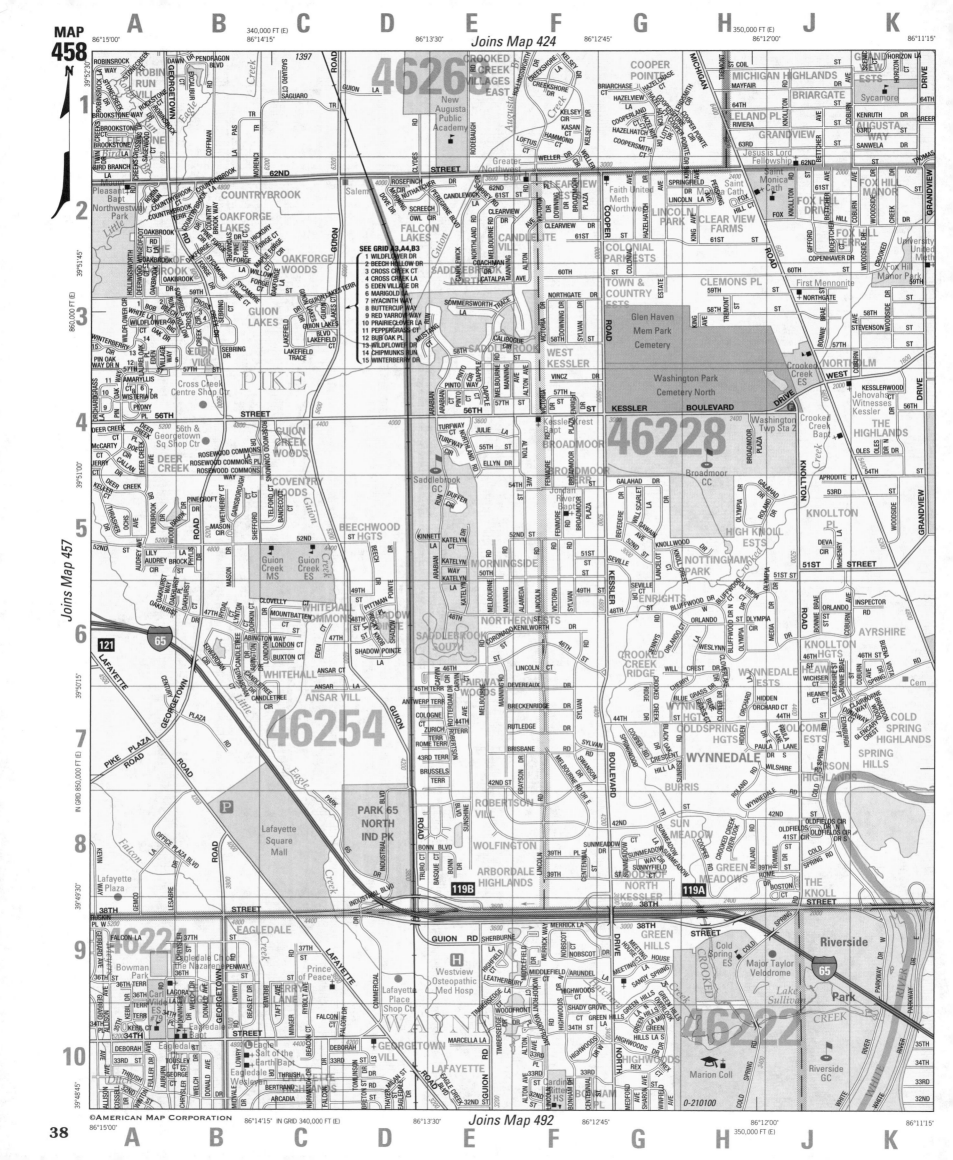

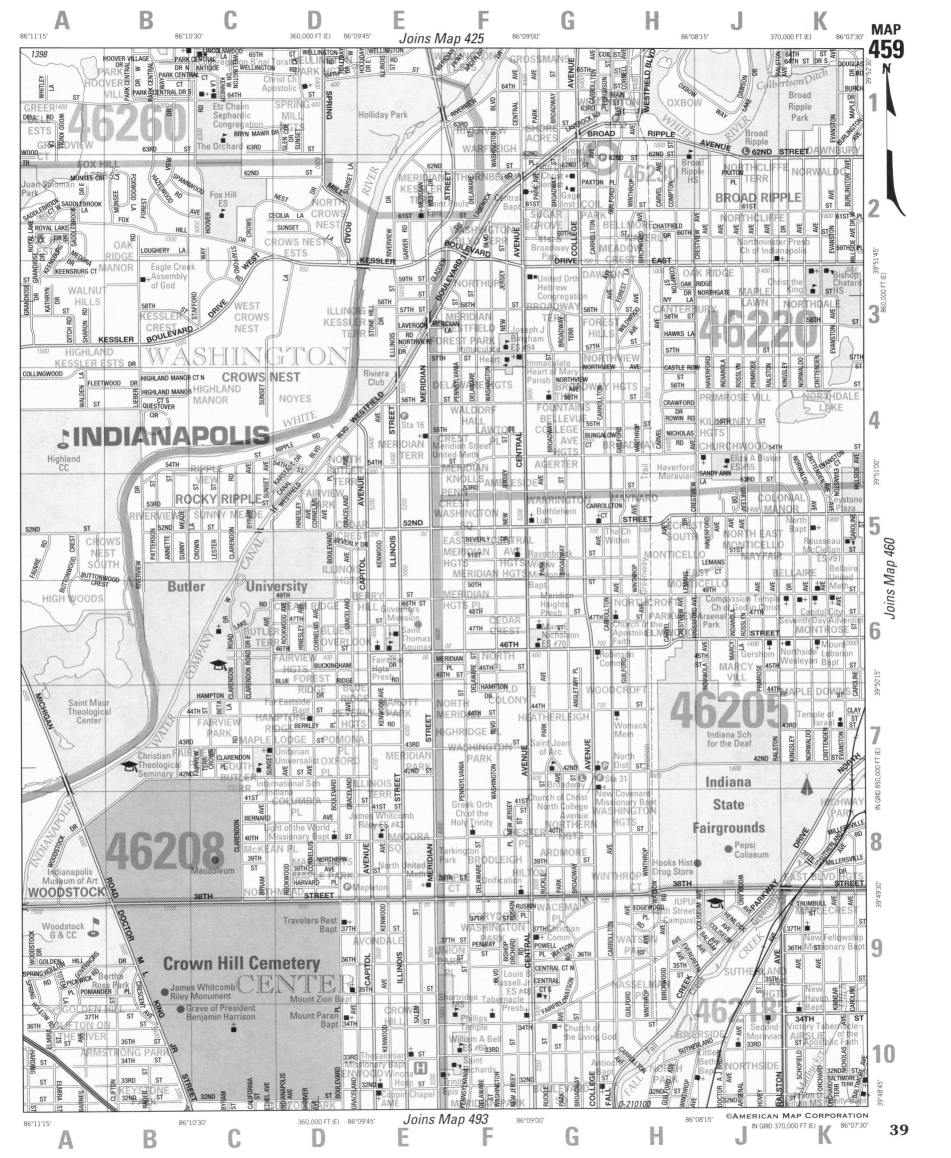

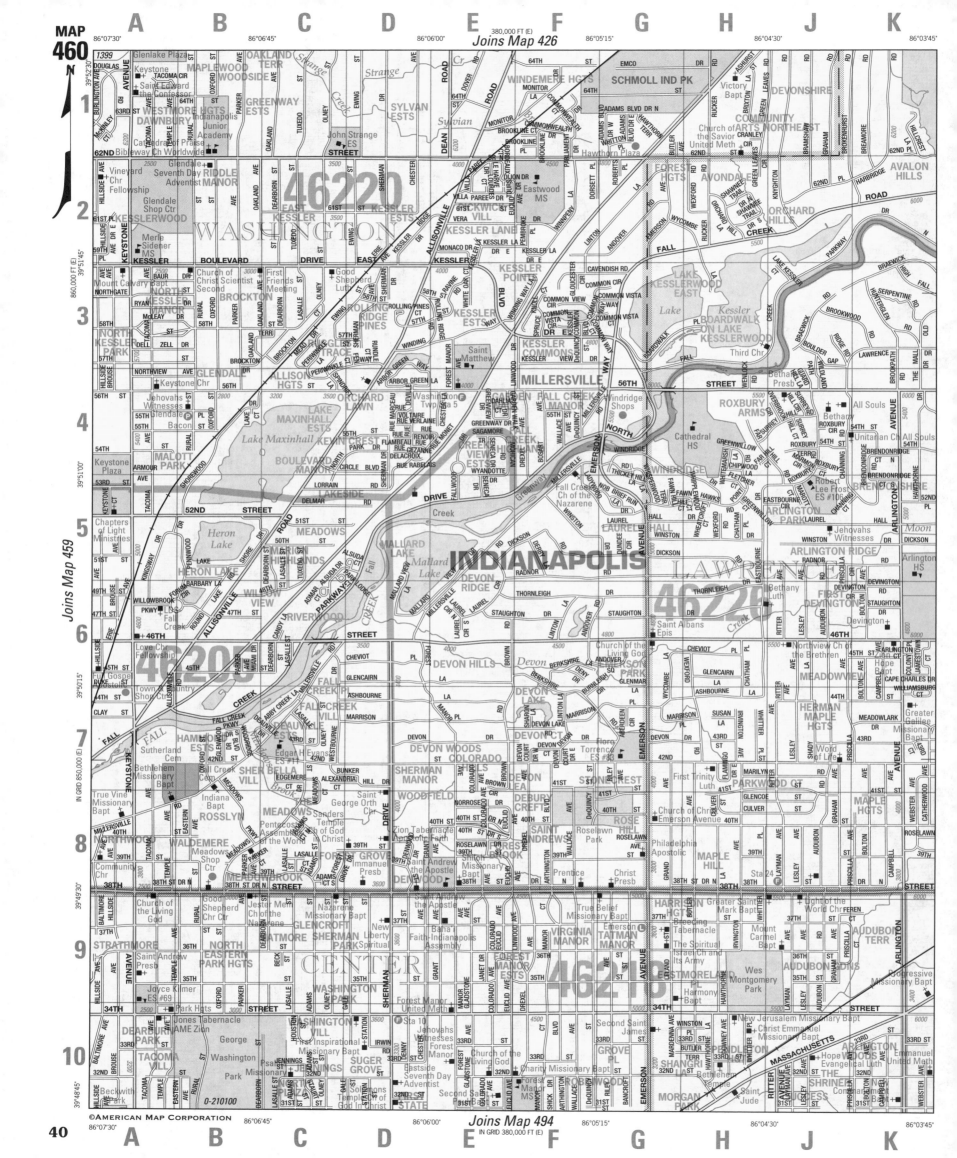

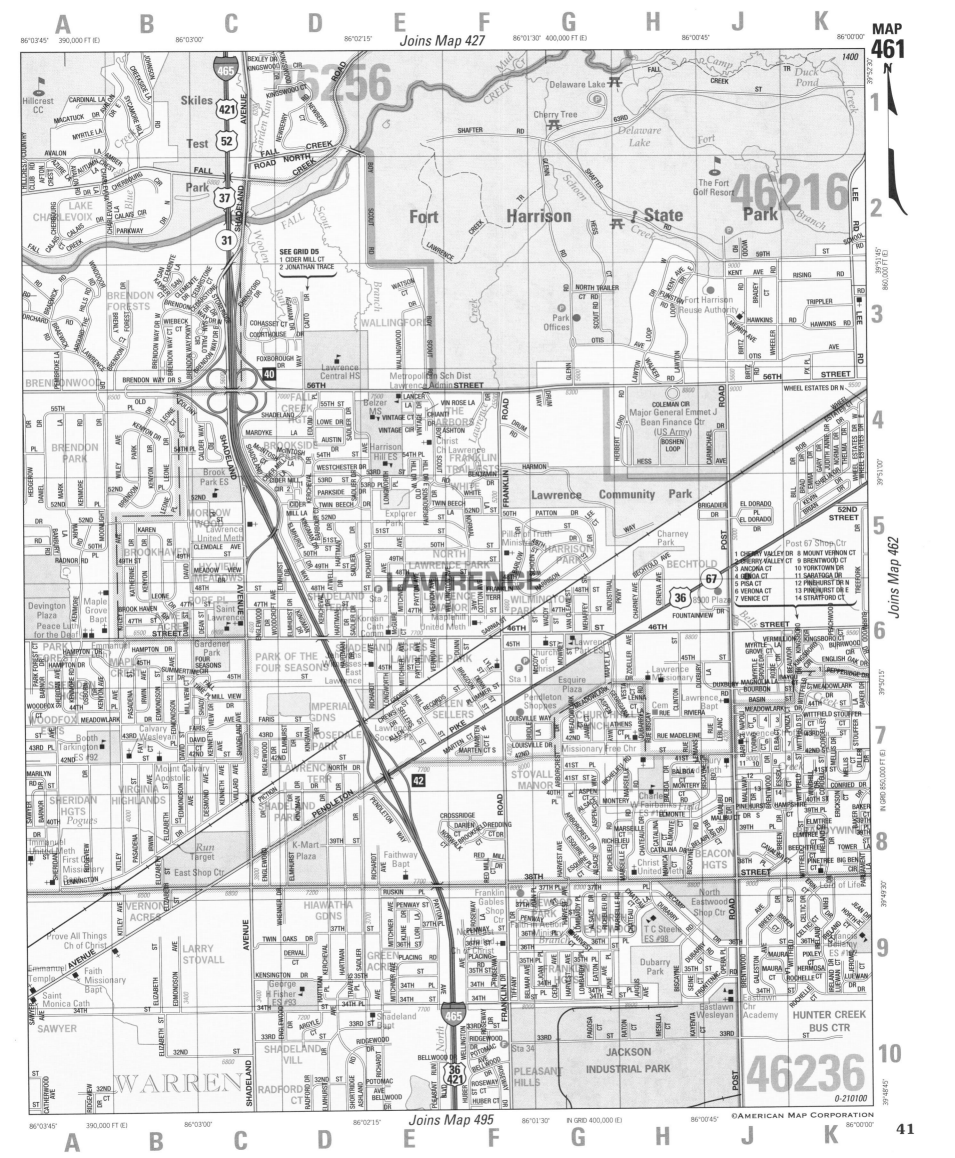

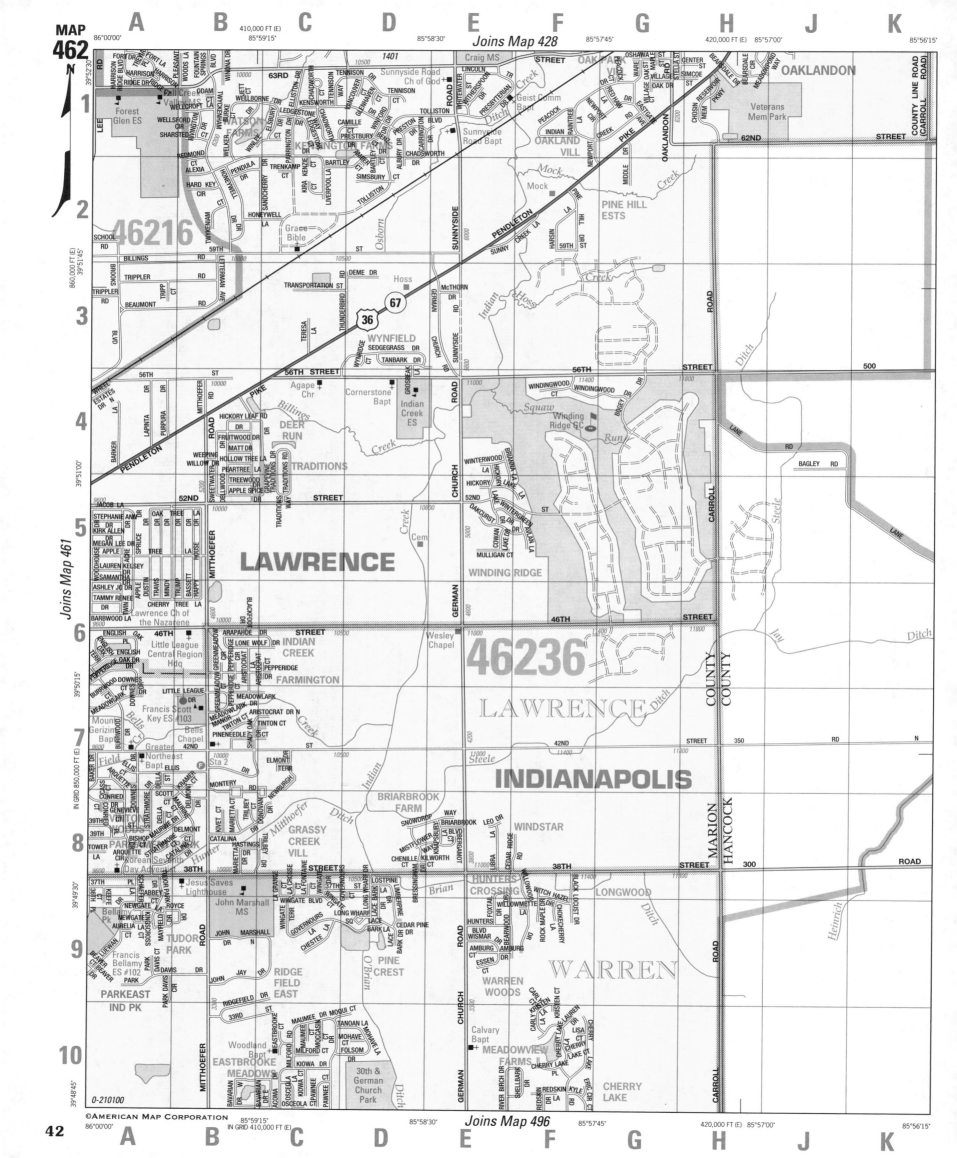

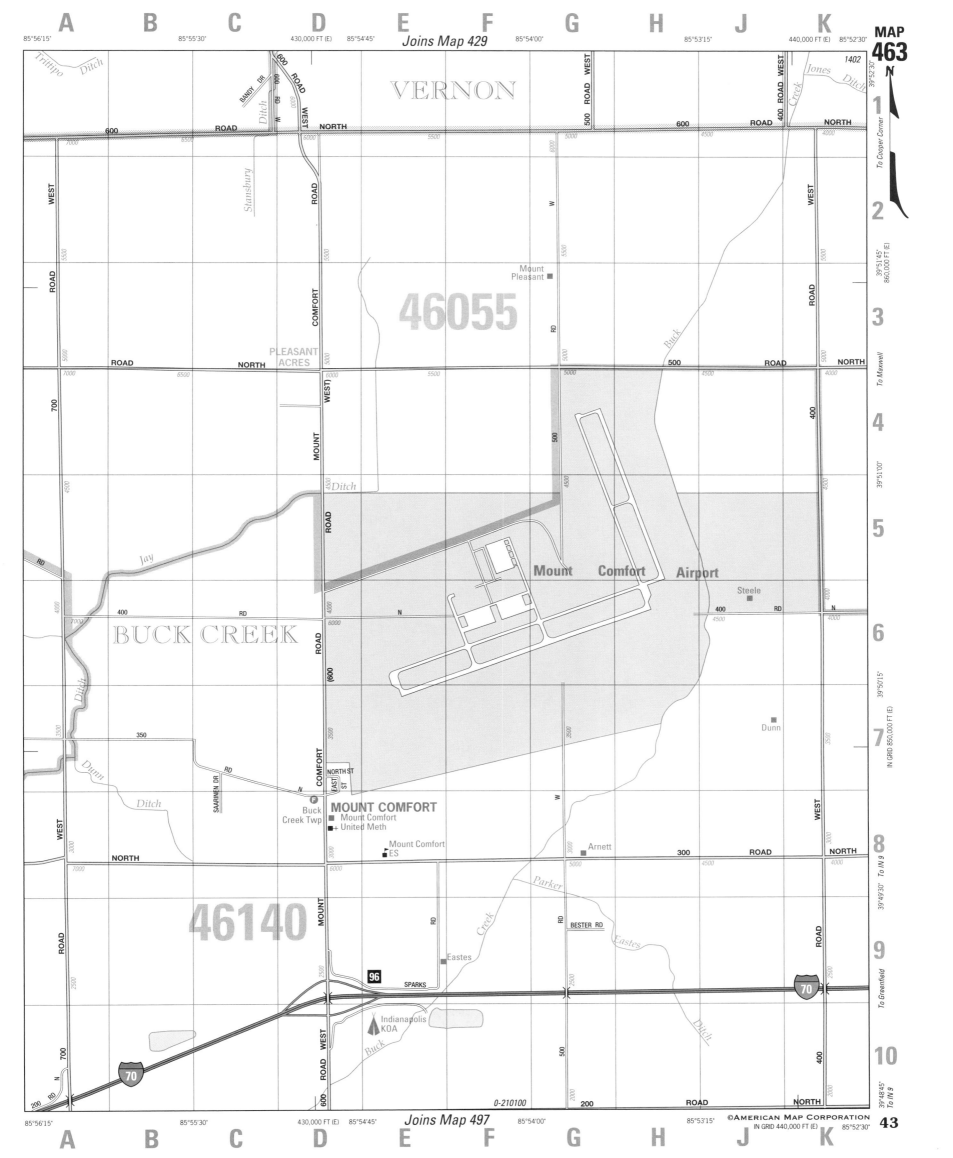

MAP
463

Joins Map 429

VERNON

46055

PLEASANT
ACRES

Mount
Pleasant ■

BUCK CREEK

Mount   Comfort   Airport

Steele ■

Dunn ■

NORTH ST

EAST ST

Buck
Creek Twp

MOUNT COMFORT
■ Mount Comfort
■+ United Meth

Mount Comfort
ES ■

Arnett ■

46140

96

Eastes

BESTER RD

SPARKS

Indianapolis
KOA

70

70

To Maxwell

To Greenfield
To IN 9

To IN 9

NOTES

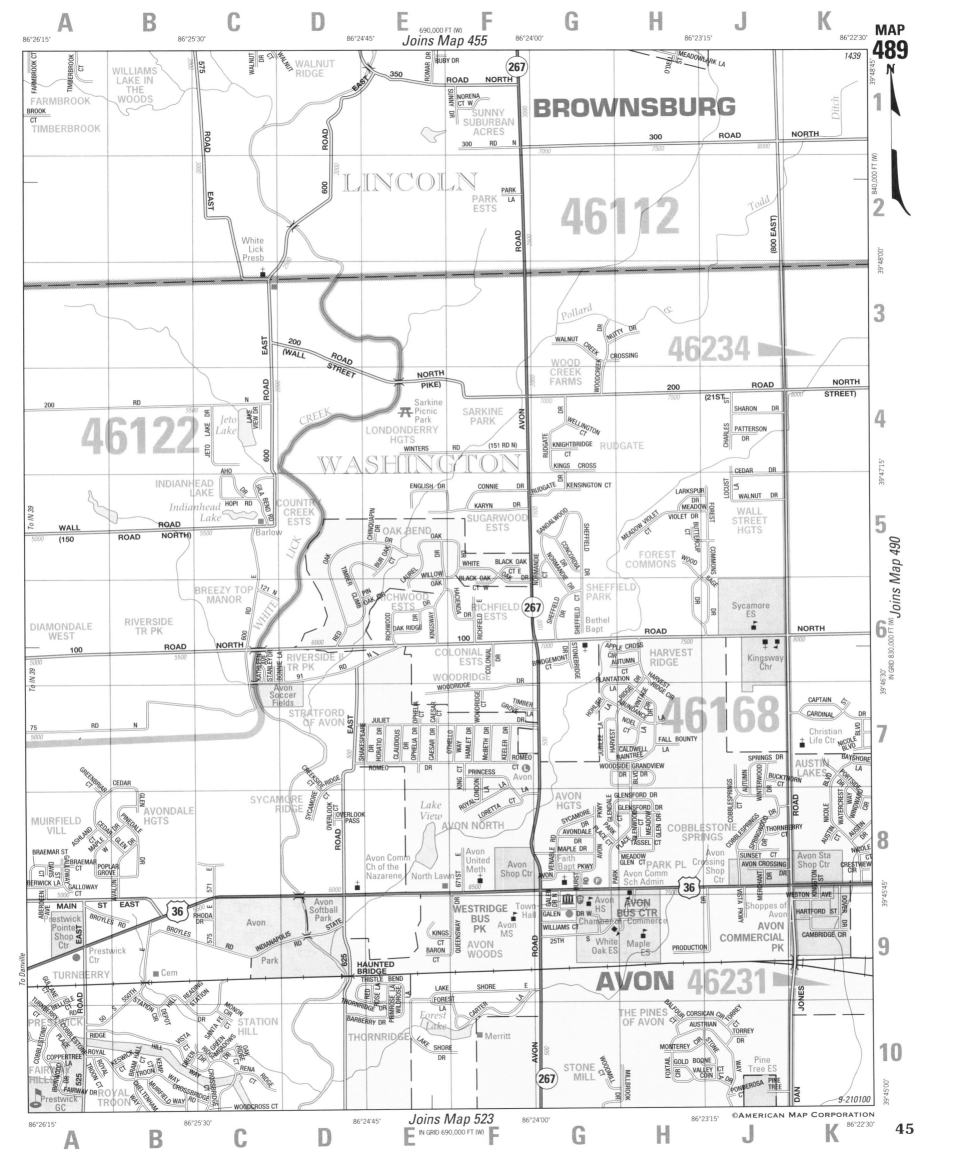

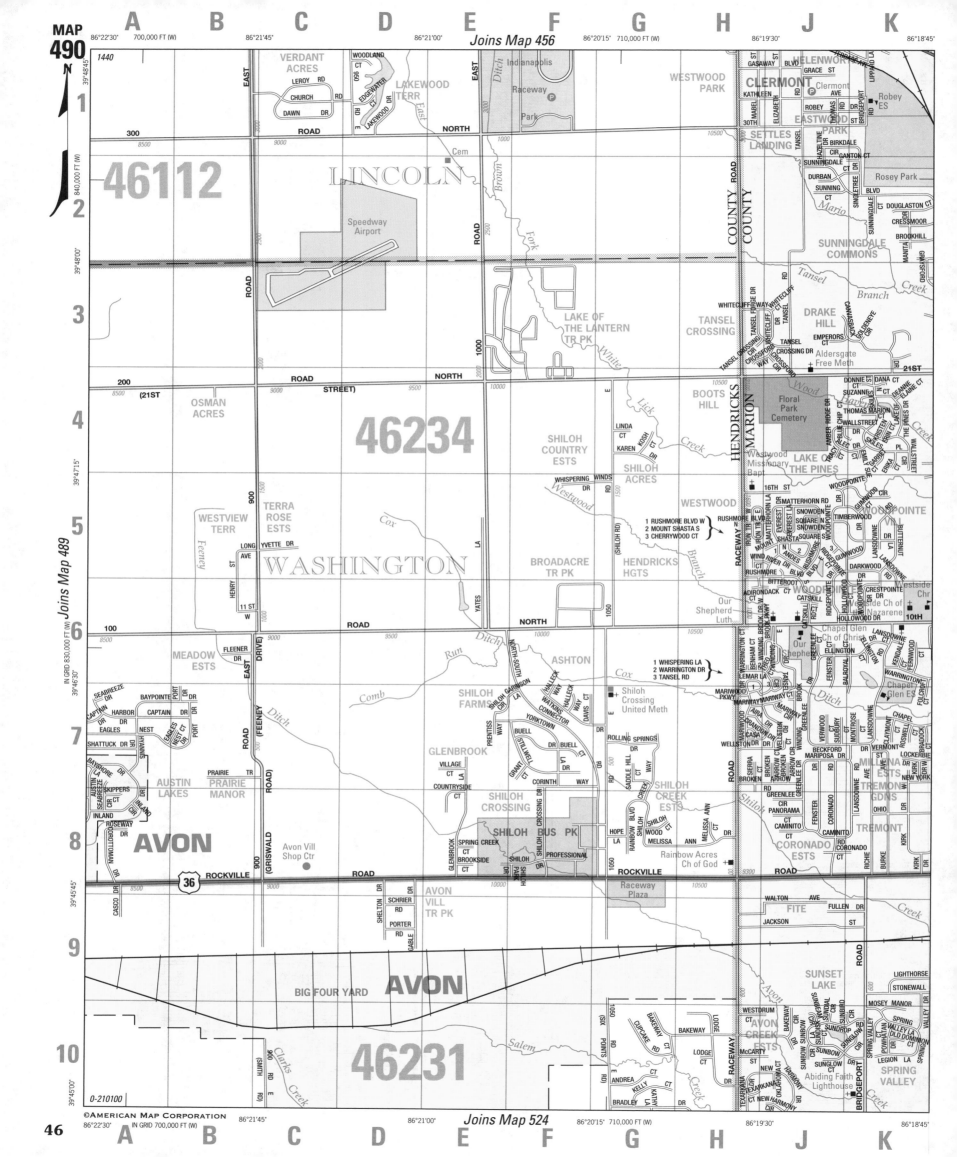

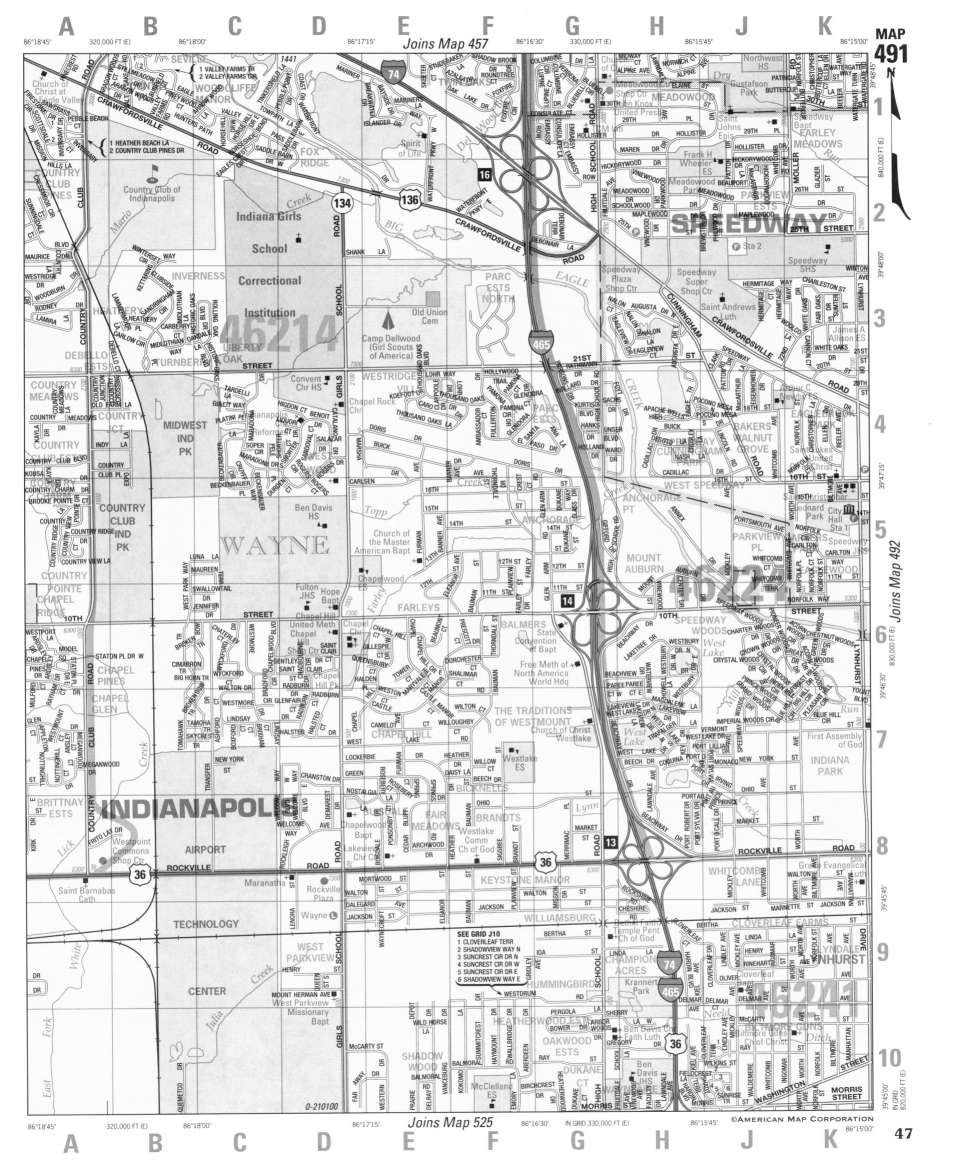

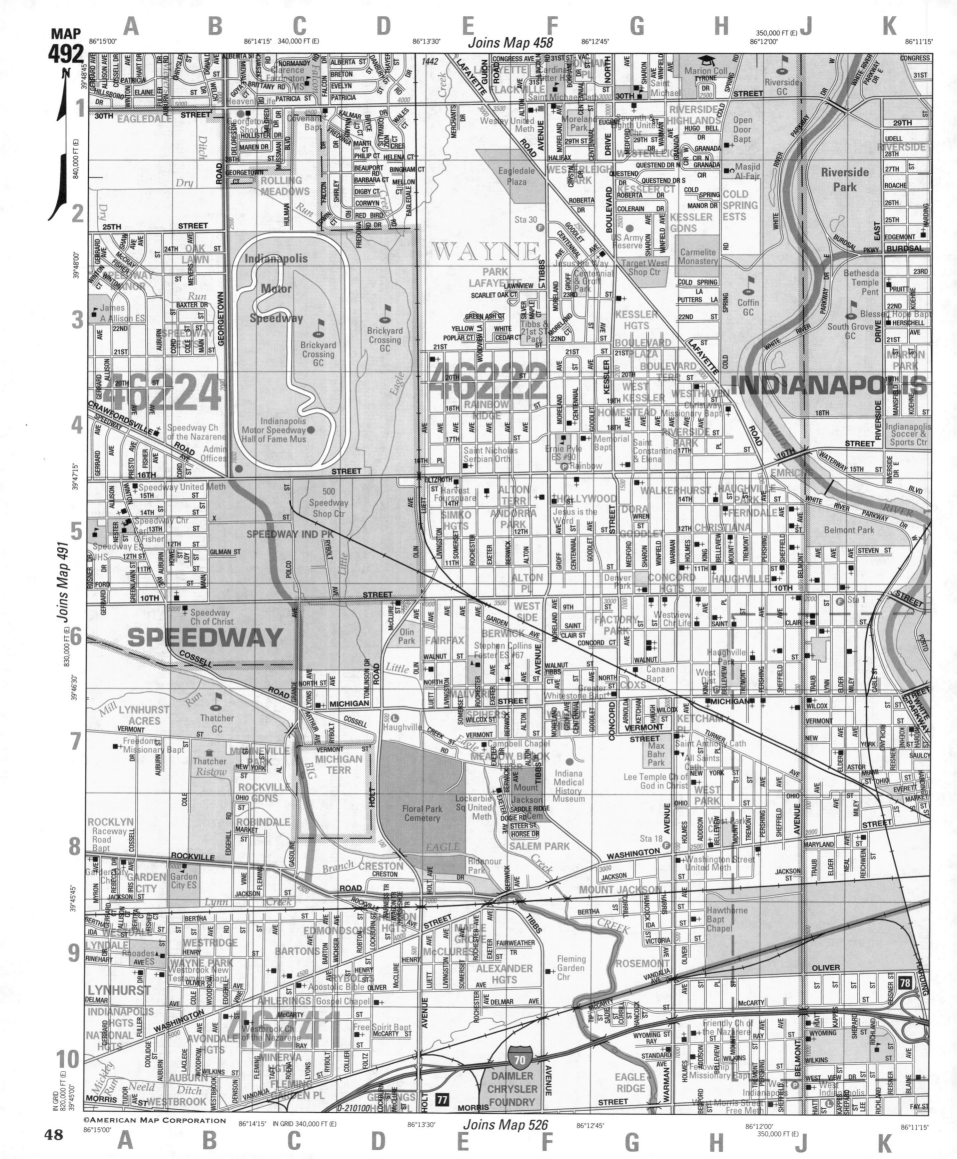

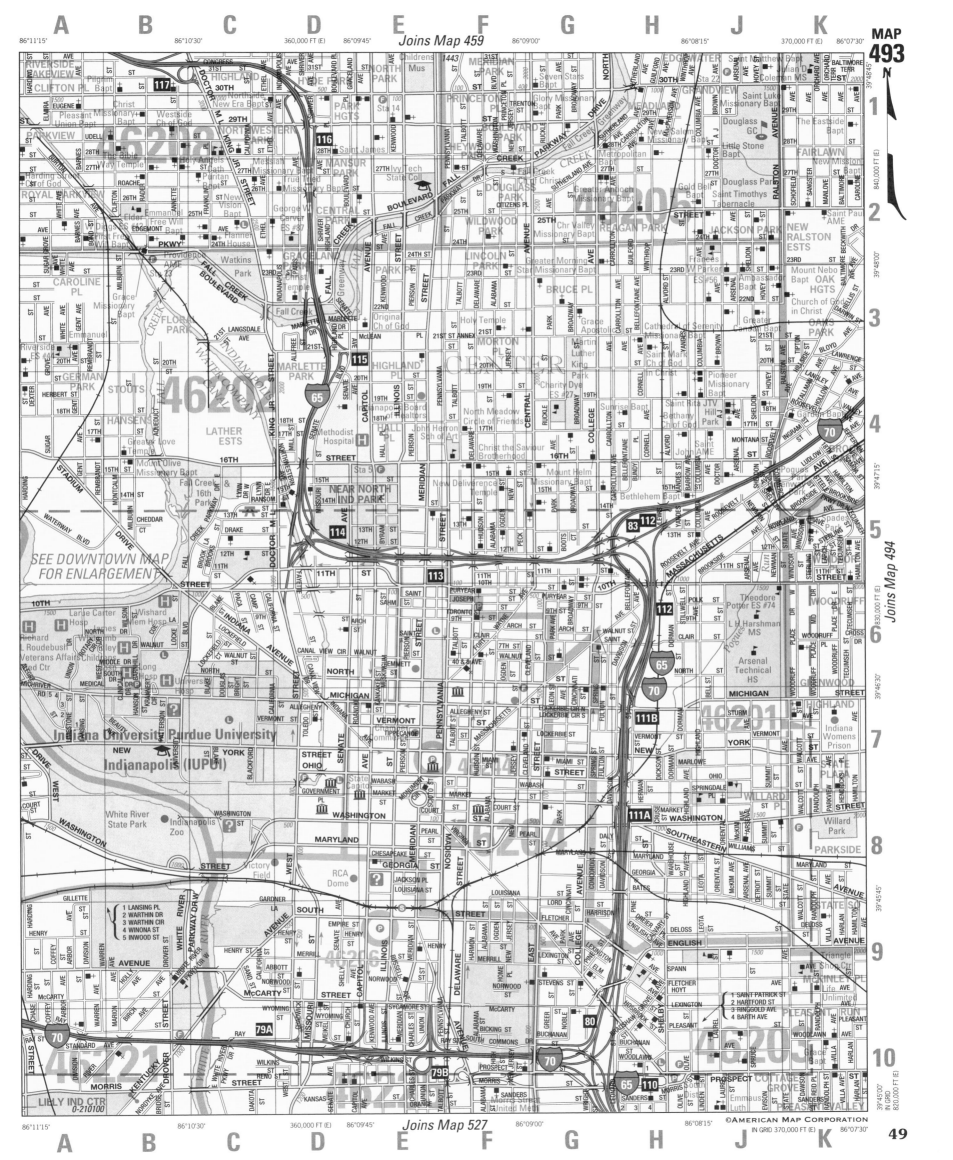

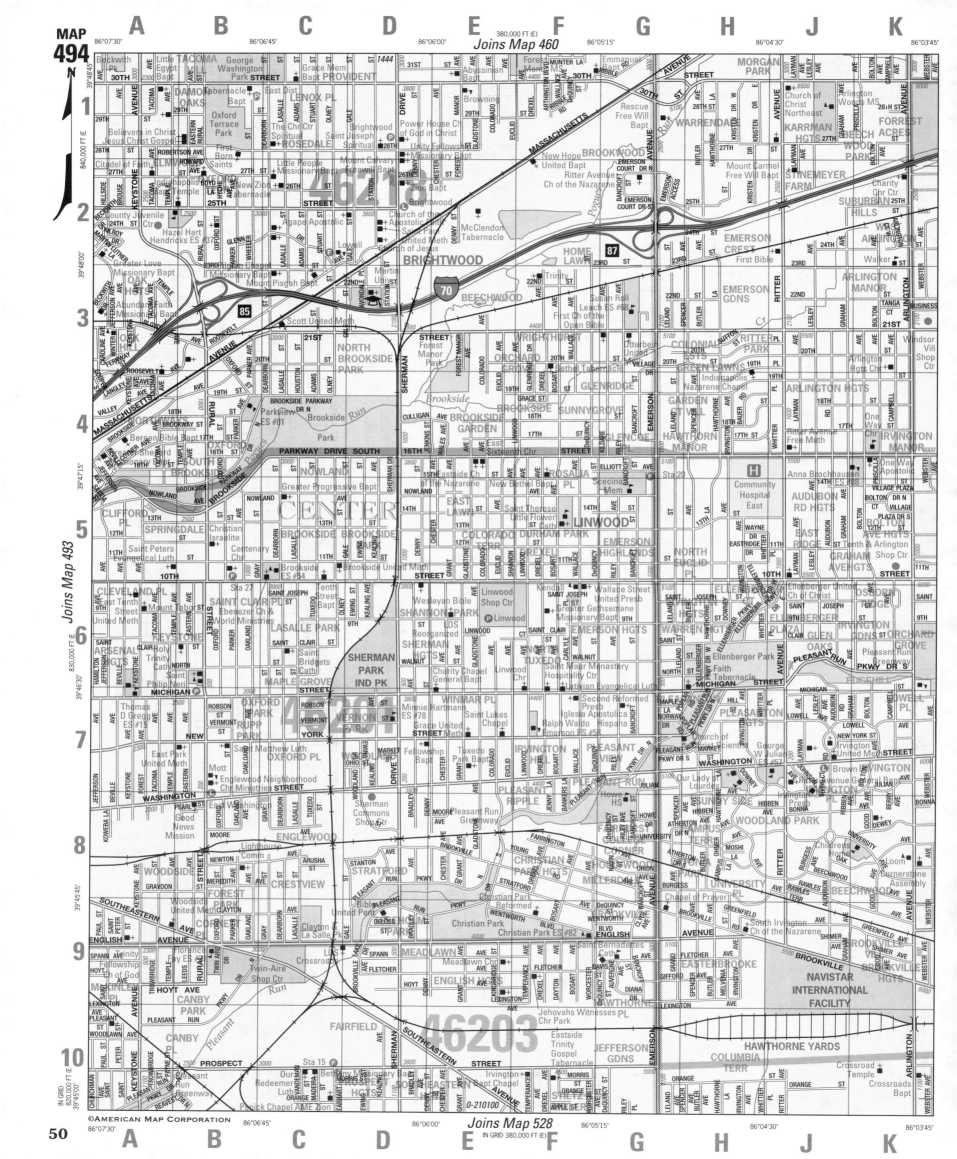

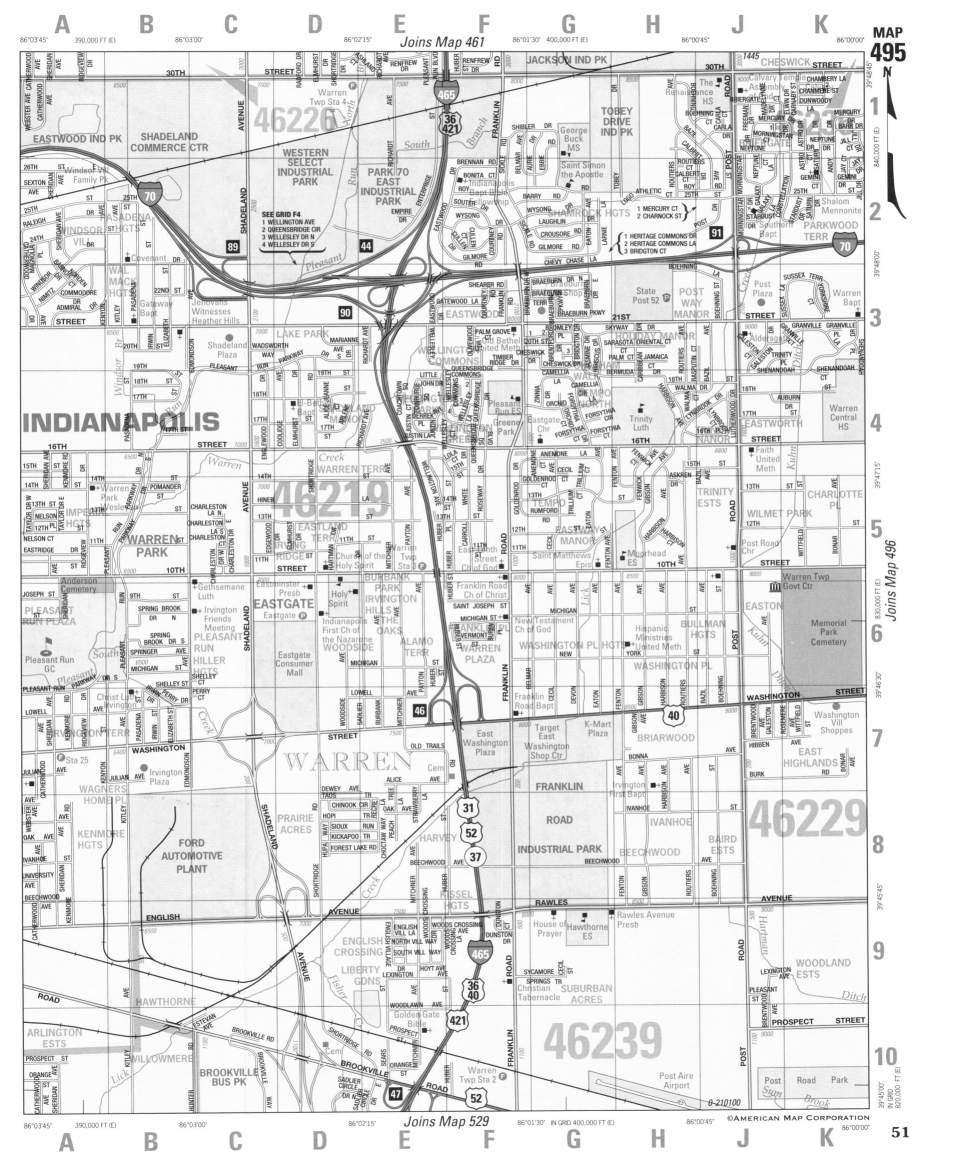

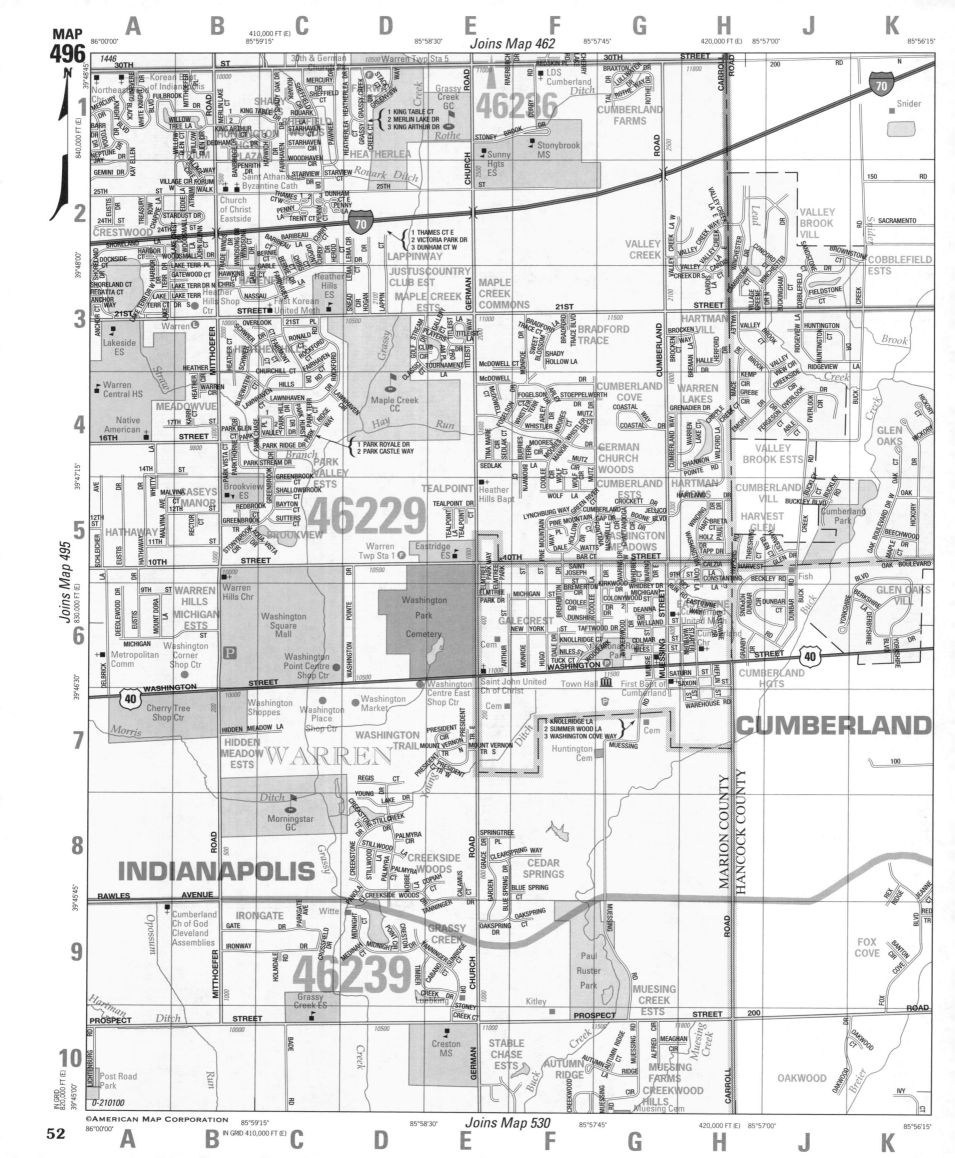

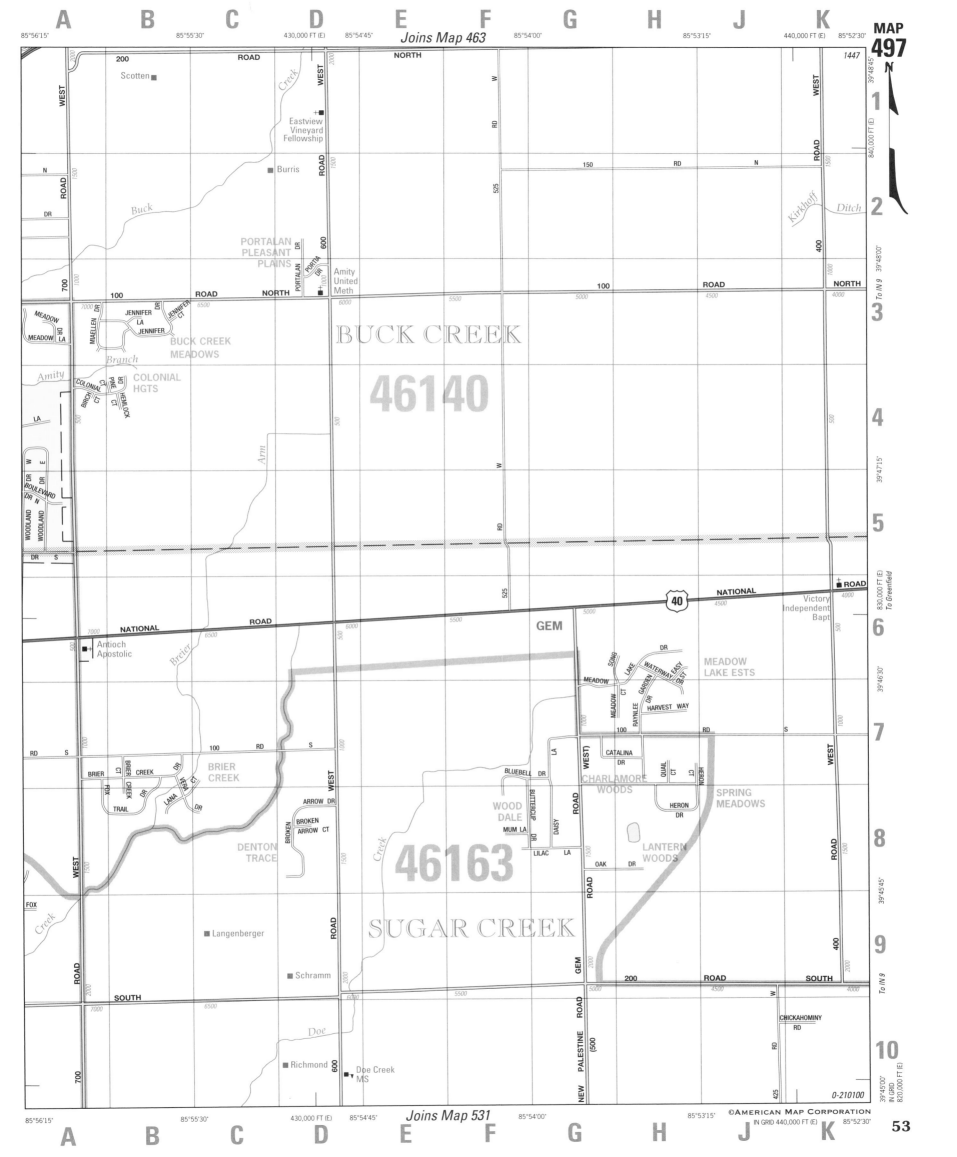

MAP 497

Joins Map 463

BUCK CREEK

46140

PORTALAN PLEASANT PLAINS

Eastview Vineyard Fellowship

Burris

Scotten

BUCK CREEK MEADOWS

COLONIAL HGTS

Amity United Meth

Antioch Apostolic

NATIONAL ROAD

40 NATIONAL

Victory Independent Bapt

GEM

MEADOW LAKE ESTS

BRIER CREEK

DENTON TRACE

46163

SUGAR CREEK

CHARLAMORE WOODS

SPRING MEADOWS

LANTERN WOODS

WOOD DALE

Langenberger

Schramm

Richmond

Doe Creek MS

CHICKAHOMINY RD

Joins Map 531

©AMERICAN MAP CORPORATION

53

0-210100

NOTES

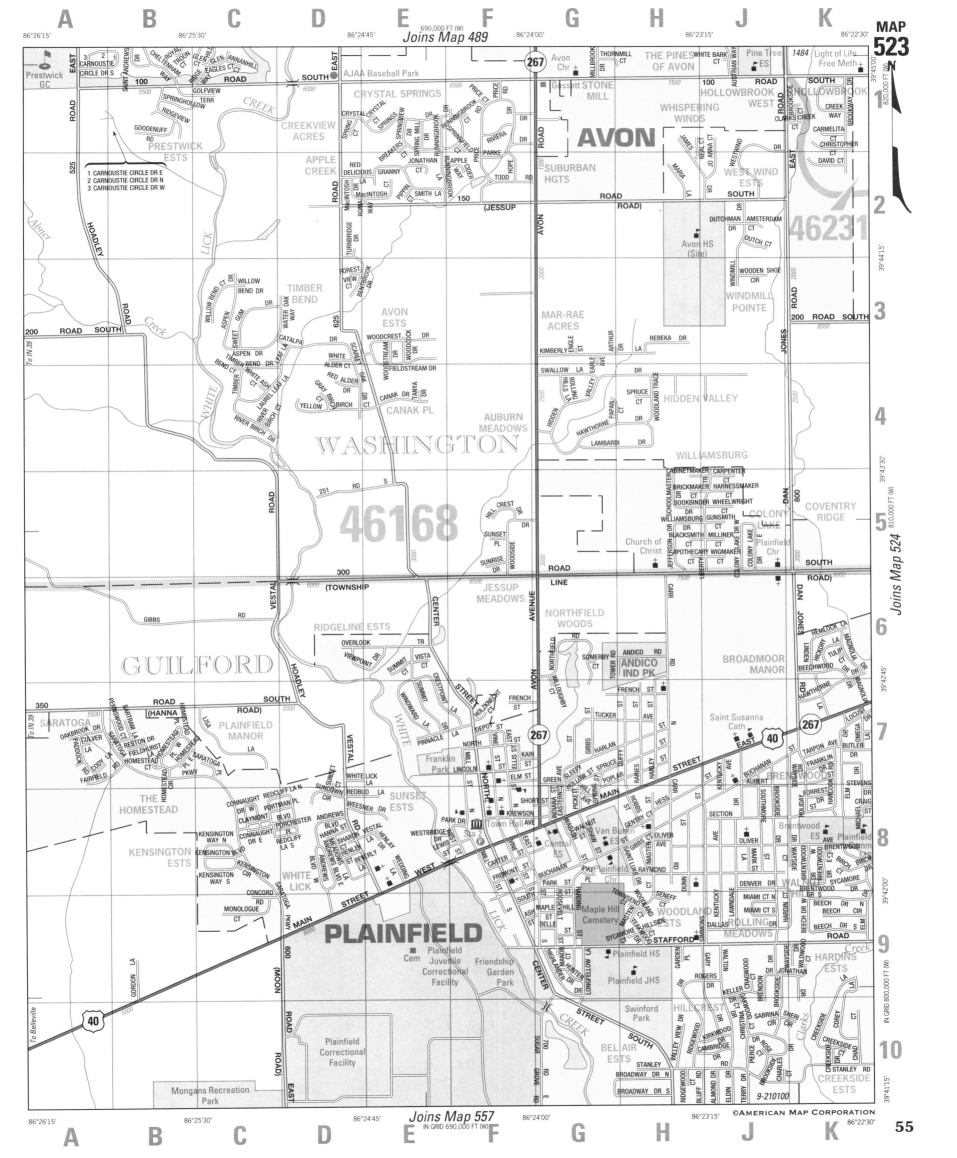

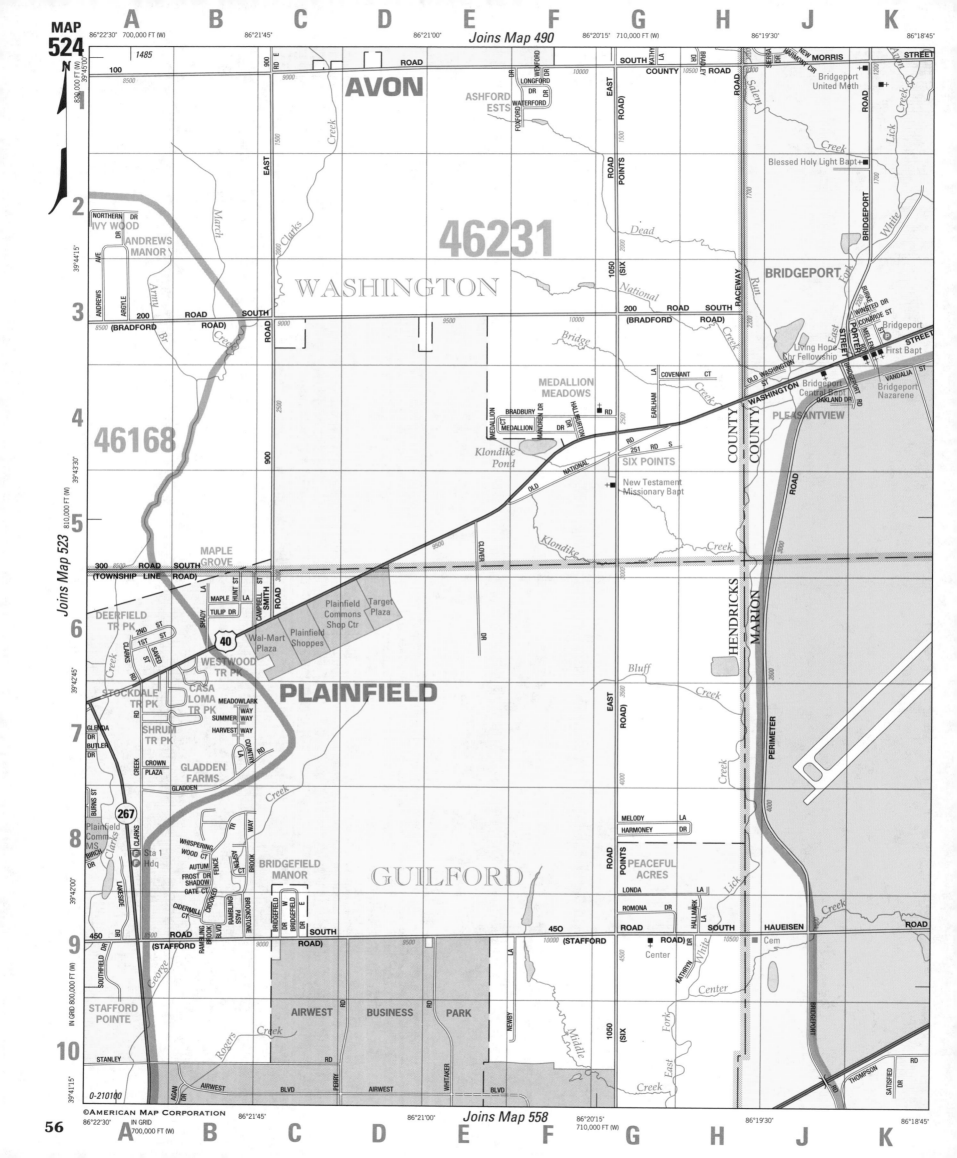

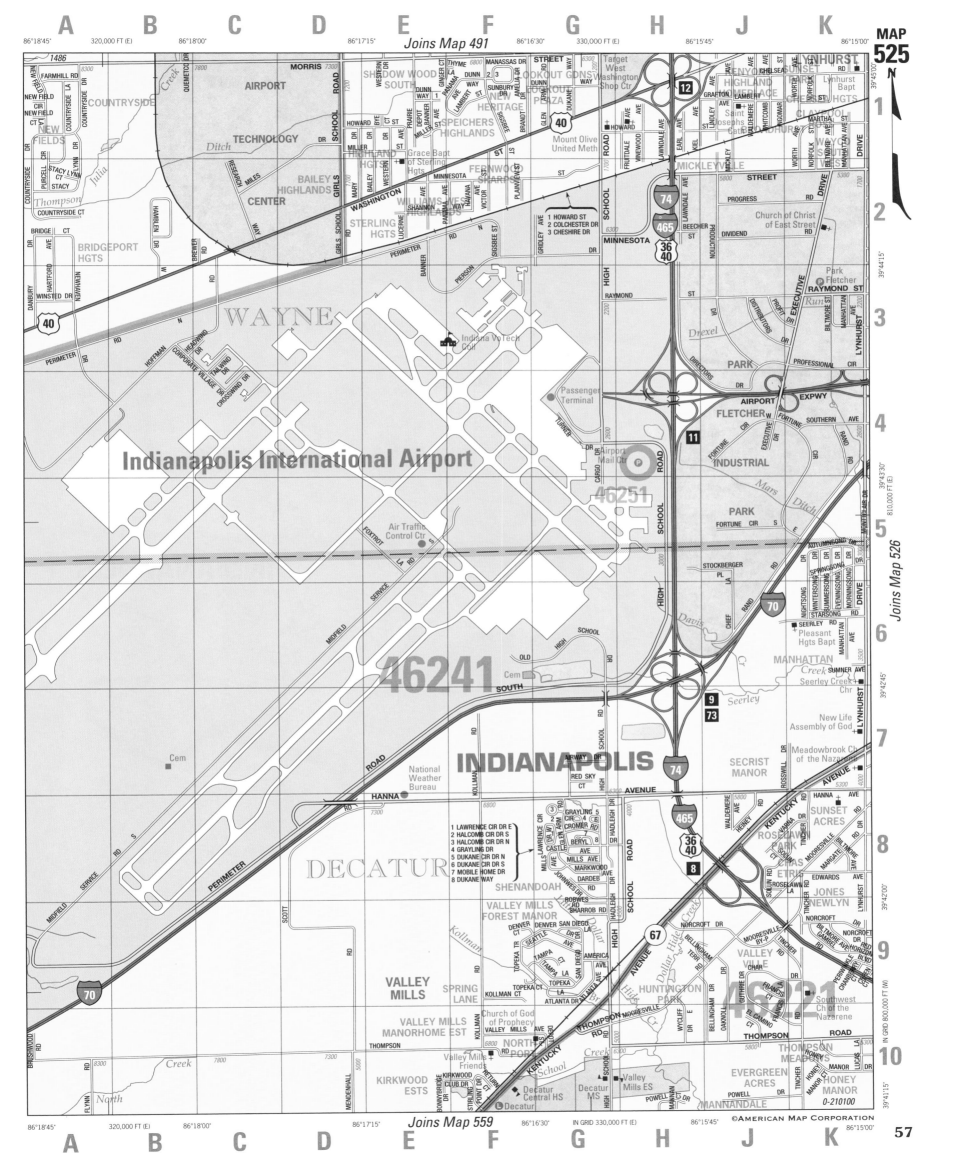

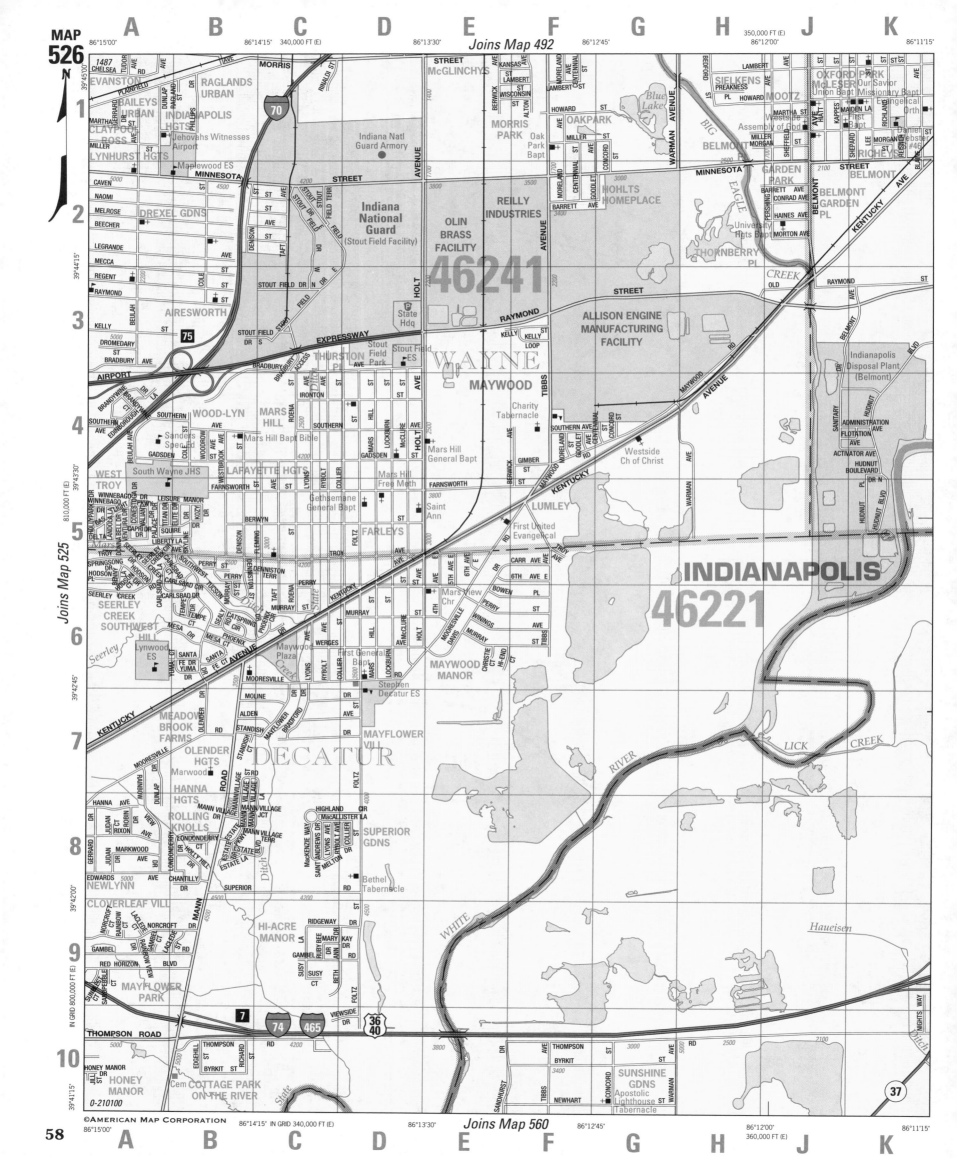

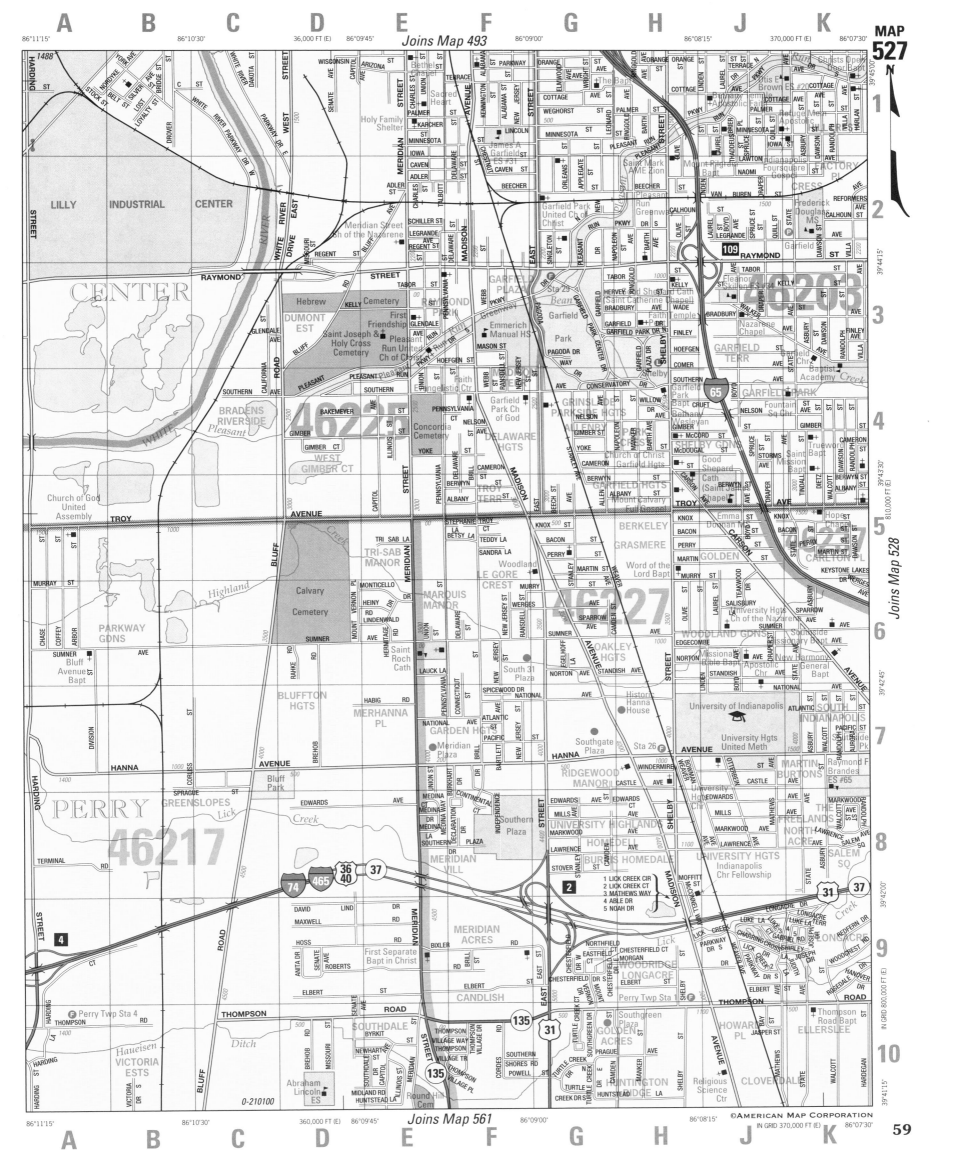

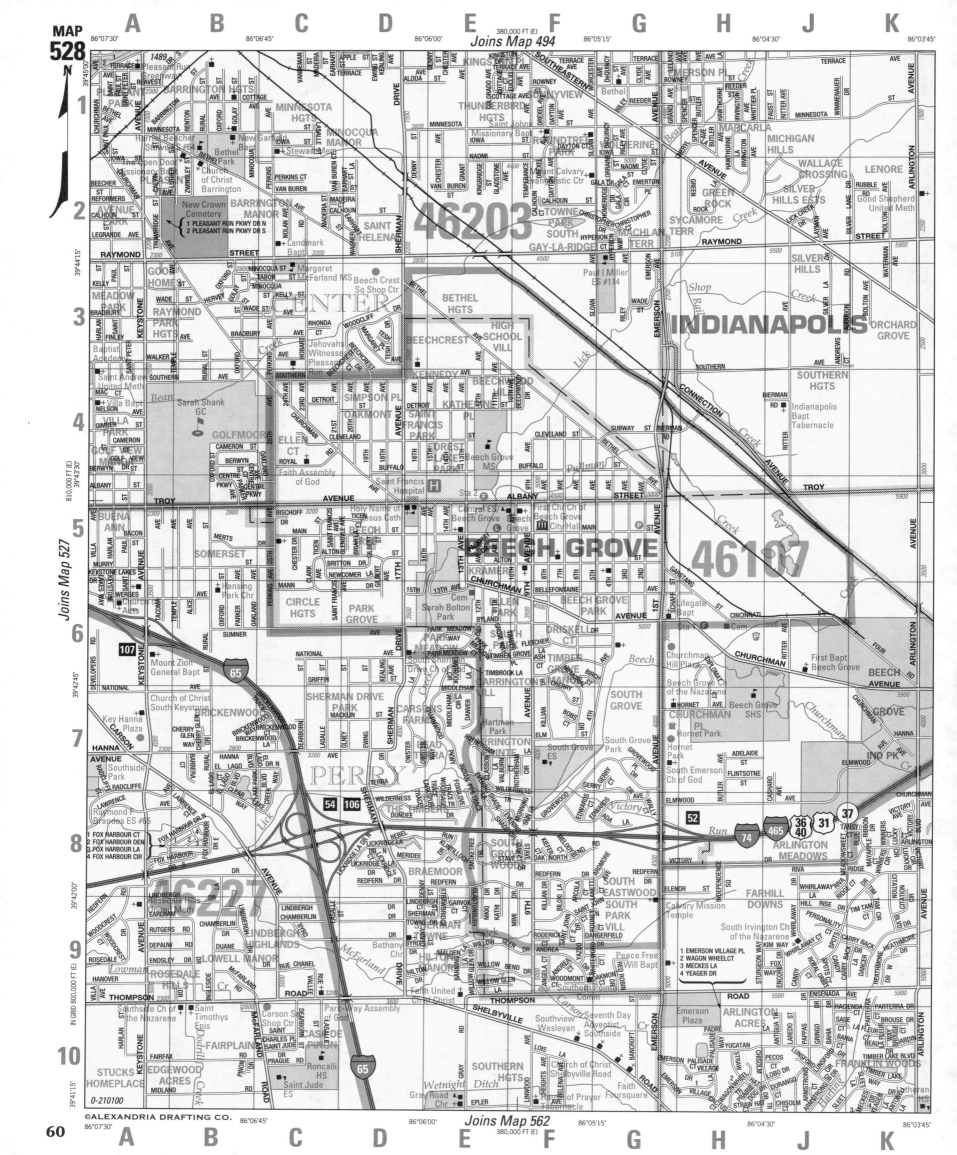

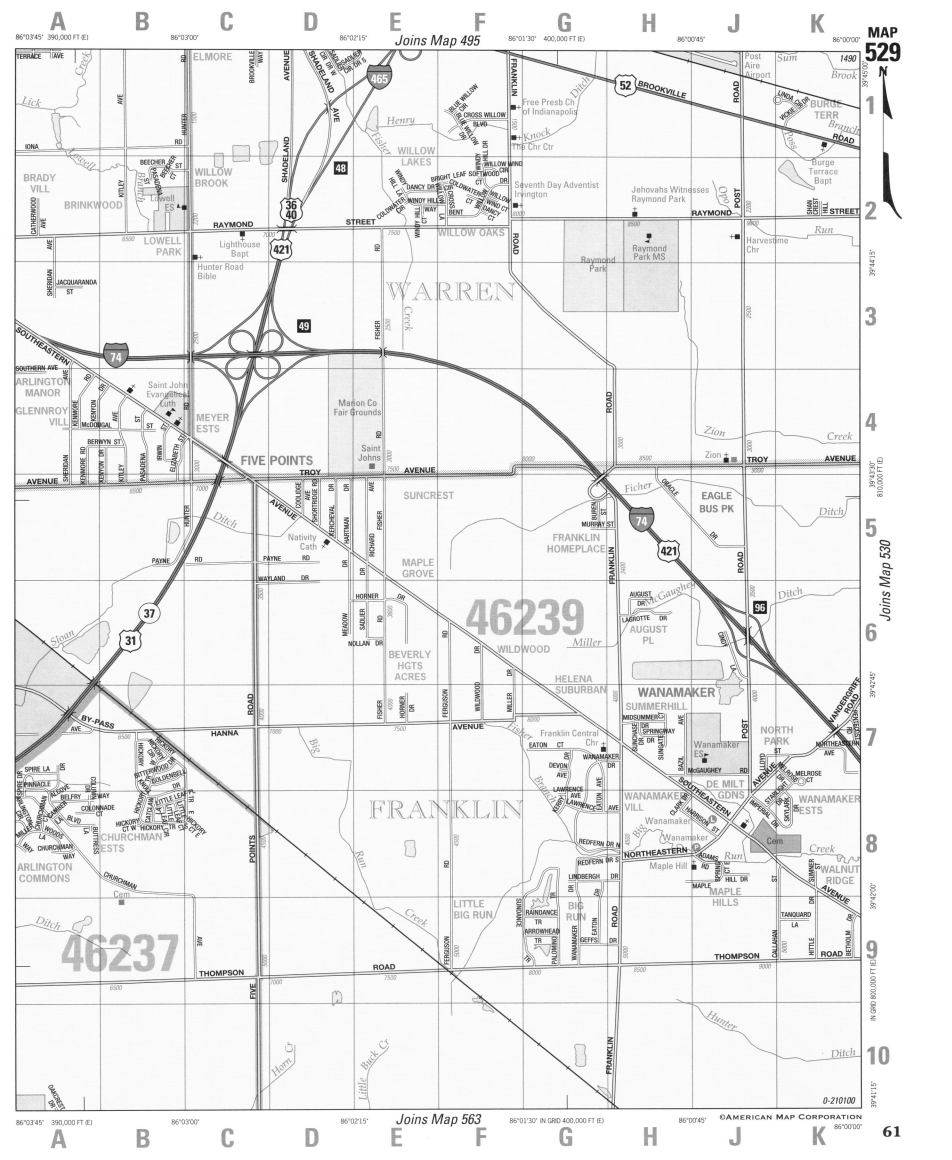

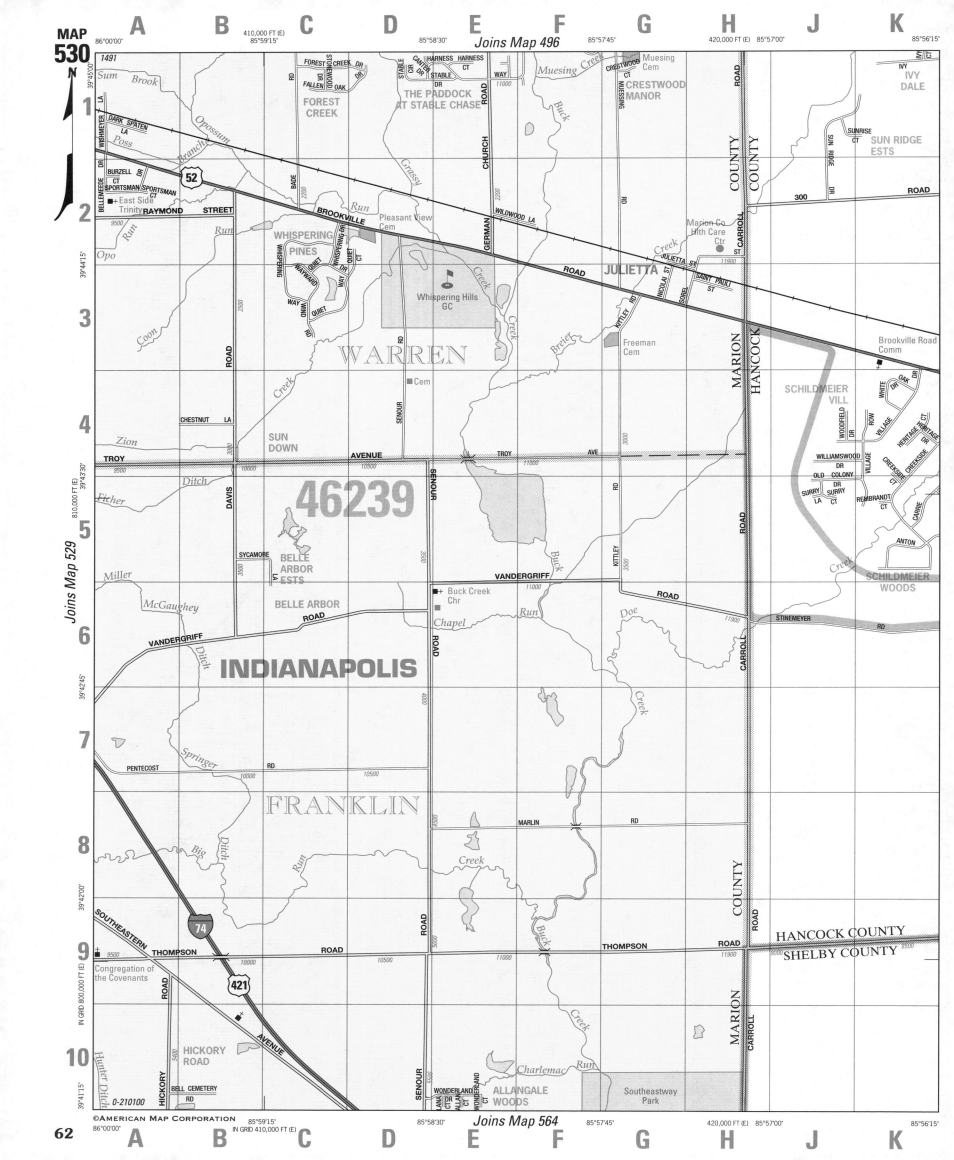

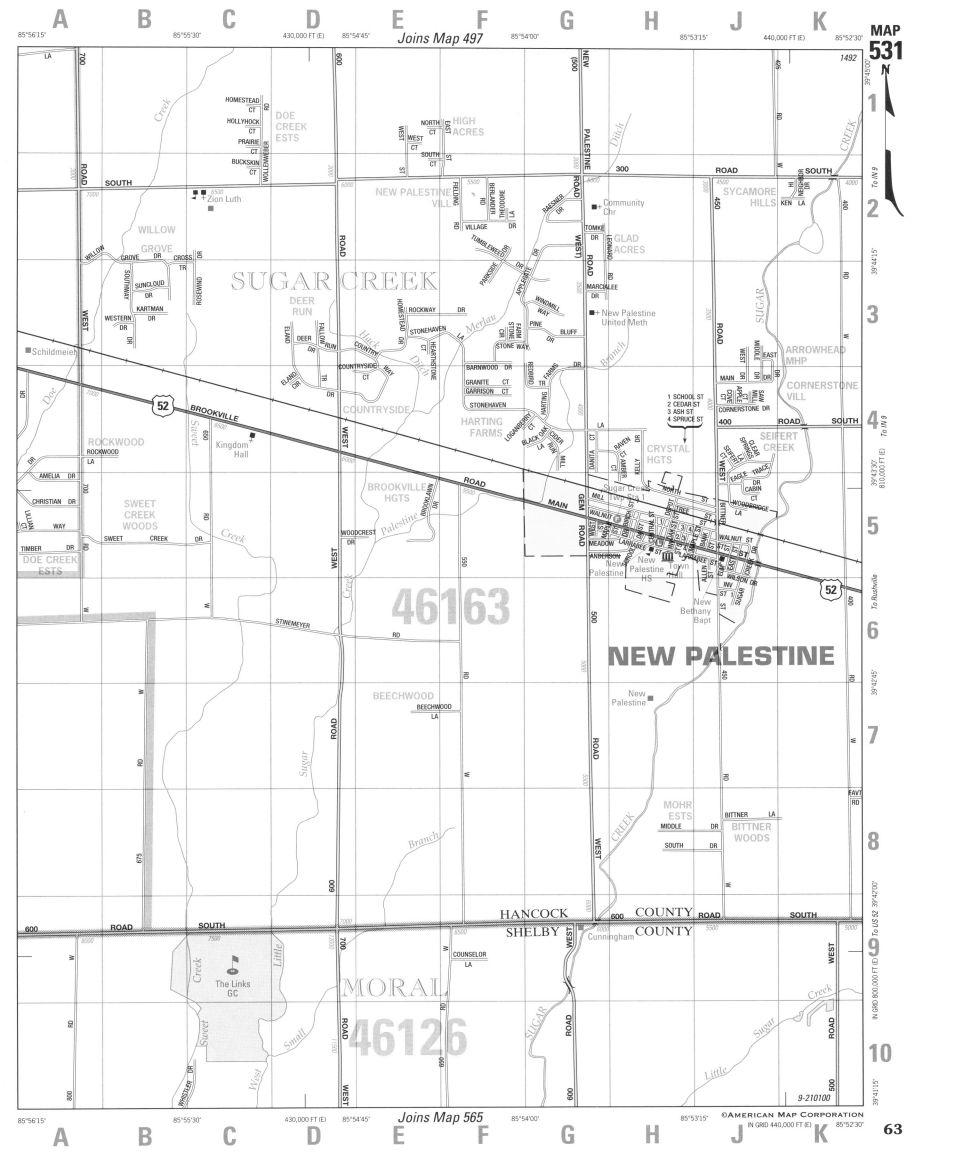

NOTES

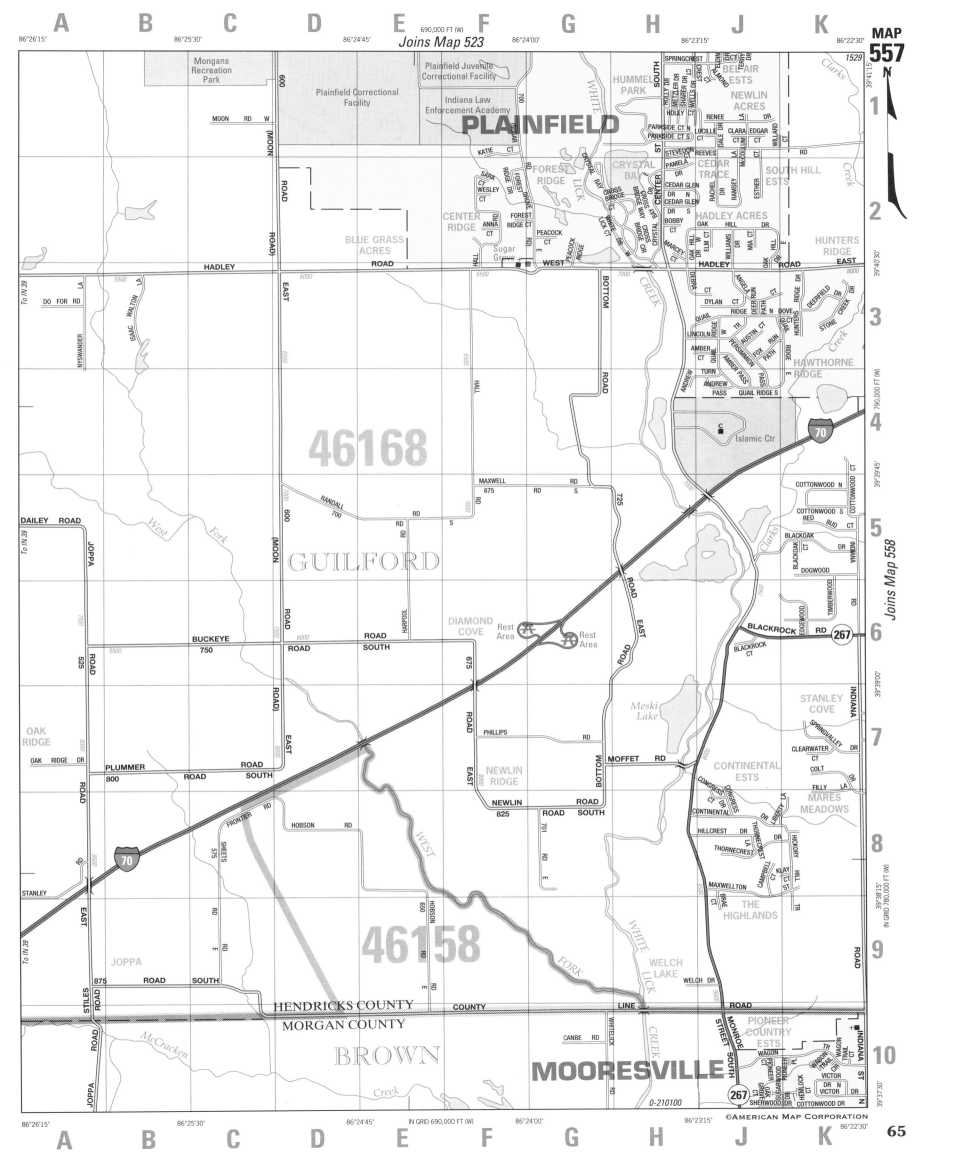

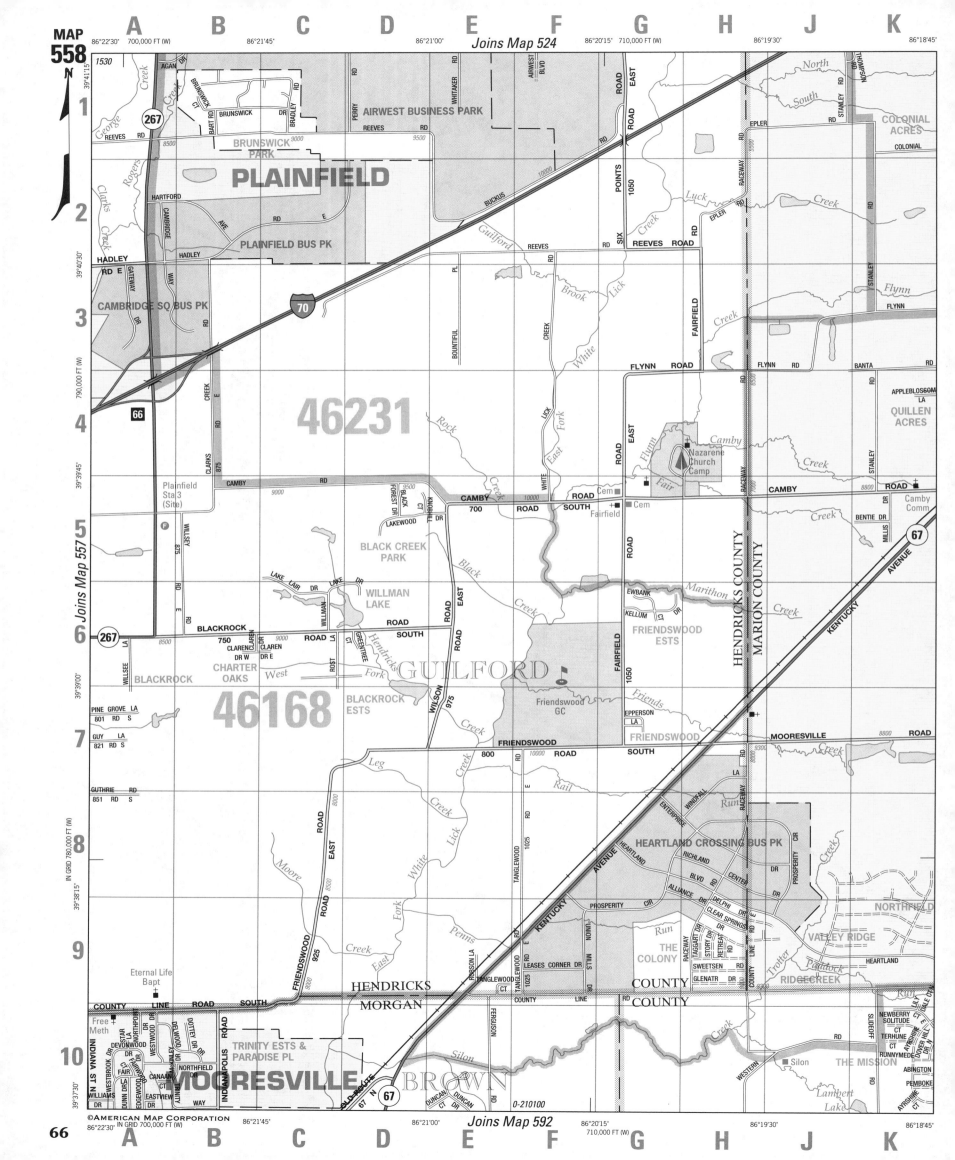

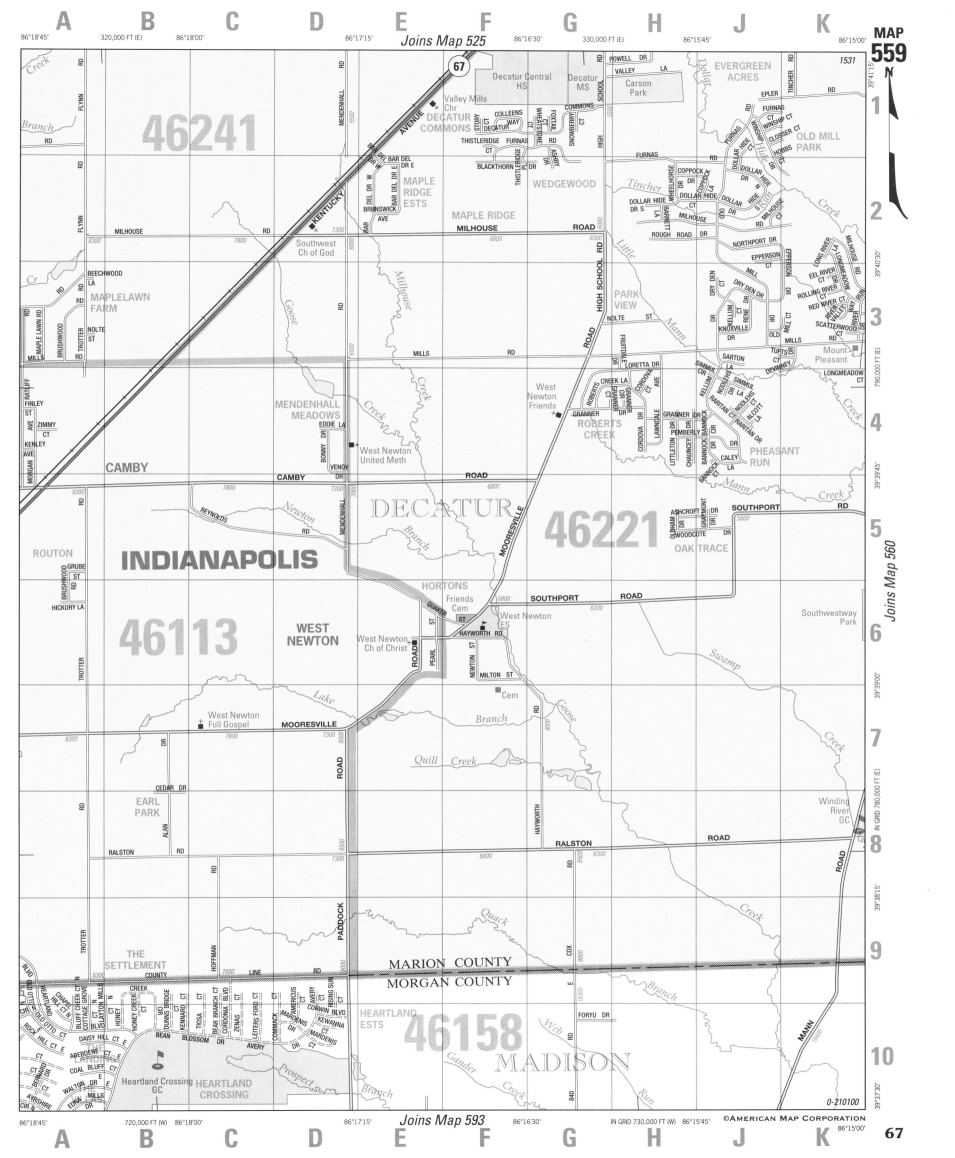

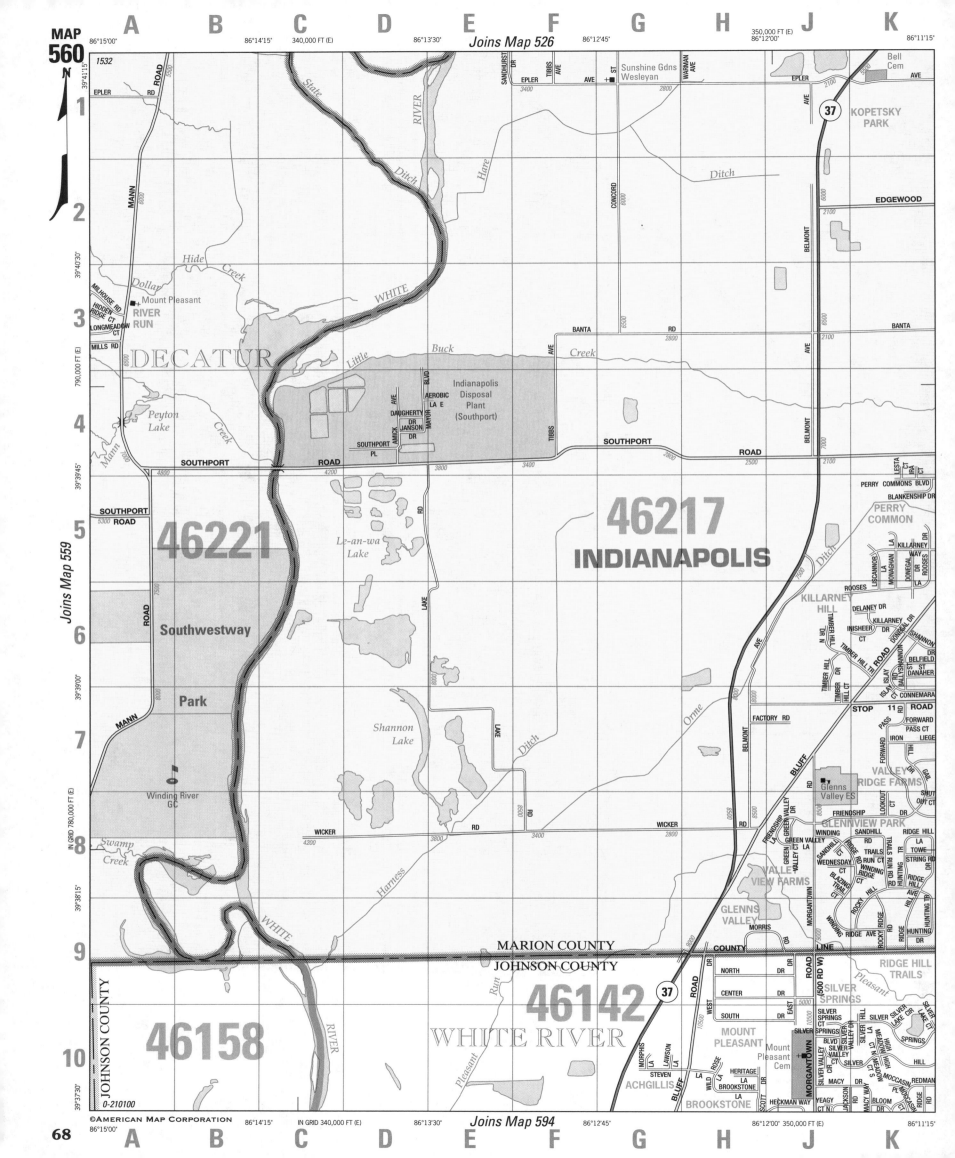

MAP
560
N

Joins Map 526

350,000 FT (E)

A B C D E F G H J K

1532

EPLER   RD

86°15'00"   86°14'15"   340,000 FT (E)   86°13'30"   86°12'45"   86°12'00"   86°11'15"

39°41'15"

1

Bell
Cem

Kopetsky
Park

37

EPLER

Sunshine Gdns
Wesleyan

SANDHURST DR

EPLER

TIBBS AVE

AVE

ST

WARMAN AVE

AVE

3400   2800

2100

MANN

ROAD

6000

Edgewood

BELMONT

2100

2

Ditch

CONCORD

6000

Hide   Creek

State   RIVER

Dollar

Mount Pleasant

RIVER
RUN

MILHOUSE RD

HIDDEN
RIDGE CT

LONGMEADOW
CT

Ditch

WHITE

RIVER

BANTA

RD

BANTA

6500   2800   6500   2100

3

DECATUR

MILLS RD

6500

790,000 FT (E)

Little   Buck   Creek

Peyton
Lake

Creek

MANN

6000

SOUTHPORT   Indianapolis
Disposal
Plant
(Southport)

AVE   BLVD
AEROBIC
LA E

DAUGHERTY
DR   JANSON
DR

AMICK

MAYOR

SOUTHPORT
PL

TIBBS

AVE

BELMONT

7000

4

39°39'45"

SOUTHPORT   ROAD   SOUTHPORT   ROAD

4800   4200   3800   3400   2800   2500   2100

5300

SOUTHPORT
ROAD

ROAD

7500

46221

Le-an-wa
Lake

RD

LAKE

46217
INDIANAPOLIS

Ditch

7500

LESTA
CT   IRA
CT

PERRY COMMONS BLVD

BLANKENSHIP DR

PERRY
COMMON

5

39°39'00"

Southwestway

MANN

8000

Park

Winding River
GC

8000

LAKE

Shannon
Lake

8000

ORME

BELMONT

AVE

4000

8000

KILLARNEY
HILL

LISCANNOR
LA   MONAGHAN
LA   KILLARNEY
WAY   DONEGAL
DR   ROOSES
LA

ROOSES

DELANEY DR

INISHEER
CT   KILLARNEY
DR

TIMBER
HILL   N
RD   DONEGAL DR

SHANNON
DR

BELFIELD
CT   ST
DANAHER

BALLYSHANNON

ISLAY
ST
CONNEMARA

6

780,000 FT (E)

IN GRID 780,000 FT (E)

Swamp
Creek

WHITE

Harness   Ditch

FACTORY RD

BLUFF

RD

8500   6500

0

STOP   11   ROAD

FORWARD
PASS   FORWARD
PASS CT

IRON   LIEGE

TIH

GAIL   SHUT
OUT CT

VALLEY
RIDGE FARMS

Glenns
Valley ES

7

39°38'15"

WICKER   RD   WICKER   RD

4200   3800   3400   2800

MORGANTOWN

BLUFF

LOOKOUT
CT

Friendship

GLENNVIEW PARK

WINDING
RIDGE

RIDGE HILL

SANDHILL
RD

TRAILS RUN RD

SANDHILL
CT

WEDNESDAY
CT   GREEN VALLEY
LA   GREEN VALLEY
CT   RIDGE
RUN CT

BLAZING
TRAIL
CT

WINDING
RIDGE
CT

LA
TOWE

STRING RD

RIDGE
HILL
RD

HUNTING
LA

AVE

8

39°37'45"

VALLEY
VIEW FARMS

GLENNS
VALLEY

MORGANTOWN

MORRIS

MORRIS
DR

WINDING
RIDGE AVE

ROCKY
HILL

ROCKY
RIDGE

RIDGE

HUNTING
DR

RIDGE HILL
TRAILS

9

MARION COUNTY

JOHNSON COUNTY

COUNTY   LINE

37

JOHNSON COUNTY

46158

Pleasant   Run

WHITE RIVER

46142

Pleasant   Run

NORTH   DR

CENTER   DR

SOUTH   DR

WEST   EAST
DR   DR

ROAD

(500 RD W)

SILVER
SPRINGS

SILVER
SPRINGS

10500

Pleasant   Run

SILVER
SPRINGS
BLVD

SILVER
VALLEY

SILVER HILL
LA   SILVER
VALLEY   SILVER
LAKE CIR   SILVER
LAKE CT

SILVER
SPRINGS

10

39°37'30"

0-210100

MORPHIS
LA

LAWSON
LA

STEVEN
LA   WILD
ROSE
LA   HERITAGE
LA
BROOKSTONE

MOUNT
PLEASANT

BLUFF

Mount
Pleasant
Cem

SCOTT

MORGANTOWN

HECKMAN WAY

YEAGY

SILVER VALLEY

HIGH
MEADOW
CT

SILVER
VALLEY
S   MOCCASIN
DR   MACY
WAY   MACY
LA

JACKSON

BLOOM

MORGANTOWN

RIDGE

REDMAN

MACY

RIDGE
DR

ACHGILLIS

BROOKSTONE

©American Map Corporation   86°14'15"   IN GRID 340,000 FT (E)   86°13'30"   Joins Map 594   86°12'45"   86°12'00"   350,000 FT (E)   86°11'15"

86°15'00"

A B C D E F G H J K

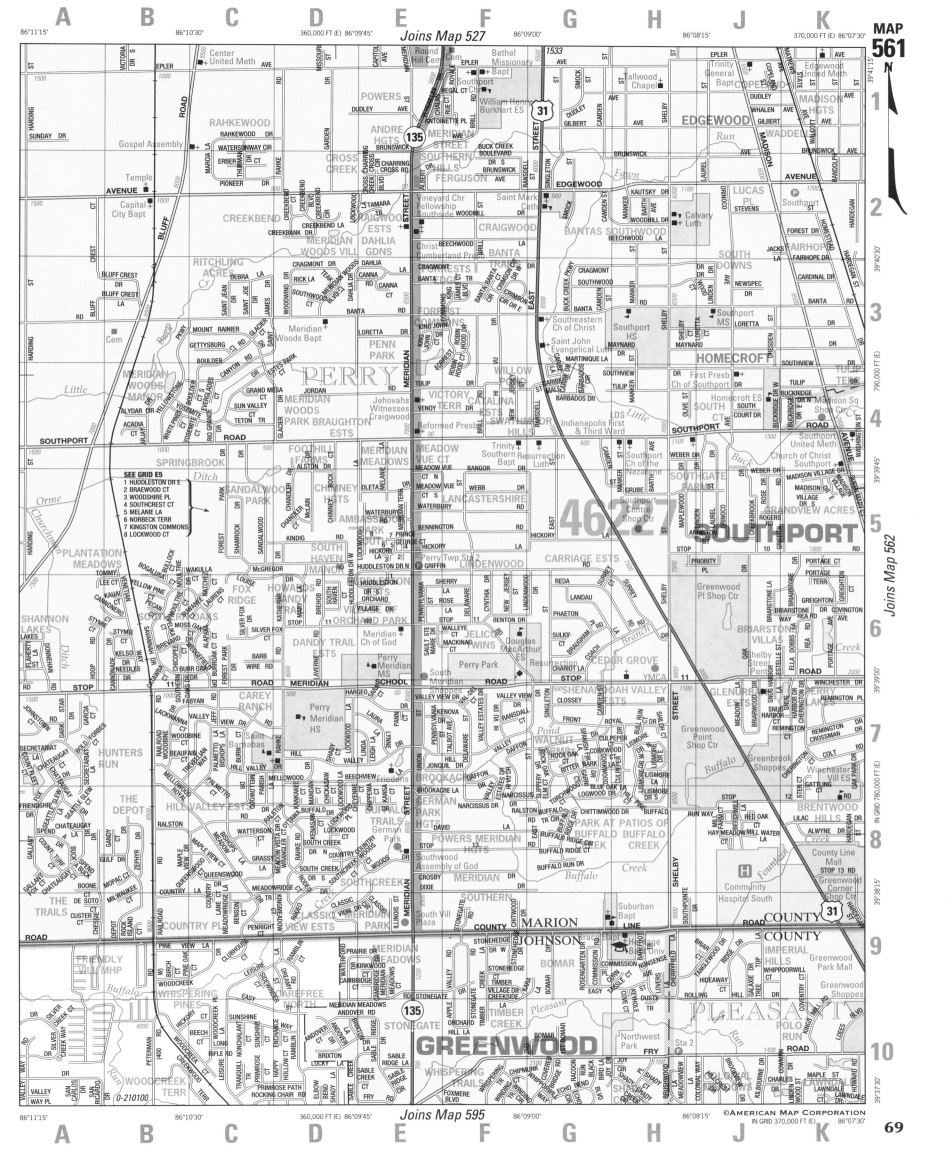

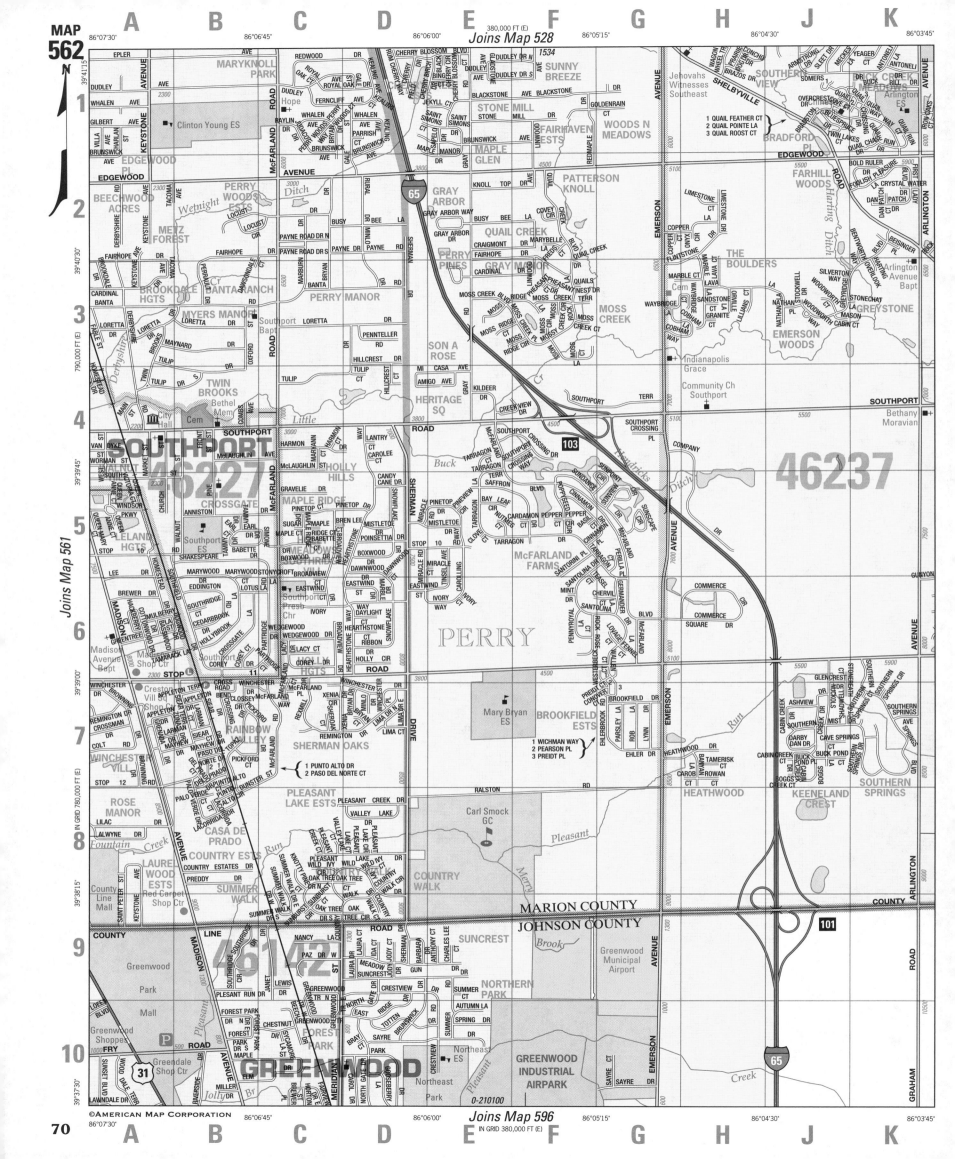

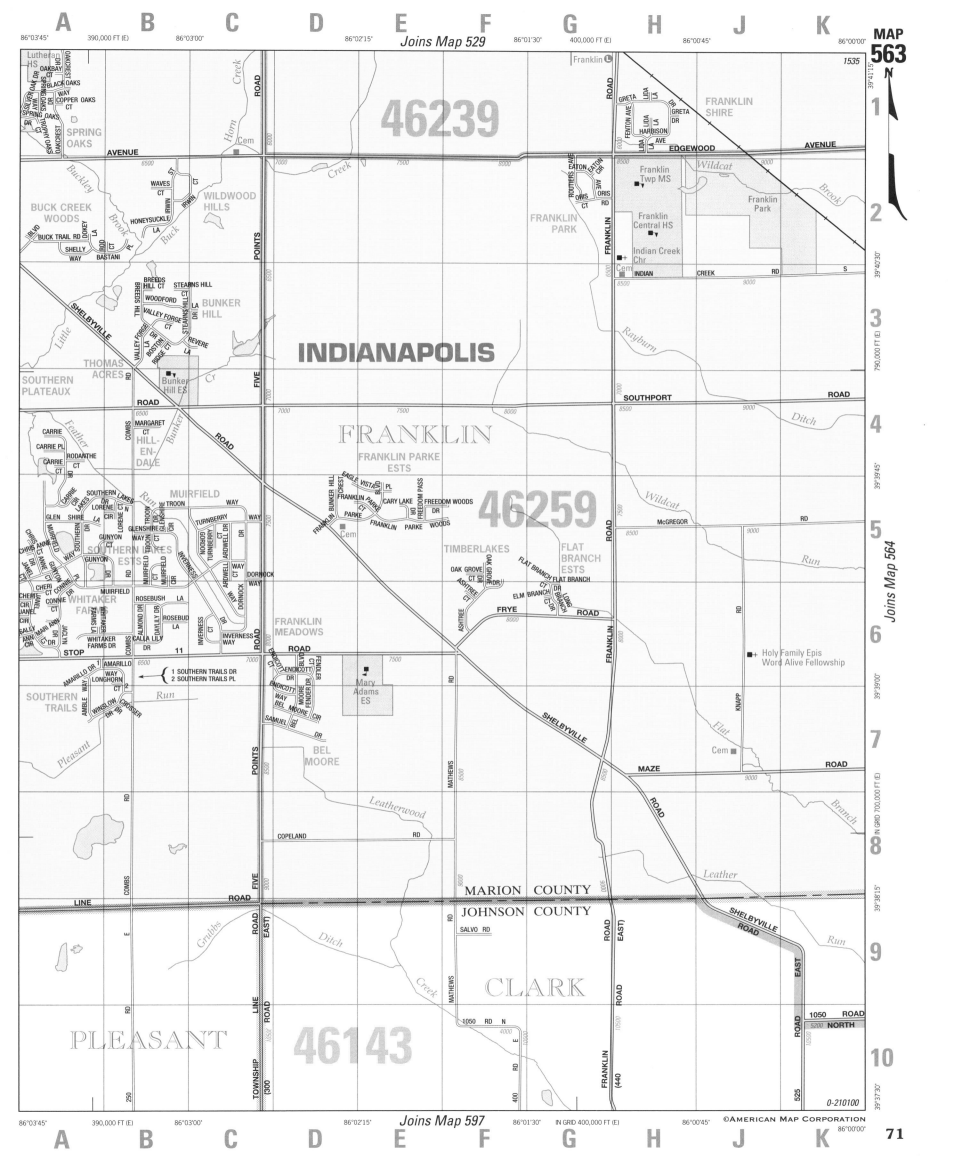

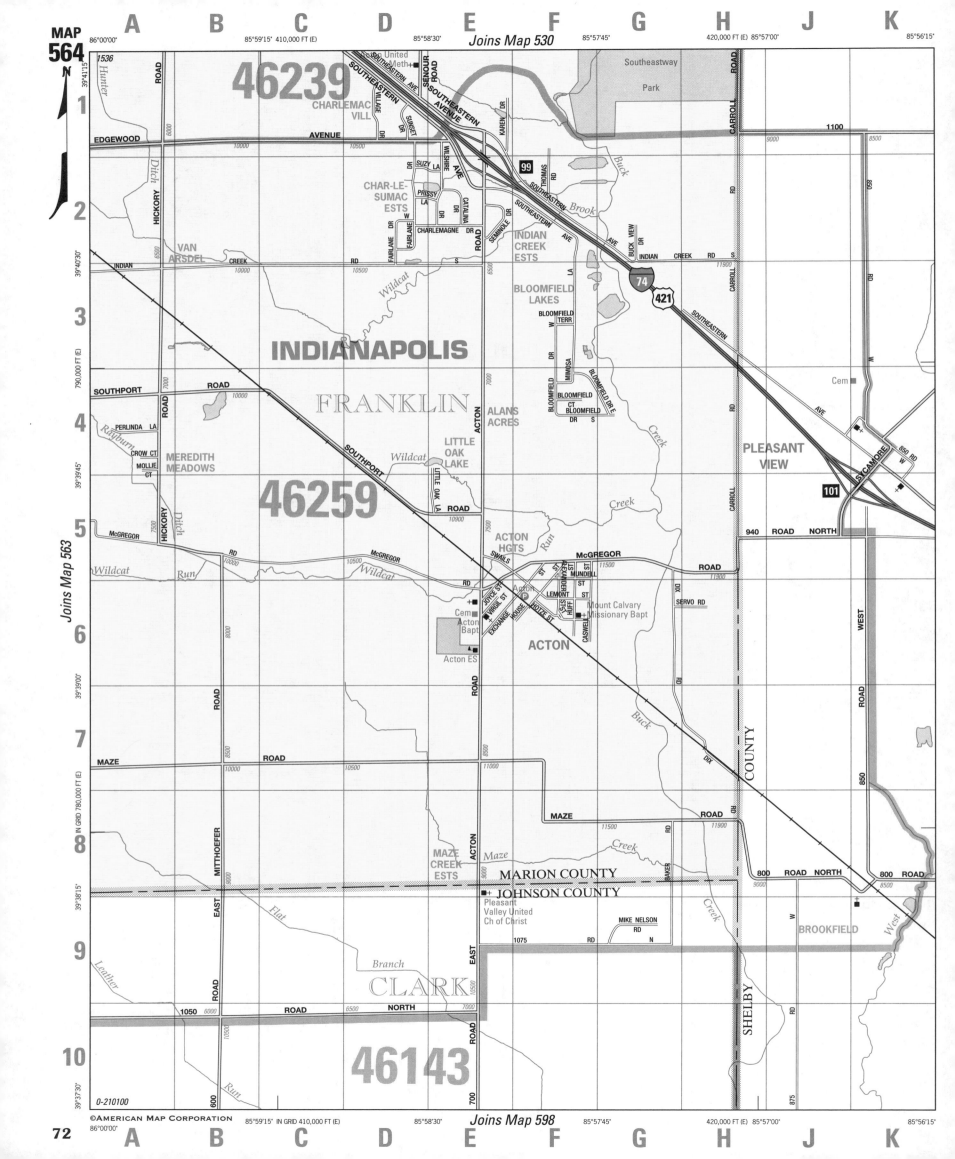

MAP
564
N

Joins Map 530

46239

CHARLEMAC VILL

EDGEWOOD AVENUE

CHAR-LE-SUMAC ESTS

VAN ARSDEL

INDIAN CREEK ESTS

INDIANAPOLIS

FRANKLIN

46259

SOUTHPORT ROAD

MEREDITH MEADOWS

PERLINDA LA

CROW CT

MOLLIE CT

RAYBURN

LITTLE OAK LAKE

LITTLE OAK LA

ALANS ACRES

BLOOMFIELD LAKES

BLOOMFIELD TERR

BLOOMFIELD

BLOOMFIELD CT BLOOMFIELD DR S

MIMOSA

PLEASANT VIEW

CEM

SYCAMORE

101

McGREGOR RD

ACTON HGTS

SWAILS

McGREGOR ROAD

940 ROAD NORTH

Wildcat Run

JOYCE ST
WRIGHT ST
EXCHANGE
HOUSE
HOTZE ST
ALEXANDER ST
LEMONT ST
MUNDELL ST
HUFF ST
CASWELL ST

Mount Calvary Missionary Bapt

DIX

SERVO RD

Cem
Acton Bapt

ACTON

Acton ES

MAZE ROAD

Buck

MAZE ROAD

MAZE CREEK ESTS

Maze Creek

MARION COUNTY

JOHNSON COUNTY

Pleasant Valley United Ch of Christ

MIKE NELSON RD

1075 RD

WEST ROAD

BROOKFIELD

SHELBY COUNTY

800 ROAD NORTH 800 ROAD

Branch

CLARK

1050 ROAD NORTH

46143

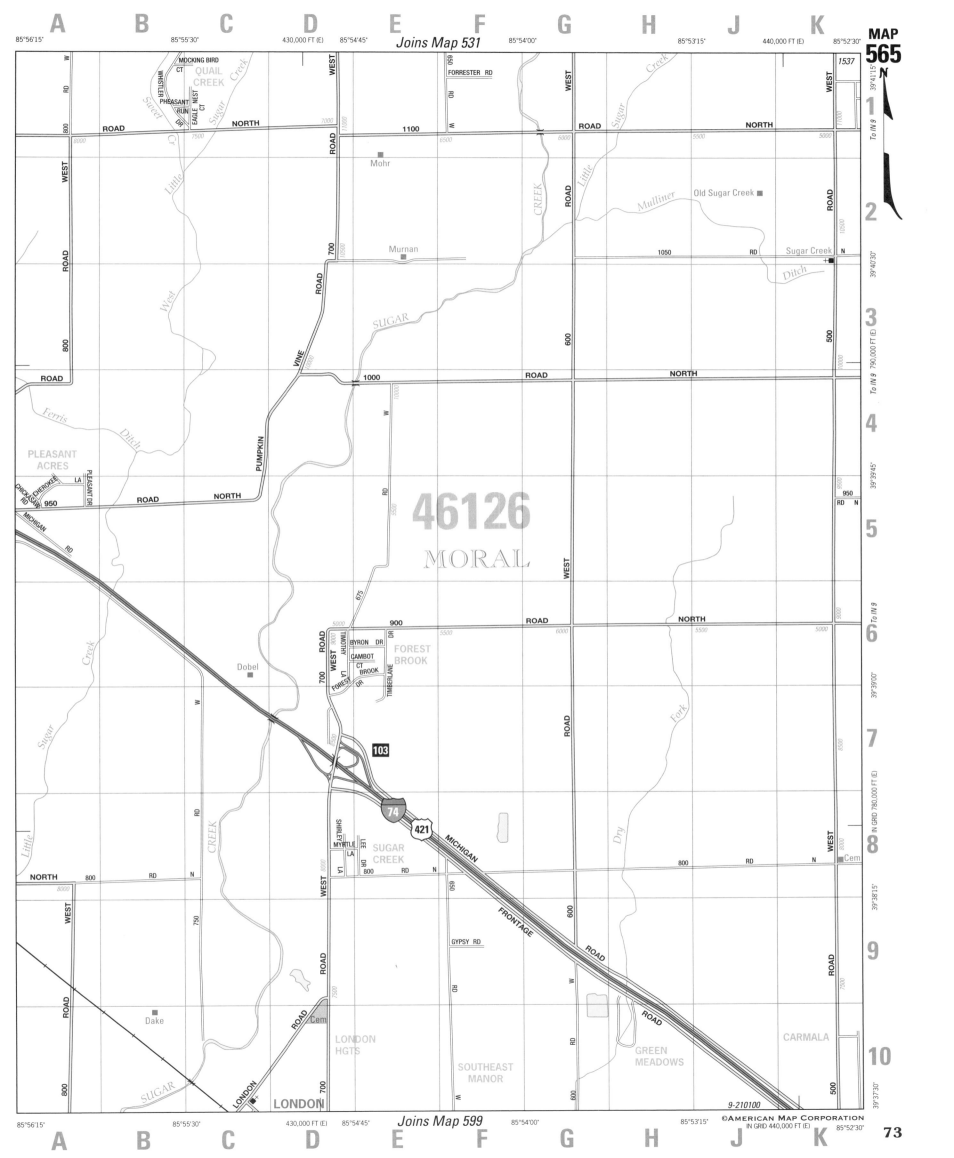

MAP
565

N

73

QUAIL
CREEK

MOCKING BIRD

WHISTLER

PHEASANT
RUN

EAGLE NEST

FORRESTER RD

WEST

ROAD   NORTH

1100

Mohr

Murnan

VINE   ROAD

SUGAR

CREEK

ROAD

Little

Mulliner

Old Sugar Creek

Sugar Creek

Ditch

WEST   ROAD   NORTH

Ferris   Ditch

PLEASANT
ACRES

CHICKASAW RD

CHEROKEE

PLEASANT DR

MICHIGAN

PUMPKIN

ROAD   NORTH

950

46126

MORAL

WEST

Dobel

WEST   ROAD

900

BYRON DR

AHLOWIL

GAMBOT
CT

FOREST
DR

BROOK

TIMBERLANE

FOREST
BROOK

ROAD   NORTH

Sugar

Creek

103

74
421

MICHIGAN

SHIRLEY

MYRTLE

LEE

SUGAR
CREEK

NORTH   800   RD   N

WEST

800   RD

FRONTAGE

GYPSY RD

ROAD

Cem

SOUTHEAST
MANOR

GREEN
MEADOWS

CARMALA

Dake

LONDON
HGTS

LONDON

London

Little

Sugar

Creek

West

Sweet Cr

Dry   Fork

CREEK

SUGAR

Cem

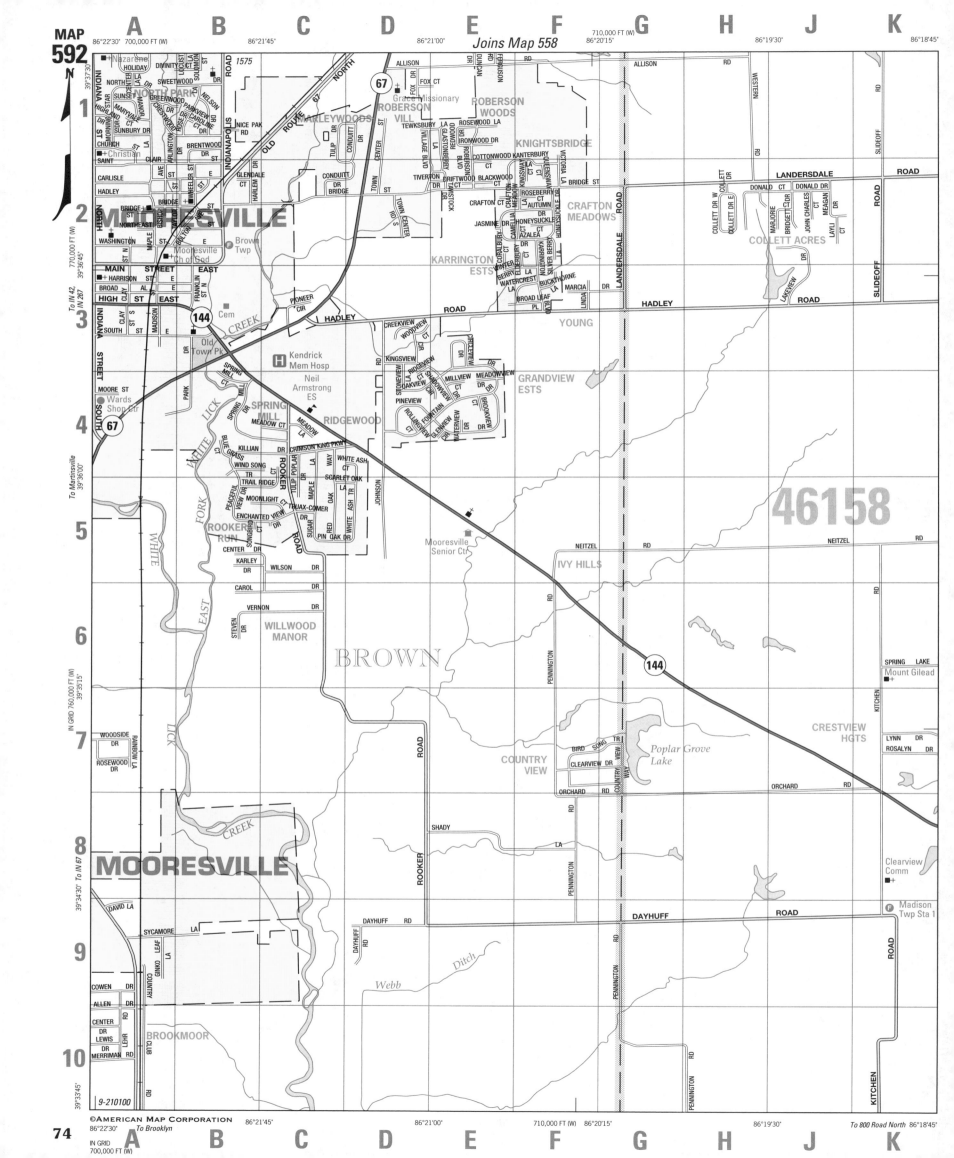

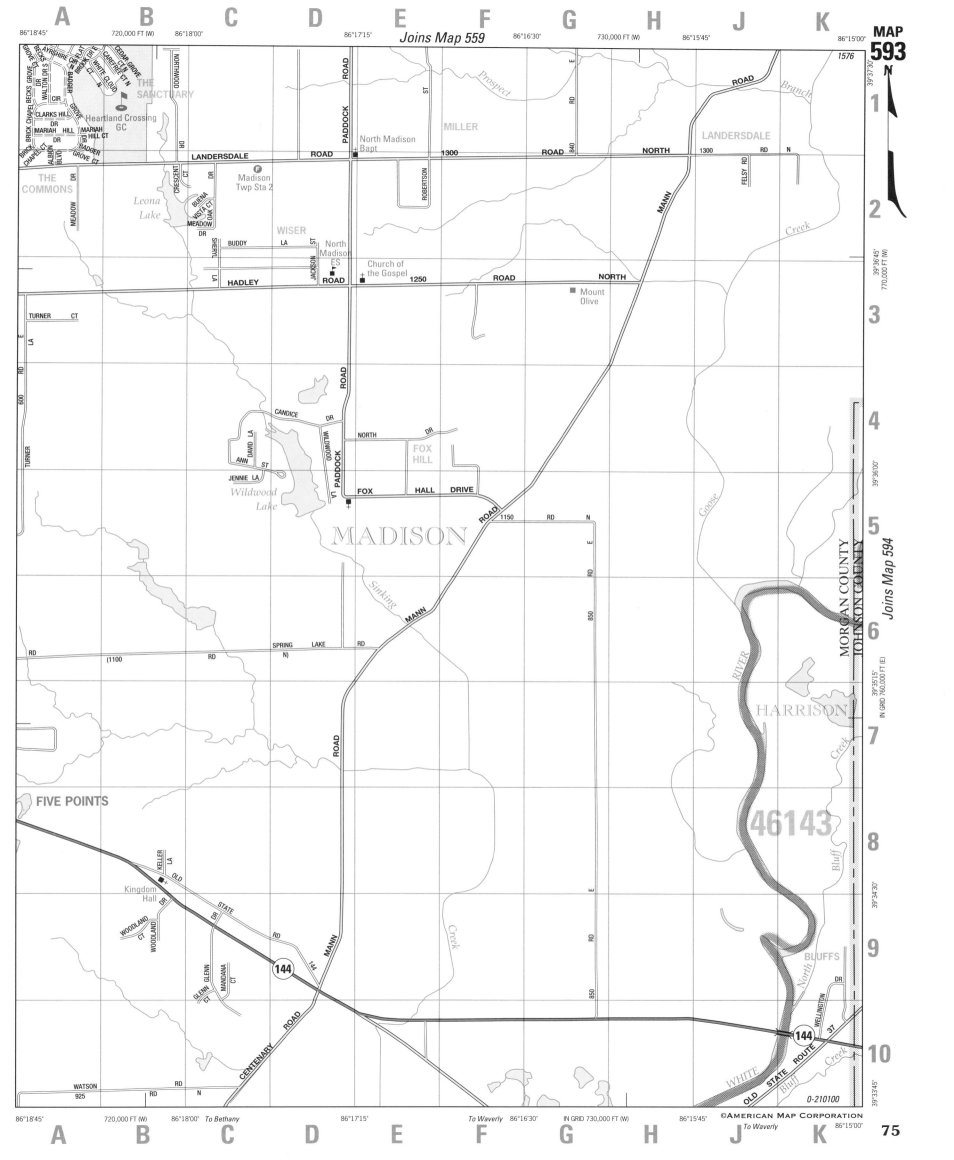

MAP
593
N

Joins Map 559

A B C D E F G H J K

86°18'45" 720,000 FT (W) 86°18'00" 86°17'15" 86°16'30" 730,000 FT (W) 86°15'45" 86°15'00"

1576

1

THE SANCTUARY

Heartland Crossing GC

THE COMMONS

Leona Lake

Madison Twp Sta 2

MILLER

LANDERSDALE

LANDERSDALE ROAD

ROAD

North Madison Bapt

1300 ROAD 840 NORTH 1300 RD N

FELSY RD

2

WISER

BUDDY LA

North Madison ES

HADLEY ROAD

Church of the Gospel

1250

ROAD NORTH

Mount Olive

MANN

Creek

3

TURNER CT

ROAD

CANDICE DR

ANN DAVID LA ST

JENNIE LA

Wildwood Lake

NORTH DR

WILDWOOD

PADDOCK LA

FOX HILL

FOX HALL DRIVE

ROAD 1150 RD N

4

MADISON

Sinking

MANN

RD E

Goose

HARRISON

5

RD E 600

TURNER

925

WATSON RD N

RD

(1100) RD

SPRING LAKE RD (N)

ROAD

MANN

Creek

850 RD E

RIVER

6

Creek

7

FIVE POINTS

46143

Bluff

8

KELLER LA

Kingdom Hall

OLD STATE DR

WOODLAND CT

WOODLAND DR

GLENN GLENN CT

MANDANA CT

144 144

MANN

CENTENARY ROAD

RD

850 RD E

BLUFFS

North

WELLINGTON DR

9

144

37

WHITE OLD STATE ROUTE

Bluff Creek

10

MORGAN COUNTY
JOHNSON COUNTY

Joins Map 594

IN GRID 760,000 FT (E)

39°37'30"
39°36'45"
770,000 FT (W)
39°36'00"
39°35'15"
39°34'30"
39°33'45"

A B C D E F G H J K

86°18'45" 720,000 FT (W) 86°18'00" *To Bethany* 86°17'15" *To Waverly* 86°16'30" IN GRID 730,000 FT (W) 86°15'45" 86°15'00"

0-210100

©AMERICAN MAP CORPORATION

To Waverly

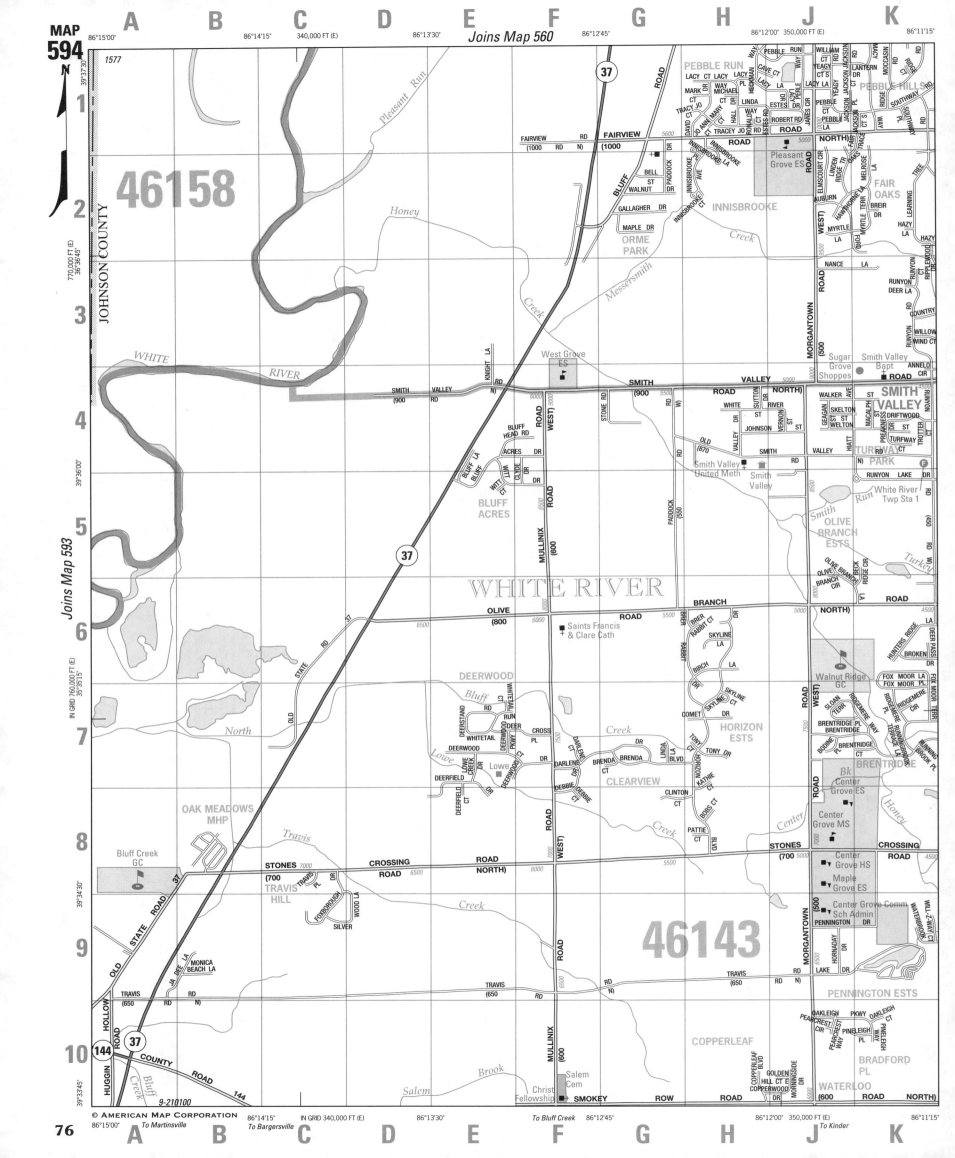

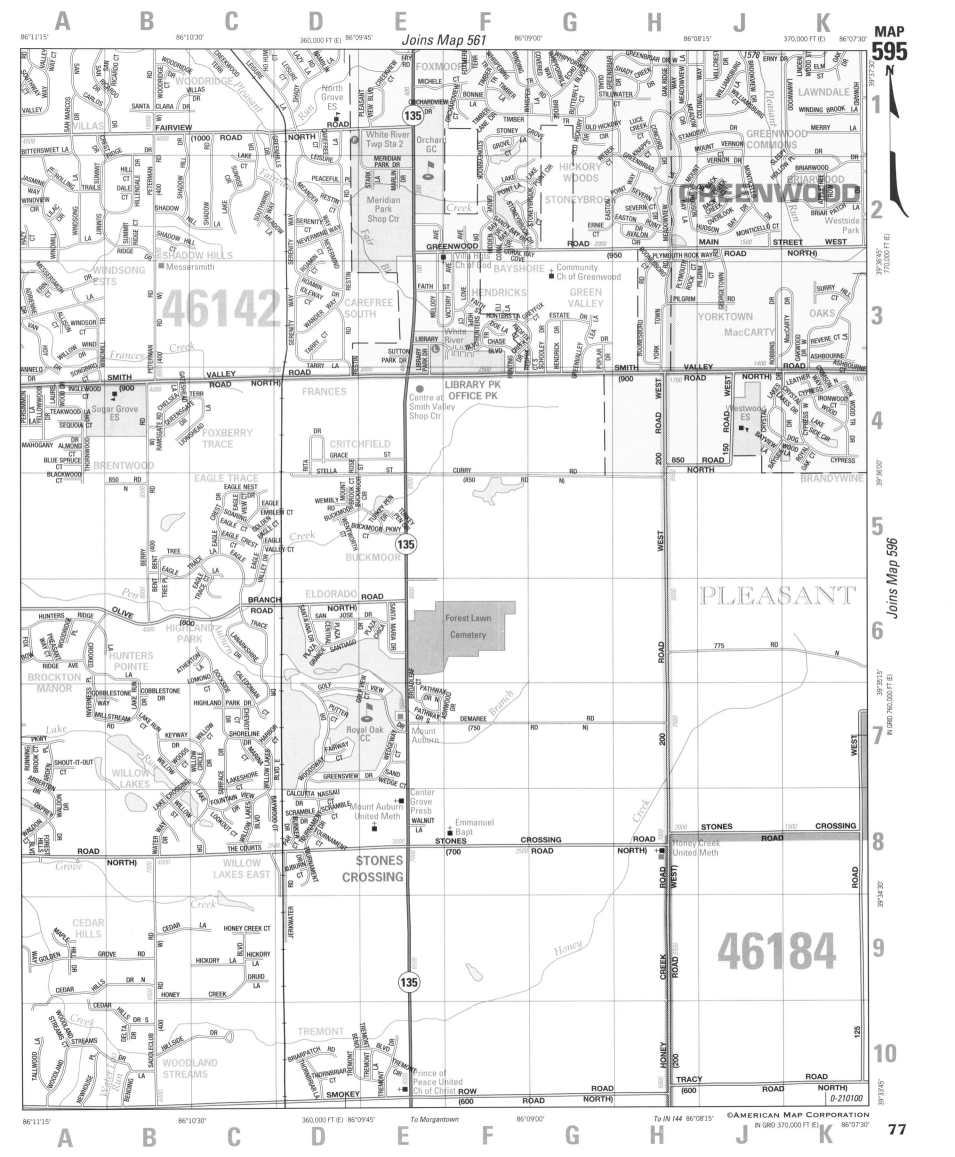

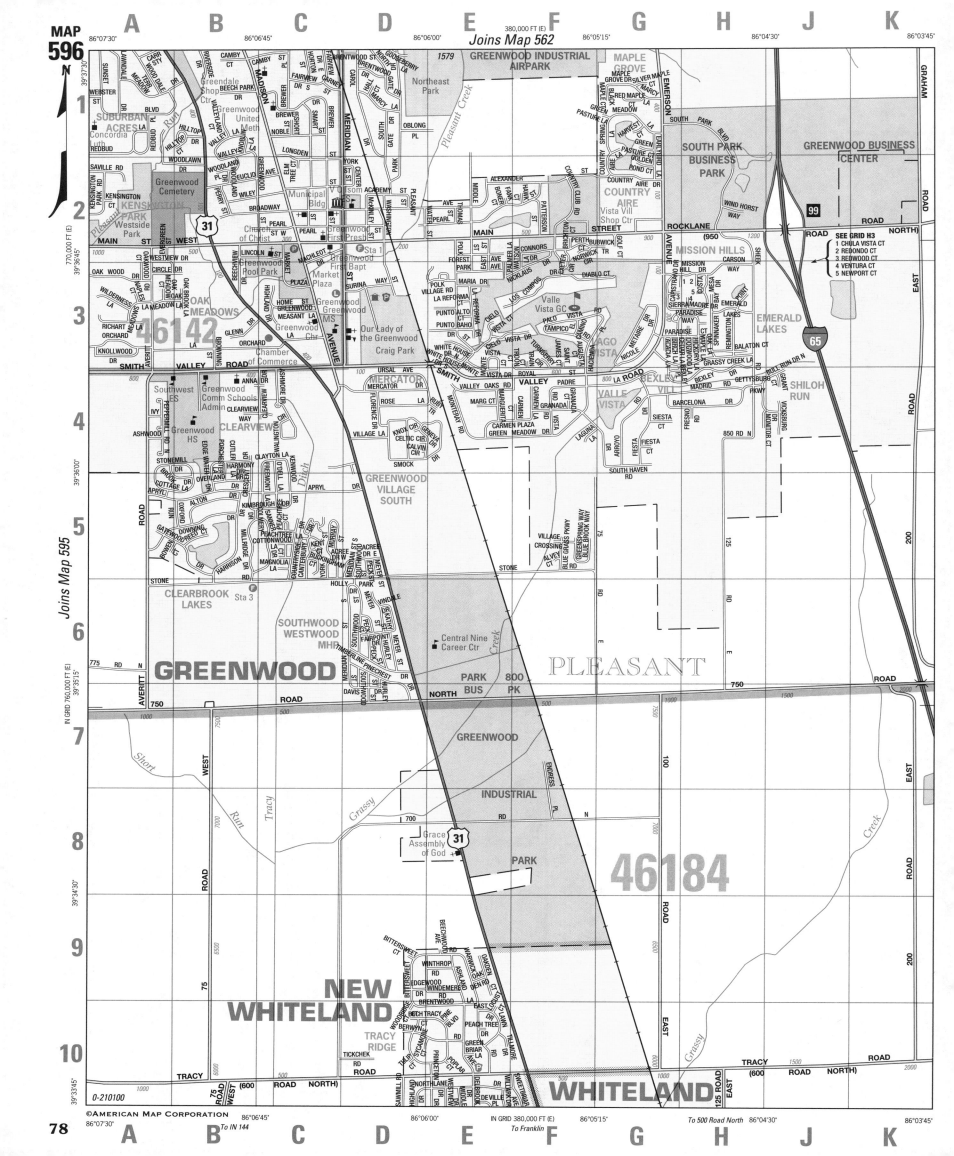

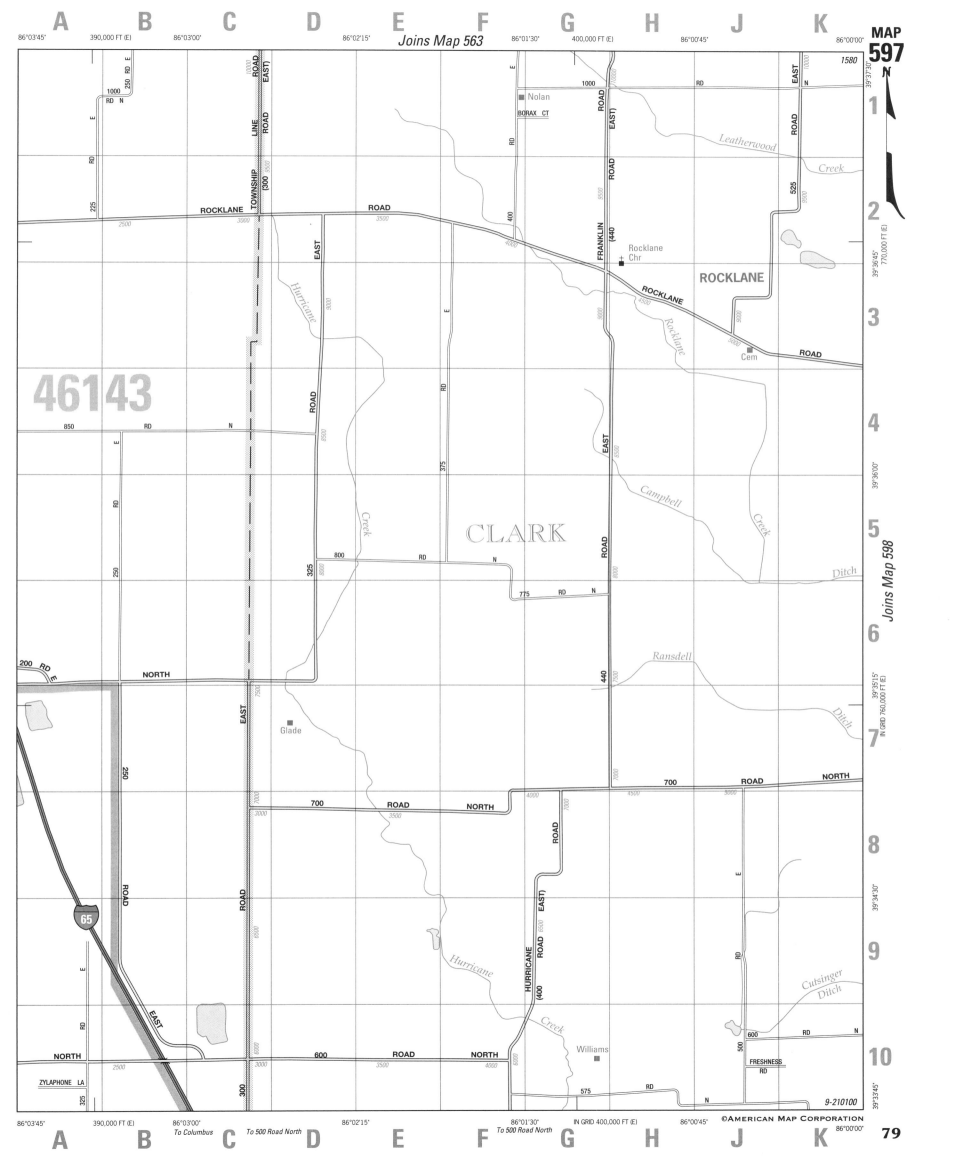

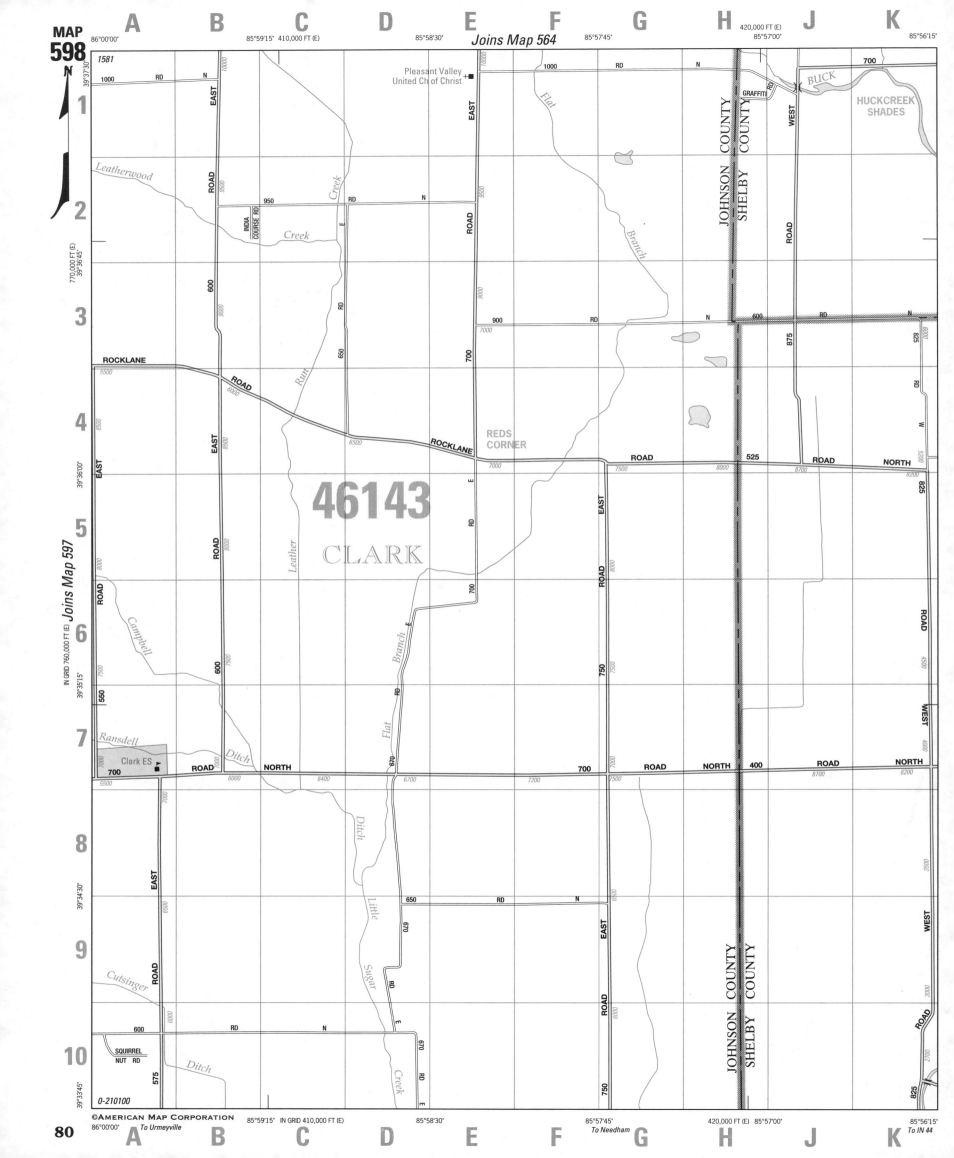

MAP
598

Joins Map 564

46143

CLARK

REDS CORNER

ROCKLANE ROAD

HUCKCREEK SHADES

Pleasant Valley United Ch of Christ

JOHNSON COUNTY
SHELBY COUNTY

BUCK

GRAFFITI

Leatherwood

Campbell

Ransdell

Clark ES

Cutsinger

SQUIRREL NUT RD

To Urmeyville   To Needham   To IN 44

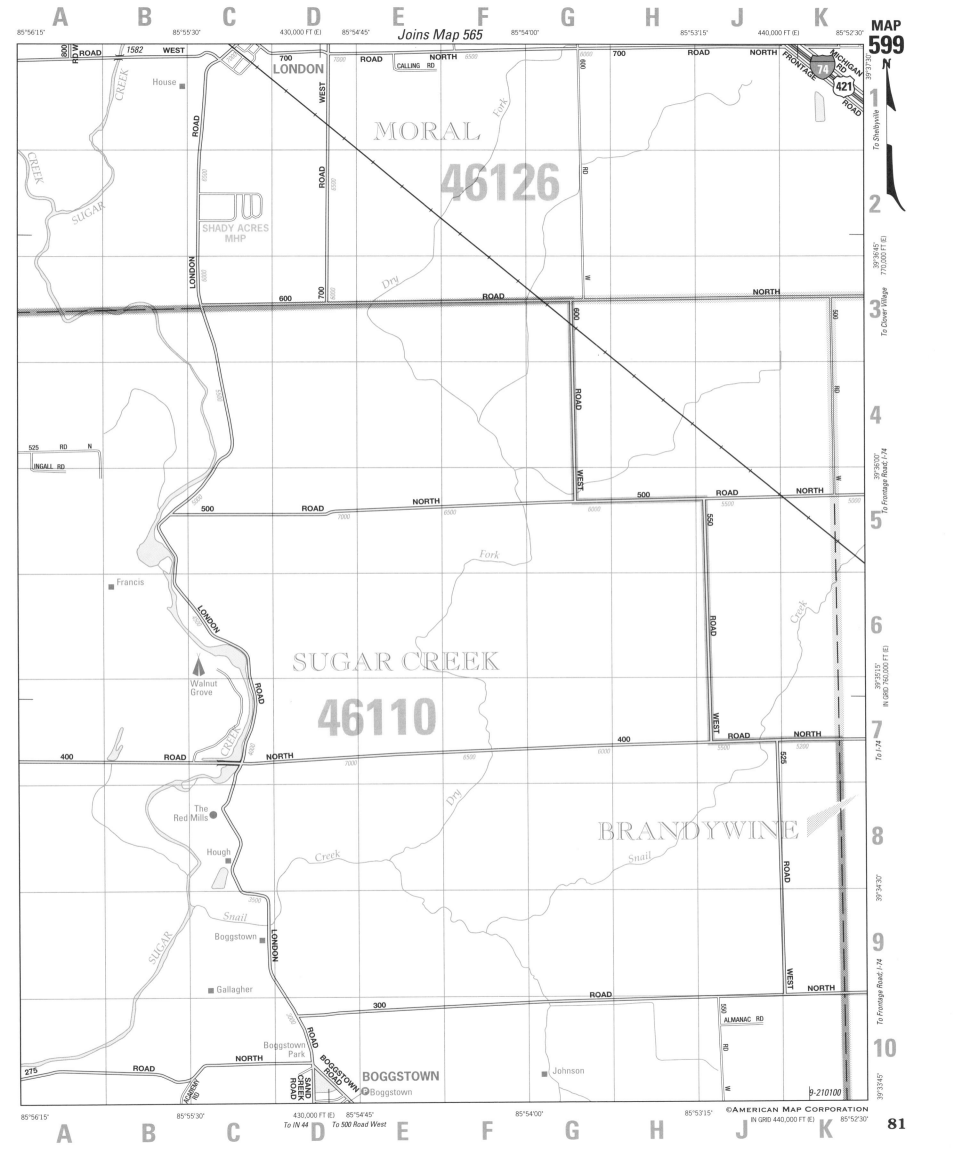

Pages 1, 2 and 3 provide you a Table of Contents, Key to Abbreviations, complete Step-by-Step Guide to using your Street Map Book and Map Legend. Take a few minutes to familiarize yourself with this time saving information.

© American Map Corporation

ZIP CODE AREAS SHOWN IN THIS PUBLICATION

Alphabetical Listing by Post Office

POST OFFICE	ZIP CODE	MAP
Beech Grove, Marion Co., IN	46107	528
Boggstown, Shelby Co., IN	46110	598,599
Brownsburg, Hendricks Co., IN	46112	422,455,456,489,490
Camby, Marion Co., IN	46113	558,559
Carmel, Hamilton Co., IN	46032	357,390-392,424-426
Carmel, Hamilton Co., IN	46033	357-359,391-393,426
Cicero, Hamilton Co., IN	46034	323-326
Danville, Hendricks Co., IN	46122	489
Fairland, Shelby Co., IN	46126	530,531,564,565,598,599
Fishers, Hamilton Co., IN	46038	392-395,427,428
Fortville, Hancock Co., IN	46040	395
Greenfield, Hancock Co., IN	46140	462,463,496,497
Greenwood, Johnson Co., IN	46142	560-562,594-596
Greenwood, Johnson Co., IN	46143	562-564,593-598
Indianapolis (Acton), Marion Co., IN	46259	563,564
Indianapolis (Airport Mail Center), Marion Co., IN	46251	525
Indianapolis (Bacon), Marion Co., IN	46205	459,460,493
Indianapolis (Bacon), Marion Co., IN	46220	425-427,459-461
Indianapolis (Bridgeport), Marion Co., IN	46231	489-491,523-525,558
Indianapolis (Brightwood), Marion Co., IN	46218	459,460,493,494
Indianapolis (Broad Ripple), Marion Co., IN	46230	459
Indianapolis (Castleton), Marion Co., IN	46250	426,427
Indianapolis (Castleton), Marion Co., IN	46256	393,427,428,461
Indianapolis (Circle City), Marion Co., IN	46202	492,493
Indianapolis (Circle City), Marion Co., IN	46204	493
Indianapolis (Circle City), Marion Co., IN	46244	493
Indianapolis (Clermont), Marion Co., IN	46234	456,457,489-491
Indianapolis (Cumberland), Marion Co., IN	46229	495-497
Indianapolis (Eagle Creek), Marion Co., IN	46214	457,491
Indianapolis (Eagle Creek), Marion Co., IN	46253	457
Indianapolis (Eagle Creek), Marion Co., IN	46254	457,458
Indianapolis (Eastgate), Marion Co., IN	46219	494,495
Indianapolis (Garfield), Marion Co., IN	46203	493-495,527-529
Indianapolis (Lawrence), Marion Co., IN	46216	427,428,461,462
Indianapolis (Lawrence), Marion Co., IN	46226	460,461,494,495
Indianapolis (Linwood), Marion Co., IN	46201	493,494
Indianapolis (Main), Marion Co., IN	46206	493
Indianapolis (Main), Marion Co., IN	46225	493,526,527
Indianapolis (Mapleton), Marion Co., IN	46208	458,459,492,493
Indianapolis (Mapleton), Marion Co., IN	46228	458,459
Indianapolis (New Augusta), Marion Co., IN	46268	423,424,457,458
Indianapolis (New Augusta), Marion Co., IN	46278	422,423,456,457
Indianapolis (Nora), Marion Co., IN	46240	425,426
Indianapolis (Nora), Marion Co., IN	46260	424,425,458,459
Indianapolis (Nora), Marion Co., IN	46280	391-393,425-427
Indianapolis (Nora), Marion Co., IN	46290	425
Indianapolis (Oaklandon), Marion Co., IN	46236	428,429,461-463,495,496
Indianapolis (Park Fletcher), Marion Co., IN	46241	491,524-526,558,559
Indianapolis (Rainbow), Marion Co., IN	46222	458,492,493
Indianapolis (Southport), Marion Co., IN	46217	526,527,560,561
Indianapolis (Southport), Marion Co., IN	46227	527,528,561,562
Indianapolis (Southport), Marion Co., IN	46237	527-529,562,563
Indianapolis (Speedway), Marion Co., IN	46224	457,458,491
Indianapolis (Wanamaker), Marion Co., IN	46239	495-497,529-531,563,564
Indianapolis (West Indianapolis), Marion Co., IN	46221	492,493,525-527,559,560
Lebanon, Boone Co., IN	46052	388,422
McCordsville, Hancock Co., IN	46055	394,395,428,429,462,463
Mooresville, Morgan Co., IN	46158	557-560,592-594
New Palestine, Hancock Co., IN	46163	496,497,530,531
Noblesville, Hamilton Co., IN	46060	324-327,358-361,393-395
Plainfield, Hendricks Co., IN	46168	489,523,524,557,558
Sheridan, Hamilton Co., IN	46069	322,323,356,357
Westfield, Hamilton Co., IN	46074	322-324,356-358,390,391
Whiteland, Johnson Co., IN	46184	595-597
Whitestown, Boone Co., IN	46075	388
Zionsville, Boone Co., IN	46077	356,388-390,422-424

Numerical Listing by ZIP Code

ZIP CODE	POST OFFICE	MAP
46032	Carmel, Hamilton Co., IN	357,390-392,424-426
46033	Carmel, Hamilton Co., IN	357-359,391-393,426
46034	Cicero, Hamilton Co., IN	323-326
46038	Fishers, Hamilton Co., IN	392-395,427,428
46040	Fortville, Hancock Co., IN	395
46052	Lebanon, Boone Co., IN	388,422
46055	McCordsville, Hancock Co., IN	394,395,428,429,462,463
46060	Noblesville, Hamilton Co., IN	324-327,358-361,393-395
46069	Sheridan, Hamilton Co., IN	322,323,356,357
46074	Westfield, Hamilton Co., IN	322-324,356-358,390,391
46075	Whitestown, Boone Co., IN	388
46077	Zionsville, Boone Co., IN	356,388-390,422-424
46107	Beech Grove, Marion Co., IN	528
46110	Boggstown, Shelby Co., IN	598,599
46112	Brownsburg, Hendricks Co., IN	422,455,456,489,490
46113	Camby, Marion Co., IN	558,559
46122	Danville, Hendricks Co., IN	489
46126	Fairland, Shelby Co., IN	530,531,564,565,598,599
46140	Greenfield, Hancock Co., IN	462,463,496,497
46142	Greenwood, Johnson Co., IN	560-562,594-596
46143	Greenwood, Johnson Co., IN	562-564,593-598
46158	Mooresville, Morgan Co., IN	557-560,592-594
46163	New Palestine, Hancock Co., IN	496,497,530,531
46168	Plainfield, Hendricks Co., IN	489,523,524,557,558
46184	Whiteland, Johnson Co., IN	595-597
46201	Indianapolis (Linwood), Marion Co., IN	493,494
46202	Indianapolis (Circle City), Marion Co., IN	492,493
46203	Indianapolis (Garfield), Marion Co., IN	493-495,527-529
46204	Indianapolis (Circle City), Marion Co., IN	493
46205	Indianapolis (Bacon), Marion Co., IN	459,460,493
46206	Indianapolis (Main), Marion Co., IN	493
46208	Indianapolis (Mapleton), Marion Co., IN	458,459,492,493
46214	Indianapolis (Eagle Creek), Marion Co., IN	457,491
46216	Indianapolis (Lawrence), Marion Co., IN	427,428,461,462
46217	Indianapolis (Southport), Marion Co., IN	526,527,560,561
46218	Indianapolis (Brightwood), Marion Co., IN	459,460,493,494
46219	Indianapolis (Eastgate), Marion Co., IN	494,495
46220	Indianapolis (Bacon), Marion Co., IN	425-427,459-461
46221	Indianapolis (West Indianapolis), Marion Co., IN	492,493,525-527,559,560
46222	Indianapolis (Rainbow), Marion Co., IN	458,492,493
46224	Indianapolis (Speedway), Marion Co., IN	457,458,491
46225	Indianapolis (Main), Marion Co., IN	493,526,527
46226	Indianapolis (Lawrence), Marion Co., IN	460,461,494,495
46227	Indianapolis (Southport), Marion Co., IN	527,528,561,562
46228	Indianapolis (Mapleton), Marion Co., IN	458,459
46229	Indianapolis (Cumberland), Marion Co., IN	495-497
46230	Indianapolis (Broad Ripple), Marion Co., IN	459
46231	Indianapolis (Bridgeport), Marion Co., IN	489-491,523-525,558
46234	Indianapolis (Clermont), Marion Co., IN	456,457,489-491
46236	Indianapolis (Oaklandon), Marion Co., IN	428,429,461-463,495,496
46237	Indianapolis (Southport), Marion Co., IN	527-529,562,563
46239	Indianapolis (Wanamaker), Marion Co., IN	495-497,529-531,563,564
46240	Indianapolis (Nora), Marion Co., IN	425,426
46241	Indianapolis (Park Fletcher), Marion Co., IN	491,524-526,558,559
46244	Indianapolis (Circle City), Marion Co., IN	493
46250	Indianapolis (Castleton), Marion Co., IN	426,427
46251	Indianapolis (Airport Mail Center), Marion Co., IN	525
46253	Indianapolis (Eagle Creek), Marion Co., IN	457
46254	Indianapolis (Eagle Creek), Marion Co., IN	457,458
46256	Indianapolis (Castleton), Marion Co., IN	393,427,428,461
46259	Indianapolis (Acton), Marion Co., IN	563,564
46260	Indianapolis (Nora), Marion Co., IN	424,425,458,459
46268	Indianapolis (New Augusta), Marion Co., IN	423,424,457,458
46278	Indianapolis (New Augusta), Marion Co., IN	422,423,456,457
46280	Indianapolis (Nora), Marion Co., IN	391-393,425-427
46290	Indianapolis (Nora), Marion Co., IN	425

EXPLANATION OF THE ABOVE CHART

EXAMPLE: Whitestown Post Office is physically located in Boone County and serves ZIP Code 46075. ZIP Code 46075 is shown on map 388 of this publication.

MARION COUNTY STREET ADDRESSING & DIRECTIONAL SYSTEM

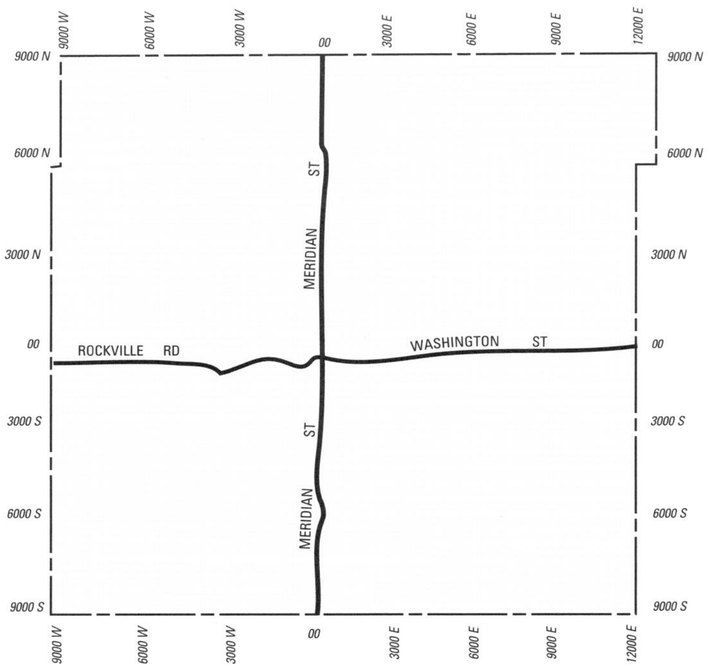

In Marion County, streets that intersect MERIDIAN STREET and exist both east and west of that street are designated as East or West.

In Marion County, streets that intersect WASHINGTON STREET or ROCKVILLE ROAD and exist both north and south of those street are designated as North and South.

TERRITORY CODES

Use the code letters behind each name and location to find the vicinity in which the street is located. The codes are as follows:

A	Avon, Hendricks Co., IN	MTM	Madison Township, Morgan Co., IN
AT	Adams Township, Hamilton Co., IN	MTS	Moral Township, Shelby Co., IN
B	Brownsburg, Hendricks Co., IN	N	Noblesville, Hamilton Co., IN
BCT	Buck Creek Township, Hancock Co., IN	NP	New Palestine, Hancock Co., IN
BG	Beech Grove, Marion Co., IN	NT	Noblesville Township, Hamilton Co., IN
BTH	Brown Township, Hendricks Co., IN	NW	New Whiteland, Johnson Co., IN
BTM	Brown Township, Morgan Co., IN	P	Plainfield, Hendricks Co., IN
BTS	Brandywine Township, Shelby Co., IN	PeT	Perry Township, Marion Co., IN
C	Cicero, Hamilton Co., IN	PTB	Perry Township, Boone Co., IN
Ca	Carmel, Hamilton Co., IN	PTJ	Pleasant Township, Johnson Co., IN
CTH	Clay Township, Hamilton Co., IN	PTM	Pike Township, Marion Co., IN
CTJ	Clark Township, Johnson Co., IN	S	Speedway, Marion Co., IN
CTM	Center Township, Marion Co., IN	SCT	Sugar Creek Township, Hancock Co., IN
Cu	Cumberland, Marion, Hancock Counties, IN	Spt	Southport, Marion Co., IN
DTH	Delaware Township, Hamilton Co., IN	STS	Sugar Creek Township, Shelby Co., IN
DTM	Decatur Township, Marion Co., IN	UT	Union Township, Boone Co., IN
ET	Eagle Township, Boone Co., IN	VT	Vernon Township, Hancock Co., IN
F	Fishers, Hamilton Co., IN	W	Westfield, Hamilton Co., IN
FCT	Fall Creek Township, Hamilton Co., IN	WaT	Washington Township, Hendricks Co., IN
FT	Franklin Township, Marion Co., IN	Wh	Whitestown, Boone Co., IN
G	Greenwood, Johnson Co., IN	Whl	Whiteland, Johnson Co., IN
GT	Guilford Township, Hendricks Co., IN	WnT	Wayne Township, Marion Co., IN
HT	Harrison Township, Morgan Co., IN	WRT	White River Township, Hamilton Co., IN
JT	Jackson Township, Hamilton Co., IN	WrT	Warren Township, Marion Co., IN
L	Lawrence, Marion Co., IN	WTB	Worth Township, Boone Co., IN
LTH	Lincoln Township, Hendricks Co., IN	WTH	Washington Township, Hamilton Co., IN
LTM	Lawrence Township, Marion, IN	WTJ	White River Township, Johnson Co., IN
M	Mooresville, Morgan Co., IN	WTM	Washington Township, Marion Co., IN
McC	McCordsville, Hancock Co., IN	WyT	Wayne Township, Hamilton Co., IN
MTB	Marion Township, Boone Co., IN	Z	Zionsville, Boone Co., IN
MTH	Middle Township, Hendricks Co., IN		

Example: Adirondack Ct 490-H6 WnT would be on map 490, grid square H6 in Wayne Township.

Example: Abbott St DN-C4 CTM would be on the Downtown Map, grid square C4 in Center Township.

STREETS

A

AA Dr 324-K4 N
AAA Way 392-B7 Ca
Abbedale Ct 357-D10 WTH
Abberton Dr 595-A7 WTJ
Abbey Ct 359-K7 N; 462-A8 WrT
Abbey Dr 392-E4 Ca
Abbey Rd 359-K7 N
Abbots Pl 392-F3 Ca
Abbott St DN-C4; 493-C9 CTM
Abby Cr La 460-C7 WTM
Abercon Tr 359-B1 N
Abercromby Cir 457-J4 PTM
Abercrumb La 428-C8 L
Aberdare Dr 427-B3 LTM
Aberdeen 391-H6 Ca
Aberdeen Ave 489-A9 WaT
Aberdeen Ct 460-G7 WTM
Aberdeen Ct 394-A4 F
Aberdeen Dr 491-F10 WnT
Aberdene Ct E 559-A10 MTM
Abington Ct 558-K10 MTM
Abington Dr 458-B6 PTM
Abington Pl 393-C10 F
Abington Way 458-B6 PTM
Able Ct 496-J4 Cu
Able Dr 527-G9 PeT
Abraham Williams Run 393-B5 Ca
Abundance La 489-H7 A
Acacia Dr 457-F10 WnT
Acacia La 596-G3 G
Academy Dr 389-G8 Z
Academy Rd 599-B10 STS
Academy St 596-D2 G
Acadia Ct 561-B4 PeT
Acadia Pl 393-H3 F
Acoma Dr 462-C10 WrT
Acorn La 457-K3 PTM
Acorn Woods Cir 491-K6 WnT
Acorn Woods Dr 491-K6 WnT
Acre Ave 455-F6 B
Acre La 457-D1 PTM
Acree Dr E 596-D5 G
Acree Dr W 596-C5 G
Activator Ave 526-J4 CTM
Acton Rd 564-E4, E8 FT
Ada La 528-G8 BG
Adam Ct 393-J10 F
Adams Blvd Dr E 460-G1 WTM
Adams Blvd Dr N 460-G1 WTM
Adams Blvd Dr W 460-G1 WTM
Adams Ct N 460-C8 WTM
Adams Ct S 460-C8 WTM
Adams Rd 529-J8 FT
Adams St 455-G5, G6 B; 460-C10; 494-C1, C2, C4 CTM; 391-G6 Ca; 460-C8 WTM
Adamson Ct 424-A10 PTM
Addison St 492-H8, H10 WnT
Adelaide St 528-H7 BG
Adenoid Pass 356-D9 WTH
Adios Ct 357-F10 WTH
Adios Pass 391-F1, F2, G2 CTH; 357-F10 WTH
Adirondack Ct 490-H6 WnT
Adler St 527-E2 CTM
Admar Ct 460-C6 WTM
Administration Ave 526-J4 CTM
Admiral Dr 495-A3 WrT
Admiral Way 357-E10 WTH
Admirals Bay Dr 428-J4 LTM
Admirals Cove 428-J5 L
Admirals Ct 428-G7 L
Admirals La 428-G7 L
Admirals Landing Blvd 428-H5 L
Admirals Landing Pl 428-J5 L
Admirals Landing Way 428-H5, J6 L
Admirals Pointe Cir 428-H3 LTM
Admirals Pointe Ct 428-H3 LTM
Admirals Pointe Dr 428-G4 LTM
Admirals Woods Cir 428-H4 LTM
Admirals Woods Dr 428-G4 LTM
Admiralty La 426-C8 WTM
Adonis Dr 423-J10 PTM
Adrienne Dr 595-A3 WTJ
Advisory Way 426-D2 WTM
Aegean Rd 394-G10 FCT
Aerie La 457-E6 PTM
Aerobic La E 560-D4 PeT
Aeronca La 395-C10 FCT
Afton Crest 461-A2 LTM
Agan Dr 524-B10; 558-A1 P
Agawam Ct 425-B6 WTM
Agawam Dr 461-D3 L
Aho Dr 489-C4 WaT
Aigner Ct 423-D9 PTM
Ainsley Cir 427-H5 LTM
Aintree Ct 427-B3 LTM
Aintree Dr 427-B3 LTM
Aintree Pl 427-B3 LTM
Aintree Terr 427-B3 LTM
Aira Dr 490-H7 WnT
Airport Dr 457-D8 PTM
Airport Expwy 525-J4; 526-A4 WnT
Airport Rd 455-F9 B; 455-F9 LTH
Airway Dr 525-G7 DTM
Airwest Blvd 558-F1 GT; 524-B10, D10 P
Alabama St DN-D4, E1, E2, E3, E4; 493-F3, F5, F8, F9, F10; 527-F1 CTM
Alameda St 458-F6 PTM
Alamosa Dr 428-K6 L
Alan Dr 559-B8 DTM
Alapaka Ct 561-C6 PeT
Albany Ct 358-G3 N
Albany St 528-E5 BG; 527-F5, G5, K5; 528-A5 CTM
Albemarle Cir 325-C10 N
Albert Ct 392-A4 Ca
Albert Dr 561-E2 PeT
Alberta St 492-B1, C1 WnT
Albion Blvd 593-A2 MTM
Albion Dr 427-D10 LTM
Albright Ct 424-F3 PTM
Albury Dr 462-D2 L
Alcott La 559-J4 DTM
Alcove Dr 529-A8 FT
Alden Ave 526-B7 DTM
Alden La 426-J6 LTM
Aldenham Blvd 394-H10 F
Alder Ct 424-A10 PTM
Alderly Rd 425-A4 WTM
Aldersgate Dr 392-F6 Ca
Alderwood Ct 392-K10 F
Aldgate La 427-A9 LTM
Alec Dr 490-J4 WnT
Alexander La 427-A2 F
Alexander St 564-F5 FT; 596-E2 G
Alexandria Ct 460-C7 WTM
Alexia Dr 462-B2 L
Alfred Cir 496-G10 WrT
Algeciras Dr 426-G4 WTM
Algonquin Sta Rd 361-H1 WyT
Alibeck Ct 428-A4 LTM
Alice Ave 528-B6 PeT; 495-E7 WrT
Alice Jeanne Ct 495-D4 WrT
Alimingo Dr 424-K9; 425-A9 WTM
Allan Ct 530-E10 FT
Allayna Pl 393-H3 F
Allegheny St DN-C2, D2; 493-D7, F7 CTM
Allen Ave 527-G5 CTM
Allen Ct 357-G7 WTH
Allen Dr 592-A10 BTM; 392-E3 Ca; 456-E8 LTH
Allen St 461-E7 L; 359-G3 N; 531-J6 NP
Allendale Dr 457-H9 WnT
Allenwood Cir 424-E7 PTM
Allenwood Ct 424-E8 PTM
Allfree St 493-D3 CTM
Alliance Dr 558-G8 GT
Allison Ave 423-K6 PTM; 492-A4, A5 S; 458-A10; 492-A1 WnT
Allison Ct 392-C1 Ca; 595-A3 WTJ; 492-A9 WnT
Allison Dr 392-C1 Ca
Allison Pointe Blvd 426-G6 WTM
Allison Pointe Tr 426-G6 WTM
Allison Rd 592-D1 BTM; 592-D1 M; 592-G1 MTM
Allison Way 324-H6 N
Allisonville Rd 393-B10, D7, G2 DTH; 393-B10, D7, G2 F; 326-A9; 359-J2 N; 325-J10; 326-A9; 359-G10, J2 NT; 426-F10, H4; 460-A7, B6, D2 WTM
Allisonwood Ct 426-K3 LTM
Allisonwood Dr 426-K3 LTM
Allport Dr 457-G6 PTM
Almaden Ct 423-D8 PTM
Almaden Dr 423-D8 PTM
Alman Dr E 392-A6 Ca
Alman Dr W 392-A6 Ca
Almanac Rd 599-J10 STS
Almond Ct 557-J1 P; 595-A4 WTJ
Almond Dr 563-B6 FT; 523-J10 P
Alnwick Ct 427-B10 LTM
Aloda St 528-D1 CTM
Aloysius Ct 325-B9 N
Alpha Ave 455-E7 B
Alpha Dr 357-F3 WTH
Alpine Ave 491-H1 WnT
Alpine Dr 324-H6 N
Alpine Pl 461-G9 WrT
Alsace Ct 461-G8 LTM
Alsace Dr 461-G9 WrT
Alsace Pl 461-G8 LTM
Alsong Ct 357-E10 WTH
Alston Dr 561-D4 PeT
Alsuda Ct 460-C5 WTM
Alsuda Dr 460-C6 WTM
Altam Ave 392-A4 Ca
Alton Ave 424-F7; 458-F3, F4 PTM; 458-F10; 492-F1, F5, F7; 526-F1 WnT
Alton Ct 427-J1 F
Alton Dr 596-B5 G; 492-F7 WnT
Alton St 528-C5, E5 BG
Alvamar Pl 393-A4 Ca
Alverna Dr 425-C5 WTM
Alvey Ct 596-F5 G
Alvord St 493-H3, H4 CTM
Alwayne Rd 392-B4 Ca
Alwyne Dr 561-K8; 562-A8 PeT
Alydar Cir 561-B4 PeT
Alyssa La 427-B5 LTM
Alyssa Way 393-J10 F
Amanda Ct 455-H8 B
Amandas Way 427-C5 LTM
Amarillo Dr 563-A6 FT
Amarillo Way 563-B6 FT
Amaryllis Ct 458-A4 PTM
Ambassador Ct 491-F4 WnT
Amber Crest 461-B1 WrT
Amber Ct 462-D1 L; 557-H3 P; 531-H4 SCT
Amber Glow Ct 427-J2 F
Amber Pass 557-J3 P
Amber Ridge Dr 490-J4 WnT
Amber Way 326-B10 N
Amberleaf Tr 358-A4 W
Amberwood Dr 358-B3 WTH
Amble Way 563-A7 FT
Amburg Ct 462-E9 WrT
Amburg Dr 462-E9 WrT
Amelia Dr 531-A5 SCT; 525-F1 WnT
Amerherst Dr 424-J8 WTM
America Ave 525-G9 DTM
American Way 427-C7 LTM
Americana Blvd 423-K4 PTM
Americus Ct 559-D10 MTM
Amethyst Ave 424-G7 PTM
Amethyst Cir 391-A6 CTH
Amherst Dr 393-A8 F
Amherst St 424-F3 PTM
Amhurst Cir 325-A7 N
Amick Ave 560-D4 PeT
Amigo Ave 562-D4 PeT
Amkey Ct 357-F10 WTH
Amkey Way 357-E10 WTH
Amos Dr 388-J6 ET
Amsterdam Ct 523-J2 WaT
Amy Ct 427-H5 LTM
Amy La 427-H5 LTM
Amys Run Dr 392-A5 Ca
Anchor Bay Ct 428-K4 LTM
Anchor Bay Dr 428-K3 LTM; 325-E4 N
Anchor Ct 496-A3 WrT
Anchor Mark Dr 428-K3 LTM
Anchor Way 496-A3 WrT
Anchorage Ct 428-H5 L
Anchorage Dr 428-J4 LTM
Anchorage Way 394-J10 FCT
Ancona Ct 461-J5 LTM
Andalusia Grove 425-F4 WTM
Anderson St 531-G5 NP; 456-H10 WnT
Andes Dr 490-J5 WnT
Andico Rd 523-H6 P
Andiron Dr 427-C3 LTM
Andiron Way 427-C3 LTM
Andorra Dr 393-G3 F
Andover Ct 392-E4 Ca; 561-D10 G
Andover Dr 392-E4 Ca; 561-D10 G
Andover La 359-J7 N
Andover Rd 561-D10 G; 460-G2 LTM; 460-F6, G2 WTM
Andover Sq 460-F6 WTM
Andrade Dr 390-A10 ET
Andre Ct 423-E8 PTM
Andre Dr 423-E8 PTM
Andrea Ct 528-F9 BG; 490-G10 WaT
Andrea Dr 528-F9 BG
Andrew Pass 557-J4 P
Andrew Turn 557-H4 P
Andrews Ave 524-A3 WaT
Andrews Blvd 523-D8 P
Andrews Blvd E 523-D8 P
Andrews Blvd W 523-D8 P
Andrews Ct 528-J3 WrT
Andrews Pl 394-A9 F
Andscott Cir 455-G9 B
Andscott Dr 455-H8 B; 457-E7 PTM
Andy Dr 495-K2 WrT
Anemone Ct 495-G4 WrT
Anemone La 495-G4 WrT
Angel Way 324-H7 N
Angela Ct 528-F9 BG; 359-A7 NT; 557-J3 P
Angela La 391-G2 CTH
Angelique Ct 391-A6 CTH
Angletary Pl 459-G7 WTM
Angola Ct 424-E3 PTM
Anita Dr 527-D9 PeT
Ann Marie Way 457-H3 PTM
Ann St 593-C4 MTM
Anna Ct 557-F2 P
Anna Dr 596-B4 G
Annally Dr 390-F10 CTH
Annandale Dr 393-A3 Ca
Annanhill Ct 523-C1 WaT
Annapolis Ct 423-G5 PTM
Annapolis Dr 457-J3 PTM
Anne La 428-B9 L
Annelo Cir 594-K4 WTJ
Annelo Dr 595-A4 WTJ
Annette St 493-B2 CTM; 459-B5 WTM
Annex Dr 491-H5 WnT
Annie La 395-C8 FCT
Anniston Dr 562-B5 Spt
Anniston St 561-H5 PeT
Ansar Ct 458-C6 PTM
Ansar La 458-C7 PTM
Ansley Ct 491-A7 WnT
Anson St 394-A5 F
Antelope Blvd 423-E10 PTM
Antelope Cir 423-E10 PTM
Antelope Ct 423-F10 PTM
Antelope Dr 423-E10 PTM
Antelope La 423-E10 PTM
Anthony Cir 428-J8 L
Anthony Ct 562-E9 G
Anthony Rd 324-C3 JT; 324-C6 WTH
Antietam Cir 423-D10 PTM
Antietam Ct 423-E10 PTM
Antietam Pl 423-D10 PTM
Antigua Tr 528-J10 FT
Antique Ct 459-C1 WTM
Antler Ct 389-D8 ET
Antler Way 457-D8 PTM
Antoinette Pl 561-E1 PeT
Anton Way 530-K5 SCT
Antoneli Dr 562-K1 FT
Antoneli La 528-J10; 562-K1 FT
Antwerp Terr 458-D7 PTM
Anvil Ct 393-G8 F
Apache Ct 360-B7 NT
Apache Dr 457-G6 PTM
Apache Moon 392-J3 Ca
Apache Wells High 491-H4 S
Apalachian Way 394-K7 F
Apilita Ct 426-C1 Ca
Apollo Pkwy 357-G8 WTH
Apollo Way 423-H10; 457-H1 PTM
Apothecary Ct 523-H5 P
Appaloosa Way 423-G9 PTM
Appel Dr 393-H8 F
Apple Blossom Dr 455-B8 LTH
Apple Cider Way 523-F2 WaT
Apple Cove Ct 531-J4 SCT
Apple Cross Cir 489-G6 A
Apple Cross Dr 457-E7 PTM
Apple Gate Ct 393-A3 Ca
Apple La 455-J3 B
Apple Spice Dr 462-B5 L
Apple Spruce Dr 462-A6 L
Apple St 494-F10; 528-C1 CTM
Apple Tree Cir 393-E6 F
Apple Tree Ct 393-E5 F
Apple Tree Dr 393-E6 F
Apple Tree La 462-A5 L
Apple Valley Rd 561-F10 G
Appleblossom La 558-K4 DTM
Appleby La 427-H3 LTM
Applecrest Dr 455-E4 B
Applegate Dr 531-F3 SCT
Applegate St 527-G2 CTM
Applehorn La 427-G3 LTM
Appleton Ct 491-A7 WnT
Appleton Dr 562-A7, B7 PeT
Appleton Terr 562-A7 PeT
Appletree Row 595-K2 G
Applewood La 427-G3 LTM
Apryl Dr 596-A5, C5 G
Aqua Vista Dr 496-B5 WrT
Aqueduct St 493-B4 CTM
Aqueduct Way 391-J9 CTH
Aqueous La 457-C10 WnT
Ar-Les Dr 325-J10 NT
Arabian Ct 458-E4 PTM
Arabian Run 458-E4, E5 PTM
Aragon Woods Ct 491-A1 WnT
Aragon Woods Dr 491-B1 WnT
Arapahoe Dr 462-B6 LTM
Arbor Ave DN-B4; 493-A9, A10 CTM
Arbor Dr 391-G5 Ca
Arbor Green La 460-D4 WTM
Arbor Green Way 460-D4 WTM
Arbor Lake Ct 424-H4 PTM
Arbor Lake Dr 424-G4 PTM
Arbor Lake La 424-K1 PTM
Arbor Springs Dr 455-H1 B
Arbor St 527-A6 PeT
Arbor Woods Dr 491-G10 WnT
Arborcrest Dr 461-G7, G8 LTM
Arborhill Ct 390-A4 ET
Arborhill Way 390-A4 ET
Arborview Dr 428-F6 L
Arborway Ct 424-K1 PTM
Arborway Dr 424-K1 PTM
Arborway La 424-H4 PTM
Arborwood Tr 391-G8 CTH
Arbutus Dr 457-G10 WnT
Arcadia St 458-C10 WnT
Arch St DN-D1, E1; 493-D6, F6, G6 CTM
Archwood Dr 491-E8 WnT
Arcola Ct 528-F9 BG
Arden Ct 392-E3 Ca
Arden Dr 425-F10; 459-F1 WTM
Arden Pl 595-A7 WTJ
Ardennes Dr 393-H3 F
Ardmore Ave 528-G8 BG
Ardsley Dr 491-A6 WnT
Ardwell Ct 563-C6 FT
Ardwell Dr 563-C5 FT
Argus Ave 461-H9 WrT
Argyle Ct 461-D10 WrT
Argyle Dr 524-A3 WaT
Aristocrat Ct 462-B6 LTM
Aristocrat Dr N 462-B7 LTM
Aristocrat La 462-B6 LTM
Arizona St 527-E1 CTM
Arjay Dr 561-B4 PeT
Arlene Dr 495-D4 WrT
Arley Dr 496-F4 WrT
Arlington Ave 528-K6 BG; 528-K10; 562-K2, K9 FT; 460-K5, K9 LTM; 460-K9; 494-K3, K10; 528-K2, K6 WrT
Arlington Cir 529-A8 FT
Arlington Ct 391-H9 CTH; 460-K6 LTM
Arlington Ct W 494-K2 WrT
Arlington Dr 592-A2 M
Arlington Way 528-K8 FT
Armada Ct 428-G1 FCT
Armadale Ct 428-H5 L
Armon Ct 392-E8 Ca
Armon Dr 392-E9 Ca
Armour Ave 460-A4 WTM

Armstrong Ct 528-J10 FT
Armstrong Dr 528-J10; 562-J1 FT
Arnolda Ave 492-G7 WnT
Aronson Dr 426-C3 WTM
Around the Hills Rd 461-A3 LTM
Arquette Cir 462-A8 LTM
Arquette Dr 462-A7 LTM
Arrodite Ct 458-J5 WTM
Arrodite Rd 393-H5 DTH
Arrow Ave 392-B5 Ca
Arrow Wood La 491-C1 WnT
Arrowhead Tr 529-G9 FT
Arrowwood Ct 325-B6 N
Arrowwood Dr 392-E1 Ca
Arroyo Rd 596-G4 G
Arsenal Ave DN-F1, F3; 459-J10; 493-J1, J3, J4, J5, J8 CTM
Arthington Blvd 460-F10; 494-F1 CTM; 460-F8 WTM
Arthur Ave 492-C7 WnT
Arthur Dr 391-F10 CTH; 523-G3 WaT
Arthur St 496-E6 Cu
Aruba La 457-D9 WnT
Arundel La 392-K1 Ca; 458-F9 WnT
Arusha St 494-C8 CTM
Arvada Pl 428-K6 L
Asbury St 527-K2, K3 CTM; 527-K6, K7, K8 PeT
Ascot Ct 424-J3 WTM
Ascot S 357-J9 WTH
Ash Cir 325-B9 N
Ash Ct 528-F6 BG; 456-J9 WnT
Ash Dr 392-B5 Ca
Ash Rd 456-J9 PTM
Ash St 531-H4 NP; 523-F9 P; 389-H8 Z
Ashbourne Cir 359-H9 N
Ashbourne Ct 595-K3 G
Ashbourne Dr 359-H9 N
Ashbourne La 595-K3 G; 460-H7 LTM; 460-D7 WTM
Ashbrook Dr 358-G3 N
Ashbury Cir 428-C1 F
Ashby Dr 559-G1 DTM
Ashcroft Dr 559-H5 DTM
Ashcroft Pl 390-G6 CTH
Ashford Ct 325-B7 N; 491-C7 WnT
Ashlake La 393-K2 F
Ashland Ave 596-E9 NW; 461-D10 WrT; 389-D8 Z
Ashland Ct 489-A8 WaT; 495-D1 WrT
Ashley Ct 393-F9 F
Ashley Jo Dr 462-A6 L
Ashley La 393-E9 F; 457-K10 WnT
Ashley Pl 393-F8 F
Ashmore Dr 596-C4 G
Ashton Dr 393-G7 F; 461-E4 L
Ashton La 393-F7 F
Ashton Pl 392-C6 Ca; 393-F7 F
Ashtree Ct 563-F6 FT
Ashtree Dr 563-F6 FT
Ashurst St 426-J10 LTM; 426-J10; 460-H1 WTM
Ashvale Dr 426-J2 LTM
Askview Dr 394-D3 F; 562-J7 FT
Ashway Ct 457-H10 WnT
Ashway Dr 457-G10 WnT
Ashwood 596-A4 G
Ashwood Cir 455-J6 B
Ashwood Ct 424-C6 PTM; 389-F5 Z
Ashwood Dr 424-B6, C6 PTM; 595-F7 WTJ
Ashwood La 393-K2 F
Ashworth Ct 425-A4 WTM
Askren Dr 495-H4 WrT
Aspen Crest La 457-E6 PTM
Aspen Ct 461-G8 LTM; 325-C10 N; 524-B8 P
Aspen Dr 394-D6 F; 456-F8 LTH; 523-C3 WaT
Aspen Grove Dr 427-A3 LTM
Aspen Grove La 427-A4 LTM
Aspen Talon Ct 457-E6 PTM
Aspen Way 392-A5 Ca; 461-G7, G8 LTM; 325-C10 N
Assembly La 457-K3 PTM
Association Ct 426-D2 Ca
Astor St DN-A2; 492-K7 CTM
Astro Ct 495-K2 WrT
Astro Dr 495-K1 WrT
Atcheson La 388-H6 ET
Athalene La 395-C10 FCT
Athens Ct 461-G7 LTM
Atherton Ct 455-H10 LTH
Atherton Dr 391-J5 Ca
Atherton Dr N 494-G8 WrT
Atherton Dr S 494-G8 WrT
Atherton La 595-B6 WTJ
Atlanta Ave 525-G9 DTM
Atlanta Dr 525-G9 DTM
Atlantic St 527-F7, K7 PeT
Atrium Boardwalk S 427-C8 LTM
Atrium Boardwalk W 427-C8 LTM
Atrium Way 496-B2 WrT
Attleboro Ct 426-J9 WTM
Atwell Dr 461-D6 L
Atwood Ct 393-H6 F
Atwood Pl 393-H6 F
Aubert St 523-J7 P
Auburn Ct 595-D8 WTJ
Auburn Dr 455-J2 B; 495-J4 WrT
Auburn Ford 594-J2 WTJ
Auburn La 325-K10; 359-K1 N
Auburn Rd 458-A10; 492-A1 WnT
Auburn St 492-A3, A5 S; 492-A7, A10 WnT
Audobon Dr 392-A3 Ca
Audrey Ave 458-A5 PTM
Audrey Cir 458-A5 PTM
Audrie Ct 393-K9 F
Audubon Ct 359-K6 N
Audubon Dr 455-J3 B
Audubon Rd 460-J6, J8 LTM; 426-J7, J9 WTM; 460-J10; 494-J5, J7, J9; 528-J3 WrT
August Dr 529-H6 FT
Augusta Blvd 394-D10 F
Augusta Ct 596-F3 G
Augusta Dr 455-A1 B
Augusta Dr E 491-H3 S
Augusta Dr N 424-E2 CTH; 491-H3 S
Augusta La 390-H9 CTH
Aulton Dr 359-K5 N
Aurelia Ct 462-A9 WrT
Aurie Dr 495-G2 WrT
Aurora St 527-K7 PeT
Austin Ct 489-K8 A; 557-J3 P
Austin Dr 489-K8; 490-A8 A; 461-D4 L
Austin Pl 395-C10 FCT
Austin Trace 390-A5 ET
Austral Dr 457-F5 PTM
Austrian Ct 358-A5 WTH
Austrian Pine Dr 424-B7 PTM
Austrian Pine Way 357-E4 WTH
Austrian Way 489-H10; 523-J1 A
Autum Frost Dr 524-B8 P
Autumn Ct 489-G6 A
Autumn Dr 592-F2 M
Autumn Harvest Dr 393-J8 F
Autumn La 562-E10 G; 461-A2 LTM
Autumn Leaf Ct 424-D5 PTM
Autumn Mill Ct 427-G5 LTM
Autumn Mill La 427-G6 LTM
Autumn Ridge Ct 496-G10 WrT
Autumn Ridge La 496-F10 WrT
Autumn Springs Dr 489-J8 A
Autumn Way 389-D4 Z
Autumn Woods Dr 426-H3 WTM
Autumn Woods La 426-H3 WTM
Autumnsong Dr 525-K5 DTM
Auvergne Ave 494-G9 CTM
Avalon Cir 595-H2 G
Avalon Dr 489-B8 WaT
Avalon Dr E 461-A1 LTM
Avalon Forest Dr 427-B8 LTM
Avalon La 461-A1 LTM
Avalon Rd 461-A2 LTM
Avalon Tr Ct 427-C9 LTM
Avalon Tr Dr 427-B9 LTM
Avalon Tr Rd 427-C8 LTM
AVDA Pk Rd 358-A6 WTH
Avenel Ct 424-G2 CTH
Averitt Rd 596-A3, A7 G; 596-A7 PTJ
Avery Cir 393-F8 F
Avery Ct 559-D9 MTM
Avery Dr 559-C10 MTM
Avery Dr E 424-B6 PTM
Avery Dr W 424-B6 PTM
Avery Row 393-F9 F
Avian Way 392-H2, J2 Ca
Aviara Dr 358-H3 N
Avlan La 462-F5 L
Avon Ave 523-G7 GT; 523-G7 P
Avon Crossing Dr 489-J8 A
Avon La 325-C6 N
Avon Pkwy 489-G8 A
Avon Rd 489-G10; 523-G2 A; 489-F4 LTH; 489-F4, G10; 523-G2 WaT
Avondale Dr 489-G8 A
Avondale Pl 494-D3 CTM
Ayrshire Cir N 558-K10; 559-A10; 593-A1 MTM
Ayrshire Ct 558-K10 MTM
Ayrshire St 458-J7 WTM
Azalea Dr 592-F2 M; 491-F1 WnT
Azionaqua St 395-D7 FCT
Azure La 461-A2 LTM

B

Babette Ct 562-C5 PeT
Babette Dr 562-B5 PeT; 562-B5 Spt
Babson Ct 393-H2 F; 424-F3 PTM
Baccus Ct 424-C6 PTM
Back Bay Ct 457-D9 WnT
Back Cr Cir 595-J2 G
Back Cr Overlook 595-J2 G
Backbay La 428-E6 LTM
Backwater Dr 427-C3 LTM
Bacon St 527-G5, H5, J5; 528-A5 PeT
Bade Rd 496-C10; 530-C2 WrT
Baden Dr 423-E9 PTM
Badger Ct 425-A9 WTM
Badger Dr 425-A8 WTM
Badger Grove Ct 593-A1 MTM
Badger Grove Dr 593-A1 MTM
Bagley Rd 462-J4 BCT
Bahama Ct 457-D9 WnT
Bahamas Cir 394-G10 FCT
Bahamas Ct 394-G10 FCT
Bahia Ct 528-J10 FT
Bahia Dr 528-J10 FT
Bailey Ct 391-D5 Ca; 389-H8 Z
Bailey Dr 525-E2 WnT
Bailey Way 393-J9 F
Bakemeyer St 527-D4 CTM
Baker Ct 461-K8 LTM
Baker Dr 461-K7, K8; 462-A7 LTM
Baker Rd 564-G8 FT
Baker St 323-E7 WTH
Bakeway Cir 490-J10 WnT
Bakeway Ct 490-G10 WaT
Bakeway Dr 490-H10 WaT
Balaton Ct 596-H3 G
Balboa Ct 461-H7 LTM
Balboa Dr 461-H8 LTM
Bald Eagle Ct 456-J8 PTM
Balfour Ct 489-H10 A; 427-B10 LTM
Balihai Ct 357-F9 WTH
Ballew Blvd 393-H5 F
Ballinshire N 457-C5 PTM
Ballinshire S 457-C6 PTM
Ballyshannon St 560-K6 PeT
Balmoral Ct 389-F9 Z
Balmoral Rd 491-E10, F10 WnT
Balroyal Cir 394-F10 F
Balroyal Ct 490-J6 WnT
Balsam Ave 459-J9 CTM
Baltimore Ave 459-K10; 460-A9, A10; 493-K2, K3 CTM; 460-A9 WTM
Baltimore Ct 393-A5 Ca
Baltimore Terr 459-K10; 493-K1 CTM
Banbridge Dr 496-B2 WrT
Banbury Cir 392-E5 Ca
Banbury Rd 461-A5 LTM; 324-K6; 325-A7 N
Banbury Rd N 324-K5 N
Bancaster Cir 424-D7 PTM
Bancaster Dr 424-D8 PTM
Bancroft St 460-G10; 494-G2, G4, G5, G7, G8, G9 CTM; 528-G10 PeT
Bandecoot Ct 458-B5 PTM
Bando Ct E 426-C10 WTM
Bando Ct W 426-C10 WTM
Bandy Dr 463-C1 VT
Bangalore Rd 390-J9 CTH
Bangor Dr 561-F4 PeT
Bank St 531-J5 NP
Bankers La 494-F8 CTM
Banner Ave 491-E5, F5; 525-E1, E3 WnT
Banning La 528-E9 PeT
Bannock Cir 559-J4 DTM
Bannock Ct 559-J5 DTM
Bannock Dr 559-J4 DTM
Banta Cir 561-F3 PeT
Banta Ct 561-F3 PeT
Banta Rd 558-K3 DTM; 560-F3, K3; 561-D3, G3, K3; 562-A3, C3 PeT
Banta Tr 561-E3 PeT
Banton Cir 496-K9 SCT
Bantry Ct 457-C5 PTM
Banyan La 562-H7 FT
Bar Del Dr E 559-E2 DTM
Bar Del Dr W 559-E1, E2 DTM
Barb Wire Rd 561-C6 PeT
Barbados Cir 561-G4 PeT
Barbados Dr 561-G4 PeT
Barbara Ct 492-D2 WnT
Barbara Dr 455-J3 BTH; 562-D9 G
Barbary La 460-B6 WTM
Barbee La 391-F10 CTH
Barbera Ct 528-B7 PeT
Barberry Dr 489-D10 A
Barbour Ct 461-D5 L
Barbwood La 462-A6 L
Barcelona Dr 596-G4 G
Barclay Ct 426-E3 WTM
Barcroft Dr 425-H3 WTM
Barcroft La 425-H3 WTM
Barefoot Tr 561-H9 G
Bari Ct 461-J7 LTM
Baribeau Ct 496-C2 WrT
Baribeau La 496-C2 WrT
Barker La 462-A4 L
Barkwood Ct 391-G8 CTH
Barley Cir 357-H10 WTH
Barlow Dr 461-F5 L
Barlum Dr 425-H6 WTM
Barmore Ave 391-G10 CTH
Barnard St 424-F4 PTM
Barnegat La 429-A1 FCT
Barnes Ave 459-A10; 493-A2 CTM
Barnett La 559-H2 DTM
Barnett Pl 393-H2 F
Barnhill Dr DN-B2; 493-B6 CTM
Barnor Dr 461-A7, A8 LTM; 495-A2 WrT
Barnstable Ct 426-J8 WTM
Barnstable Rd 390-E10 CTH
Barnstone Ct 394-J6 F
Barnwood Dr 531-F4 SCT
Barnwood Rd 424-A10 PTM
Barnwood Trace 424-B10 PTM
Baron Ct 489-E9 A; 426-J4 LTM
Baron Field Cir 424-H8 WTM
Baron Field Ct 424-H8 WTM
Baron Field Dr 424-K7 WTM
Barr Dr 495-K1; 496-A1 WrT
Barr Will Dr 426-F10 WTM
Barrett Ave 526-F2, H2 WnT
Barrhill Ct 394-A5 F
Barrington Ave 528-A1 CTM
Barrington Dr 392-E10 Ca
Barrington Pl 393-C7 F
Barrow Ave 493-H5 CTM
Barry Rd 495-F2 WrT
Barstow Dr 393-G2 F
Bart Rd 558-B1 GT
Barth Ave 493-J10; 527-H1, H2, H4 CTM; 561-H2, H5 PeT
Barth Dr 389-E4 Z
Bartlett Ave 527-F7 PeT
Bartley Ct 462-D2 L
Bartley Dr 462-C2 L
Barton Ave 492-C9 WnT
Bartram La 523-B7 P
Bash St 427-B6, C4 LTM
Basil Ct 562-F5 PeT
Basin St 461-J7 L; 461-J7 LTM
Basque Ct 458-E8 PTM
Bassett Dr 462-B6 L
Basswood Ct 391-G8 CTH
Basswood Dr 424-F5 PTM; 562-A6 PeT
Bastani Pl 563-A2 FT
Bastille Dr 457-F3 PTM
Bastille La 457-F4 PTM
Bastille Way 457-F4 PTM
Bates St DN-E3, F3; 493-H8 CTM
Battell Rd 322-B1 AT
Batten Dr 428-D3 LTM
Bauer Dr 426-D2 Ca
Bauer Dr W 426-C2 Ca
Bauer Rd 494-H4 WrT
Bauman St 491-F6, F7, F8, F9 WnT
Baur Dr 460-A3 WTM
Bavarian Dr E 462-C10 WrT
Bavarian Dr W 462-B10 WrT
Baxter Dr 492-B3 S
Bay Bk Dr 427-F7 LTM
Bay Breeze Ct 428-F3 LTM
Bay Cir Dr 424-G2 PTM
Bay Colony Dr 456-K5 PTM
Bay Colony La 456-K4 PTM
Bay Cove 427-F6 LTM
Bay Ct 424-G1 CTH
Bay Ct W 424-K6 WTM
Bay Forrest Dr 428-K3 LTM
Bay Harbor Dr 457-G5 PTM
Bay Harbor La 457-G5 PTM
Bay Hill Cir 455-A1 B
Bay La 393-K9 F
Bay Landing Cir 457-C4 PTM
Bay Landing Dr 457-C4 PTM
Bay Leaf Cir 562-E5 PeT
Bay Pointe Cir 428-K4 LTM
Bay Port Cir 428-K3 LTM
Bay Pt Ct 457-D10 WnT
Bay Pt Dr 426-C5 WTM
Bay Pt Way 428-K4 LTM; 457-E10 WnT
Bay Rd Dr N 426-C6 WTM
Bay Rd Dr S 426-C7 WTM
Bay Ridge Ct 428-H4 LTM
Bay Run Cir 428-K4 LTM
Bay Run Ct 428-K3 LTM
Bay Shore Dr 426-A7 WTM
Bay St 527-J10 PeT
Bay Tree Ct 428-G4 LTM
Bay View Dr 457-E10 WnT
Bay Vista Ct 427-A3 LTM
Bay Vista Dr E 427-A2 LTM
Bay Vista Dr W 427-A2 LTM
Bayberry Ct 426-G6 WTM
Bayberry Ct E 392-C7 Ca
Bayberry Ct W 392-B8 Ca
Bayberry La 389-J5 Z
Baycreek Dr 428-E7 L
Bayhead Dr 457-E9 WnT
Bayhill Ct 325-C5 N
Bayhill Dr 392-G5 Ca; 428-E8 L
Bayhill Way 428-F6 LTM
Bayley Cir 325-C7 N
Bayou Ct 461-J6 L
Baypointe Dr 490-A7 WaT
Bayridge Cir E 428-E8 L
Bayridge Cir W 428-E8 L
Bayridge Dr 428-E8 L
Bays Dr 359-A8 NT
Bays Water Blvd 457-F6 PTM
Bays Water Rd 422-K3 PTM
Bayshore Ct 392-D9 Ca
Bayshore La 489-K7 A; 490-A7 WaT
Bayside Ct 428-J1 FCT; 427-A2 LTM
Bayside Dr 595-J4 G; 491-E1 WnT
Bayside Dr N 427-A2 LTM
Bayside Dr S 427-A2 LTM
Bayside Way 427-A2 LTM
Bayswater La 325-E2 C
Bayton Ct 496-C5 WrT
Baytree Ct 391-D1 CTH
Bayview Ct 428-H1 FCT; 427-G6 LTM
Bayview La 595-J4 G
Bayview Pt 427-G7 LTM
Baywood Cir 427-H3 LTM
Baywood Ct 324-J6 N; 595-C8 WTJ
Baywood Dr 428-F8 L; 324-J6 N
Baywood La 428-E7 L
Bazil Ave 529-H7 FT; 495-H1, J4, J5, J7 WrT
Beach Ave 425-J8, K7; 426-A7 WTM
Beach Blvd 325-E4 C
Beachview Dr 491-G6 WnT
Beachway Ct 325-E2 C
Beachway Dr 491-G7, H6, H8 WnT
Beacon Blvd 357-J10 WTH
Beacon Ct 357-J10 WTH; 458-C10 WnT
Beacon La 325-F1 C; 428-C2 LTM
Beacon Pk Dr 357-J10 WTH
Beacon Way 357-J10 WTH
Beaconfield Ct 392-D1 Ca
Beagletown Rd 356-H7 WTH
Beals 391-J6 Ca
Beam Ridge Dr 395-C10 FCT; 428-A4 LTM
Bean Blossom Dr 559-B10 MTM
Beanblossom Cir 427-H7 LTM
Bear Branch Ct 559-C10 MTM
Beardon Ct 325-D10 N
Bearing Dr 424-C5 PTM
Bears Case Ct 392-C3 Ca
Bearsdale Cir 462-H1 L
Bearsdale Dr 462-H1 L
Bearsdale Way 324-G7 N
Bearwood Dr 462-E9 WrT
Beasley Dr 458-B10 WnT
Beau Jardin Dr 528-K10 FT
Beaufain Ct 561-B7 PeT
Beaufort La 457-J3 PTM
Beaumont Ct 389-F10 ET; 491-E6 WnT
Beaumont Green Dr E 426-G6 WTM
Beaumont Green Dr W 426-G7 WTM
Beaumont Green Pl 426-G7 WTM
Beaumont Rd 462-A3 L
Beaumont Way Dr 426-G6 WTM
Beaumont Way Dr N 426-G6 WTM
Beauport Rd 491-J2 S; 492-D2 WnT
Beauty Ave DN-B2; 493-B7 CTM
Beauvior Dr 461-K6 L
Beaver Ct 462-A9 WrT
Beaver Dr 462-A9 WrT
Beaverbrook Dr 391-F8 CTH
Beazle St 323-J7 WTH
Bech Tracy Ct 596-D10 NW
Bechtel Rd 424-J4 WTM
Bechtold Ave 461-H5 L
Beck Ridge Cir 594-K6 WTJ
Beck St 460-C9 CTM
Beckeits Ct 394-D8 F
Beckenbauer La 491-C5 WnT
Beckenbauer Pl 491-C5 WnT
Beckenbauer Way 491-C4 WnT
Becker Ct 392-K10 F; 389-J6 Z
Becker Dr 389-J6 Z
Beckford Dr 490-J7 WnT
Beckham Ct 391-H6 CTH
Beckinhill Ct 427-H5 LTM
Beckley Rd 496-H5 Cu
Becks Grove Ct 593-A1 MTM
Becks Grove Dr 593-A1 MTM
Beckwith Dr 493-K2; 494-A2, A3 CTM
Bedford Ct 392-F3 Ca
Bedford Dr 392-F3 Ca
Bedford St 492-H10 WnT
Bee Camp Ct 429-B1 FCT
Beech Cir 523-K9 P
Beech Ct 561-C10 WTJ; 456-K9 WnT
Beech Dr 393-C9 F; 562-C10 G; 458-D5 PTM; 491-F7, H7 WnT
Beech Dr N 523-K9 P
Beech Dr S 523-K9 P
Beech Dr W 523-K9 P
Beech Hollow Dr 458-A3, D3 PTM
Beech Knoll 427-G9 LTM
Beech Pk Dr 596-B1 G
Beech Pl 424-E2 CTH
Beech St 527-G5 CTM; 389-H8 Z
Beechcrest Ct 528-C4 CTM
Beechcrest Dr 528-D3 CTM
Beecher Ct 529-B2 WrT
Beecher St 527-F2, H2; 528-A2 CTM; 525-H2; 526-A2 WnT; 529-B2 WrT
Beechmill La 561-J8 PeT
Beechmont Dr 392-B4 Ca
Beechtree Cir 392-G3 CTH
Beechtree Ct 461-K8 LTM
Beechview Dr 596-B3 G
Beechview La 561-D7 PeT
Beechwood Ave 596-E9 NW; 494-J8; 495-A8, E8, G8 WrT
Beechwood Ct 359-G2 N
Beechwood Dr 455-J9 B; 528-F4 BG; 391-J9; 392-C3 CTH; 392-D9 Ca; 496-K5 Cu; 359-G1 N; 523-K6 P; 357-K2; 358-A2 W
Beechwood La 559-A3 DTM; 561-E2, G2 PeT; 531-E7 SCT; 389-G8 Z
Beeler Ave 491-K4 S; 457-K9, K10; 491-K1 WnT
Behner Bk Ct 427-A3 LTM
Behner Bk Dr 427-A3 LTM
Behner Cir 427-A3 LTM
Behner Crossing 427-A3 LTM
Behner La 427-A2 LTM
Behner Reach 427-A3 LTM
Behner Way 427-A2, A3 LTM
Beisinger Pl 562-K2 FT
Bel Air Dr 391-H9 CTH
Bel Moore Blvd 563-D7 FT
Bel Moore Cir 563-D7 FT
Belair Ct 461-J8 LTM
Belair Dr 461-H8 LTM
Belden Dr 392-B4 Ca
Belfield St 560-K6 PeT
Belford Ct 457-H7 PTM
Belfry Way 529-A8 FT
Bell Cem Rd 530-A10 FT
Bell Ct 392-H9 Ca
Bell St DN-F2; 493-J7 CTM; 594-G2 WTJ
Belle Forch Ct 357-H9 WTH
Belle Manor Ct 425-E2 WTM
Belle Manor La 425-E2 WTM
Belle St 523-G9 P
Bellefontaine Ave 528-F6 BG; DN-E1; 493-H3, H5, H6 CTM
Bellefontaine St 391-G9, G10 CTH
Bellemeede Dr 530-A2 WrT
Belleview Pl 492-H5, H7, H8, H10 WnT
Bellingham Dr 525-J10 DTM
Bellingham Terr 525-H9 DTM
Bellis St 493-K3 CTM
Bellisle Ct 489-A10 WaT
Bells Cr 461-J6 LTM
Bellwood Dr 461-F10 LTM; 461-E10 WrT
Belmar Ave 461-F9; 495-F2, G7 WrT
Belmar Ct 359-K1 N
Belmont Ave DN-A2, A4; 492-J5, J10; 526-J2, J3 CTM; 560-H7, J4, J5 PeT; DN-A2, A4; 492-J5, J10; 526-J2 WnT
Belmont Cir 390-H8; 391-H9 CTH
Belt St 527-B1 CTM
Beluga La 457-E9 WnT
Ben Hur Ave 456-J10 WnT
Benchmark Dr 425-H3 WTM
Benchview Dr 425-J2 WTM
Bend Rd N 528-F8 BG
Benderfield Dr 389-F8 Z
Bending La 595-B10 WTJ
Benham Ct 490-H6 WnT
Benjamin Dr 461-F4 L
Bennett Cir 391-H1 CTH
Bennett Ct 457-J8 PTM
Bennett Dr 457-H8 PTM
Bennett Rd 391-F1, G1 CTH
Bennington Dr 389-G6 Z
Bennington Rd 561-E5 PeT
Bennington Trace 390-H6 CTH
Benny La 526-A6 DTM
Benoit Dr 491-D4 WnT
Benson Ct 561-C9 PeT
Bent Bk Dr 426-K3 LTM
Bent Cr Ct 428-D1 F
Bent Oak Ct 428-K5 L
Bent Oak Dr 428-J5 L
Bent Oak La 428-J5 L
Bent Tree Ct 425-D5 WTM
Bent Tree La 428-B1 F; 595-B5 WTJ; 425-D5 WTM
Bent Tree Pl 595-B6 WTJ
Bent Willow Dr 529-F2 WrT
Bentbrook Dr 358-F3 N; 523-D3 WaT
Bentie Dr 558-K5 DTM
Bentley Blvd 393-G5 F
Bentley Dr 392-F6 Ca; 491-C6 WnT; 389-D9 Z
Bentley Way 391-F3 CTH
Benton Dr 561-F6 PeT
Benton Oak Dr 359-D2 N
Bentwater La 394-D8 F
Bentwood Cir Dr E 424-F6 PTM
Bentwood Cir Dr N 424-F6 PTM
Bentwood Cir Dr S 424-F6 PTM
Bentwood Cir Dr W 424-F6 PTM
Bentworth Way 562-K2 FT
Benz Ct 462-D1 L
Bergamot Ct 462-E8 LTM
Bergeson Dr 423-G4 PTM
Bergeson Way 423-F4 PTM
Beringer La 391-C2 CTH
Berkley Cir 393-F8 F
Berkley Ct 393-E8 F
Berkley Rd 459-D7 WTM
Berkshire La 496-K6 Cu; 325-A6 N; 460-F6 WTM
Berkshire Rd 460-F6 WTM
Berlander Rd 531-F2 SCT
Bermuda Dr 495-G4 WrT
Bernard Ave 459-C8 WTM
Bernard Dr 559-A10 MTM
Bernie Ct 496-C2 WrT
Bernie Dr 496-C2 WrT
Berry Ave 494-K8 WrT
Berry Rd 595-B5 WTJ
Bertha Ct 492-A9 WnT
Bertha St 491-G9, H9; 492-A9, B9, F9 WnT
Bertrand Rd 458-C10 WnT
Berwick Ave 492-E5, E7, F8; 526-E1, E5 WnT
Berwick La 489-A8 WaT
Berwick Pl 492-E7 WnT
Berwyn Rd 596-D10 NW
Berwyn St 527-F5, J5, K5; 528-A4, B4 CTM; 526-B5 WnT; 529-A4 WrT
Beryl Dr 525-G8 DTM
Best Way 357-J2 W
Bester Rd 463-G9 BCT
Beta La 459-C7 WTM
Beth Ann Dr 526-C9 DTM
Bethel Ave 528-D3, G4 BG; 528-A1, B1, D3 CTM
Bethel Morris Tr 393-B5 Ca
Bethel Rd 457-K6 PTM
Bethesda La 457-J2 PTM
Bethesda Way 457-J2 PTM
Betholm Dr 529-K9 FT
Betsy La 527-F5 PeT
Bettcher Ave 424-J10; 458-J2 WTM
Beulah Ave 526-A3, A4 WnT
Beulahland Pl 427-D3 LTM
Bevedere Dr 458-G5 WTM
Beverly Dr 459-D5, F5 WTM; 389-J5 Z
Beverly Hills Dr 424-B7 PTM
Beverly La 523-D8 P
Beville Ave 494-A4, A6, A8 CTM
Bevington La 426-E2 WTM
Bexhill Dr 392-B4 Ca
Bexley Dr 392-J1 Ca; 596-H4 G; 427-D10; 461-C1 LTM
Bexley Pl 596-H4 G
Bicking St DN-E4; 493-F10 CTM
Bierman Rd 528-G4 BG; 528-G4 CTM; 528-H4 WrT
Big Ben Cir 461-K8 LTM
Big Four Rd 529-H3 FT
Big Hill Cir 491-K7 WnT
Big Horn Dr 456-D10 LTH
Big Horn Rd 491-B6 WnT
Big Oak Dr 458-A3 PTM
Big Pine Dr 457-C2 PTM
Bighorn Ct 393-G2 F
Bill Dr 461-K5 L
Billie La 425-D8 WTM
Billings Rd 462-A2 L
Billingsgate Pl 393-C10 F
Billy Cr Cir 391-C1 CTH
Biloxi La 528-F9 BG
Biltmore Ave 525-K8, K9 DTM; 491-K5 S; 491-K8, K10; 525-K2 WnT

Biltmore St 525-K3 WnT
Bimini La 457-D9 WnT
Bing Ct 562-E1 PeT
Bingham Ct 492-D2 WnT
Birch Ave DN-B4; 493-B10 CTM
Birch Canyon Dr 392-C10 CTH
Birch Ct 497-A4 BCT; 523-K8 P; 561-B9 WTJ
Birch Dr 523-K8; 524-A8 P
Birch La 596-G3 G; 428-J9 L; 594-H6 WTJ
Birch St 528-F6 BG; 393-H8 F; 531-H5 NP; 358-A3 W
Birch Tree Cir 428-D8 L
Birch Tree Ct 428-D9 L
Birch Tree La 428-D8 L
Birchcrest Dr 491-F10 WnT
Birchwood Ave 459-H9 CTM; 459-H3 WTM
Bird Branch La 458-A2 PTM
Bird Song Tr 592-F7 BTM
Birdsong La 391-C1 CTH
Birkdale Cir 490-J1 WnT
Birmingham La 393-H3 DTH
Birnam Woods Tr 425-H1 CTH
Biron Way 457-H3 PTM
Birtz Rd 461-J3, J4 L
Biscay Sq 424-H10 WTM
Biscayne Rd 461-H8, J8 LTM; 461-H9 WrT
Bischoff Dr 528-C5 BG
Bishop Ave 592-A2 M
Bishop Cir 390-J10 CTH
Bishop Ct 462-A8 LTM
Bishop Orchard Rd 459-F9 CTM
Bishops Gate 392-F5 Ca
Bishops La 561-C7, C8 PeT
Bison Ct 424-C6 PTM
Bitter Bark La 561-G7 PeT
Bittern La 427-F7 LTM
Bitternut Dr 428-H7 L
Bitteroot Ct 490-J6 WnT
Bittersweet Ct 325-B10 N; 596-D9 NW
Bittersweet La 393-E9 F; 428-K10 L; 595-A1 WTJ
Bittersweet Rd 596-D9 NW
Bitterwood Dr 529-B7 FT
Bittner La 531-J8 SCT
Bittner St 531-J5 NP
Bixler Rd 527-E9 PeT
Black Bird La 561-G10 G
Black Cherry Cir 562-E1 PeT
Black Forest Dr 558-D5 GT
Black Hawk La 456-J9 WnT
Black Knight Blvd 496-A1 WrT
Black Locust Dr 462-F8 WrT
Black Maple Ct 596-G1 G
Black Oak Ct E 489-F5 A
Black Oak Ct W 489-F6 A
Black Oak Dr 458-G7 WTM
Black Oak La 531-G4 SCT
Black Oaks Way 563-A1 FT
Black Pine Ct 394-A10 F
Blackburn Dr 357-J1 W
Blackfoot Dr 462-B6 LTM
Blackford St DN-C2; 493-C7 CTM
Blackgum Ct 428-J6 L
Blackhawk Sta 429-C3 McC
Blackley Ct 457-H3 PTM
Blackley La 457-H3 PTM
Blackoak Cir 557-K5 GT
Blackoak Dr 557-K5 GT
Blackpool Dr 359-H10 N
Blackrock Ct 557-J6 GT
Blackrock Rd 557-J6; 558-B6 GT
Blacksmith Ct 393-G8 F; 523-H5 P
Blackstone Ave 562-E1 PeT
Blackstone Ct 391-F9 CTH
Blackstone Dr 562-F1 PeT
Blackstone Pl 389-F6 Z
Blacktern Way 392-H3 Ca
Blackthorn Cir 428-H7 L
Blackthorn Ct 393-E10 F; 428-H7 L
Blackthorn Dr 559-F2 DTM; 428-H7 L
Blackwalnut Pt 428-F6 LTM
Blackwood Ct 592-E2 M; 595-A5 WTJ
Blain Way 457-C5 PTM
Blaine Ave DN-B4; 492-K10; 526-K2 CTM
Blairsden Ave 392-B4 Ca
Blake St DN-C1, C2; 493-C6, C7 CTM
Blakeview Dr 428-H10 L
Blanchard Way 324-H6 N
Blankenship Dr 560-K5 PeT
Blazing Tr Ct 560-J8 PeT
Blixen Ct 393-B9 F
Bloom Dr 560-K10 WTJ
Bloomfield Ct 564-F4 FT; 357-E9 WTH
Bloomfield Dr E 564-F4 FT
Bloomfield Dr S 564-F4 FT
Bloomfield Dr W 564-F4 FT
Bloomfield La E 357-F8 WTH
Bloomfield Terr 564-F3 FT
Bloor La 389-G7 Z
Blossom La N 423-F7 PTM
Blossom La S 423-F7 PTM
Bloyd Ave 493-K3; 494-A3 CTM
Blue Bk Way 596-F5 G
Blue Chip Ct 490-J4 WnT
Blue Cr Dr 392-E10 Ca
Blue Cr Dr S 427-D8 LTM
Blue Cr Dr W 427-D9 LTM
Blue Fin Dr 428-C2 LTM
Blue Grass Ct 592-B4 M; 458-H7 WTM
Blue Grass Dr 458-G7 WTM
Blue Grass Pkwy 596-F5 G
Blue Heron Dr 392-H2 Ca
Blue Hill Cir 491-J7, K7 WnT
Blue Jay Ct 424-J7 WTM
Blue Jay La 424-H8 WTM
Blue Oak La 561-G8 PeT
Blue Ribbon Dr 528-K8 FT
Blue Ridge Rd 459-D6 WTM
Blue Sky Ct 391-F1 CTH
Blue Spring Ct 496-F8 WrT
Blue Spring Dr 496-E9 WrT
Blue Spruce Ct 595-A4 WTJ
Blue Spruce Dr 394-A10 F
Blue Willow Cir 529-F1 WrT
Blue Willow Dr 529-F1 WrT
Bluebell Cir 491-G1 WnT
Bluebell Ct 457-G10 WnT
Bluebell Dr 497-F7 SCT
Bluebell La 457-G10; 491-G1 WnT
Blueberry La 394-E9 F
Bluebird Ct 457-D8 PTM
Bluefin Cir 428-G4 LTM
Bluefin Ct 428-G5 LTM
Bluegrass Ct 393-F9 F
Bluespruce Dr 562-J1 FT
Bluestem Ct 326-C9 N
Bluestone Cir 428-G3 LTM
Bluestone Dr 428-H3 LTM
Bluestone Way 393-D9 F
Bluewater Ct 496-B4 WrT
Bluff Acres Dr 594-E5 WTJ
Bluff Ave 527-E2 CTM
Bluff Cr Ct N 559-A10 MTM
Bluff Crest Ct 561-A3 PeT
Bluff Crest Dr 561-A3 PeT
Bluff Crest La 561-A3 PeT
Bluff Dr 394-A10 F
Bluff Head Dr 594-E4 WTJ
Bluff La 594-E5 WTJ
Bluff Rd 527-C5, D3 CTM; 523-H10 P; 527-C5, C10; 560-J7; 561-B2 PeT; 560-G10; 594-G2 WTJ
Bluffgrove Cir 423-F10 PTM
Bluffgrove Dr 423-E10 PTM
Bluffgrove La 423-F10 PTM
Bluffridge Blvd 423-E10 PTM
Bluffridge Ct 423-E10 PTM
Bluffridge Dr 423-E10 PTM
Bluffridge La 423-E10 PTM
Bluffridge Pkwy 423-E10 PTM
Bluffridge Pl 423-E10 PTM
Bluffridge Way 423-E10 PTM
Bluffs Cir 324-J6 N
Bluffwood Ct 455-B2 BTH; 458-H6 WTM
Bluffwood Dr N 458-H6 WTM
Bluffwood Dr W 458-G6 WTM
Boardwalk La 394-B7 F
Boardwalk Pl 460-G3 LTM; 460-G3 WTM
Bob Dr 461-K4 L
Bob White La 458-A3 PTM
Bobby Ct 557-H2 P
Bobs Ct 528-F7 BG; 594-H8 WTJ
Boden Rd 360-K6, K10 WyT
Bodine Pl 594-J7 WTJ
Bodner La 392-B6 Ca
Boehning Ct 495-H1 WrT
Boehning La 495-H3 WrT
Boehning St 495-H1, J3, J7, J8 WrT
Boettcher Ct 458-J2 WTM
Bogalusa Ct 561-B5 PeT
Bogey Dr 462-G4 L
Boggs Cr Ct 562-J7 FT
Boggs Cr Dr 562-J7 FT
Boggstown Rd 599-D10 STS
Boine Cir 426-D1 Ca
Bold Forbes Ct 561-A7 PeT
Bold Ruler Dr 562-K2 FT
Bolin Ct 391-D4 Ca
Bolton Ave 460-K6, K7, K8 LTM; 592-B2 M; 460-K10; 494-K1, K2, K3, K5, K7; 528-K2, K3 WrT
Bolton Ct 494-K5 WrT
Bomar Dr 561-G9 G
Bonanza La 457-G6 PTM
Bonar Ave 495-K5, K7 WrT
Bond St 493-A2 CTM
Bonham Dr 458-F10; 492-F1 WnT
Bonita Ct 495-F2 WrT
Bonn Blvd 458-D8 PTM
Bonn Dr 458-E8 PTM
Bonna Ave 494-J8, K8; 495-H7 WrT
Bonnie Brae St 458-J3, J6, J7 WTM
Bonnie La 595-F1 G; 489-D6 WaT
Bonny Dr 559-D4 DTM
Bonnybridge Dr 525-E10 DTM
Bookbinder Dr 523-H5 P
Boone Ct 561-A8 PeT
Boone Dr 496-G5 WrT
Boone Ridge Rd 389-C8 ET
Boone St 394-A4 F
Boone Valley Ct 489-H10 A
Boonesboro Ct 595-H2 G
Boonesboro Rd 595-H3 G
Boots Ct DN-E1 CTM
Boots Dr 493-H2 CTM
Borax Ct 597-F1 CTJ
Bordeaux Ct 460-E1 WTM
Bosart Ave 494-F4, F5, F7, F9 CTM; 460-F4 WTM
Boshen Loop 461-H4 L
Bosinney Cir 427-E8 LTM
Bosloe Dr 424-D1 CTH
Bosman Ct 424-E1 CTH
Boston Ct 458-J8 WTM
Boston Ridge Ct 563-B3 FT
Boston Way 393-G8 F
Bottom Rd 557-G3, G7 GT
Boulder Ct 391-J2 Ca
Boulder Ct S 561-C4 PeT
Boulder Dr 325-J9 NT; 424-J7 WTM
Boulder Gap 460-J3 LTM
Boulder La 424-J8 WTM
Boulder Rd 561-C3 PeT
Boulevard Dr N 497-A5 Cu
Boulevard Pl 493-D1, D2 CTM; 459-D5, D8, D10 WTM
Bountiful Pl 558-E3 GT
Bounty Ct 428-C6 LTM
Bourbon St 461-J7 L
Bow La 425-F9 WTM
Bowen Ct 596-A5 G
Bowen Pl 526-E6 DTM
Bower Dr 491-G10 WnT
Bowers St 388-E2 Wh
Bowie La 457-H3 PTM
Bowline Ct 428-D5 LTM
Bowline Dr 428-D6 LTM
Bowman Ave 527-H7 PeT
Box Elder Ct 424-K4 WTM
Boxford Ct 491-C7 WnT
Boxwood Ct 394-A10 F
Boxwood Dr 562-C5, D5 PeT
Boy Scout Rd 461-E2, E3, E4 L
Boyd Ave 527-J2, J4, J5 CTM; 527-J5, J7 PeT
Boyd La 494-B2 CTM
Bracken Ct 426-E1 Ca
Brackenwood Blvd 425-B8 WTM
Brackenwood Cir 425-C8, C9 WTM
Brackenwood Dr 425-C8 WTM
Brad Dr 461-K5 L
Bradbury Access 526-C4 WnT
Bradbury Ave 527-G3, J3; 528-A3, B3 CTM; 526-A3, B3 WnT
Bradbury Pl 392-G9 Ca
Bradbury Rd 524-E4 WaT
Braddock Rd 424-D6 PTM
Bradey Ct 461-J3 L
Bradford Cir 491-C7 WnT
Bradford Ct 455-H1 B; 394-J9 F
Bradford Dr 526-C7 DTM
Bradford Knoll Dr 428-A1 F
Bradford Meadows Cir 457-K2 PTM
Bradford Pl 392-D7 Ca
Bradford Rd 524-A3 P; 524-A3, G3 WaT
Bradford Trace Blvd 496-F3 WrT
Bradford Trace Ct 496-F3 WrT
Bradford Woods La 424-D9 PTM
Bradford Woods Way 424-D9 PTM
Bradley Ave 494-D8, D9, D10 CTM
Bradley Dr 490-G10; 524-H1 WaT
Bradley Rd 558-C1 GT
Bradock Ct 490-K7 WnT
Bradshaw St DN-E4; 493-G10 CTM
Bradston Way 562-J1 FT
Bradwell Pl 427-H1 F
Brae Ct 557-J8 GT
Braeburn Dr E 495-G3 WrT
Braeburn Dr N 495-G3 WrT
Braeburn Dr W 495-G3 WrT
Braeburn Pkwy 495-G3 WrT
Braeburn Terr 495-G3 WrT
Braedon Wood 458-K7 WTM
Braemar Ct 390-H8 CTH; 489-A8 WaT
Braemar Dr 457-E7 PTM
Braemar St 489-A8 WaT
Braeside Ct 425-C3 WTM
Braeside Dr N 425-C3 WTM
Braeside Dr S 425-C4 WTM
Braewick Cir 428-D1 F
Braewick Ct 392-D9 Ca
Braewick Dr 392-D10 Ca
Braewick Pl 392-D10 Ca
Braewick Rd 460-J3, K3; 461-A3 LTM
Braewood Ct 561-B5 PeT
Bragdon St 461-F6 L
Braided Stream Way 424-D6 PTM
Brairway Ct 429-B2 McC
Brairwood Dr 426-D9 WTM
Bram Hall Ct 489-B10 WaT
Bramblewood Cir 457-C6 PTM
Bramblewood La 457-D6 PTM
Bramblewood Way 424-J2 CTH
Bramford Ct 427-D10 LTM
Bramshaw Rd 426-J10; 460-J1 LTM; 460-J1 WTM
Bramwood Ct 426-G6 WTM
Branch Cr Dr 424-D7 PTM
Branch Cr Way 424-E7 PTM
Branch Way 424-D7 PTM
Brandon Ct 425-A2 CTH
Brandon St 428-H10 L
Brandt Dr 525-F1 WnT
Brandt Rd 426-F2 WTM
Brandt St 491-F8 WnT
Brandy Wine Ct 390-E9 CTH
Brandywine Cir 455-E4 B
Brandywine Ct 455-E4 B; 526-A4 WnT
Brandywine Dr 526-A4 WnT
Brangton Dr 428-J1 F
Brantford Ct 425-B3 WTM
Brantly Dr 428-K9 L
Braugham Rd 561-G6 PeT
Brave Ct 428-E10 L
Brave Tr 428-E10 L
Braxton Dr 496-G1 WrT
Bray Ct 562-D10 G
Brazos Dr 562-H1 FT
Breakers Ct 523-E2 WaT
Breakers Way 392-K3 Ca
Breakwater Dr 394-K9 FCT; 491-E1 WnT
Breamore Rd 426-K10; 460-K1 LTM
Breckenridge Cir 426-E1 Ca
Breckenridge Ct 392-E10 Ca; 428-G10 L
Breckenridge Dr 392-E10; 426-E1 Ca; 428-G9 L; 458-E7 PTM; 458-E7 WTM
Breeds Hill Ct 563-B3 FT
Breeds Hill Dr 563-B3 FT
Breen Ct 461-J9 WrT
Breen Dr 461-J8 LTM; 461-J9 WrT
Breezy Pt Dr 394-B7 F
Brehob Rd 527-D7, D10; 561-D6 PeT
Breir Dr 594-K2 WTJ
Breman La 496-H4 WrT
Bremerton Cir 496-F6 Cu
Bremerton Dr 496-F6 Cu
Bren Lee Ct 562-C5 PeT
Brenandow Ct 359-J6 N
Brenda Blvd 594-G7 WTJ
Brenda Ct 395-J9 FCT; 594-F7 WTJ
Brendon Dr 523-J10 P
Brendon Forest Dr 461-B4 LTM
Brendon Pk Dr 461-B5 LTM
Brendon Way 389-G9 Z
Brendon Way Ct 461-B4 LTM
Brendon Way Dr E 461-C4 LTM
Brendon Way Dr N 461-B3 LTM
Brendon Way Dr S 461-B4 LTM
Brendon Way Dr W 461-B3 LTM
Brendon Way Pkwy 461-C4 LTM
Brendonridge Ct N 460-K4 LTM
Brendonridge Ct S 460-K5 LTM
Brendonridge Rd 460-K5 LTM
Brenly Ct 461-B3 LTM
Brennan Ct 393-G1 F
Brennan Rd 495-F2 WrT
Brent Ave 425-K6 WTM
Brentford Dr 495-G3 WrT
Brentridge Ct 594-J7 WTJ
Brentridge Pkwy 594-J7 WTJ
Brentridge Pl 594-J7 WTJ
Brentwood Ave 461-J9; 495-J7, J10 WrT; 389-J4 Z
Brentwood Ct 461-K5 LTM; 523-K8 P; 389-K4 Z
Brentwood Dr 392-C3 Ca; 596-D1 G; 461-J8 LTM; 592-B1 M
Brentwood Dr E 523-K8 P
Brentwood Dr S 523-K8 P
Brentwood Dr W 523-K8 P
Brentwood La 596-D10 NW
Brentwood St 596-C1 G
Brer Rabbit Ct 594-H6 WTJ
Brer Rabbit Dr 594-G6 WTJ
Bressingham Dr 462-D9 LTM
Breta Ct 496-H5 WrT
Breton St 458-D10; 492-C1 WnT
Bretton Cir 424-F9 PTM
Bretton Ct 424-F9 PTM
Bretton Wood Dr 424-F10 PTM
Brevard Dr 393-H2 F; 561-B6 PeT
Brewer Dr 596-C1 G; 562-A6 PeT; 458-C9 WnT
Brewer Pl 562-C10; 596-C1 G
Brewer Rd 525-C2 WnT
Brewer St 596-C1 G
Brewster Dr 491-J2 S
Brewster Rd 424-H4 PTM; 424-J4; 425-A4 WTM
Brewton St 394-A5 F
Brian Dr 461-K5 L
Brian Pl 392-D8 Ca
Brianna La 462-E4 L
Briar Cir 392-C10 Ca
Briar Cr La 426-C1 Ca
Briar Ct Pl 392-D10 Ca
Briar Ct 561-J9 G
Briar Dr 392-C10 Ca
Briar La 528-D5 BG
Briar Patch Ct 426-F9 WTM
Briar Patch La 595-K2 G
Briar Pl 392-C10 Ca
Briar Stone La 393-F9 F
Briarbrook Blvd 462-E8 LTM
Briarchase Ct 458-G1 PTM
Briarclift Rd 427-J9 LTM
Briarhill Dr 428-K5 L
Briarhill La 428-K5 L
Briarhill Way 428-K5 L
Briarpatch Rd 595-D10 WTJ
Briarstone Dr 561-K6 PeT
Briarstone La 561-J6 PeT
Briarstone Tr 392-G3 Ca
Briarstone Way 561-J6 PeT
Briarway La 429-C2 McC
Briarwood Ct 455-F8 B; 426-F9 WTM
Briarwood Dr 455-F8 B; 595-K2 G; 561-J7 PeT; 426-E9 WTM
Briarwood Trace 392-E4 Ca
Brichton Ct 596-F2 G
Brick Chapel Cir 593-A1 MTM
Brick Chapel Ct 593-A2 MTM
Brickenwood Ct 528-C7 PeT
Brickenwood La 528-B7 PeT
Brickenwood Trace 528-C7 PeT
Brickenwood Way 528-B7 PeT
Brickmaker Ct 523-H5 P
Bridal Cir 391-H1 CTH
Bridal Ct 391-H1 CTH
Bridge Ct 525-A2 WnT
Bridge Field Dr 392-D1 Ca
Bridge St 592-F2 BTM; 493-B10; 527-B1 CTM; 592-A2, C2, F2 M
Bridgefield Dr 457-F6 PTM
Bridgefield Dr E 524-C9 GT
Bridgefield Dr W 524-C9 GT
Bridgefield Way 457-F6 PTM
Bridgemont Ct 489-G6 WaT
Bridgeport Rd 524-J10 DTM; 490-K1, K10; 524-K2 WnT
Bridger Ct 424-A10 PTM
Bridger Dr 426-C1 Ca
Bridger Dr N 426-D1 Ca
Bridger Dr S 426-D1 Ca
Bridgett Dr 592-J2 MTM
Bridgeview Ct 429-A2 FCT
Bridgeview Way 426-A10 WTM
Bridgewater Cir 427-A4 LTM
Bridgewater Rd 428-J2 FCT
Bridgewood Ct 424-G9 PTM
Bridgewood Dr 424-G9 PTM
Bridgton Ct 495-H2 WrT
Bridgton Dr 495-G3 WrT
Bridle La 461-G7 L
Bridlewood Cir 358-B10 WTH
Bridlewood Ct 389-J1 ET
Bridlewood Dr 358-B10 WTH
Bridlewood La 358-B9 WTH
Bridlewood Tr 389-J2 ET
Brief Run 460-G5 WTM
Brier Cr Ct 497-B7 SCT
Brier Cr Dr 497-A7 SCT
Brier Pl 527-J1 CTM
Briergate Ct 495-J1 WrT
Brierley Way 392-B4 Ca
Brierwood Cir 392-F3 CTH
Brierwood Tr 392-F3 CTH
Brigadier Dr 461-J5 L
Brigantine Ct 428-E2 LTM
Brigantine Dr 428-D2 LTM
Bright Leaf Cir 529-E2 WrT
Bright St DN-C2; 493-C7 CTM
Brighton Ave 391-B5 CTH
Brighton Cir 391-B5 CTH; 393-D10 F
Brighton Ct 391-B5 CTH
Brighton La 391-B4 CTH
Brightwater Dr 394-A2 F
Brigs Ct 428-C4 LTM
Brigs Way 428-C4 LTM
Brill Rd 561-F1, F4 PeT
Brill St 527-F5 CTM; 527-F7, F9; 561-F2 PeT
Brinton St 325-H1 C
Brinwood Dr 425-K4 WTM
Brisbane Dr 393-H2 F
Brisbane Rd 458-E7 PTM; 458-E7 WTM
Bristlecone Dr 392-K10 F
Bristol Ct 392-F4 Ca
Bristol La 392-F4 Ca
Bristol Rd 425-H1 CTH; 425-A3 WTM
Brittany Cir 455-H3 B
Brittany Ct N 428-G5 L
Brittany Ct S 428-G5 L
Brittany Dr 389-K4 ET
Brittany Rd 492-B1 WnT
Brittany Way 393-D9 F
Britton Dr 528-C5 BG; 393-J4 DTH
Britton Pk Dr 393-J4 F
Britton Ridge 394-B4 F
Brixham Ct 393-H3 DTH; 491-C7 WnT
Brixton Dr 561-D10 G
Brixton La 394-C8 F; 561-D10 G; 460-H1 WTM
Broad Al E 592-A3 M
Broad Leaf La 393-E8 F
Broad Leaf Pl 592-F3 M
Broad Ripple Ave 459-F6 WTM
Broadleaf Ct 595-E7 WTJ
Broadmoor Plaza 458-F2, F5, H4 WTM
Broadview Ct 562-C5 PeT
Broadview Dr 562-C5, C6 PeT
Broadway 391-G10; 425-G1 CTH
Broadway Ave 596-B2 G
Broadway Dr N 523-G10 P
Broadway Dr S 523-G10 P
Broadway St DN-E1; 459-G10; 493-G1, G3, G4, G5, G6 CTM; 428-H10 L; 425-G3, G5, G6, G10; 459-G1, G2, G4, G5, G8 WTM
Broadway Terr 459-G3 WTM
Brobeck Ct 457-H3 PTM
Brobeck La 457-H3 PTM
Brock St 458-A5 PTM
Brocken Ct 496-G3 WrT
Brocken Way 496-G3 WrT
Brockford Ct 391-H7 CTH
Brockton Ct 460-C3 WTM
Brockton Dr 460-B3 WTM
Broken Arrow Cir 490-J7 WnT
Broken Arrow Ct 497-D8 SCT; 490-J7 WnT
Broken Arrow Dr 497-D8 SCT
Broken Arrow Rd 490-H7 WnT
Broken Bow Dr 594-K6 WTJ
Broken Bow Tr 491-B6, B7 WnT
Broken Cr Cir 392-B10 Ca
Brokenhurst Rd 460-J1 LTM; 426-J10 WTM
Bromley Pl 495-G3 WrT
Brompton Ct 427-A9 LTM; 359-J8 N
Brompton Rd 392-F5, F6 Ca
Bronson Dr 393-H2 F
Bronwyn Ct 496-F4 WrT
Brook Blvd W 359-E4 N
Brook Cir W 359-E4 N
Brook Ct 489-A1 LTH; 427-H5 LTM
Brook Dr 596-A4 G
Brook Haven Dr 461-B6 L
Brook La DN-C1; 493-C5 CTM
Brook Mill Ct 391-E3 CTH
Brook Vista 392-B10 Ca
Brookacre La 561-E8 PeT
Brookdale Dr 562-A2 PeT
Brooke Pointe Ct 491-A5 WnT
Brookfield Ct 461-F8 LTM
Brookfield Dr 562-G7 PeT
Brookhill Ct 490-K2 WnT
Brookhollow Blvd 457-G7 PTM
Brooklawn Dr 531-E5 SCT
Brookline 391-H6 Ca
Brookline Ct 460-E1 WTM
Brookline Dr 460-F2 WTM
Brookline Pl 460-E1 WTM
Brookpath Rd 460-K4 LTM
Brookridge Ct 394-C8 F
Brooks Bend 455-G1 B
Brooks Bend Dr 426-B1 Ca
Brooks Blvd 462-A3 L
Brooks Crossing 394-J10 F
Brooks Ct 392-E7 Ca
Brooks Sch Rd 394-J10 F; 360-K10; 394-J10, K4; 428-J1 FCT; 360-K10 WyT
Brooks St DN-C1; 493-C5 CTM
Brookshire Dr 455-A4 LTH
Brookshire Pkwy 392-E4, E5, E6 Ca
Brookside Ave DN-F1; 493-J5, K5; 494-A4 CTM
Brookside Ct 523-K1 A; 490-E8 WaT
Brookside Dr 523-J8, J10 P
Brookside Pkwy Dr N 493-K5; 494-A5, C4 CTM
Brookside Pkwy Dr S 494-B5 CTM
Brookstone Ct 458-A1 PTM
Brookstone Dr 391-C3 CTH
Brookstone La 458-A1 PTM; 560-H10 WTJ
Brookstone Pass 524-B9 P
Brookstone Way 458-A1 PTM
Brookton Ct 425-A7 WTM
Brookview Cir 426-H8 WTM
Brookview Ct 592-E4 M; 426-H7 WTM
Brookview Dr 392-B10 Ca; 561-J10; 595-J1 G
Brookview La 426-H7 WTM
Brookville Ave 494-D9 CTM
Brookville Rd 494-E8 CTM; 531-C4 SCT; 494-G9, J9; 495-C10, D10; 529-H1; 530-C2 WrT
Brookville Way 495-C10; 529-C1 WrT
Brookway Dr 523-K1 A
Brookway St 494-A4 CTM
Brookwood Rd 460-J3 LTM
Brothers Ct 394-A10; 428-A1 F
Brotherwood Ct 424-F10 PTM
Brouse Ave 460-A10; 494-A2 CTM; 426-A10; 460-A4, A6 WTM
Brouse Ct 528-K10 FT
Brouse Dr 528-K10 FT
Brown Cir 460-E7 WTM
Brown Rd 460-E6, E7 WTM
Brown St 359-F2 N
Browning Dr 562-A7 PeT
Browning St 596-B3 G
Brownsburg Crossing 455-K5 B
Brownstone Ct 496-J2 Cu
Brownswood Dr 455-J9 B
Broyles Rd 489-A9, B9 WaT
Bruce Ct 455-J1 BTH
Bruddy Dr 394-A2 F
Brumley Mews 392-C5 Ca
Brumley Way 392-C5 Ca
Brunson Run 427-J3 LTM
Brunswick Ave 559-E2 DTM; 561-E1, F2, H2, K1; 562-A1, C1, D1, E1 PeT
Brunswick Ct 392-E9 Ca; 558-B1 GT
Brunswick Dr 392-D9 Ca; 393-G8 F; 562-D10 G; 558-B1 GT
Brush Run 457-K1 PTM
Brushfield La 394-J10; 428-H1 F
Brushwood La 561-H10 G
Brushwood Rd 525-A10; 559-A3, A6 DTM
Brussels Terr 458-D7 PTM
Bruton Dr 427-D10 LTM
Bryan Ct 562-D7 PeT
Bryan Dr 562-C1, C3, D7 PeT
Bryant Ct 426-H3 WTM
Bryant La 426-J3 WTM
Bryce Ct 492-D1 WnT
Bryce Manor Dr 424-H8 WTM
Bryce Way 393-J10 F
Bryden Dr 393-F7 F
Bryden Pl 393-F7 F
Bryn Mawr 393-G1 DTH
Bryn Mawr Dr 459-C1 WTM
Bubwick Tr 596-F2 G
Buchanan St DN-E4; 493-G10, H10 CTM; 523-G8, J7 P
Buck Blvd 562-K2 FT
Buck Cr Blvd Dr S 561-F1 PeT
Buck Cr Pkwy 561-G3 PeT
Buck Cr Rd 496-K4 BCT; 496-J6, K4 Cu; 496-J6 SCT
Buck Ct 428-J8 L
Buck Dr 324-J5 N
Buck Pond Ct 562-J7 FT
Buck Pond Pl 562-J7 FT
Buck Rill Dr 562-K1 FT
Buck St 388-E1 Wh
Buck Tr Rd 563-A2 FT
Buck View Dr 564-G2 FT
Buckeye Ct 392-G3 Ca; 325-B9 N; 424-K4 WTM
Buckeye Rd 557-C6 GT
Buckhaven Dr 427-H3 LTM
Buckhorn Dr 391-C2 CTH
Buckingham Ct 392-E6 Ca; 496-J3 Cu; 393-J3 DTH; 596-C5 G
Buckingham Dr 459-D6 WTM
Buckley Blvd 496-J5 Cu
Buckley Ct 496-J5 Cu
Buckley Rd 496-J5 Cu
Buckmoor Cir 595-D5 WTJ
Buckmoor Ct 595-D5 WTJ
Buckmoor Pkwy 595-D5 WTJ

Buckridge Dr E 561-K4 PeT; 561-K4 Spt
Buckridge Dr N 561-K4 PeT
Buckridge Dr W 561-J4 PeT
Buckskin Cir 426-K7 LTM
Buckskin Ct 393-B3 Ca; 426-K6, K7 LTM; 531-C2 SCT
Buckthorn Ct 489-J7 A
Buckthorne Ct 424-J4 WTM
Buckthorne La 592-F3 M
Buckus Rd 558-E2 GT; 558-E2 P
Budd Run Ct 426-K3 LTM
Budd Run Dr 426-K3 LTM
Buddy La 593-C2 MTM
Buell Ct 490-F7 WaT
Buell Dr 490-F7 WaT
Buell La 457-J2 PTM
Buena Vista Ct 593-C2 MTM
Buena Vista Dr 357-J8 WTH; 458-K6 WTM
Buffalo Dr 561-D8 PeT
Buffalo Ridge Cir 561-G8 PeT
Buffalo Ridge Ct 561-G8 PeT
Buffalo Ridge Dr 561-G8 PeT
Buffalo Run Dr 561-G8 PeT
Buffalo Run Way 561-H8 PeT
Buffalo St 528-D4, F4 BG
Buffalo Tr Cir 561-G8 PeT
Buffett Pkwy 393-H3 F
Buick Dr 491-H4 S; 491-E4 WnT
Buisdale Dr 491-E8 WnT
Bull Run Ct 561-H7 PeT
Bull Run Dr N 596-J4 G
Bullock Ct 561-B5 PeT
Bundy Pl 493-H5 CTM
Bungalow Ct 459-G4 WTM
Bunker Dr 595-D8 WTJ
Bunker Hill Crest 563-D5 FT
Bunker Hill Dr 390-C9 CTH; 460-C7 WTM
Buntin Ct 324-K5 N
Bunty La 392-J6 CTH
Bur Oak Ct 489-E5 A; 326-D10 N
Bur Oak Pl 458-D3 PTM
Burbank Ave 495-E7 WrT
Burch Dr 459-K1 WTM
Burdsal Pkwy 492-J2, K2 CTM
Buren Pl 495-F6 WrT
Buren St 529-G5 FT
Burgess Ave 494-G8, J8 WrT
Burk Rd 495-J7 WrT
Burke Ave 490-K8 WnT
Burke Ct 462-B1 L
Burke St 524-K3 WnT
Burkhart Dr 527-F8 PeT
Burkwood Dr 392-G8 Ca
Burkwood Way 457-C4 PTM
Burlington Ave 459-K1, K2; 460-A1 WTM
Burmaster Ct 457-E10 WnT
Burn Ct 561-C7 PeT
Burnett Ct 392-A3 Ca
Burnham Cir 427-C10 LTM
Burning Ridge La 394-B10 F
Burning Tree La 390-H9 CTH
Burnleigh Cir 460-F7 WTM
Burns Dr 455-H1 BTH
Burns Dr N 455-H1 BTH
Burns Dr S 455-H1 BTH
Burns St 524-A8 P
Burr Oak Dr 391-F8 CTH; 561-B6 PeT
Burrell La 427-H4 LTM
Burries Terr 496-F4 WrT
Burroak Ct 561-C6 PeT
Burrwood Cir 461-K6 L
Burrwood Ct 462-A7 LTM
Burrwood Dr 461-K6 L; 462-A7 LTM
Burton Ave 493-A1 CTM
Burwick Dr 427-H3 LTM
Burzell Ct 530-A2 WrT
Bushs Run 423-G8 PTM
Business Dr 494-K3 WrT
Busseron La 426-C10 WTM
Busy Bee La 562-C2, E2 PeT
Butler Ave 528-H8 BG; 460-H9 LTM; 426-H10; 460-G1 WTM; 494-H2, H3, H6, H8, H9, H10; 528-H1 WrT
Butler Dr 523-K7; 524-A7 P
Butler Terr 460-H10 WrT
Buttercup Ct 489-H5 WaT; 491-K1 WnT
Buttercup Dr 497-G8 SCT
Buttercup La 491-J1 WnT
Buttercup Pl 491-K1 WnT
Buttercup Way 458-D3 PTM
Butterfield Dr 426-A10 WTM
Butterfly Ct 595-G1 G
Butternut Ct 424-H4 WTM
Butternut Dr 325-B10 N
Butternut La 490-K5 WnT
Buttonbush Ct 457-D8 PTM
Buttonwood Crest 459-A5, A6 WTM
Buttonwood Dr 392-C7 Ca; 324-J8; 325-A9 N
Buttress La 529-A8 FT
Buxton Ct 458-C6 PTM
Bye Ct 525-E1 WnT
Byland Dr 528-E6 BG
Byram Ave 459-C5, C8 WTM
Byram Pl DN-D1; 493-E5 CTM
Byram St 459-C10 CTM
Byrd Dr 528-C9, D9 PeT
Byrkit St 526-B10 DTM; 526-F10; 527-E10 PeT
Byron Dr 565-D6 MTS
Bywood Dr 426-J10 LTM; 426-J10 WTM

C

C St 527-B1 CTM
Cabano Ct 496-E9 WrT
Cabernet Way 423-E7 PTM
Cabin Cr Dr 562-H7 FT
Cabin Cr Dr 562-J7 FT
Cabin Ct 531-J5 SCT
Cabinetmaker 523-H5 P
Cable Dr 428-G9 L
Cable St DN-A2; 492-K7 CTM
Caboose Ct 427-D8 LTM
Cabot Cir 455-J2 B
Cactus Ct 528-H10 FT
Cadbury Cir 424-K3 WTM
Caddy Way 424-D9 PTM
Cadillac Dr 491-H4 S
Caerhays Ct 424-D1 CTH
Caesar Ct 489-E7 A
Caesar Dr 489-E7 A
Caisson St 427-C7 LTM
Caito Dr 461-D3 L
Calais Cir 461-B2 LTM
Calais Ct 461-A2 LTM
Calais Dr 461-A2 LTM
Calamus Ct 496-E8 WrT
Calaveras Way 426-A6 WTM
Calbert Ct 495-H2 WrT
Calbert Dr 495-H1 WrT
Calcutta Dr 595-D8 WTJ
Calder Way 461-C4 L
Caldwell La 489-H7 A
Caledonia Cir 457-E7 PTM
Caledonia Way 457-E7 PTM
Caledonian Ct 595-C6 WTJ
Caley La 559-J4 DTM
Calgary Ct 424-E6 PTM
Calhoun Ct 528-F2 CTM
Calhoun St 527-H2, K2; 528-A2, C2, F2 CTM; 528-G2 WrT
Calibogue Cir 458-E3 PTM
Calibouge Dr 394-C8 F
Caliburn Ct 394-B4 F
Calico Aster Dr 325-E10 N
Calico Ct 455-J7 B
California St DN-C1, C2, C4; 459-C10; 493-C1, C6, C7, C9; 527-C4 CTM
Calla Lily Dr 563-B6 FT
Callahan St 529-K9 FT
Callan Dr 458-A4 PTM
Callaway Ct 395-B7 F
Calling Rd 599-E1 MTS
Calluna Ct 394-J8 F
Calumet Ct 389-F9 Z
Calumet Dr 428-G4 LTM
Calvary St DN-F4; 493-H9 CTM
Calvin Cir 596-D4 G
Calvin Fletcher Tr 393-B4 Ca
Calvin St 528-A2 CTM
Calzia La 496-H5 Cu
Camargue Dr 389-D9 Z
Camber La 529-A8 FT
Camberley La 392-F5 Ca
Camberwood Ct 424-E9 PTM
Camberwood Dr 424-D8 PTM
Cambot Ct 565-D6 MTS
Cambourne Ct 392-F4 Ca
Cambourne Dr 392-E4 Ca
Cambria Ct 456-H9 WnT
Cambridge Cir 489-K9 A
Cambridge Ct 392-D6 Ca; 496-H3 Cu; 561-D9 G; 359-H9 N
Cambridge Dr 393-E8 F; 561-E10 G; 523-H10 P
Cambridge La 426-B10 WTM
Cambridge Pl 455-A5 LTH
Cambridge Way 558-A2 P
Camby Ct 596-B1 G
Camby Rd 558-J5; 559-D5 DTM; 558-B5, E5 GT
Camby St 596-B1 G
Camden Ct 393-A9 F
Camden Dr 389-E6 Z
Camden St 527-G6, G8, G10; 561-G1, G2, G3, G4, G7 PeT
Camel Back Ct 426-K7 LTM
Camel Back Dr 426-K7 LTM
Camellia Cir 495-G4 WrT
Camellia Ct 592-E2 M
Camellia La 495-G4 WrT
Camelot Ct 360-A3 N; 491-E7 WnT
Camelot La 392-E6 Ca
Cameron Dr 393-F7 F
Cameron Pl 393-F7 F
Cameron St 527-F4, G4, K4; 528-A4, B4 CTM
Camfield Ct 428-H7 L
Camfield Dr 428-G7 L
Camfield Way 428-H7 L
Camille Ct 462-C1 L
Caminito Ct 490-J8 WnT
Caminito Rd 490-J8 WnT
Cammack Rd 324-H3 JT
Camp Cr Ct 395-C10 FCT
Camp St DN-C1; 493-C6 CTM
Campbell Ave 426-K6; 460-K7, K8 LTM; 460-K10; 494-K1, K4, K7 WrT
Campbell Ct 557-J8 GT
Campbell St 524-C6 P
Campfire Cir 428-D8 L
Campfire Run 428-D8 L
Campus La 494-H8 WrT
Camwood Ct 424-H9 PTM
Camwood Dr 424-G9 PTM
Camwood La 424-H9 PTM
Canaan Ct 558-A10 M
Canak Dr 523-E4 WaT
Canal Blvd 459-D5 WTM
Canal View Cir DN-C1; 493-D6 CTM
Canal View Dr DN-C2; 493-D6 CTM
Canal Way 326-B10 N
Canary Ct 392-J2 Ca; 424-J6 WTM
Canary La 424-J7 WTM
Canbe Rd 557-G10 BTM
Canberra Cir 427-A10 LTM
Candice Dr 593-C4 MTM
Candle Ct 457-H6 PTM
Candletree Cir 458-B7 PTM
Candletree Dr 458-B6 PTM
Candlewick Dr 458-E3 PTM
Candlewick La 458-E2 PTM
Candlewick Rd 324-J5 N
Candlewood Ct 358-F3 N
Candlewood La 426-E7 WTM
Candlwood Ct 455-J8 B
Candy Cane Dr 562-D5 PeT
Candy La 460-C6 WTM
Candy Spots Ct 528-J9 FT
Candy Spots Dr 528-J9 FT
Cane Ridge Ct 457-K1 PTM
Cane Ridge Rd 457-K1 PTM
Canna Ct 561-E3 PeT
Canna Rd 561-E3 PeT
Cannon Ct 491-K3 S
Cannonade Dr 561-B7 PeT
Cannonero Ct 561-A6 PeT
Canoe Ct 428-D5 LTM
Canopy La 393-K2 F
Canter Dr 530-D1 WrT
Canterbury Ct 392-D5 Ca; 359-H9 N; 425-B5 WTM
Canterbury Dr 596-C5 G
Canterbury La 426-B10 WTM
Canterbury Pl 425-F4 WTM
Canterbury Sq E 425-F4 WTM
Canterbury Sq N 425-F4 WTM
Canterbury Sq S 425-F4 WTM
Canterbury Sq W 425-B5, F4 WTM
Canton Dr 392-J1 Ca
Canvasback Dr 393-C8 F; 490-J3 WnT
Canyon Ct 394-J7 F
Canyon Rd 561-C4 PeT
Cape Charles Ct 325-E3 C
Cape Charles Dr 460-K6 LTM
Cape Cod Cir 426-K8 LTM
Cape Cod Ct 426-J8 LTM
Cape Cod La 426-J8 WTM
Cape Dr 427-G4 LTM
Cape Dr E 427-G4 LTM
Cape Henry Ct 325-E3 C
Capistrano Cir 428-F5 LTM
Capistrano Ct 428-F6 LTM
Capistrano Dr 596-G3 G; 428-G5 LTM
Capitol Ave DN-D1, D4; 459-E9; 493-D9, D10, E4; 527-D1, E5 CTM; 527-E10; 561-E1 PeT; 459-E6, E9 WTM
Caplock La 427-H4 LTM
Capri Dr 392-E3 Ca; 526-A5 WnT
Captain Dr 489-K7; 490-A7 WaT
Captains Ct 428-D5 LTM
Captains Landing Ct 428-G7 L
Carberry Ct 491-B3 WnT
Carbon St 359-H6 N
Cardamon Ct 562-E5 PeT
Cardiff Ct 456-J9 WnT
Cardiff La 456-G9 WnT
Cardigan Rd 424-G7 PTM
Cardinal Cove Dr 427-E6 LTM
Cardinal Cove E 427-F6 LTM
Cardinal Cove N 427-E6 LTM
Cardinal Cove S 427-E7 LTM
Cardinal Cove W 427-F7 LTM
Cardinal Ct 326-C5 NT
Cardinal Dr 389-C6 ET; 429-A3 McC; 561-K3; 562-A3, E3 PeT
Cardinal La 455-H10 B; 392-A8 CTH; 461-A1 LTM
Cardinal St 489-K7 WaT
Cardis Ct 496-H3 WrT
Cardis La 496-H3 WrT
Carefree Cir 428-F5 LTM
Carefree Ct 595-D1 WTJ
Carefree Ct N 593-A1 MTM
Carefree Dr 428-E1 FCT
Carey Ct 391-E3 CTH
Carey Dr 359-F3 N
Carey Rd 392-C2 Ca
Cargo Dr 525-G5 WnT
Caribbean Dr 495-H4 WrT
Caribe Dr 561-G4 PeT
Caribe La 561-G3 PeT
Caribe Mall 561-G4 PeT
Caribou Cir 423-F10 PTM
Caribou Ct 423-E10 PTM
Caribou Dr 423-E10 PTM
Caribou Pl 423-E10 PTM
Caring Cove 457-K2 PTM
Carla Ct 495-J1 WrT
Carla Dr 495-J1 WrT
Carlin Ct 392-B4 Ca
Carlin Dr 392-B4 Ca
Carlisle St E 592-A2 M
Carlow Cir 491-B3 WnT
Carloway Rd 428-H6 L
Carlsbad Cir 526-A5 DTM
Carlsbad Ct 526-A5 DTM
Carlsbad Dr 526-A6 DTM
Carlsbad La 526-A6 DTM
Carlsen Ave 491-D5 WnT
Carlton Arms Dr 427-C7, C8 LTM
Carlton Arms Plaza 427-C8 LTM
Carlton Arms Rd 427-D7, D8 LTM
Carlton Ct 491-K5 S
Carlton Way 491-K5 S
Carly Ct 393-G6 F; 462-F9 WrT
Carly La 462-F10 WrT
Carly Pl 393-G6 F
Carlyle Dr 425-H2 WTM
Carlyle La 425-H2 WTM
Carlyle Pl 494-F6 CTM
Carmel Dr 391-F5, J7; 392-A7, C6 Ca
Carmel Garden 391-J6 Ca
Carmel View Dr 392-A4 Ca
Carmelaire Dr 391-K5; 392-A5 Ca
Carmelita Ct 523-K1 A
Carmen Ct 596-F4 G
Carmen La 596-F4 G
Carmen Plaza 596-E4 G
Carmichael Dr 461-J4 L
Carnaby Ct 455-E5 B
Carnaby Dr 455-F4 B
Carnaby St 495-K1 WrT
Carnation Ct 457-D10 WnT
Carnation La 457-D10 WnT
Carney Dr 427-G1 F
Carney St 596-C1 G
Carnoustie Cir Dr E 523-A2 WaT
Carnoustie Cir Dr N 523-A2 WaT
Carnoustie Cir Dr S 523-A1 WaT
Carnoustie Cir Dr W 523-A2 WaT
Caro Dr 491-E4 WnT
Carob Ct 562-G7 PeT
Carol Dr 592-B6 BTM; 562-D10; 596-D1 G
Carolee Ct 562-D4 PeT
Carolina Ct 394-B2 F
Caroline Ave 459-K10; 493-K2; 494-A3 CTM; 425-K8, K10; 426-A9; 459-K10 WTM
Caroline Ct 592-B1 M
Caroline St 459-K5, K7 WTM
Carolling Way 562-E6 PeT
Carpenter Ct 523-J5 P
Carr Ave 526-F5 DTM
Carr Rd 523-H7 P
Carr Rd N 523-H6 GT; 523-H6 P
Carr Sty 596-A1 G
Carriage La 427-J9 LTM
Carriage Lake Dr 455-H1 B
Carriage Stone Dr 394-J6 F
Carrie Cir 563-A5 FT
Carrie Ct 563-A4 FT
Carrie Dr 563-A4 FT; 530-K5 SCT
Carrie Pl 563-A4 FT
Carrigan Crossing 325-C5 N
Carrigan Rd 324-J5 N; 325-B5 NT
Carrington Ct 392-H5 Ca
Carrington Dr 462-D1 L
Carrington Pl 392-H5 Ca
Carroll Rd 462-H10; 496-H1 BCT; 530-H6, H10; 564-H2, H3, H5 FT; 428-K7; 462-A3, K5, K1 L; 530-H10; 564-H2, H3, H5 MTS; 428-K7 McC; 496-H10; 530-H2, H6 SCT; 462-K1 VT; 462-H10; 496-H1, H10; 530-H2 WrT
Carroll White Dr 495-F5 WrT
Carrollton Ave 425-G2 CTH; 459-G9, H10; 493-G4, H1, H2, H3, H5 CTM; 425-G10, H4; 459-G1, G2, G4, G6, G9 WTM
Carrollton Ct 459-G5 WTM
Carrousel Dr 457-F4 PTM
Carrow Dr 427-B8 LTM
Carry Back Dr 528-J9 FT
Carry Back La 528-J9 FT
Carson Ave 527-H5 CTM; 527-J5; 528-A7 PeT
Carson Ct 392-E3 Ca
Carson Way 596-H2 G
Carter Dr 389-G8 Z
Carter La 489-F10 WaT
Carter St 523-F8 P
Carters Grove 425-B5 WTM
Carters Grove Dr 359-B1 N
Carthay Cir 393-F4 DTH
Carvel Ave 459-H2, H4, H6 WTM
Carvin Cir 458-E6 PTM
Carvin Ct 458-E7 PTM
Carwinion Way 390-C10; 424-D1 CTH
Cary Lake Dr 563-E5 FT
Casa Dr 490-H7 WnT
Casco Bay Cir 325-F2 C
Casco Dr 490-A9 WaT
Casey Rd 323-B10; 357-B1, B4 WTH
Cashard Ave 528-J8 BG
Casper Ct 426-G9 WTM
Cass Ct 462-A8 LTM
Cassidy La 424-K7 WTM
Castetter Ct 393-H5 F
Castle Ave 525-G8 DTM; 527-H7, J7 PeT
Castle Cove Rd 427-F6 LTM
Castle Cr Pkwy E 426-K4 LTM
Castle Cr Pkwy N 426-J4 WTM
Castle Ct 392-E6 Ca; 360-A3 N
Castle Dr 427-H6 LTM
Castle Farms Ct 427-F5 LTM
Castle Farms Rd 427-F5 LTM
Castle Knoll Blvd 427-A3 LTM
Castle Knoll Ct 427-A3 LTM
Castle La 427-F10 LTM
Castle Lake Rd 427-G6 LTM
Castle Manor Ct 491-E7 WnT
Castle Manor Dr 491-E7 WnT
Castle Overlook 392-E6 Ca
Castle Pk Dr 427-F4 LTM
Castle Ridge Ct 427-E6 LTM
Castle Ridge La 427-E5 LTM
Castle Rock Ct 427-E5 LTM
Castle Row St 459-H4 WTM
Castlebar Cir 426-K10 LTM
Castlebay Way 457-E7 PTM
Castlebrook Ct 427-H6 LTM
Castlebrook Dr 427-H5 LTM
Castlegate Dr 427-F2 LTM
Castleplace Dr 427-A6 LTM
Castleton Blvd 427-G6 LTM
Castleton Corner Dr 426-J4 WTM
Castleton Corner La 426-J5 WTM
Castleton Corner Way 426-J5 WTM
Castleton Farms Dr N 427-D7 LTM
Castleton Farms Dr W 427-D8 LTM
Castleton Rd 427-B6 LTM
Castleway Ct 427-A6 LTM
Castleway Ct W 427-A6 LTM
Castleway Dr 427-A7, B6 LTM
Castleway Dr W 426-K6; 427-A6 LTM
Castlewood Dr 427-C5 LTM
Caswell St 564-F6 FT
Catalano Dr 491-D4 WnT
Catalina Ct 461-H8 LTM; 389-D7 Z
Catalina Dr 564-E2 FT; 461-H8; 462-A8, B8 LTM; 497-G7 SCT
Catalina Way 389-E7 Z
Catalpa Ave 458-E3 PTM
Catalpa Ct 325-B10 N
Catalpa Dr 523-D3 WaT
Catamaran Cir 325-E1 C
Catamaran Ct 428-E5 LTM
Catamaran Dr 428-E5 LTM
Catawba Ct 561-B7 PeT
Catboat Ct 393-D9 F
Catclaw La 529-B8 FT
Catherine Dr 391-G4 CTH; 357-K3; 358-A3 W
Catherwood Ave 460-K8 LTM; 461-A10; 495-A1, A2, A8, A9, A10; 529-A2 WrT
Catskill Ct 490-J6 WnT
Catskill Rd 490-J6 WnT
Catspring Cir 526-B6 DTM
Cattail La 455-H10 B
Causeway Dr 457-E9 WnT
Cavalier Ct 461-J8 LTM
Cave Ct 594-H1 WTJ
Cave Springs Ct 562-J7 FT
Caven St 527-E2, F2 CTM; 526-A2 WnT
Cavendish Rd 460-F3 WTM
Cawi Ct 424-B10 PTM
Caye Ct 392-H7 Ca
Cayman Dr 392-G1 Ca
Caymen Ct 392-G1 Ca
Cayuga Ct 423-J10; 457-J1 PTM
Cecil Ave 461-G9; 495-G5, G7 WrT
Cecil Ct 495-G4 WrT
Cecil St 495-G9 WrT
Cecilia La 459-C2 WTM
Cedar Bluff Dr 491-E8 WnT
Cedar Cove La 426-K2 F
Cedar Cr Ct 424-D6 PTM
Cedar Crest 389-F7 Z
Cedar Dr 455-F8 B; 559-B7 DTM; 394-C7 F; 489-J4 WaT
Cedar Glen 489-A8, B7 WaT
Cedar Glen Dr N 557-H2 P
Cedar Glen Dr S 557-H2 P
Cedar Grove Ct N 593-B1 MTM
Cedar Hills Dr N 595-A9 WTJ
Cedar Hills Dr S 595-A10 WTJ
Cedar Key Dr 427-H3 LTM
Cedar La 596-H3 G; 325-C4 JT; 595-B9 WTJ
Cedar Lake Ct 391-H1 Ca
Cedar Mill Ct 389-F5 Z
Cedar Pine Dr 462-D9 WrT
Cedar Pl 425-C1 CTH
Cedar Pt Dr 425-B2 CTH
Cedar Ridge 425-B1 CTH
Cedar Ridge La 422-H8 BTH
Cedar Ridge Rd 462-E8 LTM
Cedar Springs Dr 425-B2 WTM
Cedar St 395-D7 FCT; 531-H4 NP; 389-H8 Z
Cedar Wood Dr 425-C1 CTH
Cedar Wood Pl 425-B2 CTH
Cedarbrook Dr 562-B6 Spt
Cedarstone Ct 395-C8 FCT; 461-C3 LTM
Cedarstone Dr 461-C3 LTM
Celtic Cir 596-D4 G
Celtic Ct 461-K9 WrT
Celtic Dr 461-K9 WrT
Centenary Rd 593-C10 MTM
Centennary Dr 426-A1 CTH
Centennial Ct 392-E4 Ca
Centennial Rd 322-F10; 356-F3 WTH
Centennial St 458-F8 WTM; 458-F10; 492-F1, F2, F4, F5, F7; 526-F1, F2, G4 WnT
Center Dr 592-A10, B5 BTM; 359-H2 N; 560-H9 WTJ; 491-H5 WnT
Center La 592-A1 M
Center Run Rd 427-A5 LTM
Center St 596-D2 G; 462-G1 L; 429-C8 McC; 456-J10 WnT
Center St N 523-E6 GT; 523-E6 P
Center St S 523-F9; 557-H2 P
Centerpoint Dr 427-F1 F
Central Ave 391-F10; 425-F1 CTH; DN-E1; 459-F9; 493-G4 CTM; 392-J9 N; 425-F3, F6, F8, F10; 459-F1, F4 WTM
Central Ct 391-G8 CTH; 426-C1 Ca
Central Ct N 459-G9 CTM
Central Ct S 459-G9 CTM
Central Dr E 391-G8 CTH
Central Dr W 391-F8 CTH
Central St 531-H5 NP
Centre Ct 528-B4 CTM
Centre Pkwy 528-B5 CTM
Centurion Cir 424-K6 WTM
Centurion Pkwy 424-K6 WTM
Century Cir E 424-K6 WTM
Century Cir N 424-K6 WTM
Century Cir S 424-K6 WTM
Century Cir W 424-H7 WTM
Century Dr 392-A7 Ca; 424-J6 WTM
Century Oaks Dr 389-J5 Z
Century Plaza Rd 458-A6 PTM
Century Way 424-K6 WTM
Cerulean Dr 326-C9 N
Chablis Cir 423-D8 PTM
Chablis Ct 423-D8 PTM
Chad Ct 523-K10 P
Chadbourne Dr 491-D6 WnT
Chadsworth Dr 462-D1 L
Chadwell Ct 393-J10 F
Chadwick Ct 392-E9 Ca; 325-C6 N
Chadwick Dr 392-E9 Ca
Chadwick St DN-C4; 493-D10 CTM
Chadwood La E 424-F5 PTM
Chadwood La N 424-F5 PTM
Chadwood La W 424-F5 PTM
Chadworth Ct 462-C1 L
Chadworth Way 462-C1 L
Chalan Rue Ct 561-E1 PeT
Chalcot Cir 427-B9 LTM
Chaldean Cir 427-J2 F
Challenge Ct 428-H4 LTM
Challenge La 427-B5 LTM
Chalmers St 394-A5 F
Chamberlain Cir 325-C6 N
Chamberlin Dr 528-B9, C9 PeT
Chambery La 495-K1 WrT
Chamomile Ct 326-C10 N
Champions Dr 427-G4 LTM
Champton Dr 427-G3 LTM
Chandler Ct 561-D5 PeT
Chandler Dr 561-D5 PeT
Channing Cir 426-D9 WTM
Channing Ct 460-J5 LTM
Channing Rd 460-J5 LTM
Chantilly Dr 526-B8 DTM
Chapel Glen Dr 490-K7 WnT
Chapel Hill Ct 491-E6 WnT
Chapel Hill Ct N 559-A9 MTM
Chapel Hill Dr E 491-E6 WnT
Chapel Hill Dr W 491-D7 WnT
Chapel Hill Rd 491-E6 WnT
Chapel Pines Dr 491-A6 WnT
Chapelwood Blvd 491-C6 WnT
Chapelwood Ct 457-K1 PTM
Chappie La 496-A2 WrT
Char Dr 525-J9 DTM
Chardonnay Dr 457-E8 PTM
Charing Cross Ct 359-K7 N
Charing Cross Rd 392-E6 Ca
Charing Dr 424-J8 WTM
Chariot La 561-G6 PeT
Charlecot Dr 424-G7 PTM
Charlemagne Dr 564-D2 FT
Charles Ct 455-J1 BTH; 392-H2 Ca; 523-J10 P
Charles Dr 561-J10 G; 456-E8 LTH
Charles Lee Ct 562-E9 G
Charles St DN-D4; 493-E10; 527-E1, E2 CTM; 489-J4 WaT
Charleston Ct 495-C5 WrT
Charleston Dr E 495-C5 WrT
Charleston Dr W 495-C6 WrT
Charleston La N 495-C5 WrT
Charleston La S 495-B5 WrT
Charleston Pkwy 393-F7 F
Charleston St 491-K3 S
Charlevoix La 461-A2, B2 LTM
Charlie Dr 359-E4 N
Charliewood Ct 359-A1 NT
Charney Ave 461-H6 L
Charnock St 495-H2 WrT
Charnwood Pkwy 528-E7 PeT
Charring Cross Cir 561-E2 PeT
Charring Cross Lick Dr 527-J9 PeT
Charring Cross Rd 561-E2 PeT
Charrington Cir 457-C6 PTM
Charrington Ct 457-D6 PTM
Charter Dr 427-B3 LTM
Charter Oak Cir 424-K5 WTM
Charter Oak Dr 424-K6 WTM
Charter Oaks 424-J1 CTH
Charter Woods Dr 491-J6 WnT
Chase Blvd 595-F3 G
Chase Ct 391-H7 Ca; 394-J9 F
Chase Oak Dr 390-B4 ET
Chase St DN-B4; 493-A10 CTM; 527-A6 PeT
Chaseway Ct 424-G2 PTM
Chateau Ct 394-D6 FCT; 461-H8 WrT
Chateau Dr 461-H8 LTM
Chateau La 461-H9 WrT
Chateaugay Ct 561-A7 PeT
Chateaugay Dr 561-A7, A8 PeT
Chateaugay La 561-A8 PeT
Chaterley Ct 491-C6 WnT
Chatfield Dr 459-H2 WTM
Chatham Ct 390-J10 CTH
Chatham Ct N 427-E5 LTM
Chatham Ct S 427-E5 LTM
Chatham Dr 456-G8 LTH
Chatham Pl 460-H5, H6 LTM
Chatsbee Ct 457-G9 WnT
Chatsworth Ct 425-A5 WTM
Chattanooga Cir 496-G5 WrT
Chatterton Cir 457-B6 PTM
Chatterton Dr 457-B6 PTM
Chaucer Cir 325-B7 N
Chaucer Ct 427-B10 LTM
Chauncey Dr 559-H4 DTM
Chauncy 391-H6 Ca
Checotah Dr 428-B10 L
Cheddar Ct DN-B1; 493-B5 CTM
Cheddar Tr 360-B7 NT
Chelsea Ct 392-J1 Ca; 393-G7 F; 359-H10 NT; 426-E9 WTM
Chelsea Dr 359-G10 NT
Chelsea Rd 525-J1; 526-A1 WnT
Chelsea Terr 595-B4 WTJ
Chelsea Vill Ct 424-J3 WTM
Chelsea Vill Dr 424-J3 WTM
Cheltenham Rd 427-H5 LTM

Cheltenham Way 489-B10; 523-B1 WaT
Chenille Ct 462-D8 LTM
Chensford Dr 461-C3 L
Cherbourg Cir 461-B2 LTM
Cherbourg Dr 461-A2 LTM
Cheri Cir 563-A6 FT
Cheri Ct 563-A6 FT
Cherington Ct 561-K7 PeT
Cherington Dr 561-K7 PeT
Cherokee Dr 428-A9 L
Cherokee La 565-A5 MTS; 325-D7 N
Cherry Birch Dr 562-D1 PeT
Cherry Blossom Blvd 562-D1 PeT
Cherry Blossom Ct 562-E1 PeT
Cherry Blossom Dr E 393-C8 F
Cherry Blossom Dr W 393-B8 F
Cherry Blossom La 455-C7 LTH
Cherry Field Dr 562-D1 PeT
Cherry Glen Dr 528-B7 PeT
Cherry Glen Way 528-B7 PeT
Cherry Hill Blvd 393-C8 F
Cherry Hill Ct 393-C8 F
Cherry Hill Dr 457-D6 PTM
Cherry La 458-G7 WTM
Cherry Lake Ct 462-F10 WrT
Cherry Lake La 462-F10 WrT
Cherry Lake Pl 462-F10 WrT
Cherry Lake Rd 462-F10 WrT
Cherry Laurel La 393-B8 F
Cherry Ridge Rd 392-K1 Ca
Cherry St 528-F6 BG; 359-H3, J3; 360-A3 N; 358-A4 W; 358-A4 WTH
Cherry Tree Ave 392-K2 CTH; 392-H4 Ca; 359-D6 N; 359-D6 NT
Cherry Tree La 462-A6 L
Cherry Tree Rd 359-A10 N; 359-A10, E4 NT
Cherry Valley Ct 461-J5 LTM
Cherry Valley Dr 461-J5 L; 461-J5 LTM
Cherrybark Ct 428-J6 L
Cherrybark Dr 428-J7 L
Cherryfield La 561-H9 G
Cherryhill Ct 457-C6 PTM
Cherrywood Ct 357-J5 W; 490-G5 WnT
Cherub Pl 427-E5 LTM
Chervil Ct 562-F6 PeT
Cheryl Ct 392-B9 Ca
Cheryl La 389-C7 ET; 528-G2 WrT
Chesapeake Dr E 428-D7 L
Chesapeake Dr N 428-D7 L
Chesapeake Dr S 428-C7 L
Chesapeake Dr W 428-D7 L
Chesapeake St DN-D3; 493-E8 CTM
Chesham Ct 427-C9 LTM
Cheshire Cir 325-B7 N
Cheshire Ct 457-H7 PTM
Cheshire Dr 525-G2 WnT
Cheshire Rd 491-H9 WnT
Chessie Dr 561-A9 PeT
Chessington Rd 425-A4 WTM
Chestee La 462-C9 WrT
Chester Ave 460-D10; 494-E2, E5, E7, E8, E10; 528-E1, E2 CTM; 426-D7, D9, D10; 460-D2 WTM
Chester Dr 528-C5 BG; 392-A10; 426-B1 CTH
Chester Dr E 426-D10 WTM
Chester Dr W 426-D10 WTM
Chester La 460-E4 WTM
Chester Rd 392-C10; 426-C1 Ca
Chesterbrook Ct 425-H3 WTM
Chesterfield Ct 359-J8 N; 527-H9 PeT
Chesterfield Dr 359-J7 N
Chesterfield Dr E 527-G9 PeT
Chesterfield Dr S 527-G9 PeT
Chesterfield Dr W 527-G9 PeT
Chesterton Dr 426-A2 CTH
Chestnut Cir 392-G3 Ca
Chestnut Ct 324-K7 N; 424-K4 WTM; 389-F9 Z
Chestnut Dr 562-C10 G
Chestnut Hill Cir 394-H10 F
Chestnut Hill Ct 394-H10 F
Chestnut Hills Blvd 423-G9 PTM
Chestnut Hills Dr 423-G8 PTM
Chestnut La 455-H3 B; 530-B4 WrT
Chestnut St 527-F1 CTM; 359-G5 N
Chestnut Woods Dr 491-K6 WnT
Cheswick Blvd 391-B3 CTH
Cheswick Dr 495-F3, G3 WrT
Cheswick La 394-D10; 428-D1 F
Cheval Ct 392-E4 Ca
Cheval Pl 392-E4 Ca
Cheviot Ct 595-C7 WTJ
Cheviot Pl 460-H6 LTM; 460-D6 WTM
Chevy Chase Dr 393-F4 DTH
Chevy Chase La 425-H1 CTH; 495-G2 WrT
Cheyenne Ct 561-D8 PeT
Cheyenne Moon 392-J3 Ca
Chianti Dr 461-E4 L
Chickahominy Rd 497-J9 SCT
Chickasaw Ct 561-D8 PeT
Chickasaw Rd 565-A5 MTS
Chicopee Ct 561-B6 PeT
Chief La 525-J6 DTM
Chiltern Dr 424-G7 PTM
Chimney Rock Ct 561-D5 PeT
Chinook Cir 495-D8 WrT
Chinquapin Ct 426-C1 Ca
Chinquapin Dr 489-E5 A
Chipendale Ct 424-H8 WTM
Chipendale La 424-H8 WTM
Chipmunk Crossing 393-B8 F
Chipmunk Ct 561-F10 G
Chipmunks Run 458-D4 PTM
Chippenham La 393-J3 DTH
Chippewa Ct 561-E8 PeT
Chipping Ct 424-B10 PTM
Chipwood Dr 325-D9 N
Chipwood La 460-H4 LTM
Chisolm Ct 528-J10 FT
Chisolm Tr 528-H10 FT
Chittimwood Dr 561-G8 PeT
Chitwood Dr 561-F9 PeT
Chloe Ct 428-F5 LTM
Choate Ct 457-C6 PTM
Choctaw Way 495-E8 WrT
Chokecherry La 462-F9 WrT
Cholla Ct 425-K4 WTM
Cholla Rd 425-K4 WTM
Cholla Terr 425-J4 WTM
Chosin Res Mem Pkwy 462-H1 L
Chris Anne Ct 563-A5 FT
Chris Anne Dr 563-A5 FT
Chris Ct 325-C6 N; 496-C2 WrT
Chris Dr 496-B3 WrT
Chrisfield La 429-B1 FCT
Christian Dr 531-A5 SCT
Christian St 359-H5 N
Christiana La 427-F5 LTM
Christiana Way 427-F4 LTM
Christie Ct 526-E6 DTM
Christina Ct 523-J10 P
Christopher Ct 523-K1 A; 528-G2 CTM
Christopher Dr 528-F2 CTM
Christopher La 491-K4 S; 457-K8, K10; 491-K1 WnT
Chrysanthemum Ct 457-F10 WnT
Chrysler St 424-A10 PTM; 458-B9, B10; 492-B1 WnT
Chula Vista Ct 596-J2 G
Church Dr 360-B1 N
Church Rd 490-C1 LTH
Church St DN-D4; 493-D10 CTM; 592-A1 M; 562-A5 Spt; 456-H10, J10 WnT
Churchill Ct 391-H10 CTH; 393-F8 F; 496-C4 WrT
Churchman Ave 528-C4, E5, H6, K7 BG; 494-K10; 528-A1, A2 CTM; 528-K8; 529-B8 FT
Churchman Ct 529-A8 FT
Churchman Way 529-A8 FT
Chyverton Cir 391-A5 CTH
Cicero Rd 325-H4 JT; 359-G3, H1 N; 325-H9 NT
Cider Mill Cir 461-C5 L
Cider Mill Ct 393-E8 F; 461-D2 L
Cider Mill La 461-C5, D5 L
Cider Mill Run 531-G4 SCT
Cidermill Ct 524-B9 P
Cielo Vista Ct 596-E3 G
Cielo Vista Dr 596-E3 G
Cimarron Tr 491-B6 WnT
Cincinnati St 528-H6 BG; DN-E2, E3; 493-G7, G9 CTM
Cindy Dr 429-A8 McC
Cindy La 422-F8 BTH; 529-J6 FT
Cinnamon Ct 455-J7 B
Cinnamon Dr 562-F5 PeT
Cinnamon Pl 562-F5 PeT
Cinnebar Dr 424-H4 PTM
Circle Blvd 460-C4 WTM
Circle Ct 390-G10 CTH
Circle Dr 391-J2 Ca; 393-H6 DTH; 596-A3 G; 426-D10 WTM
Circleview Dr 592-E3 M
Citadel Ct 424-F3 PTM
Citation Blvd 528-K8 FT
Citation Cir 528-K9 FT
Citation Ct 357-G9 WTH
Citation Rd 357-G9 WTH
Citizens Pl 493-F2 CTM
Civic Sq 391-K6 Ca
Claffey Dr 425-D6 WTM
Clairborne Ct 391-H10 CTH
Clairborne Way 458-K7 WTM
Clara Ct 557-J1 P
Clara St 427-B6 LTM
Clare Ave 326-F5 NT
Claren Dr 558-B6 GT
Claren Dr E 558-C6 GT
Claren Dr W 558-B6 GT
Clarendon Dr 325-C6 N
Clarendon Pl 459-C7 WTM
Clarendon Rd 425-C7, C8; 459-C5, C8 WTM
Clarendon Rd Dr E 459-C7 WTM
Clarendon Rd Dr W 459-C7 WTM
Claret Dr 423-D9 PTM
Claridge Ct 425-B6 WTM
Claridge Rd 425-B6 WTM
Claridge Way N 390-K6 CTH
Clarion Dr 428-H7 L
Clark Ave 528-C6 BG
Clark Dr 394-C6 F; 529-H8 FT
Clark Rd 491-J3 S; 457-H10 WnT
Clark St 391-H6 Ca
Clarks Cr Ct 523-J1 A
Clarks Cr Rd 558-B4 GT; 524-A8; 558-B4 P
Clarks Hill Dr 593-A1 MTM
Clarks Rd 524-A6 P
Clarkston Ct 389-J5 Z
Clarkston Rd 389-J5 Z
Classic Cir 561-E9 PeT
Classic Ct 496-D4 WrT
Classic View Dr 561-D9 PeT
Classon La 528-E7 BG
Claudious Dr 489-E7 A
Clay Ct 389-E8 Z
Clay Ctr Rd 391-B7 CTH
Clay Springs Dr 391-A6 CTH
Clay St 459-K7; 460-A7 WTM
Clay St N 592-A3 M
Clay St S 592-A3 M
Clayburn Ct 424-C7 PTM
Clayburn Dr 424-C6 PTM
Clayburn Dr S 424-B6 PTM
Claymont Blvd 523-C8 P
Claymont Ct 490-K7 WnT
Claymore Dr 394-A4 F
Claymount La 394-A9 F
Claypoole Dr 491-E4 WnT
Clayton Ave 494-B9 CTM
Clayton La 596-C4 G
Clear Lake Ct 392-H7 Ca
Clear Lake Way 528-B7 PeT
Clear Oak Cir 359-C2 N
Clear Springs Dr 558-H9 GT
Clear Springs La 531-J4 SCT
Clearspring Way 496-E8 WrT
Clearview Cir 428-J7 L
Clearview Dr 592-F7 BTM; 596-C4 G; 458-E2 PTM; 458-F2 WTM
Clearview La 428-J7 L
Clearview Way 596-B4 G
Clearvista Dr 427-D7 LTM
Clearvista Pkwy 427-D6, E5 LTM
Clearvista Pl 427-D5 LTM
Clearvista Way 427-D6 LTM
Clearwater Cir 426-C6 WTM
Clearwater Cove Dr 426-D6 WTM
Clearwater Ct 391-E2 CTH; 557-K7 GT; 427-F7 LTM
Clearwater Dr 427-F6 LTM
Clearwater Pkwy 426-C6 WTM
Clearwater Pointe 426-D6 WTM
Cleat Ct 428-E5 LTM
Clemdale Ave 461-C5 L
Clemson St 424-F4 PTM
Cleveland St 528-C4, F4 BG; DN-E2; 493-F7, G6 CTM
Clew Ct 428-E5 LTM
Clifden Pond Rd 389-E10 Z
Cliff Overlook 359-E4 N
Clifford Cir 391-E5 Ca
Clifford Ct 456-F8 LTH
Clifford Rd 456-F8 LTH
Clifton St 459-B10; 493-B2 CTM
Clifty Falls Dr 391-E3 Ca
Clinical Dr DN-B2; 493-B7 CTM
Clinton Ct 594-G8 WTJ
Clinton St 461-H7 L; 359-H3 N
Clipper Ct 428-C4 LTM
Cloister Dr 424-K2 WTM
Closser Ct 559-J1 DTM
Clossey Dr 561-G7; 562-B7 PeT
Cloud Bay Ct 428-F4 LTM
Clove Ct 562-E5 PeT
Clovelly Ct 458-C6 PTM
Clover Dr 524-E5 P; 458-H7 WTM
Clover Leaf La 394-A2 F
Clover Rd 360-A5 N
Cloverlake Dr 458-H6 WTM
Cloverleaf Ct 491-H9 WnT
Cloverleaf Dr 491-J9 WnT
Cloverleaf Terr 491-F9, H10 WnT
Club Chase 394-J9 F
Club Cir 496-D3 WrT
Club House Dr 393-C6 F
Club House Rd 424-J7 WTM
Club Pt 394-J9 F
Clubhouse Ct 391-K2 Ca; 561-C9 WTJ
Clubside Pl 491-B3 WnT
Clune La 427-K4 LTM
Clyde Ave 494-G9 CTM; 528-G1 PeT
Clyde Dr 594-F5 WTJ
Clyde St 528-G2 CTM
Clydes Rd 458-D2 PTM
Clymer La 426-E6 WTM
Coach Rd 561-G6 PeT
Coachman Dr 392-D9 Ca; 458-E2 PTM
Coachtown Sq 495-E4 WrT
Coal Bluff Ct E 559-A10 MTM
Coast Dr 457-D10; 491-D1 WnT
Coastal Dr 496-G4 WrT
Coastal Way 496-G4 WrT
Coastline Ct 429-A1 FCT
Coatbridge Cir 457-F7 PTM
Coatbridge Way 457-F7 PTM
Cobalt Dr 394-A2 F
Cobb Is Ct 428-C8 L
Cobblefield Ct 394-J6 F
Cobblefield Dr 496-J3 Cu
Cobblesprings Ct 489-J8 A
Cobblesprings Dr 489-J8 A
Cobblestone Ct 428-J8 L
Cobblestone Dr 394-J6 F; 595-B7 WTJ
Cobblestone Dr E 428-J8 L
Cobblestone Dr S 428-J8 L
Cobblestone Dr W 428-J8 L
Cobblestone Pl 489-A10 WaT
Cobblestone Rd 489-A10 WaT
Cobblestone Way 595-A7 WTJ
Cobden Ct 457-F7 PTM
Cobden La 457-F7 PTM
Cobham La 562-G3 FT
Cobham Way 562-G3 FT
Coburn Ave 458-K1, K2, K4 WTM; 458-J6 WTW
Cody La 394-E9 F; 523-A7 P
Coe La DN-C1; 493-B6 CTM
Coffee Tree Ct 324-J7 N
Coffey St DN-B4; 493-A9, A10 CTM; 527-A6 PeT
Coffman Rd 424-B10; 458-B1 PTM
Cohasset Ct 461-C3 L
Coil St 458-H1 PTM; 458-H1; 459-G1 WTM
Colbarn Ct 393-E7 F
Colbarn Dr 393-E7, F7 F
Colbarn Pl 393-F6 F
Colby Blvd 424-F4 PTM
Colby Ct 391-F1 CTH
Colchester Dr 424-D7 PTM; 525-G2 WnT
Cold Spring La 492-G3 WnT
Cold Spring Manor Dr 492-H2 WnT
Cold Spring Rd 458-H9, H10, J7, J8 WTM; 458-H9; 492-H1, H3 WnT
Coldstream La 426-A10 WTM
Coldwater Cir 529-E2 WrT
Coldwater Ct 529-F2 WrT
Coldwater Dr 391-C2 CTH
Cole Porter La 392-F5 Ca
Cole St 492-B3 S; 492-B8, B9; 526-B3, B4 WnT
Colebrook Dr 427-A10 LTM
Coleman Cir 461-H4 L
Colemery Dr 425-D1 CTH
Colerain Dr 492-G2 WnT
Colfax Cir 392-F5 Ca
Colgate St 424-G4 PTM
Coliseum Ave 459-J9 CTM
Colitamore Ct 457-E7 PTM
Colleens Way 559-F1 DTM
College Ave 391-G10; 425-G1 CTH; DN-E2, E4; 459-G10; 493-G4, G9 CTM; 357-K4 W; 425-G1, G6, G9; 459-G2, G10 WTM
College Ave E 455-G6 B
College Ave W 455-F6 B
College Dr 391-F7 Ca; 425-G3 WTM
College La 425-G5 WTM
College Pl Dr 391-G9 CTH
College Way 391-H5 Ca
Collett Dr 592-H2 MTM
Collett Dr E 592-H2 MTM
Collett Dr W 592-H2 MTM
Collier St 526-C6, D8 DTM; 492-D10; 526-D5 WnT
Colliers Ct 393-A4 Ca
Collingswood La 394-C10 F
Collingwood Dr 459-A4 WTM
Collins Dr 360-A1 NT
Colmar St 496-G6 Cu
Colmery Dr 596-C5 G
Cologne Ct 458-D7 PTM
Colonial Ave 458-G3 WTM
Colonial Cir 393-G9 F
Colonial Ct 393-F8 F
Colonial Dr 497-A4 BCT; 489-F6 WaT
Colonial Rd 558-K1 DTM
Colonial Way 561-J10; 595-J1 G
Colonist Cir 457-J4 PTM
Colonnade Ct 529-A8 FT
Colony Cir 425-B8 WTM
Colony Ct 426-B1 CTH; 426-B1 Ca; 389-G7 Z
Colony Lake Dr E 523-J5 P
Colony Lake Dr W 523-J6 P
Colony Mill La 457-J2 PTM
Colony Pl 460-K6 LTM
Colony Pointe Dr E 427-A4 LTM
Colony Pointe Dr S 427-B3 LTM
Colony Pointe Dr W 427-A4 LTM
Colony Way 389-F7 Z
Colonywood Dr 496-G6 Cu
Colorado Ave 460-E9, E10; 494-E1, E4, E5, E7; 528-E1 CTM; 460-E8, E9 WTM
Colt Dr 557-K7 GT
Colt Rd 561-K7; 562-A7 PeT
Columbia Ave DN-F1; 493-J1, J3, J4, J5 CTM
Columbia Cir 393-A9 F
Columbine Cir 491-G1 WnT
Columbine Ct 457-G10 WnT
Columbine Dr 491-G1 WnT
Columbine La 357-E9 WTH
Columbine La E 357-E9 WTH
Column Dr 529-A7 FT
Comanche La 457-F6 PTM
Combs Ave 391-H10 CTH; 562-B4 PeT; 562-B4 Spt
Combs Rd 562-B4, B6, B8 FT
Comer Ave 527-H3 CTM
Comet Dr 594-H7 WTJ
Commack Ct 559-D10 MTM
Commander Cir 427-J4 LTM
Commerce Ave DN-F1; 493-J4 CTM
Commerce Cir 562-H6 FT
Commerce Crossing 426-C4 WTM
Commerce Pk Pl 424-C5 PTM
Commerce Sq Dr 562-H6 FT
Commercial Dr 393-J8 F; 458-D10 WnT
Commercial St 356-J4 WTH
Commission Pl 561-G9 G
Commission Rd 561-G9 G
Commodore Dr 495-A3 WrT
Common Cir 460-F3 WTM
Common View Cir 460-F3 WTM
Common Vista Cir 460-F3 WTM
Common Vista Ct 460-F3 WTM
Common Vista Way 460-G3 WTM
Common Way 460-F3 WTM
Common Way Ct 460-F3 WTM
Commons Dr 457-G7 PTM
Commonwealth Ct 460-F1 WTM
Commonwealth Dr 460-F1 WTM
Company Dr 562-G4 FT
Compass Ct 428-D3 LTM
Compton Ct 425-J2 WTM
Compton St 425-H4, H5, J3; 459-H2, H3 WTM
Conaroe St 524-K3 WnT
Conarroe Rd 423-F7 PTM
Concho Dr 562-H1 FT
Concord Cir 389-E9 Z
Concord Ct 392-A5 Ca; 496-H2 Cu; 393-G9 F; 492-F6 WnT
Concord Dr 595-H1 G
Concord La 392-A5 Ca; 393-E8 F
Concord Pl 392-A5 Ca
Concord Rd 523-C8 P
Concord St 526-G10; 560-G2 PeT; 492-G7; 526-G2, G4 WnT
Concordia Dr 489-G5 WaT
Concordia St 493-E3; 493-G8 CTM
Condit La 427-J4 LTM
Conduitt Dr 592-C2 BTM; 592-C2, D1 M
Conestoga Dr 526-A5 WnT
Congress Ave 492-K1; 493-C1 CTM; 492-E1 WnT
Congress Ct 557-J7 GT
Congress Dr 557-J7 GT
Congressional Dr 391-F7 Ca
Conifer Ct 394-A9 F; 426-E7 WTM
Connaught Dr 390-F10 CTH
Connaught Dr E 523-C8 P
Connaught Dr W 523-C8 P
Connecticut Ave 425-H2 CTH; 395-K10 FCT
Connection Ave 528-G4 BG; 528-G4 WrT
Connemara Rd 560-K7 PeT
Conner Cr Dr 393-D8 F
Conner Knoll Pkwy 393-H3 F
Conner St 359-H3 N
Connerwood Dr 393-F2 DTH
Conneticut St 527-F7 PeT
Connie Ct 563-A6 FT
Connie Dr 563-A6 FT; 489-F5 WaT
Connors Dr 596-F2 G
Conover Ct 562-F7 PeT
Conrad Ave 526-J2 WnT
Conried Ct 462-A8 LTM
Conried Dr 461-K7; 462-A8 LTM
Conservatory Dr 527-G4 CTM
Constantino La 496-H5 Cu
Constellation Dr 495-J2 WrT
Constitution Dr 390-C9 CTH; 427-C8 LTM
Consulate Ct 491-G1 S
Consulate La 491-G1 S
Continental Ct 527-F8 PeT
Continental Dr 557-H8 GT; 389-E9 Z
Continental Way 391-F3 CTH
Conway Ct 427-J1 F
Cool Cr Blvd 391-K2; 392-A2 Ca
Cool Cr Cir 357-K7; 358-A7 WTH
Cool Cr Ct 392-C4 Ca
Cool Cr Dr 392-D4 Ca
Cool Ridge 391-J4 Ca
Coolee Cir 496-F6 Cu; 496-F5 WrT
Coolee La 496-F6 Cu
Coolidge Ave 529-D5 FT; 495-D4 WrT
Coolidge St 492-A10 WnT
Cooper La 423-A1 ET
Cooper Pointe Cir 458-G1 PTM
Cooper Pointe Dr 458-G1 PTM
Cooper Rd 389-A10; 423-A2 ET; 423-A4 PTM; 458-G2, G7 WTM
Cooper St 494-A4 CTM
Cooperland Ct 458-G1 PTM
Coopers Hawk Dr 392-H3 Ca
Coopersmith Ct 458-G1 PTM
Cooperstone Ct 458-G1 PTM
Copeland Dr 455-G5 B
Copeland Rd 563-D8 FT
Copeland St 561-J1 PeT
Copen Ct 525-K9 DTM
Copenhaver Dr 458-J2 WTM
Copiah Ct 496-D8 WrT
Copley Dr 425-C2 CTH; 425-C2 WTM
Copley Pl 425-C2 CTH
Copper Ct 562-G2 PeT
Copper La 562-G2 PeT
Copper Mountain Ct 428-G9 L
Copper Mountain Dr 428-F10 L
Copper Oaks Ct 563-A1 FT
Copper Tree Way 358-B10 WTH
Copperfield Dr 427-E8 LTM
Copperfield Way 427-F8 LTM
Coppergate Dr 390-K10 CTH
Copperleaf Blvd 594-H10 WTJ
Copperleaf Dr 457-D10 WnT
Coppermill Cir 457-D6 PTM
Coppermill Ct 457-D5 PTM
Coppertree La 489-A10 WaT
Copperwood Cir E 392-E1 Ca
Copperwood Cir W 392-D1 Ca
Copperwood Dr 594-H10 WTJ
Copperwood Pl 392-E1 Ca
Coppock Dr 559-H2 DTM
Coppock La 559-J2 DTM
Coquina Key Dr 491-H7 WnT
Coral Bay Cove 595-F2 G
Coral Bay Ct 428-J5 L
Coral Bay Dr 595-F2 G
Coral Reef Ct 428-C5 LTM
Coral Reef Way 428-B5 LTM
Coralbury Ct 592-E2 M
Corbin Dr 393-F7 F
Cord St 492-B3, B4 S
Corday Ct 393-G5 F
Cordell St 461-K7, K8 LTM
Cordes Rd 527-F10 PeT
Cordonia Blvd 559-C10 MTM
Cordova Ct 559-H4 DTM
Cordova Dr 559-H4 DTM
Cordwood La 457-C10 WnT
Corey Ct 562-B6 Spt
Corey Dr 562-C6 PeT; 562-B6 Spt
Corey La 523-K10 P
Corinth Way 490-F7 WaT
Corinthian La 428-J4 LTM
Corkwood Ct 455-J8 B; 561-G7 PeT
Corkwood Dr 561-G7 PeT
Corliss St 527-B7 PeT
Corn Tassle Ct 561-G9 G
Cornelian Ct 326-C10 N
Cornelius Ave 459-D5, D6, D8 WTM
Cornell Ave 391-H10 CTH; 493-H4 CTM; 425-H10; 459-H1 WTM
Cornell St 391-G10, H9 CTH
Cornerbrook Ct 425-K4 WTM
Cornerstone Dr 531-J4 SCT
Cornflower Ct 357-E9 WTH
Cornhusker Rd 388-A4 WTB
Corniche Dr 389-D9 Z
Cornsilk Row 357-J10 WTH
Cornucopia Dr 424-K1 PTM
Cornwall Cir 427-D10 LTM
Cornwall Ct 391-C5 CTH
Cornwallis La 390-C9 CTH
Coronado Ct 490-J8 WnT
Coronado Rd 490-J8 WnT
Coronado St 458-E6 PTM
Corottoman Dr 490-A8 WaT
Corporate Dr 423-H10; 457-H2 PTM
Corporate Vill Dr 525-B3 WnT
Corporate Way 457-H1 PTM
Corporation Dr 427-D4 LTM
Corral Berry Ct 393-A3 Ca
Corral Ct 393-B9 DTH; 357-H10 WTH
Corrill St 492-G8, G10 WnT
Corsican Cir 489-H10 A; 358-A5 WTH
Corvallis Cres 492-D1 WnT
Corwin Blvd 559-D10 MTM
Corwyn Rd 492-D2 WnT
Cossell Dr 458-A10; 492-A1, A8 WnT
Cossell Rd 492-B6 S; 492-B6, D7 WnT
Costa Mesa Dr 596-H3 G
Costwold La 392-K1 Ca
Cotherstone Ct 427-F8 LTM
Cotta La 429-C1 FCT
Cottage Ave 527-G1, H1, J1, K1; 528-B1, E1 CTM
Cottage Ct 528-E1 CTM
Cottage Grove Ct N 559-A10 MTM
Cottage La 596-A5 G
Cotton Ave 461-F6 L
Cotton Bay Dr W 457-F4 PTM
Cotton Cr Ct 423-F4 PTM
Cottonwood Cir 324-K7 N
Cottonwood Ct 596-B5 G; 557-K5 GT; 592-E1 M; 389-G5 Z
Cottonwood Dr 392-C2 Ca; 557-K10 M; 562-A6 PeT; 389-G4 Z
Cottonwood La 596-B5 G
Cottonwood N 557-K5 GT
Cottonwood S 557-K5 GT
Counselor La 531-F9 MTS
Counselors Row 426-D3 WTM
Count Fleet Ct 561-A7 PeT
Count Turf Ct 561-A8 PeT
Countfleet Ct 357-F9 WTH
Country Aire Dr 596-G2 G
Country Aire La 596-G2 G
Country Bk Dr 425-A9 WTM
Country Bk Way 458-B2 PTM
Country Charm Dr 491-A5 WnT
Country Club Blvd 491-A4 WnT
Country Club La 457-A10 WnT
Country Club Pines Dr 491-B1 WnT
Country Club Pl 491-A4 WnT
Country Club Rd 592-A9 BTM; 596-F2 G; 592-A9 M; 491-A3, A8 WnT
Country Crossing 491-B4 WnT
Country Ests Dr 562-B8 PeT
Country Jct 491-A4 WnT
Country La 456-C10 LTH; 524-B7 P; 561-B8 PeT; 594-K3 WTJ; 491-A2 WnT
Country La Ct 561-C9 PeT
Country Meadows Dr 491-A4 WnT
Country Meadows La 491-A4 WnT
Country Pine Ct 324-H7 N
Country Pl Dr 356-D9 WTH
Country Pointe Dr 491-A5 WnT
Country Ridge Dr 491-A5 WnT
Country Ridge La 491-A5 WnT
Country View Ct 491-A5 WnT
Country View La 491-A5 WnT
Country View Way 592-G7 BTM; 592-G7 MTM
Country Walk Cir 562-D8 PeT
Country Walk Ct 455-J7 B; 562-D8 PeT
Country Walk Dr 455-J7 B; 562-C9 G
Country Way 531-E3 SCT
Country Woods Ct 561-E8 PeT
Country Woods Dr 561-D8 PeT
Countrybrook Ct 458-A2 PTM
Countrybrook Dr 458-B2 PTM
Countrybrook La 458-B2 PTM
Countrybrook Terr 458-A2 PTM
Countryside Ct 531-D4 SCT; 490-E7 WaT; 525-A2 WnT
Countryside Dr 596-C5 G; 525-A1, A2 WnT
Countryside La 525-A1 WnT
Countrywood Dr 326-G6 NT; 326-G6 WyT
County Line Rd 557-F10; 558-F9 BTM; 558-F9; 559-B9; 560-H9 DTM; 562-K9 FT; 561-F9; 562-A9 G; 557-F10 GT; 428-K5, K10; 462-K1 L; 558-F9; 559-B9 MTM; 428-K10 McC; 562-K9 PTJ; 560-H9; 561-F9; 562-A9 PeT; 428-K10; 462-K1 VT; 560-H9 WTJ

County Line Rd E 558-H9 DTM; 558-H9 GT
County Line Rd N 422-E3 BTH; 422-E3 ET
County Line Rd S 558-A10 GT; 558-A10 M
County Rd 524-G1 WaT
County Rd 144 594-A10 WTJ
County Rd 700th W 429-A2 McC
Courageous Dr 428-C7, D6 LTM
Court St DN-B3, D3, E3; 493-A8, E8, F8 CTM
Courthouse Dr 461-C3 L
Courtney Dr 393-G3 F
Courtney Rd 495-F2, F3 WrT
Courtyard Way 393-D9 F
Cove Ct 457-C5 PTM
Cove Trace 427-G7 LTM
Covenant Ct 524-G4 WaT
Coventry Ct 561-K10 G
Coventry Rd 425-C4 WTM
Coventry Way 392-D6 Ca; 325-A7 N
Covered Bridge Rd 561-G10; 595-G1 G; 424-B10 PTM
Covey Cir 562-F2 PeT
Covey La 424-J6 WTM
Covington Ave 561-K6 PeT
Covington Blvd 427-H1 F
Covington Cir 427-J1 F
Covington St 455-G10 B
Cowan Lake Dr 462-E5 L
Cowen Dr 592-A9 BTM
Cowman Dr 561-K10 G
Cox Rd 559-G9 DTM
Coyner Ave 494-A4 CTM
Coyote Cir 394-D4 F
Coyote Run 394-D4 F
Cozy La 388-C9 PTB
Crabapple Ct 393-K2 F
Crabtree Farm Rd 395-F3 FCT
Crafton Ct 592-E2 M
Crafton Meadow La 592-E2 M
Cragmont Dr 561-D3, E3, G3 PeT
Cragwood Ct 523-J9 P
Craig Ave 326-K1; 327-A2 WRT
Craig St 427-B5, B7, C5 LTM; 523-K8 P
Craigmont Dr 562-E2 PeT
Cranberry Ct 525-K9 DTM; 394-A2 F
Cranbrook Ct 426-E9 WTM
Cranbrook Dr 426-D9 WTM
Crandon Dr 490-H7 WnT
Crane Ct 457-E6 PTM
Crane La 392-H2 Ca
Cranley Cir 460-H1 WTM
Cranmere St 495-K1 WrT
Cranston Dr 491-D7 WnT
Crawford Dr 459-H4 WTM
Crawfordsville Rd 456-D8 LTH; 491-J3; 492-A4 S; 491-A1, F2 WnT
Cree Tr 360-B7 NT; 426-E8, F8 WTM
Creed Ct 424-B6 PTM
Creek Pkwy Dr S 527-J9 PeT
Creek Rd 326-H5, H8 WyT
Creek Ridge Tr 427-G10 LTM
Creek Side La 392-G8 Ca
Creek St 492-E7 WnT
Creek View Dr 562-E4 PeT
Creek Way 523-K1 A; 528-C8 PeT
Creekbank Dr 561-C2 PeT
Creekbend Blvd 561-D2 PeT
Creekbend Cir 561-D2 PeT
Creekbend Ct 561-D2 PeT
Creekbend Dr 392-J1 Ca
Creekbend La 561-D2 PeT
Creekbrook Dr 561-J5 PeT
Creeks Crossing Dr 458-A2 PTM
Creekshore Dr 458-F1 PTM
Creekshore La 458-F1 PTM
Creekside Cir 496-J4 Cu
Creekside Ct 393-F6 F; 523-K10 P; 530-K4 SCT; 489-D7 WaT
Creekside Dr 455-F2 BTH; 393-F6 F; 523-K10 P; 530-K4 SCT
Creekside La 391-K8 Ca; 393-E6 F; 561-F10 G; 427-B9, B10; 461-B1 LTM; 523-K10 P
Creekside Pass 390-A4, B4 ET
Creekside Woods Dr 496-D8 WrT
Creekstone Ct 496-D8 WrT
Creekstone Dr 496-D8 WrT
Creekstone Way 390-A5 ET
Creekview Cir 426-K7 LTM; 592-D3 M
Creekview Ct 595-E1 G
Creekview Dr 325-D9 N
Creekview La 393-A10 F; 428-F7 L
Creekwood Cir 496-F10 WrT
Creekwood Ct 455-B2 BTH; 428-K4 LTM
Creekwood Dr 455-B1 BTH; 357-J3 W
Creekwood La 391-D6 CTH; 428-K4 LTM
Creekwood Terr 561-B10; 595-C1 WTJ
Crenshaw Ct 392-J4 Ca
Crescent Ave 459-B9 CTM
Crescent Ct 428-F5 LTM; 593-B2 MTM
Crescent Dr 391-J5 Ca; 596-B5 G
Crescent Hill La 458-G7 WTM
Crescent Ridge 455-A8 LTH
Cresco St 427-B6 LTM
Cressida Way 394-J10 F
Cressmoor Cir 491-A2 WnT
Cressmoor Ct 490-K2 WnT
Crest Ct 557-J1 P; 491-F5 WnT
Crest Dr 595-A1 WTJ
Crest Hill Dr 427-E9, F9 LTM
Crest La 427-F9 LTM
Creston Dr 492-D8 WnT
Creston Pt Cir 496-D9 WrT
Crestpoint La 523-E6 P
Crestpointe Dr 490-K6 WnT
Crestridge Ct 394-A10 F
Crestview Ave 459-H5, H6, J2 WTM
Crestview Cir 489-K8 A
Crestview Ct 393-F8 F; 324-B10; 358-B1 WTH
Crestview Dr 393-G9 F; 562-D9 G; 425-J3, J4 WTM
Crestview Rd 562-E10 G
Crestway Dr 428-F7 L
Crestwell Dr 424-E10 PTM
Crestwood Ct 530-G1 WrT
Crestwood Dr 392-D6 Ca; 592-A1 M
Crews Dr 461-E7 L
Cricket Cir 392-B4 Ca
Cricket Knoll La 392-C4 Ca
Cricket Ridge 426-J2 WTM
Cricket Tree La 425-B4 WTM
Cricklewood Cir 426-K9 LTM
Cricklewood Ct 392-D4 Ca
Cricklewood Rd 426-K10 LTM
Cricklewood Way 389-E9 Z
Crickwood Cir 424-E8 PTM
Crickwood Ct 424-E8 PTM
Crickwood Dr 424-D8 PTM
Crickwood La 424-D8 PTM
Crickwood Pl 424-E8 PTM
Crimson Cir Dr E 561-F3 PeT
Crimson Cir Dr W 561-F3 PeT
Crimson Ct E 392-B7 Ca
Crimson Ct W 392-B7 Ca
Crimson King Ct 427-E10 LTM
Crimson King Pkwy 592-C4 M
Crimson Way 595-K3 G
Cripple Cr Ct 496-H4 WrT
Crittenden Ave 425-K10; 459-K4, K7 WTM
Crockett Dr 496-G5 WrT
Croft Ct 425-A5 WTM
Cromarty Cir 359-B1 N
Cromer Rd 525-G8 DTM
Cromwell Cir 359-G10 NT
Cromwell Rd 427-A9 LTM
Crook Dr N 427-G3 LTM
Crooked Cr Dr 458-K3 WTM
Crooked Cr Overlook 458-H8 WTM
Crooked Cr Ridge Dr 458-G6 WTM
Crooked Fence Tr 524-B9 P
Crooked La 595-A6 WTJ
Crooked Stick La 390-K9 CTH
Crosby Dr 561-E8 PeT
Crosley La 491-H4 S
Cross Bridge Cir 557-H2 P
Cross Bridge Ct 557-G2 P
Cross Bridge Way 557-H2 P
Cross Cr Blvd 561-E2 PeT
Cross Cr Cir 458-B3 PTM; 358-B3 WTH
Cross Cr Ct 458-D3 PTM
Cross Cr Dr 458-B3 PTM
Cross Cr La 458-D3 PTM
Cross Dr 493-K6 CTM
Cross Key Ct 424-A10 PTM
Cross Key Dr 424-A10 PTM
Cross Rd Bend 562-B6 PeT
Cross Roads La 394-C6 F
Cross St 392-C5 Ca
Cross Tr 531-B2 SCT
Cross Willow Blvd 529-F1 WrT
Cross Willow La 529-F2 WrT
Cross Winds Dr 428-D2 F
Crossbridge Ct 489-C10 WaT
Crossbridge Rd 489-B10 WaT
Crosser Dr 563-B7 FT
Crossfield Dr 496-C9 WrT
Crossfield Tr 429-C3 McC
Crossfields Ct 390-H7 CTH
Crossfields Dr 390-G8 CTH
Crossford Cir 490-J3 WnT
Crossford Way 490-H3 WnT
Crossgate La 562-B6 Spt
Crossing Dr 562-B7 PeT
Crossman Dr 561-K7; 562-A7 PeT
Crosspoint Blvd 393-G10; 427-F2 F
Crosspoint Commons 427-E2 F
Crossridge Dr 461-E8 LTM
Crosswind Dr 525-C4 WnT
Croton Cir 457-H3 PTM
Crousore Rd 495-G2 WrT
Crow Ct 564-A4 FT
Crowley Ct 324-K5 N
Crown Cir 390-G10 CTH
Crown Dr 455-K3 BTH
Crown Plaza 524-A7 P
Crown Pt 389-F6 Z
Crown Pt Rd 423-A8 PTM
Crown St 459-C5, C7 WTM
Crown Vetch Pl 457-K4 PTM
Crown Woods Cir 491-J6 WnT
Crowndale Ct 359-K7 N
Crows Nest 393-B8 F
Crows Nest Dr 459-C2 WTM
Cruft St 527-H4 CTM
Cruse Rd 389-C7, E7 ET; 389-E7 Z
Cruse St DN-F3; 493-H8 CTM
Cruyff Cir 491-C4 WnT
Crystal Bay Dr 424-J9 WTM
Crystal Bay Dr E 557-H2 P
Crystal Bay Dr W 557-G1 P
Crystal Cr Dr 361-H10; 395-G1 FCT
Crystal Ct 523-E1 WaT
Crystal Dr 492-F2 WnT
Crystal Lakes Dr 595-J4 G
Crystal Pointe Cir 428-J6 L
Crystal Pointe Dr 428-K5 L
Crystal Pointe La 428-J5 L
Crystal Springs Dr 523-D1 WaT
Crystal Water Dr 562-K2 FT
Crystal Woods Cir 491-J6 WnT
Crystal Woods Dr 491-J6 WnT
Cullen Ct 495-F2 WrT
Cullen Dr 495-F2 WrT
Culligan Ave 494-D4 CTM
Culpeper Ct 561-G7 PeT
Culpeper Dr 561-H7 PeT
Culpepper Dr 424-K1 CTH
Culver La 523-A7 P
Culver St 460-H8 LTM
Cumberland Gap Dr 496-F5 WrT
Cumberland Pk Dr 394-A10 F
Cumberland Rd 428-A2 DTH; 394-A3, A7, A9, A10 F; 394-A3; 428-A2 FCT; 326-A4 JT; 326-A10; 360-A2, A4; 394-A3 N; 326-A10; 360-A4, A9 NT; 326-A4 WRT; 496-G4 WrT
Cumberland Ridge Ct 394-B10 F
Cumberland Ridge La 394-A10 F
Cumberland Way 496-G4 WrT
Cunion Ct 324-K5 N
Cunningham Rd 491-H3 S
Cupcake Ct 490-G10 WaT
Currant Dr 325-B9 N
Currey La 358-C10 WTH
Curry Ct 496-C2 WrT
Curry Dr 496-C2 WrT
Curry Rd 595-F4 WTJ; 496-F1 WrT
Custer Ct 561-A9 PeT
Cutback Ct 324-G7 N
Cutler La 596-B4 G
Cycling La 424-J10 WTM
Cyntheanne Ave 395-K9; 429-J2 FCT
Cyntheanne Rd 395-K1, K5 FCT; 327-J1 WRT; 327-J8; 361-J1, K8 WyT
Cynthia Ct 357-H9 WTH
Cynthia Dr 561-F6 PeT
Cypress 595-K4 G
Cypress Dr 394-B2 F
Cypress N 595-K4 G
Cypress W 595-K4 G

D

Dabny Cir 457-H7 PTM
Dabny Ct 457-H7 PTM
Dabny Dr 457-H8 PTM
Daffodil Ct 428-J9 L
Daffon Dr 561-F7 PeT
Dahlia Ct 460-E4 WTM
Dahlia Dr 561-D3 PeT
Dahlia La 561-E3 PeT
Dailey Rd 557-A5 GT
Daisy Hill Ct E 559-A10 MTM
Daisy La 497-G8 SCT; 491-E7 WnT
Dakota Dr 325-D8 N
Dakota St 493-C10; 527-C1 CTM; 457-J7 PTM
Dale Ct 595-B2 WTJ
Dale Dr 496-F6 Cu; 557-J1 P
Dale Hollow Dr 496-F5 WrT
Dale Schrier Dr 455-J4 B
Dalegard Ave 491-D9 WnT
Dallas Ct 392-E3 Ca
Dallas Dr 392-E3 Ca; 523-J9 P
Dallas La 392-E3 Ca
Dalton Ct 359-F4 N
Dalton St 427-B6 LTM
Daly St DN-E3; 493-G8 CTM
Dan Dr 359-E5 N
Dan Jones Rd 489-K10; 523-K5 A; 523-K6 GT; 523-K6 P; 489-K10; 523-K5 WaT
Dan Patch Ct 562-K2 FT; 357-F9 WTH
Dan Patch Dr 562-K2 FT
Dana Ct 394-B10 F; 490-K4 WnT
Danaher St 560-K6 PeT
Danbury Ct 389-E7 Z
Danbury Dr 392-A1 Ca; 525-A3 WnT; 389-E7 Z
Danbury Rd 492-D1 WnT
Dancer Dr 528-K9 FT
Dancy Ct 529-F2 WrT
Dancy Dr 529-E2 WrT
Dandy Cr Dr 456-J4 PTM
Dandy Ct 457-C5 PTM
Dandy Tr 423-B9; 457-B8, C6 PTM; 457-B8 WTM
Daneby Cir 427-A10 LTM
Danford Sq 424-H10 WTM
Dangerfield Dr 528-F9 BG
Daniel Ct 455-H8 B
Daniel Dr 461-A5 LTM
Danita Ct 531-G4 SCT
Danny Dr 389-J5 Z
Dansk Ridge Ct 426-J3 WTM
Danver La 528-E7 PeT
Daphne Dr 423-H10 PTM
Dapple Ct 458-E4 PTM; 389-F9 Z
Dapple Trace 458-E4 PTM
Darby Cir 324-J5 N
Darby Ct 425-B5 WTM
Darby Dan Dr 562-J7 FT
Darby La 455-F4 B; 425-A5 WTM
Dardeb Rd 525-G8 DTM
Daredevil Tr 428-G10 L
Darien Ct 461-F8 LTM
Dark Spaten La 530-A1 WrT
Dark Star Dr 561-A7 PeT
Darkwood Dr 490-K5 WnT
Darlene Ct 594-F7 WTJ
Darlene Dr 594-F7 WTJ
Darnley Ct 425-D6 WTM
Darrow Dr 425-D10 WTM
Dartmoor Ct 457-G7 PTM
Dartmoor Dr 457-G7 PTM
Dartmouth Ct 425-A7, A8 WTM
Dartmouth Rd 425-B6, B8 WTM
Darton Rd 357-F4 WTH
Dartown Rd 357-F4 WTH
Darwin St 493-K3 CTM
Daugherty Dr 390-B6 ET; 560-D4 PeT
David Ct 523-K2 A; 461-B7 LTM
David Dr 455-J1 BTH; 324-B10 WTH; 594-H1 WTJ
David La 592-A9 BTM; 593-C4 MTM; 561-E8 PeT
David Lind Dr 527-D9 PeT
David Pl 392-B4 Ca
David St 461-B5, B6 L; 461-B7 LTM
Davidson St DN-E2, E3; 493-G8, H6 CTM
Davis Ct 489-A8; 490-F7 WaT
Davis Dr 526-E6 DTM; 596-D7 G
Davis La 428-G7 L
Davis Rd 530-B5 FT; 530-B5 WrT
Davis St 494-F9 CTM
Dawn Ct 392-B7 Ca
Dawn Dr 490-C1 LTH; 424-B10; 458-A1 PTM
Dawnwood Ct 562-D5 PeT
Dawnwood Dr 562-D5 PeT
Dawson Dr 393-F6 F
Dawson Lake Dr 425-J10; 459-J1 WTM
Dawson St DN-F4; 493-K10; 527-K1, K2, K3, K4 CTM; 527-K5 PeT
Dawsondale Ct 562-B3 PeT
Day Dr 426-B2 CTH
Dayflower Dr 325-D10 N
Dayhuff Rd 592-D9 BTM; 592-G9 MTM
Daylight Ct 562-D6 PeT
Daylily Dr 563-B6 FT
Dayton Ave 494-F9; 528-F1, F2 CTM
Dayton Ct 528-F1 CTM
Dayton Dr 392-D3 Ca
De Shane Ave 327-A10; 360-H3 WyT
De Soto Ct 561-A9 PeT
De Vault Dr 426-E9 WTM
De Ville Pl 596-E10 NW
Deacon 391-J6 Ca
Dean Rd 426-E6, E10; 460-E1 WTM
Dean St 325-G1 C; 461-C6 L
Deandra Dr 390-B10 ET
Deanna Dr 496-G6 Cu
Deanne Elaine Ct 490-K4 WnT
Dearborn Cir 394-C2 F
Dearborn St 460-C9, C10; 494-C1, C4, C5, C8, C9 CTM; 528-C7, C10 PeT; 426-C9; 460-C2, C3, C6 WTM
Deauville Dr 460-B7 WTM
Debbie Ct 357-K3 W; 594-F8 WTJ
Debbie Dr 594-F8 WTJ
Debello Ct 491-B3 WnT
Debonair La 491-G2 S
Debonair Terr 491-G2 S
Deborah St 458-A10, C10 WTM
Debra Ct 557-H3 P
Debra La 561-C3 PeT
Decamp Dr 461-H8 WrT
Decatur Commons 559-F1 DTM
Decatur Dr 428-E2 FCT
Declaration Dr 527-F8 PeT
Dedham Dr 496-B1 WrT
Deedlewood Dr 496-A6 WrT
Deep Well 394-C4 F
Deer Cr Ave 458-A4 PTM
Deer Cr Ct 458-A4 PTM
Deer Cr Dr 458-A5 PTM
Deer Cr Pl 458-A4 PTM
Deer Cross Pl 594-E7 WTJ
Deer Pass 594-K6 WTJ
Deer Path Dr 457-E8 PTM
Deer Ridge 457-E8 PTM
Deer Ridge Cross 392-G2 Ca
Deer Ridge Ct 392-G2 Ca
Deer Ridge Dr 389-D8 ET
Deer Ridge Dr N 392-F2 Ca
Deer Ridge Dr S 392-G2 Ca
Deer Ridge Pl 392-F2 Ca
Deer Run 427-H4 LTM
Deer Run Cir 428-B1 F
Deer Run Ct 427-H3, J4 LTM
Deer Run Dr 531-D3 SCT
Deer Run Path 557-J3 P
Deer Skip Cir 358-A3 WTH
Deer Stone La 395-D8 FCT
Deer Walk Tr 358-A2 WTH
Deer Way 428-J8 L
Deerberry Ct 324-J8 N
Deerberry Dr 324-K7 N
Deerbrook Ct 457-E10 WnT
Deerbrook Cir 427-A1 F
Deerfield Cir 424-K2; 425-A2 CTH
Deerfield Ct 594-E8 WTJ
Deerfield Dr 557-K3 P; 594-E7 WTJ
Deerfield La 429-B2 FCT
Deerfield Mall 425-A2 CTH
Deering St 394-B9 F
Deerstand Rd 594-E7 WTJ
Deerview Ct 424-C6 PTM
Deerview Dr 424-C6 PTM
Deerwood Ct 458-A3 PTM; 594-E7 WTJ
Deerwood Dr 594-E8 WTJ
Deerwood Pkwy 594-E7 WTJ
Del Prado Ct 562-B7 PeT
Del Prado Dr 562-B7 PeT
Delaine Ct 457-C5 PTM
Delaney Dr 393-H1 F; 560-K6 PeT
Delaware Commons Dr N 426-C9 WTM
Delaware Commons Dr S 426-C10 WTM
Delaware Pkwy 393-K10 F
Delaware St 391-F10; 425-F1 CTH; DN-D4; 459-F10; 493-F1, F3, F4, F9; 527-F2, F5 CTM; 527-F6; 561-F6, F7 PeT; 425-F3, F10; 459-F2, F4, F7, F8 WTM
Delbrick La 496-A6 WrT
Delbrook Cir 425-A7 WTM
Delbrook Ct 425-A7 WTM
Delbrook Dr 596-E10 NW; 425-A7 WTM
Delegates Row 426-E2 WTM
Delight Cr Rd 393-B8 F
Dell Zell Dr 460-A3 WTM
Della Ct 462-A8 LTM
Della St 462-A7 LTM
Dellinger Dr 394-B4 F
Dellingham Dr 425-C8 WTM
Dellwood Dr 462-B5 L
Delmar Ave 491-H9, J9; 492-A9, E9 WnT
Delmar Ct 491-J9 WnT
Delmar Rd 460-C5 WTM
Delmont Ct 462-B8 LTM
Delmont Dr 462-B8 LTM
Delores Dr 492-B1 WnT
Deloss St DN-F3; 493-H9, K9; 494-D9 CTM
Delphi Dr 558-H8 GT
Delray Dr 491-E10 WnT
Delta Dr 595-B10 WTJ; 526-A5 WnT
Delwood Dr 558-B10 M
Demaree Rd 595-F7 WTJ
Demarest Dr 491-D8 WnT
Deme Dr 462-D3 L
Deming Rd 324-E1, E3 JT
Democracy Dr 457-K3 PTM
Deneen St 326-A10 N; 326-A10 NT
Denison St 492-B10; 526-B2, B5 WnT
Denniston St 526-B5 DTM
Denniston Terr 526-B5 DTM
Denny St 460-D10; 494-D2, D5, D8, D9, E2, E10; 528-D2, E1 CTM; 528-D8, D9 PeT
Denton Cir 427-H8 LTM
Denver Ct 525-F9 DTM
Denver Dr 525-G9 DTM; 523-J8 P
Denwood Dr 460-D8 WTM
Deny Dr 460-F6 WTM
DePauw Blvd 424-D3 PTM
Depauw Rd 528-A9 PeT
Depot Cir 489-B10 WaT
Depot Dr 561-B9 PeT
Depot St 525-G10 DTM; 531-H5 NP; 523-F7 P
DeQuincy St 460-F10; 494-F1, F4, F5, F7, G8, G9, G10 CTM; 528-G1 PeT; 460-F3, F4, F8 WTM
Derby Ct 427-F4 LTM; 357-E9 WTH
Derby La 460-F5 WTM
Derby Way 423-G8 PTM
Derbyshire Ct 392-G4 Ca
Derbyshire Dr 496-K6 Cu
Derbyshire Rd 562-A2, A3 PeT; 562-A3 Spt
Derrek Pl 495-E4 WrT
Derstan Rd 427-A9 LTM
Derval Ct 461-D9 WrT
Derwyn Ct 427-D10 LTM
Desert Wind Ct 391-G3 CTH
Desmond Ave 461-C8 LTM
Desoto La 491-H4 S
Destry Pl 393-H5 F
Detroit St 528-C4, D4 BG; DN-F3; 493-J9 CTM
Deva Cir 458-J5 WTM
Developers Rd 528-A7 PeT
Devereaux Dr 458-E6 PTM; 458-E6 WTM
Deville Ct 427-E8 LTM
Devin Dr 455-H9 B
Devington Cir 460-J6 LTM
Devington Rd 460-K6 LTM
Devinney Dr 559-J4 DTM
Devon Ave 529-G7 FT; 495-G7 WrT
Devon Ct 391-C5 CTH; 393-B9 F; 460-F7 WTM
Devon Ct Dr E 460-F7 WTM
Devon Ct Dr W 460-F7 WTM
Devon Dr 460-G7 LTM; 460-D7, F7 WTM
Devon La 391-C5 CTH
Devon Lake Rd 460-F7 WTM
Devonshire Ct 324-K6 N; 424-K5 WTM
Devonwood Dr 558-A10 M
Dew Cir 425-A3 WTM
Dewberry Ct 424-J4 WTM
Dewester Dr 428-K9 L
Dewey Ave 494-K8; 495-D7 WrT
Dexter St 493-A4 CTM
Diablo Ct 596-F3 G
Diamond Ct 457-H8 PTM
Diamond Dr 390-G9 CTH
Diamond La 457-H8 PTM
Diamond Pointe Ct 428-G4 LTM
Diamond Pointe Dr 428-G3 LTM
Diamond Way 325-D9 N
Diana Dr 494-G9 CTM; 423-H10 PTM
Dianna Dr 455-H1 BTH
Dickinson Ct 393-H1 F
Dickson Rd 460-G5, K5 LTM; 460-E5 WTM
Dickson St DN-F2; 493-H7 CTM
Dietz St 527-K5 CTM; 527-K5 PeT
Digby Ct 492-D2 WnT
Dijon Dr 460-E2 WTM
Diller Dr 461-K7 LTM
Dior Ct 423-E9 PTM
Diplomat Ct 528-H6 BG
Directors Dr 525-H3 WnT
Discovery Cir 428-G4 LTM
Discovery Dr S 427-B3 LTM
Discovery Dr W 427-A4 LTM
Distributors Dr 525-J3 WnT
Ditch Rd 391-A3, A10; 425-A4 CTH; 357-A6, A10 WTH; 425-A4, A7, A8; 459-A3 WTM
Divers Cove Ct 428-E5 LTM
Dividend Rd 525-J2 WnT
Divinity Ct 592-A1 M
Division St DN-B4; 493-A9, A10 CTM; 359-G4, K4; 360-A4 N; 527-A7 PeT
Dix Rd 564-G6, H7 FT; 564-G6, H7 MTS
Dixie Dr 561-E8 PeT
Dixon Ct 325-E8 N
Dobbs Ferry Dr 457-J3 PTM
Dobson St 424-B9 PTM
Dockside Ct 496-A2 WrT
Dockside Dr 595-C6 WTJ
Doctor A J Brown Ave 459-J10; 493-J2 CTM
Doctor M L King Jr St DN-C1; 459-B9; 493-C1, D5 CTM
Doe Cir 458-A4 PTM
Doe La 595-F3 G; 428-J8, K8 L
Doe Ridge Ct 427-G5 LTM
Doe Spring Dr 422-J4 PTM
Doe Way 324-H4 N
Dofor Rd 557-A3 GT
Dog Wood La 595-K4 G
Dogie Rd 492-A8 WnT
Dogwood 557-K5 GT
Dogwood Cir E 424-F6 PTM
Dogwood Cir N 424-E6 PTM
Dogwood Cir S 424-E6 PTM
Dogwood Ct 455-J9 B; 427-J8 LTM; 325-A9 N
Dogwood Dr 562-B6 PeT
Dogwood La 424-F2 CTH; 596-H3 G; 455-C8 LTH
Dokey La 563-A2 FT
Dolittle Tr 326-C1 WRT
Dollar Hide Cir 559-H2, J2 DTM
Dollar Hide Dr N 559-J2 DTM
Dollar Hide Dr S 559-H2, J2 DTM
Dolphin La 428-C3 LTM
Dominion Dr 389-E9 Z
Dona Ct 392-E8 Ca
Dona Dr 392-E8 Ca
Donald Ave 458-B10; 492-B1 WnT
Donald Ct 592-H2 MTM
Donald Dr 592-J2 MTM
Doncaster Ct 394-H10 F
Donegal Dr 560-K5, K6 PeT
Donna Bell Dr 526-A5 WnT
Donnehan Rd 561-A6 PeT
Donnely Dr 455-F10 LTH
Donner La 424-A10 PTM
Donnie Ct 490-J4 WnT
Donny Bk Dr 391-J8 CTH
Donovan Dr 462-C8 LTM
Dora Ct 427-E8 LTM
Doral Cir 394-F10 F
Doral Ct 427-D3 LTM
Doral Dr E 427-C4 LTM
Doral Dr N 427-C3 LTM
Doral Dr S 427-C4 LTM
Doral Dr W 427-C4 LTM
Dorchester Ct 491-E6 WnT
Dorchester Dr 325-A6 N
Dorchester Pl 392-D1 Ca
Dori La 425-A4 WTM
Doris Dr 491-E4, F4 WnT
Dorkin Ct 458-B6 PTM
Dorman St DN-F1, F2; 493-H6, H7 CTM
Dornock Dr 563-C6 FT
Dornock Way 563-C5 FT
Dorothy Dr 424-J8 WTM
Dorset Blvd 391-C5 CTH; 391-C5 Ca
Dorsett Pl 460-F2 WTM
Dottey Dr 558-B10 M
Doty La 426-D1 Ca
Double Eagle Dr 393-A4 Ca
Double Tree Blvd 424-E6 PTM
Double Tree La 391-E1 CTH
Doubloon Rd 424-H3 PTM
Douglas Ct 455-H5 B; 428-H6 L
Douglas Dr 455-H5 B; 392-D5 Ca
Douglas Rd 459-K1; 460-A1 WTM
Douglas St DN-C2; 493-C7 CTM
Douglaston Ct 490-K2 WnT
Dove Ct 427-G7 LTM; 557-J3 P
Dove Dr 392-H2 Ca
Dover Blvd N 455-F7 B
Dover Blvd S 455-F7 B
Dover Cir 392-J1 Ca
Dover Ct 393-A9 F
Dover Dr 489-K8 A; 392-J1 Ca; 426-F9 WTM
Dover Hill Dr N 558-K10 MTM
Dover Rd 455-E8 B; 359-H8 N; 426-E10; 460-E1 WTM
Doverton Dr 324-J5 N
Doves Ct 359-F4 N
Dowitch Ct 424-J6 WTM
Dowitch La 424-J6 WTM
Downes Ct 462-A6 LTM
Downes Dr 462-A7, A8 LTM
Downey Ave 460-H10; 494-H6, H7 WrT
Downing Ct 359-H8 N
Downing Dr 596-B5 G; 458-F2, F3 WTM
Downing St 392-D10 Ca
Dowser Drain Rd 422-H8 BTH

Drake St DN-C1; 493-C5 CTM
Drakeford Dr 424-K2 WTM
Draper St 527-J2, J3, J5 CTM; 527-J6 PeT
Drawbridge Cir 427-A3 LTM
Drawbridge Ct 427-A4 LTM
Drawbridge La 427-A3 LTM
Drayton Ct 457-H6 PTM
Dream Ct 391-F2 CTH
Dreamy St 561-D9 WTJ
Dreier Pl DN-E3; 493-H9 CTM
Dresden St 561-J3 PeT
Drexel Ave 460-F10; 494-F1, F4, F5, F7, F8, F9, F10; 528-F1, F2 CTM; 460-F4, F8 WTM
Driftstone Dr 394-K7 F
Driftwood Ct 392-B2 Ca; 592-E2 M
Driftwood Dr 392-C2 Ca; 426-A4 WTM
Driftwood La 594-K4 WTJ
Droll Way 394-B5 F
Dromedary St 526-A3 WnT
Drover St DN-C3, C4; 493-B10; 527-B1 CTM
Druid La 595-C9 WTJ
Drum Rd 461-F4 L
Drum Way 461-G4 L
Drummond Way 422-G8 BTH
Dry Branch Ct 428-H8 L
Dry Den Ct 559-J3 DTM
Dry Den Dr 559-J3 DTM
Dry Run Rd 326-C8 NT
Duane Dr 528-B9 PeT
Dubarry Ct 461-H9 WrT
Dubarry Rd 461-H7 L; 461-H7 LTM; 461-H9 WrT
Dublin Dr 392-A1 Ca
Dubonnet Ct 423-E8 PTM
Dubonnet Way 423-E8 PTM
Duck Pond Dr 393-B8 F
Dudley Ave 561-D1, G1, J1; 562-A1, C1, E1 PeT
Dudley Dr N 562-E1 PeT
Dudley Dr S 562-E1 PeT
Duffer Cir 458-E5 PTM
Duffy St 523-H7 P
Dugan Ct 358-H1 N
Dugan Dr 424-H6 WTM
Dukane Cir Dr N 525-F8 DTM
Dukane Cir Dr S 525-F8 DTM
Dukane Ct 491-G10 WnT
Dukane St 491-G5 WnT
Dukane Way 525-F8 DTM; 457-G10; 491-G5; 525-G1 WnT
Duke Dr 456-E9 LTH
Duke St 460-A6 WTM
Dunaway Ct 458-J7 WTM
Dunbar Cir 496-H6 Cu
Dunbar Ct 496-H6 Cu
Dunbar Rd 323-H1 AT; 496-J6 Cu; 323-J5 WTH
Dunbarton Ct E 424-H8 WTM
Dunbarton Ct W 424-H8 WTM
Duncan Ct 558-E10 BTM
Duncan Dr 558-E10; 592-E1 BTM
Duncaster Ct 427-H5 LTM
Dundee Cir 460-G5 WTM
Dundee Ct 359-K8 N
Dundee Dr 528-D8 PeT
Dunes Dr 391-E3 Ca
Dunham Ct E 496-C2 WrT
Dunham Ct W 496-D2 WrT
Dunk Dr 457-J9 WnT
Dunlap Ave 526-A1 WnT
Dunlap Dr 526-A8 DTM
Dunmore Ct 457-J3 PTM
Dunn Dr 558-A10 M
Dunn St 461-F6 L; 523-H8 P
Dunn Way 525-E1, F1, G1 WnT
Dunns Bridge Ct 559-B10 MTM
Dunsany Ct 457-F7 PTM
Dunsany La 457-F7 PTM
Dunsay Cir 457-E7 PTM
Dunseth Ct 457-H7 PTM
Dunshire Dr 496-F6 Cu
Dunsmuir Dr 425-D4 WTM
Dunster St 562-B8 PeT
Dunston Ct 495-F9 WrT
Dunston Dr 495-F9 WrT
Dunwoody La 392-J3 Ca; 495-K1 WrT
Dupont Ct 496-C2 WrT
Durango Ct 528-J10 FT
Durban Ct 490-J2 WnT
Durbin Ct 390-G7 CTH
Durbin Dr 390-H7 CTH
Durbin Rd 327-E5, E10; 361-E1, E5 WyT
Durden Ct 491-C5 WnT
Durham Dr 425-K10; 426-A10 WTM
Dusk Ct 457-F7 PTM
Dustin Dr 462-A6 L
Dusty Tr 561-H10 G
Dutch Ct 523-J2 WaT
Dutchman Dr 523-J2 WaT
Duxbury La 461-J7 L
Duxbury Rd 461-J7 L
Dylan Ct 557-J3 P

E

Eads St 358-A10 WTH
Eagle Bay Cir 457-E7 PTM
Eagle Bay Dr N 457-D7 PTM
Eagle Bay Dr S 457-D8 PTM
Eagle Bay Dr W 457-D8 PTM
Eagle Beach Dr 457-C4 PTM
Eagle Cove Cir 457-E8 PTM
Eagle Cove Ct 457-D8 PTM
Eagle Cove Dr 457-E8 PTM
Eagle Cove Dr E 457-E8 PTM
Eagle Cove Dr N 457-E8 PTM
Eagle Cove Dr S 457-E8 PTM
Eagle Cove Dr W 457-D8 PTM
Eagle Cr Ave 356-C10, F6 WTH
Eagle Cr Blvd 458-E10 WnT
Eagle Cr Cir 389-K8 Z
Eagle Cr Ct 389-K8 Z
Eagle Cr Overlook Dr 457-B5 PTM
Eagle Cr Pkwy 423-C10; 457-C3, E2, E7 PTM; 457-E9 WnT
Eagle Crest Ct 595-C5 WTJ
Eagle Crest Dr 455-H5 B; 595-C5 WTJ
Eagle Crest La 456-K6 PTM
Eagle Ct 456-H1, H2 BTH; 389-C6 ET
Eagle Dr 456-G4 LTH
Eagle Emblem Ct 595-C5 WTJ
Eagle Lake Cir 457-D8 PTM
Eagle Lake Ct 457-D7 PTM
Eagle Lake Dr 457-D8 PTM
Eagle Meadow Dr 456-H6 PTM
Eagle Nest Ct 565-C1 MTS
Eagle Nest Dr 595-C5 WTJ
Eagle Pkwy Condos 455-H4 B
Eagle Pointe Dr 457-F7 PTM
Eagle Pointe Dr N 457-F6 PTM
Eagle Pointe Dr S 457-F7 PTM
Eagle Pointe La 457-F6 PTM
Eagle Rd 456-H2 BTH
Eagle Talon Ct 457-E6 PTM
Eagle Tr 491-H4 S
Eagle Trace Ct 595-C6 WTJ
Eagle Trace Dr 531-J5 SCT; 595-C5 WTJ
Eagle Trace La 595-B5 WTJ
Eagle Valley Ct 595-C5 WTJ
Eagle Valley Dr 595-C5 WTJ
Eagle Valley Pass 491-B1 WnT
Eagle View Ct 595-C5 WTJ; 389-H9 Z
Eagle View Dr 457-F9 PTM
Eagle Vill Dr 456-H4 LTH
Eagle Vista Pl 563-D5 FT
Eagledale Dr 458-D10; 492-D2 WnT
Eagles Crest Cir 491-C2 WnT
Eagles Ct 457-E10 WnT
Eagles Landing Blvd 457-D8 PTM
Eagles Nest Ct 490-A7 WaT
Eagles Nest Dr 490-A7 WaT
Eagles Perch Dr 457-F10 WnT
Eagles Roost Dr 456-K8 PTM
Eagles Watch 393-C8 F
Eagles Watch Dr 457-E6, E7 PTM
Eagles Watch La 457-E6 PTM
Eagles Way 457-E10 WnT
Eagles Wing Dr 457-F10 WnT
Eagletown Rd 322-J10; 356-J3, K6 WTH
Eagleview Ct 491-H3 S
Eagleview Dr 491-G3 S
Eaglewood Dr 388-K8 ET
Eaker Ct 455-C1 BTH
Earhart St 528-C1, D2 CTM
Earl Ave 457-H9; 525-H1 WnT
Earl Ct 562-B5 Spt
Earl Dr 562-B5 Spt
Earle Ave 523-G4 WaT
Earlham Dr 528-A9 PeT
Earlham La 524-G4 WaT
Earlybird La 596-G1 G
East 4th Ave 526-E6 DTM
East 4th Ct 392-D3 Ca
East 5th Ave 526-E6 DTM
East 6th Ave 526-E5, F5 DTM
East 26th St 495-A2 WrT
East 75 Rd 596-G5 G; 596-G5 PTJ
East 77th St 425-D8 WTM
East 100 Rd 596-G7 PTJ
East 101st St 425-G1 CTH
East 106th St 391-F10; 392-A10, F10 CTH; 391-F10; 392-A10 Ca
East 110th St 391-K9 CTH
East 111th St 391-D9, J9 CTH; 391-D9 Ca
East 121st St 394-C6 F
East 125 Rd 596-H5 G; 596-H5, H10 PTJ; 596-H10 Whl
East 131st St 392-C4, J4 Ca
East 146th St 359-E10 CTH; 358-A10, G10 Ca; 359-E10 DTH; 361-A10, H10 FCT; 358-G10; 360-A10 N; 358-G10; 359-E10 NT; 357-K10; 358-A10 WTH; 361-A10, H10 WyT
East 147th St 358-A10 WTH
East 151st St 357-K9; 358-A9, E9 WTH
East 156th St 358-G8 N; 358-G8; 360-F8 NT; 360-F8; 361-F8 WyT
East 161st St 358-K7 NT; 358-A7 WTH
East 166th St 360-B6 N; 360-B6 NT; 360-K6 WyT
East 169th St 358-H5 NT; 358-C5 WTH; 361-K5 WyT
East 176th St 358-C4 WTH; 361-H3 WyT
East 179th St 361-B3 WyT
East 181st St 360-F2 NT; 360-F2 WyT
East 186th St 360-B1 N; 360-B1 NT; 358-A1, E1 WTH; 361-A1, J1 WyT
East 191st St 324-G10; 325-K10; 326-B10 N; 324-G10; 325-K10; 326-B10 NT; 323-D10, J10 WTH; 326-H10; 327-G10 WyT
East 192nd St 325-K10 NT
East 196th St 325-E9; 326-F9 N; 325-E9; 326-F9 NT; 323-J9; 324-A9, D9 WTH; 326-F9; 327-G9 WyT
East 200 Rd 596-K9 G; 596-K5, K9; 597-A6 PTJ
East 201st St 327-C8 WyT
East 202nd St 323-K7; 324-A7 WTH
East 206th St 326-F6 N; 325-F7; 326-A7, C6 NT; 326-F6; 327-G6 WyT
East 209th St 325-E6 N
East 211th St 324-J5 N; 325-A5, F5; 326-C5, G5 NT; 326-G5; 327-G5 WyT
East 216th St 323-J4 AT; 324-A4, H4; 325-F4 JT; 324-H4 N; 324-H4; 325-F4; 326-G4 NT; 326-G4; 327-D4, J4 WRT; 324-A4 WTH; 326-G4; 327-D4, J4 WyT
East 220th St 325-A4 JT
East 221st St 325-J3; 326-A3 JT; 326-D3 WRT
East 225 Rd 597-A2 PTJ
East 225th St 324-F3 JT
East 226th St 323-D2, J2 AT; 324-A2, J2; 325-C2, J2; 326-A2 JT; 326-A2, K2; 327-G2 WRT
East 231st St 323-E1 AT; 324-F1; 325-B1 JT
East 250 Rd 563-B10; 597-B1, B5, B7 PTJ
East 300 Rd 597-C2, C10 CTJ; 563-C10; 597-C10 PTJ
East 325 Rd 597-D5 CTJ; 597-A10 PTJ
East 375 Rd 597-F4 CTJ
East 400 Rd 563-F10; 597-F2, G9 CTJ
East 440 Rd 563-H10; 597-G6, H2 CTJ
East 500 Rd 597-J10 CTJ; 388-A2, A4 WTB
East 525 Rd 563-K10; 597-K2 CTJ; 557-A6 GT; 388-A10; 422-A1 PTB; 489-A10; 523-A2 WaT
East 550 Rd 455-B4 BTH; 598-A7 CTJ; 455-B4 LTH; 455-B4 MTH
East 575 Rd 598-A10 CTJ; 557-C8 GT; 455-C10; 489-C1 LTH; 388-C2, C5 WTB
East 600 Rd 455-C6 B; 564-B10; 598-B3, B6 CTJ; 523-D9; 557-D1, D5 GT; 455-C6; 489-D2 LTH; 593-A4 MTM; 523-D9; 557-D1 P; 489-C4, C6 WaT
East 625 Rd 489-D9 A; 455-D4 B; 489-D9; 523-D3 WaT
East 650 Rd 455-E2 BTH; 598-C3 CTJ; 388-E8, E10; 422-E1 ET; 557-E9 GT; 388-E4 WTB
East 670 Rd 598-D7, D9, D10 CTJ
East 675 Rd 557-F6 GT
East 700 Rd 564-E10; 598-E3, E6 CTJ; 388-G7, G9 ET; 523-G10; 557-F1 P; 388-G1, G5 WTB
East 701 Rd 557-G8 GT
East 725 Rd 557-H5 GT
East 725 St 456-A1 BTH
East 750 Rd 598-G6, G10 CTJ
East 775 Rd 388-J10; 422-J2 ET; 388-H4, J1 WTB
East 800 Rd 523-K5 A; 455-J2 BTH; 388-K3, K8 ET; 489-J2 LTH; 388-K3 WTB; 523-K5 WaT
East 840 Rd 559-G10; 593-G1 MTM
East 850 Rd 389-A10 ET; 593-G6, G9 MTM
East 875 Rd 389-B5, B7 ET; 558-A5, B4 GT; 558-B4 P
East 900 Rd 490-C10 A; 422-B10; 456-B1 BTH; 456-B1, B8 LTH; 490-B5, C8; 524-C1, C4 WaT
East 900 Rd E 422-B3 BTH
East 925 Rd 422-C7 BTH; 558-C9 GT
East 950 Rd 422-D3 BTH; 456-D9; 490-D1 LTH
East 975 Rd 389-E6 ET; 558-E7 GT; 389-E6 Z
East 1000 Rd 422-E3; 456-D1, D2 BTH; 456-D2, E8; 490-E3 LTH; 490-E3 WaT
East 1025 Rd 422-F3; 456-F2 BTH; 558-F8, F9 GT
East 1050 Rd 422-G8 BTH; 524-G10; 558-G2, G6 GT; 524-G10 P; 490-G6, G8, G10; 524-G3 WaT
East 1075 Rd 422-H5, H6 BTH
East 550th 489-B9 WaT
East 571 489-C8 WaT
East 575 489-C9 WaT
East 671st 489-F8 A
East Aberdene Ct 559-A10 MTM
East Acree Dr 596-D5 G
East Adams Blvd Dr 460-G1 WTM
East Aerobic La 560-D4 PeT
East Alman Dr 392-A6 Ca
East Andrews Blvd 523-D8 P
East Augusta Dr 491-H3 S
East Avalon Dr 461-A1 LTM
East Avery Dr 424-B6 PTM
East Bando Ct 426-C10 WTM
East Bar Del Dr 559-E2 DTM
East Bavarian Dr 462-C10 WrT
East Bay Vista Dr 427-A2 LTM
East Bayberry Ct 392-C7 Ca
East Bayridge Cir 428-E8 L
East Beaumont Green Dr 426-G6 WTM
East Bentwood Cir Dr 424-F6 PTM
East Black Oak Ct 489-F5 A
East Bloomfield Dr 564-F4 FT
East Bloomfield La 357-F8 WTH
East Braeburn Dr 495-G3 WrT
East Branch 455-G1 B
East Brendon Way Dr 461-C4 LTM
East Brentwood Dr 523-K8 P
East Bridgefield Dr 524-C9 GT
East Broad Al 592-A3 M
East Buckridge Dr 561-K4 PeT; 561-K4 Spt
East Canterbury Sq 425-F4 WTM
East Cape Dr 427-G4 LTM
East Cardinal Cove 427-F6 LTM
East Carlisle St 592-A2 M
East Carnoustie Cir Dr 523-A2 WaT
East Castle Cr Pkwy 426-K4 LTM
East Central Dr 391-G8 CTH
East Century Cir 424-K6 WTM
East Chadwood La 424-F5 PTM
East Chapel Hill Dr 491-E6 WnT
East Charleston Dr 495-C5 WrT
East Cherry Blossom Dr 393-C8 F
East Chesapeake Dr 428-D7 L
East Chester Dr 426-D10 WTM
East Chesterfield Dr 527-G9 PeT
East Claren Dr 558-C6 GT
East Clarendon Rd Dr 459-C7 WTM
East Coal Bluff Ct 559-A10 MTM
East Cobblestone Dr 428-J8 L
East College Ave 455-G6 B
East Collett Dr 592-H2 MTM
East Colony Lake Dr 523-J5 P
East Colony Pointe Dr 427-A4 LTM
East Columbine La 357-E9 WTH
East Connaught Dr 523-C8 P
East Copperwood Cir 392-E1 Ca
East County Line Rd 558-H9 DTM; 558-H9 GT
East Crimson Cir Dr 561-F3 PeT
East Crimson Ct 392-B7 Ca
East Crystal Bay Dr 557-H2 P
East Daisy Hill Ct 559-A10 MTM
East Devon Ct Dr 460-F7 WTM
East Dogwood Cir 424-F6 PTM
East Doral Dr 427-C4 LTM
East Dr 531-J3 SCT; 357-J2 W; 560-J10 WTJ
East Dunbarton Ct 424-H8 WTM
East Dunham Ct 496-C2 WrT
East Eagle Cove Dr 457-E8 PTM
East Ellenberger Pkwy Dr 494-H6 WrT
East Fairview Dr 562-C10 G
East Fairway Cir Dr 428-H8 L
East Fairwood Ct 427-F9 LTM
East Fall Cr Pkwy Dr DN-C1; 493-B5 CTM
East Farm View Cir 427-E8 LTM
East Flamingo Dr 460-H7 LTM
East Flat Brook Dr 593-A1 MTM
East Forest Park Dr 562-B10 G
East Fortune Cir 525-J4 WnT
East Fox Cir 360-B7 NT
East Fox Harbour Dr 528-B8 PeT
East Frederick Dr 425-B8 WTM
East Garden Cir 393-G7 F
East Geist Woods Dr 428-F2 FCT
East Glen Arm Dr 457-G10 WnT
East Glenview Dr 426-E8 WTM
East Golden Hill Ct 594-H10 WTJ
East Golden Oaks 424-J3 WTM
East Green Braes Dr 456-K6; 457-A5 PTM
East Greenwood Tr 562-C10 G
East Gulfstream Dr 428-G1 FCT
East Hadley Rd 557-J3 GT; 557-J3; 558-A2, B2 P
East Hampton Cir 428-A5 LTM
East Harrison St 592-A3 M
East Hickory Ct 529-C8 FT
East Hickory La 457-D10 WnT
East Hickory Tr 529-B7 FT
East High Dr 455-B8 LTH
East High St 592-A3 M
East Hill Dr 461-E4 L
East Hillside Ave Dr 460-A2 WTM
East Holiday La 455-G9 B
East Holliday Dr 425-E10; 459-E1 WTM
East Holly Springs Dr 457-F5 PTM
East Homestead Pl 523-B7 P
East Horse Hill Dr 491-C1 WnT
East Horsehoe La 392-C7 Ca
East Huddleston Dr 561-B5 PeT
East Hunters Dr 392-A7 Ca
East Iron Tr 490-H5 WnT
East Ironwood Dr 455-K8 B; 392-D3 Ca
East Jaffa Ct Dr 425-E4 WTM
East Jefferson Dr 392-A8 Ca
East Jessman Rd Dr 427-D9 LTM
East Kessler Blvd Dr 459-E3; 460-A2, E2 WTM
East Kessler La Dr 460-E2, F2 WTM
East Keystone Way 392-B7 Ca
East Kincardine Ct 424-J7 WTM
East Kirk Dr 491-A8 WnT
East Kristen Dr 494-H1 WrT
East Lake Dr 455-G8 B
East Lake Nora Dr 425-H4 WTM
East Lake Shore 489-E9 WaT
East Lakeshore Dr 392-D9, D10; 426-D2 Ca
East Lakewood Dr 426-C1 Ca
East Lawn Dr 596-E10 NW
East Lawrence Cir Dr 525-F8 DTM
East Lawton Loop Dr 461-H4 L
East Lima Dr 562-D7 PeT
East Lismore Dr 561-H7 PeT
East Lynn Dr 493-C5 CTM
East Madison Vill Dr 561-K5 PeT
East Main St 455-H6 B; 592-A3 M; 523-G8 P; 489-A9 WaT
East Marten Ct 461-F7 L
East Marwood Trail Dr 425-H1 CTH
East Melbourne Rd Dr 458-F7 WTM
East Menlo Ct Dr 426-A6 WTM
East Moray Ct 424-J7 WTM
East Newberry Ct 558-K10 MTM
East Northfield Dr 455-H3 B
East Oak Hill Dr 557-J3 P
East Oak Run Dr 424-J3 WTM
East Old Oakland Blvd Dr 428-G7 L
East Old Otto Ct 559-A10 MTM
East Old Town Dr 425-B4 WTM
East Olde Mill Dr 425-E5 WTM
East Paree Ct 491-H6 WnT
East Paula Lane Dr 458-J7 WTM
East Pebblebrooke Dr 428-J8 L
East Pine Ridge Dr 427-A2 F
East Pine Springs Dr 427-G8 LTM
East Pinehurst Dr 461-K6 LTM
East Pineview Ct 423-G2 ET
East Port Ct 325-E3 C
East President Tr 496-E7 WrT
East Quail Ridge 557-K3 P
East Red Bud La 427-K6 LTM
East Richfield 489-F6 WaT
East Ridge Dr 562-D10 G
East Ridgegate Dr 424-C7 PTM
East Rimwood Dr 427-D3 LTM
East River Bay Dr 426-B7 WTM
East Riverside Dr 492-K4, K5 CTM
East Riviera Dr 459-H1 WTM
East Robin Run 457-K1 PTM
East Rock Hill Ct 559-A10 MTM
East Rushmore Blvd 490-J5 WnT
East Russell Lake Dr 389-B9 ET
East S St 592-A3 M
East Saddle Barn Dr 491-D1 WnT
East Saddlebrook Dr 459-A2 WTM
East Sadlier Cir Dr 495-D10 WrT
East Salem Dr 392-J2 Ca
East Sandpiper Dr 424-F3 PTM
East Scarborough Blvd Dr 427-F8 LTM
East Scarsdale Dr 427-G5 LTM
East Seven Oaks Dr 428-H9 L
East Shadow Lakes Dr 357-K10 WTH
East Shadowview Way 491-F9 WnT
East Shady Hills Dr 423-B8 PTM
East Shore Walk 357-H9 WTH
East Shore Way 357-H10 WTH
East Smallwood La 457-B9 WnT
East Spring Ct 529-J8 FT
East St 463-D7 BCT; DN-E2, E4; 493-G9; 527-G2, G5 CTM; 596-E3 G; 531-J5 NP; 527-G9, G10; 561-G3, G5, G8 PeT; 531-F1 SCT
East St N 523-F7 P
East St S 523-F8 P
East Staton Pl Dr 491-A6 WnT
East Stonebranch Dr 427-F6 LTM
East Stout Field Dr 526-C2, C3 WnT
East Summer Walk Dr 562-C8 PeT
East Suncrest Cir Dr 491-F9 WnT
East Susan Dr 426-H6 WTM
East Tara Ct 457-K10 WnT
East Taylor Dr 495-A5 WrT
East Thames Ct 496-D2 WrT
East Thistlewood Dr 391-F3 CTH
East Tilden Dr 455-G7 B
East Timber Springs Dr 393-F9 F
East Turtle Cr Dr 527-G10 PeT
East Valley Cr La 496-H2 WrT
East Villa Ave Dr 528-A6 PeT
East Village Cir 496-B1 WrT
East Village Dr 391-F3, G1 CTH
East Village Pk 358-B10 WTH
East Village Pkwy Cir 457-D7, E7 PTM
East Walton Dr 559-A10 MTM
East Waring Dr 496-G5 Cu
East Washington Blvd Dr 425-F4 WTM
East Washington St 592-A2 M
East Waterfront Pkwy 491-F2 WnT
East Watermans Dr 360-B8 NT
East Welcome Way Blvd 491-D8 WnT
East Westbury Dr 491-H7 WnT
East Westmont La 359-D4 NT
East Wheel Ests Dr 461-K5 L
East White River Dr 527-D2 CTM
East White River Pkwy Dr DN-C4; 458-K10; 492-J3, K1; 493-C10; 527-C1 CTM; 492-J3 WTM
East Williamshire Dr 425-B4 WTM
East Willow Lakes Blvd 595-C7 WTJ
East Wilson Dr 391-J5 Ca
East Wind Drift Dr 457-D8 PTM
East Winding Brook Dr 490-J7 WnT
East Windsor Dr 393-K6 F
East Wisteria Way 357-E8 WTH
East Woodland Dr 497-A5 Cu
East Woodruff Pl Dr 493-K6 CTM
East Woods Edge Dr 427-A5 LTM
East Woodview Dr 391-H8 CTH
East Wycliff Dr 525-H10 DTM
Eastbay Dr 428-H5 L
Eastbourne Cir 460-H5 LTM
Eastbourne Dr 460-H6 LTM
Eastbrooke Ct 462-C10 WrT
Eastcreek Ct 428-J4 L
Eastern Ave 455-H6 B; 460-B10; 494-B1, B6, B7 CTM; 523-G8 P; 460-B8 WTM
Eastfield Ct 527-G9 PeT
Eastgate Ave 462-G1 L
Eastham Ct 393-C10 F
Easton Dr 455-E8 B
Easton Pt Dr 595-H2 G
Easton Pt Way 595-G2 G
Eastowne Dr 496-H6 Cu
Eastowne Way 496-H6 Cu
Eastridge Dr 494-H5; 495-A5 WrT
Eastside Dr 455-E8 LTH
Eastview Ct 426-J7 LTM
Eastview Dr 558-A10 M
Eastwick Cir 427-D9 LTM
Eastwick La 427-C9 LTM
Eastwind Ct 428-B3 LTM; 562-C6 PeT
Eastwind Dr 428-B3 LTM
Eastwind La 428-B2 LTM
Eastwind St 562-D6 PeT
Eastwood Dr 495-E2, E3 WrT
Easy St 393-D9 F; 561-G9 G; 497-H6 SCT; 561-C9 WTJ
Easy Way 456-D10 LTH
Eaton Ave 529-G8; 563-G2 FT; 461-G9; 495-G2, G5, G7 WrT
Eaton Cir 563-G2 FT
Eaton Ct 393-B9 F; 529-G7 FT
Eaton Dr 529-G9 FT
Ebbie Rd 495-G2 WrT
Echo Bend Blvd 561-G10; 595-G1 G
Echo Cir 561-G10 G
Echo Crest Dr 391-K8 CTH
Echo Ct 457-H1 PTM
Echo Grove Cir 428-D6 L
Echo Grove Ct 428-E7 L
Echo Grove La 428-E6 L
Echo Grove Pl 428-E6 L
Echo La 423-H10 PTM
Echo Ridge Ct 428-E6 L
Echo Ridge La 428-E6 L
Echo Spring Cir 428-D6 L
Echo Tr 428-D7 L
Echo Tr Cir 428-E7 L
Echo Way 457-H1 PTM
Ecole St 425-J6 WTM
Eddie La 559-D4 DTM; 496-B2 WrT
Eddington Rd 562-B6 Spt
Eddy Ct 457-C10 WnT
Eden Ct 392-C7 Ca; 458-C6 PTM
Eden Ests Dr 392-C7 Ca
Eden Glen Dr 392-D7 Ca
Eden Hollow Pl 392-C6 Ca
Eden Pk Dr 392-C6 Ca
Eden Pk Pl 392-C6 Ca
Eden Ridge Ct 428-G6 L
Eden Roc Crest 427-A10 LTM
Eden Vill Ct 392-C5 Ca
Eden Vill Dr 392-C5 Ca; 458-D3 PTM
Eden Vill Pl 392-C5 Ca
Eden Vill Way 458-A3 PTM
Eden Way 392-C6 Ca
Eden Way Cir 392-C6 Ca
Eden Way Pl 392-C6 Ca
Eden Woods Pl 392-D5 Ca
Edgar Ct 557-J1 P
Edge Water Dr 596-B4 G
Edgecombe Ave 527-H6 PeT
Edgehill Rd 492-B8, B9 WnT
Edgehill St 526-B10 DTM
Edgemere Ct 460-C7 WTM
Edgemere Dr 425-C10 WTM
Edgemont Ave 492-K2; 493-B2 CTM
Edgewater Ct 325-E3 C; 490-D1 LTH
Edgewater Dr 325-D7 N; 425-H8 WTM
Edgewater Pl 425-J9 WTM
Edgewood 557-K6 GT
Edgewood Ave 562-J2; 563-H1; 564-A1 FT; 560-K2; 561-G2; 562-A2 PeT
Edgewood Ct 325-K9 NT
Edgewood Dr 558-A10 M; 596-D9 NW; 495-C5 WrT
Edgewood La 325-K10 NT
Edgewood Pl 459-H9 CTM
Edgewood Rd 456-E8 LTH
Edinborough La 526-A4 WnT
Edinburge Sq 495-E4 WrT
Edinburgh Dr 392-D1 Ca
Edinburgh Pt 458-J7 WTM
Edith Rd 325-K7 NT
Edlou Pl 461-D4 L
Edmondson Ave 461-B7, B8 LTM; 461-B9; 495-B7, C4 WrT
Edmondson St 461-B7 LTM
Edna Mills Dr 559-A10 MTM
Edward Ct 455-H1 BTH; 392-H7 Ca
Edwardian Cir 458-B6 PTM
Edwardian Ct 458-B6 PTM
Edwards Ave 528-F8 BG; 525-K8; 526-A8 DTM; 527-D8, G8, J8 PeT
Edwards Cir 392-G2 Ca
Edwards Ct 528-F8 BG; 527-G8 PeT

Edwin Ct 492-C2 WnT
Eel River Ct 559-K3 DTM
Effingham Ct 393-J3 DTH
Effingham Sq 424-H9 WTM
Egelhoff La 527-G6 PeT
Eglin Dr 391-H3 CTH
Egret Ct 424-J6 WTM
Egret La 424-J6 WTM
Ehler Dr 562-G7 PeT
Ehlerbrook Rd 562-G7 PeT
Eisenhower Dr 457-J8 PTM; 491-J4 S; 457-J10 WnT
El Beulah Blvd 427-E5 LTM
El Beulah Way 427-E5 LTM
El Camino 596-F3 G
El Camino Ct 525-J10 DTM
El Dorado Dr 461-J5 L
El Dorado Pl 461-J5 L
El Lago Blvd 528-B8, C7 PeT
El Lago Ct 528-B8 PeT
El Lago Dr N 528-B7 PeT
El Paso Dr 491-F4 WnT
Elaine St 491-H1 S; 492-A1 WnT
Eland Cir 531-D4 SCT
Eland Dr 531-D3 SCT
Elba Ct 461-J7 LTM
Elbert St 527-D9, F9, H9, J9 PeT
Elbow Bend 561-D10 WTJ
Elden Dr 392-B5 Ca
Elder Ave DN-A2, A3; 492-J7, J8 CTM
Elderberry Cir 324-K8 N
Elderberry Rd 324-J7 N
Elderbury Ct 592-F3 M
Eldin Dr 523-J10; 557-J1 P
Eleanor Ave 491-E6 WnT
Eleanor St 491-E9 WnT
Electric Ave 424-K3 WTM
Electric Ct 424-K3 WTM
Elenor St 528-G8 FT
Eli La 595-F3 G
Elias Ct 428-K9 L
Elise Ct 425-H10 WTM
Elite Dr 526-B5 WnT
Elizabeth Dr 455-E5 B
Elizabeth St 461-B8 LTM; 490-J1 WnT; 461-B9, B10; 495-B3, B7; 529-B4 WrT
Ella Dobbs La 561-K6 PeT
Ellen Dr 491-K4 S; 457-K9, K10; 491-K1 WnT
Ellenberger Ct 494-H5 WrT
Ellenberger Pkwy Dr E 494-H6 WrT
Ellenberger Pkwy Dr W 494-H6 WrT
Eller Rd 393-A8, A10 DTH; 393-A8, A10; 427-A1 F
Ellington Ct 490-K6 WnT
Ellington Dr 490-J6 WnT
Elliott Ave 494-G4 CTM
Elliott Dr 391-G5 Ca
Ellipse Pkwy 393-G6 F
Ellis Ct 462-A7 LTM
Ellis Dr 462-A7 LTM
Ellis St 523-F7 P
Elliston Dr 462-C1 L
Ellyn Dr 458-E4 PTM
Elm Branch Ct 563-F6 FT
Elm Ct 557-J2 P
Elm Ct Dr 389-J7 Z
Elm Dr 424-F2 CTH; 562-B10 G; 523-K8, K9 P
Elm La 428-H9 L
Elm Ridge Ct 428-D8 L
Elm Ridge Dr 428-D8 L
Elm St 528-F7 BG; DN-E4; 493-G9 CTM; 595-K1 G; 531-J5 NP; 523-F7 P; 357-J4 W; 388-D1 Wh; 389-J7, J8 Z
Elm Tree Ct 596-C2 G
Elmhurst Dr 461-D5, D6, D7, D8 L; 461-D8 LTM; 461-D10; 495-D1, D4, D5 WrT
Elmierry La 393-K2 F
Elmira St 459-A10; 493-A1 CTM
Elmont Terr 462-C7 LTM
Elmonte Ct 461-H8 LTM
Elmonte Dr 461-H8 LTM
Elmscourt Cir 594-J2 WTJ
Elmtree Cir 461-K8 LTM
Elmtree Ct 461-K8 LTM
Elmtree Pk Dr 496-E6 Cu
Elmtree Pk Pl 496-E6 Cu
Elmtree Pk Way 496-E6 Cu
Elmwood Ave 528-G8, J7 BG; 527-G1 CTM
Elmwood Cir 325-C10 N
Elrico Dr 425-K4 WTM
Elsbury Dr 462-C1 L
Elster Ct 427-D3 LTM
Eltzroth St 492-E5 WnT
Elwin Dr 495-K1 WrT
Elwood Ct 455-J8 B
Emanuel Ct 393-H8 F
Embassy Ct 491-G1 S
Embassy Row 491-G1 S
Ember Ct 428-D9 L
Embers Way 427-C3 LTM
Emco Dr 460-G1 WTM
Emerald Bluff 428-H4 LTM
Emerald Ct 358-A5 WTH
Emerald Green Cir 357-K5 W
Emerald La 326-F9 NT; 425-C4 WTM
Emerald Lakes 596-H3 G
Emerald Pines La 357-K5 W; 358-A5 WTH
Emerson Access 494-G2 WrT
Emerson Ave 528-G10 BG; 460-G10; 494-G4, G10; 528-G3 CTM; 528-G10; 562-G2, G7 FT; 562-G10; 596-G1 G; 460-G2, G7 LTM; 562-G10 PTJ; 528-G10; 562-G2, G7 PeT; 460-G7 WTM; 460-G10; 494-G4, G10; 528-G3 WrT
Emerson Ct Dr N 494-G2 CTM
Emerson Ct Dr S 494-G2 CTM
Emerson Rd 391-J4 Ca
Emerson Vill Dr 528-G10 FT
Emerson Vill La 528-G10 FT
Emerson Vill Pl 528-H9 FT
Emerson Way 460-F4 WTM
Emerton Pl 528-G2 CTM
Emery Way 393-K10 F
Emily Dr 424-J3; 425-A3 WTM
Emily Sue Ct 490-K4 WnT
Emily Way 392-D8 Ca
Emma Dr 461-K5 L
Emmett St DN-D2; 493-E6 CTM
Emory Dr 496-H4 Cu
Emory La 491-F10 WnT
Emperors Ct 490-J3 WnT
Empire Dr 495-E2 WrT
Empire St DN-D3; 493-D9 CTM
Enchance Ct 561-D10 WTJ
Enchanted View Dr 592-B5 M
Enclave Cir 392-B5 Ca
Enclave Ct 392-B5 Ca
Encore Dr 528-J9 FT
Enderly Ave 455-H5 B
Enderly Ct 455-H5 B
Endicott Ct 563-C6 FT
Endicott Dr 563-D6 FT
Endicott Way 563-C6 FT
Endress Pl 596-F7 G
Endsley Dr 528-A9 PeT
England Ct 325-K10 N
Engle St 523-G3 WaT
Englewood Dr 461-C6, C7, C8 L; 461-C8 LTM; 461-D10; 495-C4 WrT
Englewood Rd 425-J7 WTM
English Ave DN-E3, F4; 493-H9; 494-A9, G9 CTM; 494-G9; 495-B9 WrT
English Ct 391-J2 Ca
English Dr 489-E5 WaT
English Oak Dr 461-K6; 462-A6 L; 359-C2 N
English Oak Pl 462-A6 L
English Oak Terr 462-A6 L
English Vill Dr 495-E9 WrT
English Vill La 495-E9 WrT
Enright Dr 458-F4 WTM
Ensenada Ave 528-J9 FT
Ensley Ct 393-F5 F
Ensley Dr 393-F6 F
Ensley Pl 393-F5 F
Enterprise Dr 558-G8 DTM; 558-G8 GT; 357-F3 WTH
Enterprise St 495-E2 WrT
Epler Ave 528-E10; 560-F1, J1; 561-B1, F1, J1; 562-A1 PeT
Epler Rd 558-H1; 559-J1; 560-A1 DTM; 558-H2 GT
Epperson Ct 559-J2 DTM
Epperson Dr 559-K2 DTM
Epperson La 558-G7 GT
Equestrian Ct 424-J10 WTM
Equestrian La 424-J10 WTM
Erber Ct 561-C2 PeT
Eric Cir 462-F10 WrT
Eric Ct 393-J10 F
Erickson Ct 461-K8 LTM
Erie Ave 460-A6, D2 WTM
Erika Ct 490-K4 WnT
Erin Ct 595-A3 WTJ; 461-K8 WrT
Erin Dr 461-K9 WrT
Ernie Ct 595-G2 G
Erny Dr 595-J1 G
Esquire Ct 461-G8 LTM
Esquire Pl 461-G8 LTM
Essen Ct 462-E9 WrT
Essex Ct 392-F4 Ca; 461-J7 LTM; 324-K6 N
Essex Dr 392-G4 Ca
Essig Ave 326-H2 WRT
Estancia Way 391-B10 CTH
Estate Ave 458-G3 WTM
Estate Blvd 526-B8 DTM
Estate Dr 526-B8 DTM; 595-G3 WTJ
Estate La 526-B8 DTM
Estate Pkwy 526-B8 DTM
Estelle St 561-J6 PeT
Estes Dr 594-J1 WTJ
Estes Pk Ct 561-C4 PeT
Estes Rd 594-J1 WTJ
Estevan Ave 495-C10 WrT
Esther Ct 557-J2 P
Ethan Allen La 324-A9 WTH
Ethel Ave 459-C10; 493-C1, C2 CTM
Ethel St 391-H10 CTH
Euclid Ave 460-E9, E10; 494-E1, E4, E5, E7; 528-E1 CTM; 596-B2 G; 460-E2, E8 WTM
Eugene St 493-A1 CTM; 492-G1 WnT
Eustis Dr 496-A2, A5, A6 WrT
Evans Ave 359-J2 N
Evans Dr 392-G9 Ca
Evanston Ave 425-K8, K10; 459-K1, K2, K3, K4, K7 WTM
Evanston Ct 459-K4 WTM
Evanston Rd 425-J7 WTM
Evelyn St 492-C1 WnT
Evening Rose Way 357-E8 WTH
Evening Shade Cir 528-E8 BG
Evening Shade La 528-E7 BG
Eveningsong Dr 525-K6 DTM
Everest Dr 490-J5 WnT
Everest La 490-J5 WnT
Everett St DN-B2; 492-K7 CTM
Everglades Ct 561-C4 PeT
Evergreen Ave 459-H9 CTM; 425-H3, H5 WTM
Evergreen Ct 425-H4 WTM
Evergreen Pt 394-G10 F
Evergreen St 596-A2 G
Evian Ct 428-H7 L
Evian Dr 428-H7 L
Evison St 493-J10 CTM
Ewbank Ct 558-G6 GT
Ewing St 494-D5, D6, D7, D10; 528-D1 CTM; 528-D7 PeT; 426-C10; 460-C3, D1, D2 WTM
Excalibur Ct 458-B1 PTM
Exchange St 394-A5 F; 564-E6 FT
Executive Dr 391-K6 Ca; 525-J4, K3 WnT
Exeter Ave 492-E5, E7, E8, E9 WnT
Exeter Cir 596-F3 G
Exeter Dr 492-E7 WnT
Exit 5 Pkwy 393-K7; 394-A6 F
Exmoor Ct 457-H7 PTM
Expo La 491-B5 WnT
Eyford Ct 428-E7 L
Eyford La 428-E7 L

F

Fable St 562-A3 PeT
Fabyan Rd 561-B7 PeT
Factory Rd 560-H7 PeT
Faculty Dr 457-H8 PTM; 457-H9; 491-H10 WnT
Fair La 558-A10 M
Fair Oaks Dr 491-K3 S
Fair Oaks Trace 594-K1 WTJ
Fairbanks Ct 392-D5 Ca
Fairbanks Dr 392-C5 Ca
Fairend Ct 390-H10 CTH
Fairfax Ct 429-A2 FCT
Fairfield Ave 459-G10 CTM
Fairfield Blvd 325-K10 N
Fairfield Dr 455-J8 B
Fairfield Rd 558-G6, H3 GT; 523-A7 P
Fairhaven Ct 496-C4 WrT
Fairhaven Dr 496-C2, C3 WrT
Fairhope Dr 561-K2; 562-A2, B2, E2 PeT
Fairlane Dr 455-K9 B; 564-D2 FT
Fairlane Dr W 564-D2 FT
Fairmont Ct 496-C3 WrT
Fairpoint Dr 596-D6 G
Fairport Cir 428-F4 LTM
Fairview Blvd 359-K1; 360-A1 N
Fairview Dr E 562-C10 G
Fairview Dr S 596-C1 G
Fairview Pkwy 359-J1 N; 359-J1 NT
Fairview Rd 595-B1 G; 594-F1, G1; 595-B1 WTJ
Fairview Terr 459-C7 WTM
Fairway Ave 427-B5 LTM
Fairway Cir Dr E 428-H8 L
Fairway Cir Dr N 428-H8 L
Fairway Cir Dr S 428-H8 L
Fairway Cir Dr W 428-H8 L
Fairway Ct 428-H8 L; 595-D7 WTJ
Fairway Dr 424-F2 CTH; 358-J2 N; 424-K9; 425-B9, D9 WTM; 489-A10 WaT
Fairway Ridge La 394-E9 F
Fairway Tr 427-B5 LTM
Fairweather Tr 492-E9 WnT
Fairwind Ct 427-H5 LTM
Fairwood Cir 427-F8 LTM
Fairwood Ct 558-A10 M
Fairwood Ct E 427-F9 LTM
Fairwood Ct W 427-F9 LTM
Fairwood Dr 455-J9 B; 429-B1 FCT; 427-F10 LTM
Fairwoods Dr 394-D10; 428-E1 F
Faith St 595-E3, F3 G
Falcon Cr Blvd 457-K7 PTM
Falcon Ct 458-C10 WnT
Falcon Dr 458-C10; 492-C1, C2 WnT
Falcon Grove Ct 457-H5 PTM
Falcon Grove Dr 457-H5 PTM
Falcon La 457-H9, K9; 458-A9 WnT
Falcon Ridge 423-F5 PTM
Falcon Talon La 457-D6 PTM
Falkirk Ct 427-J2 LTM
Falkirk Dr 427-H3 LTM
Fall Bounty La 489-H7 A
Fall Cr Blvd 493-C2, D3 CTM
Fall Cr Dr 428-B7 L
Fall Cr Pkwy Dr E DN-C1; 493-B5 CTM
Fall Cr Pkwy Dr N 459-G10; 493-F2 CTM; 460-G3; 461-A2 LTM; 459-G10; 460-A7, G3 WTM
Fall Cr Pkwy Dr S 493-E2 CTM; 460-B7 WTM
Fall Cr Rd 428-E1 FCT; 428-A7; 461-C2 L; 427-F10; 428-A7; 461-C2 LTM; 460-G2 WTM
Fall Cr Rd N 461-C2 LTM
Fall Cr Tr 427-H10; 461-H1 L
Fall Rd 394-D10 F
Fall Time Pl 461-C6 LTM
Fall View Dr 393-K8 DTH; 393-K8 F
Fallen Oak Dr 530-C1 WrT
Fallingbrook Dr 427-A1 F
Fallow Tr 531-D3 SCT
Fallwood Dr 460-E5 WTM
Fallwood Way 424-H2 CTH
Fanchon Dr 423-C4 PTM
Fank Boner Ct 596-E2 G
Far Away Dr 491-D10 WnT
Far Hill Ct 460-H4 LTM
Far Hill Rd 460-H4 LTM
Faris Ave 461-B7 LTM
Faris St 461-C7 L
Farley Dr 393-H6 F; 491-F5, F6 WnT
Farley Pl 393-G6 F
Farm Stone Cir 531-F3 SCT
Farm View Cir E 427-E8 LTM
Farm View Cir W 427-E8 LTM
Farmbrook Ct 455-A10; 489-A1 LTH
Farmhill Rd 525-A1 WnT
Farmhurst La 428-G6 LTM
Farmington Rd 425-F4 WTM
Farmleigh Dr 427-A10 LTM
Farmview Ct 357-H10 WTH
Farmview La 357-H10 WTH
Farnsworth St 526-B5, E5 WnT
Farr Hills Dr 357-J7 WTH
Farragut Cir 428-E2 FCT
Farrington Ave 494-F8 CTM
Fathom Cir 428-C4 LTM
Fathom Crest 428-B4 LTM
Fathom Ct 428-B4 LTM
Fauna La 457-A6 PTM
Faust St 528-J1 WrT
Fauvre Rd 459-A5 WTM
Favt Rd 531-K8 SCT
Fawn Dr 457-E8 PTM
Fawn Hill Ct 460-G5 LTM
Fawn Hill Terr 460-G5 LTM
Fawn Lake Cir 422-J5 PTM
Fawn Lake Dr 422-H5 BTH; 422-H5 PTM
Fawn Meadow Dr 427-G5 LTM
Fawn Ridge La 428-C9 L
Fawns Dell Pl 393-F4 F
Fawns Ridge 393-F4 F
Fawns Run 393-F4 F
Fawnsbrook Dr 393-F4 F
Fawnsbrook Pl 393-F4 F
Fay Ct 461-B7 LTM
Fay St 492-K10 CTM
Fayette St DN-C1; 493-D5 CTM
Feather Grass Way 394-A2 F
Feather Rock Ct 394-K7 F
Federalist Ct 457-J3 PTM
Feeney Dr 490-C7 WaT
Feldspar Rd 428-K9 L
Felsy Rd 593-J2 MTM
Fen Ct 460-D3 WTM
Fender Dr 563-D7 FT
Fendler Ct 563-D6 FT
Fenmore Rd 458-F5 WTM
Fennel Ct 562-G6 PeT
Fennway Ave 424-H8 WTM
Fenster Ct 490-J6 WnT
Fenster Dr 490-J8 WnT
Fenton Ave 563-H1 FT; 495-G5, H5, H7, H8 WrT
Fenwick Ave 495-H5 WrT
Fenwick Ct 495-H4 WrT
Feren Ct 460-J9 WrT
Fergeson Ct 496-H4 Cu
Fergus Ave 424-F1 CTH
Ferguson Rd 558-E10; 592-E1 BTM; 529-F7, F9 FT
Ferguson St 425-G10; 459-G1 WTM
Fern Ct 424-K6 WTM
Fern Dr 356-J4 WTH
Ferncliff Ave 562-C1 PeT
Fernway St 494-A3 CTM
Fernwood Ct 490-K6 WnT
Ferrell La 425-C7 WTM
Ferry Rd 423-A3 PTM
Field Dr 359-J1; 360-A1 N; 359-J1; 360-A1 NT
Fieldcrest La 491-H10 WnT
Fieldgrass Run 357-D9 WTH
Fieldhurst La 523-B7 P
Fielding Rd 531-F2 SCT
Fieldstone Ct 455-E1 BTH; 392-G8 Ca; 496-J3 Cu; 457-C6 PTM
Fieldstone Pl 393-E5 F
Fieldstone Tr 457-D6 PTM
Fieldstream Dr 523-E4 WaT
Fiesta Ct 596-G4 G
Fiesta Dr 596-G4 G
Fife Tr 393-B3 Ca
Filly La 557-K7 GT
Finch Ct 392-J2 Ca
Finchley Rd 427-B9 LTM
Finley Ave 527-H3, K3; 528-A3 CTM
Finley St 559-A4 DTM
Fir Ct 426-E8 WTM
Fireberry Ct 428-H7 L
Firelight Ct 326-D9 N
Fireside Cir 427-B3 LTM
Fireside Ct 427-B3 LTM
Fireside Dr 427-B3 LTM
Firestone Cir 491-A1 WnT
Firestone La 390-H9 CTH
Firethorn Cir 324-J7 N
Firethorn Dr 428-J9 L
First Lady Blvd 562-K2 FT
Fishback Hill La 422-J9 PTM
Fishback Rd 422-J7 PTM
Fisher Ave 492-A2, A4 S
Fisher Ct 492-A9 WnT
Fisher Rd 529-E5, E7 FT; 529-E3, E5 WrT
Fisher St 428-J10 L
Fishermans Ct 428-D7 L
Fishers Crossing Dr 393-D7 F
Fishers Dr 393-D8 F; 360-E1 NT
Fishers Landing Dr 393-D8 F
Fishers Pointe 393-G7 F
Fishers Pointe Blvd 393-G8 F
Fishers Sch Rd 393-G10 F
Fishers Sta Dr 393-D7 F
Fishers Sta Way 393-D7 F
Fishersburg Ave 360-E3 NT; 361-D2 WyT
Fishkill Rd 422-G2 ET
Fitch Ave 425-J9 WTM
Fitch Pl 389-H8 Z
Fitness La 427-H2 F
Five Points Rd 529-C9; 563-C4, C8 FT
Fjord Dr 426-J3 WTM
Flagger Pl 428-K6 L
Flagship Cir 428-C4 LTM
Flaherty La 561-A6 PeT
Flame Way 457-H6 PTM
Flamingo Dr E 460-H7 LTM
Flat Bk Dr E 593-A1 MTM
Flat Branch Ct 563-F5 FT
Flat Branch Dr 563-G5 FT
Flatrock Ct 427-H7 LTM
Fleener Dr 490-B6 WaT
Fleet St 359-H10 N
Fleetwood Ct 391-D4 Ca
Fleetwood Dr 459-A4 WTM
Fleetwood Dr N 391-D4 Ca
Fleetwood Dr S 391-D5 Ca
Fleming St 492-C8, C10; 526-C5 WnT
Fletcher Ave DN-E3, F4; 493-G9, H9; 494-D9, F9 CTM; 494-H9 WrT
Fletcher Ct 460-H4 LTM
Fletcher La 528-F6 BG
Flintlock Ct 427-H4 LTM
Flintridge Pass 393-A3 Ca
Flintstone Dr 562-G3 FT
Flintstone St 528-H7 BG
Flippens Rd 324-A4 JT; 324-A10 WTH
Florence Dr 455-J2 BTH; 596-D4 G
Florida Rd 395-H7, H10 FCT
Flotation Ave 526-J4 CTM
Fluvia Terr 426-H4 WTM
Flynn Mills Rd 558-K3 DTM
Flynn Rd 525-A10; 558-H3; 559-A2 DTM; 558-G3 GT
Fogelson Ct 496-F4 WrT
Fogelson Dr 496-E4 WrT
Foggy Ct 424-K3 WTM
Foggy Dr 424-K3 WTM
Folcroft Ct 490-K7 WnT
Folkstone Rd 424-F6 PTM
Folsom Dr 462-D10 WrT
Foltz St 526-D7, D9 DTM; 492-D10; 526-D5 WnT
Fontana Ct 496-F5 WrT
Fonthill Dr 428-F6 LTM
Foolish Pleasure La 562-K2 FT
Ford Cir 393-J5 F
Ford Dr 393-J5 F
Ford Rd 389-F10; 423-F2 ET; 389-F8, F10 Z
Ford St 492-A6 S
Ford Valley La 389-E10; 423-F1 ET
Fordham La 424-F2 PTM
Fordham St 424-F3, F4 PTM
Fordham Way 393-A8 F
Forest Ave 494-A8 CTM; 596-E2 G
Forest Bay La 325-B3, C2 JT
Forest Bend Dr 565-D7 MTS
Forest Blvd 425-F6 WTM; 389-K8 Z
Forest Blvd Dr N 425-G6 WTM
Forest Blvd Dr S 425-G6 WTM
Forest Commons Dr 489-J5 WaT
Forest Cr Dr 530-C1 WrT
Forest Ct 392-D7 Ca
Forest Dr 392-D7 Ca; 393-F9 F; 455-D9 LTH; 561-K2 PTM
Forest Grove Dr 460-C8 WTM
Forest Hills Blvd 595-A8 WTJ
Forest Hills Dr 491-K7 WnT
Forest Hollow Dr 325-D2 JT
Forest Knoll Cir 395-B8 FCT
Forest Knoll Ct 395-A7 FCT
Forest Knoll La 395-A8 FCT
Forest La 392-K7 CTH; 359-G2 N; 425-G7, H5; 459-H3 WTM; 489-E9 WaT
Forest Lake Ct 456-H1 BTH
Forest Lake Rd 495-D8 WrT
Forest Manor Ave 460-E10; 494-E2, E4 CTM; 460-D6, E4 WTM
Forest Pk Dr 359-G2 N; 561-C5, C7 PeT
Forest Pk Dr E 562-B10 G
Forest Pk Dr N 562-B10 G
Forest Pk Dr S 562-B10 G
Forest Pk La 392-H7 Ca
Forest Pl 392-D7 Ca
Forest Ridge Ct 393-K10 DTH; 557-F2 P
Forest Ridge Dr 557-F2 P
Forest Ridge Rd 359-G1 N; 359-G1 NT
Forest Terr 391-E2 CTH
Forest View Cir 325-C3 JT
Forest View Ct 523-D3 WaT
Forest View Dr 459-B2 WTM
Form St 429-C8 McC
Forrest Commons Blvd 561-E4 PeT
Forrest Dr 523-K8 P
Forrester Rd 565-F1 MTS
Forreston Oak Dr 359-C3 N
Forsythia Cir 495-G4 WrT
Forsythia Ct 495-G4 WrT
Forsythia Dr 495-G4 WrT
Fort Dr 462-A1 L
Fort La 462-A1 L
Fort Wayne Ave DN-D1; 493-F6 CTM
Fortune Cir E 525-J4 WnT
Fortune Cir S 525-J5 WnT
Fortune Cir W 525-J4 WnT
Fortune Dr 394-A9 F
Forum Cir 460-A6 WTM
Forum Meadows Dr 393-B3 Ca
Forum Walk 496-B2 WrT
Forward Pass Ct 560-K7 PeT
Forward Pass Rd 560-K7 PeT
Foryu Dr 559-G10 MTM
Foster Ct 392-E4 Ca
Foster Dr 392-E4 Ca
Foster Ridge 392-C1 Ca
Founders Club Cir 394-F10 F
Founders Pl 393-G8 F
Founders Rd 424-E4 PTM
Fountain Cove Ct 428-B10 L
Fountain Curve Rd 455-A4 LTH
Fountain Dr 592-D4 M
Fountain La 427-B5 LTM
Fountain Springs Blvd 428-B10; 462-B1 L
Fountain Springs Ct 428-B10 L
Fountain View Ct 428-A10 L
Fountain View Dr 428-A10 L; 360-B1 N; 595-C8 WTJ
Fountain View La 393-H8 F; 428-A10 L
Fountainhead Dr 424-H7 WTM
Fountainview Dr 461-H6 L
Four Seasons Cir 461-C6 LTM
Fourwinds Ct 455-F2 BTH
Fox Cir E 360-B7 NT
Fox Cir W 360-B7 NT
Fox Cove Blvd 496-K9 SCT
Fox Cr La 394-C10 F
Fox Ct 592-D1 BTM; 357-D9 WTH
Fox Dr 592-D1 BTM; 360-B7 NT
Fox Glove Cir 392-C4 Ca
Fox Glove La 325-D9 N
Fox Hall Dr 593-E5 MTM
Fox Harbour Cir 528-A8 PeT
Fox Harbour Ct 528-A8 PeT
Fox Harbour Den 528-A8 PeT
Fox Harbour Dr E 528-B8 PeT
Fox Harbour Dr N 528-A8 PeT
Fox Harbour Dr S 528-A8 PeT
Fox Harbour La 528-A8 PeT
Fox Hill Ct 458-H2 WTM
Fox Hill Dr 458-J2; 459-B3 WTM
Fox Hollow Ct 456-H2 BTH
Fox Hollow La 456-H2 BTH
Fox Hollow Ridge 389-E10; 423-E1 ET
Fox Hunt Ct 456-H1 BTH
Fox Lake Ct 423-E6 PTM
Fox Lake N 423-E6 PTM
Fox Lake S 423-E6 PTM
Fox Moor La 594-K6 WTJ
Fox Moor Pl 594-K7 WTJ
Fox Moor Terr 594-K6 WTJ
Fox Orchard Cir 457-D10 WnT
Fox Orchard Ct 457-E10 WnT
Fox Pointe Ct 424-B10 PTM
Fox Rd 428-E6 L; 456-F9 LTH; 428-E6 LTM
Fox Ridge Ave 595-A6 WTJ
Fox Ridge La 427-H4 LTM
Fox Run Cir 423-E7 PTM
Fox Run Ct 428-C1 F
Fox Run Path 557-J3 P
Fox Run Rd 423-E7 PTM
Fox Tr Dr 497-A7 SCT
Fox Valley Pl 424-G2 PTM
Fox Way 528-J9 FT
Foxboro La 427-A2 F
Foxborough Dr 461-C3 L; 594-C9 WTJ
Foxchase Cir 428-B6 LTM
Foxchase Dr 428-B6 LTM
Foxfire Cir 391-B3 CTH; 491-F1 WnT
Foxfire Ct 457-F10 WnT
Foxfire Dr 457-F10; 491-F1 WnT
Foxfire La 455-B7 LTH
Foxford Dr 524-F1 WaT
Foxglove La 457-K4 PTM
Foxglove Trace 528-E7 PeT
Foxmere Blvd 561-F10 G
Foxmere Terr 595-F1 G
Foxtail Cir 489-H10 A
Foxtail Ct 559-G1 DTM; 393-G9 F
Foxtail Dr 462-E9 WrT
Foxtrail Cir 455-G4 B
Foxtrot La 525-E5 DTM; 525-E5 WnT
Foxwood La 459-B2 WTM
Foxwood Pl 392-C7 Ca
Foyt Dr 491-G4 S
Framington Ct 457-C6 PTM
Frances St 393-H8 F
Francis Ct 525-J9 DTM
Francis La 525-J10 DTM
Frankie Ct 455-A9 LTH
Franklin Ct 393-A8 F
Franklin Dr 523-K7 P
Franklin Hall Tr 393-C4 Ca
Franklin Parke Blvd 563-D5 FT
Franklin Parke Ct 563-D5 FT
Franklin Parke Woods 563-E5 FT
Franklin Pl 493-C2 CTM
Franklin Rd 563-G10; 597-G2 CTJ; 529-H6, H10; 563-G2, G6 FT; 461-F5 L; 461-F10 LTM; 461-F10; 495-F1, F3, F7, F10; 529-F1, H6 WrT
Franklin St 455-G5 B
Franklin St N 592-B3 M
Franklin Terr 461-F6 L
Franklin Trace 389-F7 Z
Fraser Ct 457-G3 PTM
Frederick Dr E 425-B8 WTM
Frederick Dr S 425-B9 WTM
Fredonia Rd 492-C1, D2 WnT
Freds Ct 562-F2 PeT
Freedom Ct 457-J4 PTM
Freedom Pass 563-E5 FT
Freedom Woods Dr 563-E5 FT
Freeman Dr 495-J1 WrT
Freemen Ct 390-C9 CTH
Freemont La 596-C4 G
Freemont Rd 322-K5 AT; 322-K5, K9 WTH

Freeport La 457-D9 WnT
Fremont Ct 427-J9 LTM
Fremont St 523-F8 P
French St 523-F7 GT; 523-H7 P
Freshness Rd 597-J10 CTJ
Fresno Rd 596-H4 G
Freyn Dr 457-J6 PTM
Friar Ct 425-J3 WTM
Friendship Cir 457-K1 PTM
Friendship Dr 560-J8; 561-A8 PeT
Friendship La 560-H8 PeT
Friendswood Rd 558-C9, E7 GT
Frisco Pl 426-A6 WTM
Frisco Way 426-A6 WTM
Frito Lay Dr 491-A8 WnT
Front Royal Dr 561-G7 PeT
Front St 562-B4 Spt
Frontage Rd 391-E6 CTH; 393-E6 F; 565-F9; 599-K1 MTS; 357-K9 WTH
Frontenac Rd 461-H9 WrT
Frontier Rd 557-C8 GT
Frontier St 394-A2 F
Fruitdale Ave 491-G2 S; 491-G10; 525-H2 WnT
Fruitdale Dr 559-H3 DTM
Fruitwood Dr 462-B4 L
Fry Rd 561-E10, H10; 562-A10; 595-E1 G
Frye Rd 563-F6 FT
Fulbrook Dr 496-A1 WrT
Fulham Dr 427-A9 LTM
Fullen Dr 490-J9 WnT
Fullenwider Ave 528-B2 CTM
Fuller Ct 393-H5 F
Fuller Dr 458-A10; 492-A1, A10 WnT
Fullerton Dr 491-F4 WnT
Fulton St DN-E2; 493-G7 CTM
Funston Rd 461-H3 L
Furgus Ave 390-F10 CTH
Furman Ave 491-E5, E7 WnT
Furnas Ct 559-J1 DTM
Furnas Rd 559-F1, H1, J1 DTM

G

Gable Ct 496-C3 WrT
Gable Dr 490-D9 WaT; 496-B3 WrT
Gable Ends Ct 391-J7 Ca
Gables Dr 393-C8 F
Gabriel Rd 527-J9 PeT
Gadsden St 526-A4, D4 WnT
Gainsborough Ct 458-B5 PTM
Gala Cir 528-G2 CTM
Gala Ct 528-G2 CTM
Gala Dr 528-F2 CTM
Galahad Dr 458-G5, H5 WTM
Galaxie Dr 561-J9 G
Galaxy La 495-J2 WrT
Galburgh Ct N 456-H9 WnT
Galburgh Ct S 456-H9 WnT
Gale St 460-D10; 494-D1, D2, D3, D5, D9 CTM; 562-D1, D2 PeT; 426-C8 WTM
Galen Dr N 489-G9 A
Galen Dr W 489-G9 A
Galeston Ave 461-J9; 495-J7 WrT
Galeston Ct 495-J3 WrT
Galeston Dr 495-J4 WrT
Gallagher Dr 594-G2 WTJ
Gallant Fox Ct 561-A8 PeT
Gallant Fox Dr 561-A8 PeT
Gallery Ct 496-E3 WrT
Galley Ct 428-E5 LTM
Galloway Ave 426-G9 WTM
Galloway Cir 394-A4 F
Galloway Ct 426-G8 WTM; 489-A8 WaT
Galloway St 489-A8 WaT
Gamay La 457-E8 PTM
Gambel Ct 526-A9 DTM
Gambel Rd 525-K9; 526-A9, C9 DTM
Gandy Ct 561-B8 PeT
Gann Ct 428-J8 L
Ganton Ct 490-J1 WnT
Garcia Ct 561-A7 PeT
Garden Ave 492-E6 WnT
Garden Cir E 393-G7 F
Garden Cir W 393-G7 F
Garden Ct 561-D1 PeT
Garden Grace Dr 496-E8 WrT
Garden Grove Dr 457-C10 WnT
Garden Pl 523-H9 P; 389-F5 Z
Garden Rock Ct 427-H6 LTM
Garden Walk Dr 460-E4 WTM
Gardner La DN-C3; 493-C8 CTM
Garfield Dr 527-G3 CTM
Garfield Pk Ctr Dr 527-G3 CTM
Garfield Pk Dr N 527-G3 CTM
Garfield Plaza Dr 527-H4 CTM
Garner Rd 455-H2 B
Garni Ct 561-G7 PeT
Garonne Terr 426-H4 WTM
Garret Ct 490-K4 WnT
Garrick Ct 393-E8 F
Garrick St 393-F8, F9 F
Garrison Ct 531-F4 SCT
Garrison Dr 425-H3 WTM
Garrison La 490-E7 WaT
Garstang St 528-G5 BG
Garver Rd 459-E2 WTM
Garvok Ct 528-E9 PeT
Garway La 457-F6 PTM
Gary Dr 461-K4 L; 523-J9 P
Gary Pl 427-J4 LTM
Gas Light Pkwy 526-A5 WnT
Gasaway Blvd 490-H1 WnT
Gasoline Al 492-C8 S; 492-C8 WnT
Gate Cir 393-C9 F
Gate Dr 496-B9 WrT
Gateshead La 595-B4 WTJ; 426-A10 WTM
Gateway Ave 324-G6 N
Gateway Ct 457-H8 PTM
Gateway Dr 393-K10 F; 558-A2 P; 457-G8, J8 PTM
Gatewood Ct 496-A3 WrT
Gatewood Dr 596-A5 G
Gatewood La 393-C9 F; 495-E3 WrT
Gattling Ct 561-K8 PeT
Gavin Ave 324-J7 N
Gawain Ave 458-G5 WTM
Geagan St 594-J4 WTJ
Geffs Dr 529-G9 FT
Geist Bay Ct 395-F8 FCT
Geist Bluff Cir 428-F7 L
Geist Bluff Ct 428-F7 L
Geist Bluff Dr 428-F7 L
Geist Cove Dr 428-H5 L
Geist Ests Cir 428-F8 L
Geist Ests Ct 428-F7 L
Geist Ests Dr 428-F8 L
Geist Pointe Cir 428-H8 L
Geist Rd 394-G10; 428-G1 F; 428-G1 FCT
Geist Valley Blvd 428-H8 L
Geist Valley Ct 428-F7 L
Geist Valley Dr 428-F7 L
Geist Woods Cir 428-E2 FCT
Geist Woods Ct 428-E1 FCT
Geist Woods Dr 428-D2 FCT
Geist Woods Dr E 428-F2 FCT
Geist Woods Dr N 428-F2 FCT
Geist Woods Dr S 428-F2 FCT
Geist Woods Trace 428-D2 FCT
Geist Woods Way 428-D2 FCT
Gem Rd 531-G5 NP; 497-G9 SCT
Gemco La 458-A9 PTM
Gemini Ct 495-K2 WrT
Gemini Dr 495-K2; 496-A2 WrT
Geneva Ave 461-H6 L
Geneva Dr 596-D4 G
Genevieve Ct 462-A8 LTM
Genoa Ct 461-J6 LTM
Gent Ave 493-A3, A4 CTM
Gentry Ct 523-H8 P
Gentry St 427-C6 LTM
George Ct 391-H2 Ca; 458-A10 WnT
George Kirkedall Tr 393-C4 Ca
George St 461-E7 L
Georgetown Ct 492-B2 WnT
Georgetown Rd 595-J3 G; 424-A10, B6; 458-A1, A7, B10 PTM; 492-B3 S; 458-B10 WnT
Georgia Rd 395-G10; 429-G2 FCT
Georgia St DN-D3, E3; 493-E8, H8 CTM
Georgiana La 461-G7 LTM
Gerald Morris Dr 426-K6 LTM
Gerald St 359-H5 N
Gerking Ct 427-G4 LTM
Germaine Rd 323-B10 WTH
German Ch Rd 462-E3, E6 L; 462-E10; 496-E3, E10; 530-E2 WrT
Germander La 562-G6 PeT
Gerrard Ave 492-A2, A4 S; 457-K9; 458-A9; 492-A1 WnT
Gerrard Ct 492-A9 WnT
Gerrard Dr 526-A7, A8 DTM; 492-A6 S; 492-A10; 526-A1 WnT
Gerry Ct 528-G7 BG
Gerry Dr 528-F7 BG
Gettysburg Ct 561-C3 PeT
Gettysburg Pkwy 596-H4 G
Gettysburg Pl 390-C9 CTH
Getz La 457-H8 PTM
Gibbes St 394-A5 F
Gibbs Ct 523-H8 P
Gibbs Rd 523-B6 GT
Gibbs St 523-G7 P
Gibson Ave 495-H5, H7, H8 WrT
Gifford Ave 324-D3 JT; 494-G9 WrT
Gifford Dr 491-G5 WnT
Gifford St 458-J2 WTM
Gila Bend Rd 489-C5 WaT
Gilbert Ave 528-D6 BG; 561-G1, J1; 562-A1 PeT
Gilbert St 528-D5 BG
Gillespie Ct 491-E6 WnT
Gillette St DN-B3; 493-A8 CTM
Gillingham Pl 393-H3 DTH
Gilman St 492-B5 S
Gilmore Rd 495-F2, G2 WrT
Gimber Ct 527-D4 CTM
Gimber St 527-D4, G4, H4, K4; 528-A4 CTM; 526-F4 WnT
Ginger Ct 525-E1 WnT
Ginko Leaf La 592-A9 M
Ginnylock Dr 427-H3 LTM
Girls Sch Rd 491-D4, D10; 525-D2 WnT
Glacier Ct 561-C3 PeT
Glacier Dr 561-D4 PeT
Gladden Dr 459-E3 WTM
Gladden Rd 524-B8 P
Gladesend Ct 426-A10 WTM
Gladstone Ave 460-E10; 494-E1, E5, E6, E8; 528-E2 CTM; 562-E1 PeT
Glaser Way 428-H1 FCT
Glasgow Ct 359-J7 N
Glasgow La 359-J7 N
Glass Chimney La 427-H2 F
Glass Dr 491-G5 WnT
Glastonberry La 592-E1 M
Glastonbury Ct 528-E8 BG
Glazier St 491-K2 S
Gleannloch Dr 427-J8 LTM
Glen Arm Ct 457-G10 WnT
Glen Arm Dr 457-F7 PTM
Glen Arm Dr E 457-G10 WnT
Glen Arm Dr W 457-G10 WnT
Glen Arm Rd 525-G8 DTM; 457-F8 PTM; 457-G9; 491-G5, G6; 525-G1 WnT
Glen Coe Dr 459-D1 WTM
Glen Cove Ct 428-H5 L
Glen Cove Dr 428-H5 L
Glen Ct 523-C1 WaT
Glen Eagles Ct 523-C1 WaT
Glen Highlands Dr 428-G5 L
Glen Hill Dr 426-A4 WTM
Glen Scott Dr 428-H5 L
Glen Scott La 428-H5 L
Glen Shire La 563-A5 FT
Glen Stewart Way 457-B5 PTM
Glen View Dr 428-G6 L
Glenatr Dr 558-H9 GT
Glenbrook Ct 391-H6 CTH
Glenbrook La 490-E8 WaT
Glenburr Ct 394-B5 F
Glencairn La 460-H6 LTM; 460-D6 WTM
Glencary Crest 458-K7 WMT
Glencoe St 460-H8 LTM
Glencrest Dr 562-J6 FT
Glenda Dr 524-A7 P
Glendale Ave 527-C3, E3 CTM
Glendale Ct 489-G8 A; 592-B2 M
Glendora Ct 491-F4 WnT
Glendora Dr 491-F4 WnT
Glendurgan Dr 391-A6 CTH
Glenfair Ct 491-C7 WnT
Glengarry Ct 428-G5 L
Glengary Dr 394-B5 F
Glengyle Ave 528-D5 BG
Glenhaven Ct 428-B1 F; 462-D1 L
Glenmar La 460-G6 WTM
Glenmora Ridge Rd 426-G8 WTM
Glenn Abbey La 428-D1 F
Glenn Cairn Ct 428-D1 F
Glenn Ct 593-C9 MTM
Glenn Dr 494-B2 CTM; 596-B3 G; 593-C9 MTM
Glenn Rd 461-G2, G4 L
Glennmore Dr 427-J8 LTM
Glenridge Dr 494-F4 CTM
Glensford Dr 489-G8 A
Glenshire Ct 563-B5 FT
Glenshire Way 563-B5 FT
Glenside Ct 427-D5 LTM
Glentrace Dr 428-F6 L
Glenview Cir 592-E4 M
Glenview Dr 426-D8 WTM
Glenview Dr E 426-E8 WTM
Glenview Dr S 426-E8 WTM
Glenview Dr W 426-E8 WTM
Glenvista Pl 393-D6 F
Glenway Dr 428-F6 L
Glenwood Ct 489-H8 A
Glenwood Dr 460-B7 WTM
Glenwood La 393-E6 F
Glossbrenner Ct 428-J9 L
Gloucester Cir 460-F3 WTM
Gloucester Ct 359-J7 N
Glowing Flame Dr 427-J2 F
Glynis Rd 323-E1 AT
Golay St 528-B1, B3 CTM
Gold Coin Dr 489-H10 A
Golden Ash Ct 394-D3 F
Golden Bluff Ct 428-H4 LTM
Golden Eagle Ct 595-C5 WTJ
Golden Eagle Dr 456-K8 PTM
Golden Grove Rd 595-A9 WTJ
Golden Hill Ct E 594-H10 WTJ
Golden Hill Dr 459-A9 CTM
Golden Leaf Way 424-H3 WTM
Golden Meadow Way 326-C10 N
Golden Oaks E 424-J3 WTM
Golden Oaks N 424-H3 WTM
Golden Oaks W 424-H3 WTM
Golden Pond Ct 422-H10 BTH; 596-G2 G
Golden Ridge La 395-C10 FCT
Golden Woods Dr 424-G3 PTM
Goldenbell 529-B7 FT
Goldeneye Cir 490-K3 WnT
Goldenrain Ct 562-F1 PeT
Goldenrod Ct 495-F5 WrT
Goldenrod Dr 495-F5 WrT
Goldenrod La 393-E6 F
Goldfinch Cir 427-G6 LTM
Goldfinch Dr 391-F2 CTH
Golf Club Ct 428-G7 L
Golf Course Dr 428-G8 L
Golf Ct 596-G2 G
Golf La 425-B10 WTM
Golf Stream Dr 496-D3 WrT
Golf View Ct 595-D7 WTJ
Golf View Dr 528-A4 CTM; 392-B6 Ca; 456-G3 LTH; 595-D7 WTJ
Golfview Terr 523-C1 WaT
Good Ave 494-K8, K9 WrT
Goodenuff Rd 523-B1 WaT
Goodlet Ave 492-F2, F4, F5; 526-F2, F4 WnT
Goodtime Ct 357-F9 WTH
Goodway Ct 427-K6 LTM
Goodway Dr 427-K7 LTM
Gooseberry La 562-D10; 596-D1 G
Gordon Ct 455-G7 B
Gordon Dr 423-G7 PTM
Gordon La 523-B9 GT
Gordon Way 563-C5 FT
Gordonshire Ct 423-B5 PTM
Gordonshire Dr 423-B5 PTM
Gorham Ct 392-B7 Ca
Goshawk Ct 457-D8 PTM
Gotta La 457-J7 PTM
Gould Dr 426-D1 Ca
Government Pl DN-C2; 493-D7 CTM
Governors La 394-F10 F; 389-F5 Z
Governors Rd 459-A9 CTM
Governours Ct 462-D9 WrT
Governours La 462-C9 WrT
Gower Ct 424-G6 PTM
Goya Ct 492-B1 WnT
Grace Ct 391-G1 Ca
Grace Dr 391-H2 Ca
Grace St 494-F4 CTM; 595-D4 WTJ; 490-J1 WnT
Grace Terr 428-F5 LTM
Graceland Ave 493-D1 CTM; 459-D5, D6, D8, D10 WTM
Gradle Dr 391-J6 Ca
Graffiti Rd 598-H1 MTS
Grafton Ave 525-J1 WnT
Graham Ave 460-J8 LTM; 460-J9; 494-J1, J3, J5, J9, K7 WrT
Graham Ct 426-J7 LTM
Graham Rd 596-K1 G; 426-J7, J10; 460-J1 LTM; 562-K10; 596-K1 PTJ; 426-J7, J10; 460-J1 WTM
Grampian Way 457-E7 PTM
Granada Cir 492-H2 WnT
Granada Cir N 492-H1 WnT
Granada Cir W 492-G1 WnT
Granada Ct 596-F4 G
Granada Dr 596-F4 G
Granby Dr 496-H6 Cu
Grand Ave 460-G8 LTM; 426-G9 WTM; 494-G9; 528-G1 WrT
Grand Mesa Ct 561-C4 PeT
Grand Natl Rd 424-E10 PTM
Grand Woods Dr 491-J6 WnT
Grande Ave 492-C7 S; 492-C7 WnT
Grandiose Dr 459-A3 WTM
Grandview Ct 325-K10 N
Grandview Dr 489-H7 A; 424-K10; 458-K2, K5 WTM
Granger Ct 393-E7 F; 424-A10 PTM
Granger La 424-A10 PTM
Granite Ct 391-J2 Ca; 562-H3 FT; 531-F4 SCT
Granite Dr 391-J1 Ca
Granner Cir 559-H4 DTM
Granner Ct 559-H4 DTM
Granner Dr 559-G4, H4 DTM
Granny Smith La 523-E2 WaT
Grant Ave 460-E9; 494-E5, E7, E8, E9, E10; 528-E2 CTM; 460-D8 WTM
Grant Cir 325-F3 C
Grant Ct 596-J4 G; 490-F7 WaT
Grant St 455-H5, H7 B; 359-J2 N; 356-D4 WTH
Grant Wood Ct 427-D10 LTM
Grantham Way 427-H1 F
Granville Ct 495-J3 WrT
Granville La 495-K3 WrT
Granville Pl 495-K3 WrT
Grapevine Dr 462-C5 L
Grapevine La 394-C3 F
Grasshopper Ct 326-C9 N
Grassy Branch Rd 324-C10; 358-C3, C9 WTH
Grassy Cr Ct 496-D1 WrT
Grassy Cr Dr 496-D1 WrT
Grassy Cr La 596-H3 G
Grassy La 561-C8 PeT
Grattan La 426-G10 WTM
Gravelie Dr 562-C5 PeT
Gray Arbor Dr 562-E2 PeT
Gray Arbor Way 562-D2 PeT
Gray Birch Ct 523-D4 WaT
Gray Eagle Dr 395-B6 F
Gray Rd 392-F2, F10 CTH; 392-F2, F7, F10; 426-F2 Ca; 358-F5, F10 NT; 528-E10; 562-E2, E4 PeT; 358-F5, F10 WTH
Gray St 494-B5, C8, C9 CTM
Graydon St 494-A8 CTM
Graylan Pl 359-D10 NT
Grayling Cir 525-G8 DTM
Grayling Dr 525-F8 DTM
Graymont Dr 559-J5 DTM
Graysford Rd 490-K2 WnT
Grayson Dr 458-F8 WTM
Graystone Ct 389-E8 Z
Graystone La 389-E8 Z
Great Woods Dr 491-K6 WnT
Grebe Cir 496-H4 Cu
Grebe Way 392-G3 Ca
Greely Pl 428-K6 L
Green Acre Ct 455-G6 B
Green Acre Dr 455-G6 B
Green Ash Ct 492-E3 WnT
Green Belt Ct 392-K1 Ca
Green Braes Dr E 456-K6; 457-A5 PTM
Green Braes Dr N 456-K5 PTM
Green Braes Dr S 456-K5 PTM
Green Branch La 428-B4 LTM
Green Briar La 596-E10 NW
Green Ct 392-E8 Ca
Green Hills Dr 455-E7 LTH
Green Hills La 458-F10 WnT
Green Hills La Mid 458-G10 WnT
Green Hills La N 458-G10 WnT
Green Hills La S 458-G10 WnT
Green Hills Overlook 458-G9 WnT
Green Leaves Cir 460-H2 LTM
Green Leaves Ct 326-A10 N; 326-A10 NT
Green Leaves Rd 426-H10; 460-H1 WTM
Green Meadow Ct 326-A10 NT
Green Meadow Dr 596-E4 G
Green Meadows Dr 489-C10 WaT
Green Pasture Ct 596-G1 G
Green Pasture La 596-F1 G
Green Pl 392-F8 Ca
Green Ridge Dr 489-B10 WaT
Green River Ct 496-F5 WrT
Green Rock La 528-H2 WrT
Green Springs Rd 491-D7 WnT
Green St 392-E8 Ca; 523-G7 P
Green St N 455-G5 B
Green St S 455-F7 B
Green Valley Ct 560-J8 PeT
Green Valley Dr 560-J8 PeT
Green Valley La 326-A10 NT; 560-J8 PeT
Green Woods Dr 491-K6 WnT
Greenbriar Ct 489-A7 WaT
Greenbriar Dr 394-D9 F; 595-G1, H1 G
Greenbriar W 595-H1 G
Greenbrier Dr 390-H9 CTH
Greenbrook Ct 496-C4 WrT
Greenbrook Dr 496-C5 WrT
Greenbrook Tr 496-B5 WrT
Greenfield Ave 395-B1, H5 FCT; 359-J5; 360-A6 N; 360-A6, G9 NT; 494-H9, K9 WrT; 360-G9 WyT
Greenfield Rd 390-A6 ET
Greenhills Dr 595-D1 WTJ
Greenlawn St 492-A6 S
Greenlee Cir 490-J8 WnT
Greenlee Ct 490-J6 WnT
Greenlee Dr 490-J7, J8 WnT
Greenmeadow Cir 462-B6 LTM
Greenmeadow Ct 462-B7 LTM
Greenridge Dr 423-E5 PTM
Greenridge Way 423-G4 PTM
Greenshire Dr 426-J10 WTM
Greenslope Ct 393-K2 F
Greenspire Dr 392-F8 Ca
Greenspring Way 596-F5 G
Greensview Dr 595-D7 WTJ
Greentree Ct 558-D6 GT
Greentree Dr 390-F10; 424-F1, F2 CTH
Greentree St 562-A6 PeT
Greenvalley Dr 595-G4 WTJ
Greenview Dr 460-E4 WTM
Greenview Way 496-D1 WrT
Greenway Dr 428-C1 F; 460-E4 WTM
Greenwillow Ct 460-H5 LTM
Greenwillow Rd 460-H4 LTM
Greenwood Dr 592-A1 M
Greenwood Measant La 596-C3 G
Greenwood Rd 595-E2 G; 595-E2 WTJ
Greenwood St 596-C2 G
Greenwood Tr 562-C10 G
Greenwood Tr E 562-C10 G
Greenwood Tr N 562-C9 G
Greenwood Tr W 562-C9 G
Greer Dell Rd 458-K1 WTM
Greer St DN-E4; 493-G10 CTM
Gregg Rd 425-E6 WTM
Gregory Cir 325-D8 N
Gregory Dr 491-G10 WnT
Greighton Ct 561-K6 PeT
Greighton Dr 561-K6 PeT
Grenada Dr 562-A7 PeT
Grenadier Dr 496-G4 WrT
Greta Dr 563-H1 FT
Gretna Green La 359-B1 N
Greybudd Ct 424-F9 PTM
Greybudd Dr 424-F9 PTM
Greyfox Ct 595-F3 WTJ
Greyfrair Ct 426-A10 WTM
Greyhound Ct 357-G9 WTH
Greyhound Pass 357-F9, J9; 358-A10 WTH
Greyridge Blvd 562-J3 FT
Greystone Ct 390-J8 CTH; 394-A5 F; 456-J9 WnT
Greywell Cir 427-H5 LTM
Gridley Ave 491-F9; 525-G2 WnT
Griffin Rd 561-E5 PeT
Griffin Shaw Run 393-B3 Ca
Griffin St 528-C6 PeT
Griffith Rd 561-J5 PeT
Grindstone Dr 394-D8 F
Gringo Dr 528-J10 FT
Grinnel St 424-G2 PTM
Grinnell La 424-G2 PTM
Grinnell St 424-G4 PTM
Griswald Rd 490-G8 WaT
Groff Ave 492-F3, F5, F7 WnT
Grosbeak Ct 393-B4 Ca
Grosbeak La 462-D4 L
Grosvenor Pl 427-A10 LTM
Groton La 425-B6 WTM
Grouse Ct 457-J7 PTM
Grouse Pt Tr 393-A4 Ca
Grove Ave DN-E4; 493-H10 CTM
Grove Ct 595-F1 G
Grovewood Dr 528-F8 BG
Grovewood Pl 528-G7 BG
Grube St 559-A5 DTM; 561-H5 PeT
Gryfalcon Pl 392-H3 Ca
Guard Hill La 460-J4 LTM
Guildhall Ct 424-K4 WTM
Guilford Ave 425-H2 CTH; 459-H10; 493-H1, H2 CTM; 425-H4; 459-H2, H4, H6 WTM
Guilford Dr 425-H2 WTM
Guilford Rd 391-H7 CTH; 391-H4, H7 Ca
Guinevere Dr 496-A1 WrT
Guion La 458-C1 PTM
Guion Lakes Blvd 458-C3 PTM
Guion Lakes Ct 458-C3 PTM
Guion Lakes Dr 458-C3 PTM
Guion Lakes Terr 458-C3 PTM
Guion Rd 424-C7, C10, D5, D9; 458-C2, D7 PTM; 458-E9, E10; 492-E1 WnT
Gulf Dr 561-A8 PeT
Gulfstream Ct 428-G1 FCT
Gulfstream Dr E 428-G1 FCT
Gull Ct 325-F3 C; 427-G7 LTM
Gullane Ct 489-A9 WaT
Gullit Way 491-C4 WnT
Gumwood Ct 490-K5 WnT
Gumwood Dr 490-J5 WnT
Gunnery Cir 423-F7 PTM
Gunnery Rd 423-E6 PTM
Gunnison Dr 428-K6 L
Gunpowder Ct 427-H4 LTM
Gunpowder Dr 427-H4 LTM
Gunsmith Ct 523-J5 P
Gunwale Dr 428-E6 LTM
Gunyon Ct 563-A5 FT
Gunyon Dr 563-A5 FT
Gunyon Way 562-K6 FT
Gurley St 358-A4 WTH
Guthrie Dr 525-J9 DTM
Guthrie Rd 558-A7 GT
Guy La 558-A7 GT
Gwin Way 427-G4 LTM
Gwinnett Pl 426-E6 WTM
Gwymere Run 390-K6 CTH
Gwynn Ct 492-D1 WnT
Gypsy Hill Rd 425-G8 WTM
Gypsy Rd 565-F9 MTS

H

Habig Rd 527-E7 PeT
Hacienda Ct 528-J10 FT
Hacienda Dr 489-F6 WaT
Hacienda Pl 596-F4 G
Hackberry Ct 562-A6 PeT
Hackleberry 392-A10 CTH
Haddington Dr N 427-H2 LTM
Haddington Dr W 427-H3 LTM
Hadleigh Dr 525-G8, G9 DTM
Hadley Rd 592-C3 BTM; 592-C3 M; 592-G3; 593-C3 MTM
Hadley Rd E 557-J3 GT; 557-J3; 558-A2, B2 P
Hadley Rd W 557-C3 GT; 557-C3 P
Hadley St 592-A2 M
Hadway Dr 427-G2, H3 LTM
Hague Rd 393-E10 DTH; 393-E10; 427-E2 F; 427-E4, E9 LTM; 325-E5, E10 N; 325-E5, E10; 359-E1 NT
Haines Ave 526-J2 WnT
Hal Sharp Rd 389-F7 Z
Halcomb Cir Dr N 525-F8 DTM
Halcomb Cir Dr S 525-F8 DTM
Haldale Dr 391-F2 CTH
Halden Pl 491-D6 WnT
Halfmoon La 426-K10 LTM
Halifax Dr 492-F2 WnT
Hall Ct 596-D1 G; 326-F6 NT
Hall Dr 594-H1 WTJ
Hall Pl 493-E4 CTM
Hall Rd 557-F4 GT; 557-F3 P
Halla Pl 393-D7 F
Halle Dr 496-H3 WrT
Halleck Way 490-F7 WaT
Halliburton Dr 524-F4 WaT
Hallmark La 524-H9 P
Hallwood Ct 457-C5 PTM
Halsey Dr 428-F1 FCT
Halsted Ct 491-D7 WnT
Halsted Dr 491-D7 WnT
Halyard Way 428-E5 LTM
Hamble Blvd 394-J7 F
Hamblen Dr W 525-B2 WnT
Hamburg Ct 428-A5 LTM
Hamden Rd 455-E7 B
Hamilton Ave 493-K4, K5, K8, K9; 494-A6 CTM; 456-H10 WnT
Hamilton Boone Rd 322-B3 AT; 390-B1 CTH; 390-B1 ET; 322-B3 MTB; 322-B10; 356-B3, B10; 390-B1 UT; 322-B10; 356-B3, B10; 390-B1 WTH
Hamilton Crossing Blvd 391-E5 Ca
Hamilton Dr 359-J1 N
Hamilton Ests 359-D10 NT
Hamilton Hills Dr 427-B2 DTH
Hamilton Hills La 427-B1 DTH
Hamilton La 392-A9 CTH
Hamilton Pass 394-B10, E8 F
Hamilton St 455-G7 B
Hamlet Dr 489-F7 A
Hammary Dr 361-A10 WyT
Hammon Dr 455-B4 LTH
Hammond Ct 458-F1 PTM
Hamner Ct 455-F4 B
Hamp Ct 391-G1 CTH
Hampshire Ct 461-J8 LTM; 325-B7 N
Hampstead Ct 427-D10 LTM
Hampstead La 427-C10, D10 LTM
Hampsted Ct 359-J8 N
Hampton Cir E 428-A5 LTM
Hampton Cir N 428-A5 LTM
Hampton Cir S 428-A6 LTM
Hampton Cir W 428-A6 LTM
Hampton Ct 392-C6 Ca; 425-F4 WTM
Hampton Dr 461-A6, B6 LTM; 459-C7, F7 WTM; 389-E9 Z
Hampton Pl 393-F7 F
Hampton Rd 357-D10 WTH
Hampton Way 428-A5 LTM
Hancock St 391-F6 Ca; 492-G8, G10 WnT
Hancook Rd 523-K8 P
Handball La 424-K3; 425-A3 WTM
Hangdog Dr 360-E2 NT
Hanks Dr 491-G4 WnT
Hanley St 523-H7 P
Hanna Ave 528-K7 BG; 525-E8, K8; 526-A8 DTM; 529-C7 FT; 527-B7, G7; 528-A7, B7 PeT

Hanna Rd 523-B7 GT; 523-B7 P
Hanna St 429-C8 McC; 523-D8 P
Hannah Ct 426-E2 Ca
Hannibal St 359-H4 N
Hanover Ct 393-A8 F
Hanover Dr 527-K9; 528-A9 PeT
Hanson Ave DN-B2 CTM
Hanson St DN-B2; 493-B7 CTM
Happy Hollow 457-K1 PTM
Happy Hollow Ct 561-D10 WTJ
Happy House Dr 462-B6 L
Harbinger Ct 326-C9 N
Harbison Ave 563-H1 FT; 495-H4, H5, H7, H8 WrT
Harbison Ct 495-H5 WrT
Harbor Ct 595-C7 WTJ; 496-A2 WrT
Harbor Dr 490-A7 WaT; 496-A3 WrT
Harborton Way 428-D7 L
Harbour Cir 394-K9 FCT
Harbour Dr N 325-B7 N
Harbour Dr S 359-B1 N
Harbour Isle 426-C8 WTM
Harbour Pines Ct 428-A4 LTM
Harbour Pointe Dr 426-B8 WTM
Harbour Town Ct 324-J6 N
Harbour Town Dr 324-J6 N
Harbour Trees La 325-B7 N
Harbridge Rd 426-K10; 460-K2 LTM
Harcourt Rd 424-J9, K5 WTM
Harcourt Springs Blvd 424-H9 WTM
Harcourt Springs Ct 424-J7 WTM
Harcourt Springs Dr 424-J7 WTM
Harcourt Springs Pl 424-J7 WTM
Harcourt Springs Terr 424-H9 WTM
Hard Key Cir 462-B2 L
Hardegan St 527-K10; 561-K2, K8, K9 PeT
Hardin Blvd 491-H9, H10 WnT
Hardin Ct 523-J9 P
Hardin Oak Dr 359-D3 N
Harding Ct 527-A10 PeT
Harding La 527-A10 PeT
Harding St DN-B2, B4; 459-A10; 492-K2, K7, K9; 493-A1, A5, A9; 527-A1 CTM; 523-G8 P; 527-A7, A10; 561-A1, A3, A5 PeT
Hardwick Ct 393-F7 F
Hardwick Dr 393-F7 F
Hardwood Ct 427-A4 LTM
Hardwood Dr 427-C3 LTM
Hare Dr 324-H5 N
Harfield Dr 424-K7 WTM
Hargeo Dr 561-D7 PeT
Harlan St 493-K9, K10; 527-K1; 528-A3, A5 CTM; 523-G7 P; 528-A5, A10; 562-A1 PeT
Harlem Dr 592-B2 M
Harlequin La 393-C8 F
Harlescott Rd 426-K10; 427-A10 LTM
Harlowe Dr 394-C4 F
Harmon Ct 562-C4 PeT
Harmon Dr 422-F2 ET; 562-C4 PeT
Harmon St DN-D4; 493-F9 CTM
Harmon Way 461-F4 L
Harmoney Dr 524-G8 WaT
Harmonridge Ct 423-G4 PTM
Harmony Dr 596-B4 G
Harmony Rd 391-F1 CTH
Harness Ct 530-E1 WrT
Harness Tr 492-D9 WnT
Harness Way 530-D1 WrT
Harnessmaker Ct 523-J5 P
Harper Rd 426-C3 WTM
Harpers La 424-A10 PTM
Harpool Rd 557-E6 GT
Harrier Cir 457-E6 PTM
Harrington Ct 427-J5 LTM
Harrington La 393-G8 F
Harrington Rd 427-H5 LTM
Harris Ave 492-B8 WnT
Harris St 455-J7 B
Harrison Ave 388-E1 Wh
Harrison Cir 392-G4 Ca
Harrison Dr 392-F3, G4 Ca; 596-B5 G; 461-G6 L
Harrison Pkwy 393-H2 F
Harrison Ridge Blvd 428-A10; 462-A1 L
Harrison Ridge Ct 462-A1 L
Harrison Ridge Dr 462-A1 L
Harrison St DN-E3; 493-G9 CTM; 529-H8 FT; 359-J3 N
Harrison St E 592-A3 M
Harriston Dr 394-E9 F
Harrow Pl 391-H10 CTH
Harrowgate Dr 392-C4 Ca
Harsin La 462-F2 L
Hart Dr 492-A1 WnT
Hartford Ave 558-A2 P; 525-A3 WnT
Hartford La 393-F8 F
Hartford St 489-K9 A; 493-J9 CTM
Harting Farms Dr 531-G4 SCT
Harting Overlook 562-K3 FT
Hartland Dr 496-G5 WrT
Hartman Dr 529-D5 FT; 461-D5, D6, D9 L; 461-D9 LTM; 461-D9; 495-D5 WrT
Hartman Pl 461-D9 WrT
Harvard Pl 459-D8 WTM
Harvest Ave 461-G8 LTM; 461-G9 WrT
Harvest Ct 596-G1 G; 357-H10 WTH; 461-G9 WrT
Harvest Dr 357-H10 WTH
Harvest Glen Ct 496-J5 Cu
Harvest Glen Dr 496-H5 Cu
Harvest La 427-F5 LTM
Harvest Ridge Cir 489-H6 A
Harvest Ridge Dr 489-G7 A
Harvest Way 524-B7 P; 497-H7 SCT
Harwich Dr 496-C2 WrT
Hastings Ct 394-E10 F
Hastings Dr 462-B8 LTM
Hastings Trace 456-H5 PTM
Hathaway Dr 496-A5 WrT
Hatherley Way 394-H10; 428-H1 F
Hatteras Dr 427-A8 LTM
Hatteras La 457-E9 WnT
Haueisen Rd 524-J9 DTM
Haugh St 492-G7 WnT
Havana Ave 525-F2 WnT
Haven Ct 390-C8 CTH
Haver Way 426-B3 WTM
Haverford Ave 459-J4, J5, J6 WTM
Haverhill Ct 426-E9 WTM
Haverhill Dr 426-B9, D8 WTM
Haverstick Rd 426-B2 CTH; 392-E9 Ca; 426-A5, A6, B3 WTM
Haverton Way 393-A4 Ca
Hawes Ct 427-E5 LTM
Hawk Ct 596-F2 G
Hawkesbury La 424-J9 WTM
Hawkins Ct 496-B3 WrT
Hawkins Rd 461-J3, K3 L
Hawks Cres Ct 457-F5 PTM
Hawks Hill Rd 428-H9 L
Hawks La 459-H3 WTM
Hawks Lake Dr 428-C1 F
Hawks Landing Pl 457-D8 PTM
Hawks Pt Rd 460-H5 LTM
Hawks Ridge Ct 428-C1 F
Hawthorn Pk Dr 426-H10 WTM
Hawthorn Pl 324-J7 N
Hawthorn Ridge 394-G9, J8, J10 F
Hawthorn Terr 460-G1 WTM
Hawthorne Ct 392-D4 Ca; 427-F9 LTM
Hawthorne Dr 392-D2, D3 Ca; 460-K5 LTM; 523-K7 P; 523-G4 WaT
Hawthorne Dr W 392-C2 Ca
Hawthorne La 455-J2 B; 460-H9 LTM; 594-J2 WTJ; 426-H8, H9 WTM; 460-H10; 494-H2, H4, H6, H8, H10; 528-H1, H2 WrT
Hawthorne Rd 427-F9 LTM
Hawthorne St 389-H9 Z
Hay Meadow Ct 561-J8 PeT
Hayden St 428-K7 L
Haydon Ct 393-F6 F
Hayford Ct 457-H5 PTM
Hayford Way 457-H6 PTM
Haymount Dr 491-F10 WnT
Haynes Ave 425-J9, K9; 426-A9, F9 WTM
Haynes Ct 426-G9 WTM
Hayworth Rd 559-F6, G8 DTM
Hazel Dell Pkwy 392-H10, J3, J7; 426-H2 CTH; 392-J3, J7 Ca
Hazel Foster Ct 392-C1 Ca
Hazel Foster Ct W 392-C1 Ca
Hazel Foster Dr 392-B1 Ca
Hazel Hatch Dr 458-G1 PTM
Hazelchase Ct 458-G1 PTM
Hazelhatch Ct 458-K1 WTM
Hazelhatch Dr 458-G2 WTM
Hazelnut Ct 458-G1 PTM
Hazeltine Dr 490-J2 WnT
Hazelview La 458-G1 PTM
Hazelwood Ave 425-B8, B10; 459-B2 WTM
Hazelwood Cir 392-E3 Ca
Hazelwood Ct 392-F4 Ca; 425-B10 WTM
Hazelwood Dr 392-F4 Ca
Hazledale Rd 358-J10 N; 358-J5, J10 NT
Hazy Cir 424-K3 WTM
Hazy Ct 595-A2 WTJ
Hazy La 594-K2 WTJ
Headwind Dr 525-B3 WnT
Heady Ct 393-E6 F
Heady La 393-E6 F
Heaney Ct 458-J7 WTM
Hearthside Ct 455-J8 B
Hearthstone Ct 562-D6 PeT; 531-E3 SCT
Hearthstone Dr 395-A7 F
Hearthstone Way 562-D5, D6 PeT
Heartland Bay 423-G8 PTM
Heartland Blvd 558-G8, K9 DTM; 558-G8 GT; 559-A9 MTM
Heartland Ct 423-G8 PTM
Heartland Rd 423-G8 PTM
Heartwood Ct 392-K1 Ca
Heath Cir 357-E9 WTH
Heath Row Ct 392-D1 Ca
Heather Beach La 491-B1 WnT
Heather Cir 496-B4 WrT
Heather Ct 496-B3 WrT
Heather Dr 392-A5 Ca; 491-E7, F8 WnT
Heather Hills Rd 496-B3 WrT
Heather La 393-F9 F; 326-B9 NT
Heather Ridge Dr 457-E10 WnT
Heatherglen Cir 428-B1 F
Heatherlea Ct 496-D1 WrT
Heatherlea Dr 496-D1 WrT
Heatherstone Pl 392-F6 Ca
Heatherton Cir 427-D5 LTM
Heatherton Ct 427-D5 LTM
Heatherton Dr 427-D5 LTM
Heatherwood Ct 325-B9 N
Heatherwood Dr 491-G10 WnT
Heathery Pl 491-B3 WnT
Heathmore Dr 528-K9 FT
Heathmore Dr W 528-K9 FT
Heathwood Dr 562-G7 FT
Heckman Way 560-J10; 594-H1 WTJ
Hedback Dr 426-B10 WTM
Hedback Way 426-C10 WTM
Hedgerow Dr 461-A5 LTM
Heflin St 496-H6 Cu
Heights Ave 528-F10 PeT
Heiney Rd 525-J8 DTM
Heiny Rd 527-E6 PeT
Helen Dr 425-H8 WTM
Helen Keen Ct 391-H5 Ca
Helena Ave 528-F10 PeT
Helena Ct 492-D2 WnT
Helford La 391-A6 CTH
Helmsdale Dr 427-J3 LTM
Helmsman Cir 428-C5 LTM
Hemlock Ave 459-J9 CTM
Hemlock Ct 455-H1 B; 497-B4 BCT; 557-K10 M; 324-J8 N
Hemlock La 523-K6 P
Hemlock St 392-C2 Ca
Henderson Dr 455-D5 LTH
Hendrick Dr 595-G3 WTJ
Hendricks Pl 493-K8 CTM
Henlay Dr 523-E8 P
Henley St 523-D8 P
Henry St DN-B3, C3, C4, D3, D4; 493-A9, C9, D9, E9 CTM; 490-B6 WaT; 491-D9, J9; 492-B9, D9 WnT
Hensel Cir 392-E10 Ca
Hensel Ct 392-C9 Ca
Hensel Dr 392-C9 Ca
Hensel La 392-E10 Ca
Herald Sq 394-B4 F
Heraldine Ct 357-E9 WTH
Herbert Lord Rd 461-H4 L
Herbert St 493-A4 CTM
Herford Dr 496-H3 WrT
Heritage Commons Dr 495-H2 WrT
Heritage Commons La 495-H2 WrT
Heritage Ct 393-E8 F; 427-J8 LTM; 530-K4 SCT
Heritage Dr 530-K4 SCT
Heritage Green Dr 428-C1 F
Heritage La 389-D6 ET; 560-H10 WTJ
Heritage Pl 455-H6 B
Herman St DN-E3; 493-H8 CTM
Hermitage Ct 491-J3 S
Hermitage Rd 527-E6 PeT
Hermitage Way 491-J3 S
Hermosa Ct 461-K9 WrT
Hermosa Dr 428-B7 L
Herod Ct 496-C2 WrT
Heron Ct 427-G6 LTM; 497-J7 SCT
Heron Dr 497-H8 SCT
Herriman Blvd 359-K7, K10 N
Herriman Ct 359-J9 N
Herschell Ave 492-K3 CTM
Hervey St 527-G3; 528-B3 CTM
Hess Ave 461-H4 L
Hess Ct 461-G2 L
Hess St 523-H8 P
Hewes Ct 359-C1 N
Hewes Pl 426-E6 WTM
Hewlet Dr 424-D5 PTM
Heyward Dr 426-F6 WTM
Heyward La 426-E6 WTM
Heyward Pl 426-E6 WTM
Hi Neighbor Dr 531-K2 SCT
Hi Vu Dr 561-F4, F7, F8 PeT
Hi-End Ct 526-E6 DTM
Hialeah Ct 391-H10 CTH
Hiatt Ave 594-J4 WTJ
Hiatt St DN-A4; 492-J10; 526-J1 CTM
Hiawatha Dr 326-F4 NT
Hibben Ave 494-H8, J8; 495-J7 WrT
Hibiscus Dr 495-G4 WrT
Hickory Cir 529-B7 FT
Hickory Ct 392-E10 Ca; 496-K4 Cu; 561-B10 WTJ; 389-F5 Z
Hickory Ct E 529-C8 FT
Hickory Ct W 529-B8 FT
Hickory Dr 496-K5 Cu
Hickory Forge Ct 458-B2 PTM
Hickory Hill Tr 557-K8 GT
Hickory Knoll Dr 529-B7 FT
Hickory La 496-K4 Cu; 559-A6 DTM; 596-H3 G; 455-A4 LTH; 523-K6 P; 561-E5, G5 PeT; 595-C9 WTJ; 457-D10 WnT; 389-F9 Z
Hickory La E 457-D10 WnT
Hickory La W 457-D10 WnT
Hickory Lake Dr 462-E4 L
Hickory Lake La 462-E5 L
Hickory Leaf Rd 462-B4 L
Hickory Rd 530-A10; 564-A2, A5 FT
Hickory Ridge 391-E2 CTH
Hickory Ridge Cir 325-D2 JT
Hickory Ridge Dr 389-F4 Z
Hickory Tr E 529-B7 FT
Hickory Tr S 529-B8 FT
Hickory Tr W 529-B8 FT
Hickory Way 325-A9 N
Hickory Woods Dr 393-E9 F
Hickorynut Cir 393-K2 F
Hickorywood Ct 455-F8 B; 491-J2 S
Hickorywood Dr 491-G2, J2 S
Hicory Dr 392-B5 Ca
Hidden Bay 428-F7 L
Hidden Bay Dr 595-F2 G
Hidden Bay Dr N 457-G4 PTM
Hidden Lake Dr 427-B5 LTM
Hidden Meadow La 496-B7 WrT
Hidden Orchard Ct 458-H7 WTM
Hidden Orchard La 458-H7 WTM
Hidden Pt Dr 427-K6; 428-A6 LTM
Hidden Ridge 393-F9 F
Hidden Ridge Ct 560-A3 DTM
Hidden Valley Dr 523-G4 WaT
Hideaway Ct 561-J9 G
Hideaway Dr N 424-G6 PTM
Hideaway Dr S 424-H6 PTM
Higdon Ct 491-D4 WnT
High Ct 392-C5 Ca
High Dr 392-A8 CTH; 392-C5 Ca; 425-F6 WTM
High Dr E 455-B8 LTH
High Dr W 455-A8 LTH
High Fall Rd 460-K3 LTM
High Grove Dr 424-J1 CTH
High Meadow Ct N 560-K10 WTJ
High Meadow Ct S 560-K10 WTJ
High Pt Cir 394-C3 F
High Rd 392-C5 Ca
High Sch Rd 525-G7, G9, G10, H6; 559-G1, G3 DTM; 457-G2, G4, G8 PTM; 491-G2, G4 S; 491-G2, G4, G5, G10; 525-G3, H6 WnT
High St DN-E4; 493-F10 CTM
High St E 592-A3 M
High View Cir 428-K7 L
High View Ct 428-J7 L
High View Dr 428-J7 L
High Woods 422-G8 BTH
Highburry Ct 427-D10 LTM
Highburry Dr 427-D10 LTM
Highfield Ct 458-E9 WnT
Highgate Cir 427-A2 F
Highland Ave DN-F2, F3; 493-H8, H9, J7 CTM
Highland Cir 526-C8 DTM
Highland Dr 391-J10 CTH; 393-D6 F; 596-C3 G; 592-A1 M; 596-D10 NW
Highland La 429-B3 McC
Highland Manor Ct N 459-B4 WTM
Highland Manor Ct S 459-B4 WTM
Highland Pk Dr 595-C7 WTJ
Highland Pl 493-D2, D3 CTM; 393-D5 F
Highland Rd 424-F9 PTM
Highland Springs Dr 429-B2 FCT
Highland Springs Dr N 429-C1 FCT
Highlander Dr 523-G9 P
Highmount Ct 424-H10 PTM
Highwood Dr 357-J3 W
Highwoods Ct 458-F9 WnT
Highwoods Dr 458-G10 WnT
Highwoods Dr N 458-F10 WnT
Highwoods Dr W 458-F10 WnT
Hiland Dr 424-G8 PTM
Hilda Ct 391-J5 Ca
Hill Ave 523-G8 P
Hill Crest Ct 391-E2 CTH
Hill Crest Dr 523-F5 WaT
Hill Ct 595-B2 WTJ
Hill Dr 455-E8 LTH
Hill Dr E 461-E4 L
Hill Dr W 461-E4 L
Hill Gail Dr 560-K7 PeT
Hill Pine Ct 561-H8 PeT
Hill Rise Dr 528-J9 FT
Hill St 494-H7 WrT; 361-D5 WyT
Hill Valley Dr 561-C7, D7, F7 PeT
Hillcrest CC Rd 461-A2 LTM
Hillcrest Ct 562-D4 PeT
Hillcrest Dr 392-C5 Ca; 561-J10; 595-J1 G; 557-J8 GT; 359-K5 N; 562-D3 PeT; 358-A3, A4 W
Hillcrest La 460-K1 LTM
Hillcrest Rd 425-F7 WTM
Hillendale Dr 595-B2 WTJ
Hillsboro Dr 492-A1 WnT
Hillsborough Dr 394-C10 F
Hillsdale Ct 427-B7 LTM
Hillsdale Dr 392-A2 Ca
Hillside Ave 460-A9, A10; 493-K3; 494-A2 CTM; 426-A10; 459-K5; 460-A2, A4, A6, A9 WTM
Hillside Ave Dr E 460-A2 WTM
Hillside Ave Dr W 459-K2 WTM
Hillside Ct 523-H9 P
Hillside Dr 392-A10; 426-A1 CTH; 595-B10 WTJ
Hilltop Ct 596-A1 G
Hilltop Dr 596-B1 G; 457-A10 WnT
Hilltop La 427-F9 LTM
Hillview Cir 393-B10 F
Hilton Dr 528-D9 PeT
Hiner La 495-C5 WrT
Hines Dr 456-D10 LTH
Hinesley Ave 459-D5, D6 WTM
Hinkle Rd 392-F2, F10; 426-F1 CTH; 392-F2, F7, F10 Ca; 324-F4 JT; 324-F8 WTH
Hintocks Cir 390-E8, E9 CTH
Historic Oaks Blvd 491-B3, C3 WnT
Hittle Dr 529-K9 FT
Ho Hum Ct 595-C1 WTJ
Hoadley Rd 523-A2 WaT
Hoadley Vestal Rd 523-D6 GT; 523-D6 P
Hobart Rd 528-C3 CTM
Hobbs Ct 559-J1 DTM
Hobbs St 523-H8 P
Hobson Rd 557-D8, E9 GT
Hodson Ct 526-A6 DTM
Hodson Dr 526-A5 DTM
Hodson Pl 526-A5 DTM
Hoefgen St 527-E3, H3 CTM
Hoff Ct 427-H4 LTM
Hoffman Rd 559-C9 DTM; 525-B3 WnT
Hogan Dr 496-D3 WrT
Hohlier La 489-G7 A
Holaday Dr W 392-A10; 426-A1 CTH
Holiday Ct 389-E6 Z
Holiday Dr 523-K8 P
Holiday La 592-A1 M
Holiday La E 455-G9 B
Holiday La W 455-G9 B
Holland Dr 393-G7 F; 491-G4 WnT
Holland St 359-J5 N
Hollaway Blvd 455-A2 B
Holliday Cir 425-D2 WTM
Holliday Dr 425-D3, D4, E9 WTM
Holliday Dr E 425-E10; 459-E1 WTM
Holliday Dr W 425-D9, D10; 459-D1 WTM
Holliday La 425-C7 WTM
Hollingsworth Dr 424-E9; 458-F1 PTM
Hollingsworth Rd 458-A3 PTM
Hollister Dr 491-G1, H1, J1 S; 492-B1 WnT
Hollow Ave 493-K4 CTM
Hollow Bk Ct 358-G3 N
Hollow Cr Ct 424-D6 PTM
Hollow Cr Dr 424-D6 PTM
Hollow Dr 357-K3; 358-A3 W
Hollow Oak Ct 456-H3 WTM
Hollow Reed Ct 325-D9 N
Hollow Ridge Cir 427-E6 LTM
Hollow Run Cir 457-F9 WnT
Hollow Run Dr 457-F10 WnT
Hollow Run Pl 457-F9 WnT
Hollow Tree La 462-B4 L
Hollowood Ct 490-J6 WnT
Hollowood Dr 490-J6 WnT
Hollowview Ct 359-F2 N
Hollowview Dr 359-F2 N
Holly Ave DN-B4; 493-B9 CTM
Holly Cir 562-D6 PeT
Holly Cr La 425-J7 WTM
Holly Ct 359-G1 N; 557-H1 P
Holly Ct S 359-G1 N
Holly Dr 557-H1 P
Holly Hill Dr 526-B8 DTM
Holly Pk Dr 596-C6 G
Holly Springs Cir 457-F5 PTM
Holly Springs Dr E 457-F5 PTM
Holly Springs Dr W 457-E5 PTM
Holly Springs Pl 457-E5 PTM
Hollybrook Ct 426-F6 WTM
Hollybrook La 562-B6 Spt
Hollyhock Ct 531-C1 SCT
Hollyhock Dr 395-A7 F
Hollypark Dr 526-A5 WnT
Hollywood Tr 491-F4 WnT
Holmdale Rd 496-C9 WrT
Holmes Ave 492-H5, H8, H10 WnT
Holt Ave 526-D6 DTM; 492-E8, E10; 526-D3, D4 WnT
Holt Rd 492-D8 WnT
Holyoke Ct 424-G3 PTM
Holz Dr 496-H5 WrT
Holzknecht Ct 523-F7 P
Home Dr 393-E8 F
Home Pl DN-E4; 493-F9 CTM
Home St 596-C3 G
Homeridge Dr 528-G2 CTM
Homeside Dr 427-C3 LTM
Homestead Cir 523-B8 P
Homestead Ct 523-B7 P; 531-C1 SCT
Homestead Dr 561-K2; 562-A3, A5 PeT; 531-E3 SCT; 562-A3 Spt
Homestead Pl 523-B7 P
Homestead Pl E 523-B7 P
Homestead Pl W 523-B7 P
Homestead Way 455-J7 B
Homeward Dr 391-G9 CTH
Honey Cr Blvd 595-B9 WTJ
Honey Cr Cir 559-B10 MTM
Honey Cr Ct 559-B10 MTM; 595-C9 WTJ
Honey Cr Rd 595-H10 PTJ; 595-H10 WTJ
Honey Manor Ct 525-K10 DTM
Honey Manor Dr 525-K10; 526-A10 DTM
Honeylocust Dr 428-H7 L
Honeysuckle Ct 592-F2 M
Honeysuckle Dr 592-F2 M
Honeysuckle La 563-B2 FT
Honeysuckle Way 427-G5 LTM
Honeywell Dr 462-B2 L
Honeywell La 462-B2 L
Honnen Dr N 427-E9 LTM
Honnen Dr S 427-E10 LTM
Honnen Dr W 427-E10 LTM
Hoop Rd 561-A6 PeT
Hooper Pl 426-E6 WTM
Hoosier Rd 394-F10 F; 394-F7 FCT
Hoover Cir 425-B5 WTM
Hoover Ct 425-B7 WTM
Hoover La 425-B6 WTM
Hoover Rd 390-K5, K7 CTH; 425-C8, C10; 459-C2 WTM
Hoover St 357-J2, K2; 358-A2 W
Hoover Vill Dr 459-B1 WTM
Hope Ct 595-F3 G
Hope Dr 523-F2 WaT
Hope La 490-G8 WaT
Hopi Rd 489-C5 WaT
Hopi Tr 495-D8 WrT
Hopkins La 426-F6 WTM
Hopkins Rd 496-H5, H6 Cu
Hopkinson Dr 359-C1 N
Horatio Dr 489-E7 A
Horizon Blvd 594-H7 WTJ
Horizon Ct 428-G1 FCT; 458-K1 WTM
Horizon La 458-K1 WTM
Hornaday Dr 594-J9 WTJ
Hornady Rd 455-J10 B; 455-J10 LTH
Hornbill Pl 392-H3 Ca
Horner Dr 529-E6, E7 FT
Hornet Ave 528-G7 BG
Horse Dr 492-F8 WnT
Horse Hill Dr E 491-C1 WnT
Horse Hill Dr W 491-C1 WnT
Horseback Tr 356-J9 WTH
Horses La 358-B10 WTH
Horseshoe Bend 491-C1 WnT
Horseshoe Dr 456-D10 LTH
Horseshoe La E 392-C7 Ca
Horseshoe La W 392-C7 Ca
Horseshoe Tr 492-D9 WnT
Horseshow Dr 389-B2 ET
Horth Ct 461-K9 WrT
Horton Rd 323-E4 AT; 323-E9 WTH
Horton St 562-C10 G
Hosbrook St DN-E4; 493-H9 CTM
Hoss Rd 527-D9 PeT
Hoster Rd 392-K7 CTH
Hotze St 564-F6 FT
Hounds Crossing 390-E10 CTH
House St 564-E6 FT
Houston St 460-C10; 494-C4 CTM
Hovey St 459-J10; 493-J1, J3, J4 CTM
Howard St 525-D1 WnT
Howard Ave 494-B2 CTM
Howard Rd 561-K10; 595-K1 G
Howard St 526-H1 CTM; 525-G1, G2; 526-F1, H1 WnT
Howe Dr 391-H1 CTH; 494-G8 CTM; 391-G2 Ca
Howe Rd 394-D3, D4 F; 360-D8 NT
Howe St 492-B5 S
Howell La 491-H7 WnT
Hoyt Ave DN-F4; 493-H9; 494-A9, D9 CTM; 495-E9 WrT
Huber Ct 461-F10 WrT
Huber Pl 495-E5 WrT
Huber St 461-F10; 495-E6, F1, F5, F6, F8, F10 WrT
Huckleberry Ct 424-J4 WTM
Huddleston Dr E 561-B5 PeT
Huddleston Dr N 561-E5 PeT
Huddleston Dr S 561-E6 PeT
Huddleston Dr W 561-D6 PeT
Hudnut Blvd 526-K4, K5 CTM
Hudnut Blvd Dr N 526-K4 CTM
Hudnut Pl 526-K5 CTM
Hudson Bay Dr 595-J2 G
Hudson Bay La 595-H2 G
Hudson St DN-D2, E1; 493-F5, F7 CTM
Huff Blvd 394-D4 F
Huff St 564-F6 FT
Huggin Hollow Rd 594-A10 WTJ
Hugo Bell Dr 492-H1 WnT
Hugo St 496-F6 Cu
Hull Rd 389-E10; 423-E1 ET
Hull St 461-E7 L; 388-E1 Wh
Hulman Blvd 492-C2 S; 492-C2 WnT
Humber Ct 391-E9 CTH
Hume Dr 393-D9 F
Hummingbird Cir 392-H2 Ca
Hummingbird Cir 427-G7 LTM
Humvee La 325-C4 JT
Hunnewell Dr 457-G3 PTM
Hunt Club Ave 422-G1, G2 ET
Hunt Club Dr 389-C10; 423-C1 ET
Hunt Club La 423-C1 ET
Hunt Club Rd 388-F10, H10; 389-D10; 422-G1 ET; 389-D10 Z
Hunt Country La 422-H2 ET
Hunt Country Pl 422-H3 ET
Hunt Master Ct 424-B9 PTM
Hunt St 524-B6 P
Hunter Ct 357-D10 WTH
Hunter Dr 523-G9 P
Hunter Rd 529-C5 FT; 495-B10; 529-C1, C5 WrT
Hunterglen Rd 460-K3 LTM
Hunters Blvd 462-E9 WrT
Hunters Cove Ct 428-D6 LTM
Hunters Cove Dr 428-D6 LTM
Hunters Cove Pl 428-C6 LTM
Hunters Dr 392-A7 Ca
Hunters Dr E 392-A7 Ca
Hunters Dr W 392-A7 Ca
Hunters Glen 389-E9 Z
Hunters Green Cir 423-F10; 457-F1 PTM
Hunters Green Ct 457-F1 PTM
Hunters Green La 423-E10; 457-E1 PTM
Hunters Green Pl 457-E1 PTM
Hunters Green Way 457-E1 PTM
Hunters La 595-F3 G
Hunters Path 491-B1 WnT
Hunters Pt Dr 389-D8 Z
Hunters Ridge Dr 557-K3 P
Hunters Ridge La 594-K6; 595-A6 WTJ
Hunters Tr 455-H10 B; 595-F3 G; 389-F9 Z
Huntersfield Dr 390-E10 CTH
Hunting Cr Dr 595-F4 G
Hunting Dr 560-K9 PeT
Hunting Tr 560-K8, K9 PeT
Huntington Ave 326-B10 N; 326-B10 NT; 326-G3 WRT
Huntington Ct 392-H9 Ca; 496-J3 Cu
Huntington Dr 392-G9 Ca; 496-J3 Cu; 425-A2 WTM
Huntington La 425-A3 WTM
Huntington Rd 426-D8 WTM

Huntington Woods Pt 389-F10 Z
Huntington Woods Rd 423-F1 Z
Huntsmen Ct 427-B3 LTM
Huntstead La 527-D10, G10 PeT
Hupa Way 495-D8 WrT
Hurley St 596-D6 G
Hurricane Rd 597-G9 CTJ
Hurst Rd 489-G8 A
Hurstborne Ct 423-E1 ET
Hussey La 391-C10; 425-C1 CTH
Hyacinth Ct 326-C10 N
Hyacinth Dr 394-J8 F
Hyacinth Way 391-A7 CTH; 458-D3 PTM
Hyannis Dr 490-A7 WaT
Hyannis Port Dr 457-D9 WnT
Hyche Ave 494-B2 CTM
Hyde Pk 390-J10 CTH
Hyde Pk Ct 426-E3 WTM
Hyde Pk Row 455-F8 B
Hyde Pk Way 426-E3 WTM
Hyperion Ct 528-F2 CTM
Hyperion Way 528-G2 CTM
Hythe Rd 426-K9; 427-A9 LTM

I

Ida Ct 562-D9 G
Ida St 491-G9; 492-A9, G9 WnT
Idleway Ct 595-D3 WTJ
Idlewild La 392-E10 Ca
Idlewood Dr 425-K6; 426-A6 WTM
Illinois St DN-D1, D4; 459-E9; 493-E4, E9, E10; 527-E4 CTM; 391-E10; 425-E1 Ca; 527-E10; 561-E9 PeT; 425-E3, E6, E9, E10; 459-E1, E3, E5, E9 WTM
Imperial Dr 529-J8 FT
Imperial Woods Cir 491-J7 WnT
Independence Dr 527-F8 PeT
Independence Sq 528-H9 FT
Independence Way 390-D10 CTH
India Course Rd 598-B2 CTJ
Indian Cove Rd 457-J1 PTM
Indian Cr Rd 462-F1 L
Indian Cr Rd S 563-H3; 564-A3, G2 FT
Indian Lake Blvd 428-E10 L
Indian Lake Blvd N 428-B9 L
Indian Lake Blvd S 428-B10 L
Indian Lake Blvd W 428-B9 L
Indian Lake Rd 428-C8, D9 L
Indian Pipe Trace 528-E7 PeT
Indian Pointe Dr 428-C7 L
Indian Tr 392-B6 Ca
Indiana Ave DN-D2; 493-C6, D7 CTM
Indiana Rd 557-K5, K7 GT
Indiana St 523-G8 P
Indiana St N 557-K10; 558-A10; 592-A1 M
Indiana St S 592-A3 M
Indianapolis Ave 493-D1, D3 CTM; 459-D10 WTM
Indianapolis Rd 388-B8; 422-E1 ET; 558-B10; 592-B2 M; 388-B8 PTB
Indianapolis State Rd 489-C9 A; 489-C9 WaT
Indianola Ave 425-J8; 459-J4, J6, J7 WTM
Indianpipe Cir 392-C5 Ca
Indigo Ct 393-F9 F
Indigo La 394-A2 F
Indigo Way 425-B10 WTM
Industrial Blvd 458-D8, D9 PTM
Industrial Dr 391-J4 Ca
Industrial Pkwy 461-G6 L
Indy La 491-A4 WnT
Ingall Rd 599-A5 STS
Ingleside La 528-B9 PeT
Inglewood Ct 595-A4 WTJ
Ingomar St 491-J9, J10; 525-J1 WnT
Ingram St 493-J4 CTM
Inisheer Ct 560-J6 PeT
Inland Cir 490-A8 A
Inland Dr 490-A8 A; 457-E7, F7 PTM
Inlet Dr 325-E4 C
Inlove Ct 456-G8 LTH
Innisbrooke Ave 594-H2 WTJ
Innisbrooke Ct 594-G2 WTJ
Innisbrooke La 394-E10 F; 594-H1 WTJ
Innisbrooke Pl 594-H1 WTJ
Innisbruck Blvd 424-E1 CTH
Insignia Ct 457-C9 WnT
Inspector Rd 458-K6 WTM
International Dr 424-F2 CTH
International La 424-F3 PTM
Inv St 531-H5 NP
Inv St 1 531-J6 NP
Inv St 2 357-K3 W
Inv St 4 358-A3 W
Inverness Blvd 424-E1, G2 CTH
Inverness Ct 394-E10 F; 563-C6 FT
Inverness Dr 563-B5 FT
Inverness Pl 595-A7 WTJ
Inverness Way 563-C6 FT
Inverrary Ct 491-A1 WnT
Inverrary Dr 491-A1 WnT
Inwood La 426-F7 WTM
Inwood St DN-B2; 493-B9 CTM
Iona Rd 529-A1 WrT
Iowa St 527-E1, J1; 528-A2, C1, E1, G1 CTM
Ipswich Ct 457-G7 PTM
Ira Ct 560-K4 PeT
Ira Way 391-D3 Ca
Ireland Ct 461-K9 WrT
Ireland Dr 461-K8 LTM; 461-K9 WrT
Iris Ave 492-A8 WnT
Iris Ct 326-C9 N
Irish Hill Dr 389-C8 ET
Irishman Run La 423-D1 ET
Iron Horse La 427-E8 LTM
Iron Liege Rd 560-K7 PeT
Iron Oaks Ct 562-K1 FT
Iron Rock Rd 428-K8 L
Iron Springs Ct 425-H6 WTM
Iron Tr E 490-H5 WnT
Iron Tr W 490-H5 WnT
Iron Wood Tr 595-K4 G
Irongate Cir 389-E9 Z
Irongate Ct 424-B7 PTM
Irongate Dr 389-E9 Z
Ironton St 526-C4 WnT
Ironway Dr 496-B9 WrT
Ironwood Cir 428-F1 F; 324-K7 N
Ironwood Ct 455-J7 B; 392-E4 Ca; 595-K4 G; 424-J4 WTM
Ironwood Dr 455-J7 B; 392-D3 Ca; 592-E1 M; 489-A10 WaT
Ironwood Dr E 455-K8 B; 392-D3 Ca
Ironwood Dr W 455-J8 B; 392-D2 Ca
Iroquois Ct 428-D2 FCT
Irving Ct 494-J8 WrT
Irving St 359-H5 N
Irvington Ave 460-H7, H9 LTM; 426-H9 WTM; 460-H9; 494-H4, H6, H7, H9, H10; 528-H1, H2 WrT
Irwin Ave 461-B7, B8 LTM
Irwin Ct 563-B2 FT
Irwin Dr 495-B6 WrT
Irwin Rd 460-D10 CTM
Irwin St 563-B2 FT; 495-B3, B7; 529-B4 WrT
Irwin Way 391-D4 Ca
Isaac Walton La 557-B3 GT
Isenhour Hills Dr 389-H7 Z
Island Ct 457-C10 WnT
Island Dr 428-J2 FCT; 457-C10 WnT
Island Way 457-C10 WnT
Island Woods Dr 425-H10 WTM
Islander Dr 491-E1 WnT
Islay Ct 560-K7 PeT
Islay Rd 560-K6 PeT
Ivanhoe St 495-A8, H8 WrT
Ivory Ct 562-E6 PeT
Ivory Way 562-C6, E6 PeT
Ivy 596-A4 G
Ivy Ct 496-K10; 530-K1 SCT
Ivy Hill Dr 392-K3 Ca
Ivy Knoll Ct 426-J6 LTM; 426-J6 WTM
Ivy Knoll Dr 426-J6 LTM; 426-J6 WTM
Ivy Knoll La 426-J6 WTM
Ivy La 530-K1 SCT; 459-H3 WTM
Ivy Tech Dr 423-K5 PTM
Ivydale Dr 427-A7 LTM
Ivywood Cir 427-A8 LTM
Ivywood Ct 389-F5 Z
Ivywood Dr 427-A8 LTM

J

Ja Dee La 594-A9 WTJ
Jack St 323-E7 WTH
Jacks La 561-J2 PeT; 357-J7 WTH
Jackson Ct 455-H7 B; 594-J1 WTJ
Jackson Ct S 594-K1 WTJ
Jackson Pl DN-D3; 493-E8 CTM; 594-J1 WTJ
Jackson Rd 560-J10; 594-J1 WTJ
Jackson St 455-G7 B; 593-D3 MTM; DN-A3; 490-J9; 491-D9, F9, J9, K9; 492-A8, B8, G8, J8 WnT
Jaclyn Dr 563-A6 FT
Jacob La 462-A5 L
Jacquaranda St 529-A3 WrT
Jade Cir 424-D6 PTM
Jade Ct 424-D6 PTM
Jaffa Ct Dr E 425-E4 WTM
Jaffa Ct Dr W 425-E4 WTM
Jagged Rock Ct 394-K7 F; 427-H4 LTM
Jamaica Ct 495-H3 WrT
James Ct 455-F7 B; 392-H1 Ca; 389-F8 Z
James Dr 359-K3 N; 523-H1 WaT; 389-F8 Z
James Rd 325-G6, G9 NT
Jameson La 391-C2 CTH
Jamestown Ct 460-K6 LTM
Jamestown Dr 393-F8 F
Jamestown Dr N 393-F7 F
Jamie Ct 461-G7 LTM
Jamieson La 424-F3 PTM
Janean Dr 455-J1 BTH
Janel Cir 563-A6 FT
Janel Ct 563-A5 FT
Janel Dr 563-A6 FT
Janes Cir 594-J1 WTJ
Janet Dr 455-E7 B; 460-E9 CTM; 562-C9 G
Janie Dr 392-B1 Ca
Janson Dr 560-D4 PeT
Jardiniere Rd 429-A10 VT
Jasmine Ct 393-H2 F
Jasmine Dr 592-E2 M; 495-G3 WrT
Jasmine Way 595-A2 WTJ
Jason La 359-E5 N
Jason St 392-B1 Ca
Jasper St 527-J10 PeT
Jay Ct 495-K2 WrT
Jay Dr 495-K2; 496-A2 WrT
Jaywick Dr 393-J10 F
Jean Ann Ct 455-J1 BTH
Jean Dr 461-K9 WrT
Jeanne Ct 496-K8 SCT
Jebediah Rd 423-B6 PTM
Jeff Rd 561-C7 PeT
Jefferson Ave 493-K4; 494-A3, A4, A6, A8 CTM
Jefferson Dr 392-A7 Ca; 523-H5 P
Jefferson Dr E 392-A8 Ca
Jefferson Roundabout 392-H2 Ca
Jefferson St 455-G5, G6, G7, G9 B; 356-D4 WTH
Jeffery Ct 391-H1 Ca
Jeffries Pl 392-H6 Ca
Jekyll Ct 562-D1 PeT
Jellico Blvd 496-G5 WrT
Jemima La 358-H1 N
Jena Dr 325-D9 N
Jene Ct 456-J9 WnT
Jenkins St 494-D4 CTM
Jennie La 593-C5 MTM
Jennifer Ct 497-B3 BCT
Jennifer Dr 497-B3 BCT; 491-C6 WnT
Jennifer La 497-B3 BCT; 455-H1 BTH
Jennings Dr 392-F4 Ca
Jennings St 460-C10 CTM
Jenny La 494-F8 CTM; 392-B5 Ca
Jennys Rd 458-G6 WTM
Jeremy Ct 392-B1 Ca
Jeremy Dr 392-B1 Ca
Jerkwater Rd 595-D9 WTJ
Jerome Ct 461-K9 WrT
Jerry Ct 457-K4; 458-A4 PTM
Jersey St 357-J4 W
Jessman Rd Dr E 427-D9 LTM
Jessman Rd Dr N 427-D9 LTM
Jessman Rd Dr S 427-D9 LTM
Jessman Rd Dr W 427-D9 LTM
Jessup Blvd 391-G10 CTH
Jessup Rd 523-F2 A; 523-F2 WaT
Jester Ct 457-H2 PTM
Jet Stream Blvd 357-D8 WTH
Jeto Lake Dr 489-C4 WaT
Jett Ct 462-B1 L
Jewel La 390-G10 CTH
Jewell La 426-E8 WTM
Jib Ct 428-E5 LTM
Jill Ct 495-K1 WrT
Jill Dr 495-K1, K2 WrT
Jill St 526-A10 DTM
Jo Ann Ct 594-H1 WTJ
Jo Anna Ct 523-J2 WaT
Joan Ave 455-E7 B
Joan Pl 461-G9 WrT
Joann Ct 391-H1 Ca
Jody Ct 562-D9 G
Jody Dr 562-D9 G
John Ambers La 424-J5 WTM
John Charles Ct 592-J2 MTM
John Glenn Ct 496-B2 WrT
John Jay Dr 462-B9 WrT
John Marshall Dr N 462-B9 WrT
John Muir Dr 426-A6 WTM
John St 391-J1 Ca; 395-D7 FCT; 359-G3 N
Johns Dr 456-K9 WnT
Johnson Ave 494-J7 WrT
Johnson Ct 455-J2 BTH
Johnson Dr 455-E5 B; 392-E2 Ca
Johnson Rd 592-D5 BTM; 427-B9, B10; 461-B1 LTM; 592-D5 M
Johnson St 594-H4 WTJ
Johnstown Ct 561-A7 PeT
Johnwes Dr 525-G8 DTM
Joliet Rd 322-C10; 356-C2, C8 WTH
Jonathan Ct 523-E2 WaT
Jonathan Dr 523-J9 P
Jonathan Trace 461-D3 L
Jonquil Dr 561-E7 PeT
Joppa Rd 557-A10 BTM; 557-A5 GT
Jordan Ct 392-B10 CTH
Jordan Rd 392-B9 CTH; 561-D4 PeT
Joseph Cir 527-K9 PeT
Joseph Dr 527-K9 PeT
Joseph Way 391-D3 Ca
Joshua Dr 392-B1 Ca
Joy Cir 561-H10 G
Joy Dr 561-G10 G
Joyce St 564-E6 FT
Jubilee La 489-G7 A
Judaco Dr 562-C1 PeT
Judan Ct 526-A8 DTM
Judan Dr 526-A8 DTM
Judith Anne Dr 461-K4 L
Judith La 527-D4 PeT
Jules La 422-H7 BTH
Julian Ave 494-G7 CTM; 494-G7, K7; 495-A7, B7 WrT
Julie La 458-E4 PTM
Juliet Dr 489-F7 A
Julietta St 530-G2 WrT
Jumper La 391-C10 CTH
Juniper Ct 426-E7 WTM
Justin Ave 495-E4 WrT
Justin Ct 495-E4 WrT
Justin La 495-E4 WrT
Justin Morgan Dr 323-K9 WTH
Jutland Ct 426-J3 WTM

K

Kain St 523-F7 P
Kalmar Dr 492-C1 WnT
Kane Ct 393-G5 F
Kankakee Ct 561-D8 PeT
Kankakee St DN-D2; 493-E7 CTM; 326-F4 NT
Kansa Ct 561-E8 PeT
Kansas St 493-D10 CTM; 526-E1 WnT
Kanterbury La 592-E1 M
Kappes St DN-A4; 492-J10; 526-J1 CTM
Kara La 561-F9 G
Karcher St 527-E1 CTM
Karen Dr 389-C8 ET; 564-E1 FT; 461-B5 L; 490-G4 WaT
Karley Dr 592-B5 BTM
Karri Ct 496-B4 WrT
Karrington Blvd 592-F2 M
Karstadt Dr 459-D5 WTM
Kartman Dr 531-B3 SCT
Karyn Dr 489-F5 WaT
Kasan Ct 458-F1 PTM
Kasteel Way 426-K4 LTM
Katelyn Ct 458-E5 PTM
Katelyn Dr 458-E6 PTM
Katelyn La 458-E6 PTM
Katelyn Way 458-E5 PTM
Kathcart Way 457-C5 PTM
Katherine Dr 461-B6 L; 561-D6 PeT
Kathi Dr 528-E9 BG
Kathie Ct 594-H7 WTJ
Kathleen Ave 489-C6 WaT; 490-H1 WnT
Kathryn Dr 524-H9 GT; 459-A3 WTM
Kathy Dr 455-H1 BTH
Kathy La 490-G10; 524-G1 WaT
Kathy St 596-D6 G
Katie Ct 557-F1 P
Kauai Ct 561-B6 PeT
Kautsky Dr 561-H2 PeT
Kay Ellen Dr 496-A2 WrT
Kayak Ct 428-F5 LTM
Kayenta Ct 461-H10 WrT
Kayla Dr 491-A4 WnT
Kayser Ct 461-B3 LTM
Kealing Ave 494-D5, D6, D7, D10; 528-D1 CTM; 528-D6; 562-D1 PeT
Kealing Ct 562-D1 PeT
Keating Dr 425-A8 WTM
Kebil Ct 458-A10 WnT
Kebil Dr 458-A10 WnT
Keefe Ct 462-A8 WrT
Keeler Dr 489-F7 A
Keeley Ct 393-K6 F
Keeneland Ct 391-H9 CTH; 423-G8 PTM
Keensburg Ct 459-A3 WTM
Keensburg Dr 459-A3 WTM
Keevers Dr 456-J5 PTM
Keith Ct 389-F8 Z
Keith Dr 389-F8 Z
Keller Ct 458-A5 PTM
Keller Dr 523-J9 P
Keller La 593-B8 MTM
Kellum Ct 559-J3 DTM
Kellum Dr 559-J4 DTM; 558-G6 GT
Kelly Ann Way 324-H6 N
Kelly Ct 490-G10 WaT
Kelly Dr 531-H4 SCT
Kelly La 326-E7 NT; 426-G5 WTM
Kelly Loop 526-F3 WnT
Kelly Pl 393-E6 F
Kelly St 527-D3, H3, J3; 528-A3, C3 CTM; 526-A3, E3 WnT
Kelsey Cir 458-F1 PTM
Kelsey Ct 427-J1 F
Kelsey Dr 458-F1 PTM
Kelsey La 393-G3 F
Kelso Dr 561-B6 PeT
Kemble Ct 393-F6 F
Kemp Cir 496-H4 Cu
Kemp Ct 489-B10 WaT
Kempton Pl 393-C10 F
Ken La 531-K2 SCT
Kenasaw Ct 561-D8 PeT
Kendale Ct 490-K6 WnT
Kenetta Ct 393-F6 F
Kenilworth Dr 458-F6 PTM; 458-F6 WTM
Kenley Ave 559-A4 DTM
Kenmore Rd 461-A5, A6, A7 LTM; 495-A5, A7, A9; 529-A4, A5 WrT
Kennard Ct 559-B10 MTM
Kennedy La 425-C10; 459-C1 WTM
Kenneth Ave 461-C7, C8 LTM
Kennington St 527-F1 CTM
Kenny Stewart La 359-K1 N
Kenova Dr 561-E7 PeT
Kenruth Dr 458-K1 WTM
Kensington Blvd 523-C8 P
Kensington Cir 523-C8 P
Kensington Ct 596-A2 G; 489-G5 WaT
Kensington Dr 359-H10 NT; 461-C9 WrT
Kensington Pk Rd 596-A2 G
Kensington Pl 391-J3 Ca
Kensington Rd 392-F6 Ca
Kensington Way N 523-C8 P
Kensington Way S 523-C8 P
Kensworth Dr 462-C1 L
Kent Ave 461-H3, J3 L
Kent Ct 391-C5 CTH; 596-C5 G
Kent La 391-H1 Ca
Kentallen Ct 428-H5 L
Kentstone Dr 424-E10 PTM
Kentucky Ave 558-F9 BTM; DN-B4; 493-B10; 526-K2 CTM; 525-F10, J8; 526-A7, C6; 558-J6; 559-D2 DTM; 558-F9 GT; 523-J8, J9 P
Kenwood Ave DN-D4; 459-E9, E10; 493-E1, E3, E10 CTM; 425-E3, E4, E6; 459-E5, E7, E9 WTM
Kenwood Cir 425-E4 WTM
Kenwood Ct 425-E4 WTM
Kenwood Dr 596-C4 G; 425-D3 WTM
Kenwood Pl 393-A6 Ca
Kenyon Ave 461-A7 LTM; 495-A3 WrT
Kenyon Dr 461-B6 L; 461-B4, B5 LTM; 529-A4, B5 WrT
Kenyon St 495-A7 WrT
Kenzie Ct 462-C2 L
Keough Ct 428-E7 L
Keough Dr 428-E7 L
Kercheval Dr 529-D5 FT; 461-D5, D6, D9 L; 461-D9 LTM; 461-D9 WrT
Kerria Ct 392-F8 Ca
Kerry Ct 357-F10 WTH
Kerry Dr 529-G8 FT
Kerwood Dr 426-A3 WTM
Kerwood La 455-E5 LTH
Kessler Blvd Dr E 459-E3; 460-A2, E2 WTM
Kessler Blvd Dr N 458-G5 WTM; 458-G5; 492-G4 WnT
Kessler Blvd Dr W 458-G4; 459-A3 WTM
Kessler Common Blvd 460-F3 WTM
Kessler La 460-E3 WTM
Kessler La Dr E 460-E2, F2 WTM
Kessler Ridge Dr 460-D2 WTM
Kessler View Dr 460-F3 WTM
Kesslerwood Ct 458-K4 WTM
Keston Cir 427-C10 LTM
Kestrel Ct 457-D7 PTM
Keswick Ct 489-B10 WaT
Keswick Rd 492-C1 WnT
Ketcham St 492-G7 WnT
Kettering Way 491-B3 WnT
Kevin Ct 389-F8 Z
Kevin Dr 461-K5 L; 389-F8 Z
Kevin Way 457-K8; 458-A8 PTM
Kewanna Ct 559-D10 MTM
Key Harbour Dr 428-F4 LTM
Key La 456-J9 WnT
Keyhole Cove Ct 561-H9 G
Keystone Ave 392-B2, B8 CTH; 460-A7; 494-A2, A3, A4, A6, A8, A9, A10; 528-A3 CTM; 392-B2, B8; 426-B4 Ca; 528-A6, A10; 562-A1, A2, A3, A9 PeT; 426-A10, B4; 460-A2, A7 WTM
Keystone Crossing 426-B5, C5 WTM
Keystone Ct 460-A5 WTM
Keystone Lakes Dr 527-K5; 528-A5 PeT
Keystone Lakes Way 528-A5 PeT
Keystone Way 392-B7 Ca
Keystone Way E 392-B7 Ca
Keyway Dr 595-B7 WTJ
Kickapoo Tr 495-D8 WrT
Kiefer Ct 528-F8 BG
Kiel Ave 457-H9; 491-H9, H10; 525-H1 WnT
Kilbourne Dr 561-J10 G
Kildare Ave 494-G4 CTM
Kildeer Ct 389-C6 ET
Kildeer Dr 562-E4 PeT
Kileen Rd 428-J9 L
Kilkenny Ct 457-C6 PTM
Killarney Ct 455-A1 B
Killarney Dr 560-K6 PeT
Killarney Way 560-K5 PeT
Killdeer Pl 392-G4 Ca
Killian Dr 528-F7, F9 BG; 592-B4 M
Killington Cir 394-E9 F
Killingworth Ct 428-A5 LTM
Kilmer La 427-E7 LTM; 426-H7 WTM
Kilroy Dr 494-A2 CTM
Kilworth Ct 462-D8 LTM
Kim Way 528-J9 FT
Kimberly Dr 427-E6 LTM
Kimberly La 523-G3 WaT
Kimbrough Dr 596-B5 G
Kimbrough La 455-H10 B; 391-J5 Ca
Kimcoe La 457-B5 PTM
Kimkris Ct 423-E8 PTM
Kimlough Cir 425-H6 WTM
Kimlough Dr 425-H6, H7 WTM
Kincaid Dr 393-H10; 427-G1 F
Kincardine Ct E 424-J7 WTM
Kinder Oak Dr 359-C2 N
Kindig Rd 561-D5 PeT
King Arthur Ct 392-E7 Ca; 496-B1 WrT
King Arthur Dr 496-D1 WrT
King Ave 458-H2, H3 WTM; 492-H5, H7 WnT
King Ct 489-F7 A
King Dr 425-C7 WTM
King George Dr 425-D9 WTM
King James Ct 561-F3 PeT
King John Ct 561-E3 PeT
King John Dr 561-E3 PeT
King Lear Ct 457-H2 PTM
King Lear Dr 457-G2 PTM
King Lear La 457-H2 PTM
King Table Ct 496-D1 WrT
King Table Dr 496-B1 WrT
Kingbridge St 494-E9; 528-E2 CTM
Kingfisher Cir 428-H4 LTM
Kingfisher Ct 428-H4 LTM
Kingfisher Pl 392-H4 Ca
Kinglet Ct 457-D8 PTM
Kingman Cir 427-D10 LTM
Kingman Dr 461-D5, D6, D7, D8 L; 427-D10 LTM
Kingmeadow Ct 561-D9 PeT
Kingrail Way 392-H3 Ca
Kings Cove Ct 425-A4 WTM
Kings Cross 489-G4 WaT
Kings Cross Ct 359-K7 N
Kings Ct 489-E9 A; 425-B5 WTM
Kings Mill Dr 390-G10 CTH
Kings Mill Rd 561-K10 G
Kings Pt Ct 357-D9 WTH
Kingsbee Ct 457-G10 WnT
Kingsboro Cir 461-K6 L
Kingsboro Ct 461-K6 L
Kingsboro Dr 461-K6 L
Kingsbury Dr 391-D4 Ca
Kingscross Ct 462-A9 WrT
Kingsford Dr 424-J9 WTM
Kingslane Dr 360-A2 N
Kingsley Dr 425-K9, K10; 459-K4, K7 WTM
Kingsley La 393-J10 F
Kingsport Rd 427-C8 LTM
Kingston Cir 455-J3 B
Kingston Commons 561-B5 PeT
Kingston Ct 394-B9 F
Kingston Dr 528-E1 CTM; 395-B10 FCT
Kingston St 489-K9 A
Kingsview Dr 592-D3 M
Kingsway Ct 592-F2 M
Kingsway Dr 489-E6 A; 460-A5 WTM; 489-E6 WaT
Kingswood Cir 461-C1 LTM
Kingswood Ct 461-C1 LTM
Kingswood Dr 392-F9 Ca; 427-C10, D10; 461-D1 LTM
Kingussie Ct 457-E7 PTM
Kinlock Dr 427-J8 LTM
Kinnear Ave 459-K10 CTM; 459-K10 WTM
Kinnerton Dr 457-F5 PTM
Kinnett La 458-D5 PTM
Kinser Ct 393-E7 F
Kinsey Ave 357-F2 WTH
Kinzer Ave 392-B5 Ca
Kiowa Ct 462-C10 WrT
Kiowa Dr 462-C10 WrT
Kiowa La 428-E1 FCT
Kira Ct 462-C2 L
Kirk Allen Dr 462-A5 L
Kirk Dr 490-K8 WnT
Kirk Dr E 491-A8 WnT
Kirk Dr W 490-K7, K8 WnT
Kirk Gate Ct 392-D1 Ca
Kirkham Ct 425-A3 WTM
Kirkham La 425-A4 WTM
Kirkham Rd 425-A4 WTM
Kirkwood Club Dr 525-E10 DTM
Kirkwood Ct 561-E9 G
Kirkwood Dr 496-G6 Cu; 523-J10 P
Kirsch Dr 456-D10 LTH
Kiser Pointe 427-G4 LTM
Kissel Rd 388-K10 ET; 422-J3 PTM
Kitchen Rd 592-K7, K10 MTM
Kitley Ave 461-B6 L; 427-B9; 461-B8 LTM; 461-B9; 495-B3, B8, B10; 529-B2, B5 WrT
Kittley Rd 530-G5 FT; 530-G3 WrT
Kittrell Ave 425-K2 CTH
Kitty Hawk Ct 392-E9 Ca
Kivet Ct 462-B8 LTM
Klay Ct 557-J8 GT
Klepfer Sch Rd 394-F10 F; 394-F7 FCT
Kline Dr 461-E9 WrT
Klintilloch Ct 528-E8 PeT
Knaphill Ct 392-E2 Ca
Knapp Rd 563-J7 FT
Knapps Ct 595-H1 G
Knapsbury La 462-E8 LTM
Knickerbocker Pl 426-D4 WTM
Knickerbocker Way 426-D4 WTM
Knight Dr 390-G9 CTH
Knight La 594-E4 WTJ
Knightbridge Ct 489-G4 WaT
Knights Bridge Blvd 426-E3 WTM
Knights Ct 426-K3 LTM
Knightsbridge La 394-B8, B9 F
Knob Cr Overlook 456-K8 PTM
Knobhill Ct 558-E5 GT
Knoblin La 596-B1 G
Knobwood Dr 424-J9 WTM
Knoll Crest Ct 458-G5 WTM
Knoll Crossing 393-G3 F
Knoll Ct 324-J6 N
Knoll La 455-G10 B
Knoll Ridge 393-H4 F
Knoll Top Dr 562-E2 PeT
Knoll Valley La 427-G9 LTM
Knollcreek Cir 427-G10 LTM
Knollcreek Ct 427-G10 LTM
Knollgate Ct 424-C7 PTM
Knollridge Ct 496-F6 Cu
Knollridge La 496-F7 Cu
Knollton Ct 393-G4 F
Knollton Rd 424-J10; 458-J1, J2, J4 WTM
Knollview Ct 427-G10 LTM
Knollway Ct 393-H3 F
Knollwood Dr 596-A3 G; 458-G5 WTM
Knollwood Pl 393-H4 F
Knotty Pine Ct 562-C8 PeT
Knox Cir 596-D4 G
Knox St 527-G5, H5, J5 PeT
Knoxville Dr 559-J3 DTM
Knue Rd 427-A6, A8 LTM
Knyghton Rd 460-J2 LTM; 426-J10; 460-J2 WTM
Koefoot Dr 491-E4 WnT
Koehne St DN-B2; 492-K3, K4, K7 CTM
Kokomo La 491-F10 WnT

Kolby Ct 324-H6 N
Koldyke Dr 393-C6 F
Kollman Ct 525-F9 DTM
Kollman Rd 525-F8, F10 DTM
Kosh Ct 490-G4 WaT
Koster Dr 457-G3 PTM
Kousa Dr 491-A4 WnT
Koweba La 494-A8 CTM
Kozy Dr 526-B5 WnT
Kramer Ct 462-B7 LTM
Krannert Cir DN-B2; 493-B7 CTM
Krewson Ave 523-F8 P
Kristen Ct 462-F10 WrT
Kristen Dr 494-H2 WrT
Kristen Dr E 494-H1 WrT
Kristen Dr W 494-H1 WrT
Kristen Erin Ct 490-K4 WnT
Kristen La 462-F10 WrT
Kruggle Ct 427-H4 LTM
Kungsholm Dr 426-J2 WTM
Kurtis Blvd 491-G4 WnT
Kylan Ct 393-G5 F
Kyle Ct 393-K10 F; 462-F10 WrT

L

La Canada Blvd 393-G4 DTH
La Crosse Ct 462-C8 WrT
La Fleur Ct 528-K10 FT
La Fleur Way 528-K10 FT
La Fontaine Ct 462-C8 WrT
La Grange Ct 462-C9 WrT
La Habra Cir 428-G6 LTM
La Habra La 428-F5 LTM
La Pas Tr 458-B1 PTM
La Reforma Ct 596-E3 G
La Reforma Dr 596-E3 G
La Tour Cir 423-F7 PTM
Lace Bark Dr 462-D9 WrT
Lace Bark La 462-D9 WrT
Lackwanna Ct 561-B7 PeT
Laclede Ct 526-A9 DTM
Laclede St 526-A9 DTM; 492-B10 WnT
Lacorrida Ct 562-B8 PeT
Lacorrida Dr 562-B8 PeT
Lacosta La 358-H3 N
Lacy Ct 455-G8 B; 562-C6 PeT; 594-H1 WTJ
Lacy Dr 562-C6 PeT; 594-J1 WTJ
Lacy La 594-H1, J1 WTJ
Lacy Pl 594-H1 WTJ
Lacy Way 594-H1 WTJ
Ladson St 394-A5 F
Ladywood Dr 460-F4 WTM
Lafayette Rd 359-F2 N; 422-H3; 423-A5, C9; 457-F1, J5; 458-A6 PTM; 458-C9; 492-E1, H3 WnT
Lafayette St 326-J1 WRT
Lagora La 458-A9 WnT
Lagrotte Dr 529-H6 FT
Laguna Dr 424-K6 WTM
Laguna La 596-F4 G
Lahr Ct 427-G4 LTM
Lakawanna Rd 324-C10 WTH
Lake Cir 393-G7 F
Lake Cir Dr 424-G5 PTM
Lake Crest Dr 496-A2 WrT
Lake Crossing 595-B8 WTJ
Lake Ct 595-C2 WTJ; 460-B4 WTM
Lake Dr 494-D9 CTM; 594-J9; 595-C2 WTJ
Lake Dr E 455-G8 B
Lake Dr N 455-F8 B
Lake Dr S 455-F8 B
Lake Dr W 455-F8 B
Lake Forest Dr 424-C2 PTM
Lake Forest Pkwy 392-H7 Ca
Lake Front Dr 428-E4 LTM
Lake Kessler Ct 460-J2 LTM
Lake Lair Dr 558-C5 GT
Lake Nora Ct N 425-G4, H3 WTM
Lake Nora Ct S 425-G4, H4 WTM
Lake Nora Dr E 425-H4 WTM
Lake Nora Dr N 425-G3 WTM
Lake Nora Dr S 425-G4 WTM
Lake Nora Dr W 425-G4 WTM
Lake of the Pines Dr 490-K4 WnT
Lake Pk Blvd 528-B8 PeT
Lake Plaza Dr 426-J10 LTM
Lake Pointe Dr 392-H6 Ca
Lake Pt Cir 595-G2 G
Lake Pt Ct 427-G6 LTM
Lake Pt La 595-F2 G
Lake Pt Way 427-G6 LTM; 324-J7 N
Lake Rd 560-D6, E7 PeT; 459-C6 WTM
Lake Run 393-C9 F
Lake Run Ct 595-B7 WTJ
Lake Run Dr 595-B7 WTJ
Lake Shore Dr 460-B5 WTM; 489-E10 WaT
Lake Shore E 489-E9 WaT
Lake Side Cir 595-K4 G
Lake Springfield Rd 423-D9 PTM

Lake St 455-J10 LTH
Lake Terr Ct 324-J7 N; 496-A3 WrT
Lake Terr Dr 496-A3 WrT
Lake Terr Dr N 496-A3 WrT
Lake Terr Dr S 496-A3 WrT
Lake Terr Dr W 496-A3 WrT
Lake Terr Pl 496-A3 WrT
Lake Valley Ct 324-J7 N
Lake View Dr 389-C8 ET; 489-C4 WaT
Lakefield Ct 458-C3 PTM
Lakefield Dr 458-C3 PTM
Lakefield Trace 458-C3 PTM
Lakeknoll Dr 426-K10 LTM
Lakeland Blvd 456-G3 LTH
Lakeland Ct 391-G2 CTH; 456-G3 LTH
Lakeland Dr 428-B2 F; 426-J10 LTM; 426-J10 WTM
Lakeland La 456-G3, G4 LTH
Lakemore St 455-J6 B
Lakeridge Dr 456-K7 PTM
Lakeshire La 424-G2 PTM
Lakeshore Cir 455-K7 B; 426-F6 WTM
Lakeshore Ct 392-C8 Ca; 595-C7 WTJ; 426-G5 WTM
Lakeshore Dr E 392-D9, D10; 426-D2 Ca
Lakeshore Dr W 392-C10 Ca
Lakeshore Pl 455-K8 B; 392-D10 Ca; 426-F5 WTM
Lakeshore Tr E 426-G6 WTM
Lakeshore Tr W 426-G6 WTM
Lakeside Dr 393-D7 F; 524-A8 P; 423-D9, F9 PTM
Lakeside Green Dr 428-B2 F
Lakeside Pl 393-E7 F
Lakeside Woods Cir 423-F9 PTM
Lakeside Woods Dr 423-F9 PTM
Laketon Dr 426-K10 LTM
Laketree Dr 491-H6 WnT
Lakeview Ct 392-C10 Ca
Lakeview Dr 392-C9 Ca; 592-J3 MTM; 359-E1, G2 N; 359-E1 NT; 491-G7, H7 WnT
Lakeview La 491-H7 WnT
Lakeview Pkwy 393-K9 F
Lakeview Pkwy Dr S 423-J9 PTM
Lakeview Pkwy Dr W 423-J9 PTM
Lakevista Dr 393-E6 F
Lakewind Ct 428-B3 LTM
Lakewind Dr 428-B3 LTM
Lakewood Cir 389-F4 Z
Lakewood Dr 455-K7 B; 558-D5 GT; 490-D1 LTH; 428-B5 LTM; 389-E4 Z
Lakewood Dr E 426-C1 Ca
Lakewood Dr N 426-C1 Ca
Lakewood Dr S 455-K8 B
Lakewood Dr W 426-C2 Ca
Lakeworth Dr 426-J10 WTM
Lambardi Dr 523-G4 WaT
Lambert St 526-H1 CTM; 525-F1, J1; 526-E1, F1, H1 WnT
Lambeth Walk 392-F6 Ca
Lamboll St 394-A4 F
Lamira La 491-A3 WnT
Lammermoor La 491-B3 WnT
Lamong Rd 322-H3 AT; 322-H9 WTH
Lana Ct 530-E10 FT; 497-B8 SCT
Lanarkshire Dr 595-C6 WTJ
Lancashire Ct 425-A5 WTM
Lancaster Ct 392-F7 Ca; 424-K4 WTM
Lancaster La 389-E7 Z
Lancaster Rd 424-K5 WTM
Lancelot Dr 458-G5 WTM
Lancelot La 392-E5 Ca
Lancer La 461-E4 L
Landau La 561-G6 PeT
Landborough Dr N 427-A10 LTM
Landborough Dr S 427-A10 LTM
Landersdale Rd 592-G3 BTM; 592-G3, J2; 593-C2 MTM
Landings Cir 426-A8 WTM
Landings Dr 428-G1 FCT; 426-A7 WTM
Landmark Dr 424-J8 WTM
Landmark Tr 394-C5 F
Landola La 526-A5 WnT
Landover La 394-H10 F
Lands End Cir 325-D5 N
Lands End La 427-A10 LTM
Landsdowne Dr 359-K7 N
Landsdowne La 392-C4 Ca
Landser Ct 392-F3 Ca
Landser Pl 392-F3 Ca
Lane Rd 462-H4, K5 BCT
Lanett Ct 528-F8 BG
Langley Ave 493-K4; 494-A4 CTM
Langley Ct 391-H2 CTH
Langley Dr 391-H2 CTH

Langsdale Ave 493-C3 CTM
Langston Dr 424-D8 PTM
Langwood Ct 424-C7 PTM
Langwood Dr 424-D7 PTM
Lansburgh Cir 456-G9 WnT
Lansburgh Ct 456-G9 WnT
Lansdowne Ct 490-K6 WnT
Lansdowne Dr 393-G4 F
Lansdowne Rd 490-K5, K7, K8 WnT
Lansing Pl DN-B2; 493-B9 CTM
Lansing St DN-B2; 493-A7 CTM
Lantern Dr 594-K1 WTJ
Lantern Farm Ct 393-H4 F
Lantern Farm Dr 393-H4 F
Lantern Forest Ct 427-H8 LTM
Lantern La 391-H4 Ca; 427-H8 LTM
Lantern Rd 393-H4, H7 DTH; 393-H7, H9 F; 427-H8, H9, J7 LTM
Lantern Rd N 393-H5 DTH; 393-H5 F
Lantern Rd S 393-H10; 427-H2 F
Lantry Ct 562-D4 PeT
Lanyard Ct 325-F1 C
Lanyard Dr 325-F1 C
Lapinta Dr 462-A4 L
Lappin Ct 496-D3 WrT
Larch St 493-K5 CTM
Laredo Ct 357-E10 WTH
Laredo Dr 391-H2 CTH
Laredo St 528-J10 FT
Laredo Way 357-E10 WTH
Laredo Way N 357-F10 WTH
Larissa Pl 392-K6 Ca
Lark Ct 391-J4 Ca
Lark Dr 391-J4 Ca
Lark Spurn La 390-E8 CTH
Larkfield Ct 424-K7 WTM
Larkshall Rd 427-B9 LTM
Larkspur Cir 392-B4 Ca
Larkspur Dr 489-H5 WaT
Larkspur Trace 528-E7 PeT
Larman Ct 562-B7 PeT
Larman Dr 562-A7 PeT
Larnie La 495-G2 WrT
Larrabee St 531-H5 NP
Lasalle Ct 460-C8 WTM
Lasalle La 392-C10 Ca
Lasalle St 460-C10; 494-C1, C2, C4, C5, C8, C9; 528-C1 CTM; 528-C7, C9, C10 PeT; 426-C8; 460-C3, C5, C6, C7, C8 WTM
Lasso Dr 456-D10 LTH
Latona Ct 457-J1 PTM
Latona Dr 423-J10 PTM
Latonia La 391-H9 CTH
Lattice Ct 424-D2 CTH
Lauck La 527-E6 PeT
Laughlin Dr 495-G2 WrT
Laughner St 388-E2 Wh
Laura Ct 562-D9 G
Laura Dr 562-D9 G
Laura Lynne La 561-E7 PeT
Laureate Ct N 457-B9 WnT
Laureate Ct S 457-B9 WnT
Laurel Ave 389-G9 Z
Laurel Cir 460-E6 WTM
Laurel Cir N 460-E6 WTM
Laurel Cir S 460-E6 WTM
Laurel Ct 393-G4 F
Laurel Dr 561-J5 PeT
Laurel Hall Dr 460-G5, J5 LTM; 460-G5 WTM
Laurel La 325-A8 N
Laurel Lakes Pl 390-H6 CTH
Laurel Leaf La 523-C4 WaT
Laurel Oak Dr 489-E6 A; 428-G8 L
Laurel Oak Pl 458-A4 PTM
Laurel St DN-F4; 493-J10; 527-J1, J2 CTM; 527-J6; 561-J2 PeT
Laurel Valley 455-A3 B
Laurel Valley Dr 427-B5 LTM
Laurel Wood Dr 391-B10; 425-B1 CTH; 595-A4 WTJ
Laurelwood Ct 428-J7 L
Laurelwood Dr 428-H7 L
Lauren Dr 462-F10 WrT
Lauren Kelsey Dr 462-A5 L
Lauren Pass 428-B2 F
Laurens Ct 561-C6 PeT
Laurey Ct 457-C10 WnT
Lava Ct 562-H3 FT
Lava La 562-H3 FT
Laverne Rd 561-D6 PeT
Laverock Rd 459-E3, F2, G1 WTM
Lavonnie Ave 325-H9 NT
Lawndale Ave 559-H4 DTM; 457-H9 PTM; 491-H1 S; 457-H10; 491-H1, H8, H10; 525-H2 WnT
Lawndale Ct 561-K10 G
Lawndale Dr 561-K10; 562-A10; 596-A1 G; 523-J9 P

Lawnhaven Cir 496-C4 WrT
Lawnhaven Ct 496-B4 WrT
Lawnhaven Dr 496-C4 WrT
Lawnview La 492-E3 WnT
Lawnwood Dr 595-K1 G
Lawrence Ave 529-G8 FT; 527-G8, J8, K8; 528-A8 PeT
Lawrence Cir Dr E 525-F8 DTM
Lawrence Cir Dr W 525-G8 DTM
Lawrence Cr 461-E2 L
Lawrence Ct 528-B8 PeT
Lawrence Dr 460-K3; 461-A3 LTM
Lawrence Rd 392-C5 Ca
Lawrence St 493-K3 CTM
Lawson La 560-G10 WTJ
Lawton Ave 527-J2 CTM
Lawton Loop Dr E 461-H4 L
Lawton Loop Dr W 461-H4 L
Layli Ct 592-J2 MTM
Layman Ave 460-J8 LTM; 426-J9 WTM; 460-J10; 494-J1, J4, J5, J7; 528-J2 WrT
Layton Mills Ct N 559-A10 MTM
Lazy Hollow Dr 455-J6 B
Lazy Hollow La 391-D1 CTH
Lazy La 595-D1 WTJ
Le Harve Dr 460-E2 WTM
Lea La 595-G3 WTJ
Leaf La 523-D3 WaT
Leander La 428-F6 LTM
Learning Tree Rd 594-K2 WTJ
Leases Corner Dr 558-F9 GT
Leather Wood Dr 595-K4 G
Leatherbury La 458-E9 WnT
Ledgerock Ct 394-J7 F
Ledgestone Cir 394-J7 F
Ledgestone Ct 462-C1 L
Ledgestone Dr 462-C1 L
Ledyard Ct 425-J8 LTM
Lee Ct 325-E3 C; 461-G5 L
Lee Dr 565-E8 MTS; 562-A5 PeT
Lee Rd 428-A10; 461-K2, K3; 462-A1 L
Lee St DN-A4; 492-K10; 526-K1 CTM
Leeds Ave 494-B9 CTM
Leeds Cir 391-D4 CTH
Leeds Ct 389-F6 Z
Leeward Blvd 428-A3, B3 LTM
Leeward Ct 428-C3 LTM
Legacy Ct 393-H9 F
Legare St 394-A5 F
Legend La 457-G7 PTM
Legion La 490-K10 WnT
Legrande Ave 527-E2, J2; 528-A2 CTM; 526-A2 WnT
Lehigh Ct 424-F3 PTM
Lehr Rd 592-A10 BTM
Lehr St 361-D6 WyT
Leichester Ct 359-J10 NT
Leisure Ct 595-D1 WTJ
Leisure La 561-C9, C10; 595-C1, D2 WTJ
Leisure Manor 526-A5 WnT
Leiters Ford Ct 559-C10 MTM
Leland Ave 494-G10; 528-G1 WrT
Leland St 460-G9; 494-G3, G4, G6 WrT
Lema Cir 496-D2 WrT
Lema Ct 496-D3 WrT
Lemans Ct 459-J5 WTM
Lemans Dr 459-H6 WTM
Lemar La 490-H6 WnT
Lemode Ct 424-F4 PTM
Lemont St 564-F6 FT
Lendsmith Cir 458-G1 PTM
Lenna Ct 461-H7 LTM
Lennington Dr 461-A8 LTM
Lenora St 491-D9 WnT
Lenox La 391-G7 CTH; 424-G5 PTM
Lenwood St 394-A5 F
Leo Dr 462-E8 LTM
Leon St DN-E2; 493-G7 CTM
Leonard Rd 531-G2 SCT
Leonard St DN-E4; 493-G10; 527-G1 CTM
Leone Ct 461-B4 LTM
Leone Dr 461-B6 L; 461-B5 LTM
Leone Pl 461-B5 L
Leota St DN-F3, F4; 493-J8, J9 CTM
Lepart Ct 423-G5 PTM
Leroy Rd 490-C1 LTH
Lesabre Dr 458-A9 PTM
Lesley Ave 460-J6, J7, J8 LTM; 426-J9 WTM; 460-J10; 494-J1, J3, J5, J7 WrT
Lesley La 422-G7 BTH
Lesta Ct 560-K4 PeT
Lester St 459-C5 WTM
Letterman Ave 462-B2 L
Lewis Dr 592-A10 BTM; 562-C9 G
Lewis Rd 427-E10 LTM
Lewis St DN-F1; 493-H5 CTM; 523-E8 P

Lexington Ave DN-E4, F4; 493-G9, H9; 494-A10, E9 CTM; 494-G10; 495-E9, J9 WrT
Lexington Blvd 392-A5 Ca
Lexington Ct 389-E9 Z
Lexington Dr 391-H9 CTH; 389-D9 Z
Lexington La 392-E10 Ca
Lexington St DN-E4; 493-G9 CTM
Liberty Cr Dr 457-J3, J4 PTM
Liberty Cr Dr N 457-J3 PTM
Liberty Cr Dr W 457-J4 PTM
Liberty Cr Pkwy 457-J4 PTM
Liberty Crossing Dr 457-H4 PTM
Liberty Crossing Way 457-H4 PTM
Liberty La 557-J8 GT; 526-A5 WnT
Liberty Tr 523-J6 P
Libra La 462-E8 LTM
Library Blvd 595-E3 G
Library Pk Dr 595-E4 G
Lichtenburg Rd 496-A10 WrT
Lick Cr Cir 527-G8 PeT
Lick Cr Ct 527-G8 PeT
Lick Cr Dr 528-J2 WrT
Lick Cr Pkwy Dr S 527-H9 PeT
Lickridge Ct 528-D8 PeT
Lickridge La Dr N 528-D8 PeT
Lickridge La Dr S 528-D8 PeT
Lida La 563-H1 FT
Lieber Rd 425-B7, B8; 459-B4 WTM
Lighthorse Dr 490-K9 WnT
Lighthouse Pt 325-F1 C
Lighthouse Way 428-C3 LTM
Lightship Ct 393-D9 F
Lilac Cir 595-A2 WTJ
Lilac Ct 324-J6 N
Lilac Dr 561-K8; 562-A8 PeT
Lilac La 497-G8 SCT
Lillian Ct 531-A5 SCT
Lillians Ct 562-H3 FT
Lilly Lake Dr 457-C1 PTM
Lilly Lake Tr 457-C1 PTM
Lily Dale Ct N 558-K10 MTM
Lily La 458-A5 PTM
Lima Ct 562-D7 PeT
Lima Dr E 562-D7 PeT
Lima Dr N 562-D7 PeT
Limbach Cir 428-E8 L
Limbach Ct 428-E8 L
Limberlost Dr 392-G5 Ca
Limberlost Trace 392-G4 Ca
Limberpine Dr 462-D8 WrT
Limerick Ct 427-A4 LTM
Limestone Ct 562-H2 FT
Limestone Dr 394-J6 F; 562-H2 FT
Limestone St DN-B2; 493-A7 CTM
Lin Rd 395-J9 FCT
Lincoln Ave 455-G6 B
Lincoln Blvd 426-A2 CTH; 425-K7 WTM
Lincoln Cir 456-J8 PTM
Lincoln Ct 392-A5 Ca; 393-H8 F; 458-F6 PTM; 458-F6 WTM
Lincoln Dr 455-G6 B; 325-F3 C; 359-J1 N
Lincoln La 458-G2 WTM
Lincoln Rd 458-F6, F8 PTM; 491-J4 S; 458-F6, F8 WTM; 458-F10; 492-F1 WnT
Lincoln St 527-F1 CTM; 596-B2 G; 523-F7 P
Lincoln Tr 462-E1 L; 557-H3 P
Lincolnwood La 459-C1 WTM
Linda 592-F3 BTM
Linda Cir 529-K1 WrT
Linda Ct 490-G4 WaT
Linda La 594-G7 WTJ; 491-G9, J9 WnT
Linda Leigh La 561-E7 PeT
Linda Way 594-H1 WTJ
Lindbergh Ct 528-D9 PeT
Lindbergh Dr 529-G8 FT; 528-A8, B9, C9 PeT
Lindel Ct 424-F10 PTM
Lindel La 424-E10 PTM
Linden Cir 325-A8 N
Linden Ct 393-E10 F
Linden Dr 561-J3, J5 PeT
Linden Hill Cir 491-J6 WnT
Linden La 392-C2 Ca; 523-K6 P
Linden Ridge Tr 594-J2 WTJ
Linden St 493-J10; 527-J1, J2 CTM; 527-J7 PeT; 389-H8 Z
Linden Wood St 561-K10; 595-K1 G
Lindenwald Dr 527-E6 PeT
Lindenwood Dr 561-G6 PeT
Lindley Ave 491-J9, J10; 525-J1 WnT
Lindsay Ct 491-C7 WnT
Lindsay Dr 491-C7 WnT
Linton La 460-F2 LTM; 460-F2, F6, F7 WTM

Linville Ave 388-F1 Wh
Linwood Ave 460-F9; 494-F4, F5, F7 CTM; 528-F10; 562-F1, F3 PeT
Linwood Dr 460-F4 WTM
Lions Cr Blvd 324-J5 N
Lions Head Dr 425-C8 WTM
Lions Head La 425-C8 WTM
Lionshead La 595-B4 WTJ
Lippard La 456-K10; 490-K1 WnT
Lippincott Way 424-E8 PTM
Liquori Ct 491-D4 WnT
Lisa Ct 462-F10 WrT
Lisa La 523-C7 GT
Liscannor La 560-K6 PeT
Lisering Cir 427-F4 LTM
Lismore Dr E 561-H7 PeT
Lismore Dr N 561-H7 PeT
Lismore Dr S 561-H8 PeT
Lismore Dr W 561-H8 PeT
Lismore La 561-H7 PeT
Little Chicago Rd 324-J7, J10; 358-J3 N; 324-J10; 358-J3 NT
Little Cr Ct 457-K3 PTM
Little Cr Dr 324-H7 N; 457-K4 PTM
Little Eagle 360-B7 NT
Little John Dr 495-E4 WrT
Little Leaf Cir 529-B8 FT
Little Leaf Ct 529-B8 FT
Little Leaf Pl 529-B8 FT
Little League Dr 462-A7 LTM
Little Oak La 564-E4 FT
Little Rock Ct 395-A7 F
Littleton Dr 559-H4 DTM
Live Oak Ct 457-F10 WnT
Live Oak Rd 457-F10 WnT
Liverpool La 462-C2 L
Livingston Ave 492-E5, E7, E9 WnT
Lloyd St 529-J7 FT
Lobo Dr 528-J10 FT
Lochmere Dr 393-A5 Ca
Lockburn Pl 393-H4 F
Lockburn St 526-D6 DTM; 492-D9, D10; 526-D4 WnT
Locke St DN-C1; 493-B6 CTM
Lockefield Ct DN-C2; 493-C6 CTM
Lockefield St DN-C1; 493-C6 CTM
Lockerbie Cir 392-F5 Ca
Lockerbie Cir N DN-E2; 493-G7 CTM
Lockerbie Cir S DN-E2; 493-G7 CTM
Lockerbie Ct 392-F5 Ca
Lockerbie Dr 490-K7; 491-D7 WnT
Lockerbie La 394-B5 F
Lockerbie St DN-E2; 493-G7 CTM
Lockwood Ct 561-B5, D8 PeT
Lockwood La 561-D2, D7, D8, E5 PeT
Lockwood Pl 561-D8 PeT
Locust Cir 562-B2 PeT
Locust Ct 596-E10 NW
Locust Dr 523-K7 P; 562-B2 PeT
Locust La 455-F9 B; 455-F9 LTH; 592-B1 M; 489-J5 WaT
Locust St 389-H8 Z
Lodge Ct 490-H10 WaT
Lodge Dr 490-H10 WaT
Loees Blvd 561-K10; 562-A10 G
Loftus Ct 458-F1 PTM
Log Run Dr N 456-H8, J8 PTM
Log Run Dr S 456-H8 PTM
Logan La 427-J1 F
Logan St 455-J7 B; 359-F3, H3 N
Loganberry Ct 531-F4 SCT
Logo Athletic Ct 495-H2 WrT
Logwood Dr 561-G8 PeT
Lohr Dr 491-F4 WnT
Lohr Way 491-E4 WnT
Lois La 528-F10 PeT
Lois Way 391-D3 Ca
Lola Ct 495-F4 WrT
Loma Ct 393-E10 DTH
Lombard Ct 393-H4 F
Lombardy Pl 461-G9 WrT
Lomond Ct 595-B6 WTJ
Londa La 524-G8 P
London Ct 458-C6 PTM
London Dr 458-C6 PTM
London La 489-F8 A
London Rd 565-C10; 599-C3 MTS; 599-C6, C9 STS
Londonderry Ct 526-B8 DTM
Londonderry Dr 526-B8 DTM
Lone Wolf Dr 462-B6 LTM
Long Ave 490-B5 WaT
Long Boat Dr 427-D3 LTM
Long Branch Dr 563-G6 FT
Long Meadow Ct 424-B10 PTM
Long Meadow Dr 394-B2 F
Long Rifle Rd 561-C10 WTJ

Long River La 559-K3 DTM
Long Run Dr 424-C10 PTM
Long St 389-K4 ET
Long Wharf Dr 462-D9 WrT
Long Wharf Sq 462-C9 WrT
Longacre Dr 527-J9 PeT
Longacre Terr 527-K9 PeT
Longden St 596-C1 G
Longest Dr 393-B4 Ca
Longfellow La 523-G9 P
Longford Dr 524-F1 WaT
Longford Way 325-C6 N
Longhorn Ct 563-A6 FT
Longleaf La 394-A5 F
Longleat Rd 426-C8 WTM
Longmeadow Ct 559-K4; 560-A3 DTM
Longmeadow Dr 559-K2 DTM
Longstone Roundabout 392-G1 Ca
Longstraw Dr 428-H6 L
Longview Bend 455-J5 B
Longview Ct 455-J6 B
Longview Dr 358-H3 N
Longwell Dr 425-H2 WTM
Longwell La 425-H2 WTM
Longwell Pl 425-H2 WTM
Longwood Fountain La 426-F6 WTM
Longwoods Cir 457-F5 PTM
Longwoods Ct 457-F5 PTM
Longwoods Dr 457-F4 PTM
Longworth Ave 461-E7 L
Longworth Pl 461-E7 L
Lookout Ct 560-K8 PeT; 595-C8 WTJ
Lord St DN-E3; 493-G9 CTM
Lorene Cir 563-A5 FT
Lorene Ct 563-B5 FT
Loretta Ct 489-F8 A; 561-J3 PeT
Loretta Dr 559-H3 DTM; 561-E3, J3; 562-A3, B3, C3 PeT
Lori La 461-E9 WrT
Loring Ct 424-A9 PTM
Lorrain Rd 460-C5 WTM
Lorraine St 528-G2 CTM
Los Compos Dr 596-E3 G
Los Robles Rd 393-F4 DTH
Lost Loyalty St 527-B1 CTM
Lost Tree Ct 424-B10 PTM
Lost Tree Dr 424-B10 PTM
Lostpine La 462-D8 WrT
Lothbury Cir 394-H10; 428-H1 F
Lott Dr 458-G1 PTM
Lotus Dr 392-A2 Ca
Lotus La 562-B6 Spt
Loughery La 459-B2 WTM
Louise Ave 456-K10 WnT
Louise Dr 359-K1 N; 561-C6 PeT
Louisiana St DN-D3, E3; 493-E8, F8 CTM
Louisville Dr 461-F7 L
Louisville Way 461-F7 L
Lourdes Ct 460-E2 WTM
Lovage Ct 562-G6 PeT
Love Ave 595-F3 G
Love Ct 391-F2 CTH
Love La 457-K1 PTM
Lovers La 561-H9 G
Lowanna Ct 427-B10 LTM
Lowanna Way 427-B10 LTM
Lowe Cr Dr 594-E7 WTJ
Lowe Dr 461-D4 L
Lowell Ave 494-J7; 495-A7, D7 WrT
Lowell Ct 455-H10 B
Lowell Dr 359-K5 N
Lower Bay La 428-E6 LTM
Lowry Rd 458-B10 WnT
Loy St 492-B5 S
Loyola Ct 393-A9 F
Luann St 325-H9 NT
Lucann St 392-C8 Ca
Lucas Cir 358-B3 WTH
Lucas Dr 358-B3 WTH
Lucas La 525-K10 DTM
Lucas St 388-E1 Wh
Luce Cr Ct 595-H1 G
Lucerne Ave 525-E2 WnT
Lucia Ct 394-E9 F
Lucille Ct 394-A2 F; 557-J1 P
Lucky Cir 528-K8 FT
Lucky Ct 528-K8 FT
Lucky La 561-D10 WTJ
Ludlow Ave 493-K4 CTM
Luett Ave 492-E5, E7, E9 WnT
Luewan Ct 461-K9 WrT
Luewan Dr 461-K9; 462-A9 WrT
Luke Ct 527-J9 PeT
Luke La 527-J9, K9 PeT
Lullwater Dr 496-G1 WrT
Luna La 491-B5 WnT
Lunsford Cir 528-J10 FT
Lunsford Dr 528-J10 FT
Lupine Ct 326-B10 N; 491-G1 WnT
Lupine Dr 457-G10; 491-G1 WnT
Lupine Terr 457-G10 WnT

Luther St 528-A2 CTM
Lutherwood Dr 495-J4 WrT
Lux Rd 395-H9 FCT
Lyle St 461-F6 L
Lynbrook Ct 495-J4 WrT
Lynbrook Dr 495-H4 WrT
Lynch La 426-E6 WTM
Lynchburg Way 496-F5 WrT
Lynhaven Pl 427-E5 LTM
Lynhurst Dr 525-K7, K9 DTM; 491-K3 S; 457-K9; 491-K6; 525-K3 WnT
Lynn Ave 393-H1 DTH
Lynn Ct 357-C10 WTH; 389-E6 Z
Lynn Dr 394-A7 F; 592-K7 MTM; 562-G7 PeT
Lynn Dr E 493-C5 CTM
Lynn Dr W 493-C5 CTM
Lynn St DN-A2; 492-J7 CTM
Lynne La 391-B5 CTH
Lynnfield Ct N 457-F6 PTM
Lynnfield Ct S 457-F6 PTM
Lynnfield Rd 457-F6, G6 PTM
Lynnwood Blvd 392-K6 Ca
Lynton Ct 458-B6 PTM
Lyons Ave 526-C6, C8 DTM; 492-C7, C10; 526-C5 WnT
Lypham Rd 359-H9 N

M

Mabel St 490-H1 WnT
Mabi Way 391-D3 Ca
Mac Ct 528-A4 CTM
MacAllister La 526-C8 DTM
MacAlph St 594-K4 WTJ
MacArthur Ave 457-J10 WnT
MacArthur Ct 457-J10 WnT
MacArthur La 491-J2, J4 S; 457-J10 WnT
MacAtuck Dr 461-A1 LTM
Macaw Pl 392-G3 Ca
Mace Dr 496-H4 Cu
Machleot Dr 596-C3 G
MacKell Ct 424-E8 PTM
MacKenzie Way 526-C8 DTM
Mackinac Ct 561-F6 PeT
MacKlin St 528-C7 PeT
Macy Dr 560-J10 WTJ
Macy Way 560-K10; 594-K1 WTJ
Madden Dr 393-E7 F
Madden La 393-F7 F
Madden Pl 393-E7 F
Madeira Ct 528-C2 CTM
Madeira St 494-C10; 528-C1, C2 CTM
Madeline 393-J9 F
Madelynne Dr 495-J1 WrT
Madison Ave 527-H8 PeT
Madison Ave DN-D4; 493-F8; 527-F2, F4 CTM; 562-B9; 596-B1 G; 527-F4; 561-J1; 562-A6 PeT; 561-J1 Spt
Madison Dr 392-A7 Ca
Madison St 592-A3 M; 326-J1 WRT; 356-D4 WTH
Madison Vill Dr 561-K5 PeT
Madison Vill Dr E 561-K5 PeT
Madison Vill Dr S 561-K5 PeT
Madrid Rd 596-H4 G
Madrone Ct 428-H6 L
Madrone Dr 428-H6 L
Mae Cir 358-B10 WTH
Mae Dr 392-H1 Ca
Magdalene La 491-H7 WnT
Magenta Dr 326-C9 N
Magnolia Ct 455-C7 LTH; 324-J5 N
Magnolia Dr 523-K6 P
Magnolia La 596-C5 G; 461-J6 L
Magnolia Pl 495-A3 WrT
Mahogany Dr 595-A4 WTJ
Maiden La 526-J1 CTM
Maidstone Rd 457-G6 PTM
Main Dr 531-J4 SCT
Main St 528-C5, F5 BG; 391-H4; 392-A4 Ca; 389-K4 ET; 596-E2 G; 324-E2 JT; 531-G5 NP; 492-B3, B6 S; 562-A4 Spt; 357-H4; 358-A4 W; 323-E7 WTH; 459-H1 WTM; 388-E2 Wh; 389-H8 Z
Main St E 455-H6 B; 592-A3 M; 523-G8 P; 489-A9 WaT
Main St W 455-D4 B; 595-J2; 596-A2 G; 455-D4 LTH; 523-D9 P
Mainsail Ct 394-C8 F
Maisons Ct 423-D8 PTM
Major Run 427-J4 LTM
Malaga Dr 426-G4 WTM
Malden La 528-E9 PeT
Malibu Ct 461-J8 LTM
Malibu Dr 461-J8 LTM
Mallard Ct 422-H9 BTH; 391-D6 CTH; 393-C8 F; 429-B3 McC; 425-A8 WTM
Mallard La 429-B2 McC
Mallard Landing 422-H10 BTH; 393-B9 F
Mallard Manor 422-G10 BTH
Mallard View Dr 460-D6 WTM
Mallard View La 460-D6 WTM
Mallard Way 422-H10 BTH; 427-G7 LTM
Mallery Dr 326-A10 NT
Mallory Rd 326-F10; 360-F2 NT
Mallway Dr 461-J8 LTM
Maloney Rd 422-B9, G9 BTH
Malvina Ave 496-A5 WrT
Malvina Ct 496-A5 WrT
Manassas Dr 525-F1 WnT
Manchester Ct 391-E9 CTH; 359-J9 N
Manchester Dr 393-A9 F; 424-J8 WTM
Manchester La 424-J9 WTM
Mandan Ct 561-D8 PeT
Mandana Ct 593-C9 MTM
Manderley Dr 426-A4 WTM
Mandren Dr 524-F4 WaT
Manhattan Ave 525-K6 DTM; 491-K8, K10; 525-K2, K3 WnT
Manita Dr 490-K2 WnT
Manitou Ct 428-F4 LTM
Manker St 527-H4 CTM; 527-H10; 561-H2, H3, H4, H5 PeT
Manlove Ave 493-K2 CTM
Mann Dr 528-C6 BG
Mann Rd 526-B9; 559-K10; 560-A2, A7 DTM; 559-K10; 593-D9, E6, H2 MTM
Mann Vill Dr 526-B8 DTM
Mann Vill Jct 526-B8 DTM
Mann Vill La 526-B8 DTM
Mann Vill Rd 526-B8 DTM
Mann Vill St 526-B8 DTM
Mann Vill Terr 526-B8 DTM
Mannan Ct 525-H10 DTM
Manning Ave 458-E4 PTM
Manning Rd 458-E3, E6, E7 PTM
Manor Ct 460-F9, F10 CTM; 523-G9 P
Manor Dr N 455-F9 LTH
Manor Dr S 455-F10 LTH
Mansfield Ct 389-A8 ET
Mansfield Pl 390-H7 CTH
Mansfield St 492-K4 CTM
Manship Dr 393-G9 F
Manship La 393-H8 F
Manti Ct 492-D1 WnT
Maple Ave 359-H3 N
Maple Bk Dr 455-G7 B
Maple Crest Ct 392-C4 Ca
Maple Ct 455-J7 B; 496-K5 Cu
Maple Dr 489-G8 A; 426-A2 CTH; 393-G7 DTH; 594-G2 WTJ; 459-K1 WTM
Maple Dr W 489-A8 WaT
Maple Forge Cir 458-B3 PTM
Maple Forge Ct 458-B3 PTM
Maple Glen Dr 427-B5 LTM
Maple Grove Dr 596-G1 G
Maple Grove La 427-B5 LTM
Maple Hill Dr 529-J8 FT
Maple Hill St 523-G9 P
Maple La 455-F7, G7, H7 B; 596-H3 G; 461-G6 L; 592-A2 M; 524-B6 P; 357-K2; 358-A2 W; 494-G7 WrT
Maple Lawn Rd 559-A3 DTM
Maple Leaf Ct 424-E6 PTM
Maple Leaf Dr 427-B5 LTM
Maple Leaf La 427-B5 LTM
Maple Manor 455-A3 LTH
Maple Manor Dr 562-D1 PeT
Maple Pk Dr 357-K1, K2; 358-A2 W
Maple Ridge Ct 562-C5 PeT
Maple Ridge Dr 562-C5 PeT
Maple St 392-D3 CTH; 393-H7 F; 561-K10; 562-B10 G; 428-G10; 462-G1 L; 360-A3 N; 531-G5, H5 NP; 357-J4 W; 389-J8 Z
Maple Tree Dr 427-B5 LTM
Maple View Ct 561-C8 PeT
Maple View Dr 561-B8 PeT
Maple Way 424-H2 PTM
Maplebrook Dr 427-A1 F
Maplehurst Dr 455-G3 B
Mapleton Ct 428-C1 F; 457-E10 WnT
Maplewood Ct 455-J9 B
Maplewood Dr 324-K8 N; 561-H5 PeT; 491-H2, J2 S
Maqua Ct 426-C1 Ca
Marabou Mills Dr 457-C10 WnT
Marabou Mills Way 457-C10 WnT
Maradona Dr 491-C4 WnT
Maradona Dr S 491-C4 WnT
Maralice Dr 392-B2 Ca
Marana Dr 391-H2 CTH
Marble Ct 562-G3 FT
Marble Dr 562-D6 PeT
Marble La 562-H2 FT
Marblehead Ct 428-H3 LTM
Marborough La 424-K7 WTM
Marbro Rd 391-K9 CTH
Marburn Dr 562-C3 PeT
Marcella La 458-E10 WnT
Marcey Ct 557-H2 P
Marcia Dr 592-F3 BTM
Marcia La 455-J7 B; 561-C2 PeT
Marcialee Dr 531-G3 SCT
Marco Pt 393-A6 Ca
Marcy La 596-D1, G1 G; 459-J6 WTM
Mardenis Ct 559-D10 MTM
Mardenis Dr 559-D10 MTM
Mardenna Ave 460-G10 WrT
Mardyke La 461-C4 L
Maren Dr 491-H1 S; 492-B1 WnT
Marg Ct 596-E4 G
Margaret Ave 528-D3 CTM
Margaret Ct 523-B4 FT
Margate Ct 394-A4 F
Margate Rd 525-K8 DTM
Margene Dr 422-F7 BTH
Margie Dr 455-J3 BTH
Marguerita 596-E4 G
Mari Ann Ct 563-A6 FT
Maria Dr 596-E3 G
Maria La 523-H2 WaT
Mariah Hill Ct 593-A1 MTM
Mariah Hill Dr 593-A1 MTM
Marian Dr 425-K3 WTM
Mariana Ct 455-E7 B
Marianne Ave 495-D3 WrT
Marie Ct 325-E8 N
Marie Dr 426-C2 Ca
Mariesi Dr 423-G5 PTM
Marietta Ct 462-B8 LTM
Marietta Dr 462-B8 LTM
Marigold Cir 393-G7 F
Marigold La 458-D3 PTM
Marilyn Ct 391-F2 CTH
Marilyn Dr 457-F2 PTM
Marilyn Rd 394-H3 FCT; 460-H7; 461-A7 LTM; 360-H10 WyT
Marina Ct 595-C7 WTJ
Marina Dr 426-A7 WTM
Mariner Ct 429-A2 FCT
Mariner Way 491-D1 WnT
Mariners La 491-E1 WnT
Marion Ave DN-B4; 493-B10 CTM
Mariposa Dr 490-J7 WnT
Maritime Dr 457-B10 WnT
Mariway Cir 490-J7 WnT
Mariway Ct 490-H7 WnT
Mariway Rd 490-H7 WnT
Mariwood Dr 455-J3 BTH; 490-H7 WnT
Mariwood Pkwy 490-H7 WnT
Marjorie Ct 592-J2 MTM
Mark Ct 594-H1 WTJ
Mark La 461-A5 LTM; 523-J8 P
Markay Dr 393-J5 DTH
Market Plaza 596-C2 G
Market St DN-B2, D2, E3, F3; 492-K8; 493-E8, F8, H8; 494-D7 CTM; 562-A5 Spt; 491-G8, J8; 492-B8 WnT; 494-H7 WrT
Marksman Ct 424-J10 WTM
Markwood Ave 525-G8; 526-A8 DTM; 527-G8, J8, K8 PeT
Marla Dr 427-F9 LTM
Marlette Dr 493-D3 CTM
Marlin Ct 428-C3 LTM
Marlin Dr 595-E2 G
Marlin Rd 530-F8 FT
Marlowe Ave DN-F2; 493-H7 CTM
Marmon Cir 460-J4 LTM
Marmont Cir 427-B10 LTM
Marmont Ct 427-B10 LTM
Marnette St 491-J9 WnT
Maroon Ct 390-D9 CTH
Marott Ct 460-J5 LTM
Marquette Cir 424-H6 PTM
Marquette Ct 424-F3 PTM
Marquette Dr 389-H5 Z
Marquis La 424-J7 WTM
Marrison Pl 460-G7 LTM; 460-D7, F7 WTM
Mars Hill St 526-D6 DTM; 526-D4 WnT
Marseille Ct 461-G8 LTM
Marseille Rd 461-H8 LTM; 461-H9 WrT
Marsh Dr 393-D8 F
Marsh Rd 423-G9 PTM
Marsha Dr 491-D4 WnT
Marten Ct E 461-F7 L
Marten Ct S 461-F7 L
Marten Ct W 461-E7 L
Martha St 395-H9 FCT; 525-K1; 526-A1, J1 WnT
Martin Luther La 494-A2 CTM
Martin Pike 394-B6 F
Martin St 527-G5, H5, K5 PeT
Martinique La 561-G3 PeT
Marwood Tr Dr E 425-H1 CTH
Marwood Tr Dr N 425-H1 CTH
Marwood Tr Dr W 425-H1 CTH
Mary Ct 422-G9 BTH; 394-A2 F; 594-H1 WTJ
Mary Dr 525-D2 WnT
Mary Ellen Ct 391-D5 Ca
Mary Kay Dr 526-C9 DTM
Mary La 561-D6 PeT
Mary Ralls La 424-J5 WTM
Maryann Ct 562-C4 PeT
Marybelle La 562-F2 PeT
Maryland Ct 393-K9 F
Maryland St DN-A3, C3, E3, F3; 492-J8; 493-D8, G8, H8, K8 CTM
Maryvale Ct 592-A1 M; 491-E7 WnT
Marywood Ct 562-B5 Spt
Marywood Dr 562-B5 Spt
Mason Cabin Ct 562-J3 FT
Mason Cir 458-B5 PTM
Mason Dr 458-B6 PTM
Mason St 527-F3 CTM; 361-D5 WyT
Massachusetts Ave DN-D2, F1; 493-F7, H5; 494-A4, F1 CTM; 460-J10; 494-F1 WrT
Masten Ct 523-H9 P
Masten St 523-H8 P
Masters Cir 455-A2 B
Masters Rd 427-C4, C5 LTM
Maswa Ct 426-C1 Ca
Match Pt Ct 428-B4 LTM
Matchlock Ct 427-H3 LTM
Mathews Ave 527-J8, J10, K10; 561-K1 PeT
Mathews Rd 563-F9 CTJ; 563-F7 FT
Mathews Way 527-G8 PeT
Matrea More Ct 457-E7 PTM
Matt Dr 462-B4 L
Matterhorn La 490-J5 WnT
Matterhorn Rd 490-J5 WnT
Mattock Chase 393-B3 Ca
Maumee Ct 462-C10 WrT
Maumee Dr 462-C10 WrT
Maura Ct 461-J9 WrT
Maura La 461-J9 WrT
Maureen Terr 491-B5 WnT
Maurice Dr 491-A2 WnT
Maurine Ct 462-B8 LTM
Maurine Dr 462-B8 LTM
Max Ct 393-J10 F
Maxine Dr 455-E7 B
Maxine Manor 455-E7 B
Maxine Rd 425-J8 WTM
Maxwell Ct N 389-F5 Z
Maxwell Ct S 389-G6 Z
Maxwell La 389-F5 Z
Maxwell Rd 557-F5 GT; 527-D9 PeT
Maxwells Dr 455-K3 BTH
Maxwellton St 557-J8 GT
May Apple Cir W 357-D9 WTH
May Ridge La 457-H6 PTM
Mayapple Ct 528-K8 FT; 326-C10 N
Mayfair Dr 458-H1 PTM; 458-H1 WTM
Mayfair La 391-B5 CTH
Mayfield Dr 462-A9 WrT
Mayfield La 389-K8; 390-A8 ET
Mayflower Dr 526-C7 DTM
Mayhew Dr 562-A7, B7 PeT
Maynard Dr 561-G3, H3; 562-A3 PeT
Mayor Blvd 560-E4 PeT
Maywood Rd 526-F5, H4 WnT
Maze Rd 563-H7; 564-A7, F8 FT
McBeth Ct 457-H2 PTM
McBeth Dr 489-F7 A
McBeth Way 457-H2 PTM
McCarty Ct 458-A4 PTM
McCarty Dr 595-K3 G
McCarty St DN-A4, B4, C4, E4; 493-A9, C9, F10 CTM; DN-A4; 490-H10; 491-D10, J10; 492-C10, D10, G10, H9 WnT
McClellan Ct 457-J2 PTM
McCloud Ct N 457-J3 PTM
McCloud Ct S 457-J3 PTM
McClure St 526-D6 DTM; 492-D6 S; 492-D9, D10; 526-D4 WnT
McCollough Ct 424-K7 WTM
McCollough Dr 424-K7 WTM
McCollum La 557-J2 P
McConnell Way 527-H8 PeT
McCord La 428-J9 L
McCord Rd 429-E4 VT
McCord St 527-H4 CTM; 429-C8 McC
McCoy St 461-G6 L
McCray St 492-A2 S
McCurdy Rd 456-K7 PTM
McDoogle Dr 359-A5 NT
McDougal St 527-H4 CTM; 529-A4 WrT
McDowell Dr 496-E3, E4 WrT
McDowell Dr 496-E4 WrT
McFadden Way 392-F6 Ca
McFarland Blvd 562-G5 FT; 562-E4 PeT
McFarland Ct 562-C7 PeT
McFarland La 562-G6 PeT
McFarland Pl 562-C7 PeT
McFarland Rd 528-B9, B10; 562-C2, C5, C7 PeT; 562-C5 Spt
McFarland Way 562-B7 PeT
McGaughey Rd 529-H7 FT
McGregor Rd 563-H5; 564-A5, D5, F5 FT; 562-C5 PeT
McGuire Ct 461-E6 L
McHenry La 458-J5 WTM
McIlvain Dr 424-H9 LTM
McIntosh Ct 461-C4 L; 523-D2 WaT
McIntosh Dr 523-D2 WaT
McIntosh La 461-D4 L
McKean La 426-E6 WTM
McKim Ave DN-F3; 493-J8 CTM
McKinges Cir 393-C4 Ca
McKinley Ct 460-A1 WTM
McKinley Dr 558-A10 M
McKinley St 596-D2 G
McKinstray Ct 394-C10 F
McLain Dr 561-D5 PeT
McLaughlin Ave 562-B4 Spt
McLaughlin St 562-C4 PeT
McLean Pl 493-E3 CTM
McLeay Dr 460-A3 WTM
McNutt Cir 427-H4 LTM
McPherson Ave 493-H1 CTM
McPherson St 391-H10 CTH
McThorn Dr 462-E3 L
Mead Ct 394-B5 F
Mead Dr 460-C3 WTM
Meadow Bk Dr 393-H8 F
Meadow Cir 595-H1 G
Meadow Cresent 391-H1 Ca
Meadow Ct 592-B4 M; 389-J6 Z
Meadow Dr 497-A3 BCT; 529-D6 FT; 596-A1 G; 593-A2, C2 MTM; 531-G5 NP
Meadow Glen Ct 489-H8 A
Meadow Glen Dr 489-H8 A
Meadow Grass Way 394-A2 F
Meadow Gun Dr 562-D9 G
Meadow La 497-A3 BCT; 592-C4 BTM; 391-J4 Ca; 393-E6 F; 596-G1 G; 428-H10 L; 561-J7 PeT; 595-C2 WTJ; 389-J5, J6 Z
Meadow Lake Dr 497-G6 SCT
Meadow Ridge Dr 393-E9 F
Meadow Song Ct 497-H7 SCT
Meadow View Dr 461-C5 L
Meadow Violet Ct 489-H5 WaT
Meadow Violet Dr 489-H5 WaT
Meadow Vista Dr 561-D8 PeT
Meadow Vue Ct N 561-E4 PeT
Meadow Vue Ct S 561-E5 PeT
Meadowbrook Ct 425-H7 WTM
Meadowbrook Dr 425-H6, H7 WTM
Meadowcreek Dr 358-C10 WTH
Meadowfield Blvd 428-J10 L
Meadowfield Dr 428-J10 L
Meadowgate Ct 424-C6 PTM
Meadowgreen Dr 428-F9 L
Meadowlark Cir 393-B8 F
Meadowlark Ct 461-G7 LTM
Meadowlark Dr 461-G7 L; 460-K7; 461-A7, G7, J7, K7; 462-A7, B7 LTM
Meadowlark La 455-H10; 489-H1 B; 456-C10 LTH
Meadowlark Manor 462-B7 LTM
Meadowlark Pl 392-G3 Ca
Meadowlark Way 524-B7 P
Meadowood Dr 491-G2, J2 S
Meadowpond Way 428-H10; 462-H1 L
Meadowridge La 561-C9 PeT
Meadowridge Tr 561-C8 PeT
Meadows Blvd 326-C9 N
Meadows Ct 460-C8 WTM
Meadows Dr 393-H9 F; 460-B8 WTM
Meadows La 596-A3 G; 523-D8 P
Meadows Pkwy 460-B7 WTM
Meadowsweet Ct 528-J8 FT
Meadowview Ct 391-F2 CTH
Meadowview Dr 592-E4 M
Meadowview La 561-H10; 595-H1, H2 G
Meagan Dr 592-J2 MTM
Meaghan Cir 496-G10 WrT
Meander Bend 455-B1 BTH; 424-D6 PTM
Meander Way 595-D2 WTJ
Mecca St 526-A2 WnT
Meckes Dr 528-K10 FT
Meckes La 528-H9; 562-J1 FT
Medalist Pkwy 393-B6 Ca
Medallion Ct 524-E4 WaT
Medallion Dr 424-J10 WTM; 524-E4 WaT
Medford Ave 458-G10; 492-G1, G5 WnT
Media Dr 458-J6 WTM
Medical Dr DN-B2; 493-A6 CTM; 391-K7; 392-A7 Ca
Medina Ct 527-E8 PeT
Medina Dr 527-E8 PeT
Medina La 527-E8 PeT
Medina Way 527-E8 PeT
Medinah Ct 496-D9 WrT
Medora Dr 459-A2 WTM
Meek St 359-K4 N
Meeting House Ct 458-G9 WnT
Meeting House La 458-G9 WnT
Meeting St 394-A5 F
Megan Ct 427-E5 LTM
Megan Dr 427-E5 LTM
Megan La 427-E5 LTM
Megan Lee Dr 462-A5 L
Meganwood Ct 491-A7 WnT
Meganwood Dr 491-A7 WnT
Mehaffey St 461-G6 L
Meikel St DN-D4; 493-D10 CTM
Meith St 395-H9 FCT
Melanie La 561-B5, E5 PeT
Melark Dr 392-B5 Ca
Melbourne Ct 357-D10 WTH
Melbourne Rd 424-E7; 458-E2, E4, E6, E7 PTM
Melbourne Rd E 458-F7 WTM
Melissa Ann Ct 490-H8 WaT
Melissa Ann Dr 490-G8 WaT
Mellen Rd 524-K3 WnT
Mellis Ct 461-K7 LTM
Mellis Dr 461-K7 LTM
Mellon Ct 492-D2 WnT
Mellowood Dr 561-B7, C7 PeT
Melody Ave 595-E3 G
Melody Ct 528-F8 BG
Melody La 524-G8 WaT
Melrose Ave 526-A2 WnT
Melrose Cir 393-J5 F
Melrose Ct 529-K7 FT
Melrose Dr 529-K7 FT
Melrose La 594-K2 WTJ
Melt Water Dr 424-C6 PTM
Melton Dr 526-C8 DTM
Melvenia St 494-H9 WrT
Memorial Dr 528-F6 BG
Memory La 391-G3 CTH
Mendenhall Rd 525-D10; 559-D1, D5 DTM
Menlo Ct Dr E 426-A6 WTM
Menlo Ct Dr W 425-K6 WTM
Menlo La 426-A6 WTM
Mercator Dr 596-D4 G
Mercedes Dr 424-H7 PTM
Mercer Rd 424-F5 PTM
Merchant Dr 489-J9 A
Merchants Dr 492-E1 WnT
Mercury Ct 357-E10 WTH; 495-H2 WrT
Mercury Dr 495-J1, K1; 496-A1, C1 WrT
Meredith Ave 494-B8 CTM
Merganser Dr 393-C8 F; 425-A8 WTM
Meridee Dr 528-D8 PeT
Meridian Corners Blvd 391-F3 CTH; 391-E5 Ca
Meridian Hills Blvd 425-E9 WTM
Meridian Hills Ct 425-C9 WTM
Meridian Hills La 425-E7 WTM
Meridian La 459-E3 WTM
Meridian Meadows Ct 561-E9 G
Meridian Meadows Rd 561-D10 G
Meridian Pk Dr 595-E2 G
Meridian Pkwy 459-E1 WTM
Meridian Pl 459-E6 WTM
Meridian Sch Rd 561-D7 PeT
Meridian St 391-E6, E10, G3 CTH; DN-D1, D4; 493-E5, E8, E9, E10; 527-E2, E6 CTM; 391-E10 Ca; 562-C10; 596-D1 G; 527-E6, E9, E10; 561-E1, E4, E9 PeT; 425-E3, E10; 459-E4, E8 WTM
Meridian St S 596-D5, D6 G
Meridian Terr 561-E5 PeT
Meridian West Dr 459-E2 WTM
Meridian Woods Blvd 561-D3 PeT
Merlin Lake Ct 496-B1 WrT
Merlin Lake Dr 496-D1 WrT
Merom Ct 457-J1 PTM
Merriam Rd 426-D9 WTM
Merrick La 458-F9 WnT
Merrick Way 458-F9 WnT
Merrill St DN-C4, E4; 493-D9, F9 CTM
Merrimac Dr 357-C10 WTH
Merrimac Pl 491-G8 WnT
Merriman Rd 592-A10 BTM
Merrit Ave 461-J3 L
Merry La 595-K1 G
Mersey Ct 391-E9 CTH
Mersey La 359-H10 N
Merts Dr 528-B5 PeT
Mesa Ct 526-B6 DTM
Mesa Dr 526-A6 DTM
Mesilla Ct 461-H10 WrT
Mesquite Ct 457-D10 WnT
Messersmith Dr 595-A7 WTJ
Messiah Pl 427-D3 LTM
Messina Cir 394-B4 F
Metaire Dr 596-G3 G
Metzger Ct 427-G4 LTM
Metzger La 359-D4 NT
Metzler Dr 557-H1 P
Meyer St 596-D5, D6 G
Meyers Ave 492-B3 S
Mi Casa Ave 562-D4 PeT
Mia Ct 557-J2 P
Miaellen Dr 497-A3 BCT
Miami Ct N 523-J9 P
Miami Ct S 523-J9 P
Miami Dr 460-B6 WTM
Miami St DN-A2, D2, E2; 492-K7; 493-F7, G7 CTM; 326-E5 NT
Micawber Cir 427-E8 LTM
Micawber Ct 427-E7 LTM
Michael Ct 455-D6 LTH; 594-H1 WTJ
Michael Dr 523-K8 P
Michele Ct 595-E1 G
Michigan Rd 424-C1 CTH; 389-J3; 390-A7 ET; 565-A5, F8; 599-K1 MTS; 424-G8; 458-H1 PTM; 458-H1; 459-A7 WTM; 389-J3; 390-A7 Z
Michigan St DN-A2, C2, F2; 492-H7; 493-D7, J7; 494-A7 CTM; 496-F6, G6 Cu; DN-A2; 492-C7, H7 WnT; 494-H6, J7; 495-B6, D6, F6, G6; 496-A6 WrT
Michriver Rd DN-B2; 493-A6 CTM
Mickley Ave 491-J5 S; 491-J5, J8, J9, J10; 525-J2 WnT
Middle Bay La 428-E6 LTM
Middle Dr 391-K10 CTH; DN-B2; 493-A6 CTM; 462-G2 L; 325-H6 NT; 596-E10 NW; 531-H8, J3 SCT
Middle St 596-E2 G
Middlebrook Ct 395-C10 FCT
Middlebury Rd 426-C3 WTM
Middlefield Ct 458-F9 WnT
Middlefield Dr 458-F9 WnT
Middleham Cir 528-E7 PeT
Middleham La 528-E7 PeT
Middleton Ct 424-A10 PTM
Middletown Ave 361-A4, F2 WyT
Midfield Service Rd S 525-A9, D6 DTM; 525-D6 WnT
Midland Rd 527-A10; 528-A10 PeT
Midlothian La 491-B3 WnT
Midlothian Way 491-B3 WnT
Midnight Ct 496-D9 WrT
Midnight Dr 496-D9 WrT
Midnight Pass 394-E9 F
Midsummer Dr 529-H7 FT
Midvale Dr 458-B10; 492-B1 WnT
Midway Ct 491-H1 WnT
Mignon Dr 457-H3 PTM
Mignon La 457-H3 PTM
Mikco La 426-K2 LTM
Mike Nelson Rd 564-G9 CTJ
Mikesell Dr 424-K8, K9 WTM
Milan St 458-D10 WnT
Milburn Ct 455-J10 B
Milburn St DN-B1; 493-B3, B5 CTM
Mildred Dr 492-C1 WnT
Miles Dr 525-C2 WnT
Miley Ave DN-A2, A3; 492-K7, K8 CTM
Milford Ct 462-C10 WrT
Milford Rd 462-C10 WrT
Milhouse Ct 559-J2 DTM
Milhouse Rd 559-B2, F2, H2, K2; 560-A3 DTM
Mill Cr Cir 457-F9 WnT
Mill Cr Dr 457-F9 WnT
Mill Cr Dr N 359-A1 NT
Mill Cr Pl 425-B2 CTH
Mill Cr Rd 325-A4 JT; 325-A6, A10 N; 359-A3, A6 NT
Mill Ct 391-D9 CTH
Mill Farm Ct 561-J8 PeT
Mill Farm Rd 359-A1 NT
Mill Pond La 423-B7 PTM
Mill Run 425-B1 CTH; 393-G2 DTH
Mill Run Cir 457-F9 WnT
Mill Run Dr 359-B2 NT; 457-F9 WnT
Mill Run Overlook 359-A2 NT
Mill St 493-D4 CTM; 531-G5 NP; 357-K4 W
Mill St N 523-F7 P
Mill St S 523-F8 P
Mill Stream Cir 423-A7 PTM

Mill Stream Ct 391-D2 CTH
Mill View Ct 461-B7 LTM
Mill View Dr 461-C7 LTM
Mill Water La 561-J8 PeT
Millbrook Dr 489-H10; 523-G1 A
Miller Ct 360-B2 N
Miller Dr 529-F7 FT; 562-B10 G
Miller St 526-H1 CTM; 525-D1, E1; 526-A1, F1, H1 WnT
Miller Woods La 529-A8 FT
Millersville Dr 459-K8 WTM
Millersville Rd 459-K8; 460-A8, C7, E6, F4, F5 WTM
Milliner Ct 523-J5 P
Million Mile Rd 456-J5 PTM
Millis Dr 558-K5 DTM
Millridge Dr 391-D10 CTH; 391-D9 Ca; 596-B5 G
Millrtone Ct 391-F2 CTH
Mills Ave 525-G8 DTM; 527-G8, J8 PeT
Mills Rd 559-A3, E3, K3; 560-A3 DTM
Millstone Ct 457-D6 PTM
Millstream Rd 595-A7 WTJ
Millview Ct 592-E4 M
Millwood Cir 358-B3 WTH
Millwood Ct 425-F4 WTM
Millwright Ct 457-E6 PTM
Milton St 559-F6 DTM
Milwaukee Ct 561-B9 PeT
Mimi Dr 528-F9 BG
Mimosa Ct 326-C9 N
Mimosa La 564-F4 FT
Mindy Dr 462-A6 L
Mindy La 455-G10 B
Minger Rd 458-C10 WnT
Minlo Dr 562-D2, D7 PeT
Minnesota St 526-H2; 527-E1, G1, J1; 528-A1, E1 CTM; 525-E2, G2; 526-B2, H2 WnT; 528-J1 WrT
Minocqua St 528-B2, B3 CTM
Mint Dr 562-F6 PeT
Minton Ct 392-F5 Ca
Minturn La 424-K8; 425-A8 WTM
Minuteman Cir 390-C10 CTH
Miracle Ct 562-E5 PeT
Miracle Rd 562-D5, D6 PeT
Mirafield La 429-C2 McC
Miramar Ct 427-B2 LTM
Miranda Cir 394-B4 F
Mispillion St 391-F10 CTH
Mission Dr 457-G6, G8 PTM; 457-G9, G10; 491-G9 WnT
Mission Hill Dr 596-H3 G
Mission Hills La 491-A1 WnT
Mission Terr 457-F8 PTM
Missouri St DN-D4; 493-D5, D10; 527-D2 CTM; 527-D10; 561-D1 PeT
Mistflower La 325-E10 N
Mistflower Way 462-D8 LTM
Mistletoe Dr 562-D5, E5 PeT
Misty Cir 425-A3 WTM
Misty Cove 428-J5 L
Misty Ct 425-A3 WTM
Misty Dr 428-H5 L
Misty Hollow La 393-F10 F
Misty La 425-A3 WTM
Misty Lake Cir 424-K3 WTM
Misty Lake Ct 424-K3 WTM
Misty Lake Dr 424-K3 WTM
Misty Pine Ct 391-D2 CTH
Misty Way 428-H6, J5 L
Mistyknoll Ct 428-B1 F
Mitchner Ave 461-E6 L; 461-E9; 495-E5, E7, E9, E10 WrT
Mitthoefer Pl 496-B1 WrT
Mitthoefer Rd 564-B8 FT; 462-B5 L; 462-B10; 496-B4, B9 WrT
Mobile Home Dr 525-F8 DTM
Moccasin Ct 560-K10 WTJ; 462-C10 WrT
Moccasin Pl 560-K10 WTJ
Moccasin Rd 594-K1 WTJ
Mockernut Ct 428-H6 L
Mocking Bird Ct 565-B1 MTS
Mockingbird La 427-G6 LTM
Model Sq 491-A6 WnT
Modesto Ct 423-F5 PTM
Moffet Rd 557-G7 GT
Moffitt St 527-H8 PeT
Mohave Ct 462-D10 WrT
Mohave La 462-D10 WrT
Mohawk Dr 392-G5 CTH; 391-K5; 392-A5, G5 Ca; 428-C9 L
Mohawk Hill Dr 392-B6 Ca
Mohawk La 425-B7, B8, B9, B10 WTM
Mohawk St 392-D5 Ca
Mohican Rd 460-E4 WTM
Moline Dr 526-B7 DTM
Moll Dr 393-H8 F
Mollenkopf Rd 394-D10; 428-D1 F; 428-D2 LTM
Moller Ct 457-J9 WnT
Moller Rd 423-J5, J8; 457-J6, J8, K2, K5 PTM; 491-K2 S; 457-J10; 491-K2 WnT
Moller Way 457-K8 PTM
Mollie Ct 564-A4 FT
Molly Ct 393-G8 F
Monaco Dr 460-E2 WTM
Monaghan La 560-K6 PeT
Monahan Rd 389-E10 Z
Monarch Cir 457-G9 WnT
Monarch Ct 326-C10 N
Monarch Dr 457-G9 WnT
Monica Beach La 594-B9 WTJ
Monica Ct 461-H8 LTM
Monica Dr 457-J4 PTM
Monitor Ct 596-J4 G
Monitor Dr 460-E1 WTM
Monitor La 390-C9 CTH; 460-F1 WTM
Monninger Dr 458-B10 WnT
Monologue Ct 523-C9 P
Monon Cir 427-D8 LTM; 489-C10 WaT
Monon Ct 427-D8 LTM
Monon Greenway Tr 391-J8 CTH; 391-J5 Ca; 425-H7, J4 WTM
Monroe Dr 392-A7 Ca; 496-F4 WrT
Monroe St 496-F6 Cu
Monroe St S 557-J10 BTM
Montana Ave 327-K7 WyT
Montana St 493-J4 CTM
Montauk Ct 457-D9 WnT
Montcalm St 493-B5 CTM
Monte La 427-H3 LTM
Monte Vista Ct 596-E4 G
Monte Vista Dr 596-E3 G
Monteray Rd 596-E4 G
Monterey Cir 489-H10 A
Monterey Ct 359-F2 N
Monterey Dr 359-F2 N
Montery Ct 461-H7 LTM
Montery Rd 461-G8; 462-B7 LTM
Monticello Ct 595-J2 G; 359-J6 N
Monticello Dr 595-J2 G; 527-E6 PeT
Montroff Cir 427-C10 LTM
Montrose Ct 490-K7 WnT
Montrose La 357-G7 WTH
Monttclair Dr 525-K5 WnT
Monty Cir 424-E1 CTH
Monument Cir DN-D3; 493-E8 CTM
Monument St 359-J2; 360-A2 N
Moon Bay Cir 428-G4 LTM
Moon Rd 523-C9; 557-C1, D5 GT; 523-C9; 557-C1 P
Moon Rd W 557-C1 GT
Moonlight Ct 592-B5 M
Moonlight Dr 461-A5 LTM
Moonstone Pl 429-C3 McC
Moontown Rd 324-F10; 358-F3 NT; 324-F10; 358-F3 WTH
Moore Ave 494-B8, E8 CTM; 423-E2 ET
Moore Dr 455-K7 B
Moore Rd 423-B7, D4 PTM
Moore St 393-H8 F; 592-A4 M
Moores Cir 496-F4 WrT
Moores Ct 496-F4 WrT
Moores Manor 496-F4 WrT
Mooresville By-P 525-J9 DTM
Mooresville Ct 360-A3 N
Mooresville Rd 525-H10, K8; 526-A7, B6, E6; 558-J7; 559-D7, F5 DTM; 526-E6 WnT
Moorgate Ct 359-J6 N
Moorgate Rd 427-B9 LTM
Moorhead Dr 424-C2 PTM
Moorings Blvd 428-C3 LTM
Mopac Ct 561-B8 PeT
Moqui Ct 462-C10 WrT
Moraine Ct 393-A3 Ca
Moran Ct 424-E8 PTM
Moray Ct E 424-J7 WTM
Moray Ct W 424-H8 WTM
Moreland Ave 492-F1, F3, F4, F6, F7; 526-F1, F2 WnT
Moreland Ct 492-F3 WnT
Moreland St 526-F4 WnT
Morenci Tr 458-C2 PTM
Morgan Ave 559-A5 DTM
Morgan Dr 393-H8 F; 527-H9 PeT
Morgan St 526-K1 CTM; 526-H1 WnT
Morgantown Rd 560-J9 PeT; 560-J10; 594-J3, J9 WTJ
Mornay Dr 457-F4 PTM
Mornay Pl 457-F4, H4 PTM
Mornay Way 457-F4 PTM
Morning Dove Dr 458-D2 PTM
Morning Glory Ct 428-J9 L
Morning Star Dr 592-A1 M
Morning Sun La 528-F8 BG
Morningbird Ct 391-D1 CTH
Morningside Ct 389-F10 Z
Morningside Dr 455-E4 B; 594-J10 WTJ; 425-F6, G6, G8 WTM; 389-F10 Z
Morningside La 425-G7 WTM
Morningsong Dr 525-K6 DTM
Morningstar Ct 495-J1 WrT
Morningstar Dr 495-J2 WrT
Morphis La 560-G10 WTJ
Morris Rd 560-H9 PeT
Morris St 493-A10, F10, H10; 494-C10, F10 CTM; 491-G10, H10, K10; 492-A10, E10; 524-J1; 525-D1; 526-C1 WnT
Morrison Way 325-K10 N
Morristown Cir 390-C10 CTH
Morse Landing Dr 325-E1 C
Morton Ave 526-J2 WnT
Morton Pl 392-F5 Ca
Morton St 359-J2 N
Mortwood St 491-D8 WnT
Mosey Manor 490-K9 WnT
Moshi La 494-H8 WrT
Moss Cir 562-F3 PeT
Moss Cr Blvd 562-E3 PeT
Moss Cr Cir 562-F3 PeT
Moss Cr Ct 562-F3 PeT
Moss Cr Pl 562-F3 PeT
Moss Cr Terr 562-F3 PeT
Moss Ct 562-F3 PeT
Moss Dr 392-F8 Ca
Moss La 562-F3 PeT
Moss Oak Ct 561-B6 PeT
Moss Ridge Cir 562-E3 PeT
Moss Ridge Ct 562-E3 PeT
Moss Ridge La 562-E3 PeT
Moss Rock Ct 394-K7 F
Moss Wood Dr 392-K10 F
Mosswood Ct 457-C5 PTM
Mosswood Dr 457-C5 PTM
Mossy Rock La 562-F3 PeT
Motif Blvd 455-G4 B
Moultrie Ct 561-B6 PeT
Moultrie Dr 561-B6 PeT
Mounds Ct 391-D3 Ca
Mount Auburn Dr 491-H6 WnT
Mount Bk Ct 595-D5 WTJ
Mount Comfort Rd 463-D4, D9 BCT; 429-C5 McC
Mount Dora La 496-A6 WrT
Mount Herman Ave 491-C9, D9 WnT
Mount Rainier Dr 561-C3 PeT
Mount Shasta N 490-H5 WnT
Mount Shasta S 490-G5 WnT
Mount St DN-A3, A4; 492-H5, H8, H10 WnT
Mount Vernon Ct 595-H1 G; 461-K5 LTM
Mount Vernon Dr 595-H2 G; 527-G9 PeT
Mount Vernon Pl 527-D6 PeT
Mount Vernon Tr N 496-D7 WrT
Mount Vernon Tr S 496-E7 WrT
Mountain Ash Ct 392-E2 Ca
Mountbatten Ct 458-C6 PTM
Mowrey St 461-G6 L
Mud Cr Ct 394-E8 F
Mud Cr Rd 428-A3, A5 LTM
Muessing Rd 496-G7 Cu; 496-G7, G9, G10; 530-G1 WrT
Muessing St 496-G6 Cu
Mugo Dr 428-J10 L
Muirfield Cir 563-B6 FT
Muirfield Ct 455-H3 B; 563-B6 FT
Muirfield Dr 455-H3 B
Muirfield Pl 563-A5 FT
Muirfield Tr 428-F1 F
Muirfield Way 424-G2 CTH; 563-A6 FT; 489-B10 WaT
Mulberry Cir 324-K7 N
Mulberry Ct 455-H2 B
Mulberry La 562-A6 PeT
Mulberry St 359-H4, J4, K4; 360-A4 N; 389-F6, H7 Z
Mule Barn Rd 322-E4 AT; 322-E10; 356-E3 WTH
Mulford Ct 491-A7 WnT
Mullet Ct 428-C2 LTM
Mulligan Ct 462-E5 L
Mulligan Way 424-C9 PTM
Mullinix Rd 594-F5, F10 WTJ
Mulsanne Dr 389-D9 Z
Mum La 497-F8 SCT
Mundell St 564-F5 FT
Municipal Dr 393-H7 F
Munsee Cir 459-A2 WTM
Munsee Ct 425-A8 WTM
Munsee La 425-A10, B9; 459-B2 WTM
Munsie St 496-G6 Cu
Munter La 494-F1 CTM
Murphy Cir 455-J6 B
Murphy Ct 455-H6 B; 427-F9 LTM
Murphy Dr 427-F9 LTM
Murphy La 455-H6 B
Murray St 526-B6, C6, D6, E6 DTM; 529-G5 FT; 596-C5 G; 527-A6 PeT
Murry St 527-F6, H5; 528-A5 PeT
Musket St 427-C7 LTM
Muskingum St DN-D2; 493-E6 CTM
Mussman Dr 492-C2 WnT
Mustang Ct 458-D3 PTM
Mutz Cir 496-F4 WrT
Mutz Ct 496-F4 WrT
Mutz Dr 496-F5 WrT
Myers Lake Dr 324-H7 N
Myron Ave 492-A9 WnT
Myrtle Grove Ct 461-J6 L
Myrtle Grove Dr 461-J6 L
Myrtle La 461-A1 LTM; 565-D8 MTS; 594-J2 WTJ
Myrtle Terr 594-K2 WTJ
Mystic Bay Dr 425-K7 WTM
Mystic Rd 327-C8; 361-C5 WyT

N

Naab Rd 424-J6 WTM
Nafanee St 326-E4 NT
Nakomis St 326-F4 N; 326-F4 WRT
Nalon Ct 491-G3 S
Nalon Dr 491-H3 S
Nalon La 491-H3 S
Nambler Way 324-E3 JT
Nance La 594-J3 WTJ
Nancy La 562-C9 G
Nansmond Cir 391-G2 CTH
Nansmond Ct 391-G2 CTH
Nansmond Dr 391-G2 CTH
Nantucket Ct 457-D9 WnT
Nantucket Dr 325-F1 C
Naomi St 527-J2; 528-E2, G2 CTM; 526-A2 WnT
Naples Ct 596-A3 G
Naples Dr 394-B2 F
Napoleon St 527-H2, H4 CTM
Napoli Ct 461-J7 LTM
Nappanee Dr 391-K6; 392-A6 Ca
Narcissus Dr 561-F8 PeT
Narragansett Ct 428-A6 LTM
Nash Cir 455-G8 B
Nash Ct 455-G8 B
Nash La 491-H4 S
Nashua Ct 425-A5 WTM
Nashua Dr 425-A6 WTM
Nashville Cir 496-G5 WrT
Nassau Ct 595-D8 WTJ
Nassau La 496-B3 WrT
Natalie La 425-A8 WTM
Natasha Ct 359-E4 N
Natasha Dr 359-E4, E5, F5 N
Natchez Ct 561-C6 PeT
Nathan La 562-J3 FT
Nathan Pl 562-J3 FT
Nathaniel Cir 428-H8 L
National Ave 527-E7, F7, J7; 528-A7, C6 PeT
National Rd 497-B6, J6 SCT
Nature Dr N 422-K4 PTM
Nature Dr W 422-K4 PTM
Nautical Watch Dr 428-E4 LTM
Nautilus Cir 428-F1 FCT
Navajo Ct 360-B7 NT
Navajo Tr Dr S 425-B8 WTM
Navajo Tr Dr W 425-A8 WTM
Navigate Way 427-B2 LTM
Navin St 494-G8 CTM
Neal Ave DN-A3; 492-K8 CTM
Neal Ct 523-J2 WaT
Needles Dr 561-B6 PeT
Neitzel Rd 592-F5 BTM; 592-F5, J5 MTM
Nekton La 428-F6 LTM
Nellis Ct 391-H2 CTH
Nelson Ave 527-F4, G4, J4; 528-A4 CTM
Nelson Cir 455-J5 B; 360-A2 N
Nelson Ct 495-A5 WrT
Nelson Dr 592-B1 M
Nelson Pl 495-A5 WrT
Nelson St 455-H4 B
Neptune Ct 495-J2 WrT
Neptune Dr 495-J1, K1; 496-A1 WrT
Nero Ct 391-G2 CTH
Nesbitt Rd 426-D10 WTM
Nesse St 388-E1 Wh
Nester St 492-A5 S
Neva La 426-E1 Ca
Nevele La 391-G2 CTH
Nevermind Ct 595-D2 WTJ
Nevermind Way 595-D2 WTJ
New Augusta Rd 424-C9 PTM
New Britton Dr 393-G4 F
New Castle Pl 393-D5 F
New Field Cir 525-A1 WnT
New Field Ct 525-A1 WnT
New Field La 525-A1 WnT
New Harmony Cir 490-H10; 524-J1 WnT
New Harmony Dr 490-J10 WnT
New Jersey St 391-F10; 425-F1 CTH; DN-E1, E2, E3, E4; 459-F10; 493-F1, F5, F8, F9, F10; 527-F1, F4 CTM; 527-F6, F7; 561-F4, F6 PeT; 459-F3, F5, F8 WTM
New London Ct 428-A5 LTM
New Palestine Rd 497-G10; 531-G1 SCT
New Salem Overlook 456-J8 PTM
New St 527-G2 CTM
New York St DN-A2, B2, F2; 492-J7; 493-B7, H7; 494-B7 CTM; 496-F6 Cu; 490-K7; 491-C7, J7; 492-H7 WnT; 494-J7; 495-G6 WrT
Newberry Ct 461-D1 LTM
Newberry Ct E 558-K10 MTM
Newberry Rd 461-D1 LTM
Newbridge Ct 390-J8 CTH
Newburgh Dr 462-C8 LTM
Newbury Ct 393-D9 F
Newby Ct 357-J3 W
Newby La 524-F10 GT
Newcomer La 528-C5 BG
Newgate La 462-A9 WrT
Newhart St 526-F10; 527-D10 PeT
Newhaven Dr 525-A3 WnT
Newhouse Pl 595-A10 WTJ
Newlin Rd 557-F8 GT
Newman St DN-F1; 493-J5 CTM
Newport Bay Dr 426-B8 WTM
Newport Cir 462-F1 L
Newport Ct 596-J3 G
Newport Dr 462-F2 L; 325-C6 N; 357-D10 WTH
Newport La 389-E9 Z
Newport Way 427-C7, D8 LTM
Newspec Dr 561-J3 PeT
Newton Ave 494-B8 CTM
Newton St 559-F6 DTM
Nice Pak Rd 592-B1 M
Nicholas Ave 459-K10 CTM
Nicholas Rd 459-H4 WTM
Nichole Ct 390-F8 CTH
Nicklaus Dr 596-E3 G
Nicolai St 530-G3 WrT
Nicole Blvd 489-K8 A; 489-K7 WaT
Nicole Ct 489-K8 A; 428-G5 LTM
Nicole Dr 596-G3 G
Night Hawk Dr 428-C1 F
Nightingale Ct 427-F7 LTM
Nights Way 526-K10 PeT
Nightsong Dr 525-K6 DTM
Nikki Dr 528-E9 BG
Nile Ridge Ct 428-D9 L
Niles St 496-F6, G6 Cu
Niman Ct 425-J1 CTH
Nimitz Dr 495-A3 WrT
Nixon St 359-G3 N
Noah Dr 527-G9 PeT
Nob La 460-G5 WTM
Nobbe La 496-D8 WrT
Noble Cir 426-K4 LTM
Noble Run 360-A3 N
Noble St DN-E4; 493-G10 CTM; 596-C1 G
Noblesville Dr 360-A1 N
Noblet Ct 456-J5 PTM
Nobscot Ct 458-F9 WnT
Nobscot Dr 458-F9 WnT
Nodlehs Ct 559-J4 DTM
Nodlehs Dr 559-J4 DTM
Noel Ct 489-H7 A
Noel Forest Ct 423-C8 PTM
Noel Forest La 423-C9 PTM
Noel Rd 423-D9 PTM
Nogales St 428-G10 L
Nolan Ave 528-C2 CTM
Nolan Dr 393-H1 F
Nolen Dr 456-K10 WnT
Nollan Dr 529-D6 FT
Nolte St 559-A3, G3 DTM
Nonchalant Ct 561-C10 WTJ
Nonsense Ave 561-H9 G
Nora La 425-J2, J3, J4 WTM
Nora Woods Ct 425-H4 WTM
Nora Woods Dr 425-J4 WTM
Norbeck Terr 561-B5 PeT
Norcroft Ct 526-A9 DTM
Norcroft Dr 525-H9, K9; 526-A9 DTM
Norcross Cir 424-J3 WTM
Norcross Ct 424-J3 WTM
Norcross Dr 424-J3 WTM
Norden Ct 495-A3 WrT
Nordyke Ave 493-B10; 527-A1 CTM
Norena Ct W 489-F1 LTH
Norfolk Cir 391-B5 CTH; 491-K5 S
Norfolk Ct 491-K4, K6 S
Norfolk Dr 389-D8 Z
Norfolk La 391-B6 CTH
Norfolk Pl 491-K6 S
Norfolk St 423-K6 PTM; 491-K4, K6 S; 457-K10; 491-K1, K9, K10; 525-K1, K2 WnT
Norfolk Way 491-K6 S
Norma Dr 461-K4 L
Normal Ave 461-F5 L
Norman Ct 456-F3, F8 LTH
Norman Rd 456-E8 LTH
Normandie Ct 489-G6 WaT
Normandie Dr 489-G5 WaT
Normandy Blvd 423-E8 PTM
Normandy Rd 458-C10; 492-C1 WnT
Normandy Way 423-D9 PTM
Norrison Dr 425-J1 CTH
Norrose Dr 460-E8 WTM
North 38th St Dr 460-G8, H8 LTM; 460-A8, B8, E8 WTM
North 40th St Dr 460-E8 WTM
North 51st Dr 457-J6 PTM
North 75 Rd 489-A7 WaT
North 77th St Dr 425-B7, C7 WTM
North 91 Rd 489-D6 A; 489-D6 WaT
North 100 Rd 489-F6 A; 497-B3, G3 BCT; 356-A1 UT; 489-A6, F6; 490-A6 WaT
North 150 Rd 496-K2; 497-G2 BCT; 489-A5 WaT
North 151 Rd 489-F4 WaT
North 200 Rd 463-A10, G10; 496-J1; 497-B1 BCT; 322-A9 MTB; 322-A9; 356-A8 UT; 489-A4, D3, H4; 490-A4 WaT
North 275 Rd 599-A10 STS
North 300 Rd 463-H8 BCT; 489-F1, H1; 490-A1 LTH; 322-A7 MTB; 599-E10 STS
North 350 Rd 462-H7; 463-B7 BCT; 455-A10; 489-E1 LTH
North 375 Rd 322-A5 MTB
North 400 Rd 455-J9 B; 463-B6, J6 BCT; 455-J9; 456-A9 LTH; 322-A5 MTB; 598-H7; 599-A7, H7 STS
North 425 Rd 455-F9 B; 455-F9 LTH
North 450 Rd 455-A8; 456-F8 LTH
North 500 Rd 462-K3; 463-H3 BCT; 322-A2 MTB; 599-C5, H5 STS
North 525 Rd 598-H4; 599-A4 STS
North 550 Rd 455-A6 LTH
North 575 Rd 597-G10 CTJ
North 600 Rd 455-H4 B; 597-D10, J10; 598-A10 CTJ; 456-C4 LTH; 598-H3; 599-D3 MTS; 595-H10; 596-B10, H10 PTJ; 598-H3; 599-D3 STS; 463-A1, H1 VT; 594-J10; 595-F10 WTJ; 596-H10 Whl
North 650 Rd 456-E3 BTH; 598-D9 CTJ; 429-A10 VT; 594-A10, E9, H9 WTJ
North 700 Rd 455-F2, B; 455-B2, F2; 456-C2 BTH; 597-D8, H7; 598-A7, F7 CTJ; 596-D8 G; 599-D1, H1 MTS; 429-D9, J9 VT; 594-C8, J8; 595-F8 WTJ
North 750 Rd 456-A1, F1 BTH; 596-A7 G; 429-A8 McC; 596-A7, H7 PTJ; 456-F1 PTM; 595-F7 WTJ
North 775 Rd 597-F6 CTJ; 595-J6; 596-A6 PTJ
North 800 Rd 597-D5 CTJ; 564-H8, K8; 565-E8, H8 MTS; 429-A7 McC; 429-F7 VT; 594-E6; 595-B6 WTJ
North 850 Rd 595-H4; 596-H4 G; 595-H4; 597-A4 PTJ; 595-B5, F5 WTJ
North 870 Rd 594-H4 WTJ
North 875 Rd 422-A8 BTH
North 900 Rd 598-E3 CTJ; 595-H4 G; 565-E6 MTS; 429-A4 McC; 429-E4, J4 VT; 594-D4, G4; 595-B4, H4 WTJ
North 925 Rd 593-A10 MTM
North 940 Rd 564-H5 MTS
North 950 Rd 422-C6, G6 BTH; 598-C2 CTJ; 595-G2; 596-H2 G; 565-A5, K5 MTS
North 1000 Rd 422-A5, F5 BTH; 597-G1; 598-A1, F1 CTJ; 565-E4 MTS; 597-B1 PTJ; 594-F1, G1; 595-C1 WTJ
North 1050 Rd 563-F10, K10; 564-B10 CTJ; 565-H2 MTS
North 1075 Rd 564-F9 CTJ
North 1100 Rd 593-B6 MTM; 564-J1; 565-E1 MTS
North 1150 Rd 593-F5 MTM
North 121 489-C6 WaT
North 1250 Rd 593-E3 MTM
North 1300 Rd 593-F1, J1 MTM
North Adams Blvd Dr 460-G1 WTM
North Adams Ct 460-C8 WTM
North Aristocrat Dr 462-B7 LTM
North Atherton Dr 494-G8 WrT
North Augusta Dr 424-E2 CTH; 491-H3 S
North Ayrshire Cir 558-K10; 559-A10; 593-A1 MTM
North Ballinshire 457-C5 PTM
North Bay Road Dr 426-C6 WTM
North Bayside Dr 427-A2 LTM
North Beaumont Way Dr 426-G6 WTM
North Beech Dr 523-K9 P
North Bend Rd 528-F8 BG
North Bentwood Cir Dr 424-F6 PTM
North Blossom La 423-F7 PTM
North Bluff Cr Ct 559-A10 MTM
North Bluffwood Dr 458-H6 WTM
North Boulevard Dr 497-A5 Cu
North Braeburn Dr 495-G3 WrT
North Braeside Dr 425-C3 WTM
North Brendon Way Dr 461-B3 LTM
North Brendonridge Ct 460-K4 LTM
North Bridger Dr 426-D1 Ca
North Brittany Ct 428-G5 L
North Broadway Dr 523-G10 P
North Brookside Pkwy Dr 493-K5; 494-A5, C4 CTM
North Buckridge Dr 561-K4 PeT
North Bull Run Dr 596-J4 G
North Burns Dr 455-H1 BTH
North By Northeast Blvd 427-F2 F
North Canterbury Sq 425-F4 WTM
North Cardinal Cove 427-E6 LTM
North Carefree Ct 593-A1 MTM
North Carnoustie Cir Dr 523-A2 WaT
North Carr Rd 523-H6 GT; 523-H6 P
North Castle Cr Pkwy 426-J4 WTM
North Castleton Farms Dr 427-D7 LTM
North Cedar Glen Dr 557-H2 P
North Cedar Grove Ct 593-B1 MTM
North Cedar Hills Dr 595-A9 WTJ
North Center St 523-E6 GT; 523-E6 P
North Central Ct 459-G9 CTM
North Century Cir 424-K6 WTM
North Chadwood La 424-F5 PTM
North Chapel Hill Ct 559-A9 MTM
North Charleston La 495-C5 WrT
North Chatham Ct 427-E5 LTM
North Chesapeake Dr 428-D7 L
North Claridge Way 390-K6 CTH
North Clay St 592-A3 M
North Cottage Grove Ct 559-A10 MTM
North Cottonwood 557-K5 GT
North County Line Rd 422-E3 BTH; 422-E3 ET
North Ct 531-E1 SCT
North Cypress 595-K4 G
North Deer Ridge Dr 392-F2 Ca
North Delaware Commons Dr 426-C9 WTM
North Dogwood Cir 424-E6 PTM
North Dollar Hide Dr 559-J2 DTM
North Doral Dr 427-C3 LTM
North Dover Blvd 455-F7 B
North Dover Hill Dr 558-K10 MTM
North Dr 325-E4 C; DN-B1; 493-A6 CTM; 461-D7 L; 592-A1 M; 593-E4 MTM; 359-H2 N; 325-H6 NT; 560-H9 WTJ
North Dudley Dr 562-E1 PeT
North Dukane Cir Dr 525-F8 DTM
North Eagle Bay Dr 457-D7 PTM
North Eagle Cove Dr 457-E8 PTM
North Eagle Pointe Dr 457-F6 PTM
North East St 523-F7 P; 358-A3 W
North El Lago Dr 528-B7 PeT
North Emerson Ct Dr 494-G2 CTM
North Fairway Cir Dr 428-H8 L
North Fall Cr Pkwy Dr 459-G10; 493-F2 CTM; 460-G3; 461-A2 LTM; 459-G10; 460-A7, G3 WTM
North Fall Cr Rd 461-C2 LTM
North Fleetwood Dr 391-D4 Ca
North Forest Blvd Dr 425-G6 WTM
North Forest Pk Dr 562-B10 G

North Fox Harbour Dr 528-A8 PeT
North Fox Lake 423-E6 PTM
North Franklin St 592-B3 M
North Galburgh Ct 456-H9 WnT
North Galen Dr 489-G9 A
North Garfield Pk Dr 527-G3 CTM
North Gate Dr 562-D10; 596-D1 G
North Geist Woods Dr 428-F2 FCT
North Golden Oaks 424-H3 WTM
North Granada Cir 492-H1 WnT
North Green Braes Dr 456-K5 PTM
North Green Hills La 458-G10 WnT
North Green St 455-G5 B
North Greenwood Tr 562-C9 G
North Haddington Dr 427-H2 LTM
North Halcomb Cir Dr 525-F8 DTM
North Hampton Cir 428-A5 LTM
North Harbour Dr 325-B7 N
North Hidden Bay Dr 457-G4 PTM
North Hideaway Dr 424-G6 PTM
North High Meadow Ct 560-K10 WTJ
North Highland Manor Ct 459-B4 WTM
North Highland Springs Dr 429-C1 FCT
North Highwoods Dr 458-F10 WnT
North Honnen Dr 427-E9 LTM
North Huddleston Dr 561-E5 PeT
North Hudnut Blvd Dr 526-J4 CTM
North Indian Lake Blvd 428-B9 L
North Indiana St 557-K10; 558-A10; 592-A1 M
North Jamestown Dr 393-F7 F
North Jessman Rd Dr 427-D9 LTM
North John Marshall Dr 462-B9 WrT
North Kensington Way 523-C8 P
North Kessler Blvd Dr 458-G5 WTM; 458-G5; 492-G4 WnT
North Lake Dr 455-F8 B
North Lake Nora Ct 425-G4, H3 WTM
North Lake Nora Dr 425-G3 WTM
North Lake Terr Dr 496-A3 WrT
North Lakewood Dr 426-C1 Ca
North Landborough Dr 427-A10 LTM
North Lantern Rd 393-H5 DTH; 393-H5 F
North Laredo Way 357-F10 WTH
North Laureate Ct 457-B9 WnT
North Laurel Cir 460-E6 WTM
North Layton Mills Ct 559-A10 MTM
North Liberty Cr Dr 457-J3 PTM
North Lickridge La Dr 528-D8 PeT
North Lily Dale Ct 558-K10 MTM
North Lima Dr 562-D7 PeT
North Lismore Dr 561-H7 PeT
North Lockerbie Cir DN-E2; 493-G7 CTM
North Log Run Dr 456-H8, J8 PTM
North Loop 357-J2 W
North Lynnfield Ct 457-F6 PTM
North Manor Dr 455-F9 LTH
North Marwood Tr Dr 425-H1 CTH
North Maxwell Ct 389-F5 Z
North McCloud Ct 457-J3 PTM
North Meadow Cir 457-J1 PTM
North Meadow Dr 457-J1 PTM
North Meadow Vue Ct 561-E4 PeT
North Miami Ct 523-J9 P
North Mill Cr Dr 359-A1 NT
North Mill St 523-F7 P
North Mount Shasta 490-H5 WnT
North Mount Vernon Tr 496-D7 WrT
North Nature Dr 422-K4 PTM
North Oak Blvd Dr 496-K5 Cu
North Oak Lake Cir 424-D5 PTM
North Oak Run Dr 424-J3 WTM
North Oak Tree Dr 562-C8 PeT
North Old Oakland Blvd Dr 428-F7 L
North Old Otto Ct 559-A9 MTM
North Old Route 67 592-C1 BTM; 592-C1 M
North Old Rte 67 558-D10 BTM
North Old Town Dr 425-A4 WTM
North Olde Mill Cir Dr 425-D5 WTM
North Oldfields Cir Dr 458-J8 WTM
North Oles Dr 458-K4 WTM
North Orchard Pk Dr 391-J10 CTH
North Paddington La 424-D7 PTM
North Park Bend 424-K7 WTM
North Park Central Dr 459-B1 WTM
North Park Cir 424-K7 WTM
North Park Ct 424-K7 WTM
North Park Dr 460-C4 WTM
North Park La 424-K7 WTM
North Park Lake Dr 424-H8 WTM
North Park Way 424-K7 WTM
North Parkside Ct 557-H1 P
North Pathway Dr 595-E7 WTJ
North Payne Rd Dr 562-C2 PeT
North Peppermill Rd 596-A4 G
North Perimeter Rd 525-A3, E2 WnT
North Pin Oak Way Dr 457-K3; 458-A3 PTM
North Pine Ridge Dr 427-A2 F
North Pinehurst Dr 461-K6 LTM
North Pleasant Run Pkwy Dr 494-A10, D8, F8; 527-D4, G1; 528-B2 CTM; 494-H7; 495-B5 WrT
North Pocono Mesa 491-H4 S
North Port Rd 325-E3 C
North Quail Ridge 557-J3 P
North Questend Dr 492-G2 WnT
North Racquet Club Dr 425-A3 WTM
North Railroad St 429-C7 McC
North Ransburg Dr 391-G5 Ca
North Reavest Dr 494-A10 CTM
North Redcliff La 523-C8 P
North Redfern Dr 529-G8 FT
North Rippling Way 424-K1 WTM
North River Bay Dr 426-B6 WTM
North Roxburgh Ct 456-G9 WnT
North Rushmore Blvd 490-H5 WnT
North Sadlier Cir Dr 495-D10 WrT
North Saint John Ct 528-F9 BG
North Salem Dr 392-J1 Ca
North Sandpiper Dr 424-F2 PTM
North School Rd 455-H5 B
North Settlement Dr 427-B2 LTM
North Seven Oaks Dr 428-G9 L
North Shadow Lakes Dr 357-J10 WTH
North Shadowview Way 491-F9 WnT
North Shawnee Trail Dr 460-H2 LTM
North Skiles St 490-K4 WnT
North Snowden Sq 490-J5 WnT
North Southcreek Dr 561-D8 PeT
North Southern Lakes Dr 563-A5 FT
North Spring Bk Dr 495-B6 WrT
North Spring Side La 424-K1 WTM
North St 463-D7 BCT; DN-C2, D2, F2; 493-C6, D6, H6; 494-A6 CTM; 359-J2 N; 531-H5 NP; 523-F7 P; 358-A3 W; 492-C6, E6, G6 WnT; 494-G6 WrT
North Steinmeier Dr 426-H9 WTM
North Stonebranch Dr 427-F6 LTM
North Stonehinge Ct 424-H7 WTM
North Stout Field Dr 526-C3 WnT
North Stratford Dr 393-A8 F
North Summerfield Dr 457-E9 WnT
North Suncrest Cir Dr 491-F9 WnT
North Sundown Dr 457-F7 PTM
North Tamarack Cir Dr 425-B3 WTM
North Tara Ct 457-K10 WnT
North Timber Hill Dr 560-J6 PeT
North Tocovi Ct 455-F3 B
North Trailer Ct Rd 461-G3 L
North Trophy Club Dr 457-C9 WnT
North Turtle Cr Dr 527-G10 PeT
North Victor Dr 557-K10 M
North Vill Way 495-E9 WrT
North Villa Paree Dr 460-E2 WTM
North Village Greene Dr 496-H3 Cu
North Village Pk 358-B10 WTH
North Village Pkwy 457-D7 PTM
North Village Plaza Dr 494-K5 WrT
North Vine St 523-F7 P
North Vinewood Dr 455-G8 B
North Walnut Cr Dr 390-F9 CTH
North Warbler Way 392-J2 Ca
North Watergate Mall 457-K10 WnT
North Wellesley Dr 495-C2 WrT
North West Lake Dr 491-G7, H7 WnT
North Westbury Dr 491-H6 WnT
North Westridge Dr 359-E4 N
North Wheel Ests Dr 461-K4; 462-A4 L
North White Cloud Ct 593-A1 MTM
North White House Dr 596-E3 G
North Willow Way 424-H4 PTM
North Wilson Dr 391-H5 Ca
North Windjammer Ct 428-F1 FCT
North Windjammer Dr 428-E1 FCT
North Woodacre Blvd Dr 456-H4 PTM
North Woodfield Dr 392-G1 Ca
North Woods Edge Dr 427-A5 LTM
North Woodview Dr 391-G8 CTH
North Yeagy Ct 560-J10 WTJ
North-South Conn Rd 490-F6 WaT
Northants Cir 391-B5 CTH
Northbrook Cir 324-B10; 358-B1 WTH
Northbrook Ct 425-A6 WTM
Northbrook Dr 424-K6 WTM
Northcrest Cir 427-D3 LTM
Northcrest Ct 427-D3 LTM
Northcrest Dr 427-D3 LTM
Northcrest Pl 427-D3 LTM
Northeast 1st Ave 391-K4 Ca
Northeast 1st St 391-K4; 392-A4 Ca
Northeast 2nd Ave 392-A3 Ca
Northeast 2nd St 391-K4; 392-A4 Ca
Northeast 3rd Ave 392-A4 Ca
Northeast 3rd St 391-K4; 392-A3 Ca
Northeast 4th Ave 392-A4 Ca
Northeast 4th St 391-K3 Ca
Northeast 5th St 391-K3; 392-A3 Ca
Northeast 7th St 391-K3; 392-A3 Ca
Northeast S Commons Dr DN-D4 CTM
Northeast St 592-A2 M; 324-A10 W
Northeastern Ave 529-H8, K7 FT
Northern Ave 459-D8 WTM
Northern Dr 524-A2 WaT
Northfield Blvd 393-E9 F
Northfield Cir 393-E9 F
Northfield Ct 527-G9 PeT
Northfield Dr 455-C4, J4 B; 558-B10 M
Northfield Dr E 455-H3 B
Northfield Dr W 455-E3 B
Northfield Pl 393-D10 F
Northfield Rd 523-G6 P
Northgate Ct 359-J1 N
Northgate Dr 458-F3 WTM
Northgate St 458-J3; 459-J3; 460-A3 WTM
Northgren Pkwy 455-G5 B
Northhampton Dr 393-D9 F
Northland Ct 393-F5 F
Northland Rd 458-E2, E4 PTM
Northland St 393-E5 F
Northlane Dr 596-D10 NW
Northpoint Dr 558-A10 M
Northport Cir 428-J4 LTM
Northport Dr 559-J2 DTM
Northridge Courts 455-G4 B
Northridge Dr 359-J1 N
Northridge Pl 359-J1 N
Northrup Rd 389-C2 ET
Northside Dr 455-E8 B; 455-E8 LTH
Northview Ave 459-G4; 460-A4 WTM
Northview Ct 429-B2 McC
Northview Dr 429-B2 McC; 459-E3 WTM
Northway La 424-G2 PTM
Northwest 1st Ave 391-K4 Ca
Northwest 1st St 391-K4 Ca
Northwest 2nd Ave 391-K4 Ca
Northwest 2nd St 391-K4 Ca
Northwest 3rd Ave 391-J4 Ca
Northwest 3rd St 391-K4 Ca
Northwest 4th St 391-K3 Ca
Northwest 5th St 391-K3 Ca
Northwest 6th St 391-K3 Ca
Northwest Blvd 423-H5 PTM
Northwestern Ave 493-D4 CTM
Northwestern Dr 390-B10; 424-B1 CTH
Northwind Cir 428-B2 LTM
Northwind Dr 428-B2 LTM
Northwood Dr 392-K6 CTH; 393-E6 F; 593-B1 MTM; 425-J7 WTM
Norton Ave 527-G6, H6 PeT
Norwaldo Ave 459-K4, K7 WTM
Norwalk Ct 461-E8 LTM
Norwalk Dr 392-J1 Ca
Norway Dr 494-G7 WrT
Norway Spruce La 357-F5 WTH
Norwich Ct 457-H10; 491-H1 WnT
Norwich La 457-H10 WnT
Norwick Cir 596-F3 G
Norwood St DN-C4, D4, E4; 493-C9, E9, F9 CTM
Nostalgia La 491-D7 WnT
Notre Dame Dr 425-G3 WTM
Nottingham Ct 391-B4 CTH; 425-G9 WTM
Nottingham Dr 425-J3 WTM
Nottingham Rd 393-J4 DTH
Nottinghill Ct 491-A7 WnT
Nottinghill Dr 491-A7 WnT
Nowland Ave DN-F1; 493-J5; 494-A5, B5, D5 CTM
Nuckols La 562-J7 FT
Nuthatch Dr 389-C6 ET
Nuthatcher Dr 458-D2 PTM
Nutmeg Ct 562-E5 PeT
Nutty Dr 489-G3 WaT
Nyswander La 557-A3 GT

O

O'Bara Ct 392-E3 Ca
O'Dell La 596-C4 G
O'Dell St 455-H10, J5, J6, J8; 489-H1 B; 455-H10 LTH
O'Hara Ct 457-K10 WnT
O'Hara La 457-K10 WnT
O'Neal Ave 389-F3, H3 ET
Oak Ave 494-J8; 495-A8, E8 WrT
Oak Bk La 596-B3 G
Oak Blvd Dr N 496-K5 Cu
Oak Blvd Dr S 496-K5 Cu
Oak Blvd Dr W 496-K5 Cu
Oak Cove La 325-D5 N
Oak Ct 496-K5 Cu
Oak Den Rd 596-E9 NW
Oak Dr 392-A8 CTH; 391-H5 Ca; 393-K8 DTH; 393-K8 F; 595-K1 G; 593-C2 MTM; 561-J6 PeT; 497-G8 SCT
Oak Grove Ct 394-A2 F; 563-F5 FT; 557-J10 M
Oak Grove Dr 563-F5 FT
Oak Harbour Cir 325-D5 N
Oak Hill Dr 557-J2 P; 426-F7 WTM
Oak Hill Dr E 557-J3 P
Oak Hill Dr W 557-H2 P
Oak Knoll La 393-K10 F
Oak La 596-H3 G; 425-F10 WTM
Oak Lake Cir 424-D5 PTM
Oak Lake Cir N 424-D5 PTM
Oak Lake Cir S 424-D5 PTM
Oak Lake Dr 491-F1 WnT
Oak Meadow Ct 596-A3 G
Oak Meadow La 596-A3 G
Oak Pk Cir 358-B7 WTH
Oak Pk Ct 358-B7 WTH
Oak Pk Dr 561-K8 PeT
Oak Pt Cir 325-C4 N
Oak Rd 358-A10, B6, B9 WTH
Oak Ridge Ct 391-G2 Ca; 489-C10 WaT
Oak Ridge Dr 557-A7 GT; 459-H3 WTM; 489-E6 WaT; 389-F5 Z
Oak Ridge Rd 323-G2 AT; 391-G3 CTH; 323-G6; 357-G5, G10 WTH
Oak Ridge Way 595-H1 G
Oak Run Cir 424-J3 WTM
Oak Run Ct 424-J3 WTM
Oak Run Dr E 424-J3 WTM
Oak Run Dr N 424-J3 WTM
Oak Run Dr S 424-J3 WTM
Oak Run Pl 424-J3 WTM
Oak St 531-H5 NP; 389-E8, G8 Z
Oak Tree Cir 562-D9 PeT
Oak Tree Ct 562-C8 PeT
Oak Tree Dr 455-A2 B
Oak Tree Dr N 562-C8 PeT
Oak Tree Dr S 562-C9 PeT
Oak Tree La 393-E9 F; 462-A5 L
Oak Tree Way 390-E7 CTH
Oak Wood Dr 596-A3 G
Oak Woods La 358-A7 WTH
Oakbay Ct 563-A1 FT; 325-C5 N
Oakbay Dr 325-C5 N
Oakbrook Ct 458-A2 PTM
Oakbrook Dr 392-F2 Ca; 523-A7 P; 458-A3 PTM
Oakbrook La 458-A3 PTM
Oakbrook Rd 458-A2 PTM
Oakcrest Ct 428-B1 F
Oakcrest Dr 529-A10; 563-A1 FT
Oakcurst Dr 462-E5 L
Oakdale La 491-B3 WnT
Oakden Ct 596-E9 NW
Oakenshaw Dr 393-C7 F
Oakforge Dr 458-B2 PTM
Oakforge La 458-C3 PTM
Oakham Pl 393-H3 DTH
Oakhaven Ct 428-A6 LTM
Oakhaven Pl 428-A7 LTM
Oakhurst Ct 458-B6 PTM
Oakhurst Dr 458-A6 PTM
Oakhurst La 456-E9 LTH
Oakhurst Pl 458-A6 PTM
Oakhurst Way 458-A6 PTM
Oakland Ave 494-B6, B8, B9; 528-C4 CTM; 528-B6 PeT; 426-C9; 460-B2, C1, C3 WTM
Oakland Dr 524-J4 WnT
Oakland Hills Cir 428-E8 L
Oakland Hills Ct 428-E8 L
Oakland Hills Dr 428-E8 L
Oakland Rd 428-K6, K7 WTM
Oakland Terr 460-B3 WTM
Oaklandon Rd 428-G7, G10; 462-G2 L
Oakleaf Dr 390-B3 ET; 459-J5 WTM
Oakleaf Way 429-B2 FCT
Oakleigh Ct 594-K10 WTJ
Oakleigh Pkwy 594-J10 WTJ
Oakmont Ct 528-G9 BG
Oakmont Dr 455-A3 B; 359-C1, C3 N
Oakmont La 425-C5 WTM
Oaknoll Dr 525-J10 DTM
Oakridge Dr 393-C9 F
Oakshot La 424-E8 PTM
Oakspring Ct 496-F9 WrT
Oakspring Dr 496-E9 WrT
Oakview Cir 325-C5 N
Oakview Dr 592-D4 M; 325-C5 N; 457-F1 PTM
Oakview Dr S 457-F1 PTM
Oakwood Cir 325-C4 N
Oakwood Ct 455-J9 B; 391-E2 CTH; 392-B10 Ca; 596-A2 G; 523-J9 P; 496-K10 SCT; 425-C5 WTM
Oakwood Dr 389-J4 ET; 496-J10 SCT; 425-C5 WTM
Oakwood Dr W 595-K3 G
Oakwood Tr 424-B10 PTM; 425-A10, B9 WTM
Oakwood Tr Dr S 425-B10 WTM
Oarmine Dr 326-B10 N
Oberlin Ct 424-F3 PTM
Oblong Pl 596-D1 G
Oceanline Dr 457-B10 WnT
Ochs Ave 458-A5 PTM
Odam Ct 462-B1 L
Office Pk Dr 424-K5 WTM
Office Plaza Blvd 458-A8 PTM
Offutt Dr 391-H2 CTH
Ogden St DN-E1, E2, E4; 493-F5, F6, F9 CTM
Oglethorpe Ct 424-G3 PTM
Ohio St DN-A2, D2, E2, F2; 492-J8, K7; 493-D7, J7; 494-D7 CTM; DN-A2, A3; 490-K8; 491-F8, J7; 492-B8, G8, J8 WnT
Ohmer Ave 494-H8 WrT
Oil Cr Ct 424-C6 PTM
Oil Cr Dr 424-C6 PTM
Oklahoma Ct 490-J10 WnT
Old Barn Cir 457-J2 PTM
Old Barn Ct 457-K1 PTM
Old Barn Dr 457-J2 PTM
Old Bridge Rd 455-C8 LTH
Old Colony Dr 530-J4 SCT
Old Colony Rd 461-B4 L; 461-B4 LTM
Old Dominion Ct 490-K10 WnT
Old Fairgrounds Dr 461-E5 L
Old Farm La 491-A4 WnT
Old Farm Rd 427-F5 LTM
Old Grayce La 391-K3 Ca
Old Hickory Cir 595-G1 G
Old Hickory Dr 595-G1 G
Old High Sch Dr 525-F6 DTM
Old House Rd 427-C7 LTM
Old Meridian St 391-F5 CTH; 391-F5 Ca
Old Mill Cir 391-D1 CTH
Old Mill Ct 391-D1 CTH; 559-J3 DTM
Old Mill Dr 559-J2 DTM
Old Natl Rd 524-F5 P; 524-F5 WaT
Old Oak Dr 393-K2 F
Old Oak Tr 428-H9 L
Old Oakland Blvd Dr E 428-G7 L
Old Oakland Blvd Dr N 428-F7 L
Old Oakland Blvd Dr W 428-F8 L
Old Oakland Cir 428-F8 L
Old Orchard Rd 428-H9 L; 460-K3 LTM
Old Otto Ct E 559-A10 MTM
Old Otto Ct N 559-A9 MTM
Old Prairie Ct 427-F5 LTM
Old Raymond St 526-J3 CTM; 526-J3 WnT
Old Rte 67 N 558-D10; 592-C1 BTM; 592-C1 M
Old Smith Valley Rd 594-H4 WTJ
Old State Rte 37 593-J10 HT; 594-A9, C7 WTJ
Old State Rte 144 593-B8 MTM
Old Stone Dr 428-F4, H4 LTM
Old Town Dr E 425-B4 WTM
Old Town Dr N 425-A4 WTM
Old Town Dr S 425-A4 WTM
Old Town Dr W 425-A4 WTM
Old Town La 425-B4 WTM
Old Trails Rd 495-E7 WrT
Old Washington St 524-H4 WnT
Olde Mill Bay 425-E5 WTM
Olde Mill Cir Dr N 425-D5 WTM
Olde Mill Cir Dr S 425-E5 WTM
Olde Mill Cir Dr W 425-D5 WTM
Olde Mill Cove 425-E5 WTM
Olde Mill Dr E 425-E5 WTM
Olde Mill Run 425-E4 WTM
Olde Mill Trace 425-D5 WTM
Oldfield Ct 392-G9 Ca
Oldfield Dr 392-G9 Ca
Oldfields Cir 458-J8 WTM
Oldfields Cir Dr N 458-J8 WTM
Oldfields Cir Dr S 458-J8 WTM
Oldham Dr 559-H5 DTM
Oldstone Pl 393-C7 F
Olender Dr 526-B7 DTM
Oles Dr 455-C9 LTH; 458-K4 WTM
Oles Dr N 458-K4 WTM
Oleta Dr 561-E5 PeT
Olin Ave 492-D5 S; 492-D5, D6 WnT
Olin Rd 422-K5 PTM
Olio Rd 395-C2, C5 F; 395-C2, C9; 429-C2 FCT; 327-C3 WRT; 327-C6; 361-C5, C9 WyT
Olive Branch Cir 594-J6 WTJ
Olive Branch La 594-J5 WTJ
Olive Branch Rd 594-E6; 595-B6 WTJ
Olive St DN-F4; 493-H10; 527-H2 CTM; 527-H6; 561-H4 PeT
Oliver Ave DN-A4, B4; 492-J9 CTM; 523-H8, J8 P; DN-A4; 491-J9; 492-B9, D9, H9 WnT
Olivewood Dr 495-F3 WrT
Olney St 494-C1, C4, C6 CTM; 528-D7 PeT; 426-C10; 460-C1, C3, C7 WTM
Olvey St 428-H10 L
Olympia Cir 458-H6 WTM
Olympia Ct 458-H6 WTM
Olympia Dr 428-C2 F; 458-H5, H6, J6 WTM
Omega La 523-K7 P
One W Dr 425-E5 WTM
Ontario Cir 424-E5 PTM
Ontario La 424-D6 PTM
Onyx Cir 562-H2 FT
Opelika Ct 561-B6 PeT
Opera Pl 461-J9 WrT
Ophelia Ct 489-E7 A
Ophelia Dr 489-E7 A
Oracle Dr 529-H5 FT
Orange St 493-E10; 494-C10, F10; 527-G1, H1 CTM; 494-G10, J10; 495-A10, E10 WrT
Orchard Ave 459-K10; 493-K1 CTM; 459-K10 WTM
Orchard Blvd 393-E6 F
Orchard Dr 428-J9 L
Orchard Hill La 561-F10 G; 460-H2 LTM
Orchard La 596-A3, B3 G
Orchard Pk Dr N 391-J10 CTH
Orchard Pk Dr S 391-J10; 425-J1 CTH
Orchard Pk Dr W 391-J10; 425-J1 CTH
Orchard Rd 592-F8 BTM; 592-J7 MTM
Orchard St 389-F5 Z
Orchard Terr 459-K10; 493-K1 CTM
Orchard Vill Dr 561-E6 PeT
Orchardgrass La 458-A4 PTM
Orchardview Ct 595-F1 G
Orchardview Dr 595-E1 G
Orchid Ct 495-G4 WrT
Orchid La 495-G4 WrT
Oriental Ct 495-H3 WrT
Oriental Oak Ct 359-C1 N
Oriental St DN-F2, F3; 493-J8 CTM
Orinoco Ave 561-J2, J5 PeT
Oriole Dr 392-H2 Ca
Orion Ave 494-G8 CTM
Oris Ct 563-G2 FT
Oris Rd 563-G2 FT
Orlando Ct 458-G6 WTM
Orlando St 458-H6, J6 WTM
Orleans Ct 359-K1 N
Orleans St 527-G2 CTM
Orville La 562-H3 FT
Osborn Dr 461-A7 LTM
Osborn St 359-G3 N
Osceola Ct 462-C10 WrT
Osceola La 462-C10 WrT
Oshawa St 462-G1 L
Osprey Cir 427-G8 LTM
Osprey Dr 595-A8 WTJ
Osprey Way 392-H3 Ca
Ossington Ct 457-F6 PTM
Ossington Dr 457-F6 PTM
Ostara Dr 394-J8 F
Oswego Rd 392-A6 Ca
Othello Way 489-F7 A
Otis Ave 461-G3, J3 L
Ottawa Dr 561-D8 PeT
Otter Cove Cir 428-E4 LTM
Otter Pl 426-C1 Ca
Otterbein Ave 527-J7 PeT
Outrigger Ct 428-E5 LTM
Outrigger La 394-C7 F
Overbrook Cir 460-J4 LTM
Overcrest Dr 394-A10 F; 562-J1 FT
Overdorf Rd 326-C7 NT; 326-C2 WRT
Overland Ct 359-J6 N; 424-A10 PTM
Overland Dr 596-B5 G
Overland Way 455-J10 LTH
Overlook Cir 325-E3 C; 496-J4 Cu
Overlook Ct 393-F9 F; 489-D8 WaT; 496-B3 WrT
Overlook Dr 496-J4 Cu
Overlook Pass 489-D8 WaT
Overlook Pkwy 425-F4 WTM
Overlook Pl 390-A5 ET
Overlook Pt 423-E1 ET
Overlook Tr 523-D6 P
Owl Ct 424-C6 PTM
Owls Nest Ct 457-E6 PTM
Owls Nest Dr 457-E7 PTM
Owls Nest Pl 457-E6 PTM
Owster La 528-D7 PeT
Owster Way 528-D7 PeT
Oxbow Way 425-H10; 459-H1 WTM
Oxford Ct 359-J8 N
Oxford Dr 325-A7 N
Oxford Pl 392-F6 Ca
Oxford Run 596-B5 G
Oxford St 460-B10; 494-B2, B3, B5, B6, B8, B9; 528-B1, B3, B4, B5 CTM; 528-B6; 562-B3 PeT; 426-B10; 460-B1, B3, B4, B7 WTM
Oyster Bay Ct 428-D7 L

P

P G A Dr 427-C4 LTM
Paca St DN-C1; 493-C6 CTM
Pacer Ct 357-D10 WTH
Pacific St 527-F7, K7 PeT
Packard Dr 394-C10 F
Paddington Cir 424-E7 PTM
Paddington La N 424-D7 PTM
Paddington La W 424-D7 PTM
Paddock Ct 422-H3 BTH; 422-H3 PTM
Paddock Dr 594-G2 WTJ
Paddock Rd 559-D9 DTM; 593-D1, D5 MTM; 523-A7 P; 594-G5 WTJ
Padre La 528-H10 FT; 596-F4 G
Pagoda Dr 527-G3 CTM
Pagoda Dr Way 527-G3 CTM
Pagosa Ct 461-G10 WrT
Painted Maple Ct 457-D4 PTM
Painter Ct 391-F2 CTH
Pake Side Ct 455-J5 B
Pakenham Dr 326-H6 WyT
Palace Ct 390-G10 CTH
Palace Dr 526-A5 WnT
Palais Cir 423-E9 PTM
Palais Ct 423-E8 PTM
Palais Dr 423-E9 PTM
Palatka Ct 428-E10 L
Palisade Ct 528-H10 FT
Palisade Way 528-H10 FT
Palm Ct 495-G3 WrT
Palm Grove Ct 495-F3 WrT
Palmaire Pl 394-C2 F
Palmbrook Blvd 358-F2 N
Palmer Dr 324-K5 N
Palmer La 596-E3 G
Palmer St 527-E1, H1, J1 CTM
Palmetto Ct 561-C7 PeT
Palmetto La 561-C7 PeT
Palmyra Cir 496-D8 WrT
Palmyra Ct 496-D8 WrT
Palmyra Dr 496-D8 WrT
Palo Verde Ct 562-B8 PeT
Palo Verde Dr 562-B7 PeT

Palo Vista Rd 596-F3 G
Palomino Ct 389-F9 Z
Palomino Run 423-G9 PTM
Palomino Tr 529-G9 FT
Pam Rd 391-F9 CTH
Pamela Dr 557-H2 P; 426-A10 WTM
Pamela Pkwy 455-G7 B
Pamona Cir 491-F4 WnT
Pamona Ct 491-F4 WnT
Pamona Dr 491-F4 WnT
Panama Ave 525-E1, E2 WnT
Pann Ct 561-E7 PeT
Panola Ct 496-D9 WrT
Panorama Ct 490-J8 WnT
Papan Ct 523-G4 WaT
Pappas Dr 528-J10 FT
Par Ct 595-D8 WTJ
Par Dr 424-C9 PTM
Paradise Ct 596-G3 G; 428-J10 L
Paradise La 428-H10 L; 326-C5 NT
Paradise Rd 428-H10 L
Paradise Way 596-G3 G
Parallel St 424-G8 PTM
Parc Chateau Dr 424-H10 WTM
Paree Ct E 491-H6 WnT
Paree Ct W 491-G6 WnT
Paris Ave 493-D3 CTM
Parish La 561-C8 PeT
Park 31 Dr 357-J3 W
Park 32 W 359-B4 NT
Park 65 Dr 458-C8 PTM
Park Ave 391-G10; 425-G1 CTH; DN-E1, E3, E4; 459-G10; 493-G1, G3, G5, G6, G8, G9 CTM; 596-E3 G; 425-G3, G5, G8, G10; 459-G1, G2, G5, G7, G8 WTM
Park Bend N 424-K7 WTM
Park Castle Way 496-D4 WrT
Park Central Ct 459-B1 WTM
Park Central Dr N 459-B1 WTM
Park Central Dr S 459-B1 WTM
Park Central Dr W 425-B10; 459-B1 WTM
Park Central Way 425-B10; 459-B1 WTM
Park Chase Pl 496-B4 WrT
Park Cir N 424-K7 WTM
Park Ct N 424-K7 WTM
Park Davis Cir 462-A10 WrT
Park Davis Ct 462-A9 WrT
Park Davis Dr 462-A9 WrT
Park Dr 562-D10; 596-D2 G; 592-B4 M; 523-E8 P
Park Forest Ct 461-A6 LTM
Park Glen Ct 496-B4 WrT
Park Guion Ct 424-D10 PTM
Park Hill Dr 496-C4 WrT
Park Hurst Dr 496-C4 WrT
Park La 391-J4 Ca; 489-F2 LTH
Park La N 424-K7 WTM
Park Lake Dr N 424-H8 WTM
Park Lodge Ct 460-C5 WTM
Park Meadow Ct 528-E6 PeT
Park Meadow Dr 528-E6 PeT
Park Meadow Way 528-E6 PeT
Park Pl 391-J3 Ca; 389-F6 Z
Park Pl Blvd 489-G8 A
Park Pl Ct 489-G8 A
Park Plaza Ct 426-J10 WTM
Park Rd 455-F5 B
Park Ridge Dr 496-C4 WrT
Park Ridge Way 496-C4 WrT
Park Royale Dr 496-D4 WrT
Park St 359-F2 N; 523-G8 P; 357-J4 W
Park Stream Dr 496-B4 WrT
Park Terr Ct 496-C4 WrT
Park Valley Dr 496-B4 WrT
Park View Rd 391-F2 CTH
Park Vista Ct 393-K9 F; 496-B5 WrT
Park Way N 424-K7 WTM
Park Way W 491-B6 WnT
Parkdale Pl 457-E8 PTM
Parke Dr 523-F2 WaT
Parker Ave 460-B10; 494-B3, B4, B6, B9; 528-B5 CTM; 528-B6 PeT; 426-B9, B10; 460-B1, B3, B6, B8 WTM
Parker Ct 460-B8 WTM
Parker La 426-B10 WTM
Parker Oaks 455-J5 B
Parkgate Ave 496-C9 WrT
Parkland Pl 427-D3 LTM
Parkshore Dr 394-B2 F
Parkside Ct N 557-H1 P
Parkside Ct S 557-H1 P
Parkside Dr 393-K4 F; 461-D5 L; 531-F3 SCT
Parkthorne Dr 496-B4 WrT
Parkview Ave 493-K8 CTM
Parkview Ct 391-F2 CTH; 393-H6 F
Parkview Dr 592-B1 M
Parkview La 393-G6 F
Parkway Ave 527-F1 CTM
Parkway Cir 357-J4 W
Parkway Dr 528-E5 BG; 428-B1 F; 389-F9 Z
Parkwood Crossing 425-F2 Ca
Parkwood Ct 457-H9 PTM
Parkwood Dr 455-K8 B; 491-H2 S
Parliament Ct 359-K6 N
Parliament Dr 460-F2 WTM
Parliament La 461-K8 LTM
Parr Dr 426-A10, B9 WTM
Parrington Dr 462-C2 L
Parrish Ct 562-D1 PeT
Parrot Ct 394-E9 F
Parsley La 562-G7 PeT
Parsons Dr 491-G3 WnT
Parterra Ct 528-K10 FT
Parterra Dr 528-K10 FT
Parthenia Ave 455-G5 B
Partridge Ct 562-B6 Spt
Partridge Pl 426-D1 Ca; 389-C6 ET
Partridge Rd 562-C6 Spt
Pasadena Rd 325-B10 NT
Pasadena St 461-B7, B8 LTM; 495-B3, B4, B7; 529-B2, B5 WrT
Pascal Ct 424-C6 PTM
Paso Del Norte Ct 562-C7 PeT
Paso Del Norte Dr 562-B7 PeT
Passage Cir 427-B3 LTM
Pathway Dr N 595-E7 WTJ
Pathway Dr S 595-E7 WTJ
Patoka Pl 391-D3 Ca
Patricia Ct 392-C7 Ca
Patricia Dr 392-C7 Ca
Patricia St 491-J1; 492-A1, C1 WnT
Patrick Ct 394-B5 F
Patrick Pl 455-J4 B; 427-C7 LTM
Patriot Ct 390-E9 CTH
Patriot Way 457-J4 PTM
Patterson Dr 489-J4 WaT
Patterson St DN-C2; 493-B7 CTM; 596-F2 G; 459-B5 WTM
Pattie Ct 594-H8 WTJ
Patton Dr 461-G5 L; 491-J2, J4 S; 457-H10, J10 WnT
Paul Dr 496-H5 WrT
Paula La Dr E 458-J7 WTM
Paula La Dr S 458-H7 WTM
Paunee Rd 391-K6 Ca
Pawnee Ct 462-C10 WrT
Pawnee Dr 462-C10; 496-C1 WrT
Pawtucket Ct 426-K8; 428-A5 LTM
Paxton Pl 459-G2, J2 WTM
Payne Branch Rd 424-D4 PTM
Payne Dr 562-C2 PeT
Payne Rd 529-B5, C5 FT; 424-D7 PTM; 562-D2 PeT
Payne Rd Dr N 562-C2 PeT
Payne Rd Dr S 562-C2 PeT
Payne St 494-A10 CTM
Payton Ave 461-E6 L; 461-E9; 495-E5, E7 WrT
Paz Dr W 562-C9 G
Peace Pl 457-K1 PTM
Peaceful Pl 595-D2 WTJ
Peaceful View Dr 592-B5 M
Peacemaker La 358-K5 NT
Peach Blossom Pl 457-C5 PTM
Peach Ct 455-H10 LTH
Peach Tree Dr 596-E10 NW
Peach Tree La 495-E8 WrT
Peachtree Ct 596-C5 G
Peachtree La 596-C5 G
Peachwood Ct 461-K6 L
Peacock Ct 462-G1 L; 557-G2 P
Peacock Dr 462-F1 L
Peacock Ridge 557-G2 P
Pearcrest Cir 594-J10 WTJ
Pearcrest Way 594-J10 WTJ
Pearl Bay Ridge 428-H3 LTM
Pearl St 325-H1 C; DN-D3, E3; 493-E8, F8; 494-B8 CTM; 391-J1 Ca; 559-E6 DTM; 596-C2, E2 G
Pearl St W 596-C2 G
Pearson Pl 562-F7 PeT
Peartree La 462-B4 L
Pebble Beach Ct 491-A1 WnT
Pebble Beach Dr 390-H9 CTH
Pebble Bk Blvd 358-H4 N
Pebble Bk Cir 358-J2 N
Pebble Bk Dr 358-H1, H2 N
Pebble Bk La 392-K7 CTH
Pebble Bk Pl 358-H2 N
Pebble Cr Ct 424-D6 PTM
Pebble Cr Dr 424-D6 PTM
Pebble Ct 594-J1 WTJ
Pebble La 594-J1 WTJ
Pebble Pt Dr 491-D1 WnT
Pebble Run 594-J1 WTJ
Pebblebrooke Ct 428-H8 L
Pebblebrooke Dr E 428-J8 L
Pebblebrooke Dr W 428-H8 L
Pebblepointe Pass 392-G5, G7 Ca
Pecan Ct 561-B6 PeT
Peck St DN-E1; 493-F5 CTM; 596-D5, D6 G
Pecos Ct 528-J10 FT
Peggy La 455-B4 LTH
Pele Pl 491-C4 WnT
Pelican Pl 392-H3 Ca
Pemberly Ct 359-K6 N
Pemberly Dr 559-H4 DTM
Pemberton Cir 424-K4 WTM
Pemberton La 424-K4 WTM
Pembroke Ct 558-K10 MTM
Pembridge Dr 457-F6 PTM
Pembridge Way 457-F6 PTM
Pembroke La 461-A4 LTM
Pembroke Pl 460-F2 WTM
Pembrook Cir 390-K6 CTH
Pendleton Ave 360-C3 NT; 360-J4; 361-J6 WyT
Pendleton Pike 428-J9; 461-D8; 462-A4, E2 L; 461-D8 LTM
Pendleton Rd 428-H10 L
Pendleton Way 461-E8 LTM
Pendragon Blvd 458-B1 PTM
Pendula Dr 392-F8 Ca; 462-B2 L
Penjerack Ct 424-D1 CTH
Penn Dr 391-F9 CTH
Penn Pl 426-E6 WTM; 389-F7 Z
Penn St 391-F10; 425-F1 CTH; 391-F10; 425-F1 Ca; 357-K3; 358-A3 W
Penneagle Dr 392-K3 Ca
Pennington Ct 457-C6 PTM
Pennington Dr 594-J9 WTJ
Pennington Rd 592-F6, F8, G9 BTM; 395-B4; 395-B4 FCT; 592-G9, H10 MTM; 361-B2 WyT
Pennridge Dr 425-E9, F9 WTM
Pennswood Ct 523-A7 P
Pennsylvania Ct 527-E4 CTM
Pennsylvania Pkwy 425-F1 Ca
Pennsylvania Rd 391-F5, F8 CTH; 391-F5, F8 Ca
Pennsylvania St DN-D1, D4; 459-F10; 493-E4, E7, E10, F2; 527-E5, F3 CTM; 391-F9 Ca; 527-E7; 561-E6, E7 PeT; 425-F3, F5, F8, F10; 459-F4, F8 WTM
Pennteller Rd 562-D3 PeT
Pennwood Ct 425-F4 WTM
Pennwood Dr 460-B5 WTM
Pennwood La 455-J6 B
Penny Ct 496-C2 WrT
Penny La 496-C2 WrT
Pennycroft Dr 428-E8 L
Pennyroyal La 562-F6 PeT
Penright Ct 561-C9 PeT
Penrith Dr 496-B2 WrT
Pentecost Rd 529-K7; 530-A7 FT
Pentwater Ct 428-J4 LTM
Penway Cir 457-H9 WnT
Penway St 459-F9 CTM; 457-H9, K9; 458-B9 WnT; 461-E9, F9 WrT
Penzance Pl 424-D1 CTH
Peony Pl 458-A4 PTM
Pepper Cir 562-F5 PeT
Pepper Ct 562-F5 PeT
Pepper Mill Ct 392-E5 Ca
Peppergrass Ct 458-D3 PTM
Pepperidge Cir 462-B6 LTM
Pepperidge Ct 462-B7 LTM
Pepperidge Dr 461-K6; 462-A6, C6 LTM
Peppermill La 394-D8 F
Peppermill Rd N 596-A4 G
Peppermint Dr 455-A5 LTH
Pepperwood Dr 428-H6 L
Peregrine Blvd 458-E2 PTM
Pergola La 491-G10 WnT
Perilla Ct 562-G5 FT
Perimeter Rd 524-J7 DTM; 524-J7 WnT
Perimeter Rd N 525-A3, E2 WnT
Perimeter Rd S 525-C8 DTM
Periwinkle Blvd 525-K9 DTM
Periwinkle La 460-C3 WTM
Periwinkle Way 460-C4 WTM
Perkins Ave 528-C4, C6 BG; 528-C2, C4 CTM; 528-C6 PeT
Perkins Ct 528-C2 CTM
Perle Way 594-J1 WTJ
Perlinda La 564-A4 FT
Perrault Dr 562-B3 PeT
Perrier Ct 423-E9 PTM
Perrier Dr 423-E9 PTM
Perrin Dr 391-H2 CTH
Perry Commons Blvd 560-K5 PeT
Perry Ct 495-C7 WrT
Perry Dr 495-B7 WrT
Perry Rd 524-C10; 558-D1 P
Perry St 526-B5, C5, E6 DTM; 596-B2 G; 527-G5, H5, K5 PeT
Perry Woods Ct 562-C1 PeT
Perry Woods Way 562-C1 PeT
Perry-Worth Rd 388-D9 ET; 388-A6 PTB
Pershing Ave 424-G9 PTM; 458-H2 WTM; DN-A2, A3, A4; 492-J5, J7, J8, J10; 526-J2 WnT
Pershing Rd 424-F8 PTM
Persimmion Pass 557-J3 P
Persimmon Dr 428-J9 L
Persimmon La 595-A4 WTJ
Persimmon Pl 324-J7 N
Personality Ct 528-J9 FT
Perth Ct 596-F2 G
Petalon Trace 394-J8 F
Pete Moore Dr 455-J8 B
Peterman Rd 561-B10; 595-B2, B4 WTJ
Peters St 388-F1 Wh
Petersburg Pkwy 457-G3 PTM
Petersen Ct 457-H3 PTM
Petra Ct 395-A8 FCT
Pewter Pl 393-G5 F
Phaeton Pl 561-G6 PeT
Phantom Ct 389-E9 Z
Pheasant Ct 393-A4 Ca; 457-J7 PTM; 562-F3 PeT
Pheasant Dr 562-F3 PeT
Pheasant Run 389-C6 ET; 565-B1 MTS
Pheasant Way Ct 595-A6 WTJ
Philadelphia Ct 457-F4 PTM
Philadelphia Dr 393-G8 F
Philip Ct 492-D1 WnT
Phillips Dr 526-B1 WnT
Phillips Pl 389-E8 Z
Phillips Rd 557-F7 GT
Philwood Dr 491-J2 S
Phoenix Cir 526-C6 DTM
Phoenix Dr 526-B6 DTM
Phylis Dr 458-B5 PTM
Picadilly Ct 455-G8 B; 427-G5 LTM
Picadilly Dr 455-F8 B
Picadilly La 427-G5 LTM
Picadilly Pl 491-J3 WTM
Pickens Ct 390-D9 CTH
Pickett St 523-G8 P
Pickford Ct 562-B7 PeT
Pickford Dr 562-B7 PeT
Pickwick Ct 325-B7 N
Pickwick Dr 425-B4 WTM
Pickwick Pl 459-A9 CTM
Piction Dr 461-C8 L
Pierce Dr 523-J10 P
Pierce St 388-E1 Wh
Pierson Dr 525-F3 WnT
Pierson St 493-E3, E4, E6 CTM
Pigeon Cr La 456-J8 PTM
Pike Pkwy 457-H4 PTM
Pike Pl 523-G8 P
Pike Plaza Rd 457-K8; 458-A7 PTM
Pike View Ct 424-A10 PTM
Pike View Dr 424-A10 PTM
Pikeside Dr 428-H10 L
Pilgrim Ct 595-J3 G
Pilgrim Dr 457-H3 PTM
Pilgrim Rd 595-H3 G; 327-D10 WyT
Pillory Cir 457-J2 PTM
Pillory Dr 457-H2 PTM
Pillory Pl 457-H2 PTM
Pimbury Ct 425-B3 WTM
Pimlico Cir 391-H9 CTH
Pin Oak Cir 489-E6 A; 429-B3 McC
Pin Oak Ct 429-B3 McC; 325-C10 N; 424-J4 WTM
Pin Oak Dr 455-G10 LTH; 592-C5 M; 429-B3 McC
Pin Oak Tr 428-H9 L
Pin Oak Way 458-A4 PTM
Pin Oak Way Dr N 457-K3; 458-A3 PTM
Pine Bluff Dr 394-A9 F; 531-G3 SCT
Pine Blvd 596-E10 NW
Pine Cone Way 424-K1 PTM
Pine Crest Rd 456-K9 WnT
Pine Ct 497-B4 BCT
Pine Dr 425-C3, E3 WTM
Pine Forge Cir 458-B2 PTM
Pine Forge Ct 458-B2 PTM
Pine Grove Ct 428-K7 L
Pine Grove La 523-E4 GT
Pine Hill Dr 462-F2 L; 324-G6, G7 N
Pine Knoll Blvd 324-H7 N
Pine Lake Rd 424-C7 PTM
Pine Lake Way 424-C6 PTM
Pine Meadow 455-A3 B
Pine Meadow Dr 389-G7 Z
Pine Mountain Pl 496-F5 WrT
Pine Mountain Way 496-F5 WrT
Pine Needle Ct 394-C9 F
Pine Oak Ct 561-B9 WTJ
Pine Pk La 424-B7 PTM
Pine Ridge Dr 357-F5 WTH; 425-C4 WTM
Pine Ridge Dr E 427-A2 F
Pine Ridge Dr N 427-A2 F
Pine Royal Dr 427-E10 LTM
Pine Springs Ct 427-G8 LTM
Pine Springs Dr 427-F8 LTM
Pine Springs Dr E 427-G8 LTM
Pine Springs Dr W 427-F8 LTM
Pine St 455-G8 B; DN-E2, E3, E4; 493-G9, H9 CTM; 455-J10 LTH; 562-B5 Spt; 389-G9 Z
Pine Tree 489-J10 A
Pine Tree Blvd 427-G4 LTM
Pine Tree La 360-E5 NT
Pine Valley Ct 394-C9 F
Pine View Dr 392-A2 Ca
Pine View La 561-B9 WTJ
Pinebrook Dr 358-F2 N; 458-A5 PTM
Pinecreek Cir 427-J3 LTM
Pinecreek Ct 427-J2 LTM
Pinecreek Dr 427-J3 LTM
Pinecreek Way 427-J3 LTM
Pinecrest Dr 596-D6 G
Pinecrest Rd 491-A1 WnT
Pinecroft Dr 458-B5 PTM
Pinedale Dr 489-B8 WaT
Pinehollow Ct 457-G7 PTM
Pinehurst Ave 394-D9 F
Pinehurst Dr 390-J9 CTH
Pinehurst Dr E 461-K6 LTM
Pinehurst Dr N 461-K6 LTM
Pinehurst Dr S 461-J8 LTM
Pineleigh Pl 594-J10 WTJ
Pineleigh Way 594-K10 WTJ
Pineneedle Ct 462-B7 LTM
Pineneedle Dr 428-J9 L
Pinetop Ct 562-C5 PeT
Pinetop Dr 562-C5, E5 PeT
Pinetree Ct 461-K8 LTM
Pineview Cir 393-B10 F; 562-E5 PeT
Pineview Ct 426-F7 WTM
Pineview Ct E 423-G2 ET
Pineview Ct W 423-G2 ET
Pineview Dr 423-G2 ET; 592-D4 M
Pineway Dr 422-F8 BTH
Pinewood Ct 425-H3 WTM
Pinewood Dr 455-E8 LTH
Piney Wood Ct 491-B1 WnT
Pinnacle Blvd 529-A7 FT
Pinnacle La 523-E7 P
Pinon Dr 528-B10 PeT
Pintail Ct 391-D6 CTH
Pintail La 393-C8 F
Pinto Cir 458-E4 PTM
Pinto Ct 458-E4 PTM
Pinto Way 458-E4 PTM
Pinyon Ct 424-H4 WTM
Pioneer Cir 592-C3 BTM; 592-C3 M
Pioneer Ct 557-J10 M
Pioneer Dr 561-C2 PeT
Pioneer Pl 557-K10 M
Pioneer Tr 393-H9 F
Pioneer Woods Dr 491-J6 WnT
Piping Rock La 457-F6 PTM
Pippin Ct 523-E2 WaT
Pisa Ct 461-J6 LTM
Pitney Dr 358-H2 N
Pittman Pl 458-D6 PTM
Pittwood Dr 425-J3 WTM
Pixley Ct 461-K9 WrT
Pixley La 325-A6 N
Placing Rd 461-E9, F9 WrT
Plainfield Ave 526-A1 WnT
Plainview St 491-F6, F9; 525-F2 WnT
Plantana Blvd 394-B2 F
Plantation Dr 426-G6 WTM
Plantation La 489-G6 A
Platini Pl 491-C4 WnT
Play View Way 393-A10 F
Player Cir 392-K4 Ca
Players Dr 496-D3 WrT
Plaza Central 595-D6 WTJ
Plaza Chica 595-E6 WTJ
Plaza Dr 424-G6 PTM
Plaza Grande 595-D6 WTJ
Plaza La 424-G6 PTM
Plaza W Dr 424-B1 CTH
Pleasant Cr Ct 562-C8 PeT
Pleasant Cr Dr 562-C8 PeT
Pleasant Dr 565-A4 MTS
Pleasant Hill Cir 491-K7 WnT
Pleasant Hill Ct 325-C2 JT
Pleasant Lake Cir 562-D8 PeT
Pleasant Lake Ct 562-D8 PeT
Pleasant Lake Dr 562-C8 PeT
Pleasant Run Blvd 461-E10; 495-E1 WrT
Pleasant Run Pkwy Dr N 494-A10, D8, F8; 527-D4, G1; 528-B2 CTM; 494-H7; 495-B5 WrT
Pleasant Run Pkwy Dr S 494-D9; 527-D4, G3, H2; 528-B2 CTM; 494-G7, J6; 495-A7, B6, C3 WrT
Pleasant St DN-F4; 493-H10, K10; 494-A10 CTM; 596-D2 G; 359-G4, J4; 360-A4 N; 495-J9 WrT
Pleasant View 392-C9 Ca
Pleasant View Blvd 595-E1 G
Pleasant View La 394-D4 F
Pleasant Way 426-B2 CTH
Pleasant Way W 426-B2 CTH
Pleasant Woods La 462-A1 L
Plesant Run Dr 562-B9 G
Plublishers Dr 393-K4 F
Plum Hollow Cir 394-E9 F
Plum St 455-K10 LTH; 359-G5 N; 389-G9 Z
Plummer Rd 557-B7 GT
Plummer St 461-F7 L
Plymouth Rock Ct 595-H3 G
Plymouth Rock Dr 392-J1 Ca
Plymouth Rock Way 595-H2 G
Pocket Hollow Ct 427-H7 LTM
Pocono Mesa N 491-H4 S
Pocono Mesa S 491-H4 S
Poinsettia Dr 562-D5 PeT
Point Bar Rd 424-D6 PTM
Pointe Ct 393-K10 F
Pointe E Ct 427-B2 LTM
Pointer Pl 393-G5 F
Pointers Ct 427-G5 LTM
Pokagon Dr 391-E3 Ca
Polco St 492-C5 S
Polk St DN-F1; 493-H6 CTM; 596-E2 G
Polk Vill Rd 596-E3 G
Pollard St 424-B9 PTM
Polonius Ct 457-H2 PTM
Polonius Dr 457-H2 PTM
Polonius La 457-H2 PTM
Pomander Pl 459-A9 CTM
Pomander St 495-B5 WrT
Pomona Ct 424-G3 PTM
Pompano Dr 428-G5 LTM
Ponderosa Blvd 426-E7 WTM
Ponderosa Ct 489-J10 A
Ponds Pointe Dr 391-C1 CTH
Pondview Ct 455-G10 B; 424-F10 PTM
Pondview Dr 391-E1 CTH
Ponsonby Ct 491-E8 WnT
Ponza Ct 461-K7 LTM
Poole Pl 324-J4 N
Poplar Byrd Ct 391-G2 CTH
Poplar Ct 324-J5 N; 596-E10 NW
Poplar Dr 324-J5 N; 595-G3 WTJ
Poplar Grove 489-A8 WaT
Poplar Rd 494-G7 WrT
Poplar St 523-G7 P; 357-J4 W; 389-G8, H8 Z
Poppyseed Dr 562-F5 PeT
Porchester La 596-B4 G
Porchester Pl 523-C8 P
Porsche Dr 424-H7 PTM
Port Au Prince 491-H8, J8 WnT
Port Ct E 325-E3 C
Port Ct W 325-E3 C
Port Dr 490-B7 WaT
Port Irving Dr 491-H7 WnT
Port Lillian Dr 491-H7 WnT
Port O Call Dr 491-J8 WnT
Port O Monaco 491-H7 WnT
Port Rd N 325-E3 C
Port Robert Dr 491-H8 WnT
Port Sylvia Dr 491-H8, J7 WnT
Portage Ave 561-K6 PeT
Portage Cir 394-K9 FCT
Portage Ct 561-K5 PeT
Portage Terr 561-K5 PeT
Portage Way 394-K9 FCT
Portalan Dr 497-D3 BCT
Porter Ave 388-E1 Wh
Porter Rd 490-D9 WaT
Porter St 524-K3 WnT
Portia Dr 497-D3 BCT
Portillo Pl 457-H3 PTM
Portland Sq 424-H9 WTM
Portman Pl 523-C8 P
Porto Alegre St DN-B1; 492-K6 CTM
Portside Ct 428-D5 LTM
Portside Dr 489-K7 A
Portside Way 428-J1 FCT
Portsmouth Ave 491-J5 WnT
Portsmouth Ct 391-D4 CTH
Portsmouth Dr 391-D5 CTH
Portwood Ct 457-H2 PTM
Portwood Pl 457-J2 PTM
Post Dr 495-J2 WrT
Post Rd 529-J7 FT; 461-J5 L; 461-J10; 495-J2, J6, J10; 529-J2 WrT
Potomac Ave 461-E10, F10 WrT
Potomac Dr 428-D7 L
Potters Bridge Rd 325-K10 N
Potters Cove Ct 456-K5 PTM
Potters Pike 456-K5 PTM
Powderhorn Ct 392-E10 Ca; 427-H3 LTM
Powderhorn La 427-H4 LTM
Powderhorn Way 427-H3 LTM
Powell Dr 525-H10, J10; 559-G1 DTM
Powell Pl 459-G9 CTM
Powell St 527-F10 PeT
Power Dr 392-D10; 426-D1 Ca
Power Pl 392-D10 Ca
Powhatan Dr 490-K10 WnT
Prague Ave 527-G10 PeT
Prague Rd 528-C10 PeT
Praire Cr 391-E2 CTH
Prairie Bapt Rd 395-F1, F4 FCT; 327-F1, F8; 361-F1, F7 WyT
Prairie Ct 531-C1 SCT
Prairie Depot 491-E10; 525-E1 WnT
Prairie Dog Dr 528-H10; 562-H1 FT
Prairie Dr 455-G7 B; 561-D9 G; 427-F5 LTM
Prairie Fox Dr 428-C1 F
Prairie Lake Dr 427-D8 LTM
Prairie Pkwy 455-G7 B
Prairie Pl 392-K7 CTH
Prairie Tr 490-B7 WaT
Prairie View Dr 427-K7 LTM
Prairie View La 427-J7 LTM
Prairieclover La 457-K4; 458-D3 PTM
Prairieview Dr 393-F5 F
Prairieview Terr 455-K4 B
Prairiewood Way 424-H2 CTH
Preakness Dr 594-K4 WTJ
Preakness Pl 526-H1 WnT
Preddy Dr 562-B8 PeT
Preidt Ct 562-F7 PeT
Preidt Pl 562-F7 PeT
Prentis Cir 457-K3 PTM
Prentiss Way 490-E7 WaT
Presbyterian Dr 462-E1 L
Prescott Ct 491-F6 WnT
President Cir 496-E7 WrT
President Ct 496-D7 WrT
President Tr E 496-E7 WrT
President Tr W 496-E7 WrT
Presidential Way 455-J9 B
Prestbury Dr 462-C1 L
Presto Ave 492-A4 S
Preston Ct 390-K9 CTH
Preston Dr 425-G1 CTH; 462-D1 L
Preston Tr 390-K9 CTH
Prestonwood Ct 457-J4 PTM
Prestonwood Dr 457-J3 PTM
Prestwick Cir 391-A8 CTH
Prestwick La 390-K8 CTH
Price Ct 457-J8 PTM; 523-F1 WaT
Price La 457-H8 PTM
Price Rd 523-F1, F2 WaT
Primrose Ave 459-J4, J7 WTM
Primrose Ct 561-C10 WTJ
Primrose La 489-E10 A
Primrose Path 359-E10 NT; 561-C10 WTJ
Prince George Ct 561-E5 PeT
Prince Regent Ct 427-A4 LTM
Prince Woods Cir 491-J6 WnT
Princess La 489-F7 A
Princeton Dr 596-E10 NW
Princeton La 357-C10 WTH
Princeton Pl 493-F1 CTM; 389-F5 Z
Priority Pl 561-H5 PeT
Priority Way Dr S 426-C3 WTM
Priority Way Dr W 426-C3 WTM
Priscilla Ave 460-K7, K8 LTM; 460-K10; 494-K1, K5 WrT
Priscilla Cir 460-J6 LTM
Priscilla Ct 460-J9 WrT
Priscilla Pl 393-G3 F
Prissy La 564-D2 FT
Pro Am Pl 496-E3 WrT
Pro Med La 391-H3 Ca
Production Dr 489-H9 A; 525-J2 WnT
Professional Cir 525-K3 WnT
Profit Dr 525-J3 WnT
Progress Rd 525-J2 WnT
Promenade Cir 325-E1 C
Promenade Ct 457-G10 WnT
Promise Rd 394-E4 FCT; 326-E10 N; 326-E10; 360-E3, E9 NT
Promontory Cir 428-H3 LTM
Promontory Ct 428-G3 LTM
Promontory Rd 428-J4 L; 428-H3, J4 LTM
Promontory Tr 390-A4 ET
Prospect St DN-D4, E4; 493-F10, J10; 494-B10 CTM; 495-A10, E10, J10; 496-A10, F10 WrT
Prosperity Cir 558-J8 DTM; 558-F9 GT
Providence Cir 426-F7 WTM
Providence Dr 393-G1 F
Provincetown Cir 426-K8 LTM
Pruitt St 492-K3 CTM

Puffin Pl 392-H3 Ca
Pullman Ct 427-E8 LTM
Pumpkin Vine Rd 565-C4 MTS
Punto Alto Cir 562-B8 PeT
Punto Alto Ct 596-E3 G; 562-B7 PeT
Punto Alto Dr 562-C7 PeT
Punto Baho Dr 596-E3 G
Purcell Cir 525-A2 WnT
Purdue Rd 424-E4 PTM
Purdy St 424-C9 PTM
Purham Dr 392-A1 Ca
Purple Lilac Cir 457-C5 PTM
Purpura Dr 462-A4 L
Pursel Dr 392-H7 Ca
Pursel La 392-H7 Ca
Puryear St DN-D1, E1; 493-F6, G6 CTM
Putnam Pl 390-C10 CTH
Putter Ct 595-D7 WTJ
Putters La 392-H3 WnT
Px Pl 461-K4 L
Pymbroke Cir 393-D6 F
Pymbroke Dr 393-D6 F
Pymbroke Pl 393-D6 F
Pymbroke Way 393-D6 F

Q

Quail 595-G1 G
Quail Chase Dr 562-K1 FT
Quail Cir 457-J1 PTM
Quail Cove Ct 562-J1 FT
Quail Cr Blvd 562-F2 PeT
Quail Cr Dr 562-F2 PeT
Quail Cres Ct 457-E6 PTM
Quail Crossing Dr 562-K1 FT
Quail Ct 427-G7 LTM; 497-H7 SCT
Quail Feather Ct 562-H1 FT
Quail Hollow Rd 425-B5 WTM
Quail Pointe Dr 391-C2 CTH
Quail Pointe La 562-H1 FT
Quail Rd 457-J1 PTM
Quail Ridge Dr 357-G5 WTH
Quail Ridge E 557-K3 P
Quail Ridge La 457-E6 PTM
Quail Ridge N 557-J3 P
Quail Ridge S 557-J4 P
Quail Ridge W 557-J3 P
Quail Roost Ct 562-H1 FT
Quail Run 393-B9 F
Quail Run Ct 562-K1 FT
Quail Run Dr 562-K1 FT
Quail Valley Dr 389-C7 ET
Quail Way 562-K1 FT
Quail Wood La 357-F5 WTH
Quails Nest Dr 562-F3 PeT
Quaker Ridge Ct 394-B10 F
Quaker St 559-E6 DTM
Quarry Dr 394-J7 F
Quarterhorse Dr 427-F4 LTM
Quartz Rock Rd 428-K8 L
Queen Anne Ct 562-A5 PeT
Queen Mary Ct 561-K5; 562-A5 PeT
Queen St S 491-D9 WnT
Queen Victoria Ct 562-A5 PeT
Queens Ct 425-A5 WTM
Queens La 360-A3 N
Queens Way 391-A8 CTH
Queens Way Cir 391-B9 CTH
Queensborough Ct 392-E1 Ca
Queensborough Dr 392-D2 Ca
Queensbridge Cir 495-C2 WrT
Queensbridge Commons 495-F4 WrT
Queensbridge Dr 495-F4 WrT
Queensbridge Sq 495-F4 WrT
Queensbury Ct 392-D10 Ca; 325-A6 N; 491-D6 WnT
Queensbury Dr 325-A6 N
Queensgate Dr 595-B4 WTJ
Queensway Ct 592-F1 M
Queensway Dr 489-F9 A
Queenswood Ct 561-B8 PeT
Queenswood Dr 561-C8 PeT
Quemetco Dr 491-B10; 525-B1 WnT
Questend Dr 492-G2 WnT
Questend Dr N 492-G2 WnT
Questend Dr S 492-G2 WnT
Questover Cir 459-B4 WTM
Quetico Dr 424-D5 PTM
Quicksilver Rd 324-G7 N
Quiet Bay Cir 325-E1 C
Quiet Ct 530-D2 WrT
Quiet Dr 530-C3 WrT
Quiet Way 530-C3 WrT
Quill St 527-J1, J2 CTM
Quincy Ct 457-D6 PTM

R

Raccoon Ct 455-H10 B; 324-J5 N
Racebrook Ct 358-F3 N
Raceway Rd 422-H10; 456-H1, H3 BTH; 558-H2, H8 DTM; 558-H2, H5, H8, H9 GT; 456-H9; 490-H5 LTH; 456-H3 LTM; 422-H10; 456-H1, H3, H9 PTM; 490-H5, H10; 524-H3 WaT; 456-H9; 490-H5, H10; 524-H3 WnT
Rachel Dr 557-J2 P
Racine La 457-F3 PTM
Racoon Run 561-G10 G
Racquet Ball Dr 425-A3 WTM
Racquet Ball La 425-A3 WTM
Racquet Ball Way 424-K3 WTM
Racquet Club Dr 425-A3 WTM
Racquet Club Dr N 425-A3 WTM
Racquet Club Dr S 425-A3 WTM
Radburn Ct 491-D7 WnT
Radburn Dr 491-D6, D7 WnT
Radcliffe Ave 528-A7 PeT
Radcliffe Ct 528-A7 PeT
Rader St 459-B10; 493-B2 CTM
Radford Dr 461-D10; 495-D1 WrT
Radnor Rd 460-J5; 461-A5 LTM; 460-F5 WTM
Raesner Dr 531-G2 SCT
Ragland St 526-A1 WnT
Rahke Rd 527-D6; 561-D2, D7, D8 PeT
Rahkewood Dr 561-C1 PeT
Rail Timber Run 393-B3 Ca
Railhead Ct 427-D8 LTM
Railroad 455-G5 B
Railroad Ave 359-G1 N
Railroad Rd 561-B7, B9 PeT
Railroad St 428-G10 L
Railroad St N 429-C7 McC
Railway Ct 427-E8 LTM
Railwood Dr 456-J9 WnT
Rainbow Blvd 490-G8 WaT
Rainbow Ct 526-A9 DTM
Rainbow La 592-A7 BTM; 428-C8 L; 425-C10 WTM
Rainbow View Dr 526-A7, A9 DTM
Raindance Tr 529-G9 FT
Raines St 523-H7 P
Rains La 457-J2 PTM
Raintree Dr 489-H7 A; 389-K8 Z
Raintree La 462-F1 L
Raleigh Dr 495-A2 WrT
Raleigh La 393-F8 F
Ralph Ct 425-H10 WTM
Ralph Rd 388-E9 ET
Ralston Ave 391-J8 CTH; 459-J10; 493-J2, K4 CTM; 425-J9, J10; 459-J4, J7, K1 WTM
Ralston Ct 561-C8 PeT
Ralston Rd 559-B8, G8 DTM; 561-B8, F8; 562-E8 PeT
Ramblewood Dr 424-F5 PTM
Ramblin Ct 561-D9 WTJ
Ramblin Rd 561-D10; 595-D1 WTJ
Rambling Bk Blvd 524-B9 P
Rambling Bk Way 524-B9 P
Ramsey La 557-J2 P
Ramsgate Ct 425-H1 CTH; 394-B5 F
Ramsgate Rd 595-B4 WTJ
Rand Rd 525-J6 DTM; 525-K4 WnT
Randall Ct 393-H5 F; 425-K8 WTM
Randall Dr 426-E1 Ca
Randall Rd 557-D5 GT; 425-H8, J8, K8; 426-A8 WTM
Randall Way 455-H8 B
Randolph St 493-K8, K9, K10; 527-K1, K3, K4 CTM; 527-K7, K8; 561-K2 PeT
Randue Ct 423-D8 PTM
Rangeline Rd 391-K3, K6 Ca
Ransburg Dr N 391-G5 Ca
Ransdall Ct 561-F7 PeT
Ransdell St 527-F4 CTM; 527-F6; 561-F2, G4 PeT
Ransom St 493-C5 CTM
Rapidan La 457-K2 PTM
Raritan Ct 559-J4 DTM
Raritan Dr 559-J4 DTM
Rasputin Ct 495-H4 WrT
Ratcliff Ct 456-H9 WnT
Rathmann Dr 491-G3 WnT
Ratliff Rd 559-A4 DTM
Raton Ct 461-H10 WrT
Ravan Ridge 389-C6 ET
Raven Ct 531-H4 SCT
Raven Rock Ct 427-H6 LTM
Raven Rock Dr 427-H6 LTM
Ravenswood Blvd 425-J8 WTM
Ravine Rd 393-G1 DTH; 460-E3 WTM
Rawles Ave 494-J8; 495-G9; 496-A8 WrT
Rawles Terr 494-J8 WrT
Rawlings Pl 394-C4 F
Rawlins Sq 424-H9 WTM
Ray Cir 427-G4 LTM
Ray St DN-B4, C4, D4; 493-A10, C10, E10 CTM; DN-A4; 491-G10, J10; 492-C10, G10, H10 WnT
Rayham Ct 491-A7 WnT
Raylin Dr 562-C1 PeT
Raymond St 527-C3, J2; 528-A2 CTM; 523-H8 P; 525-G3, K3; 526-A3, E3 WnT; 528-H2; 529-C2, J2; 530-A2 WrT
Raynlee Garden Dr 497-H7 SCT
Rea Rd 561-K6 PeT
Reading Sta 489-B9 WaT
Reavest Dr N 494-A10 CTM
Reavest Dr S 528-A1 CTM
Rebecca Dr 492-A8 WnT
Rebecca St 361-B3 WyT
Rebeka Dr 523-H3 WaT
Rebel Run 528-D8 PeT
Records St 461-E7 L
Recre La 495-E8 WrT
Rector Ct 496-B5 WrT
Red Alder Dr 523-D4 WaT
Red Berry Ct 394-G10 F
Red Bird Dr 492-D2 WnT
Red Bluff Dr 457-D10 WnT
Red Bud Ct 557-K5 GT
Red Bud La 424-F2 CTH
Red Bud La E 427-K6 LTM
Red Bud La W 427-J6 LTM
Red Cedar Ct 427-F3 LTM
Red Chalice Rd 457-K2 PTM
Red Delicious La 523-D2 WaT
Red Fox Run 393-C8 F
Red Fox Tr 496-K9 SCT
Red Haw La 462-G1 L
Red Hawk Dr 395-B7 F
Red Horizon Blvd 525-K9; 526-A9 DTM
Red Maple Ct 596-G1 G
Red Mill Ct 461-F8 LTM
Red Mill Dr 461-F8 LTM
Red Oak Ave 392-D4 Ca
Red Oak Ct 392-D4 Ca; 561-J8 PeT
Red Oak Dr 489-D6 A
Red Oak Ridge 392-D3 Ca
Red Oak Way 592-C5 M
Red Pine Dr 394-A10 F
Red River Ct 559-K3 DTM
Red Robin Dr 528-G9 BG
Red Rock Rd 428-K8 L
Red Rose La 489-E9 A
Red Sail Ct 428-D5 LTM
Red Sky Ct 525-G7 DTM
Red Tail Dr 428-C1 F
Red Yarrow Way 458-D3 PTM
Reda Rd 561-G6 PeT
Redan Dr 457-F6 PTM
Redbay Ct 324-K8 N
Redbay Dr 324-K8 N
Redberry Ct 457-C5 PTM
Redbird Tr 531-G3 SCT
Redbrook Ct 496-B5 WrT
Redbud Cir 325-A9 N
Redbud La 596-A1 G; 523-D8 P; 389-H5 Z
Redbud Pl 596-A1 G
Redcliff La N 523-C8 P
Redcliff La S 523-C8 P
Redcliff Rd 427-D9 LTM
Redcoach Cir 427-A7 LTM
Redcoach Ct 427-A7 LTM
Redcoach Dr 426-K7 LTM
Redcoach La 427-A7 LTM
Redding Ct 461-F8 LTM; 389-E6 Z
Redfern Dr 528-E8, F8, G8 BG; 527-K9; 528-A9, D8, E8 PeT
Redfern Dr N 529-G8 FT
Redfern Dr S 529-G8 FT
Redford Ct 425-B3 WTM
Redfox Ct 595-F3 WTJ
Redfox Ct S 595-E3 WTJ
Redhawk Sta 429-C3 McC
Redman Dr 560-K10 WTJ
Redmaple Dr 562-F2 PeT
Redmaple La 393-K2 F
Redmond Ct 462-B1 L
Redondo Ct 596-J2 G
Redondo Dr 428-G5 LTM
Redskin Dr 462-F10 WrT
Redskin La 462-F10 WrT
Redskin Pl 496-F1 WrT
Redwood Ct 455-J8 B; 596-J2 G
Redwood Dr 455-J9 B; 391-E2 CTH; 592-E1 M; 325-B10 N; 562-C1 PeT
Reed Ct 596-B5 G
Reed Rd 457-D6 PTM
Reeder St 528-G1 CTM; 528-G1, H1 WrT
Reef Ct 428-E5 LTM
Reel Cr Dr 422-G9 BTH
Reel Cr La 422-G9 BTH
Reese Ct 392-H1 Ca
Reeves Rd 557-J1; 558-A1, D1, F2, G2 GT; 558-A1, D1 P
Reflection Pt Dr 394-C8 F
Reformers Ave 527-K2; 528-A2 CTM
Regal Ct 561-F1 PeT
Regal Dr 391-A9 CTH
Regatta Ct 496-A3 WrT
Regency Ct 457-J10 WnT
Regency Dr 393-G6 F; 457-H10 WnT
Regency La 392-G8 Ca
Regency Pl 392-F8 Ca
Regent Cir 391-C5 CTH
Regent Ct 359-J8 N
Regent St 527-D2, E2 CTM; 526-A3 WnT
Regents Pk La 325-C6 N
Regina Cir 457-H10 WnT
Regina Dr 455-D6 LTH
Regis Ct 496-D7 WrT
Reichwein St DN-A3; 492-K8 CTM
Reid Pl 493-K10 CTM
Reisner St DN-A2, A4; 492-K7, K9, K10; 526-K1 CTM
Rembrandt Ct 530-K5 SCT
Rembrandt St 493-A3, A5 CTM
Remington Ct 561-J7 PeT
Remington Dr 561-K7; 562-A7, C7 PeT
Remington Pl 561-K7 PeT
Remington Pt 596-H3 G
Rena Ridge Ct 489-C10 WaT
Rene Dr 559-J3 DTM
Renee Dr 557-J1 P
Renfrew Dr 495-E1, F1 WrT
Renn La 457-J7 PTM
Reno St DN-C4; 493-C10 CTM
Renton St 528-B1 CTM
Research Way 525-C2 WnT
Residence Dr 423-F5 PTM
Restin Ct 595-D2 WTJ
Restin Rd 595-D3 WTJ
Reston Dr 523-B7 P
Reston La 429-B2 FCT
Retreat Rd 558-H9 GT
Return Ct 525-F10 DTM
Reunion La 427-B5 LTM
Revere Ct 595-K3 G
Revere La 563-C3 FT
Revere Pl 392-A7 Ca
Revere Run 389-F7 Z
Revere Way 427-A2 F
Revolutionary Dr 457-J3 PTM
Rex Ct 458-G10 WnT
Rex Dr 458-G10 WnT
Rex Ridge 496-K8 SCT
Rexford Rd 425-A4 WTM
Rexham La 393-H3 DTH
Rexmill Dr 562-C7 PeT
Reynolds Dr 393-K6 F
Reynolds Rd 559-C5 DTM
Rhoda Dr 489-B9 WaT
Rhonda Ct 528-C3 CTM
Rhone Terr 426-H4 WTM
Ribble Rd 494-F1 CTM
Ribbon Dr 562-D6 PeT
Richard Ave 529-E5 FT
Richard St 526-B10 DTM
Richardt Ave 461-E5, E7 L; 461-E8 LTM; 461-E10; 495-E1, E2, E3, E4 WrT
Richardt St 427-E7 LTM
Richart La 596-A3 G
Richelieu Ct 461-G8 LTM
Richelieu Rd 461-G7, G8 LTM; 461-G9 WrT
Richfield E 489-F6 WaT
Richie Ave 490-K8 WnT
Richie Cir 428-J8 L
Richland Ctr Dr 558-H8 DTM; 558-H8 GT
Richland St DN-A2, A4; 492-K7, K10; 526-K1 CTM
Richland Way 357-D10 WTH
Richlane Dr 428-K3 LTM
Richmond Ct 390-D9 CTH
Richmond Dr 389-E9 Z
Richmond La 457-J3 PTM
Richwood Dr 489-E6 WaT
Rick La 561-D3 PeT
Ridge Ct 392-C5 Ca; 393-B9 F; 428-E1 FCT; 594-K1 WTJ
Ridge Dr 428-E1 FCT; 561-J9 G
Ridge Hill Ave 560-K8 PeT
Ridge Hill Dr 560-K9 PeT
Ridge Hill La 560-K8 PeT
Ridge Hill Way 489-A10; 523-C1 WaT
Ridge Rd 392-C5 Ca; 460-J3 LTM; 560-K10; 594-K1 WTJ; 425-G7 WTM
Ridgecreek Ct 427-J2 LTM
Ridgecreek Dr 427-J2 LTM
Ridgefield Dr 462-B10 WrT
Ridgegate Dr E 424-C7 PTM
Ridgegate Dr W 424-C7 PTM
Ridgeland Dr 455-C9 LTH; 426-F7 WTM
Ridgeline Rd 455-E5 B
Ridgemere Cir 594-K7 WTJ
Ridgemere Pl 594-K7 WTJ
Ridgemere Way 594-J7 WTJ
Ridgepointe Ct 490-J5 WnT
Ridgepointe Dr 490-J6 WnT
Ridgeside Rd 428-J1 FCT
Ridgeview 523-B1 WaT
Ridgeview Cir 393-A10 F
Ridgeview Ct 592-D4 M
Ridgeview Dr 461-A8 LTM; 461-A10; 495-A1, A5, A7 WrT
Ridgeview La 496-J3 Cu
Ridgeway Ct 429-B3 McC; 359-K1 N
Ridgeway Dr 455-F4 B; 526-C9 DTM
Ridgewood Ave 357-G6 WTH
Ridgewood Ct 523-H10 P
Ridgewood Dr 523-H10 P; 461-D10, F10 WrT
Ridley Ct 425-D6 WTM
Riggers Dr 426-D5 WTM
Rigging Ct 428-C3 LTM
Riley Ave 460-G10; 494-G4, G5, G7, G8; 528-G1, G3 CTM; 426-F10, G9; 460-G7 WTM
Riley La 389-C8 ET
Riley Mews 392-F4 Ca
Riley Pl 494-G10 CTM
Riley Rd 428-J9 L
Rimwood Dr E 427-D3 LTM
Rimwood Dr W 427-D3 LTM
Rimwood La 427-E5 LTM
Rinaldi St 526-C1 WnT
Rinehart Ave 491-J9; 492-A9 WnT
Ringer Rd 395-E8 FCT
Ringgold Ave 493-J10; 527-H1, H3 CTM
Ringtail Ct 457-E6 PTM
Rio Grande Dr 561-C4 PeT
Rio Vista Rd 596-F4 G
Ripon Ct 424-G4 PTM
Ripple Rd 459-D4 WTM
Ripplewood Dr 594-K3 WTJ
Rippling Bk Way 392-K1 Ca
Rippling Way N 424-K1 WTM
Rippling Way S 424-H4 WTM
Rising Rd 461-K3 L
Rising Sun Ct 559-D10 MTM
Rita Dr 595-D4 WTJ
Ritter Ave 528-J6 BG; 460-J6, J7 LTM; 426-H9 WTM; 460-J10; 494-J3, J8, J10; 528-J1, J4 WrT
Ritterskamp Ct 426-E7 WTM
Riva Ridge Ct 528-J8 FT
Riva Ridge Dr 528-J8 FT
River Ave 393-A7, C5 CTH; DN-B4; 493-A10 CTM; 393-C3 Ca; 359-F4 N; 359-E9, F4 NT
River Bay Ct 426-B6 WTM
River Bay Dr E 426-B7 WTM
River Bay Dr N 426-B6 WTM
River Bay Dr W 426-B6 WTM
River Bend Ct 426-H4 WTM
River Bend Pkwy 426-G4 WTM
River Birch Ct 523-C4 WaT
River Birch Dr 523-C4 WaT; 462-E10 WrT
River Birch La 428-D8 L
River Crossing Blvd 426-C4 WTM
River Dr 392-K8 CTH
River Edge La 426-B7 WTM
River Glen Dr 393-C7 F
River Hgts Dr 425-H9 WTM
River Oak La 427-A2 F
River Rd 393-B6 CTH; 393-B6 Ca; 426-A8, B7, D4 WTM
River Ridge Dr 393-C7 F
River Run Dr 559-K3 DTM
River Run Pl 359-F4 N
River Valley Way 559-K3 DTM
River Wood Ct 426-J2 WTM
Riverby La 425-H8 WTM
Riverfront Ave 425-J10 WTM
Riverrock Ct 392-K1 Ca
Riverside Dr 562-B10 G
Riverside Dr E 492-K4, K5 CTM
Riverside Way 393-B7 F
Riverstone Ct 357-K1 W
Riverview Dr 425-F10, G10; 459-B6, E2, F1 WTM
Riverwood 391-E2 CTH
Riverwood Ave 325-K9; 326-A8, E6 NT
Riverwood Dr 426-J3 LTM; 326-F5 NT; 426-J3 WTM; 457-C9 WnT
Riviera Dr 523-F1 WaT
Riviera St 458-H1 WTM
Rivington Dr 462-B1 L
Rixon Ave 526-A8 DTM
Roache St 492-K2; 493-B2 CTM
Roamin Ct 595-D3 WTJ
Roamin Dr 595-D3 WTJ
Roan La 428-K9 L
Roancke Dr 389-E9 Z
Roanoke St DN-D1, D2; 493-D7 CTM
Rob La 562-G7 PeT
Robbins Dr 595-J3 G
Robbins Rd 423-K4 PTM
Roberson Blvd 592-E1 M
Robert Ct 389-F8 Z
Robert Dr 389-F8 Z
Robert Rd 594-J1 WTJ
Roberta Ct 455-J5 B
Roberta Dr 492-F2, G2 WnT
Roberts Cr La 559-G4 DTM
Roberts Dr 427-H2 F
Roberts Pl 460-G2 WTM
Roberts Rd 527-D9 PeT
Robertson Ave 494-A1 CTM
Robertson Blvd 458-E7 PTM
Robertson St 593-E2 MTM
Robey Dr 490-J1 WnT
Robin Dr 526-A8 DTM
Robin Hood Ct 561-F4 PeT
Robin Hood Dr 561-F3 PeT
Robin La 425-K3 WTM
Robin Run 458-A2 PTM
Robin Run E 457-K1 PTM
Robin Run W 457-K1 PTM
Robinson La 323-E6 WTH
Robinson Run 393-G3 F
Robinsrock Dr 458-A1 PTM
Robinsrock La 458-A1 PTM
Robinsrock Way 458-A1 PTM
Robinwood Dr 455-J9 B
Robison Rd 423-K3; 424-A3 PTM
Robson La 558-E9 GT
Robson St 494-B7, C7 CTM
Robton St 492-D9 WnT
Robwes Rd 525-G8 DTM
Rochelle Ct 461-K10 LTM
Rochelle Dr 461-J9 WrT
Rochester Ave 492-E5, E7, E9, E10 WnT
Rock Hampton Ct 423-J4 PTM
Rock Hill Ct E 559-A10 MTM
Rock Hollow Cir 427-F3 LTM
Rock Is Ct 561-B9 PeT
Rock Maple Dr 462-F9 WrT
Rock Oak Ct 561-G7 PeT
Rock Oak Dr 561-G7 PeT
Rock Rose Ct 562-G6 PeT
Rockberry 391-J1 Ca
Rockford Ct 496-C3 WrT
Rockford Rd 496-C4 WrT
Rocking Chair Rd 561-C10 WTJ
Rockingham Pl 425-A5 WTM
Rocklane Rd 597-H3; 598-A3, E4 CTJ; 596-G2 G; 597-C2 PTJ
Rockleigh Ave 491-D8 WnT
Rockne Cir 392-G5 Ca
Rockridge Ct 424-A6 PTM
Rockrose Ct 357-E8 WTH
Rockshire Rd 491-H8 WnT
Rockspray Cir 457-D4 PTM
Rockspray Ct 393-A3 Ca
Rockstone Ct 458-A1 PTM
Rockville Ave 492-D8 WnT
Rockville Rd 490-B8, G8 WaT; 490-G8; 491-B8, J8; 492-B8 WnT
Rockway Dr 531-E3 SCT
Rockwell Ct 389-E5 Z
Rockwood La 531-A4 SCT
Rocky Cay Ct 392-G7 Ca
Rocky Hill Rd 560-K9 PeT
Rocky Knob La 458-D6 PTM
Rocky Ridge Rd 560-K9 PeT
Rod Ct 563-A2 FT
Rodanthe Ct 563-A4 FT
Rodebaugh Rd 424-E10; 458-E1 PTM
Rodeo Ct 561-D8 PeT
Rodeo Dr 561-D9 PeT
Roderick Ct 528-F9 BG
Rodney Ct 528-F9 BG
Rodney Dr 491-A3 WnT
Rodney St 455-H5 B
Roena St 526-C6 DTM; 492-C10; 526-C4, C6 WnT
Rogers Cir 491-D4 WnT
Rogers Ct 491-D5 WnT
Rogers Dr 523-H9 P; 491-D4 WnT
Rogers Rd 391-J4 Ca; 561-J5 PeT
Rohan Ct 422-K4 PTM
Rohrer Rd 391-H3, J2 CTH; 391-H3, J2 Ca
Rokbury Pl 392-E6 Ca
Roland Dr 458-H5 WTM
Roland Rd 458-H8 WTM
Rolling Ct 392-C8 Ca; 357-J7 WTH
Rolling Hill Dr 391-J1 Ca; 561-H9 G
Rolling Hills La 523-G4 WaT
Rolling Oak Dr 491-C3 WnT
Rolling Pines Ct 460-D3 WTM
Rolling Ridge Dr 359-K5 N
Rolling Ridge Rd 460-E3 WTM
Rolling River Ct 559-K3 DTM
Rolling Springs Ct 392-D9, E9 Ca
Rolling Springs Dr 392-B8, D9 Ca; 490-G7 WaT
Rolling Springs Rd 392-C7 Ca
Rolling Trails 595-A2 WTJ
Rollingview Ct 592-D4 M
Rollingwood Cir 358-A3 WTH
Rollins Ct 424-G3 PTM
Rolls Dr 424-H7 PTM
Rollshore Ct 392-C8 Ca
Roma Way 523-D2 WaT
Romalong La 357-E9 WTH
Roman Ct 357-E9 WTH
Romar Dr 455-E10; 489-E1 LTH
Rome Dr 458-H8 WTM
Rome Terr 458-D7 PTM
Romeo Ct 489-F7 A
Romeo Dr 489-E7 A
Rommel Dr 458-J8 WTM
Romona Dr 524-G9 P
Ronald Ct 594-H1 WTJ; 496-C3 WrT
Rook Rd 456-K8 PTM
Rooker Rd 592-C4, D8 BTM; 592-C4 M
Rookwood Ave 459-D6, D8 WTM
Rooses Dr 560-K5 PeT
Rooses La 560-J6 PeT
Roosevelt Ave DN-F1; 493-H5, J4, J5, K4; 494-A4, B3 CTM
Roosevelt Dr 359-J2 N
Roosevelt Is Rd 426-C7 WTM
Roosevelt St 523-G8 P; 357-K4 W
Rosalyn Dr 592-K7 MTM
Roscommon Ct 457-C6 PTM
Rose Crest Dr 426-B2 CTH
Rose Ct 392-H7 Ca; 523-J10 P
Rose Dr 561-J5 PeT
Rose La 455-J3 B; 455-J3 BTH; 596-D4 G; 592-B1 M; 561-E6 PeT
Rose St 595-D4 WTJ
Rosebay Ct 425-G5 WTM
Rosebay Dr 425-H5 WTM
Roseberry Ct 592-F2 M
Rosebery Ct 491-E7 WnT
Rosebery La 491-E7 WnT
Rosebud La 563-B6 FT
Rosebury 392-F2 Ca
Rosebush La 563-B6 FT
Rosedale Ct 359-K7 N
Rosedale Dr 527-K9; 528-A9 PeT
Rosedowne Ct 359-K7 N
Rosefinch Cir 458-D2 PTM
Rosegrans Ct 455-G10 B
Rosehill Dr 424-J9 WTM
Roselawn Ave 455-K8 B; 460-G8 WTM
Roselawn Dr 460-K8 LTM; 460-E8 WTM
Roselawn La 525-J8 DTM
Rosemary Dr 426-G9 WTM
Rosemeade Dr 391-J7 Ca
Rosemeade La 425-J6 WTM
Rosemere Ave 495-K7 WrT
Rosemill Dr 357-J10 WTH
Rosemont Ct 457-K4 PTM
Rosemont Dr 457-K4 PTM
Rosemoss Crossing 357-F9 WTH
Rosengarten Dr 561-G9 G
Roses Rd 393-G3 DTH
Roseway Ct 461-F10 WrT
Roseway Dr 490-A8 WaT; 461-F9, F10; 495-F5 WrT
Roseway La 461-F9 WrT
Rosewind Dr 531-C3 SCT
Rosewood Commons Dr 458-C4 PTM
Rosewood Commons La 458-B4 PTM
Rosewood Commons Pl 458-B4 PTM
Rosewood Commons Way 458-B4 PTM
Rosewood Ct 392-C10 Ca
Rosewood Dr 592-A7 BTM
Rosewood La 592-E1 M; 426-A4 WTM
Rosner Dr 492-A6 S
Ross Crossing 394-C4 F
Ross La 424-C3 PTM
Rossi Dr 428-H8 L
Rosslyn Ave 425-J8; 459-J4, J6 WTM
Rosswill Dr 525-J7 DTM
Rost La 558-C6 GT
Roswell Ct 490-K7 WnT
Roswell Dr 391-H2 CTH
Rotary Cir DN-B2; 493-A6 CTM
Rothbury Dr 425-A5 WTM
Rothe Dr 496-G1 WrT
Rothe Way 496-G1 WrT
Rotherham Cir 528-F7 BG
Rotherham La 528-E7 BG
Rotterdam Dr 458-E7 PTM
Rouark Cir 496-C1 WrT
Rouark La 496-C1 WrT

Rough Cedar La 426-K7 LTM
Rough Rd Dr 559-H2 DTM
Round Ct 389-K8 Z
Round Hill Ct 425-C6 WTM
Round Hill Rd 425-C6 WTM
Round Lake Rd 460-B6 WTM
Round Table Ct 425-B5 WTM
Round Up Tr 393-A9 DTH
Roundtree Ct 491-F1 WnT
Routiers Ave 563-G2 FT; 495-H2, H4, H7, H8 WrT
Routiers Ct 495-H2 WrT
Rowan Ct 562-H7 FT
Rowan Ct W 357-D8 WTH
Rowan Run W 357-E9 WTH
Rowin Rd 459-H4 WTM
Rowney St 528-F1, G1 CTM; 528-G1 WrT
Roxburgh Ct N 456-G9 WnT
Roxburgh Ct S 456-J9 WnT
Roxbury Cir 460-J4 LTM
Roxbury Ct 460-J4 LTM
Roxbury Dr 427-A2 F
Roxbury La 325-A7 N
Roxbury Rd 460-J5 LTM
Roxbury Terr 460-J4 LTM
Roxie Dr 461-J6 L
Roy Rd 495-F2, H2 WrT
Royal Blvd 390-H8 CTH
Royal Cir 390-H9 CTH
Royal Ct 390-J8 CTH
Royal Dr 391-B9 CTH; 393-H8 F
Royal Fern La 325-D9 N
Royal La 489-F8 A
Royal Lake Cir 459-A2 WTM
Royal Lake Dr 459-A2 WTM
Royal Meadow Dr 561-B8 PeT
Royal Oak Ct 595-K4 G; 562-C1 PeT; 389-G6 Z
Royal Oak Dr 562-C1 PeT
Royal Oak La 392-F6 Ca
Royal Oakland Ct 428-F9, F10 L
Royal Oakland Dr 428-F8, F10 L
Royal Oakland Pl 428-F10 L
Royal Oakland Way 428-F9 L
Royal Orbit Ct 528-J9 FT
Royal Pine Blvd 426-E7 WTM
Royal Pine La 325-C4 JT
Royal Pl 390-H9 CTH
Royal Rd 528-C4 BG
Royal St 596-F4 G
Royal Troon Ct 489-A10; 523-B1 WaT
Royal Troon Way 489-A10 WaT
Royale 561-F1 PeT
Royalton Ave 422-G2 ET
Royalton Dr 424-K1 CTH
Royce Ct 392-E5 Ca
Royce Dr 462-A9 WrT
Rubble Rd 528-K2 WrT
Ruby Bee Dr 526-C9 DTM
Ruby Dr 489-E1 LTH
Ruby St 428-H10 L
Ruby Tr 596-E4 G
Rucker Cir 426-H7 WTM
Rucker Rd 460-H2 LTM; 426-G7, H6, H10; 460-H1 WTM
Ruckle Ave 391-F9, G10; 425-G1 CTH
Ruckle St 391-F8 CTH; 459-G10; 493-G1, G4 CTM; 459-G8 WTM
Ruddy St 393-C8 F
Rudgate Dr 489-G4, G5 WaT
Rudolph Rd 424-K5 WTM
Rue Biscay 461-H7 L
Rue Cezanne 460-D4 WTM
Rue Chanel 528-C9 PeT
Rue Delacroix 460-D4 WTM
Rue Demargot Dr 424-H9 WTM
Rue Deville 460-D4 WTM
Rue Flambeau 460-D4 WTM
Rue Leblanc 461-J7 L
Rue Lemans 461-H7 L
Rue Madeleine 461-H7 L
Rue Marceau 460-D4 WTM
Rue Monet 460-E4 WTM
Rue Rabelais 460-D4 WTM
Rue Renoir 460-D4 WTM
Rue Riviera 461-H7 L
Rue Vallee 528-C9 PeT
Rue Verlaine 460-D4 WTM
Rue Voltaire 460-D4 WTM
Ruelling Dr 457-K5 PTM
Rugby Ct 425-G1 CTH; 359-H10 NT
Rumford Rd 495-G5 WrT
Rundle Ct 460-D3 WTM
Runevere Dr 391-J8 CTH
Running Bk Ct 595-A7 WTJ
Running Bk Pl 594-K7 WTJ
Running Cr Ct 424-G4 PTM
Running Tide Ct 428-E6 LTM
Runningbrook Ct 457-C5 PTM; 523-E1 WaT
Runningbrook Dr 523-E2 WaT
Runningbrook La 523-F2 WaT
Runningbrook Terr La 594-K7 WTJ
Runningbrook Way 457-D5 PTM
Runnymede Ct 558-K10 MTM
Runview Cir 393-A10 F
Runyon Ct 594-K3 WTJ
Runyon Deer La 594-K3 WTJ
Runyon Lake Dr 594-K5 WTJ
Runyon Rd 594-K3, K4 WTJ
Rural Dr 562-D2 PeT
Rural St 460-B9, B10; 494-B1, B2, B4, B9; 528-B1, B4 CTM; 528-B6, B7 PeT; 426-B9; 460-B1, B3, B4, B9 WTM
Rush Ct 393-E7 F
Rush Dr 393-E7 F
Rush Pl 426-E6 WTM
Rushmore Blvd E 490-J5 WnT
Rushmore Blvd N 490-H5 WnT
Rushmore Blvd S 490-H5 WnT
Rushmore Blvd W 490-G5 WnT
Ruskin Ct 457-H9 WnT
Ruskin Pl 459-F9 CTM; 459-F9 WTM; 461-E8 WrT
Ruskin Pl W 457-H9, J9; 458-A9 WnT
Russell Ave DN-D4; 493-E9 CTM
Russell Dr 394-D4 F
Russell Lake Dr 389-B9 ET
Russell Lake Dr E 389-B9 ET
Russell Lake Dr W 389-B9 ET
Rustic Ct 428-J10 L
Rutgers La 393-B9 F
Rutgers Rd 528-A9 PeT; 327-D8 WyT
Ruth Dr 360-A1 NT; 425-H8, J8; 426-A8 WTM
Rutherglen Way 457-C5 PTM
Rutherwood Ct 425-H1 CTH
Rutledge Ct 325-C10 N
Rutledge Dr 458-E7 PTM; 458-E7 WTM
Ryan Dr 460-A3 WTM
Ryan Tr 455-G9 B
Rybald Ave 327-K2 WRT
Rybolt Ave 526-C6, C8 DTM; 492-C5 S; 458-C10; 492-C7, C10; 526-C5 WnT
Rydal Ct 458-B6 PTM
Rymark Ct 426-J3 LTM
Rymark Dr 426-K3 LTM

S

Saarinen Dr 463-C8 BCT
Saben Ct 391-E2 CTH
Sable Chase 455-J5 B
Sable Chase Ct 455-J5 B
Sable Cr Ct 561-E10 G
Sable Cr La 561-D10 G
Sable Ridge Cir 561-E10 G
Sable Ridge Dr 561-E10 G
Sable Ridge La 561-E10 G
Sable Run 391-B3 CTH
Sabrina Cir 523-J10 P
Sachems Head Ct 428-J6 L
Sachs Dr 491-G4 S
Sackett Dr 456-D10 LTH
Sacramento Dr 496-K2 BCT
Saddle Barn Dr E 491-D1 WnT
Saddle Barn Dr W 491-C1 WnT
Saddle Ct 427-F4 LTM
Saddle Hill Ct 490-G7 WaT
Saddle Horn Ct 358-C10 WTH
Saddle Horn Dr 358-B10 WTH
Saddle Pt Dr 427-K6 LTM
Saddle Ridge 492-F8 WnT
Saddleback Dr 391-G1 CTH
Saddlebrook Ct W 459-A2 WTM
Saddlebrook Dr E 459-A2 WTM
Saddlebrook La 459-A2 WTM
Saddleclub Rd 595-B10 WTJ
Sadie St 492-G10 WnT
Sadlier Cir Dr E 495-D10 WrT
Sadlier Cir Dr N 495-D10 WrT
Sadlier Cir Dr S 529-D1 WrT
Sadlier Cir Dr W 529-D1 WrT
Sadlier Dr 529-E6 FT; 461-D4, D5, D6 L; 461-D9 LTM; 461-D9; 495-E7 WrT
Saffron Dr 562-E5 PeT
Sagamore Tr 460-E4 WTM
Sage Ct 528-J10 FT; 326-C9 N
Sagewood Ct 458-C6 PTM
Saguaro Ct 458-C1 PTM
Saguaro Tr 458-C1 PTM
Sahm St DN-D1; 493-E6 CTM
Sail Pl Dr 428-H1 FCT
Sailing Ct 424-K10 WTM
Sailors La 457-B5 PTM
Saint Andrews Cir 390-J8 CTH
Saint Andrews Dr 526-C8 DTM; 523-B1 WaT
Saint Andrews La 390-J8 CTH
Saint Andrews Way 394-A4 F
Saint Armamds Cir 393-B6 Ca
Saint Charles Ct 392-F9 Ca
Saint Charles Pl 392-F9 Ca; 528-C10 PeT
Saint Clair Ct 491-D6 WnT
Saint Clair St DN-A1, D1, E1; 492-H6; 493-E6, G6; 494-A6, C6, F6 CTM; 592-A2 M; DN-A1; 491-D6; 492-F6, H6 WnT; 494-G6 WrT
Saint Croix La 457-D10 WnT
Saint Francis Ave 528-C5, C6 BG
Saint George Blvd 393-F8 F
Saint George Ct 393-E9 F
Saint James Ct 596-F3 G
Saint James Dr 561-C3 PeT
Saint James Pl 359-J8 N
Saint Jean Dr 561-C3 PeT
Saint Joe Dr 561-C3 PeT
Saint John Ct N 528-F9 BG
Saint John Ct S 528-F9 BG
Saint Joseph St DN-D1; 493-E6; 494-C6, F6 CTM; 496-F5 Cu; 494-G6, J6, K6; 495-F6 WrT
Saint Jude Dr 528-C10 PeT
Saint Luke Dr 523-H8 P
Saint Patrick St 493-J9 CTM
Saint Paul St 494-A9, A10; 528-A1, A3, A6 CTM; 528-A6 PeT
Saint Pauli St 530-H3 WrT
Saint Peter St 494-A9, A10; 528-A1, A4 CTM; 562-A9 PeT
Saint Simons Ct 562-E1 PeT
Saint Simons Dr 562-E1 PeT
Saint Thomas Blvd 457-D10 WnT
Saint Thomas La 457-D9 WnT
Saint Vail Ct 324-G6 N
Saint Vincent Dr 424-J5 WTM
Saksons Blvd 393-G6 F
Salatheal Ct 393-G8 F
Salazar Dr 491-D4 WnT
Salem Ch Rd 388-J10; 422-J2 ET
Salem Cir 392-J2 Ca
Salem Ct 326-A10 N
Salem Dr 393-A9 F
Salem Dr E 392-J2 Ca
Salem Dr N 392-J1 Ca
Salem Dr S 392-J2 Ca
Salem Dr W 392-J1 Ca
Salem Sq 527-K8 PeT
Salem St 459-E10 CTM
Salisbury La 527-J6 PeT
Sally Ann Cir 563-A6 FT
Salt Fork Way 427-H7 LTM
Salt Lake Rd 457-B10; 491-B1 WnT
Salter Ct 426-G7 WTM
Salvo Rd 563-F9 CTJ
Samantha Dr 462-A5 L
Samoa St 493-K4; 494-A5 CTM
Samuel Dr 563-C7 FT
San Carlos Ct 427-F5 LTM
San Carlos Dr 561-A10; 595-A1 WTJ
San Clemente Dr 461-B3 LTM
San Clemente La 461-B3 LTM
San Diego Dr 525-G9 DTM
San Diego La 525-G9 DTM
San Fernando Dr 424-B7 PTM
San Gabriel Dr 424-B8 PTM
San Gabriel Way 424-C8 PTM
San Jacinto Dr 426-K2 LTM
San Jose Dr 595-D6 WTJ
San Marcos Cir 427-D3 LTM
San Marcos Dr 595-A1 WTJ
San Miguel Cir 426-K3 LTM
San Miguel Ct 426-K3 LTM
San Miguel Dr 426-K3 LTM
San Paulo Cir 461-C3 LTM
San Ricardo Ct 427-F5 LTM; 595-B1 WTJ
San Ricardo Dr 561-A10; 595-A1 WTJ
San Vicente Blvd 393-G4 DTH
Sanctuary Dr 426-C8 WTM
Sand Cr Blvd 394-C7 F
Sand Cr Rd 599-D10 STS
Sand Dollar Cir 428-H1 FCT
Sand Dollar Ct 428-H1 FCT
Sand Key Cir 428-D3 LTM
Sand Key La 428-D3 LTM
Sand Pt 426-B8 WTM
Sand Shoal Ct 428-D7 L
Sand St DN-C4; 493-C9 CTM
Sand Wedge Ct 595-E7 WTJ
Sandalwood 489-G5 WaT
Sandalwood Dr 561-C5 PeT
Sandbrook Ct 358-H3 N
Sandbrook Dr 358-H3, J2 N
Sandbury Rd 427-J8 LTM
Sandcherry Dr 462-C2 L
Sanders St 493-F10, H10, K10 CTM
Sandhill Ct 560-J8 PeT
Sandhill Rd 560-K8 PeT
Sandhurst Dr 526-E10; 560-E1 PeT
Sandi Ct 425-A6 WTM
Sandi Dr 425-A6 WTM
Sandoval Ct 491-D4 WnT
Sandpebble Ct 526-A9 DTM
Sandpiper Ct 427-G6 LTM
Sandpiper Dr E 424-F3 PTM
Sandpiper Dr N 424-F2 PTM
Sandpiper Dr S 424-F3 PTM
Sandpiper Dr W 424-F3 PTM
Sandpoint Way 426-B5 WTM
Sandra La 527-F5 PeT
Sandringham Cir 491-B3 WnT
Sandstone Ct 496-J2 Cu; 562-H3 FT
Sandstone Run 392-H5 Ca
Sandy Ann La 459-J5 WTM
Sandy Bay Dr 595-F2 G
Sandy Cr Ct 391-E1 CTH
Sandy Dr 390-A7 ET
Sandy Run Ct 358-F3 N
Sandy Spring La 458-G9 WnT
Sanger Dr 394-B4 F
Sangster Ave 493-K2 CTM
Sanitary Dr 526-J4 CTM
Sanitation Plant Rd 455-E6 B; 455-E6 LTH
Sanner Ct 391-D10 CTH
Sanner Dr 596-C5 G
Santa Ana Dr 595-D6 WTJ
Santa Ana La 491-F4 WnT
Santa Anita Ct 391-H9 CTH
Santa Clara Dr 595-B1 WTJ
Santa Cruz Dr 424-B8 PTM
Santa Fe Ct 526-B6 DTM; 489-C10 WaT
Santa Fe Dr 526-B6 DTM
Santa Maria Dr 595-E6 WTJ
Santa Monica Dr 424-B8 PTM
Santana Cir 423-B5 PTM
Santana La 423-B4 PTM
Santiago Dr 595-D6 WTJ
Santolina Dr 562-F6 PeT
Santorini Pl 562-F6 PeT
Sanwela Dr 458-K1 WTM
Sapelo Dr 562-E1 PeT
Sapphire Blvd 424-F7 PTM
Sara Ct 557-F2 P; 561-E7 PeT
Sarah Ct 393-J9 F
Sarasota Ct 495-G3 WrT
Saratoga Cir 391-H10 CTH
Saratoga Dr 455-F7 B; 461-K5 LTM
Saratoga Pkwy 523-A7, C8 P
Saratoga Pl 523-B7 P
Sargent Cr Ct 427-J4 LTM
Sargent Cr Dr 427-J4 LTM
Sargent Ct 427-J4 LTM
Sargent La 427-G6 LTM
Sargent Manor Ct 427-J4 LTM
Sargent Rd 427-F10, H7, K2 LTM
Sargent Ridge 427-H6 LTM
Sarnia St 461-F6 L
Sarto Dr 426-B9 WTM
Sarton La 559-J3 DTM
Sassafras Cir 325-A9 N
Sassafras Ct 424-K4 WTM
Satisfied Dr 524-K10 DTM
Saturn Dr 495-K2 WrT
Saturn St 496-G6 Cu
Saulcy St DN-B2; 492-K7 CTM
Sault Ste Marie Dr 561-E6 PeT
Sauterne Ct 423-F8 PTM
Sauterne Dr 423-F8 PTM
Savannah Dr 561-B6 PeT
Savannah La 358-A3 WTH
Saved St 524-A6 P
Saveille Rd 359-H10 NT
Saville Rd 596-A2 G
Savin Dr 457-F8 PTM
Saw Mill Ct 531-J4 SCT
Saw Mill Rd 359-D3 N
Sawgrass Dr 394-D9 F; 491-A1 WnT
Sawleaf Rd 424-J4 WTM
Sawmill Ct 428-F3 LTM
Sawmill Rd 596-D10 NW
Sawyer Ave 461-A10 WrT
Sawyer St 461-A8 LTM
Saxon St 496-G6 Cu
Saylor Ct 389-F8 Z
Saylor Dr 389-E9, F8 Z
Sayre Ct 562-G10 G
Sayre Dr 562-D10, G10 G
Scarborough Blvd Dr E 427-F8 LTM
Scarborough Blvd Dr S 427-F8 LTM
Scarborough Cir 325-B7 N
Scarborough Cir 427-F8 LTM
Scarborough La 358-K10 NT
Scarborough Way 359-J8 N
Scarbourough La 390-H7 CTH
Scarlet Ct 457-J10 WnT
Scarlet Dr 457-J10 WnT
Scarlet Oak Ct 359-C1 N; 492-E3 WnT
Scarlet Oak Dr 523-D3 WaT
Scarlet Oak La 592-C5 M
Scarlet Terr 457-J10 WnT
Scarsdale Ct 427-G6 LTM
Scarsdale Dr 427-G5 LTM
Scarsdale Dr E 427-G5 LTM
Scarsdale Dr W 427-G5 LTM
Scatterwood Ct 559-K3 DTM
Scenic Ct 458-K1 WTM
Scenic Dr 425-D7 WTM
Schaefer La 462-A8 WrT
Schaff St 528-G6 BG
Scheiling Ct 392-K7 CTH
Schiller St 527-E2 CTM
Schleicher Ave 496-A5 WrT
Schmus Ct 457-K1 PTM
Schoen Ct 391-G5 Ca
Schoen Dr 461-G5 L
Schofield Ave 459-K10; 493-K2 CTM
School Dr 531-H5 NP
School La 491-G10 WnT
School Pkwy 391-J10 CTH
School Rd 461-K2; 462-A2 L
School Rd N 455-H5 B
School St 455-G7 B; 393-H8 F; 531-H4 NP
Schooley Dr 595-G3 WTJ
Schoolmaster Dr 523-H5 P
Schoolwood Dr 491-G2 S
Schooner Ct 428-C4 LTM
Schrier Rd 490-D9 WaT
Schubert Pl 325-K10 N
Schulley Rd 325-B3 JT; 325-B6 NT
Schwier Ct 496-B3 WrT
Schwier Dr 496-B3 WrT
Scioto St 493-E8 CTM
Scotch Pine Ct 394-A10 F
Scotch Pine La 428-A4 LTM
Scotia Ct 457-F7 PTM
Scott Ct 462-A8 LTM
Scott Dr 391-H2 CTH; 560-H10 WTJ
Scott Rd 525-D9 DTM
Scott-Ian Ct 457-J3 PTM
Scottish Bend 392-K5 Ca
Scottsdale Dr 392-A1 Ca; 491-A1 WnT
Scout Rd 461-G3 L
Scramble Ct 595-D8 WTJ
Scramble Dr 595-D8 WTJ
Scranton Ct 389-F6 Z
Screech Owl Cir 458-D2 PTM
Sea Angel La 427-J4 LTM
Sea Eagle Ct 457-E6 PTM
Sea Oats Dr 427-C3 LTM
Sea Oats La 427-C3 LTM
Sea Pine Dr 427-C3 LTM
Sea Pine La 427-D3 LTM
Sea Star Cir 394-G10 FCT
Sea Star Ct 394-G10 FCT
Sea Star Dr 428-H1 FCT
Sea Star Way 394-G10 FCT
Seabreeze Cir 490-A8 A; 428-B3 LTM
Seabreeze Ct 428-B4 LTM
Seabreeze Dr 490-A7 WaT
Seabreeze Way 428-B3 LTM
Seabridge Way 426-C5 WTM
Seabury Ct 393-C10 F
Seafan Ct 428-F5 LTM
Seagrave Dr 394-B8 F
Sealord Ct 428-D7 L
Sealy Rd 526-B6 DTM
Seaport Dr 425-K7; 426-A7 WTM
Searay Dr 428-H5 L
Sears St 495-E10 WrT
Seascape Ct 428-D3 LTM
Seascape Dr 428-D3 LTM
Seattle Ave 525-F9 DTM
Seattle Slew Ct 561-A8 PeT
Seattle Slew La 561-A8 PeT
Seaview La 428-D7 L
Seaward Ct 428-C4 LTM
Seaward La 428-C4 LTM
Seaway Ct 428-J3 LTM
Seaway Dr 457-C10 WnT
Seawood Ct 424-B6 PTM
Sebring Ct 458-B3 PTM
Sebring Dr 458-B3 PTM
Secretariat La 561-A7 PeT
Section St 523-J8 P
Sedgegrass Crossing 393-A3 Ca
Sedgegrass Dr 462-D3 L
Sedgemoor Cir 390-E9 CTH
Sedgewick Way 427-D9 LTM
Sedlak Ct 496-E4 WrT
Sedlak La 496-E4 WrT
Sedona Ct 391-E1 CTH
Sedona Dr 391-E1 CTH
Sedwick Ct 324-K6 N
Seekonk Ct 428-A5 LTM
Seerley Cr Cir 526-A5 DTM
Seerley Cr Dr 526-A5 DTM
Seerley Cr Rd 526-A6 DTM
Seerley Rd 525-K6 DTM
Seifert Ct 531-J4 SCT
Seine Ct 461-H9 WrT
Selby Ct 324-K5 N
Selkirk Ct 425-B3 WTM
Selkirk La 425-A3 WTM
Sellers St 461-E7 L
Seminole Dr 564-E2 FT
Seminole Rd 359-A7 NT
Senate Ave DN-D2, D4; 493-D3, D4, D7, D9, D10; 527-D1 CTM; 527-D9, D10 PeT
Senate Blvd 493-D4 CTM
Senator Way 357-E9, F10 WTH
Seneca Dr 460-E4 WTM
Seneff Ct 523-H9 P
Senour Rd 530-D10; 564-D1 FT; 530-D4 WrT
Sentinel Tr 426-G8 WTM
Sequoia Ct 595-A4 WTJ; 425-K6 WTM
Sequoia La 425-K6; 426-B5 WTM
Serenity Ct 595-D2 WTJ
Serenity Way 595-D3 WTJ
Serpent Cir 428-G4 LTM
Serpentine Rd 460-K3 LTM
Serve Dr 457-G1 PTM
Servo Rd 564-G6 FT
Setser St 359-J5 N
Setters Rd 358-E10 WTH
Settlement Dr N 427-B2 LTM
Settlement Dr S 427-B2 LTM
Settlement Dr W 427-B3 LTM
Settlers Ct 393-G9 F
Seven Oaks Dr E 428-H9 L
Seven Oaks Dr N 428-G9 L
Severn Ct 595-H2 G
Severn Dr 595-H2 G
Seville Ct 458-G6 WTM
Seville Dr 458-G5 WTM
Sextant Ct 394-C8 F
Sextant Dr 424-K10 WTM
Sextant Way 424-J10 WTM
Sexton Ave 495-A2 WrT
Shadeland Ave 461-C2, C4 L; 427-C9; 461-C2, C7 LTM; 461-C10; 495-C2, C6, C8; 529-D1, D2 WrT
Shadeland Sta 427-C8 LTM
Shadeland Sta Way 427-D9 LTM
Shadeland Way 461-C4 L
Shades Ct 391-D3 Ca
Shadow Bk Ct 457-E10 WnT
Shadow Bk Dr 457-F10; 491-F1 WnT
Shadow Cir 424-K6 WTM
Shadow Ct 389-F9 Z
Shadow Dr 424-K6 WTM
Shadow Gate Ct 524-B8 P
Shadow Hill Ct 595-B2 WTJ
Shadow Hill Dr 595-B2 WTJ
Shadow Hill La 595-B2 WTJ
Shadow Lakes Dr E 357-K10 WTH
Shadow Lakes Dr N 357-J10 WTH
Shadow Lawn 425-B5 WTM
Shadow Pointe Dr 458-D6 PTM
Shadow Pointe La 458-D6 PTM
Shadow Rd 595-C2 WTJ
Shadow Rock Cir 392-G7 Ca
Shadow Wood Ct 457-D5 PTM
Shadow Wood Dr 457-D5 PTM
Shadowcrest Ct 359-K8 N
Shadowlawn Dr 393-C8 F
Shadowview Cir 592-D4 M
Shadowview Way E 491-F9 WnT
Shadowview Way N 491-F9 WnT
Shadwell Ct 562-J7 FT
Shady Cr Dr 561-H10; 595-H1 G
Shady Ct 561-H10 G; 561-D7 PeT
Shady Grove Ct 458-F10 WnT
Shady Hills Dr 423-B8 PTM
Shady Hills Dr E 423-B8 PTM
Shady Hills Dr W 423-B8 PTM
Shady Hollow La 496-F3 WrT
Shady La 592-E8 BTM; 391-H5 Ca; 460-J7 LTM; 524-B6 P; 561-D10; 595-D1 WTJ
Shady Nook Rd 324-E10; 358-E3 WTH
Shady Oak Dr 462-B7 LTM; 496-C1 WrT
Shady Pl 561-H10 G
Shady Terr 491-H10 WnT
Shady Tree La 427-G3 LTM
Shady View Dr 461-C7 LTM
Shafer Ct 392-E10 Ca
Shafter Rd 461-F1, G2 L
Shagbark Rd 424-J4 WTM
Shahan Ct 428-B4 LTM
Shakamac Dr 391-E3 Ca
Shakespeare Dr 489-D7 A; 562-B5 Spt
Shale La 428-K8 L
Shalimar Ct 491-F6 WnT
Shallowbrook Ct 496-C5 WrT
Shamel Dr 423-F5 PTM
Shamrock Blvd 357-J3 W
Shamrock Dr 561-C5 PeT
Shan Crest Hill 529-K2 WrT
Shandon La 394-A4 F
Shanghai Rd 423-F10; 457-F1 PTM
Shank La 491-D2 WnT
Shanna Cir 428-J8 L
Shannon Ave 494-E5 CTM
Shannon Ct 324-K6 N
Shannon Lakes Dr 560-K6 PeT
Shannon Pointe Rd 496-H4 WrT
Shannon Rd 389-E10 Z
Shannon Way 525-E2 WnT
Sharer Dr 557-H1 P
Sharon Ave 458-G10; 492-G1, G2, G5 WnT
Sharon Ct 523-D8 P
Sharon Dr 489-J4 WaT
Sharon La 460-F7 WTM
Sharon Rd 459-A3 WTM
Sharrob Rd 525-G9 DTM
Sharsted Ct 462-A1 L
Shasta Dr 394-A3 F
Shattuck Dr 490-A7 WaT
Shaw Ave 492-A2 S
Shaw St 523-G8 P
Shawnee Rd 424-K10; 425-A10 WTM
Shawnee Tr Dr N 460-H2 LTM
Shawnee Tr Dr S 460-H2 LTM
Shearer Rd 495-F3 WrT
Sheehan La 457-G6 PTM
Sheehan Pl 457-G6 PTM
Sheek Rd 596-H2 G
Sheets Rd 389-D7 ET; 557-C8 GT; 389-D7 Z
Sheffield Ave DN-A1, A3, A4; 492-J5, J7, J8, J10; 526-J1 WnT
Sheffield Blvd 391-D5 CTH
Sheffield Ct 391-D5 CTH; 393-E9 F; 489-G6 WaT; 496-C1 WrT
Sheffield Dr 489-G5, G6 WaT; 496-C1 WrT
Shefford Ct 458-B5 PTM
Shelborne Rd 390-E3, E10; 424-E2 CTH; 356-E10 WTH
Shelbourne Ct 390-D9 CTH
Shelburne Dr 424-J9 WTM
Shelby Ct 561-H3 PeT
Shelby St DN-F4; 493-H10; 527-H3 CTM; 527-H8, H9, H10; 561-H1, H3, H6, H8 PeT
Shelbyville Rd 563-J9 CTJ; 528-E10; 562-H1; 563-A3, G7 FT; 528-E10 PeT
Sheldon St 493-J3, J4, J5 CTM
Shelia Dr 455-H1 BTH; 461-K5 L
Shellbark Dr 462-F10 WrT
Shelley Ct 495-C6 WrT
Shelley St 495-B6 WrT
Shelly Ave DN-D4 CTM
Shelly Way 563-A2 FT
Shelton Dr 490-D9 WaT
Shenandoah Ct 495-K4 WrT
Shenandoah Dr 495-J4 WrT
Shenandoah Pl 495-K3 WrT
Shepard St DN-A4; 492-K10; 526-K1 CTM
Sherborne Rd 393-D10 F
Sherburne La 458-E9 WnT
Sheri Cir 523-J10 P
Sheridan Ave 322-K1 AT; 461-A7, A8 LTM; 359-D2 N; 324-J9; 359-D2 NT; 323-J5; 324-B6 WTH; 495-A1, A2, A5, A6, A7, A8, A10; 529-A3, A5 WrT
Sheridan Ct 325-F3 C
Sherlock Dr 457-J8 PTM
Sherman Ave 460-D3 WTM
Sherman Cir 325-F3 C; 426-D10 WTM
Sherman Dr 460-D10; 494-D4, D5, D10; 528-D2 CTM; 391-H4 Ca; 562-D9 G; 528-D7; 562-D2, D5 PeT; 426-D7, D8, D10; 460-D2, D3, D4, D10 WTM
Sherman Towne Dr 528-D9 PeT
Sherrack Ct 562-C7 PeT
Sherry Ct 357-H9 WTH
Sherry La 561-E6 PeT
Sherry La W 491-G10 WnT
Sherwood Ct 392-G8 Ca; 389-E5 Z
Sherwood Dr 557-J10 M; 425-G9 WTM
Sherwood La 425-J3 WTM
Sheryl La 593-C2 MTM
Shetland Ct 422-J4 PTM
Shetland La 422-J4 PTM
Shibler Dr 495-F1 WrT
Shick Dr 460-F10 CTM
Shiloh Cir 490-E7 WaT
Shiloh Cr Way 490-G8 WaT
Shiloh Crossing Dr 490-F8 WaT
Shiloh Ct 561-H7 PeT
Shiloh Falls 392-K4 Ca
Shiloh Pk Dr 490-F8 WaT
Shiloh Prof Dr 490-F8 WaT
Shiloh Rd 490-G5 WaT
Shiloh Wood Ct 490-G8 WaT
Shimer Ave 494-J9, K9 WrT
Shireton Ct 457-C6 PTM

Shirley Dr 492-C2 WnT
Shirley La 565-D8 MTS; 527-J9 PeT
Shoal Cr La 456-C3 BTH; 456-K7 PTM
Shoe Overlook Dr 393-G4 F
Shoemaker Dr 391-D4 Ca
Shore Cir 392-C8 Ca
Shore Dr 457-E9 PTM
Shore Is Dr 425-H10 WTM
Shore La 325-G1 C
Shore Line Ct 324-J6 N
Shore Terr 457-E8 PTM
Shore Walk E 357-H9 WTH
Shore Way E 357-H10 WTH
Shoreham Ct 457-J8 PTM
Shoreham Dr 457-J7 PTM
Shoreland Ct 496-A3 WrT
Shoreland Dr 496-A3 WrT
Shoreland La 496-A2 WrT
Shoreline Blvd 429-B1 FCT
Shoreline Cir 325-G1 C
Shoreline Dr 325-G1 C; 595-C7 WTJ
Shoreridge Terr 428-F6 LTM
Shoreview Cir 428-H6 LTM
Shoreview La 428-H6 LTM
Shorevista Dr 428-K3 LTM
Shorevista La 325-E5 N
Shorewalk Dr 428-F6 LTM
Shoreway Ct 426-C5 WTM
Shoreway Dr 426-C5 WTM
Shorewood Dr 460-B5 WTM
Short St 596-C1 G; 523-F8 P
Shorter Ct 491-C4 WnT
Shorter Dr 491-D4 WnT
Shortleaf Ct 428-J6 L
Shortridge Dr 495-D1 WrT
Shortridge Rd 529-D5 FT; 461-D10; 495-D5, D8, D10 WrT
Shoshone Dr 391-K6; 392-A6 Ca
Shottery Terr 424-F6 PTM
Shout-It-Out Ct 595-A7 WTJ
Shower Ct 357-E10 WTH
Shrewsbury La 424-J9 WTM
Shrike Ct 427-F7 LTM
Shriver Ave 493-D1, D2 CTM; 459-D10 WTM
Shut Out Ct 560-K8 PeT
Siarry La 530-J5 SCT
Sickle Rd 495-F2 WrT
Sidewinder Ct 561-C9 WTJ
Siear Ct 562-B7 PeT
Siear Dr 562-B7 PeT
Siear Terr 562-B7 PeT
Sienna Dr 326-C9 N
Sierra Ct 490-H7 WnT
Sierra Dr 524-J1 WnT
Sierra Madre Dr 596-G3 G
Siesta Ct 596-G4 G
Sigmond Cir 393-B8 F
Signature Dr 424-D4 PTM
Sigsbee St 491-F8; 525-F1, F2 WnT
Silk Cir 427-F4 LTM
Silver Ave 527-B1 CTM
Silver Bay Cir 428-K4 LTM
Silver Berry La 592-F3 M
Silver Cr Ct 561-A10 WTJ
Silver Cr Way 561-A10 WTJ
Silver Ct 358-A9 WTH
Silver Dawn Ct 389-E9 Z
Silver Fox Ct 561-C6 PeT
Silver Fox Dr 561-C6 PeT
Silver Hill Dr 560-J10 WTJ
Silver Hill La 560-K10 WTJ
Silver La Dr 528-J3, K2 WrT
Silver Lake Cir 560-K10 WTJ
Silver Lake Ct 560-K9 WTJ
Silver Lakes Dr 358-A3 WTH
Silver Maple Ct 392-B7 Ca; 596-G1 G; 492-F3 WnT
Silver Oak Dr 563-A1 FT
Silver Pine Ct 426-E8 WTM
Silver Ridge Ct 392-K10 F; 423-C5 PTM
Silver Shore Ct 428-H3 LTM
Silver Springs Blvd 560-J10 WTJ
Silver Springs Ct 560-J10 WTJ
Silver Springs Dr 560-K10 WTJ
Silver Thorne Way 358-A9 WTH
Silver Tree Dr 428-G10 L
Silver Valley Cir 560-J10 WTJ
Silver Valley Ct 560-J10 WTJ
Silver Valley Dr 560-J10 WTJ
Silver Wood La 594-C9 WTJ
Silver Wraith Dr 389-D9 Z
Silverado Dr 394-J7 F
Silverleaf Ct 423-D5 PTM
Silverleaf Dr 424-H7 WTM
Silverstream Dr 391-E2 CTH
Silverton Dr 428-K7 L
Silverton Way 562-J3 FT
Simcoe St 462-G1 L
Simmerman Ct 426-E1 Ca
Simmons St 523-H9 P
Simmul Cir 559-J3 DTM
Simmul La 559-J4 DTM
Simone Dr 562-C5 Spt
Simsbury Ct 462-D2 L
Sinclair Pl 394-B4 F
Sinclair Woods Dr 426-B4 WTM
Singleton St 527-G3 CTM; 561-G2, G7 PeT
Singletree Ct 391-B3 CTH
Singletree Dr 490-K2 WnT
Sioux Cir 325-D8 N
Sioux Run 495-D8 WrT
Sioux Tr 426-F8 WTM
Six Points Rd 323-B3 AT; 391-C4 CTH; 524-G10; 558-G2 GT; 524-G10 P; 323-B9 WTH; 490-G10; 524-G3 WaT
Skeeter Ct 491-E1 WnT
Skelton St 594-J4 WTJ
Skiles Pl 490-K4 WnT
Skiles St N 490-K4 WnT
Skipjack Dr 428-D5 LTM
Skipper Ct 392-B1 Ca
Skippers Ct 490-A8 A; 428-B4 LTM
Skippers Way 428-B4 LTM
Skipping Rock Ct 392-F5 Ca
Skipton Ct 324-J4 N
Skycrest Tr 491-B7 WnT
Skyhawk Ct 395-A7 F
Skylark Ct 392-J2 Ca
Skylark Dr 529-K8 FT
Skyline Ct 594-H7 WTJ
Skyline Dr 594-H7 WTJ; 526-B5 WnT
Skyline La 594-H6 WTJ
Skyridge Dr 426-J6 WTM
Skyway Dr 495-G3 WrT
Sleepy Ct 358-A3 W
Sleepy Hollow La 391-H5 Ca
Sleepy Hollow Pl 595-J2 G
Sleepy Hollow St 523-G7 P
Sleet Dr 528-J10; 562-J1 FT
Sleet La 528-K10 FT
Slideoff Rd 558-K10; 592-K1, K3 MTM
Slippery Elm Ct 561-G8 PeT
Slippery Rock Rd 428-K9 L
Sliver Dr 455-E9 LTH
Sloan Ave 528-F1, F3 CTM
Sloan Terr 594-J7 WTJ
Sloop Cir 393-E9 F
Sloop Ct 428-E5 LTM
Sly Run 325-B10; 359-A1 NT
Sly Run Overlook 359-B2 NT
Sly Run Rd 359-K6 N; 359-K6 NT
Smallwood La E 457-B9 WnT
Smallwood La W 457-B9 WnT
Smart St 596-C1 G
Smethwick Cir 427-H5 LTM
Smith La 389-E10 ET
Smith Rd 490-C10 A; 428-G10 L; 524-C6 P
Smith St 388-E2 Wh
Smith Valley Rd 595-B4, H4; 596-A4, E4 G; 595-H4 PTJ; 594-D4, G4; 595-B4 WTJ
Smock Dr 596-D4 G
Smock St 561-G1, G2 PeT
Smoketree Dr 528-E8 BG
Smokey Hollow Ct 391-E2 CTH
Smokey Ridge Cir 392-C2 Ca
Smokey Ridge Ct 392-C3 Ca
Smokey Ridge Dr 392-C3 Ca
Smokey Ridge La 392-B2 Ca
Smokey Ridge Overlook 392-C2 Ca
Smokey Ridge Pl 392-C3 Ca
Smokey Ridge Tr 392-B2 Ca
Smokey Ridge Trace 392-B2 Ca
Smokey Ridge Way 392-C2 Ca
Smokey Row Ct 392-D3 Ca
Smokey Row La 392-D3 Ca
Smokey Row Pl 392-B3 Ca
Smokey Row Rd 391-A3, F3 CTH; 391-A3 Ca; 594-F10; 595-D10 WTJ
Snac Bary Tr 391-G9 CTH
Snapper Ct 428-C2 LTM
Snead Cir 496-D3 WrT
Snowberry Bay Ct 392-F5 Ca
Snowberry Ct 559-G1 DTM; 325-B10 N
Snowden Sq N 490-J5 WnT
Snowden Sq S 490-J5 WnT
Snowdrop Way 462-D8 LTM
Snowflake Dr 562-D5, D6 PeT
Snowowl Dr 392-H4 Ca
Snug Harbor Ct 561-J7 PeT
Snug Harbor Dr 561-K7 PeT
Snug Harbor La 561-J7 PeT
Soaring Eagle Ct 595-C5 WTJ; 457-C10 WnT
Soaring Hawk Cir 423-D2 ET
Sobax Dr 424-D5 PTM
Softwood Ct 529-F2 WrT
Solitude Ct 558-K10 MTM
Solomon St 592-B1 M
Solomons Ct 428-G1 FCT
Solun Ct 525-J8 DTM
Solun Rd 525-J8 DTM
Somebody Dr 457-A10 WnT
Somerby Ct 523-G6 P
Somers Dr 562-J1 FT
Somerset Ave 492-E5, E7, E9 WnT
Somerset Bay 426-A8, C7 WTM
Somerset Cir 455-J4 B
Somerset Ct 359-H9 N
Somerset Dr 425-C6 WTM
Somerset La 389-H6 Z
Sommersworth La 458-E3 PTM
Son St 390-K10 CTH
Sondridge Cir 427-D10 LTM
Song Ct 391-F2 CTH
Songbird Ct 392-B9 Ca; 592-B5 M; 595-A4 WTJ
Songbird La 392-C9 Ca; 393-B8 F
Sonhatsett Dr 358-A3 WTH
Sonna Dr 391-F4 CTH
Soper Cir 491-C4 WnT
Sorbonne Pl 424-F4 PTM
Sorel St 530-G3 WrT
Sorrel Ct 389-F9 Z
Sorrel Dr 424-J5 WTM
Sourwood Ct 424-K4 WTM
Souter Dr 495-F2 WrT
South 40th St Dr 460-E8 WTM
South 51st Dr 457-J6 PTM
South 64th St Dr 459-K1 WTM
South 77th St Dr 425-B8, C8 WTM
South 100 Rd 523-J1; 524-A1 A; 496-K7; 497-C7, H7 SCT; 523-B1, J1; 524-A1 WaT
South 150 Rd 523-F2 A; 523-F2 WaT
South 200 Rd 523-K3 A; 496-H10; 497-H9 SCT; 523-A3, K3; 524-A3, G3 WaT
South 251 Rd 523-D5; 524-G4 WaT
South 300 Rd 389-H1; 390-A1 ET; 523-D5; 524-A5 GT; 524-A5 P; 530-J2; 531-H2 SCT; 389-H1; 390-A1 UT; 388-A1, G1 WTB; 523-D5 WaT
South 350 Rd 389-B2 ET; 523-A7 GT
South 375 Rd 389-D3 ET
South 400 Rd 388-J3; 389-B3 ET; 531-J4 SCT; 388-C3, F3, J3 WTB
South 425 Rd 388-G3 WTB
South 450 Rd 524-A9, F9 GT; 524-A9, F9 P; 388-A4 WTB
South 500 Rd 388-B6; 390-A5 ET; 388-B6 PTB; 388-B6 WTB
South 525 Rd 388-E6 ET
South 550 Rd 388-B7, G7; 389-A7, J7; 390-A7 ET; 388-B7 PTB; 389-J7 Z
South 600 Rd 389-C7 ET; 531-A9 MTS; 531-A9, H9 SCT
South 650 Rd 388-E9 ET; 388-A9 PTB
South 675 Rd 557-F5 GT
South 700 Rd 388-J10; 389-D10, J10; 390-A10 ET; 557-D5; 558-E5 GT; 389-D10 Z
South 750 Rd 422-D2 ET; 557-C6; 558-B6 GT; 422-A2 PTB
South 800 Rd 557-B7; 558-E7 GT
South 801 Rd 558-A7 GT
South 821 Rd 558-A7 GT
South 825 Rd 557-F8 GT
South 851 Rd 558-A8 GT
South 875 Rd 557-A9 GT
South 25th 489-G9 A
South 50 489-A10 WaT
South Adams Ct 460-C8 WTM
South Ascot 357-J9 WTH
South Atherton Dr 494-G8 WrT
South Atrium Boardwalk 427-C8 LTM
South Ballinshire 457-C6 PTM
South Bay Dr 426-K2 F
South Bay Road Dr 426-C7 WTM
South Bayside Dr 427-A2 LTM
South Beech Dr 523-K9 P
South Bentwood Cir Dr 424-F6 PTM
South Bloomfield Dr 564-F4 FT
South Blossom La 423-F7 PTM
South Blue Creek Dr 427-D8 LTM
South Boulder Ct 561-C4 PeT
South Braeside Dr 425-C4 WTM
South Brendon Way Dr 461-B4 LTM
South Brendonridge Ct 460-K5 LTM
South Brentwood Dr 523-K8 P
South Bridger Dr 426-D1 Ca
South Brittany Ct 428-G5 L
South Broadway Dr 523-G10 P
South Brookside Pkwy Dr 494-B5 CTM
South Buck Cr Blvd Dr 561-F1 PeT
South Burns Dr 455-H1 BTH
South Canterbury Sq 425-F4 WTM
South Cardinal Cove 427-E7 LTM
South Carnoustie Cir Dr 523-A1 WaT
South Cedar Glen Dr 557-H2 P
South Cedar Hills Dr 595-A10 WTJ
South Center St 523-F9; 557-H2 P
South Central Ct 459-G9 CTM
South Century Cir Dr 424-K6 WTM
South Charleston La 495-B5 WrT
South Chatham Ct 427-E5 LTM
South Chesapeake Dr 428-C7 L
South Chesterfield Dr 527-G9 PeT
South Clay St 592-A3 M
South Clayburn Dr 424-B6 PTM
South Cobblestone Dr 428-J8 L
South Colony Pointe Dr 427-B3 LTM
South Commons Dr 493-F10 CTM
South Commons Dr NE DN-D4 CTM
South Cottonwood 557-K5 GT
South County Line Rd 558-A10 GT; 558-A10 M
South Court Dr 561-J4 PeT
South Creek Pkwy Dr 527-J9 PeT
South Ct 531-E2 SCT
South Deer Ridge Dr 392-G2 Ca
South Delaware Commons Dr 426-C10 WTM
South Discovery Dr 427-B3 LTM
South Dogwood Cir 424-E6 PTM
South Dollar Hide Dr 559-H2, J2 DTM
South Doral Dr 427-C4 LTM
South Dover Blvd 455-F7 B
South Dr 325-E4 C; DN-B2; 493-A6 CTM; 395-C7 FCT; 455-E8 LTH; 325-H6 NT; 531-H8 SCT; 357-J2 W; 560-H10 WTJ
South Dudley Dr 562-E1 PeT
South Dukane Cir Dr 525-F8 DTM
South E St 523-F8 P
South Eagle Bay Dr 457-D8 PTM
South Eagle Cove Dr 457-E8 PTM
South Eagle Pointe Dr 457-F7 PTM
South Emerson Ct Dr 494-G2 CTM
South Fairview Dr 596-C1 G
South Fairway Cir Dr 428-H8 L
South Fall Cr Pkwy Dr 493-E2 CTM; 460-B7 WTM
South Fleetwood Dr 391-D5 Ca
South Forest Blvd Dr 425-G6 WTM
South Forest Pk Dr 562-B10 G
South Fortune Cir 525-J5 WnT
South Fox Harbour Dr 528-A8 PeT
South Fox Lake 423-E6 PTM
South Frederick Dr 425-B9 WTM
South Galburgh Ct 456-H9 WnT
South Gate Dr 596-D1 G
South Geist Woods Dr 428-F2 FCT
South Glenview Dr 426-E8 WTM
South Green Braes Dr 456-K5 PTM
South Green Hills La 458-G10 WnT
South Green St 455-F7 B
South Halcomb Cir Dr 525-F8 DTM
South Hampton Cir 428-A6 LTM
South Harbour Dr 325-B9; 359-B1 N
South Haven Ct 561-D6 PeT
South Haven Rd 596-G4 G
South Hickory Tr 529-B8 FT
South Hideaway Dr 424-H6 PTM
South High Meadow Ct 560-K10 WTJ
South Highland Manor Ct 459-B4 WTM
South Holly Ct 359-G1 N
South Honner Dr 427-E10 LTM
South Huddleston Dr 561-E6 PeT
South Indian Cr Rd 563-H3; 564-G2 FT
South Indian Lake Blvd 428-A10, B10 L
South Indiana St 592-A3 M
South Jackson St 594-K1 WTJ
South Jessman Rd Dr 427-D9 LTM
South Kensington Way 523-C8 P
South Lake Dr 455-F8 B
South Lake Nora Ct 425-G4, H4 WTM
South Lake Nora Dr 425-G4 WTM
South Lake Terr Dr 496-A3 WrT
South Lakeview Pkwy Dr 423-J9 PTM
South Lakewood Dr 455-K8 B
South Landborough Dr 427-A10 LTM
South Lantern Rd 393-H10; 427-H2 F
South Laureate Ct 457-B9 WnT
South Laurel Cir 460-E6 WTM
South Lick Cr Pkwy Dr 527-H9 PeT
South Lickridge La Dr 528-D8 PeT
South Lismore Dr 561-H8 PeT
South Lockerbie Cir DN-E2; 493-G7 CTM
South Log Run Dr 456-H8 PTM
South Loop 357-J2 W
South Lynnfield Ct 457-F6 PTM
South Madison Vill Dr 561-K5 PeT
South Manor Dr 455-F10 LTH
South Maradona Dr 491-C4 WnT
South Marten Ct 461-F7 L
South Maxwell Ct 389-G6 Z
South McCloud Ct 457-J3 PTM
South Meadow Vue Ct 561-E5 PeT
South Meridian St 596-D5, D6 G
South Miami Ct 523-J9 P
South Midfield Service Rd 525-A9, D6 DTM; 525-D6 WnT
South Mill St 523-F8 P
South Monroe St 557-J10 BTM
South Mount Shasta 490-G5 WnT
South Mount Vernon Tr 496-E7 WrT
South Navajo Tr Dr 425-B8 WTM
South Oak Blvd Dr 496-K5 Cu
South Oak Lake Cir 424-D5 PTM
South Oak Run Dr 424-J3 WTM
South Oak Tree Dr 562-C9 PeT
South Oakview Dr 457-F1 PTM
South Oakwood Tr Dr 425-B10 WTM
South Old Town Dr 425-A4 WTM
South Olde Mill Cir Dr 425-E5 WTM
South Oldfields Cir Dr 458-J8 WTM
South Orchard Pk Dr 391-J10; 425-J1 CTH
South Park Blvd 596-G1 G
South Park Central Dr 459-B1 WTM
South Parkside Ct 557-H1 P
South Pathway Dr 595-E7 WTJ
South Paula Lane Dr 458-H7 WTM
South Payne Rd Dr 562-C2 PeT
South Perimeter Rd 525-C8 DTM
South Pinehurst Dr 461-J8 LTM
South Pleasant Run Pkwy Dr 494-D9; 527-D4, G3, H2; 528-B2 CTM; 494-G7, J6; 495-A7, B6, C3 WrT
South Pocono Mesa 491-H4 S
South Priority Way Dr 426-C3 WTM
South Quail Ridge 557-J4 P
South Queen St 491-D9 WnT
South Questend Dr 492-G2 WnT
South Racquet Club Dr 425-A3 WTM
South Reavest Dr 528-A1 CTM
South Redcliff La 523-C8 P
South Redfern Dr 529-G8 FT
South Redfox Ct 595-E3 WTJ
South Rippling Way 424-H4 WTM
South Roxburgh Ct 456-J9 WnT
South Rushmore Blvd 490-H5 WnT
South Sadlier Cir Dr 529-D1 WrT
South Saint John Ct 528-F9 BG
South Salem Dr 392-J2 Ca
South Sandpiper Dr 424-F3 PTM
South Scarborough Blvd Dr 427-F8 LTM
South Settlement Dr 427-B2 LTM
South Shawnee Tr Dr 460-H2 LTM
South Snowden Sq 490-J5 WnT
South Southcreek Dr 561-D8 PeT
South Spring Brook Dr 495-B6 WrT
South St DN-D3; 493-D9 CTM; 393-H8 F; 428-H10 L; 359-H5 N; 523-F9 P; 562-A5 Spt
South St N 592-A3 M
South Stonebranch Dr 427-E6 LTM
South Stonehinge Ct 424-H8 WTM
South Stout Field Dr 526-B3 WnT
South Stratford Dr 393-A8 F
South Sugarbush La 455-G9 B
South Summer Walk Dr 562-B9 PeT
South Sunblest Blvd 393-E7 F
South Sundown Dr 457-F8 PTM
South Susan Dr 426-J7 WTM
South Tamarack Cir Dr 425-B3 WTM
South Tara Ct 457-K10 WnT
South Tidewater Dr 428-G5 LTM
South Timber Springs Dr 393-E9 F
South Tocovi Ct 455-F3 B
South Town Ctr Rd 592-D2 M
South Trophy Club Dr 457-C9 WnT
South Tulip Dr 562-A4 PeT
South Turtle Cr Dr 527-G10 PeT
South Valley Cr Dr 496-H3 WrT
South Victoria Dr 527-B10; 561-B1 PeT
South Vill Way 495-E9 WrT
South Village Pk 358-B10 WTH
South Village Pkwy 457-D7 PTM
South Village Plaza Dr 494-K5 WrT
South Vine St 523-F8 P
South Vinewood Dr 455-H8 B
South W Lake Dr 491-H7 WnT
South Walton Dr 593-A1 MTM
South Warbler Way 392-H3 Ca
South Watergate Mall 457-K8 WnT
South Watergate Pl 457-K8 WnT
South Wellesley Dr 495-C2 WrT
South Westridge Dr 359-E4 N
South White House Dr 596-E3 G
South Windjammer Dr 428-E1 FCT
South Windsor Dr 393-J6 F
South Woodacre Blvd Dr 456-H5 PTM
South Woodfield Dr 392-H2 Ca
South Woods Edge Dr 427-A5 LTM
South Woodstone Way Dr 427-F3 LTM
South Woodview Dr 391-G8 CTH
South Yeagy Ct 594-J1 WTJ
Southampton Ct 391-C4 CTH; 359-H8 N
Southbrook Dr 425-H6 WTM
Southcreek Ct 428-H5 L; 561-D8 PeT
Southcreek Dr N 561-D8 PeT
Southcreek Dr S 561-D8 PeT
Southcrest Ct 561-B5 PeT
Southdale Dr 527-E10 PeT
Southeast 1st Ave 391-K5 Ca
Southeast 1st St 391-K4 Ca
Southeast 2nd St 391-K4 Ca
Southeast 3rd St 391-K4 Ca
Southeast 4th Ave 392-A4 Ca
Southeast 4th St 391-K4; 392-A4 Ca
Southeast 5th St 391-K5 Ca
Southeast 6th St 391-K5 Ca
Southeastern Ave DN-F3; 493-H8; 494-A9, D10; 528-F1 CTM; 529-A3, J8; 530-A9; 564-D1, E1, F2, H3 FT; 564-H3 MTS; 528-F1; 529-A3 WrT
Southern Ave 528-C4 BG; 527-C4, E4, H4; 528-A4, C4 CTM; 528-H4 PeT; 525-K4; 526-A4, C4, F4 WnT; 529-A4 WrT
Southern Lakes Dr 563-A5 FT
Southern Lakes Dr N 563-A5 FT
Southern Mist Dr 562-J7 FT
Southern Oaks Dr 561-B7 PeT
Southern Plaza Dr 527-E8 PeT
Southern Shores Rd 527-F10 PeT
Southern Springs Ave 562-K7 FT
Southern Springs Blvd 562-K6 FT
Southern Springs Cir 562-K7 FT
Southern Springs Ct 562-K7 FT
Southern Springs Dr 562-K7 FT
Southern Trails Dr 563-B6 FT
Southern Trails Pl 563-B6 FT
Southfield Dr 524-A9 P; 562-A5 Spt
Southgate Dr 424-C7 PTM
Southgreen Dr 527-G10 PeT
Southmore St 523-J8 P
Southpoint Dr 427-F1 F
Southpointe Dr 561-H9 PeT
Southport Crossing Dr 562-E4 PeT
Southport Crossing Pl 562-G4 FT
Southport Crossing Way 562-E4 PeT
Southport Pl 560-D4 PeT
Southport Rd 559-G6, J5; 560-A5, B4 DTM; 562-K4; 563-H4; 564-A4, D4 FT; 560-B4, G4; 561-A4, H4; 562-B4 PeT; 561-H4; 562-B4 Spt
Southport Terr 562-F4 PeT
Southridge Cir 562-B9 G; 428-K7 L
Southridge Ct 562-B6 Spt; 357-K5 W
Southridge Dr 562-B9 G; 455-C9 LTH
Southview Dr 561-G4, K4 PeT
Southway Ct 595-A1 WTJ
Southway Dr 531-B3 SCT
Southway Pl 594-K1 WTJ
Southway Rd 594-K1 WTJ
Southwest 1st Ave 391-K5 Ca
Southwest 1st St 391-K4 Ca
Southwest 2nd Ave 391-K5 Ca
Southwest 2nd St 391-J4 Ca
Southwest 3rd Ave 391-J4, J6 Ca
Southwest 3rd St 391-K4 Ca
Southwest 4th Ave 391-J4 Ca
Southwest 5th St 391-K5 Ca
Southwest Dr 526-B5 DTM
Southwick Ct 424-H9 PTM
Southwind Cir 428-B3 LTM
Southwind Ct 428-A3 LTM
Southwind Dr 428-A3 LTM
Southwind Way 595-C2 WTJ
Southwood Ct 561-D3 PeT
Southwood Dr 561-G3 PeT
Southwood St 596-D5, D6 G
Sovereign La 394-B5 F
Sowers Dr 393-H1 DTH
Spanish Fir La 561-G7 PeT
Spann Ave DN-F4; 493-H9; 494-A9, D9 CTM
Spannwood Rd 459-B2 WTM
Sparks Rd 463-E9 BCT
Sparrow Ave 527-G6, K6 PeT
Sparrowood Ct 428-J10 L
Sparrowood Dr 428-H10 L
Sparrows Pt Ct 428-D7 L
Speedway Ave 492-A4 S
Speedway Dr 491-J3 S
Speedway Woods Dr 491-J6, J7 WnT
Speights Dr 457-F1 PTM
Spencer Ave 494-G8, H3, H4, H9, H10; 528-H1 WrT
Spend A Buck Ct 561-A8 PeT
Spend A Buck Dr 561-A8 PeT
Spice Bush Dr 457-D4 PTM
Spice La 394-D7 F
Spicebush Ct 393-A3 Ca
Spicewood Ct 424-J4 WTM
Spicewood Dr 527-F7 PeT
Spider Bay Ct 428-E4 LTM
Spindrift La 460-C4 WTM
Spinnaker Bay 596-H3 G
Spinnaker Ct 428-D4 LTM
Spire Dr 529-A8 FT
Spire La 529-A7 FT
Split Granite Dr 394-J6 F
Split Tree Ct 427-G3 LTM
Sportsman Ct 530-A2 WrT
Sportsman Dr 530-A2 WrT
Spotted Owl Dr 455-H9 B
Sprague St 527-B8 PeT
Spring Bk Dr N 495-B6 WrT
Spring Bk Dr S 495-B6 WrT
Spring Blossom Dr 393-J8 F
Spring Cr Cir 457-K4 PTM
Spring Cr Ct 324-H7 N; 457-K5 PTM; 490-E8 WaT
Spring Cr Dr 457-J5 PTM
Spring Cr Pl 457-K5 PTM
Spring Ct 392-B8 Ca; 523-D1 WaT; 491-E7 WnT; 389-E4 Z
Spring Ct E 529-J8 FT
Spring Dale Dr 393-K8 DTH
Spring Dr 562-E10 G; 389-K7 Z
Spring Farms Dr 391-D4 Ca
Spring Forest Dr 425-B2 WTM
Spring Highland Dr 425-D1 CTH
Spring Hill Ct 424-H6 PTM
Spring Hill Dr 392-A10 CTH
Spring Hills Dr 389-D9 Z
Spring Hollow Dr 425-C3 WTM
Spring Hollow Rd 459-A9 CTM
Spring La 596-G1 G; 424-F8 PTM
Spring Lake Rd 592-K6; 593-D6 MTM
Spring Lakes Dr 425-B3 WTM
Spring Meadow Ct 424-G5 PTM
Spring Mill Blvd 391-D2 CTH
Spring Mill Ct 592-B3 M; 425-D5 WTM

Spring Mill Dr 592-B4 M; 523-E2 WaT
Spring Mill La 391-D10 CTH; 425-C8 WTM
Spring Mill Rd 323-D3 AT; 391-D3, D10; 425-D1 CTH; 391-D3 Ca; 323-D10; 357-D3, D10 WTH; 425-D6, D7, D10; 459-D1 WTM
Spring Oaks Dr 563-A1 FT
Spring Oaks Way 563-A1 FT
Spring Ridge Ct 391-D9 CTH
Spring Ridge Dr 391-D9 CTH
Spring Side La Ct 424-H4 WTM
Spring Side La N 424-K1 WTM
Spring St DN-E2; 493-G7 CTM; 523-G8 P
Spring Valley Ct 490-K10 WnT
Spring Valley Dr 490-K10 WnT
Spring Valley La 490-K10 WnT
Spring Violet Pl 392-H5 Ca
Springbrook Run 392-H6 Ca
Springcrest Ct 557-H1 P
Springdale Pl DN-F2; 493-H7 CTM
Springer Ave 495-B6 WrT
Springfield Ct 393-G6 F; 523-F1 WaT
Springfield Dr 458-G2 WTM
Springfield La 393-G7 F
Springfield Overlook 456-K9 PTM
Springhill Way 457-F7 PTM
Springhollow 523-B1 WaT
Springmeadow La 358-C10 WTH
Springmill Ponds Blvd 391-D1 CTH
Springmill Ponds Cir 391-D2, E2 CTH
Springridge Cir 428-A1 F
Springsong Dr 525-K5; 526-A5 DTM
Springston Ct 428-D1 F
Springstone Rd 395-B10; 429-B1, C1 FCT
Springtree Pl 496-E8 WrT
Springvalley Dr 557-K7 GT
Springview Ct 455-H2 B
Springview Dr 425-C5 WTM; 523-E1 WaT
Springwater Cir 427-F7 LTM
Springwater Ct 427-F7 LTM
Springwater Dr W 427-F6 LTM
Springway Dr 529-H7 FT
Springwood Ct 429-B1 FCT
Springwood Dr 489-J8 A
Springwood Tr 458-G7 WTM
Spruance Ct 428-F1 FCT
Spruce Ct 392-E2 Ca; 523-H4 WaT
Spruce Dr 392-D2, E2 Ca
Spruce Knoll Ct 460-F3 WTM
Spruce La 357-H4 WTH
Spruce La W 427-A2 F
Spruce St DN-F4; 493-J10; 527-J1, J2, J4 CTM; 455-K10 LTH; 531-H4 NP; 523-G7 P
Spurrington Cir 428-K9 L
Spurrington Way 428-K9 L
Spy Run Rd 496-G5 Cu
Spyglass Dr 424-H5 WTM
Spyglass Pl 424-H5 WTM
Spyglass Ridge Dr 394-C8 F
Squire Ct 426-K4 LTM
Squire Dr 526-A5 WnT
Squirrel Hollow 393-B8 F
Squirrel Nut Rd 598-A10 CTJ
Squirrels Run 458-A3 PTM
Stable Cir 530-D1 WrT
Stable Dr 530-D1 WrT
Stacey Dr 392-C1 Ca
Stacie Cir 428-H8 L
Stack Ct 496-D1 WrT
Stacy Lynn Ct 525-A2 WnT
Stacy Lynn Dr 525-A2 WnT
Stadium Dr 455-H7 B; DN-B1; 493-B5 CTM
Stafford Ct 425-A6 WTM
Stafford La 425-A6, A7 WTM
Stafford Rd 524-A9, F9 GT; 523-H9; 524-F9 P; 459-C2 WTM
Stafford Way 459-C3 WTM
Staffordshire Cir 457-J3 PTM
Stagg Hill Dr 392-K4 Ca
Staghorn Rd 424-K4 WTM
Stairs Pride Ct 357-F9 WTH
Stamford Ct 393-E9 F
Stamm Ave 425-J9; 426-B9 WTM
Standard Ave DN-B4; 493-A10 CTM; 492-G10 WnT
Standing Tree Way 394-B5 F
Standish 391-J6 Ca
Standish Ave 527-G6, J6 PeT
Standish Ct 526-B7 DTM
Standish Dr 526-B7 DTM; 595-H1 G
Stanford Ct 424-G3 PTM
Stanhope Dr 457-F5 PTM
Stanhope Way 457-F5 PTM
Stanley Ave 527-G4, G6 CTM; 527-G6, G8 PeT; 389-H5 Z
Stanley Dr 489-C6 WaT
Stanley Rd 558-J1, K3, K4 DTM; 523-K10; 524-A10; 557-A8 GT; 523-H10, K10; 524-A10 P
Stansbury Ct 457-C6 PTM
Stansbury La 457-C7 PTM
Stanton Ave 494-D8 CTM
Stanton Ct 392-D2 Ca
Star La 558-A10 M
Starboard Way 428-C4 LTM
Stardust Blvd 359-J1 N
Stardust Dr 495-J2, K2; 496-A2 WrT
Stargrass La 357-E8 WTH
Starhaven Cir 496-C1 WrT
Starhaven Ct 496-C1 WrT
Stark La 595-E2 G
Starkey Ave 389-F10 ET; 389-F10 Z
Starkey Ridge La 424-E10 PTM
Starlight Dr 529-J8 FT
Starsong Rd 525-K6 DTM
Starter St 496-H6 Cu
Starview Ct 496-C2 WrT
Starview Dr 496-C2 WrT
State Ave DN-F1, F3, F4; 493-K5, K8, K10; 527-K2, K4, K5 CTM; 527-K5, K6, K8, K10; 561-K1 PeT
State Grid Rd 429-K7 VT
Staten Pl 389-G6 Z
Statesman Ct 455-J9 B
Statesman Dr 455-K9 B
Statesmen Dr 426-E6 WTM
Station Dr 392-B7 Ca
Station Hill Dr 489-B9 WaT
Station St 460-D10; 494-D2, D3 CTM; 393-H7 F; 426-D8 WTM
Staton Pl Dr E 491-A6 WnT
Staton Pl Dr W 491-A6 WnT
Statuette Ct 457-C10 PTM
Staughton Dr 460-G6, K6 LTM; 460-E6, G6 WTM
Staurt St 460-C10 CTM
Stave Oak Ct 528-F8 BG
Stave Oak Dr 528-E8 BG
Steambrook Dr 426-K1 F
Stearns Hill Ct 563-B3 FT
Stearns Hill Dr 563-B3 FT
Steele St 493-K5 CTM
Steeplebush Ct 326-C9 N
Steeplechase Dr 390-E10 CTH; 427-A4 LTM
Steer St 492-F8 WnT
Stein Rd 389-J10 ET
Steinmeier Ct 426-H9 WTM
Steinmeier Dr 426-H8, H10 WTM
Steinmeier Dr N 426-H9 WTM
Steinmeier Dr W 426-H10 WTM
Steinmetz Dr 457-J8 PTM
Stella St 462-G1 L; 595-D4 WTJ
Stelor La 394-C10 F
Sten Ct 561-K8 PeT
Stephanie Ann Dr 462-A5 L
Stephanie La 527-E5 PeT
Stephanie St 392-B1 Ca
Stephen Ct 391-F10 CTH
Stephen Dr 455-F7 B
Sterling Commons 394-A4 F
Sterling Ridge Run 428-H4 LTM
Sterling St 493-K5 CTM
Stern Dr 428-H1 FCT
Sterrett Blvd 428-F8 L
Stevedon Ct 557-H1 P
Steven Dr 592-B6 BTM
Steven La 560-G10 WTJ; 425-D10 WTM
Steven St 492-K5 CTM
Stevens Dr 523-K8 P
Stevens Rd 389-J6 Z
Stevens St DN-E4; 493-G9 CTM; 561-J2 PeT
Stevenson St 458-K3 WTM
Stewart Ct 427-J9 LTM
Stiles Rd 557-A10 GT
Stillcreek Dr 496-D8 WrT
Stillman Ave 424-C2 PTM
Stillmeadow Dr 491-B1 WnT
Stillwater Ct 428-D1 F; 595-G1 G
Stillwater La 424-H10 PTM
Stillwell Dr 490-F7 WaT
Stillwell St DN-F1; 493-H6 CTM
Stillwood La 496-D8 WrT
Stinemeyer Rd 530-J6; 531-D6 SCT
Stingray Dr 428-C2 LTM
Stirling Pt Dr 525-F10 DTM
Stirrup Ct 427-G4 LTM
Stock St 527-A1 CTM
Stockberger Pl 525-J5 DTM
Stockbridge Dr 424-H9 PTM; 424-H9 WTM
Stockport Rd 457-G6 PTM
Stockton Ct 425-A7 WTM
Stockton Dr 325-C10; 359-C1 N
Stockton St 425-A7 WTM
Stockwell Dr 562-J3 FT
Stoeppelwerth Dr 496-F4 WrT
Stone Bk Pl 393-C7 F
Stone Cr Dr 557-K3 P
Stone Dr 391-C3 CTH; 428-J4 LTM
Stone Haven Dr 393-A3 Ca
Stone Hill Dr 459-E3 WTM
Stone La 489-J10 A
Stone Mill Dr 562-E1 PeT
Stone Rd 596-A6, E5 G; 596-A6, E5 PTJ; 594-G4 WTJ
Stone Ridge Dr 455-C9 LTH
Stone Ring Cir 424-D6 PTM
Stone Wall La 389-F10 Z
Stone Way 531-F3 SCT
Stonebranch Dr E 427-F6 LTM
Stonebranch Dr N 427-F6 LTM
Stonebranch Dr S 427-E6 LTM
Stonebridge Ct 394-C7 F
Stonebridge Dr 426-E3 WTM; 489-G6 WaT
Stonechat La 562-K3 FT
Stonecreek Ct 458-A1 PTM
Stonecreek Dr 458-A1 PTM
Stonegate Ct 427-E8 LTM
Stonegate Dr 561-E10 G
Stonegate Rd 561-F10 G; 561-F9 PeT
Stoneham Dr 424-J8 WTM
Stonehaven La 531-E3, F4 SCT
Stonehedge Ct 391-J1 Ca; 561-F9 G
Stonehedge Dr 391-J1 Ca; 561-F9 G
Stonehedge Dr W 561-F9 G
Stonehinge Cir 424-H7 WTM
Stonehinge Ct N 424-H7 WTM
Stonehinge Ct S 424-H8 WTM
Stonehinge Dr 424-H7 WTM
Stonehurst Ct 427-F8 LTM
Stonehurst Dr 427-F8 LTM
Stonemill Cir 391-E1 CTH
Stonemill Ct 393-F9 F
Stonemill Dr 596-A4 G
Stonereath Ct 562-J6 FT
Stoneridge Ct 426-B1 Ca
Stoneridge Dr 461-C3 LTM
Stones Crossing Rd 595-J8 PTJ; 594-C8, J8; 595-E8 WTJ
Stones Ferry Pl 423-A3 PTM
Stones Ferry Rd 422-K4 PTM
Stoneview La 592-D4 M
Stonewall Dr 490-K9 WnT
Stoneway La 426-B1 Ca
Stonewick Run 392-G8 Ca
Stonewood Dr 530-C1 WrT
Stoney Bay Cir 392-G7 Ca
Stoney Bk Dr 496-E1 WrT
Stoney Cr Cir 391-E2 CTH
Stoney Cr Ct 496-E10 WrT
Stoney Grove La 595-F1 G
Stoneybrook Ct 595-G2 G
Stoneybrook Dr 595-F2 G
Stoneybrook Grove Dr 595-F1 G
Stony Cr Cir 359-J6 N
Stony Cr Dr 327-D9 WyT
Stony Cr Overlook 359-J7 N
Stony Cr Rd 359-K5; 360-A6 N; 359-K5; 360-A6 NT
Stony Cr Way 359-J9 N
Stony La 360-F4 NT
Stony Ridge Way 425-B10 WTM
Stonybrook Cir 496-B5 WrT
Stonybrook Dr 455-F3 B
Stonycroft La 562-C5 Spt
Stop 10 Rd 561-H5; 562-A5, D5 PeT; 562-A5 Spt
Stop 11 Rd 563-A6 FT; 560-K7; 561-A7, D6, E6, G6; 562-A6 PeT; 562-A6 Spt
Stop 12 Rd 561-J8; 562-A7 PeT
Stop 13 Rd 561-E8, K8 PeT
Stormhaven Ct 428-D4 LTM
Stormhaven Way 428-C3 LTM
Storms Ave 527-J4 CTM
Stormy Ridge Ct 391-E2 CTH
Story Ct 559-F1 DTM
Story Dr 558-H9 GT
Stouffer Ct 461-K7 LTM
Stouffer La 461-K7 LTM
Stoughton Ct 457-C6 PTM
Stout Field Dr E 526-C2, C3 WnT
Stout Field Dr N 526-C3 WnT
Stout Field Dr S 526-B3 WnT
Stout Field Dr W 526-C2 WnT
Stout Field Terr 526-C2 WnT
Stover Spur 391-F3 CTH
Stover St 527-G8 PeT
Stratfield Dr 428-G7 L
Stratford Ave 494-E8 CTM
Stratford Ct 461-K6 LTM
Stratford Dr N 393-A8 F
Stratford Dr S 393-A8 F
Stratford Hall 425-F3 WTM
Stratford Pl 392-D9 Ca
Stratford Way 393-A9 F
Strathdon Pl 428-H6 LTM
Strathmore Ct 462-A8 LTM
Strathmore Dr 462-A8 LTM
Stratton Ct 427-J1 F
Stratton Sq 424-J10 WTM
Straw Hat Ct 528-H10 FT
Straw Hat Dr 528-H10 FT
Strawberry La 495-E8 WrT
Strawbridge St 528-E8 PeT
Strawtown Ave 326-H1, K1; 327-F1 WRT
Streamside Ct 457-J1 PTM
Streamside Dr 392-K2 Ca; 457-J1 PTM
Street 15 326-J1 WRT
Stribeck Rd 423-F3 PTM
Stringtown Ave 325-E5, E10 N; 325-E5, E10; 359-E1 NT
Stringtown Pike 325-F2 C
Stuart Ct 325-F2 C
Stuart Dr 456-G8 LTH
Stuart St 494-C1, C2 CTM
Studebaker Ct 457-F10 WnT
Studebaker La 491-E1 WnT
Sturbridge Rd 424-K4 WTM
Sturgen Bay La 428-F4 LTM
Sturgeon Way 528-H9 FT
Sturm Ave DN-F2; 493-J7 CTM
Stymie Ct 561-A6, B6 PeT
Suburban Dr 457-H9 WnT
Subway St 528-G4 CTM; 528-G4 WrT
Sudbury Ct 490-J7 WnT
Sue Dr 392-G1 Ca
Sue Springs Ct 392-C7 Ca
Suemin St 455-F5 B
Suffolk La 391-B6 CTH; 424-J7 WTM
Sugar Cay Ct 392-G5 Ca
Sugar Cr Dr 531-J6 NP
Sugar Grove Ave 493-A3, A4 CTM
Sugar Grove Rd 523-G10; 557-F1 P
Sugar Maple Ct 392-C7 Ca; 562-C5 PeT
Sugar Maple La 592-C5 M
Sugar Pine Pt 427-G4 LTM
Sugar Tree La 425-D4 WTM
Sugarberry Ct 428-H6 L
Sugarbush Dr 389-G10 Z
Sugarbush La 455-G8 B
Sugarbush La S 455-G9 B
Sugarbush Ridge 389-G10; 423-G1 Z
Sugarleaf Pl 394-A3 F
Sugarloaf Ct 426-C2 Ca
Sugarloaf Dr 426-C1 Ca
Sugarwood Dr 557-J10 M
Suggins Cir 359-A4 NT
Sulky Ct 561-G6 PeT
Sulky Way 357-E10 WTH
Sullivans Ridge 389-F10 Z
Sumac Ct 392-D3 Ca
Sumac La 428-B7 L
Summer Ct 562-E9 G
Summer Est Dr 427-J5 LTM
Summer Hill 391-B3 CTH
Summer Rd 562-E10 G
Summer Ridge Pl 425-A3 WTM
Summer Sweet 392-F2 Ca
Summer Walk Dr E 562-C8 PeT
Summer Walk Dr S 562-B9 PeT
Summer Walk Dr W 562-C8 PeT
Summer Way 524-B7 P; 389-E4 Z
Summer Wood La 496-F7 Cu
Summerfield Cir 457-E10 WnT
Summerfield Dr 457-E9 WnT
Summerfield Dr N 457-E9 WnT
Summerhill Blvd 457-J3 PTM
Summerlakes Ct 424-J2 CTH
Summerlakes Dr 424-J1 CTH
Summerlin Way 428-J1 FCT
Summersby La 455-J2 B
Summerset Way 392-E7, F6 Ca
Summersong Dr 525-K6 DTM
Summertime Dr 461-B6 LTM
Summertree Ct 427-F5 LTM
Summertree La 427-F5 LTM
Summerwood La 394-D3 F
Summit Cir 390-A5 ET
Summit Ct 523-E6 P
Summit Dr 523-E6 P
Summit Ridge Ct 595-B2 WTJ
Summit Ridge Dr 595-A2 WTJ
Summit St DN-F2, F3; 493-J7, J8 CTM
Summitcrest Dr 491-F10 WnT
Summitt Rd 324-G6 N
Sumner Ave 528-B6 BG; 525-K6 DTM; 527-A6, D6, G6, J6; 528-B6 PeT
Sumner Rd 360-G4, G8 NT; 360-G4, G8 WyT
Sumner St 529-K8 FT
Sumter Rd 427-A9 LTM
Sumter St 491-K3 S
Sun Brair Ct 392-G3 CTH
Sun Pk Dr 357-H4 W
Sun Ridge Cir 358-F2 N
Sun Ridge Dr 530-J1 SCT
Sun River Dr 393-C7 F
Sun Valley Ct 561-C4 PeT
Sunbeam Cir 490-J9 WnT
Sunbird Cir 490-J10 WnT
Sunblest Blvd 393-E7, H6 F
Sunblest Blvd S 393-E7 F
Sunblest Ct 526-A9 DTM; 393-E7 F
Sunbow Cir 490-J10 WnT
Sunbow Dr 490-J10 WnT
Sunbow La 490-J10 WnT
Sunburst Cir 562-C9 PeT
Sunburst Ct 562-C9 PeT
Sunbury Dr 592-A1 M; 525-F1 WnT
Sunchase Dr 529-H7 FT
Suncloud Dr 531-B3 SCT
Suncrest Cir Dr E 491-F9 WnT
Suncrest Cir Dr N 491-F9 WnT
Suncrest Cir Dr W 491-F9 WnT
Suncrest Dr 562-D9 G
Sundance Dr 562-F5 FT
Sundance Tr 529-F8 FT
Sunday Dr 561-A1 PeT
Sundew Cir 357-E8 WTH
Sundial Cir 490-J10 WnT
Sundisk Ct 490-J10 WnT
Sundown Cir 523-D7 P
Sundown Dr N 457-F7 PTM
Sundown Dr S 457-F8 PTM
Sundrop Rd 490-J10 WnT
Sunfield Ct 491-B1 WnT
Sunfish Ct 325-E1 C; 428-D6 LTM
Sunflower Ct 457-F10 WnT
Sunflower Dr 325-E10 N
Sungate Ct 529-H7 FT
Sunglow Cir 490-J10 WnT
Sunglow Ct 490-J10 WnT
Sunloch Ct 427-A4 LTM
Sunmeadow Cir 458-G8 WTM
Sunmeadow Ct 458-G8 WTM
Sunmeadow Dr 458-F8 WTM
Sunmeadow La 458-G8 WTM
Sunmeadow Way 458-G8 WTM
Sunning Ct 490-J2 WnT
Sunningdale Blvd 490-J2; 491-A2 WnT
Sunningdale Ct 490-K2 WnT
Sunny Bk Dr 455-G7 B
Sunny Bk Pl 393-C7 F
Sunny Cr La 462-E2 L
Sunny Dr 489-F1 LTH
Sunny La 426-D10 WTM
Sunny Meade La 459-B5 WTM
Sunny Ridge Dr 426-J3 WTM
Sunnybay La 428-E7 L
Sunnyfield Ct 458-G8 WTM
Sunnyhill Rd 456-K4 PTM
Sunnyside Rd 428-D8, E10; 462-E2 L; 428-D8 LTM
Sunpoint Cir 562-G4 FT
Sunray Ct 423-E6 PTM
Sunridge Ct 496-E9 WrT
Sunrise Cir 393-H6 F; 595-C2 WTJ
Sunrise Ct 530-J1 SCT
Sunrise Dr 523-F5 WaT
Sunrise Rd 458-H7 WTM
Sunrise Tr 491-J10 WnT
Sunscape Cir 562-G5 FT
Sunset Ave 459-C5, C7 WTM
Sunset Bay 428-F7 L
Sunset Blvd 562-A10; 596-A1 G
Sunset Cove Ct 428-H7 L
Sunset Cove Dr 428-H7 L
Sunset Cove La 428-G6 L
Sunset Ct 489-J8 A; 389-E10; 423-F1 ET; 523-D7 P
Sunset Dr 564-D1 FT; 456-B4 LTH; 359-E2, F2 N
Sunset La 326-C9 NT; 425-D5, D7, D8, D10; 459-D1, D2 WTM
Sunset Manor 592-A1 M
Sunset Pl 523-F5 WaT
Sunset Pt La 394-D8 F
Sunshine Ave 458-E8 PTM
Sunshine Ct 561-C10 WTJ
Sunshine Way 561-C10 WTJ
Sunview Cir 562-G5 FT
Sunwood Dr 457-H10 WnT
Sunwood Way 424-J2 CTH
Superior Rd 526-B8 DTM
Superior St 425-D1 Ca
Surface Dr 595-C8 WTJ
Surina Way 596-D3 G
Surrey Ct 561-G6 PeT
Surrey Dr 561-H6 PeT
Surrey Hill Ct 460-J4 LTM
Surrey Hill Ct 460-J4 LTM; 324-K6 N
Surrey Hill Rd 460-H4 LTM
Surrey La 392-F3 Ca
Surrey Rd 458-E2 PTM
Surry Ct 530-J5 SCT
Surry Hill Ct 595-K3 G
Susan Ct 359-A7 NT; 357-H9 WTH
Susan Dr E 426-H6 WTM
Susan Dr S 426-J7 WTM
Susan La 460-H7 LTM
Sussex Cir 325-A7 N
Sussex La 495-K3 WrT
Sussex Terr 495-K3 WrT
Susy Ct 526-C9 DTM
Susy La 526-C9 DTM
Sutherland Ave 459-H10; 493-G1, G2, H1 CTM; 459-K8 WTM
Sutters Ct 496-C5 WrT
Sutton Ave 390-H8 CTH
Sutton Dr 594-H4 WTJ
Sutton Pk Dr 595-E3 G
Sutton St 494-H3 WrT
Suwanee Ct 561-B6 PeT
Suzanne Ct 490-J4 WnT
Suzy La 564-D2 FT
Swails St 564-E5 FT
Swallow La 523-G4 WaT
Swallowtail Dr 491-C6 WnT
Swans Way 425-B5 WTM
Swanson Dr 458-F7 WTM
Sweet Bay Ct 424-J4 WTM
Sweet Blossom La 496-F3 WrT
Sweet Brair Pkwy 394-C5 F
Sweet Clover Way 394-A2 F
Sweet Cr Dr 531-B5 SCT
Sweet Gum Ct 325-B9 N
Sweet Gum Dr 424-K4 WTM; 523-C3 WaT
Sweet Gum St 455-G9 B
Sweet Spring Ct 393-G4 F
Sweetbriar Ave 529-F10 NW
Sweetsen Rd 558-H9 GT
Sweetwater Dr 462-B5 L
Sweetwood Dr 592-A1 M
Swiftsail Cir 428-C4 LTM
Swiftsail Ct 428-C4 LTM
Swiftsail La 428-C4 LTM
Sycamore Ct 455-J8 B; 389-A9 ET; 596-D10 NW; 523-G9 P
Sycamore Dr 489-G8 A; 455-F8, J8 B; 428-H9 L; 325-C10 N; 523-K8 P
Sycamore Forge Ct 458-B3 PTM
Sycamore Forge Dr 458-B2 PTM
Sycamore Forge La 458-B2 PTM
Sycamore Grove Ct 425-A8 WTM
Sycamore Hill 461-B1 LTM
Sycamore La 592-A9 BTM; 530-B5 FT; 562-C10 G; 592-A9 M
Sycamore Rd 424-E2 CTH; 392-D4 Ca; 564-K5 MTS; 425-F7 WTM
Sycamore Ridge Ct 489-D8 WaT
Sycamore Springs Tr 495-F9 WrT
Sycamore St 455-H8 B; DN-D4; 493-E10 CTM; 389-J9, K4 ET; 358-A3 W; 389-G9, J9; 390-A8 Z
Sydney Bay Ct 428-J3 LTM
Sylvan Ct 326-F6 NT
Sylvan Dr 326-F6 NT; 458-F3 WTM
Sylvan La 392-A3 Ca
Sylvan Rd 458-F6, F7 WTM
Sylvan Ridge Ct 426-C8 WTM
Sylvan Ridge Rd 426-D9, D10 WTM
Sylvan Tr 326-F6 NT

T

T C Steel La 392-G5 Ca
Tabor St 527-E3, G3, J3; 528-C3 CTM
Tacoma Ave 460-A10; 494-A1, A2, A3, A4, A6, A7 CTM; 528-A6; 562-A2 PeT; 426-A2, A3, A9; 460-A1, A3, A5, A8 WTM
Tacoma Cir 460-A1 WTM
Tade Ct 456-K9 WnT
Tade La 456-K9 WnT
Taft Ave 526-C6 DTM; 458-C10; 492-C10; 526-C2, C6 WnT
Taftwood Dr 496-F6 Cu
Taggart Dr 558-H9 GT
Tahoe Cir 325-E8 N
Tahoe Ct 426-D1 Ca
Tahoe Rd 426-C1 Ca
Tailwind Dr 525-C4 WnT
Tal Dr 496-G1 WrT
Talbot Ave 561-F7 PeT
Talbott St DN-D1, D2; 493-E10, F1, F3, F4, F6, F7; 527-E2 CTM
Tall Trees Dr 393-B9 F
Tallgrass Ct 358-G3 N
Talliho Dr 428-B6 LTM
Tallman Ave 493-K4 CTM
Tallowtree Ct 428-J7 L
Tallwood La 595-A10 WTJ
Talmadge Ct 390-B10 CTH
Talon La 456-K8 PTM
Talping Row 424-F3 PTM
Tam-O-Shanter Ct 390-H9 CTH
Tam-O-Shanter Dr 390-H9 CTH
Tamara Tr 393-G2 F; 561-E2 PeT
Tamarack Cir Dr N 425-B3 WTM
Tamarack Cir Dr S 425-B3 WTM
Tamarack Dr 425-B2, B3 WTM
Tamarack La 325-A9 N; 562-A6 PeT
Tamenend Ct 428-J1 FCT
Tamenend Terr 428-J1 FCT
Tamerisk Ct 562-H7 FT
Tammany Tr 392-J3 Ca
Tammin Dr 457-H6 PTM
Tammin La 457-H6 PTM
Tammy Dr 562-B5 Spt
Tammy Renee Dr 462-A6 L
Tamoha Tr 491-B7 WnT
Tampa Ct 525-G9 DTM
Tampa La 525-G9 DTM
Tampico Rd 596-F3 G
Tanager Ct 427-F7 LTM
Tanager La 393-A4 Ca; 427-E7, F7 LTM
Tanbark Dr 462-D3 L
Tanfield Ct 424-E10 PTM
Tanga Ct 494-K3 WrT
Tanglewood Ct 558-E9 GT
Tanglewood Dr 561-J9 G; 326-G6 NT
Tanglewood Rd 558-F8, F9 GT
Tanglewood Sq 424-H8 WTM
Tanner Dr 393-J6 F
Tanninger Dr 496-D9 WrT
Tanoan La 462-C10 WrT
Tanquard La 529-K9 FT
Tansel Cir 490-J6 WnT
Tansel Crossing Cir 490-H4 WnT
Tansel Crossing Dr 490-J3 WnT
Tansel Ct 456-J8 WnT
Tansel Forge Dr 490-H3 WnT
Tansel Rd 456-J10; 490-G6, J1, J3 WnT
Tansey Crossing W 357-D8 WTH
Tansy Ct 528-J8 FT
Tanya Dr 523-E4 WaT
Taos Tr 495-D8 WrT
Tapp Dr 496-H5 WrT
Tappan Dr 424-D9 PTM
Tara Ct 390-D2 CTH
Tara Ct E 457-K10 WnT
Tara Ct N 457-K10 WnT
Tara Ct S 457-K10 WnT
Tara Ct W 457-K10 WnT
Tara La 457-K10 WnT
Tardelli La 491-C4 WnT
Tarkington Common 392-F4 Ca
Tarpon Ave 523-K7 P
Tarpon Dr 428-C3 LTM
Tarragon Ct 393-F10 F; 562-E4 PeT
Tarragon Dr 562-E5 PeT
Tarragon La 562-E5 PeT
Tarragon Pl 562-F5 PeT
Tarragon Terr 562-E4 PeT
Tarry Ct 595-D3 WTJ
Tarry La 595-D3 WTJ
Tarrynot La 392-G7 Ca
Tartan Ct 457-E7 PTM
Tasman Cir 395-B7 F
Tassel Ct 489-H8 A
Tates Way 424-F9 PTM
Taunton Rd 425-B7 WTM
Tavistock Dr 592-E2 M
Taylor Dr E 495-A5 WrT
Taylor Dr W 495-A5 WrT
Taylor St 592-A2 M
Tayside Ct 428-G5 L
Teak Ct 561-D3 PeT
Teakwood Dr 523-H9 P; 527-J6 PeT
Teakwood La 595-A4 WTJ
Teal La 391-D6 CTH
Teal St 393-C8 F
Tealpoint Ct 496-E5 WrT
Tealpoint Dr 496-E5 WrT
Tealpoint La 496-E5 WrT
Tealwood Dr 428-K5 L
Teasel Ct 562-F5 PeT
Technology Dr 391-G7 Ca; 393-J7 F
Technology La 393-J7 F
Technology Way 423-K9 PTM
Tecumseh St 493-K5, K6 CTM
Teddy La 527-F5 PeT
Teel Way 427-G7, G8 LTM
Teesdale Ct 394-B4 F
Telegraph Rd 322-K4 AT
Telford Ct 458-C5 PTM
Telford Dr 393-J10 F
Tellum Rd 456-C3 BTH
Telluride Dr 428-K6 L
Tembroke La 425-D6 WTM
Tempe Ct 526-B6 DTM
Tempe Dr 526-B6 DTM
Temperance Ave 494-F9, F10; 528-F2 CTM

Temple Ave 460-A10, B9; 494-A2, A3, A6, A7, A9, B4; 528-B4 CTM; 528-B6 PeT; 426-A2, A3, A7, A9; 460-A1, A8 WTM; 389-H7 Z
Temple Ct 426-A3 WTM
Templin Rd 389-J6; 390-A6 ET; 389-J6 Z
Tenacious Dr 428-D6 LTM
Tennessee Walk 423-G9 PTM
Tennis Ct Cir 425-B3 WTM
Tennison Ct 462-D1 L
Tennison Dr 462-C1 L
Tennison Way 462-C1 L
Tequista Cir 428-G5 LTM
Tequista Ct 428-G5 LTM
Teresa La 462-C3 L; 359-E5 N
Terhune Ct 558-K10 MTM
Terminal Rd 527-A8 PeT
Tern Ct 427-G8 LTM
Terra Dr 528-D7 PeT
Terra La 429-C3 McC
Terra Vista La 426-C10 WTM
Terrace Ave 527-F1, J1; 528-A1, C1, E1, F1, G1 CTM; 456-J10; 490-J1 WnT; 528-G1, J1; 529-A1 WrT
Terrace Dr 359-F2 N; 389-H7 Z
Terrace Pl 393-H1 DTH
Terrents Ct 391-D4 Ca
Terri La 422-F8 BTH
Terry Dr 523-J10; 557-J1 P
Terrytown Pkwy 457-J3 PTM
Terwithen La 424-D1 CTH
Tesh Dr 528-D3 CTM
Tesh Pl 528-D3 CTM
Teton Tr 561-C4 PeT
Tewksbury La 592-D1 M
Texarkana Ct 490-H10 WnT
Texarkana Dr 490-H10 WnT
Thackery Ct 427-G5 LTM
Thaddeus St 527-J2 CTM
Thames Ct 359-H9 N
Thames Ct E 496-D2 WrT
Thames Ct W 496-C2 WrT
Thatcher Dr 427-D9 LTM
Thayer St 458-D10; 492-D1 WnT
The Courts 595-C8 WTJ
The Lenends Blvd 394-E7 F
The Mall Dr 460-K4 LTM
The Springs Dr 424-H4 WTM
Thelma Dr 461-K4 L
Theo Ct 490-H6 WnT
Theodore La 531-F2 SCT
Thicket Hill Cir 392-G6 Ca
Thicket Hill La 460-G4 LTM; 460-G4 WTM
Thickett Dr 457-E8 PTM
Thistle Bend 489-D9 A
Thistle Dr 457-G10 WnT
Thistle Ridge 393-F9 F
Thistle Wood 391-F3 CTH
Thistleridge Ct 559-F1 DTM
Thistleridge Pl 559-F2 DTM
Thistlewood Ct 391-F3 CTH
Thistlewood Dr E 391-F3 CTH
Thistlewood Dr W 391-F3 CTH
Thomas Barrow Tr 393-C4 Ca
Thomas Dr 391-D1 CTH
Thomas Marion Ct 490-J4 WnT
Thomas Morris Trace 393-C4 Ca
Thomas Rd 564-F2 FT; 490-J1 WnT
Thomas St 596-E2 G
Thomas Wood Tr 458-K2 WTM
Thompson Rd 528-E9 BG; 528-E9 CTM; 524-K10; 525-E10, G10, J10; 526-A10, B10 DTM; 528-E9; 529-C9, J9; 530-A9, G9 FT; 526-F10; 527-A10, C10, J10; 528-A9 PeT
Thompson Vill Dr 527-F10 PeT
Thompson Vill Pl 527-F10 PeT
Thompson Vill Tr 527-E10 PeT
Thompson Vill Way 527-E10 PeT
Thornapple La 426-J2 LTM
Thornberry Ct 489-J8 A
Thornberry Dr 391-J1 Ca
Thornbird La 391-F3 CTH
Thornbriar Ct 595-D10 WTJ
Thornbriar La 595-D10 WTJ
Thornburg Pkwy 455-G10 B
Thorncrest Ct 456-J9 WnT
Thorncrest Dr 456-J9 WnT
Thorndale La 394-B3 F
Thorndale St 491-F4, F6 WnT
Thorne Rd 455-K7 B
Thornecrest Dr 557-J8 GT
Thornecrest La 557-J8 GT
Thorneycroft Dr 424-F6 PTM
Thornhill Dr 427-J5 LTM
Thornleigh Ct 455-F8 B
Thornleigh Dr 455-F8 B; 460-H6 LTM; 460-F6 WTM
Thornmill Ct 523-G1 A
Thornridge Dr 489-D9 A
Thornton La 424-C2 PTM
Thornwood Ct 426-K3 LTM
Thornwood Dr 426-K3 LTM; 595-A4 WTJ
Thorny Ridge Pass 394-G9 F
Thorny Ridge Trace 394-G9 F
Thoroughbred Blvd 422-H3 BTH; 422-H3 PTM
Thoroughbred Ct 423-E6 PTM
Thoroughbred Dr 423-E5 PTM
Thoroughbred Run 427-F4 LTM
Thousand Oaks Blvd 491-E4 WnT
Thousand Oaks Dr 491-E4 WnT
Thousand Oaks La 491-E4 WnT
Thradd St 394-A5 F
Thrasher Dr 458-A5 PTM
Threel Rd 426-C3 WTM
Threshing Ct 496-H5 Cu
Thronhurst Dr 391-H4 Ca
Thrush Dr 458-A10, C10 WnT
Thrush La 392-H3 Ca
Thrushwood Cir 426-K3; 427-A3 LTM
Thrushwood Ct 426-K4 LTM
Thrushwood La 427-A3 LTM
Thunder Bay Ct 428-J3 LTM
Thunderbird Dr 390-J9 CTH
Thunderbird Rd 462-C3 L
Thurman Dr 561-C2 PeT
Thurston Ct 393-H5 F; 360-E1 NT
Thurston Dr 360-E1 NT; 457-H10 WnT
Thyme La 525-F1 WnT
Tiara Ct 457-H9 WnT
Tibbs Ave 526-F6 DTM; 526-F10; 560-F1, F4 PeT; 492-F3, F7, F9; 526-F4 WnT
Tibbs Ct 492-F6 WnT
Ticen Ct 528-D5 BG
Ticen St 528-C5 BG
Tickchek Rd 596-D10 PTJ
Ticonderoga La 457-J4 PTM
Tidewater Ct 428-G5 LTM
Tidewater Dr 394-C7 F
Tidewater Dr S 428-G5 LTM
Tidewater Dr W 428-G5 LTM
Tiffany Ct 392-B7 Ca
Tiffany Dr 461-F9 WrT
Tilbury Ct 456-J9 WnT
Tilden Dr E 455-G7 B
Tilden Dr W 455-C7 B; 455-C7 LTH
Tilden Terr 455-A7 LTH
Tiller Ct 357-F4 WTH
Tillmore Dr 596-E10 NW
Tillson Dr 390-A8 ET
Tilly Mill Rd 423-A4 PTM
Tim Tam Cir 528-K8 FT
Tim Tam Ct 528-K9 FT
Timber Bend Ct 523-C3 WaT
Timber Bend Dr 523-C4 WaT
Timber Bk Run 358-A4 W
Timber Climb 489-D5 A
Timber Cr Dr 496-D9 WrT
Timber Cr La 561-F10 G
Timber Crest Dr 392-H5 Ca
Timber Ct 426-E7 WTM
Timber Dr 531-A5 SCT
Timber Grove La 489-F7 WaT
Timber Grove Pl 528-E6 BG
Timber Grove Way 528-E6 BG
Timber Hill Ct 560-J7 PeT
Timber Hill Dr 560-J7 PeT
Timber Hill Dr N 560-J6 PeT
Timber Hill Tr 560-J6 PeT
Timber La 455-F3, F4 B; 392-B9 CTH; 595-F1 G
Timber La Cir 595-F1 G
Timber Lake Blvd 528-K10 FT
Timber Lake Way 528-K10 FT
Timber Mill La 425-C8 WTM
Timber Ridge Ct 325-C3 JT
Timber Ridge Dr 495-F3 WrT
Timber Ridge Trace 455-E6 LTH
Timber Run Ct 427-K7 LTM
Timber Springs Ct 392-D8 Ca
Timber Springs Dr 393-E9 F
Timber Springs Dr E 393-F9 F
Timber Springs Dr S 393-E9 F
Timber Tr 595-F1 G
Timber Trace 456-D3 LTH
Timber Valley Dr 426-J2 WTM
Timber View Dr 427-A2, A4 LTM
Timber Vill Dr 561-F9 G
Timberbrook Ct 455-A10; 489-A1 LTH
Timberlake Ct 393-E8 F
Timberlake La 393-E8 F
Timberlane Dr 393-E8 F; 565-E7 MTS
Timberlane Pl 393-E8 F
Timberlane St 425-B8 WTM
Timberline Ct 428-A7 LTM
Timberline Dr 596-C6 G; 427-K7; 428-A7 LTM
Timberline Way 427-K7 LTM
Timberly Dr 426-A10 WTM
Timbersedge Ct 458-E10 WnT
Timbersedge Dr 458-E10 WnT
Timberwood 557-K6 GT
Timberwood Dr 490-J5 WnT
Timbrook Cir 528-E6 PeT
Timbrook La 528-E6 PeT
Timken Ct 395-B7 F
Timothy La 565-D6 MTS; 326-C9 N
Tina Marie Cir 496-E4 WrT
Tincher Rd 525-J9, K8, K9, K10; 559-K1 DTM
Tindall St 527-K5 CTM
Tinkersfield La 491-C1 WnT
Tinsel Ave 562-E6 PeT
Tinton Ct 462-B7, C7 LTM
Tiosa Ct 559-C10 MTM
Tip St 492-G10 WnT
Tippecanoe Dr 326-F5 NT
Tippecanoe St DN-D2; 493-E7 CTM
Tipton St 493-K3 CTM
Tisbury Ct 393-C10 F
Tishman La 425-A8 WTM
Titan Dr 526-A5 WnT
Titleist La 496-E3 WrT
Titleist Way 496-E3 WrT
Tito Ct 393-J5 F
Tiverton Dr 592-D2 M
Tobermory Rd 428-H5 L
Tobey Dr 495-H2 WrT
Tocovi Ct N 455-F3 B
Tocovi Ct S 455-F3 B
Todd Rd 523-F2 WaT
Todda Dr 496-A1 WrT
Toledo St DN-C2; 493-D7 CTM
Toll House Way 394-C6 F
Tollgate Rd 325-D1 JT
Tolliston Blvd 462-D1 L
Tolliston Dr 462-D2 L
Tomahawk Tr 491-B7 WnT
Tomke Dr 531-G2 SCT
Tomlinson Dr 492-D7 WnT
Tomlinson Rd 323-J10; 357-J1 WTH
Tommy Lee Ct 561-A6 PeT
Tony Ct 594-H7 WTJ
Tony Dr 594-H7 WTJ
Tooley Ct 324-J5 N
Topaz Dr 562-B7 PeT
Topaz La 390-G9 CTH
Topeka Ct 525-F9 DTM
Topeka La 525-G9 DTM
Topeka Tr 525-F9 DTM
Torbay Cir 457-C6 PTM
Torberg Pl 393-H6 F
Torchwood Ct 561-G8 PeT
Torino Ct 461-J7 LTM
Toronto Ct 424-E5 PTM
Toronto St DN-D1; 493-F6 CTM
Torrance Pl 393-J6 F
Torrey Ct 489-J10 A; 358-A5 WTH
Torrey Dr 489-J10 A
Torrey Pine Dr 455-A3 B
Torrey Pines Cir 390-H10 CTH
Totem La 459-A9 CTM
Totten Dr 562-D10 G
Tottenham Dr 391-E9 CTH; 427-A8 LTM
Touchstone Dr 394-B4 F
Tournament Ct 595-D8 WTJ
Tournament Dr 595-D8 WTJ
Tournament La 496-D3 WrT
Tournon Dr 394-J10 F
Tours Dr 460-E2 WTM
Tousley Ct 458-A10 WnT
Tousley Dr 427-E9 LTM
Towe String Rd 560-K8 PeT
Tower Bridge Rd 426-F3 WTM
Tower Ct 491-E6 WnT
Tower La 461-K8; 462-A8 LTM
Tower Rd 523-G6 P
Town & Country Blvd 360-A5 N
Town Ctr Rd S 592-D2 M
Town Ctr St 592-D2 M
Towne Ct 457-G7 PTM
Towne Dr 390-H10; 424-G1 CTH
Towne La 424-G1 CTH
Towne Rd 390-H3, H7, H10; 424-H2 CTH; 356-H6, H10 WTH
Townsend Ct 523-G8 P
Township La 424-H6 PTM
Township Line Rd 597-C2 CTJ; 523-D6 GT; 524-A6 P; 563-C10; 597-C2 PTJ; 424-G10, H7 PTM; 424-G10, H7 WTM; 523-D6; 524-A6 WaT
Towpath La 491-C1 WnT
Trace Cir 424-K5 WTM
Trace La 424-K5 WTM
Tracey Jo Rd 594-H1 WTJ
Tracy Ct 490-J4 WnT
Tracy Jo Ct 594-G1 WTJ
Tracy La 455-H10 B
Tracy Rd 595-H10; 596-B10, H10 PTJ; 596-H10 WhI
Trade Winds Dr 496-B3 WrT
Traders Cove La 457-B5 PTM
Traders Ct 393-G8 F
Traders Hollow Ct 423-C6 PTM
Traders Hollow La 423-B6 PTM
Traders La 423-B8 PTM
Traders Landing 422-G8 BTH
Traders Pass 422-G8 BTH
Tradewinds Dr 325-D10 N
Trading Post Pl 393-B3 Ca
Traditions Dr 462-C5 L
Traditions La 360-A1 N
Traditions Rd 462-C5 L
Traditions Way 462-C5 L
Trafalger La 491-H7 WnT
Trager Ct 427-F4 LTM
Trail Cr Ct 391-E1 CTH
Trail Ridge Ct 592-B5 M
Trail View Dr 392-A2 Ca
Trailgate Dr 424-C7 PTM
Trails End 455-G1 B
Trails End Dr 392-K8 DTH
Trails Pointe Dr 428-C7 L
Trails Run Ct 560-K8 PeT
Trails Run Rd 560-K8 PeT
Trailview Dr 359-F4 N
Trailwind 455-F1 BTH
Train Ct 596-F3 G
Tranquility 393-H2 F
Tranquill Tr 561-C10 WTJ
Transfer Dr 491-C7 WnT
Transportation St 462-C3 L
Trappers Ct 393-G8 F
Traub Ave DN-A2, A3; 492-J7, J8 CTM
Travers Pl 461-D9 WrT
Traverse Pl 393-H6 F
Travis Dr 462-A6 L
Travis Pl 594-C8 WTJ
Travis Rd 594-A9, E9, H9 WTJ
Treasure Pointe 428-K3 LTM
Treasury Row 496-A2 WrT
Trebah Cir 390-D10 CTH
Tree St 531-H5 NP
Tree Top Dr 425-C5 WTM
Tree Top La 561-J9 G
Treefork Dr 461-K6 L
Treeline Ct 394-J10 FCT
Treeline Dr 427-D5 LTM
Treeline Pl 427-D3 LTM
Treewood Dr 462-B5 L
Tremont Bend 595-E10 WTJ
Tremont Blvd 595-D10 WTJ
Tremont Cir 394-C10 F; 595-E10 WTJ
Tremont Ct 325-A6 N
Tremont Dr 394-B10 F; 595-E10 WTJ
Tremont La 394-B10 F; 595-E10 WTJ
Tremont St 424-H10 PTM; 424-H10; 458-H1, H3 WTM; DN-A2, A3, A4; 492-H5, H7, H8, H10 WnT
Trenkamp Ct 462-C2 L
Trent Ct 496-C2 WrT
Trenton Ct 393-F8 F; 389-E6 Z
Trenton St 493-F1 CTM
Trerice Pl 390-D10 CTH
Trester La 393-J5 F
Trestle Way Cir 427-D8 LTM
Trestle Way Ct 427-D8 LTM
Trevellian Way 561-B7 PeT
Trevia Ct 428-B10 L
Trevia Dr 428-A10 L
Trevia Pl 462-A1 L
Trevor St 455-H5 B
Treyburn Dr 394-E10; 428-F1 F
Tri Sab La 527-E5 PeT
Trigger La 456-D10 LTH
Trilbey Ct 462-B8 LTM; 325-B8 N
Trilbey Dr 462-C8 LTM
Trillium Ct 326-C10 N; 495-G5 WrT
Trilobi Dr 428-A10 L
Trinity Pl 495-J3 WrT
Trinity Way 558-B10 M
Tripp Ct 462-A3 L
Trippler Rd 461-K3; 462-A3 L
Trittipo Way 428-H7 L
Trixie Ct 326-A7 NT
Trolley Rd 428-H10 L
Troon Ct 424-G2 CTH; 563-B5 FT; 596-F3 G
Troon Dr 563-B5 FT
Troon Way 563-B5 FT
Trophy Club Dr 457-C9 WnT
Trophy Club Dr N 457-C9 WnT
Trophy Club Dr S 457-C9 WnT
Trophy Dr 393-J5 F
Trophy Oaks Ct 563-A1 FT
Trotter Ct 357-E10 WTH; 594-K4 WTJ
Trotter Rd 559-A3, A9 DTM
Trotters Run 455-G10 B
Trotwood Cir 427-E8 LTM
Trotwood La 389-D8 Z
Trout St 388-F1 Wh
Trowbridge St 494-A9, A10; 528-A2 CTM
Troy Ave 528-A5 BG; 527-B5, H5; 528-A5 CTM; 526-A5, C5, F5 DTM; 528-J5; 529-D4, J4; 530-A4, E4 FT; 527-B5, H5; 528-A5 PeT; 526-A5, C5 WnT; 528-J5; 529-D4, J4; 530-A4, E4 WrT
Troy Ct 527-F5 PeT
Truax-Comer Dr 592-C5 M
Trullbrook Dr 358-G3 N
Trumball Ct 393-J6 F
Trumbull St 459-K9 CTM
Trump Dr 462-B6 L
Truro Ct 458-D8 PTM
Tuck Ct 496-F6 Cu
Tuckahoe 425-B5 WTM
Tucker Ave 523-G7 P
Tucson Dr 526-B6 DTM
Tudor Ave 492-A10; 526-A1 WnT
Tudor Bend 391-J2 Ca
Tudor Cir 392-G4 Ca
Tudor Dr 392-G4 Ca
Tudor La 427-H1 F
Tudor Lake Dr 391-J2 Ca
Tudor Pk Dr 462-A8 WrT
Tudor Pl 392-G4 Ca
Tufton Ct 393-G8 F
Tufton Pl 393-G9 F
Tufton St 393-F9 F
Tufts Ct 559-J3 DTM
Tulane Rd 424-G3 PTM
Tulip Ct 325-B10 N; 596-D10 NW; 523-K6 P; 562-D4 PeT
Tulip Dr 525-C8 LTH; 592-C1 M; 524-B6 P; 561-E4, H4, K4; 562-A3, C4 PeT
Tulip Dr S 562-A4 PeT
Tulip Poplar Crest 392-D3 Ca
Tulip Poplar Dr 592-C5 M
Tuliptree Tr 427-G9 LTM
Tullamore Ct 457-C5 PTM
Tumbleweed Dr 531-F2 SCT
Turfgrass Way 428-E9 L
Turfway Cir 458-E4 PTM
Turfway Ct 458-E4 PTM; 594-K4 WTJ
Turin Ct 393-H6 F
Turkel Ct 393-H6 F
Turkel Dr 393-H5 F
Turkel Pl 393-H6 F
Turkey Pen Cir 595-E5 WTJ
Turkey Pen Dr 595-E5 WTJ
Turkeyfoot Ave 389-H5 Z
Turnberry Cir 596-F3 G
Turnberry Ct 424-G2 CTH; 563-C5 FT; 489-A9 WaT
Turnberry Way 563-C5 FT
Turnbridge Ct 425-B4 WTM
Turnbridge Dr 523-D2 WaT
Turnbury La 455-J3 B
Turne Grove 394-J9 F
Turner Ave DN-A2; 492-H7 WnT
Turner Ct 593-A3 MTM
Turner Dr 525-G9 DTM
Turner La 593-A4 MTM
Turner St 388-E1 Wh
Turnstone Ct 325-K10 N
Turtle Cr Ct 527-G10 PeT
Turtle Cr Dr E 527-G10 PeT
Turtle Cr Dr N 527-G10 PeT
Turtle Cr Dr S 527-G10 PeT
Tuxedo La 426-C10 WTM
Tuxedo St 494-C6, C8 CTM; 426-C8, C9, C10; 460-C1, C2, C5 WTM
Twelve Oaks 391-B3 CTH
Twelve Oaks Blvd 423-E10 PTM
Twilight Dr 359-J1 N; 457-F8 PTM
Twin Acre Dr 462-A6 L
Twin Aire Dr 494-B9 CTM
Twin Beech Dr 461-D5 L
Twin Beech La 461-E5 L
Twin Brooks Dr 562-A4 PeT
Twin Creeks Dr 458-A2 PTM
Twin Lakes Ct 562-J1 FT
Twin Oaks Dr 391-C1 CTH; 461-C9 WrT
Twin Pointe Cir 428-F5 LTM
Twin Springs Ct 392-D8 Ca
Twin Springs Dr 392-D8 Ca
Twin St 455-G4 B
Twinshore Ct 392-C9 Ca
Twinshore St 392-C8 Ca
Twyckenham Dr 462-B1 L
Twykeniam Ct 462-B2 L
Tybalt Cir 457-G2 PTM
Tybalt Ct 457-H2 PTM
Tybalt Dr 394-B5 F; 457-G2 PTM
Tybalt La 457-H2 PTM
Tybalt Pl 457-G2 PTM
Tyler Ct 455-G8 B
Tynan Way 393-J5 F
Tyrone Dr 492-H1 WnT

U

Udell St 492-K1; 493-A1 CTM
Uitts St 388-E1 WTB; 388-E1 Wh
Underwood Ct 392-H8 Ca
Union Chapel Rd 360-D7 N; 360-D7 NT; 426-B6 WTM
Union Dr DN-B2; 493-A6 CTM
Union Mills Dr 558-F9 GT
Union St DN-D6; 493-E10; 527-E1, E4 CTM; 527-E6, E7; 561-E7 PeT
Union Traction Blvd 391-G10 CTH
Unity Tr 457-K2 PTM
University Ave 494-G8 CTM; 494-G8, J8; 495-A8 WrT
University Blvd DN-C2; 493-B7 CTM
Unser Blvd 491-G4 S
Upland Way 326-D9 N
Upper Bay La 428-E6 LTM
Ursal Ave 596-D4 G
USA Dr 393-J9 F
USA Pkwy 393-K8 DTH; 393-H9, K8 F
Ute Dr 392-A6 Ca

V

Vail Dr 426-D1 Ca
Val-Del Ct 561-F7 PeT
Valburn Ct 528-E7 BG
Vali Ct 391-F9 CTH
Vali Dr 391-F10 CTH
Valiant Dr 526-A5 WnT
Valley Ave 493-K4; 494-A4 CTM
Valley Bk Ct 496-H3 Cu
Valley Bk Dr 496-H3 Cu
Valley Cir 455-G1 B
Valley Cr Dr S 496-H3 WrT
Valley Cr La E 496-H2 WrT
Valley Cr La W 496-G3 WrT
Valley Cr Way 496-G2 WrT
Valley Ct 357-H9 WTH
Valley Dr 391-J10 CTH; 594-H4 WTJ
Valley Ests Dr 561-F7, F8 PeT
Valley Farms Cir 491-C1 WnT
Valley Farms Ct 394-A9 F; 457-B10 WnT
Valley Farms La 457-B10 WnT
Valley Farms Pl 457-B10 WnT
Valley Farms Rd 491-B1 WnT
Valley Farms Tr 491-C1 WnT
Valley Farms Way 457-B10 WnT
Valley Forge Cir 390-D8 CTH
Valley Forge Ct 563-B3 FT
Valley Forge La 563-B3 FT
Valley La 559-H1 DTM; 596-B2 G
Valley Lake Ct 562-C8 PeT
Valley Lake Dr 562-D8 PeT
Valley Meadow Dr 389-K6; 390-A6 Z
Valley Mills Ave 525-F10 DTM
Valley Oaks Rd 596-E4 G
Valley Rd 391-J10; 425-J1 CTH
Valley Ridge Cir 394-B7 F
Valley View Cir 496-J3 Cu
Valley View Ct 326-A10 NT
Valley View Dr 523-H10 P; 561-C7, E7, F7 PeT; 389-G8 Z
Valley View La 428-F6 L
Valley Way Ct 595-A1 WTJ
Valley Way Pl 561-A10 WTJ
Valley Way Rd 561-A10; 595-A1 WTJ
Valleybrook Pl 392-E7 Ca
Valleyland Ct 596-B1 G
Valleyview 455-G1 B
Valleyview Dr 393-A10 F; 357-H9 WTH
Valparaiso Ct 424-D3 PTM
Van Buren Ct 528-C2 CTM
Van Buren St 527-J2; 528-C2, E2 CTM
Van Cleave St 461-G6 L
Van Dyke St 562-A4 Spt
Van Hoy Dr 595-A3 WTJ
Van Ness Pl 426-B5 WTM
Van Ness Way 426-A6 WTM
Van Spronsen Ct 428-H9 L
Van Spronsen Way 428-J8 L
Van Tassel Dr 426-B9 WTM
Vanceburg Dr 491-E10 WnT
Vancouver Ct 462-D1 L
Vandalia Ave 492-G9 WnT
Vandalia St 492-B10; 524-K4 WnT
Vandeman St 494-C10; 528-C1 CTM
Vandergriff Rd 529-K7; 530-A6, E5 FT
Vanherp Ct 428-H8 L
Varna Dr 525-J8 DTM
Varner Rd 456-F8 LTH
Vassar La 425-G3 WTM
Vauxhall Rd 427-A9 LTM
Venable Rd 489-G8 A
Venetian Way 561-B6 PeT
Venice Ct 461-J6 LTM
Venoy Dr 559-D4 DTM; 561-E4 PeT
Ventana Ct 425-D1 CTH
Ventura Ct 596-J3 G
Ventura Dr 526-A5 WnT
Vera Dr 497-B7 SCT; 460-E2 WTM
Verbena Ct 326-C9 N; 491-G1 WnT
Verdin St 428-G10 L
Vermillion La 461-J6 L
Vermont St DN-A2, B2, C2, D2, E2, F2; 492-J7; 493-C7, E7, H7, J7; 494-B7, C7 CTM; 492-C7 S; 490-K7; 491-J7; 492-A7, C7, E7, G7 WnT; 495-F6 WrT
Vernon Ave 461-E6 L
Vernon Dr 592-B6 BTM
Vernon La 455-F6 B
Vernon St 594-J4 WTJ
Verona Ct 461-J6 LTM
Versailles Dr 391-E3 Ca; 561-E1 PeT
Vertmont St 455-G5 B
Verwood Ct 490-J7 WnT
Vesta Ct 461-H7 LTM
Vestal La 523-E8 P
Vestal Rd 523-C6 GT; 523-C6 WaT
Viburnum Ct 425-B5 WTM
Viburnum Dr 425-A5 WTM
Vickie Dr 529-K1 WrT
Vickie La 389-C7 ET
Vicksburg Dr 596-J4 G; 457-J2 PTM
Vicksburg La 457-H3 PTM
Vicky La 422-F8 BTH
Victor Dr 557-K10 M
Victor Dr N 557-K10 M
Victor St 525-F2 WnT
Victoria Ct 392-H7 Ca
Victoria Dr 458-F2, F3, F4 WTM
Victoria Dr S 527-B10; 561-B1 PeT
Victoria La 592-F1 M
Victoria Pk Dr 496-D2 WrT
Victoria Rd 458-F6 WTM
Victoria St 492-G9 WnT
Victory Ave 528-K8 FT; 595-F3 G
Victory Blvd 528-K8 FT
Victory Chapel Rd 327-B3 WRT; 327-A10, B7 WyT
Victory Cir 528-K8 FT
Victory Dr 528-G8 BG; 528-G8 FT
Viewpoint Dr 523-D6 P
Viewside Dr 526-C10 DTM
Viking Hills Ct 426-J3 WTM
Villa Ave 493-K9, K10; 527-K1, K2, K3 CTM; 528-A5, A9; 562-A2 PeT
Villa Paree Dr 460-E2 WTM
Villa Paree Dr N 460-E2 WTM
Village Blvd 592-D1 M
Village Cir 389-F8 Z
Village Cir E 496-B1 WrT
Village Cir W 496-A2 WrT
Village Crossing 596-F5 G
Village Ct 457-D7 PTM; 490-E7 WaT; 389-E9 Z
Village Dr 494-G3 CTM; 564-D1 FT; 530-K4; 531-F2 SCT
Village Dr E 391-F3, G1 CTH
Village Greene Dr N 496-H3 Cu
Village La 596-D4 G; 457-E7 PTM
Village Oak Ct 462-G1 L
Village Oak Dr 462-G1 L
Village Pk Cir 358-C10 WTH
Village Pk E 358-B10 WTH
Village Pk N 358-B10 WTH
Village Pk S 358-B10 WTH
Village Pk W 358-B10 WTH
Village Pkwy Cir E 457-D7, E7 PTM
Village Pkwy Cir W 457-D7 PTM
Village Pkwy N 457-D7 PTM
Village Pkwy S 457-D7 PTM
Village Pl 389-F8 Z
Village Pl Dr 391-G10 CTH
Village Plaza Dr N 494-K5 WrT
Village Plaza Dr S 494-K5 WrT
Village Row 530-K4 SCT
Village Walk Ct 389-D7 Z
Village Walk Dr 389-E7 Z
Village Way 427-G3, G4 LTM; 358-H3 N
Villard Ave 461-C8 LTM
Villas Dr 595-B1 WTJ
Vin Rose La 461-E4 L
Vincennes Ave 424-D4 PTM
Vincennes Cir 424-C4 PTM
Vincennes Rd 424-E4 PTM
Vincz Dr 458-F4 WTM
Vindale Dr 596-D6 G
Vine St 359-G4, H4 N; 492-B8, B9 WnT; 361-E6 WyT
Vine St N 523-F7 P
Vine St S 523-F8 P
Vinewood Ave 457-H6, H8 PTM; 491-H10; 525-H2 WnT
Vinewood Dr 491-H2 S
Vinewood Dr N 455-G8 B

Vinewood Dr S 455-H8 B
Vinewood St 491-H5 WnT
Vineyard Cir 424-K7 WTM
Vineyard Ct 424-K7 WTM
Vineyard Dr 393-D9 F; 425-A7 WTM
Vinings Dr 426-B1 Ca
Vinston Ct 325-K10 N
Vintage Cir 489-H7 A; 461-E4 L
Vintage Ct 461-E4 L
Vintage Dr 461-E4 L
Vinter Ct 428-A4 LTM
Vinter Way 428-B4 LTM
Virgil St 564-E6 FT
Virginia Ave DN-D3, E4; 493-F8 CTM
Visionary Way 393-J6 F
Vista Ct 523-E6 P; 489-B10 WaT
Vista Dr 391-F9 CTH
Vista Pkwy 489-J8 A
Vivian Dr 391-F4 CTH
Voigt Ct 457-H10 WnT
Voigt Dr 457-H10 WnT
Voilet Way 391-D3 Ca
Volta Dr 457-H3 PTM
Volunteer Dr 457-J3 PTM
Von Trapp Rd 422-A2 PTB
Voss Hiatt Ave 325-F2 C; 325-F2 JT
Voyageur Ct 428-J4 LTM

W

Wabash Dr 393-H2 F
Wabash St DN-D2, E2; 493-E7, F7 CTM; 523-G8 P
Wabesa Way 428-E9 L
Waddy St 461-G6 L
Wade Hill Ct 427-F6 LTM
Wade St 527-H3; 528-A3, B3, G3 CTM
Wadsworth Cir 427-A4 LTM
Wadsworth St 427-B6 LTM
Wadsworth Way 495-C3 WrT
Wagner La 528-D2 CTM
Wagner Rd 456-K10 WnT
Wagon Tr 557-J10 M; 492-D9 WnT
Wagon Tr Cir 557-K10 M
Wagon Tr Ct 557-K10 M
Wagon Tr Dr 326-A10 N; 326-A10, C8 NT
Wagon Wheel Ct 528-H9 FT
Wagon Wheel Tr 528-H10; 562-H1 FT
Wainwright Blvd 393-E7 F
Wakefield Ct 427-E5 LTM
Wakefield Pl 393-J2 F
Wakefield Rd 457-G6 PTM
Wakulla Ct 561-B5 PeT
Walbridge 391-J6 Ca
Walcott St DN-F3; 493-K7, K8, K9; 527-K5 CTM; 527-K7, K8, K10; 561-K1 PeT
Waldemar Dr 423-K9 PTM
Waldemar Rd 424-D3 PTM
Waldemere Ave 525-J8 DTM; 491-J10; 525-J1 WnT
Walden La 459-A4 WTM
Walden Pl 392-C6 Ca
Waldon Ct 595-A8 WTJ; 389-E9 Z
Waldon Dr 595-A8 WTJ
Waldorf La 424-H6 PTM
Wales Ave 494-E4 CTM
Wales Ct 492-D1 WnT
Walington Cir 596-C4 G
Walker Ave 527-J3; 528-A3 CTM
Walker Rd 461-H3 L
Walker St 594-J4 WTJ
Wall Rd 489-A5 WaT
Wall St Pike 489-D3 WaT
Wallace Ave 460-F10; 494-F1, F3, F5, F7 CTM; 460-F4, F8 WTM
Wallard Dr 491-G4 WnT
Wallas Turn 427-J7 LTM
Wallbridge Dr 491-F10 WnT
Wallen Ct 562-G6 PeT
Walleye Ct 561-F6 PeT
Wallingwood Dr 461-E4 L; 427-E6 LTM
Wallstreet Cir 490-K4 WnT
Wallstreet Dr 490-J4 WnT
Wally Ct 528-G8 BG
Walma Ct 495-H4 WrT
Walma Dr 495-H4 WrT
Walney Ct 394-A5 F
Walney Rd 424-F7 PTM
Walnut Bend Rd 457-E4 PTM
Walnut Cr Crossing 489-G3 WaT
Walnut Cr Ct 390-F9 CTH
Walnut Cr Dr N 390-F9 CTH
Walnut Cr Dr W 390-F10 CTH
Walnut Ct 455-D10; 489-D1 LTH; 324-J7 N
Walnut Dr 455-C10; 489-C1 LTH; 424-G8 PTM; 594-G2 WTJ; 489-J5 WaT
Walnut Grove Dr 428-K3 LTM
Walnut La 455-H5 B; 595-E8 WTJ
Walnut Pt Rd 457-B2 PTM
Walnut Ridge Pl 393-D5 F
Walnut St DN-C1, C2, D2, E1, E2; 493-B6, C6, D6, F6, G6; 494-D6, F6 CTM; 324-E2 JT; 359-H4, J4 N; 531-G5, J5 NP; 523-G8 P; 562-B5 Spt; 357-K4, K5 W; 388-D1 Wh; DN-A2; 492-E6, F6, G6 WnT; 494-F6 WrT; 389-H8 Z
Walnut Way 455-A3 BTH; 455-A3 LTH; 427-G9 LTM; 324-J7 N
Walnut Way Ct 455-A3 BTH; 455-A3 LTH
Walrond Rd 394-K4 FCT
Walsham Way 457-H7 PTM
Walston Ct 425-A7 WTM
Walter Ct 391-J1 Ca
Walter Rd 391-K1 Ca
Walter St 391-K2 Ca
Walthan Way 427-J1 F
Walton Ave 490-J8 WnT
Walton Dr 523-J9 P; 491-C6 WnT
Walton Dr E 559-A10 MTM
Walton Dr S 593-A1 MTM
Walton St 491-D8, F8, K8 WnT
Wanamaker Dr 529-G7, G9 FT
Wander Way 595-D3 WTJ
Wander Wood Ct 424-F10 PTM
Wapahani Dr 392-K8 DTH
Warbler Ct 427-F7 LTM
Warbler Dr 427-F7 LTM
Warbler Way 389-C6 ET; 427-F7 LTM
Warbler Way N 392-J2 Ca
Warbler Way S 392-H3 Ca
Ward Dr 491-G4 S
Ware St 428-G10; 462-G1 L
Wareham Ct 393-C10 F
Warehouse Rd 496-H7 Cu
Warehouse St DN-F3; 493-H8 CTM
Warf St 389-K5 ET
Waring Dr E 496-G5 Cu
Waring Dr W 496-G5 Cu
Warman Ave 526-G10; 560-H1 PeT; 492-G1, G5, G10; 526-G2, H5 WnT
Warren Ave DN-B4; 493-A9, A10 CTM
Warren Cir 496-B4 WrT
Warren La 455-B3 LTH
Warren Lake Ct 496-H4 WrT
Warrington Ct 490-H6 WnT
Warrington Dr 490-G6, K6 WnT
Warrior Tr 424-J9 WTM
Warthin Cir DN-B2; 493-B9 CTM
Warthin Dr DN-B2; 493-B9 CTM
Warwick Ct 392-D1 Ca
Warwick La 427-E5 LTM
Warwick Rd 596-E9 NW; 425-G3, G9 WTM
Washington Blvd 391-F8, F10; 425-F1 CTH; 459-F10; 493-F1 CTM; 425-F3, F5, F9, F10; 459-F2, F4, F8 WTM
Washington Blvd Dr E 425-F4 WTM
Washington Blvd Dr W 425-F4 WTM
Washington Blvd W 425-F10 WTM
Washington Cove La 496-H5 Cu
Washington Cove Way 496-F7 Cu
Washington Crossing Dr 393-K10 F
Washington Pointe Dr 496-D6 WrT
Washington St 455-F6 B; 325-H1 C; DN-A3, B3, E3; 492-G8; 493-A8, C8, D8, H8; 494-A8 CTM; 496-F6 Cu; 389-K4 ET; 596-D2 G; 359-G4 N; 496-F6 SCT; 561-K4 Spt; 356-D4, J3, J4 WTH; DN-A3; 491-J10; 492-A10, G8; 524-H4; 525-D2 WnT; 461-H7; 495-B7, J7; 496-A7 WrT
Washington St E 592-A2 M
Water Crest Dr 394-B3 F
Water Front Ct 324-J6 N
Water Oak Way 523-D3 WaT
Water Ridge Dr 429-A1 FCT
Water St 389-K5 ET; 596-E2 G
Water Trace 427-F6 LTM
Water Way Dr 595-B8 WTJ
Waterbrook Way 594-K9 WTJ
Waterbury Ct 325-E2 C
Waterbury Rd 561-E5 PeT
Watercrest Ct 457-H1 PTM
Watercrest La 392-E4 Ca
Watercrest Way 489-K8 A; 423-H10; 457-H1 PTM
Waterford Ct 389-E8 Z
Waterford Dr 561-D9 G; 524-F1 WaT; 389-E8 Z
Waterford La 392-C7 Ca
Waterford Pl 424-J9 WTM
Waterfront Dr 491-D1 WnT
Waterfront Pkwy E 491-F2 WnT
Waterfront Pkwy W 491-E2 WnT
Watergate Ct 457-K10 WnT
Watergate Mall N 457-K10 WnT
Watergate Mall S 457-K8 WnT
Watergate Pl S 457-K8 WnT
Watergate Rd 457-K8, K10; 491-K1 WnT
Watergate Turn 491-K1 WnT
Watergate Way 491-K1 WnT
Waterlily Ct 457-D8 PTM
Waterloo Dr 424-E10 PTM
Waterman Ave 528-K3 WrT
Watermans Dr E 360-B8 NT
Watermans Dr W 360-B8 NT
Watermark Ct 428-H4 LTM
Waters Edge 427-D5 LTM
Waterscape Way 325-D6 N
Waterside Cir 392-G7 Ca; 423-F4 PTM
Waterside Ct 423-E4 PTM
Waterside Dr 360-B1 N; 423-F5 PTM
Watersite Cir 457-B6 PTM
Watersonway Cir 561-C2 PeT
Waterstone Cir 424-E10 PTM
Waterstone Ct 424-E10 PTM
Waterstone Dr 424-E10 PTM
Waterstone Way 392-F7 Ca
Waterthrush Dr 457-D8 PTM
Waterton Pl 393-J2 F
Waterview Ct 429-B3 McC
Waterview Dr 592-E4 M; 491-H6 WnT
Waterview Pt 325-C5 N
Waterway Blvd DN-B1; 492-J4; 493-A5 CTM
Waterwood Dr 497-H6 SCT
Waterwood Dr 457-C9 WnT
Waterwood Pkwy 457-C9 WnT
Waterwood Way 391-G8 CTH
Watham Ct 427-B3 LTM
Watkins Dr 490-F7 WaT
Watson Ct 461-E3 L
Watson La 596-F3 G
Watson Rd 459-G9, H9 CTM; 593-A10 MTM
Watterson Ct 561-C8 PeT
Watts Bar Ct 496-F5 WrT
Waverly Ct 426-B10 WTM
Waverly Dr 392-K1 Ca
Waves Ct 563-B2 FT
Wawasee Ct 426-J7 WTM
Wawasee Dr 426-H7 WTM
Waybridge Ct 562-H3 FT
Waybridge La 562-G3 FT
Wayburn St 496-H6 Cu
Waycross Dr 393-J2 F
Wayland Dr 529-C6 FT
Waymen Dr 424-C2 PTM
Wayne Dr 494-H5 WrT
Wayne St 359-H3 N
Waynecroft St 491-E9 WnT
Waypoint Ct 426-B5 WTM
Wayside Ct 523-K8 P
Wayside Dr 523-J9, K7 P; 425-C2 WTM
Wayside Rd 428-J2 FCT
Wayward Wind Rd 530-C3 WrT
Waywing Ct 393-A3 Ca
Weatherly Ct 428-D5 LTM
Weaver Ave 527-G5, H7, J9 PeT
Weaver Woods Pl 393-G2 F
Webb Dr 561-F5 PeT
Webb St 527-F3, F4 CTM
Weber Ct 595-G2 G
Weber Dr 561-H4, J5 PeT
Webster Ave 460-K8 LTM; 460-K10; 494-K1, K3, K5, K8, K9, K10; 495-A1, A8 WrT
Webster St 596-E4 G
Wedding La 523-E8 P
Wedgefield Dr 561-C6 PeT
Wedgeway Ct 595-E7 WTJ
Wedgewood Ct 457-H7 PTM
Wedgewood Dr 392-E2 Ca; 562-C6 PeT; 562-C6 Spt
Wedgewood Way 457-G7 PTM
Wednesday Ct 560-J8 PeT
Weeping Willow Ct 392-K1 Ca
Weeping Willow Dr 462-B4 L
Weesner Dr 523-D8 P
Weghorst St 527-G1 CTM
Weil Dr 455-J3 BTH
Welch Dr 557-H9 GT; 458-B10; 492-B1 WnT
Welchwood Cir 424-H8 WTM
Welchwood Dr 424-K6 WTM
Welcome Way 491-C8 WnT
Welcome Way Blvd E 491-D8 WnT
Welcome Way Blvd W 491-C8 WnT
Welham Ct 359-K7 N
Welham Rd 427-A9 LTM
Welker Dr 462-B1 L
Well St 455-G4 B
Welland St 496-G6 Cu
Wellborne Dr 462-B1 L
Wellcroft La 462-A1 L
Weller Cir 458-F1 PTM
Weller Dr 458-F2 PTM
Wellesley Blvd 495-E3 WrT
Wellesley Commons 495-F4 WrT
Wellesley Ct 495-F4 WrT
Wellesley Dr N 495-C2 WrT
Wellesley Dr S 495-C2 WrT
Wellesley La 391-C2 CTH; 495-F4 WrT
Wellington Ave 461-F6 L; 461-F10; 495-C2, E4 WrT
Wellington Bluff Ct 359-G10 NT
Wellington Ct 489-G4 WaT
Wellington Dr 593-K10 HT; 425-C10 WTM
Wellington Dr W 459-C1 WTM
Wellington La 392-E6 Ca
Wellington Overlook 359-H9 N
Wellington Pkwy 359-J7, K8; 360-A7 N
Wellington Rd 425-E10; 459-C1, D1, E1 WTM
Wells Dr 557-H1 P
Wells St 427-B6 LTM
Wellsbrook Dr 423-F6 PTM
Wellsford Cir 462-A1 L
Wellston Ct 490-J7 WnT
Wellston Dr 490-H7 WnT
Welton St 594-J4 WTJ
Wembley Ct 425-B6 WTM
Wembly Cir 392-F4 Ca
Wembly Ct 392-F4 Ca
Wembly La 392-F5 Ca
Wembly Rd 392-F4, F5 Ca; 595-D5 WTJ
Wemouth Ct 427-G5 LTM
Wenlock Rd 460-H4 LTM
Wentworth Blvd 494-E9, F9 CTM
Wentworth Ct 424-E1 CTH; 595-D5 WTJ
Werges Ave 526-C6 DTM; 527-F6, K5; 528-A6 PeT
Wesley Cir 325-B7 N
Wesley Ct 393-J6 F; 557-F2 P; 425-H9 WTM
Wesley Pl 393-J6 F
Wesleyan Rd 424-D3 PTM
Weslynn Dr 458-H6 WTM
Wessex Cir 325-B7 N
West 4th Ct 392-D3 Ca
West 11 St W 490-B6 WaT
West 16th St 323-C4 AT
West 62nd St 457-H2 PTM
West 75 Rd 596-B10 WnT; 596-B9, B10 PTJ; 596-B10 Whl
West 106th St 390-C10; 391-B10 CTH; 391-B10 Ca; 389-J10; 390-A10 ET
West 116th St 390-C8; 391-B8 CTH
West 121st St 390-D6 CTH
West 125 Rd 595-K10 PTJ
West 126th St 390-B5, F5 CTH
West 131st St 390-B4, F4; 391-B4 CTH; 391-B4 Ca
West 136th St 390-D3, J3 CTH; 391-E3 Ca
West 141st St 390-C2; 391-B2 CTH
West 146th St 390-C1, H1; 391-A1, F1 CTH; 391-F1 Ca; 357-K10; 390-C1, H1; 391-A1, F1 WTH
West 150 Rd 595-J4 G
West 151st St 356-E9, K9; 357-J9 WTH
West 156th St 356-B8, J8; 357-G8 WTH
West 159th St 356-F8 WTH
West 161st St 356-J7; 357-G7 WTH
West 166th St 356-B6, J6 WTH
West 169th St 357-B5, F5 WTH
West 181st St 357-G2 W; 357-G2 WTH
West 186th St 356-B1; 357-D1 WTH
West 193rd St 322-D10; 323-C10 WTH
West 196th St 322-B9 WTH
West 199th St 323-F8 WTH
West 200 Rd 595-H7, H10 PTJ; 595-H7, H10 WTJ
West 203rd St 323-J7 WTH
West 206th St 322-B7; 323-C7 WTH
West 211th St 322-H6 WTH
West 216th St 322-B4 AT; 322-B4; 323-C4 WTH
West 221st St 322-H3; 323-C3 AT
West 226th St 322-B2; 323-B2 AT
West 400 Rd 463-K4, K10; 497-K2 BCT; 497-K9; 531-K2, K6 SCT; 429-J4, J10; 463-J1 VT; 561-B10; 595-B2, B3, B5, B10 WTJ
West 425 Rd 497-J10; 531-J1 SCT
West 450 Rd 531-J2, J6 SCT; 594-K5 WTJ
West 500 Rd 463-G4, G10 BCT; 599-K3 BTS; 531-K10; 565-K3, K10 MTS; 497-G10; 531-G1, G6 SCT; 599-K3 STS; 429-F5, G10; 463-G1 VT; 560-J9; 594-J3, J9 WTJ
West 525 Rd 497-F2 BCT; 497-F6 SCT; 599-K7 STS
West 550 Rd 531-F5 SCT; 599-J5, J10 STS; 594-G5 WTJ
West 600 Rd 463-D6, D10; 497-D2 BCT; 531-G10; 565-G3, G9, G10; 599-G1 MTS; 497-D10; 531-D1, D8 SCT; 599-G3 STS; 429-C10; 463-C1 VT; 594-F5, F10 WTJ
West 650 Rd 531-F10; 565-F1, F8 MTS; 531-C4 SCT
West 675 Rd 565-E6 MTS; 531-B8 SCT
West 700 Rd 463-A4, A10; 497-A3 BCT; 531-D9; 565-D2, D6, D10; 598-K1; 599-D3 MTS; 429-A2 McC; 497-A10; 531-A1, A5 SCT
West 750 Rd 565-C9 MTS
West 800 Rd 565-A1, A3, A10; 599-A1 MTS
West 800 Rd W 531-A10 MTS
West 825 Rd 598-K3, K5, K10 STS
West 850 Rd 564-K2, K4, K7 MTS
West 875 Rd 564-J10; 598-J3 MTS; 598-J3 STS
West Acree Dr 596-C5 G
West Adams Blvd Dr 460-G1 WTM
West Alman Dr 392-A6 Ca
West Andrews Blvd 523-D8 P
West Arlington Ct 494-K2 WrT
West Atrium Boardwalk 427-C8 LTM
West Avery Dr 424-B6 PTM
West Bando Ct 426-C10 WTM
West Bar Del Dr 559-E1, E2 DTM
West Bauer Dr 426-C2 Ca
West Bavarian Dr 462-B10 WrT
West Bay Ct 424-K6 WTM
West Bay Vista Dr 427-A2 LTM
West Bayberry Ct 392-B8 Ca
West Bayridge Cir 428-E8 L
West Beaumont Green Dr 426-G7 WTM
West Beech Dr 523-K9 P
West Bentwood Cir Dr 424-F6 PTM
West Black Oak Ct 489-F6 A
West Bloomfield Dr 564-F4 FT
West Blue Cr Dr 427-D9 LTM
West Bluffwood Dr 458-G6 WTM
West Braeburn Dr 495-G3 WrT
West Branch 455-G1 B
West Brendon Way Dr 461-B3 LTM
West Brentwood Dr 523-K8 P
West Bridgefield Dr 524-C9 GT
West Brook Blvd 359-E4 N
West Brook Cir 359-E4 N
West Buckridge Dr 561-J4 PeT
West Canterbury Sq 425-B5, F4 WTM
West Cardinal Cove 427-F7 LTM
West Carnoustie Cir Dr 523-A2 WaT
West Castleton Farms Dr 427-D8 LTM
West Castleway Ct 427-A6 LTM
West Castleway Dr 426-K6; 427-A6 LTM
West Central Dr 391-F8 CTH
West Century Cir 424-H7 WTM
West Chadwood La 424-F5 PTM
West Chapel Hill Dr 491-D7 WnT
West Charleston Dr 495-C6 WrT
West Chesapeake Dr 428-D7 L
West Chester Dr 426-D10 WTM
West Chesterfield Dr 527-G9 PeT
West Claren Dr 558-B6 GT
West Clarendon Rd Dr 459-C7 WTM
West Cobblestone Dr 428-J8 L
West College Ave 455-F6 B
West Collett Dr 592-H2 MTM
West Colony Lake Dr 523-J6 P
West Colony Pointe Dr 427-A4 LTM
West Connaught Dr 523-C8 P
West Copperwood Cir 392-D1 Ca
West Cotton Bay Dr 457-F4 PTM
West Crimson Cir Dr 561-F3 PeT
West Crimson Ct 392-B7 Ca
West Crystal Bay Dr 557-G1 P
West Ct 531-E1 SCT
West Cypress 595-K4 G
West Devon Ct Dr 460-F7 WTM
West Discovery Dr 427-A4 LTM
West Doral Dr 427-C4 LTM
West Dr 392-K8 CTH; DN-B2; 493-A6 CTM; 531-J3 SCT; 357-J2 W; 357-J2 WTH; 560-H10 WTJ
West Dunbarton Ct 424-H8 WTM
West Dunham Ct 496-D2 WrT
West Eagle Bay Dr 457-D8 PTM
West Eagle Cove Dr 457-D8 PTM
West Ellenberger Pkwy Dr 494-H6 WrT
West Fairlane Dr 564-D2 FT
West Fairway Cir Dr 428-H8 L
West Fairwood Ct 427-F9 LTM
West Farm View Cir 427-E8 LTM
West Fortune Cir 525-J4 WnT
West Fox Cir 360-B7 NT
West Galen Dr 489-G9 A
West Garden Cir 393-G7 F
West Glen Arm Dr 457-G10 WnT
West Glenview Dr 426-E8 WTM
West Golden Oaks 424-H3 WTM
West Granada Cir 492-G1 WnT
West Greenbriar 595-H1 G
West Greenwood Tr 562-C9 G
West Haddington Dr 427-H3 LTM
West Hadley Rd 557-C3 GT; 557-C3 P
West Hamblen Dr 525-B2 WnT
West Hampton Cir 428-A6 LTM
West Hawthorne Dr 392-C2 Ca
West Hazel Foster Ct 392-C1 Ca
West Heathmore Dr 528-K9 FT
West Hickory Ct 529-B8 FT
West Hickory La 457-D10 WnT
West Hickory Tr 529-B8 FT
West High Dr 455-A8 LTH
West Highwoods Dr 458-F10 WnT
West Hill Dr 461-E4 L
West Hillside Ave Dr 459-K2 WTM
West Holaday Dr 392-A10; 426-A1 CTH
West Holiday La 455-G9 B
West Holliday Dr 425-D9, D10; 459-D1 WTM
West Holly Springs Dr 457-E5 PTM
West Homestead Pl 523-B7 P
West Honnen Dr 427-E10 LTM
West Horse Hill Dr 491-C1 WnT
West Horseshoe La 392-C7 Ca
West Huddleston Dr 561-D6 PeT
West Hunters Dr 392-A7 Ca
West Indian Lake Blvd 428-A10, B9 L
West Iron Tr 490-H5 WnT
West Ironwood Dr 455-J8 B; 392-D2 Ca
West Jaffa Ct Dr 425-E4 WTM
West Jessman Rd Dr 427-D9 LTM
West Kessler Blvd Dr 458-G4; 459-A3 WTM
West Kirk Dr 490-K7, K8 WnT
West Kristen Dr 494-H1 WrT
West Lake Dr 455-F8 B; 491-H7 WnT
West Lake Dr N 491-G7, H7 WnT
West Lake Dr S 491-H7 WnT
West Lake Nora Dr 425-G4 WTM
West Lake Rd 491-D7 WnT
West Lake Terr Dr 496-A3 WrT
West Lakeshore Dr 392-C10 Ca
West Lakeview Pkwy Dr 423-J9 PTM
West Lakewood Dr 426-C2 Ca
West Lawrence Cir Dr 525-G8 DTM
West Lawton Loop Dr 461-H4 L
West Liberty Cr Dr 457-J4 PTM
West Lismore Dr 561-H8 PeT
West Lynn Dr 493-C5 CTM
West Main St 455-D4 B; 595-J2; 596-A2 G; 455-D4 LTH; 523-D9 P
West Maple Dr 489-A8 WaT
West Marten Ct 461-E7 L
West Marwood Tr Dr 425-H1 CTH
West May Apple Cir 357-D9 WTH
West Menlo Ct Dr 425-K6 WTM
West Moon Rd 557-C1 GT
West Moray Ct 424-H8 WTM
West Nature Dr 422-K4 PTM
West Navajo Tr Dr 425-A8 WTM
West Norena Ct 489-F1 LTH
West Northfield Dr 455-E3 B
West Oak Blvd Dr 496-K5 Cu
West Oak Hill Dr 557-H2 P
West Oakwood Dr 595-K3 G
West Old Oakland Blvd Dr 428-F8 L
West Old Town Dr 425-A4 WTM
West Olde Mill Cir Dr 425-D5 WTM
West Orchard Pk Dr 391-J10; 425-J1 CTH
West Paddington La 424-D7 PTM
West Paree Ct 491-G6 WnT
West Park 32 359-B4 NT
West Park Central Dr 425-B10; 459-B1 WTM
West Park Way 491-B6 WnT
West Paz Dr 562-C9 G
West Pearl St 596-C2 G
West Pebblebrooke Dr 428-H8 L
West Pine Springs Dr 427-F8 LTM
West Pineview Ct 423-G2 ET
West Pleasant Way 426-B2 CTH
West Point Dr 424-E3 PTM
West Point Pl 424-F3 PTM
West Port Ct 325-E3 C
West Priority Way Dr 426-C3 WTM
West Quail Ridge 557-J3 P
West Rd 322-C1 AT; 390-C3, C5, C6 CTH
West Red Bud La 427-J6 LTM
West Ridgegate Dr 424-C7 PTM
West Rimwood Dr 427-D3 LTM
West River Bay Dr 426-B6 WTM
West Robin Run 457-K1 PTM
West Rowan Ct 357-D8 WTH
West Rowan Run 357-E9 WTH
West Rushmore Blvd 490-G5 WnT
West Ruskin Pl 457-H9, J9; 458-A9 WnT
West Russell Lake Dr 389-B9 ET
West Saddle Barn Dr 491-C1 WnT
West Saddlebrook Ct 459-A2 WTM
West Sadlier Cir Dr 529-D1 WrT
West Salem Dr 392-J1 Ca
West Sandpiper Dr 424-F3 PTM
West Scarsdale Dr 427-G5 LTM
West Settlement Dr 427-B3 LTM
West Shady Hills Dr 423-B8 PTM
West Sherry La 491-G10 WnT
West Smallwood La 457-B9 WnT
West Springwater Dr 427-F6 LTM
West St DN-C2, C4; 493-D8, D10; 527-D1 CTM; 531-G5 NP; 523-E8 P; 531-E1 SCT; 562-A5 Spt
West Staton Pl Dr 491-A6 WnT
West Steinmeier Dr 426-H10 WTM
West Stonehedge Dr 561-F9 G
West Stout Field Dr 526-C2 WnT
West Summer Walk Dr 562-C8 PeT
West Suncrest Cir Dr 491-F9 WnT
West Tansey Crossing 357-D8 WTH
West Tara Ct 457-K10 WnT
West Taylor Dr 495-A5 WrT
West Thames Ct 496-C2 WrT
West Thistlewood Dr 391-F3 CTH
West Tidewater Dr 428-G5 LTM
West Tilden Dr 455-C7 B; 455-C7 LTH
West Valley Cr La 496-G3 WrT
West View Dr DN-A4; 492-J10 CTM
West Villa Ave Dr 528-A6 PeT
West Village Cir 496-A2 WrT
West Village Pk 358-B10 WTH
West Village Pkwy Cir 457-D7 PTM
West Walnut Cr Dr 390-F10 CTH
West Waring Dr 496-G5 Cu
West Washington Blvd 425-F10 WTM
West Washington Blvd Dr 425-F4 WTM
West Waterfront Pkwy 491-E2 WnT
West Watermans Dr 360-B8 NT
West Welcome Way Blvd 491-C8 WnT
West Wellington Dr 459-C1 WTM
West Westbury Dr 491-H6 WnT
West Westfield Ct 425-H9 WTM
West Westmont La 359-D4 NT
West Wheel Ests Dr 461-K5 L
West White River Pkwy Dr DN-A1, B2, C3, C4; 458-J10; 492-J2, J5; 493-B9; 527-C1 CTM; 458-J10 WTM; 492-J2, J5 WnT
West Williamshire Dr 425-B4 WTM
West Wind Cir 391-E3 CTH
West Wind Drift Dr 457-D9 WnT
West Wind La 426-H4 WTM
West Winding Brook Dr 490-H6 WnT

West Windsor Dr 393-J6 F
West Woodland Dr 497-A5 Cu
West Woodruff Pl Dr DN-F2; 493-K7 CTM
West Woods Edge Dr 427-A5 LTM
West Woodstone Way Dr 427-G4 LTM
West Woodview Dr 391-G8 CTH
West Zoo Rd 595-H4 G
West-Chester Dr 392-G9 Ca
Westbay Cir 325-C5 N
Westbourne Dr 455-F4 B; 460-C7 WTM
Westbridge Dr 523-E8 P
Westbrook Ave 492-B10; 526-B5 WnT
Westbrook Dr 558-A10 M
Westbury Dr E 491-H7 WnT
Westbury Dr N 491-H6 WnT
Westbury Dr W 491-H6 WnT
Westchester Blvd 325-B8 N
Westchester Dr 461-D4 L
Westcreek Ct 428-H4 L
Westdrum Ct 490-H10 WnT
Westdrum Rd 491-F9 WnT
Westerbeck Ct 562-F6 PeT
Western Dr 531-B3 SCT; 491-E10; 525-E1, E2 WnT
Western Rd 558-H10; 592-H1 MTM
Westfield Blvd 391-K10; 425-K2 CTH; 391-K10 Ca; 357-K2 W; 357-K8 WTH; 425-H8, H10, J6; 459-D4, D5, H1 WTM
Westfield Ct 425-J9 WTM
Westfield Ct W 425-H9 WTM
Westfield Pk Rd 357-H4, H5 W
Westfield Rd 358-G4; 359-D3 N; 358-G4; 359-D3 NT
Westfield Way 425-J4 WTM
Westhaven Dr 457-G8, H8 PTM
Westlane Rd 424-F9 PTM; 424-F9; 425-A9 WTM
Westle Dr 357-K3 W
Westleigh Dr 424-F6, G6 PTM
Westminister Dr 359-J8 N
Westminster Ct 392-F9 Ca; 427-H8 LTM
Westminster Dr 427-J9 LTM
Westminster Way 392-G9 Ca
Westmont La E 359-D4 NT
Westmont La W 359-D4 NT
Westmore Cir 491-C7 WnT
Westmore Dr 491-C6 WnT
Westmount Ct 491-A7 WnT
Weston Ave 489-J9 A
Weston Ct 491-E7 WnT
Weston Dr 390-C10, D9 CTH
Weston St 455-E7 B
Westover Cir 424-D7 PTM
Westover Dr 424-C6 PTM
Westpoint Dr 427-E1 F
Westport La 491-A6 WnT
Westridge Cir 428-J7 L; 359-E4 N
Westridge Dr 491-A3 WnT
Westridge Dr N 359-E4 N
Westridge Dr S 359-E4 N
Westside Dr 455-E8 LTH
Westview Dr 596-A2 G; 596-E10 NW
Westwind Dr 523-J2 WaT
Westwood Cir 392-G9 Ca
Westwood Dr 392-K7 CTH; 392-G9 Ca; 558-A10 M
Westwood Rd 425-F6 WTM
Wet Rock Ct 428-K9 L
Wetherby Ct 458-B5 PTM
Wexford Ct 325-A8 N
Wexford Dr 426-H9 WTM; 524-F1 WaT
Wexford Rd 460-H2, H5, H6 LTM
Whalen Ave 561-J1; 562-A1, C1, D1 PeT
Wharfside La 457-E9 WnT
Wharton La 393-B9 F
Wheat Ridge Ct 424-A6 PTM
Wheatcroft Ct 460-H5 LTM
Wheatfield Ct 357-H10 WTH
Wheatfield La 357-H10 WTH
Wheatgrass La 325-E9 N
Wheatstone Ct 559-G1 DTM
Wheel Ests Ct 461-K4 L
Wheel Ests Dr E 461-K5 L
Wheel Ests Dr N 461-K4; 462-A4 L
Wheel Ests Dr W 461-K5 L
Wheel Wright Way 393-C4 Ca
Wheeler Rd 461-J3 L; 357-H4 W; 357-H4 WTH
Wheeler St 494-B2 CTM; 592-B2 M
Wheelhorse Dr 559-H2 DTM
Wheeling Ct 393-J2 F
Wheelwright Ct 523-J5 P
Whenner Dr 461-D9 WrT
Whidbey Ct 496-G5 Cu
Whidbey Dr 496-G6 Cu
Whipplewood Ct 460-H4 LTM
Whippoorwill Ct 561-J9 G
Whippoorwill Way 392-G3 Ca
Whipporwill 595-G1 G
Whipporwill Dr 427-D5 LTM
Whipporwill Pl 427-D5 LTM
Whipporwill Way 561-G10; 595-G1 G
Whirlaway Ct 528-J9 FT
Whirlaway Dr 528-J9 FT
Whirlaway La 528-J8 FT
Whisper Bay Ct 392-G7 Ca
Whisper La 595-F1 G
Whisper Oaks Ct 457-E10 WnT
Whisper Wind Dr 391-D2 CTH
Whisper Wood Ct 455-J7 B
Whispering Dr 530-C2 WrT
Whispering La 490-G6 WnT
Whispering Tr 392-C9 Ca; 561-F10; 595-F1 G
Whispering Way 530-C2 WrT
Whispering Willow Ct 359-F1 N
Whispering Winds Dr 490-F5 WaT
Whispering Wood Ct 524-B8 P
Whisperwood La 460-G4 LTM; 460-G4 WTM
Whistler Cir 496-F4 WrT
Whistler Dr 531-B10; 565-B1 MTS; 496-F4 WrT
Whistler Terr 496-F4 WrT
Whitaker Dr 457-J8 PTM
Whitaker Farms Dr 563-A6 FT
Whitaker Farms La 563-A6 FT
Whitaker Rd 524-E10; 558-E1 P
Whitcomb Ave 491-J2, J5 S; 457-J10; 491-J8, J10, K5; 525-J1 WnT
Whitcomb Ct 491-J5 WnT
Whitcomb Pl 359-C1 N
Whitcomb Terr 491-J5 WnT
White Alder Ct 523-D3 WaT
White Ash Ct 592-C4 M; 523-C4 WaT
White Ash Dr 392-E3 Ca
White Ash Tr 592-D5 M
White Ave 455-K7 B; 493-A2, A3 CTM
White Bark Ct 523-H1 A
White Cedar Ct 492-E3 WnT
White Cloud Ct N 593-A1 MTM
White Dove Ct 427-E7 LTM
White Dove Dr 427-E7 LTM
White Fir Dr 427-G4 LTM
White Hall Cir 392-J1 Ca
White Hall Way 392-J1 Ca
White Haven Ct 359-H9 N
White Horse La 392-K9 DTH
White House Dr N 596-E3 G
White House Dr S 596-E3 G
White Knight Blvd 496-A1 WrT
White La 461-F5 L
White Lick Cr Rd 558-F5 GT
White Lick Ct 557-G2 P
White Lick La 523-D7 P
White Oak Ct 389-A8 ET; 460-E3 WTM
White Oak Dr 489-F5 A; 392-C10 Ca; 393-G2 DTH; 530-K4 SCT
White Oak Tr 428-H9 L
White Oaks Dr 491-K3 S
White Pines Ct 561-B4 PeT
White Pkwy 492-K7 CTM
White River Dr 426-B6 WTM
White River Dr E 527-D2 CTM
White River Pkwy Dr E DN-C4; 458-K10; 492-J3, K1; 493-C10; 527-C1 CTM; 492-J3 WnT
White River Pkwy Dr W DN-A1, B2, C3, C4; 458-J10; 492-J2, J5; 493-B9; 527-C1 CTM; 458-J10 WTM; 492-J2, J5 WnT
White River St 594-H4 WTJ
White Rock Ct 428-K8 L
White Sail Ct 428-E5 LTM
White Tail Cir 389-D8 ET
White Water Ct 325-E1 C
White Willow Dr 358-B3 WTH
White Willow Way 457-D5 PTM
Whitebark Ct 358-A5 WTH
Whitebark Dr 428-H6 L
Whitebirch Dr 392-K10 F
Whitebridge Dr 395-A7 F
Whitecap Cir 428-B4 LTM
Whitecap Way 428-B4 LTM
Whitecliff Ct 490-J3 WnT
Whitecliff Dr 490-J3 WnT
Whitecliffy Way 490-H3 WnT
Whitehall Dr 427-J8, J9 LTM
Whitehall Pl 392-C5 Ca
Whitehaven La 394-A4 F
Whitehaven Rd 457-F6, G6 PTM
Whitelick Rd 557-G10 BTM
Whitemarsh La 460-H5 LTM
Whiteriver Pl 393-B7 F
Whitestone Rd 427-D8 LTM
Whitestown Rd 388-K5; 389-D6 ET
Whitetail Cir 428-B1 F
Whitetail Ct 594-E6 WTJ
Whitetail La 457-E9 PTM
Whitetail Run 594-E7 WTJ
Whitethorn Ct 426-A10 WTM
Whitewater St 462-E1 L
Whitewood Ct 528-F9 BG; 424-J4 WTM
Whitley Ct 324-K6 N
Whitley Dr 426-B3 WTM
Whitley La 459-A1 WTM
Whitlock Ct 424-F8 PTM
Whitney Way 427-J1 F
Whittier Ct 426-H7 WTM
Whittier Dr 393-J2 F
Whittier La 426-H7 WTM
Whittier Pl 460-H7, H9 LTM; 426-H7 WTM; 460-H9, H10; 494-H5, H7, H10, J4; 528-H1 WrT
Whittington Dr 455-H2 B
Whitton Pl 460-G1 WTM
Whitty La 496-A5 WrT
Whitworth Dr 392-C1 Ca
Wichman Way 562-F7 PeT
Wichser Ave 492-C9 WnT
Wichser Ct 458-J6 WTM
Wicker Rd 560-C8, G8 PeT
Wickerwood Dr 496-G6 Cu
Wickfield Ct 427-F7 LTM
Wickfield Dr 427-F8 LTM
Wickfield Way 427-F7 LTM
Wickham Ct 391-G7 CTH
Wickham Rd 425-B4 WTM
Wickland Ct 427-H2 F
Wiebeck Ct 461-B3 LTM
Wigeon Dr 393-C8 F
Wigmaker Ct 523-J5 P
Wilbur Smith Pl 359-J9 N
Wilcox St DN-A2; 492-J7 CTM; 492-E7, G7 WnT
Wild Cherry Dr 393-B8 F
Wild Cherry La 426-A2 CTH
Wild Horse La 491-E10 WnT
Wild Ivy Cir 562-C8 PeT
Wild Ivy Ct 562-D8 PeT
Wild Ivy Dr 562-D8 PeT
Wild Opera Ct 360-B1 N
Wild Ridge Ct 326-G6 NT
Wild Ridge Dr 326-G6 NT; 326-G6 WyT
Wild Rose La 560-H10 WTJ
Wilderness La 596-A3 G
Wilderness Tr 528-E7 BG; 393-B8 F; 528-D8 PeT
Wildflower Cir 458-A3 PTM
Wildflower Ct 393-B8 F; 458-A3 PTM; 357-E9 WTH
Wildflower Dr 458-D2, D3 PTM
Wildflower Way La 357-E9 WTH
Wildland Path 460-J3 LTM
Wildridge Dr 427-H9 LTM
Wildrose La 489-E10 A
Wildwood Ave 459-H3 WTM
Wildwood Ct 455-J8 B; 523-K9 P; 424-B10 PTM
Wildwood Dr 391-H4 Ca; 394-C10 F; 529-F7 FT; 389-F4 Z
Wildwood La 393-E9 F; 593-D4 MTM; 530-E2 WrT
Wiley Ave 461-B4 LTM
Wiley St 596-B2 G
Wilford La 496-H4 WrT
Wilkins St DN-A4, C4, D4; 492-J10; 493-C10, E10 CTM; DN-A4; 491-J10; 492-B10, H10 WnT
Will Crest Dr 458-G6 WTM
Will Scarlet La 458-G5 WTM
Will-Z-Way Ct 594-K9 WTJ
Willa Bonn Ct 326-A7 NT
Willard Ct 557-J1 P
Willark Dr 596-E10 NW
Willcreek La 425-D6 WTM
William Conner Way 393-B4 Ca
William Ct 594-J1 WTJ
William Dr 455-E7 B; 360-A1 NT
William Penn Cir 427-J8 LTM
William Penn Dr 427-H8 LTM
William Penn Pl 427-H7 LTM
Williams Cir 392-G9 Ca
Williams Cove Dr 425-C5 WTM
Williams Cr Blvd 425-E7 WTM
Williams Cr Dr 391-C8 CTH; 425-H9 WTM
Williams Ct 489-G9 A; 392-G8 Ca; 425-D6 WTM
Williams Dr 392-G9 Ca; 558-A10 M; 557-J2 P; 425-D6 WTM
Williams La 425-D6 WTM
Williams St DN-F3; 493-J8 CTM
Williamsburg Ct 595-J1 G; 460-K7 LTM; 389-G7 Z
Williamsburg Dr 392-G2 Ca; 523-H5 P
Williamsburg La 595-J1 G; 389-F6 Z
Williamshire Dr E 425-B4 WTM
Williamshire Dr W 425-B4 WTM
Williamson Pkwy 392-D10 Ca
Williamswood Dr 530-J4 SCT
Williston Ct 425-A3 WTM
Willman Lake Dr 558-C6 GT
Willoughby Ct 523-G6 P; 491-E7 WnT
Willow Ave 389-K4; 390-A4 ET
Willow Bend Ct 428-B1 F; 523-C3 WaT
Willow Bend Dr 528-E9 BG; 528-E9 PeT; 523-C3 WaT
Willow Cir Dr 595-C7 WTJ
Willow Cr Way 358-B4 WTH
Willow Ct 393-H1 DTH; 324-K8 N; 595-C7 WTJ; 491-F7 WnT
Willow Dr 527-H4 CTM; 393-H1 DTH
Willow Forge Ct 458-B3 PTM
Willow Glen Cir 496-B1 WrT
Willow Glen Ct 496-B1 WrT
Willow Glen Dr 528-E9 BG; 528-E9 PeT
Willow Glen La 528-E9 BG; 528-E9 PeT
Willow Grove Dr 531-A2 SCT
Willow Lake Dr 424-G4 PTM; 595-B7 WTJ
Willow Lakes Blvd 595-C8 WTJ
Willow Lakes Blvd E 595-C7 WTJ
Willow Oak 489-E5 A
Willow Rd 390-B2 CTH; 389-J4; 390-B2 ET; 425-F10 WTM; 389-J4, J7 Z
Willow Ridge 393-F10 F
Willow Ridge Ct 389-G5 Z
Willow Spring Blvd 455-F8 B
Willow Spring Rd 425-F7 WTM
Willow St 595-B8 WTJ; 389-J8 Z
Willow Tree La 496-A1 WrT
Willow View Rd 393-B10; 427-B2 F; 427-B2 LTM
Willow Way 325-A8 N
Willow Way N 424-H4 PTM
Willow Wind Cir 529-F2 WrT
Willow Wind Ct 594-K3 WTJ; 529-F2 WrT
Willow Wind Dr 595-A3 WTJ
Willowbrook Dr 427-A1 F
Willowbrook Pkwy 460-A6 WTM
Willowgate Cir 425-D3 WTM
Willowgate Dr 425-D3 WTM
Willowgate La 425-D3 WTM
Willowick Rd 392-B3 Ca
Willowmere Dr 391-J9 CTH
Willowmette La 462-E9 WrT
Willowood Dr 457-C9 WnT; 462-F8 WrT
Willowrun Dr 425-E3 WTM
Willowrun Pl 425-D3 WTM
Willowrun Way 425-E3 WTM
Willowview Rd 359-B5 N; 359-B5 NT
Willowwood La 393-E6 F
Willsee La 558-A6 GT
Willsey Rd 558-B5 GT
Wilmington Cir 393-F8 F
Wilmington Dr 392-E9 Ca
Wilshire Ct 325-A7 N
Wilshire Dr 564-E1 FT; 456-G8 LTH
Wilshire Glen Dr 456-H9 WnT
Wilshire Rd 458-J7 WTM
Wilson Dr 592-C5 BTM; 531-J6 NP
Wilson Dr E 391-J5 Ca
Wilson Dr N 391-H5 Ca
Wilson Rd 422-F6, H8 BTH; 558-E7 GT; 422-H8, K9; 423-B8 PTM
Wilson St DN-B1; 493-B6 CTM
Wilson Terr 391-H4 Ca
Wilton Ct 491-F7 WnT
Wiltonwood Ct 457-D5 PTM
Wimbledon Ct 427-A4 LTM
Wimbley Way 325-K10 N
Wimmenauer Dr 528-J1 WrT
Winamac Ct 391-E3 Ca
Winchester Dr 496-H3 Cu; 561-K7; 562-A7, B7, D6 PeT
Winchester La 456-E9 LTH
Winchester Pl 425-H1 CTH; 562-D7 PeT
Wind Cir W 391-E3 CTH
Wind Drift Dr 457-D9 PTM
Wind Drift Dr E 457-D8 PTM
Wind Drift Dr W 457-D9 WnT
Wind Horst Way 596-H2 G
Wind River Ct 490-H5 WnT
Wind Run Cir 427-E6 LTM
Wind Song Tr 562-B1 PeT
Windbush Way 392-H6 Ca
Windcombe Blvd 425-G5, G6 WTM
Winddoor Rd 461-A2 LTM
Windemere Dr 390-J10 CTH
Windemere Rd 596-E9 NW
Windermere Blvd 394-E10; 428-C2, D1 F
Windermire St 527-H7 PeT
Windfall La 558-H8 GT
Windham Ct 455-F10 B
Windham Lake Cir 457-B10 WnT
Windham Lake Ct 457-B10 WnT
Windham Lake Dr 457-B10 WnT
Windham Lake Pl 457-B10 WnT
Windham Lake Rd 457-B9 WnT
Windhaven Blvd 428-F5 LTM
Windhaven Cir 455-K4 B; 428-F6 LTM
Windhaven Ct 428-F5 LTM
Windhill Dr 427-K7; 461-K8 LTM
Winding Bk Dr 391-K9 CTH
Winding Bk Dr E 490-J7 WnT
Winding Bk Dr W 490-H6 WnT
Winding Bk La 595-K1 G
Winding Bk Pkwy 490-J6 WnT
Winding Bk Way 326-G6 NT; 326-G6 WyT
Winding Cir 561-F10 G
Winding Cr Cir 428-J7 L
Winding Cr Ct 393-G5 F; 428-K7 L
Winding Cr Dr 428-K7 L
Winding Cr La 393-F5 F; 428-J7 L
Winding Cr Pl 428-J7 L
Winding Cr Tr 455-H2 B
Winding Hart Dr 496-H5 WrT
Winding Ridge Ave 560-J9 PeT
Winding Ridge Ct 560-K8 PeT
Winding Ridge Rd 560-J8 PeT
Winding Tr 561-F10; 595-F1 G
Winding Way 391-H5 Ca; 393-E10 F; 359-E10 NT; 460-D3 WTM
Winding Way La 460-E3 WTM
Windingwood Ct 462-F4 L
Windingwood Dr 462-F4 L
Windjammer Cir 428-D6 LTM
Windjammer Ct 428-C6 LTM
Windjammer Ct N 428-F1 FCT
Windjammer Dr 455-E1 BTH
Windjammer Dr N 428-E1 FCT
Windjammer Dr S 428-E1 FCT
Windjammer Trace 428-F1 FCT
Windledge Cir 390-B8 CTH
Windmill Cir 358-C9 WTH
Windmill Dr 457-J8 PTM; 358-C10 WTH; 523-J3 WaT
Windmill Tr 595-A2, A3 WTJ
Windmill Way 531-G3 SCT
Windpointe Pass 392-G6 Ca
Windrider Ct 455-F1 BTH
Windridge Dr 460-G4 LTM; 460-G4 WTM
Windridge Way 455-F1, F2 BTH
Windrift Way 392-F7 Ca
Windsong Ct 455-F2 BTH; 496-B2 WrT
Windsong Dr 496-B2 WrT
Windsong La 595-A2 WTJ
Windsor Ct 595-A3 WTJ
Windsor Dr 392-E6 Ca; 393-J6 F; 495-A3 WrT
Windsor Dr E 393-K6 F
Windsor Dr S 393-J6 F
Windsor Dr W 393-J6 F
Windsor La 359-H10 N
Windsor Pkwy 562-A5 PeT
Windsor Rd 456-G8 LTH
Windsor St DN-F1; 493-K5 CTM
Windswept Dr 394-K7 F
Windview Cir 595-A2 WTJ
Windward Cir 489-K8 A
Windward Ct 455-E1 BTH; 423-H10 PTM
Windward La 523-E7 P
Windward Pass 428-D1 F
Windward Way 390-E10 CTH; 423-H10 PTM
Windwood Cir 427-F3 LTM
Windwood Pkwy 325-E9 N
Windy Hill Ct 529-E2 WrT
Windy Hill Dr 529-F2 WrT
Windy Hill La 529-E2 WrT
Windy Hill Way 529-E2 WrT
Winfield Ave 458-G2 PTM; 458-G10; 492-G1, G2, G5 WnT
Winfield Dr 390-H6 CTH
Winford Dr 462-D1 L
Wingate Blvd 462-C9 WrT
Wingate Ct 462-C8 WrT
Wingate Dr 462-C8 WrT
Wingate Terr 462-C9 WrT
Wingedfoot Ct 458-A2 PTM
Wings Ct 455-D7 LTH
Wings Dr 455-D7 LTH
Wingstem Ct 394-A4 F
Winings Ave 526-E6 DTM
Winlee Ct 462-B1 L
Winnebago Dr 526-A5 WnT
Winners Cir 422-H3 BTH; 528-K8 FT
Winners Ct 528-K8 FT
Winnock Dr 426-K10 LTM
Winnpeny La 460-F2 WTM
Winona Dr 428-B10; 462-B1 L
Winona St DN-B2; 493-B9 CTM; 326-F4 WRT
Winonia Dr 391-K6; 392-A5 Ca
Winship Ct 559-J1 DTM
Winship Dr 559-J1 DTM
Winslow Dr 563-A7 FT
Winsted Dr 524-K3; 525-A3 WnT
Winston Dr 460-J5 LTM; 460-F5, G5 WTM
Winston La 394-C10 F
Winston Pl 460-G10 WrT
Winter Ave 494-A3 CTM
Winter Berry La 592-E3 M
Winter Ct 391-H1 CTH
Winter Way 391-G1 CTH; 389-D4 Z
Winter Wood Ct 423-F1 Z
Winter Wood Dr 391-C10 CTH
Winterberry Cir 457-K3; 458-A3 PTM
Winterberry Ct 325-E9 N
Winterberry Dr 457-K3; 458-D4 PTM
Wintercove Way 393-D9 F
Wintergreen Dr 462-E5 L; 324-J8 N
Wintergreen La 392-F3 CTH
Wintergreen Way 427-F3 LTM
Winterhazel Dr 457-D4 PTM
Winterking Pass 394-G10 F
Winters Rd 489-E4 WaT
Winterset Cir 390-G9 CTH; 491-B2 WnT
Wintersong Dr 525-K6 DTM
Winterspring Cres 390-A4 ET
Winterspring Way 390-A4 ET
Winterthur 425-B5 WTM
Winterwood Dr 489-J8 A
Winterwood La 462-E4 L
Winthrop Ave 459-H10; 493-H1, H3 CTM; 425-H5; 459-H2, H4, H6, H8 WTM
Winthrop Pl 393-H2 F
Winthrop Rd 596-D9 NW
Winton Ave 491-K3; 492-A3, A5 S; 458-A10; 492-A1 WnT
Winton Ct 492-A3 S
Winton Dr 424-A8, A9 PTM
Wisconsin St 527-D1 CTM; 526-E1 WnT
Wishbone Blvd 424-D7 PTM
Wishmeyer La 530-A1 WrT
Wismar Dr 462-E9 WrT
Wisteria Dr 458-A4 PTM
Wisteria Way E 357-E8 WTH
Wistview Ct 455-C8 LTH
Witch Hazel Ct 394-B8 F
Witch Hazel Dr 462-F8 WrT
Witherington Rd 424-G7 PTM
Witherspoon Dr 462-E1 L
Witt Ct 594-E5 WTJ
Witt Dr 594-E4 WTJ
Wittfield Ct 461-K7 LTM
Wittfield St 461-K7, K8 LTM; 461-K9; 495-K5, K7 WrT
Wixshire Ct 457-H6 PTM
Wixshire Dr 457-G7 PTM
Wixson Ct 457-H7 PTM
Woburn Dr 427-A9 LTM
Wolf Cir 496-F5 WrT
Wolf Cr Cir 426-D1 Ca
Wolf Ct 496-F5 WrT
Wolf La 496-F5 WrT
Wolfe Ave 422-A3 PTB
Wolffe Dr 393-D7 F
Wolford Ct 393-H6 F
Wolford Dr 393-H5 F
Wolford Pl 393-H5 F
Wollenweber Rd 531-C2 SCT
Wonderland Ct 530-E10 FT
Wonderland Dr 530-E10 FT
Wood Acre Dr 391-J4 Ca
Wood Bk Dr 458-A5 PTM
Wood Cr Wind River Crossing Run 429-C3 McC
Wood Ct 393-C9 F; 561-J3 PeT; 389-K7 Z
Wood Dale Terr 562-A10; 596-A1 G
Wood Duck Ct 392-G6 Ca; 457-D8 PTM
Wood Gate Cir 392-D1 Ca
Wood Gate Dr 392-D1 Ca
Wood Hollow Ct 358-A4 W
Wood Knoll La 459-A1 WTM
Wood Mill Ct 391-E3 CTH
Wood Rd 461-J2 L
Wood Ridge Ct 391-K2 Ca
Wood Ridge La 393-B9 F
Wood Sage Dr 489-H5 WaT
Wood Stream Dr 457-D5 PTM
Wood Valley Ct 423-F1 Z
Wood Valley Dr 391-K8; 392-A8 CTH
Woodacre Blvd Dr N 456-H4 PTM
Woodacre Blvd Dr S 456-H5 PTM
Woodacre Ct 456-J4 PTM
Woodacre La 456-J4 PTM
Woodale Rd 456-K10 WnT
Woodall Dr 424-D5 PTM
Woodbine Ct 392-F3 Ca; 561-B7 PeT
Woodbine Dr 392-E3, F3 Ca; 561-B7 PeT
Woodbridge Ct 390-A4 ET; 425-B4 WTM
Woodbridge La 531-J5 NP; 531-J5 SCT; 425-B3 WTM
Woodbrush Ct 427-F3 LTM
Woodburn Dr 491-A3 WnT
Woodbury Dr 392-H9 Ca
Woodcliff Dr 528-D3 CTM
Woodcock Dr 523-E3 WaT
Woodcote Dr 559-H5 DTM
Woodcote La 455-J2 B
Woodcreek Ct 392-H9 Ca; 561-B10 WTJ
Woodcreek Dr 392-F8, G8 Ca; 427-G10 LTM; 561-B9 WTJ; 489-G4 WaT
Woodcreek Pl 561-C10 WTJ
Woodcrest Ct 528-A9 PeT
Woodcrest Dr 531-D5 SCT; 523-E3 WaT
Woodcrest Rd 527-K9; 528-A9 PeT
Woodcroft Ave 461-C6 L
Woodcross Ct 489-C10 WaT
Wooded Glen Ct 424-G4 PTM
Wooden Dr 425-C7 WTM
Wooden Shoe Cir 523-J3 WaT
Woodfield Blvd 392-H1 Ca
Woodfield Cir 392-G2 Ca
Woodfield Crossing Blvd 426-A5 WTM
Woodfield Dr 392-F1, H1 Ca; 530-J4 SCT
Woodfield Dr N 392-G1 Ca
Woodfield Dr S 392-H2 Ca
Woodfield Way 392-G1 Ca
Woodford La 563-B3 FT
Woodfox Ct 461-A7 LTM
Woodfront Ct 458-F9 WnT
Woodfront Dr 458-E10 WnT
Woodfront Pl 458-F10 WnT
Woodgate Cir 393-B9 F
Woodgate Ct 424-A6 PTM
Woodgate Dr 393-C9 F
Woodglen Ct 424-H6 WTM
Woodglen Dr 424-H6 WTM
Woodglen Pl 424-H6 WTM
Woodhaven Cir 496-C1 WrT
Woodhaven Dr 390-B8 CTH
Woodhill Dr 561-F2, H2 PeT
Woodhouse Dr 462-A6 L
Woodlake Ct 391-A9 CTH
Woodland Ave 459-J8 CTM
Woodland Cir 392-A8 CTH
Woodland Ct 490-D1 LTH; 593-B9 MTM; 523-H8 P; 457-J7 PTM
Woodland Dr 391-K10; 392-A7, A8 CTH; 494-D8 CTM; 596-B2 G; 593-B9 MTM; 359-K5 N; 423-H7, H9; 457-H7, J6, J7 PTM
Woodland Dr E 497-A5 Cu
Woodland Dr W 497-A5 Cu
Woodland Pl 596-B2 G
Woodland Streams Ct 595-A10 WTJ
Woodland Streams Dr 595-A10 WTJ
Woodland Trace 523-H4 WaT
Woodland Way 424-G4 PTM
Woodlands Dr 428-B2 F
Woodlane Ct 424-F10 PTM
Woodlark Dr 496-F6 Cu; 393-H2 F
Woodlawn Ave DN-E4, F4; 493-H10, K10; 494-A10 CTM; 495-E10 WrT
Woodlawn Dr 596-A2 G
Woodlea Ct 427-D5 LTM
Woodmere Cir 425-B10 WTM
Woodmere Ct 425-B10 WTM
Woodmere Dr 425-B10, C10 WTM
Woodmill Ct 489-G10 A
Woodmill Dr 426-K1; 427-A1 F
Woodmont Ct 528-F9 BG
Woodmont La 428-D2 F
Woodmore Trace 424-J8 WTM
Woodmoss La 426-H3 WTM
Woodpointe Cir 490-J5 WnT
Woodpointe Dr 490-J5, K6 WnT
Woodpond Roundabout 392-D1 Ca
Woodridge Blvd 460-B7 WTM
Woodridge Ct 596-D10 NW; 595-B1 WTJ; 489-F7 WaT
Woodridge Dr 595-B1 WTJ; 489-E7 WaT

Woodridge Pl 595-A6 WTJ
Woodrow Ave 492-B9, B10; 526-B4 WnT
Woodruff Pl DN-F1; 493-K6 CTM
Woodruff Pl Dr E 493-K6 CTM
Woodruff Pl Dr W DN-F2; 493-K7 CTM
Woodruff Pl Mid Dr 493-K7 CTM
Woods Bay Ct 392-F6 Ca
Woods Bay La 428-F4 LTM
Woods Bay Pl 392-F6 Ca
Woods Crossing Ave 495-E9 WrT
Woods Crossing Dr 495-E9 WrT
Woods Crossing La 495-F9 WrT
Woods Ct 595-B7 WTJ
Woods Edge Ct 391-E2 CTH
Woods Edge Dr 390-A5 ET; 394-B10; 428-A1, B1 F
Woods Edge Dr E 427-A5 LTM
Woods Edge Dr N 427-A5 LTM
Woods Edge Dr S 427-A5 LTM
Woods Edge Dr W 427-A5 LTM
Woodsage Trace 528-E7 PeT
Woodshire Pl 561-B5 PeT
Woodshore Ct 392-C8 Ca
Woodside Ave 495-D7 WrT
Woodside Ct 455-H1 B; 392-G8 Ca; 389-G10 Z
Woodside Dr 489-G7 A; 592-A7 BTM; 391-K9 CTH; 357-J6 WTH; 424-K8, K9; 458-K2, K3, K5 WTM; 523-F5 WaT; 389-H5 Z
Woodsmall Dr 496-A2 WrT
Woodsmall La 496-B2 WrT
Woodstock Ct 389-F6 Z
Woodstock Dr 455-K9 B; 459-A9 CTM; 459-A8 WTM
Woodstock Way 427-J1 F
Woodstone Ct 428-B2 F; 427-H4 LTM
Woodstone Dr 427-F3 LTM
Woodstone Way Dr S 427-F3 LTM
Woodstone Way Dr W 427-G4 LTM
Woodstream Ct 357-K2 W
Woodstream Dr 523-E4 WaT
Woodsway Dr 595-D7 WTJ
Woodthrush Dr 457-H1 PTM
Woodview Ct 393-E8 F; 592-D3 M
Woodview Dr 359-F1 N
Woodview Dr E 391-H8 CTH
Woodview Dr N 391-G8 CTH
Woodview Dr S 391-G8 CTH
Woodview Dr W 391-G8 CTH
Woodview La 492-E3 WnT
Woodview Trace 424-E3 PTM
Woodville St 326-J1 WRT
Woodward Dr 394-E9 F
Woodwind Dr 561-D3 PeT
Woodworth Ct 562-J3 FT
Woodworth Way 562-J3 FT
Woolco La 491-J3 S
Woonsocket Ct 428-A6 LTM
Wooster Ct 393-J2 F
Worcester Ave 494-F9, F10; 528-F1 CTM
Worchester Ct 392-C1 Ca
Worchester Dr 392-D1 Ca
Wordsworth Ct 359-K6 N
Worman St 562-A4 Spt; 323-E7 WTH
Worth Ave 491-K5 S; 491-K8, K9, K10; 525-K1, K2 WnT
Worthington Cir 423-F4 PTM
Worthington Ct 423-F4 PTM
Wrangler Ct 561-D8 PeT
Wren Ct 392-J3 Ca
Wren St 492-G5 WnT
Wren Way 389-C6 ET
Wright St 493-G10; 527-G1 CTM
Wyandot Tr 426-D7, F7 WTM
Wyandotte Ct 360-B7 NT
Wyandotte Dr 460-E4 WTM
Wyandotte Pl 393-H3 F
Wychwood Pl 359-B1 N
Wyckfield Way 426-J10 LTM; 426-J10 WTM
Wyckford Ct 491-C6 WnT
Wyckford Dr 491-C6 WnT
Wycliff Dr E 525-H10 DTM
Wycombe La 460-G2, G7 LTM
Wyman Ct 427-B10 LTM
Wyndham Dr 455-G10 B
Wyndham La 455-G10 B
Wyndote Dr 391-E3 Ca
Wynham Ct 428-C1 F
Wynne St 428-H10 L
Wynnedale Rd 458-H8 WTM
Wynridge Ct 462-D3 L
Wynstone Way 392-G5 Ca
Wynter Way 426-K9 LTM
Wyoming St DN-A4, C4, D4; 492-J10; 493-C10, D10 CTM; 492-G10 WnT
Wysong Dr 495-F2, G2 WrT
Wysteria Ct 455-C8 LTH
Wythe Dr 325-C10; 359-C1 N
Wythe La 426-E6 WTM

X

X St 492-B5 S
Xenia Cir 562-C7 PeT
Xenia Dr 562-D7 PeT

Y

Yacht Harbor Cir 424-J10 WTM
Yale Dr 425-H3 WTM
Yandes St DN-F1; 493-H3, H5 CTM
Yardley Ct 424-G4 PTM
Yarmouth Pl 393-C10 F
Yates La 490-E6 WaT
Yazoo Dr 528-F9 BG
Yeager Ct 562-K1 FT
Yeager Dr 528-H9 FT
Yeager La 528-K10 FT
Yeagy Ct N 560-J10 WTJ
Yeagy Ct S 594-J1 WTJ
Yeagy Rd 594-J1 WTJ
Yearling Run 423-G9 PTM
Yellow Birch Ct 523-D4 WaT
Yellow Birch Way 457-D5 PTM
Yellow Pine Ct 561-B6 PeT
Yellow Poplar Ct 492-E3 WnT
Yellowstone Pkwy 561-B4 PeT
Yellowwood Cir 325-A8 N
Yellowwood Ct 424-K4 WTM
Yellowwood Dr 595-A4 WTJ
Yoke St 527-E4, G4 CTM
Yolanda Ct 428-J9 L
York Cir 325-A8 N
York Dr 391-J4 Ca; 389-F6 Z
York Pl 393-E7 F
York Rd 455-G8 B
York St 527-B1 CTM; 596-C5, D2 G
York Town Rd 595-H3 G
Yorkshire Blvd 496-J6, K6 Cu
Yorkshire Cir 359-J7, J8 N
Yorkshire Ct 495-K3 WrT
Yorkshire La 392-E7 Ca
Yorktown Crossing 390-D8 CTH
Yorktown Dr 461-K5 LTM
Yorktown La 490-F7 WaT
Yorkville Ct 457-F4 PTM
Yosemite Ct 561-D4 PeT
Yosemite Dr 561-B4 PeT
Young Ave 494-F8 CTM
Young Lake Dr 496-D8 WrT
Youngwood La 394-B2 F
Yount Blvd 491-K7 WnT
Yucatan Dr 528-H10 FT
Yuma Ct 526-B6 DTM
Yuma Dr 526-B6 DTM
Yvette Dr 490-C5 WaT

Z

Zelda St 359-J5 N
Zellwood Ct 392-K4 Ca
Zenas Ct 559-C10 MTM
Zephyr Dr 561-B8 PeT
Zephyr Way 357-C8 WTH
Zimmy Ct 559-A4 DTM
Zinfandel Way 457-E8 PTM
Zinnia Dr 495-G4 WrT
Zion Ct 492-D1 WnT
Zion La 390-A6 ET
Zionsville Ave 388-J4 WTB
Zionsville Rd 389-J9; 423-J2 ET; 423-J4, J9; 457-J2 PTM
Zoeller Ave 461-H6 L
Zoeller Cir 393-A5 Ca
Zona Dr 562-B7 PeT
Zonda Blvd 424-E1 CTH
Zuker Ct 461-E1 CTH
Zurich Terr 458-D7 PTM
Zwingley St 528-B2 CTM
Zylaphone La 597-A10 PTJ

NUMBERED STREETS

1st Ave 528-G6 BG; 456-J10 WnT
1st Ave NE 391-K4 Ca
1st Ave NW 391-K4 Ca
1st Ave SE 391-K5 Ca
1st Ave SW 391-K5 Ca
1st Bomar 561-G10 G
1st Ct 392-D4 Ca
1st St 524-A6 P; 389-H8 Z
1st St NE 391-K4; 392-A4 Ca
1st St NW 391-K4 Ca
1st St SE 391-K4 Ca
1st St SW 391-K4 Ca
2nd Ave 528-G5 BG; 456-J10 WnT
2nd Ave NE 392-A3 Ca
2nd Ave NW 391-K4 Ca
2nd Ave SW 391-K5 Ca
2nd Bomar 561-G10 G
2nd St 429-C7 McC; 359-G4 N; 524-A6 P; 389-J8 Z
2nd St NE 391-K4; 392-A4 Ca
2nd St NW 391-K4 Ca
2nd St SE 391-K4 Ca
2nd St SW 391-J4 Ca
2nd Way 392-D3 Ca
3rd Ave 528-G5 BG; 391-J3 Ca
3rd Ave NE 392-A4 Ca
3rd Ave NW 391-J4 Ca
3rd Ave SW 391-J4, J6 Ca
3rd St 429-C8 McC; 359-G5 N; 389-H8 Z
3rd St NE 391-K4; 392-A3 Ca
3rd St NW 391-K4 Ca
3rd St SE 391-K4 Ca
3rd St SW 391-K4 Ca
4th Ave 528-F7, G6 BG
4th Ave E 526-E6 DTM
4th Ave NE 392-A4 Ca
4th Ave SE 392-A4 Ca
4th Ave SW 391-J4 Ca
4th Ct E 392-D3 Ca
4th Ct W 392-D3 Ca
4th St 359-G5 N; 389-H8, H9 Z
4th St NE 391-K3 Ca
4th St NW 391-K3 Ca
4th St SE 391-K4; 392-A4 Ca
5th Ave 528-F5 BG
5th Ave E 526-E6 DTM
5th St 359-H5 N; 389-H9 Z
5th St NE 391-K3; 392-A3 Ca
5th St NW 391-K3 Ca
5th St SE 391-K5 Ca
5th St SW 391-K5 Ca
6th Ave 528-F5 BG
6th Ave E 526-E5, F5 DTM
6th St 359-H5 N; 389-H9 Z
6th St NW 391-K3 Ca
6th St SE 391-K5 Ca
7th Ave 528-F5 BG
7th St DN-E1; 493-F6 CTM; 359-H4, H5 N; 389-H9 Z
7th St NE 391-K3; 392-A3 Ca
8th Ave 528-F5 BG
8th St 359-H3, H5 N; 389-G8, G9 Z
9th Ave 528-F5, F6, F9 BG
9th St DN-C1, D1, E1, F1; 493-C6, F6, G6, H6; 494-A6, D6, G6 CTM; 496-G5 Cu; 359-H3, H5 N; 492-F6 WnT; 494-G6, J6, K6; 495-B6; 496-A6 WrT; 389-G8, G9 Z
10th Ave 528-E4, F5 BG
10th St DN-B1, D1, E1, F1; 492-J6; 493-A6, F6, G6; 494-A5 CTM; 496-E5 Cu; 359-H9, J4 N; 359-H9 NT; 492-A6 S; 490-K6; 491-A6, H6; 492-A6, J6 WnT; 494-H5; 495-B5, H5; 496-A5, E5 WrT
11th Ave 528-E4, E6 BG
11th St DN-C1, E1, F1; 493-C5, D5, F5, G5, J5, K5; 494-A5, C5, F5 CTM; 359-J2, J3, J5 N; 491-K5; 492-A5 S; 491-F6, G6; 492-E5, H5 WnT; 494-J5, K5; 495-A5, C5, D5, F5; 496-A5 WrT
11th St W 490-B6 WaT
12th Ave 528-E4, E6 BG
12th St DN-C1, D1, E1, F1; 493-C5, D5, F5, J5; 494-A5, E5 CTM; 359-J2, J4 N; 492-A5 S; 491-E6, F5, G5; 492-F5, H5 WnT; 494-K5; 495-A5, F5, J5; 496-A5 WrT
13th Ave 528-E5, E6 BG
13th St DN-C1, D1, F1; 493-C5, E5, F5, H5; 494-A5, C5, E5 CTM; 359-J3, J5 N; 492-A5 S; 491-E5 WnT; 494-H5; 495-A5, C5, E5, G5, J5 WrT
14th Ave 528-E4, E5 BG
14th St DN-E1; 493-B5, D5, G5; 494-D5, F5 CTM; 359-J2, J4, J5 N; 491-K5; 492-A5 S; 491-F5, G5; 492-E5, H5 WnT; 494-J5; 495-A5, C5, F5; 496-A4 WrT
15th Ave 528-D6, E4 BG
15th St 492-K4; 493-B4, D5, F4, G5, H5; 494-D4 CTM; 359-J2, J3, J4, J5 N; 491-K5; 492-A5 S; 491-E5 WnT; 495-A4, F4, H4 WrT
16th Ave 528-D4, D5 BG
16th Pl 492-D4 WnT; 495-J4 WrT
16th St 492-J4; 493-C4, G4; 494-A4, B4, D4 CTM; 359-K3, K4, K5 N; 491-J5, K5; 492-A4 S; 490-J5; 491-E5; 492-J4 WnT; 495-A4, H4; 496-A4 WrT
17th Ave 528-D5 BG
17th St 493-A4, D4, F4, J4; 494-B4, F4 CTM; 359-K3, K4 N; 492-E4, H4 WnT; 494-H4, J4; 495-B4, C4, D4, J4; 496-A4 WrT
18th Ave 528-D4 BG
18th Dr 359-K3 N
18th St 492-J4; 493-A4, D4, E4, J4, K4; 494-A4, F4 CTM; 359-K4 N; 491-J4 S; 492-E4, G4 WnT; 494-H4, J4; 495-B4, C4, H4, J4 WrT
19th Ave 528-D4 BG
19th Pl 494-H3 WrT
19th St 492-K4; 493-E4, F4, G4; 494-B4, E4 CTM; 359-K3, K4 N; 492-G4 WnT; 494-J4; 495-B3, D4 WrT
20th Ave 528-D4 BG
20th Pl 494-H3 WrT
20th St 493-A3, B3, D4, F3, J3; 494-B3, F3 CTM; 491-K3; 492-A4 S; 492-E4, G4 WnT; 494-G3, J3; 495-B3, F3 WrT
21st Ave 528-C4 BG
21st Pl 496-C3 WrT
21st St 492-K3; 493-C3, D3, F3, J3; 494-C3 CTM; 496-F3 Cu; 491-G3; 492-A3 S; 492-H3; 490-A4 WaT; 490-K3; 491-G3; 492-E3, F3, G3 WnT; 494-K3; 495-H3; 496-A3, F3 WrT
21st St Annex 493-E3 CTM
22nd St 492-K3; 493-E3, J3; 494-C3, F3 CTM; 491-J3; 492-A3 S; 492-F3, H3 WnT; 494-G3, J3; 495-B3 WrT
23rd Ave 528-C4 BG
23rd St 492-K3; 493-C3, F3, H3, K2; 494-B3 CTM; 492-F3 WnT; 494-G2, J2 WrT
24th Ave 528-C4 BG
24th St 493-C2, E2, F2, J2; 494-A2 CTM; 492-A2 S; 494-H2, J2; 495-A2; 496-A2 WrT
25th Ave 528-C4, C5 BG; 528-C4 CTM; 528-C5 PeT
25th S 489-G9 A
25th St 492-K2; 493-C2, F2, G2; 494-B2 CTM; 491-H2, K2; 492-A2 S; 494-H2, K2; 495-A2, B2, H2, K2; 496-A2, D2 WrT
26th St 492-K2; 493-B2, C2; 494-C2, D2 CTM; 491-K2 S
26th St E 495-A2 WrT
27th St 492-K2; 493-A2, C2, E2, G2, J2, K2; 494-A2, B2 CTM; 494-H1, J1 WrT
28th St 492-K1; 493-A1, D1, G1, K1; 494-A1, D1 CTM; 492-B2 WnT; 494-H1, K1 WrT
29th Pl 491-H1, J1 S
29th St 492-K1; 493-C1, H1, K1; 494-A1, E1 CTM; 492-F1, G1 WnT
30th St 493-C1, H1; 494-A1, F1, G1 CTM; 491-G1, K1; 492-A1 S; 490-H1; 491-K1; 492-A1, G1 WnT; 494-F1, G1; 495-B1, J1; 496-A1, G1 WrT
31st St 460-A10, C10, E10, G10; 492-K1; 493-C1, D1, F1; 494-D1 CTM; 492-F1 WnT; 460-J10, K10 WrT
31st St Vac 492-F1 WnT
32nd Ct 461-A10 WrT
32nd Pl 457-G10, K10 WnT
32nd St 458-K10; 459-B10, C10, E10, F10, H10, J10, K10; 460-A10, C10, D10, E10 CTM; 457-K10; 458-A10, E10, F10 WnT; 460-G10, J10, K10; 461-B10, D10 WrT
33rd Pl 457-H10; 458-F10 WnT
33rd St 458-K10; 459-B10, D10, F10, J10; 460-A10, D10, E10, F10, G10 CTM; 461-C10 LTM; 458-A10, C10, F10 WnT; 460-H10, K10; 461-D10, F10, G10, J10; 462-B10 WrT
34th Pl 457-K10; 458-A10 WnT; 461-D10, E9, F9, G9 WrT
34th St 458-K10; 459-B10, D10, F10, K10; 460-A10 CTM; 461-C10 LTM; 457-D10, G10, J10; 458-A10, F10 WnT; 460-G10; 461-A10, E9, F9, G9, J9 WrT
35th Pl 457-G10 WnT; 461-F9, G9 WrT
35th St 458-K10; 459-B10, D9, E9, H9, J9; 460-B9, D9, F9 CTM; 457-G10, K10 WnT; 460-J9; 461-D9, F9, H9 WrT
35th Terr 458-A10 WnT
36th Ct 457-K9 WnT
36th Pl 461-F9, G9, K9; 462-A8 WrT
36th St 459-A10, D9, D10, G9, K9; 460-B9, F9 CTM; 457-K9; 458-A9, B9 WnT; 460-J9; 461-E9, J9 WrT
36th Terr 458-A9 WnT
37th Pl 461-E9, G8; 462-A8 WrT
37th St 459-A10, D9, E9, F9, G9, K9; 460-A9, D9 CTM; 457-G9; 458-B9, C9 WnT; 460-G9, J9; 461-D9, F9; 462-C8 WrT
38th Pl 461-J8 LTM
38th St 459-C8, H8; 460-A8 CTM; 462-B8, F8 LTM; 457-C9, J9; 458-A9 PTM; 458-G9; 459-C8, H8; 460-A8 WTM; 457-G9, J9; 458-A9 WnT; 460-H8; 461-F8; 462-B8, F8 WrT
38th St Dr N 460-G8, H8 LTM; 460-A8, B8, E8 WTM
39th Pl 461-J8, K8; 462-A8 LTM; 458-F8 WTM
39th St 460-F8, H8, K8; 461-D8, K8; 462-A8 LTM; 458-F8, H8; 459-C8, D8, E8, G8, K8; 460-A8, C8, D8, E8, F8 WTM
40 & 8 Ave DN-D2; 493-F6 CTM
40th Pl 461-G8 LTM
40th St 460-H8; 461-A8, K8 LTM; 459-C8, G8; 460-A8, E8, F8, G8 WTM
40th St Dr N 460-E8 WTM
40th St Dr S 460-E8 WTM
41st Pl 461-G7, H7 LTM; 457-H8 PTM
41st St 460-H7, K8; 461-G7, K7 LTM; 458-J8; 459-C8, E8, F8; 460-D7, F7 WTM
42nd Pl 461-G7 LTM
42nd St 461-C7, F7 L; 460-G7; 461-A7, B7, F7, K7; 462-B7, F7 LTM; 456-J8; 457-J7; 458-E7 PTM; 458-G8, J8; 459-B7, E7, G7, J7; 460-B7, C7 WTM
43rd Ct 460-K7 LTM
43rd Pl 461-A7, B7 LTM
43rd St 461-C7 L; 460-H7, K7; 461-K7 LTM; 457-J7 PTM; 458-E7, F7, K7; 460-C7 WTM
43rd Terr 458-D7 PTM
44th Pl 461-A7 LTM
44th St 460-J7; 461-K7 LTM; 458-G7, J7; 459-B7, F7, G7, J7; 460-A7 WTM
44th Terr 458-E7 PTM
45th St 461-C6, E6, F6, H6 L; 460-J6; 461-B6, C6 LTM; 459-E6, F6, J6; 460-A6, B6 WTM
45th Terr 458-D7 PTM
46th St 461-F6, H6; 462-B6, F6 L; 460-J6; 462-F6 LTM; 456-J7; 457-D6, J6; 458-E6 PTM; 458-F6, J6; 459-D6, F6; 460-A6 WTM
47th St 461-B6, C6, E6, G6 L; 458-B6, C6 PTM; 459-D6, F6, G6, J6; 460-A6, B6 WTM
48th St 461-C6, D6, E5, F5, G6 L; 458-D6, E6 PTM; 458-G6; 459-E6, F6; 460-C6 WTM
49th St 461-B5, D5, E5, G5 L; 458-D6 PTM; 458-F6; 459-D6, J6; 460-A6 WTM
50 S 489-A10 WaT
50th Pl 461-A5 LTM
50th St 461-D5, E5, F5 L; 458-E5 PTM; 458-E5; 459-F6; 460-C5 WTM
51st Dr N 457-J6 PTM
51st Dr S 457-J6 PTM
51st St 461-D5, E5 L; 457-J6 PTM; 458-F5, J5; 459-F5, J5; 460-A5, C5 WTM
52nd Pl 461-C5 L; 460-K5; 461-A5, B5 LTM
52nd St 461-A5, D5, F5, K5; 462-B5, E5 L; 461-A5 LTM; 456-H5; 457-H5; 458-A5, C5, E5 PTM; 458-G5; 459-A5, B5, E5; 460-B5 WTM
53rd Pl 461-E5 L
53rd St 461-D5, E4 L; 457-K5 PTM; 458-J5; 459-B5, F5, J5; 460-A5 WTM
54th Pl 461-B4, E4 L; 460-K4; 461-B4 LTM
54th St 461-D4 L; 460-J4 LTM; 458-E5 PTM; 458-E5, K4; 459-B4, C5, E4, J4; 460-A4 WTM
55th Pl 461-A4 LTM; 460-A4 WTM
55th St 461-D4 L; 458-E4 PTM; 459-E4, G4, J4; 460-A4, C4, F4 WTM
56th St 455-G4 B; 461-D4, J4; 462-A4, F3 L; 460-G4 LTM; 456-H4; 457-A4, H4; 458-A4, E4 PTM; 458-E4, K4; 459-E4, G4, H4; 460-A4, B4, G4 WTM
57th St 458-A4, B4, E4 PTM; 458-F4, J3; 459-E3, G3, H3, K3; 460-A3, C3, D3 WTM
58th St 458-E3 PTM; 458-F3, H3, K3; 459-B3, E3, F3, G3, H3, K3; 460-A3, B3, D3 WTM
59th Pl 459-K2; 460-A2 WTM
59th St 461-J2; 462-B2, F2 L; 457-K3; 458-B3 PTM; 458-H3, K3; 459-E3 WTM
60th St 458-F3 PTM; 458-F3, J3; 459-G2, H2 WTM
61st Pl 459-K2; 460-A2 WTM
61st St 458-E2 PTM; 458-F2, J2; 459-E2, G2, J2; 460-C2, E2 WTM; 458-H2 WnT
62nd Pl 460-J2, K1 LTM; 458-E2 PTM; 458-E2; 459-G2 WTM
62nd St 455-C2 BTH; 462-H1 L; 457-C2, F2; 458-C2 PTM; 458-J2; 459-C2, E2, G2, H2, J1; 460-A1, H1 WTM
62nd St W 457-H2 PTM
63rd Pl 459-G1 WTM
63rd St 461-H1; 462-C1 L; 458-H1, K1; 459-B1, C1, F1; 460-A1 WTM
64th St 428-G10 L; 458-H1 PTM; 458-H1, K1; 459-C1, D1, F1, K1; 460-B1, E1, F1 WTM
64th St Dr S 459-K1 WTM
65th Pl 427-A10 LTM; 424-K10; 426-K10 WTM
65th St 456-H1 BTH; 428-H10, J10 L; 427-B10, D10 LTM; 424-H10; 457-C1 PTM; 424-H10; 425-D10, E10, K10; 426-A10, D10, H10; 459-C1, G1 WTM
66th St 424-G10 PTM; 424-J10; 425-G10, K10; 426-A10, B10, F10 WTM
67th Ct 426-C10 WTM
67th St 424-H10 PTM; 424-H10; 425-G10, J10; 426-B10, F10 WTM
68th Ct 426-C10 WTM
68th St 425-H10, K10; 426-A10, G10 WTM
69th St 424-D10, G10 PTM; 425-K10; 426-A10, C10, G10 WTM
70th St 425-C9, D9, E10; 426-A9, F9 WTM
71st St 427-K9; 428-H9 L; 427-D9, E9, K9 LTM; 423-D10, H9; 424-A9 PTM; 425-F9, H9, J9; 426-A9, J9 WTM
72nd Ct 426-G9 WTM
72nd Pl 424-K9; 426-G9, H9 WTM
72nd St 424-B9 PTM; 424-K9; 425-B9, C9, E9, F9, H9, J9; 426-A9, B9, F9, H9, J9 WTM
73rd Ct 426-H8 WTM
73rd Pl 424-K9 WTM
73rd St 423-H9; 424-B9 PTM; 425-E8, E9, G9, J8; 426-E8 WTM
74th Ct 426-G8 WTM
74th Pl 424-K8; 426-G8, H8 WTM
74th St 423-H8; 424-B9 PTM; 425-D8, H8, J8; 426-A8 WTM; 424-J8 WTN
75 Rd E 596-G5 G
75th Ct Terr 425-A8 WTM
75th Pl 424-J8, K8; 425-K8 WTM
75th Rd E 596-G5 PTJ
75th Rd N 489-A7 WaT
75th Rd W 596-G9, B10 PTJ
75th St 428-C8, J8 L; 427-A8, F8 LTM; 424-F8 PTM; 425-B8, E8, H8, J8; 426-A8, D8 WTM
76th Pl 424-K8; 425-A8 WTM
76th St 423-J8; 424-A8, G8 PTM; 424-J8; 425-H7; 426-C8 WTM
76th St Ct 426-G8 WTM
77th St 428-D7 L; 427-C7 LTM; 424-F8 PTM; 425-C7, D7, E8, F7, J7; 426-D8, F8, G8, H7 WTM
77th St Dr N 425-B7, C7 WTM
77th St Dr S 425-B8, C8 WTM
77th St E 425-D8 WTM
78th Pl 426-H7 WTM
78th St 423-K7; 424-A7, G7 PTM; 425-A7, G7; 426-A7, D7, F7 WTM
79th St 428-H7 L; 428-B7 LTM; 423-C7, H7; 424-A7 PTM; 424-G7; 425-C7, E7, G7, H7; 426-A7, D7, H7 WTM
80th St 427-E6 LTM; 423-H7; 424-C7 PTM; 424-K6; 425-E6, G6, H6, J6; 426-A6, F7 WTM
81st Pl 424-B6 PTM
81st St 422-J6; 423-J6; 424-A6 PTM; 425-A6, D6, G6, J6; 426-H6 WTM
82nd Pl 427-G6 LTM
82nd St 426-E5; 427-B6, J6; 428-A6 LTM; 422-J6; 423-B6, H6; 424-F6 PTM; 425-D6, F5, H6; 426-E5 WTM
83rd Pl 425-D5 WTM
83rd St 425-C5, G5, J5 WTM
84th St 423-A5, J5; 424-A5, B5 PTM; 425-D5, F5, G5 WTM
85th Pl 427-G5 LTM
85th St 423-A5, H5 PTM; 425-G5 WTM
86th St 428-H4 L; 427-D4, J4; 428-A4, H4 LTM; 422-H5; 423-C5, H5; 424-A5 PTM; 424-H5; 425-C4, H4; 426-A4, G4, J4 WTM
87th St 427-D4 LTM; 423-A5 PTM; 425-E4, G4, J4 WTM
88th Pl 427-E4 LTM
88th St 427-E4 LTM; 422-K4; 423-C4 PTM; 425-E4, J4, K4; 426-A4 WTM
89th St 427-E4 LTM
90th Pl 425-J4 WTM
90th St 427-D4 LTM; 425-H4, J4 WTM
91 Rd N 489-D6 A
91st Rd N 489-D6 WaT
91st St 427-B3 LTM; 425-C3, F3, J3; 426-A3, K3 WTM
92nd St 423-C4; 424-D3 PTM; 425-C3, D3 WTM
93rd St 423-C3; 424-C3 PTM; 425-C3, F3, G3 WTM
94th St 424-C3 PTM; 426-B3 WTM
95th St 425-F2 WTM
96th Pl 427-A2 LTM
96th St 424-H2; 426-C2 CTH; 425-F2; 426-C2 Ca; 427-B2; 428-A2 DTH; 422-K3; 423-G3; 424-A2 ET; 427-B2, J2 F; 429-B2, J2 FCT; 427-B2, J2 LTM; 429-B2 McC; 422-K3; 423-G3; 424-A2 PTM; 424-H2; 425-J2; 426-C2 WTM
97th St 424-D2 CTH; 428-D2 FCT
98th St 424-D2; 425-K2; 426-A2, B2 CTH; 426-D2 Ca; 427-A2 DTH; 428-D2 FCT
99th St 425-K1; 426-A1 CTH
100 Rd E 596-G7 PTJ
100 Rd N 489-F6 A; 497-B3, G3 BCT; 356-A1 UT; 489-A6, F6; 490-A6 WaT
100 Rd S 523-J1; 524-A1 A; 496-K7; 497-C7, H7 SCT; 523-B1, J1; 524-A1 WaT
101st St 425-K1 CTH; 429-K1 FCT
101st St E 425-G1 WTM
102nd St 425-F1 CTH
103rd St 425-D1 CTH; 425-D1, E1 Ca
104th St 391-H10; 392-C10 CTH; 395-D10, H10 FCT
105th St 391-H10 CTH
106th Pl 392-D10 Ca
106th St 393-A10, D10, H10 DTH; 393-A10, D10, H10; 394-C10, F10 F; 394-F10 FCT
106th St E 391-F10; 392-A10, F10 CTH; 391-F10; 392-A10 Ca
106th St W 390-C10; 391-B10 CTH; 391-B10 Ca; 389-J10 ET
107th St 391-D10, F10, G10 CTH
108th St 391-G9 CTH; 393-C9 DTH; 393-G9 F
109th St 392-A9 CTH
110th St 391-G9, K9; 392-A9 CTH
110th St E 391-K9 CTH
111th St 393-C8 DTH; 393-C8; 394-F9 F
111th St E 391-E9, J9 CTH; 391-E9 Ca
113th St 395-D8, J8 FCT
114th St 391-F8 CTH
115th St 391-F8 CTH; 393-F8 F
116th St 391-H7; 392-B7, J7 CTH; 391-H7; 392-B7, J7 Ca; 393-A8, F8 DTH; 393-A8, G7; 394-A7; 395-A7 F; 394-A7; 395-A7, D7 FCT
116th St W 390-C8; 391-B8 CTH
117th St 391-G7 Ca; 395-D7 FCT
118th St 395-C7 FCT
121 N 489-C6 WaT
121st St 393-H6 DTH
121st St E 394-C6 F; 394-C6 FCT
121st St W 390-D6 CTH; 390-A7 ET
122nd St 393-A6 CTH; 391-F6; 393-A6 Ca
125 Rd E 596-H5 G; 596-H5, H10 PTJ; 596-H10 Whl
125 Rd W 595-K10 PTJ
126th St 392-K5 CTH; 391-E5, H5, J5; 392-K5 Ca; 393-F5 DTH; 393-F5; 394-B5, J5 F; 394-B5, J5; 395-E5, K5 FCT
126th St W 390-B5, F5 CTH
131st St 393-G4 DTH; 390-A4 ET; 393-G4; 394-B4 F; 394-G4, J4 FCT
131st St E 392-C4, J4 Ca

131st St W 390-B4, F4; 391-B4 CTH
132nd St 393-F3 DTH
133rd St 393-J3 F
136th St 391-J3; 392-B3 CTH; 391-J3; 392-B3 Ca; 395-C3 F; 394-F3; 395-A2, G2 FCT
136th St W 390-D3, J3 CTH; 391-E3 Ca
138th St 390-B2 CTH
141st St 393-G2 DTH; 393-G2; 394-A2 F; 394-F1; 395-D1 FCT; 393-G2; 394-A2 N
141st St W 390-C2; 391-B2 CTH
146th St E 359-E10 CTH; 358-A10, G10 Ca; 359-E10 DTH; 361-A10, H10 FCT; 358-G10; 360-A10 N; 358-G10; 359-E10 NT; 357-K10; 358-A10 WTH; 361-A10, H10 WyT
146th St W 390-C1, H1; 391-A1, F1 CTH; 391-F1 Ca; 357-K10; 390-C1, H1; 391-A1, F1 WTH
147th Pl 359-H10 NT
147th St E 358-A10 WTH
150 Rd N 496-K2; 497-G2 BCT; 489-A5 WaT
150 Rd S 523-F2 A; 523-F2 WaT
150 Rd W 595-J4 G
151 Rd N 489-F4 WaT
151st St E 357-K9; 358-A9, E9 WTH
151st St W 356-E9, K9; 357-J9 WTH
156th St E 358-G8 N; 358-G8; 360-F8 NT; 360-F8; 361-F8 WyT
156th St W 356-B8, J8; 357-G8 WTH
159th St W 356-F8 WTH
160th St 359-E7 NT
161st St E 358-K7 NT; 358-A7 WTH
161st St W 356-J7; 357-G7 WTH
166th St E 360-B6 N; 360-B6 NT; 360-K6 WyT
166th St W 356-B6, J6 WTH
169th St 357-J5 W
169th St E 358-H5 NT; 358-C5 WTH; 361-K5 WyT
169th St W 357-B5, F5 WTH
171st St 359-B5 N; 359-B5 NT; 357-K5 W; 357-K5; 358-A5 WTH
175th St 357-F4 WTH
176th St E 358-C4 WTH; 361-H3 WyT
179th St E 361-B3 WyT
181st St E 360-F2 NT; 360-F2 WyT
181st St W 357-G2 W; 357-G2 WTH
186th St E 360-B1 N; 360-B1 NT; 358-A1, E1 WTH; 361-A1, J1 WyT
186th St W 356-B1; 357-D1 WTH
191st St E 324-G10; 325-K10; 326-B10 N; 324-G10; 325-K10; 326-B10 NT; 323-J10; 324-A10 W; 323-D10, J10; 324-A10 WTH; 326-H10; 327-G10 WyT
192nd St E 325-K10 NT
193rd St W 322-D10; 323-C10 WTH
194th St 325-K9 N
196th St E 325-E9; 326-F9 N; 325-E9; 326-F9 NT; 323-J9; 324-A9, D9 WTH; 326-F9; 327-G9 WyT
196th St W 322-B9 WTH
199th St W 323-F8 WTH
200 Rd E 596-K5 G; 596-K5, K9; 597-A6 PTJ
200 Rd N 463-A10, G10; 496-J1; 497-B1 BCT; 322-A9 MTB; 322-A9; 325-A8 UT; 489-A4, D3, H4; 490-A4 WaT
200 Rd S 523-K3 A; 524-A3 P; 496-H10; 497-H9 SCT; 523-A3, K3; 524-A3, G3 WaT
200 Rd W 595-H4 G; 595-H7, H10 PTJ; 595-H7, H10 WTJ
201st St E 327-C8 WyT
202nd St E 323-K7; 324-A7 WTH
203rd St W 323-J7 WTH
205th St 327-C7 WyT
206th St E 325-F7; 326-A7, C6, F6 NT; 326-F6; 327-G6 WyT
206th St W 322-B7; 323-C7 WTH
209th St E 325-E6 N
211th St 324-F5 NT
211th St E 324-J5 N; 325-A5, F5; 326-C5, G5 NT; 326-G5; 327-G5 WyT
211th St W 322-H6 WTH
214th St 323-F5 WTH
216th St E 323-J4 AT; 324-A4, H4; 325-F4 JT; 324-H4 N; 324-H4; 325-F4; 326-G4 NT; 326-G4; 327-D4, J4 WRT; 324-A4 WTH; 326-G4; 327-D4, J4 WyT
216th St W 322-B4; 323-C4 AT; 322-B4; 323-C4 WTH
220th St E 325-A4 JT
221st St E 325-J3; 326-A3 JT; 326-D3 WRT
221st St W 322-H3; 323-C3 AT
225 Rd E 597-A2 PTJ
225th St E 324-F3 JT
226th St E 323-D2, J2 AT; 324-A2, J2; 325-C2, J2; 326-A2 JT; 326-A2, K2; 327-G2 WRT
226th St W 322-B2; 323-B2 AT
231st St E 323-E1 AT; 324-F1; 325-B1 JT
250 Rd E 563-B10; 597-B1, B5, B7 PTJ
251 Rd S 523-D5; 524-G4 WaT
275 Rd N 599-A10 STS
300 Rd 462-H8 BCT
300 Rd E 597-C2, C10 CTJ; 563-C10; 597-C2, C10 PTJ
300 Rd N 463-H8 BCT; 489-F1, H1; 490-A1 LTH; 322-A7 MTB; 599-E10 STS
300 Rd S 389-H1; 390-A1 ET; 523-D5 GT; 524-A5 P; 530-J2; 531-H2 SCT; 389-H1; 390-A1 UT; 388-A1, G1 WTB; 523-D5; 524-A5 WaT
325 Rd E 597-D5 CTJ; 597-A10 PTJ
350 Rd N 462-H7; 463-B7 BCT; 455-A10; 489-E1 LTH
350 Rd S 389-B2 ET; 523-A7 GT
375 Rd E 597-F4 CTJ
375 Rd N 322-A5 MTB
375 Rd S 389-D3 ET
400 Rd E 563-F10; 597-F2, G9 CTJ
400 Rd N 455-J9 B; 463-B6, J6 BCT; 455-J9; 456-A9 LTH; 322-A5 MTB; 598-H7; 599-A7, H7 STS
400 Rd S 388-J3; 389-B3 ET; 531-J4 SCT; 388-C3, F3, J3 WTB
400 Rd W 463-K4, K10; 497-K2 BCT; 497-K9; 531-K2, K6 SCT; 429-J4, J10; 463-J1 VT; 561-B10; 595-B2, B3, B5, B10 WTJ
425 Rd N 455-F9 B; 455-F9 LTH
425 Rd S 388-G3 WTB
425 Rd W 497-J10; 531-J1 SCT
440 Rd E 563-H10; 597-G6, H2 CTJ
450 Rd N 455-A8; 456-F8 LTH
450 Rd S 524-A9, F9 GT; 524-A9, F9 P; 388-A4 WTB
450 Rd W 531-J2, J6 SCT; 594-K5 WTJ
500 Rd E 597-J10 CTJ; 388-A2, A4 WTB
500 Rd N 462-K3; 463-H3 BCT; 322-A2 MTB; 599-C5, H5 STS
500 Rd S 388-B6; 390-A5 ET; 388-B6 PTB; 388-B6 WTB
500 Rd W 463-G4, G10 BCT; 599-K3 BTS; 531-K10; 565-K3, K10 MTS; 497-G10; 531-G1, G6 SCT; 599-K3 STS; 429-F5, G10; 463-G1 VT; 560-J9; 594-J3, J9 WTJ
525 Rd E 563-K10; 597-K2 CTJ; 557-A6 GT; 388-A10; 422-A1 PTB; 489-A10; 523-A2 WaT
525 Rd N 598-H4; 599-A4 STS
525 Rd S 388-E6 ET
525 Rd W 497-F2 BCT; 497-F6 SCT; 599-K7 STS
550 Rd E 598-A7 CTJ; 455-B4 LTH
550 Rd N 455-A6 LTH
550 Rd S 388-B7, G7; 389-A7, J7; 390-A7 ET; 388-B7 PTB; 389-J7 Z
550 Rd W 531-F5 SCT; 599-J5, J10 STS; 594-G5 WTJ
550th E 489-B9 WaT
571 E 489-C8 WaT
575 E 489-C9 WaT
575 Rd E 598-A10 CTJ; 557-C8 GT; 455-B10; 489-C1 LTH; 388-C2, C5 WTB
575 Rd N 597-G10 CTJ
600 Rd E 564-B10; 598-B3, B6 CTJ; 523-D9; 557-D1, D5 GT; 455-C6; 489-D2 LTH; 593-A4 MTM; 523-D9; 557-D1 P; 489-C4, C6 WaT
600 Rd N 455-H4 B; 463-A1, H1 BCT; 597-D10, J10; 598-A10 CTJ; 456-C4 LTH; 598-H3; 599-D3 MTS; 596-B10 NW; 595-H10; 596-B10, H10 PTJ; 598-H3; 599-D3 STS; 463-A1, H1 VT; 594-J10; 595-F10 WTJ; 596-H10 Whl
600 Rd S 389-C7 ET; 531-A9 MTS; 531-A9, H9 SCT
600 Rd W 463-D6, D10; 497-D2 BCT; 531-G10; 565-G3, G9, G10; 599-G1 MTS; 497-D10; 531-D1, D8 SCT; 599-G3 STS; 429-C10; 463-C1 VT; 594-F5, F10 WTJ
625 Rd E 489-D9 A; 455-D4 B; 455-D4 BTH; 455-D4 LTH; 489-D9; 523-D3 WaT
650 Rd E 455-E2 BTH; 598-C3 CTJ; 388-E8, E10; 422-E1 ET; 557-E9 GT; 388-E4 WTB
650 Rd N 456-E3 BTH; 598-D9 CTJ; 429-A10 VT; 594-A10, E9, H9 WTJ
650 Rd S 388-E9 ET; 388-A9 PTB
650 Rd W 531-F10; 565-F1, F8 MTS; 531-C4 SCT
670 Rd E 598-D7, D9, D10 CTJ
671st E 489-F8 A
675 Rd E 557-F6 GT
675 Rd S 557-F5 GT
675 Rd W 565-E6 MTS; 531-B8 SCT
700 Rd E 564-E10; 598-E3, E6 CTJ; 388-G7, G9 ET; 523-G10; 557-F1 P; 388-G1, G5 WTB
700 Rd N 455-F2 B; 455-B2, F2; 456-C2 BTH; 597-D8, H7; 598-A7, F7 CTJ; 596-D8 G; 599-D1, H1 MTS; 596-D8 PTJ; 429-D9, J9 VT; 594-C8, J8; 595-F8 WTJ
700 Rd S 388-H10; 389-D10, J10; 390-A10 ET; 557-D5; 558-E5 GT
700 Rd W 463-A4, A10; 497-A3 BCT; 531-D9; 565-D2, D6, D10; 598-K1; 599-D3 MTS; 429-A2 McC; 497-A10; 531-A1, A5 SCT
701 Rd E 557-G8 GT
725 Rd E 557-H5 GT
725th St E 456-A1 BTH
750 Rd E 598-G6, G10 CTJ
750 Rd N 456-A1, F1 BTH; 596-A7 G; 429-A8 McC; 596-A7, H7 PTJ; 456-F1 PTM; 595-F7 WTJ
750 Rd S 422-D2 ET; 557-C6; 558-B6 GT; 422-A1 PTB
750 Rd W 565-C9 MTS
775 Rd E 388-J10; 422-J2 ET; 388-H4, J1 WTB
775 Rd N 597-F6 CTJ; 595-J6; 596-A6 PTJ
800 E 489-J2 LTH
800 Rd E 523-K5 A; 455-J2 BTH; 388-K3, K8 ET; 388-K3 WTB; 523-K5 WaT
800 Rd N 597-D5 CTJ; 564-H8, K8; 565-A8, E8, H8 MTS; 429-A7 McC; 429-F7 VT; 594-E6; 595-B6 WTJ
800 Rd S 557-B7; 558-E7 GT
800 Rd W 531-A10; 565-A1, A3, A10; 599-A1 MTS
801 Rd S 558-A7 GT
821 Rd S 558-A7 GT
825 Rd S 557-F8 GT
825 Rd W 598-K3, K5, K10 STS
840 Rd E 559-G10; 593-G1 MTM
850 Rd E 389-A10 ET; 593-G6, G9 MTM
850 Rd N 595-H4; 596-H4 G; 597-A4 PTJ; 595-B5, F5, H4 WTJ
850 Rd W 564-K2, K4, K7 MTS
851 Rd S 558-A8 GT
870 Rd N 594-H4 WTJ
875 Rd E 389-B5, B7 ET; 558-A5, B4 GT
875 Rd N 422-A8 BTH
875 Rd S 557-A9 GT
875 Rd W 564-J10; 598-J3 MTS; 598-J3 STS
900 Rd E 490-C10 A; 422-B3, B10; 456-B1 BTH; 456-B1, B8 LTH; 490-B5, C8; 524-C1, C4 WaT
900 Rd N 598-E3 CTJ; 595-H4 G; 565-E6 MTS; 429-A4 McC; 429-E4, J4 VT; 594-D4, G4; 595-B4 WTJ
925 Rd E 422-C7 BTH; 558-C9 GT
925 Rd N 593-A10 MTM
940 Rd N 564-H5 MTS
950 Rd E 422-D3 BTH; 456-D9; 490-D1 LTH
950 Rd N 422-C6, G6 BTH; 598-C2 CTJ; 595-G2; 596-H2 G; 565-A5, K5 MTS; 595-G2 WTJ
975 Rd E 389-E6 ET; 558-E7 GT; 389-E6 Z
1000 Rd E 422-E3; 456-D1, D2 BTH; 456-D2, E8; 490-E3 LTH; 490-E3 WaT
1000 Rd N 422-A5, F5 BTH; 597-G1; 598-A1, F1 CTJ; 565-E4 MTS; 597-B1 PTJ; 594-F1, G1; 595-C1 WTJ
1025 E 456-F2 BTH
1025 Rd E 422-F3 BTH; 558-F8, F9 GT
1050 Rd E 422-G8 BTH; 524-G10; 558-G2, G6 GT; 524-G10 P; 490-G6, G8, G10; 524-G3 WaT
1050 Rd N 563-F10, K10; 564-B10 CTJ; 565-H2 MTS
1075 Rd E 422-H5, H6 BTH
1075 Rd N 564-F9 CTJ
1100 Rd N 593-B6 MTM; 564-J1; 565-E1 MTS
1150 Rd N 593-F5 MTM
1250 Rd N 593-E3 MTM
1300 Rd N 593-F1, J1 MTM

ROUTE NUMBERS

I 65 422-G3 BTH; DN-D1, E4, F2; 458-J9; 493-D4, H6, H10; 527-J4 CTM; 422-G3 ET; 596-J3 G; 338-C8 PTB; 562-J10; 596-J3; 597-A9 PTJ; 422-G3; 423-C9; 457-E1, J5; 458-A6 PTM; 528-B6, D10; 562-D2 PeT
I 69 393-J8; 394-A6, K3; 427-G1 F; 395-K2 FCT; 427-C6 LTM
I 70 463-B10, K9; 496-K1 BCT; DN-B4, E4, F2; 493-A10, G10, H7, K4; 494-E3 CTM; 525-A9, J6; 558-C3 DTM; 557-B8, K4; 558-C3 GT; 558-C3 P; 492-F10; 525-J6; 526-C1 WnT; 495-B2, K2; 496-D2 WrT
I 74 455-E2 B; 528-H8 BG; 455-E2 BTH; 525-H7; 526-C10 DTM; 528-H8; 529-H5; 530-B9; 564-G3 FT; 455-E2 LTH; 565-E8; 599-K1 MTS; 456-J8; 457-B9 PTM; 527-D8 PeT; 457-B9; 491-E1, H9; 525-H2 WnT; 529-B3 WrT
I 465 528-J8 BG; 425-H2 CTH; 525-H8; 526-C10 DTM; 422-J1; 423-K2 ET; 528-J8 FT; 427-C9; 461-C1 LTM; 423-G7; 424-A3; 457-F8, G1 PTM; 527-D8 PeT; 424-A3; 426-A3 WTM; 457-F8; 491-G3, H9; 525-H2 WnT; 461-E10; 495-F1, F9; 529-E1 WrT
IN 19 325-H1 C; 359-H2 N; 325-H10 NT
IN 31 461-C2 LTM
IN 32 359-K3; 360-A3 N; 359-A4; 360-G3 NT; 356-A4 UT; 356-H4; 357-G4; 358-C4 WTH; 327-K10; 361-H1 WyT
IN 37 528-J8 BG; 527-K8 CTM; 393-H9 DTH; 393-K6; 427-G1 F; 528-J8; 529-B6 FT; 427-C6, C10 LTM; 326-B10; 359-K9; 360-A7, B1; 393-K1 N; 326-B10, F6; 359-K9; 360-A7, B1 NT; 526-K10; 527-E8; 560-J1 PeT; 326-J1 WRT; 560-G9; 594-A10, D5, G1 WTJ
IN 38 322-J1 AT; 325-A10; 359-C1, K3; 360-A3 N; 360-G4 NT; 323-H5; 324-A6 WTH; 361-H6 WyT
IN 67 558-D10; 592-D1 BTM; 525-H9; 558-K5; 559-F1 DTM; 558-D10 GT; 461-J6; 462-D3 L; 592-A4, D1 M; 429-A8 McC; 429-A8, K4 VT
IN 134 491-D2 WnT
IN 135 561-E10; 595-E1 G; 527-E10, F5, F10; 561-E1 PeT; 595-E5, E9 WTJ
IN 136 491-E2 WnT
IN 144 593-K10 HT; 592-B3 M; 593-D9 MTM; 594-A10 WTJ
IN 234 429-E7, K7 VT
IN 238 395-A1, K6 FCT; 360-A7 NT; 360-K10 WyT
IN 267 489-D10; 523-F1 A; 455-F10 B; 455-H1 BTH; 557-J10 BTM; 523-F7; 524-A8; 557-J10, K6; 558-A1, A6 GT; 455-F10; 489-F1 LTH; 557-J10 M; 523-F7, K7; 524-A8; 558-A1 P; 489-F6; 523-F1 WaT
IN 334 388-E9; 389-A9, K8 ET; 389-K8; 390-A8 Z
IN 431 391-K1; 392-A2, B9 CTH; 391-K1; 392-A2, B9; 426-B1 Ca; 426-B1 WnT
US 31 323-K1 AT; 528-J8 BG; 391-K1 CTH; 527-K8 CTM; 391-E4, E10, K1; 425-E1 Ca; 528-J8; 529-B6 FT; 562-A10; 596-B2, E8 G; 323-K1 JT; 427-C10 LTM; 596-E8 NW; 596-E8 PTJ; 527-G10; 561-G1, K9 PeT; 323-K10; 357-K1 W; 323-K10; 357-K1, K9 WTH; 425-E9 WTM; 596-E8 Whl
US 36 489-H8 A; 528-J8 BG; 525-H8; 526-D10 DTM; 528-J8 FT; 461-H6; 462-D3 L; 429-A8 McC; 527-D8 PeT; 429-A8, K4 VT; 489-B9; 490-B8 WaT; 491-B8, H10; 525-H2 WnT; 461-E10; 495-F1, F9; 529-D2 WrT
US 37 461-C2 LTM
US 40 528-J8 BG; 496-J6 Cu; 525-H8; 526-D10 DTM; 528-J8 FT; 523-A10 GT; 523-J7; 524-B6 P; 527-D8 PeT; 496-J6; 497-H6 SCT; 524-B6 WaT; 524-B6; 525-A3, G1, H2 WnT; 495-F9, H7; 496-A7; 529-D2 WrT
US 52 422-K1; 423-C2 ET; 427-C10; 461-C1 LTM; 388-C8 PTB; 423-K2; 424-B3 PTM; 531-B4, K6 SCT; 424-B3; 426-F4 WTM; 495-F10; 529-H1; 530-B2 WrT
US 136 455-K7 B; 455-C4; 456-A7 LTH; 456-K10 WnT
US 421 390-C10; 424-C1; 425-H2 CTH; 389-J2; 390-A6 ET; 529-H5; 530-B9; 564-G3 FT; 427-C9; 461-C1 LTM; 565-E8; 599-K1 MTS; 424-C1 PTM; 426-A3 WTM; 461-E10; 495-F1, F10; 529-D2 WrT

PLACE NAMES

A

A View Farm 427-K6 LTM
Achgillis 560-G10 WTJ
Acton 564-F6 FT
Acton Hgts 564-E5 FT
Adams Twp 323-A3 AT
Admirals Bay 428-K4 LTM
Admirals Cove 428-F7 L
Admirals Landing 428-H5 L
Admirals Pointe 428-H3 LTM
Admirals Sound 428-G4 LTM
Admirals Woods 428-H4 LTM
Agerter 459-G4 WTM
Ahlerings 492-C9 WnT
Airesworth 526-A3 WnT
Airslie 459-K10 CTM
Alamo Terr 495-E6 WrT
Alans Acres 564-E4 FT
Alcove at Greenbriar 425-B5 WTM
Alexander Hgts 492-E9 WnT
Allangale Woods 530-E10 FT
Allen & Sellers 461-E7 L
Allenby 527-G4 CTM
Allens Acres 389-B2 ET
Allison Hgts 460-C4 WTM
Allisonville 426-G6 WTM
Allisonville Ests 426-F10 WTM
Alpha Tau 457-G3 WTH
Alton Pl 492-F5 WnT
Alton Terr 492-E5 WnT
Alverna Ests 425-C6 WTM
Ambassador Park South 561-D5 PeT
Ambleside 459-F5 WTM
Amli at Conner Farms 393-C8 F
Anchorage 491-F5 WnT
Anchorage Pt 491-H5 WnT
Andorra Park 492-E5 WnT
Andre Hgts 561-E1 PeT
Andrews Manor 524-A2 WaT
Ansar Vill 458-C7 PTM
Apple Creek 523-D2 WaT
Arbordale Highlands 458-E8 PTM
Arden 425-F10 WTM
Ardmore 459-G8 WTM
Arlington Acres 528-H10 FT
Arlington Commons 529-A8 FT
Arlington Ests 495-A10 WrT
Arlington Hgts 494-J4 WrT
Arlington Manor 494-J3; 529-A4 WrT
Arlington Meadows 528-J8 FT
Arlington Park 460-J5 LTM
Arlington Ridge 460-J5 LTM
Arlington Woods 460-J10 WrT
Armstrong Park 459-A10 CTM
Arrowhead Ests 426-F8 WTM
Arrowhead MHP 531-K3 SCT
Arsenal Hgts 494-A6 CTM
Arsenal Park DN-F2; 493-J7 CTM
Ashford Ests 524-E1 WaT
Ashford Pointe 395-D8 FCT
Ashmore Trace 392-J1 Ca
Ashton 392-H1 Ca; 490-F6 WaT
Ashwood 455-B7 L; 394-D3 F
Aspen Ridge 457-D10 WnT
Atrium Vill 496-A1 WrT
Atwell Acres 461-B6 L
Auburn 492-B10 WnT
Auburn Meadows 523-F4 WaT
Auburn Springs 394-C2 F
Audubon Gdns 460-J9 WrT
Audubon Road Hgts 494-J5 WrT
Audubon Terr 460-K9 WrT
August Pl 529-H6 FT
Augusta 424-F8 PTM
Augusta Green 424-B9 PTM
Augusta Hgts 424-F7 PTM
Augusta Way 458-K1 WTM
Austin Lakes 489-K7 A; 490-A7 WaT
Austin Meadows 455-J5 B
Austin Oaks 390-A5 ET
Autumn Ridge 496-F10 WrT
Avalon Ests 427-A9 LTM
Avalon Hills 427-B10; 460-K2 LTM
Avalon Meadows 427-C9 LTM
Avalon Trails 427-B9 LTM
Avenue Park 528-A2 CTM
Avery Woods Ests 424-B6 PTM
Avian Glen 392-H2 Ca
Avon 489-G9; 490-A8, D9; 523-G1; 524-D1 A
Avon Creek Ests 490-H10 WnT
Avon Ests 523-E3 WaT
Avon Hgts 489-G8 A
Avon North 489-F8 A
Avon Vill Tr Park 490-E8 WaT
Avon Woods 489-F9 A
Avondale 459-D9 CTM; 460-H2 LTM
Avondale Hgts 489-B8 WaT; 492-B10 WnT
Ayrshire 458-K6 WTM

B

Backbay 428-E6 LTM
Bailey Highlands 525-D2 WnT
Baileys Urban 526-A1 WnT
Baileys Westwood Park 424-E7 PTM
Baird Ests 495-J8 WrT
Bakers Walnut Grove 491-J4 S
Ballinshire 457-B6 PTM
Balmers 491-F6 WnT
Banta Ranch 562-B3 PeT
Banta Trails 561-F2 PeT
Bantas Southwood 561-G2 PeT
Barrington Hgts 528-A1 CTM
Barrington Manor 528-B2 CTM
Barrington Ridge 393-C7 F
Bartons 492-C9 WnT
Bay Colony 456-K4 PTM
Bay Forest Ests 428-E6 LTM
Bay Landing 457-B4 PTM
Bay Pt 457-E10 WnT
Bay Ridge 428-E7 L
Bayshore 595-F3 G
Beacon Hgts 461-H8 LTM
Beamreach 428-C4 LTM
Beau Terra 528-D7 PeT
Beaumont Farms 426-F6 WTM
Beaumont on the Green 426-F6 WTM
Bechtold 461-H5 L
Beech Grove 528-E5 BG
Beech Grove Park 528-F6 BG
Beech Tree 528-D5 BG
Beech Wood Park 494-J1 WrT
Beechcrest 528-D3 CTM
Beechler Ests 427-D6 LTM
Beechwood 494-E3 CTM; 531-E7 SCT; 494-J8; 495-H8 WrT
Beechwood Acres 562-A2 PeT
Beechwood Hgts 458-E5 WTM
Beechwood Hill 528-E4 BG
Bel Air Ests 523-G10; 557-J1 P
Bel Moore 563-D7 FT
Bellaire 459-J5 WTM
Belle Arbor 530-C6 FT
Belle Arbor Ests 530-C5 FT
Belle Meade Ests 425-D3 WTM
Bellevue 459-G4 WTM
Bellmore 459-G2 WTM
Belmont 526-K2 CTM
Belmont Garden Pl 526-J2 CTM
Belmont Pl 526-H1 WnT
Benderfield 389-G8 Z
Berkeley 527-H5 PeT
Berkley Grove 393-F9 F
Berkley Ridge 393-F10 F
Berkshire Hgts 425-C9 WTM
Berry Hill 459-D6 WTM
Berwick 492-E6 WnT
Bethel Hgts 528-E3 CTM
Beverly Hgts 459-D7 WTM
Beverly Hgts Acres 529-E6 FT
Bexley Vill 596-G4 G
Bicknells 491-F7 WnT
Big Four Yard 494-C9 A
Big Run 529-G9 FT
Biltmore Gdns 491-J10 WnT
Bittner Woods 531-J8 SCT
Black Creek Park 558-D5 GT
Blackrock 558-A6 GT
Blackrock Ests 558-D7 GT
Bloomfield Lakes 564-F3 FT
Blue Creek 426-D1 Ca
Blue Grass Acres 557-D2 GT
Blue Ridge 459-D7 WTM
Blues Overlook 459-D6 WTM
Bluestone 393-C9 F
Bluff Acres 594-E5 WTJ
Bluffs 593-K9 HT; 324-J6 N
Bluffton Hgts 527-D7 PeT
Bluffwood Creek 455-B2 BTH
Boardwalk on Lake Kesslerwood 460-H3 LTM
Boggstown 599-E10 STS
Bolander Woods 427-J8 LTM
Bolton Avenue Hgts 494-K5 WrT
Bomar 561-G9 G
Bonham Pl 458-F10 WTM; 492-F1 WnT
Boots Hill 490-H4 WaT
Boulder Gate Terr 424-D4 PTM
Boulders at Geist 428-K8 L
Boulevard Manor 460-C4 WTM
Boulevard Park 493-F1 CTM
Boulevard Plaza 492-G3 WnT
Boulevard Sq 459-G10 CTM
Boulevard Terr 492-G3 WnT
Bradens Riverside 527-C4 CTM
Bradford Creek 428-J7 L
Bradford Knoll 428-A1 F
Bradford Meadows 457-J1 PTM
Bradford Pl 562-J1 FT; 594-K10 WTJ
Bradford Ridge 394-A10 F
Bradford Trace 496-F3 WrT
Bradford Woods 424-C9 PTM
Brady Vill 529-A2 WrT
Braemoor 528-D8 PeT
Braewick 425-C6 WTM
Branch Creek at Pike 424-D7 PTM
Brandts 491-F8 WnT
Brandywine 595-K5 G; 461-K8 LTM
Brandywine Twp 599-G8 STS
Braughton Ests 561-D4 PeT
Breakwater 394-K9 FCT
Breezy Top Manor 489-C6 WaT
Brendon Forests 461-B3 LTM
Brendon Park 461-A4 LTM
Brendonshire 460-K5 LTM
Brendonwood 461-A4 LTM
Brentridge 594-K7 WTJ
Brentwood 392-C3 Ca; 523-J7 P; 595-A4 WTJ; 425-C5 WTM
Brentwood Hills 561-K8 PeT
Bretton Wood 424-G9 PTM
Briar Creek 426-C2 Ca
Briar Patch 426-F8 WTM
Briarbrook Farm 462-D8 LTM
Briargate 458-J1 WTM
Briarstone Villas 561-J6 PeT
Briarwood 595-K2 G; 495-H7 WrT
Brickenwood 528-B7 PeT
Bridgefield Manor 524-C8 P
Bridgefield Villas 457-F6 PTM
Bridgeport 524-J3 WnT
Bridgeport Hgts 525-A2 WnT
Bridgewater 428-J2 FCT
Bridlewood 389-J1 ET
Brier Creek 497-C7 SCT
Briergate 495-J1 WrT
Brierwood 392-F3 Ca
Brightwood 494-D2 CTM
Brinkwood 529-A2 WrT
Brittany Chase 389-K3 ET
Brittnay Ests 491-A8 WnT
Britton Ridge 394-B4 F
Broad Ripple 459-J2 WTM
Broadacre Tr Pk 490-F5 WaT
Broadhurst 525-J1 WnT
Broadmoor 458-F4 WTM
Broadmoor Manor 523-J6 P
Broadmoor Terr 458-F4 WTM
Broadway 459-G4 WTM
Broadway Hgts 459-G4 WTM
Broadway Terr 459-G3 WTM
Brockton 460-B3 WTM
Brockton Manor 595-A6 WTJ
Brodleigh 459-F8 WTM
Brook Knoll 426-F9 WTM
Brook Park 493-K4 CTM
Brookacre 561-E7 PeT
Brookdale Hgts 562-A3 PeT
Brookfield 564-J9 MTS
Brookfield Ests 562-F7 PeT
Brookhaven 461-B5 L
Brookmoor 592-A10 BTM

Brooks Bend 426-B1 Ca
Brooks Crossing 394-K10 F
Brookshire 392-E6 Ca
Brookshire North 392-E5 Ca
Brookside 494-C5, E4 CTM
Brookside Garden 494-E4 CTM
Brookside Park 494-D5 CTM; 461-C4 L
Brookston Pl 428-H1 F
Brookstone 560-H10 WTJ
Brookview 496-C5 WrT
Brookville 494-G9 CTM
Brookville Hgts 531-E5 SCT; 494-K9 WrT
Brookville Vill 494-J9 WrT
Brookwood 494-F1 CTM
Brown Leaf 455-H5 B
Brown Twp 422-D7; 455-E1; 456-C2 BTH; 557-D10; 558-D10; 592-C6 BTM
Brownsburg 455-H6; 456-B7 B; 489-G1 LTH
Brownswood Ests 455-J8 B
Bruce Pl 493-G3 CTM
Brunson Acres 427-H2 LTM
Brunswick Park 558-B1 GT
Buck Creek Meadows 497-B3 BCT; 562-K1 FT
Buck Creek Twp 463-B6; 497-D3 BCT
Buck Creek Woods 563-A2 FT
Buckmoor 595-D5 WTJ
Bucks Creek 428-D2 FCT
Buena Ann 528-A5 PeT
Buffalo Trails 561-E8 PeT
Buisdale 491-E8 WnT
Bullman Hgts 495-H6 WrT
Bunker Hill 563-C3 FT
Burbank Park 495-E5 WrT
Burberry Pl 393-F8 F
Burge Terr 529-K1 WrT
Burns Brea Ct 427-A1 F
Burns Highland Acres 455-H1 BTH
Burris 458-G7 WTM
Burris Homedale 527-G8 PeT
Butler Terr 459-C6 WTM

C

Cabinet DN-F1; 493-H5 CTM
Cambridge Pl 455-A4 LTH
Camby 559-B4 DTM
Campus Terr 494-H8 WrT
Canak Pl 523-E4 WaT
Canal Ct DN-D2 CTM
Canby Park 494-B9 CTM
Canby Pl 494-A10 CTM
Candlelite Vill 458-E2 PTM
Candlish 527-F9 PeT
Canterbury 425-B5; 459-H3 WTM
Cape Cod Vill 427-G3 LTM
Cardinal Cove 427-E7 LTM
Cardinal Woods 429-A3 McC
Carefree Ests 428-E1 FCT
Carefree North 561-D9 WTJ
Carefree South 595-D3 WTJ
Carey Ranch 561-C7 PeT
Carlton Hgts 324-K5 N
Carlton Pl 527-K5 PeT
Carmala 565-K10 MTS
Carmel 391-F5; 392-C6; 425-E2; 426-E2 Ca
Carmel Meadows 392-B5 Ca
Carmel Sta 391-J5 Ca
Carolina Commons 392-F9 Ca
Caroline Pl 493-A3 CTM
Carpenters Home Pl DN-A3; 492-H8 WnT
Carriage Ests 561-G5 PeT
Carrigan Cove 325-D5 N
Carrington Pointe 528-E7 BG
Carrington Vill 528-E6 PeT
Carsons Farms 528-D7 PeT
Carters Park 491-K5 S
Casa De Pinon 528-C10 PeT
Casa De Prado 562-B8 PeT
Casa Loma Tr Pk 524-B7 P
Caseys Manor 496-B5 WrT
Cassell Forest 425-H7 WTM
Castillia 427-F5 LTM
Castle Cove 427-G6 LTM
Castle Ridge 427-F5 LTM
Castlebrook 427-H5 LTM
Castleton 427-B5 LTM
Castleton Ests 427-G5 LTM
Castleton Farms 427-D8 LTM
Castleton Gentry 427-B6 LTM
Castlewood 426-K3 LTM
Catalina Ests 561-F4 PeT
Cedar Bend 389-E4 Z
Cedar Cove 427-A2 F
Cedar Crest 459-D5, F6 WTM
Cedar Grove 561-G6 PeT
Cedar Hills 595-A9 WTJ
Cedar Knolls 425-D3 WTM
Cedar Ridge 422-H8 BTH
Cedar Springs 496-F8 WrT
Cedar Trace 557-J2 P
Cenal Ct 493-D6 CTM
Center Ridge 557-F2 P
Center Twp DN-B3; 460-C9; 493-F4; 494-C5; 527-A3; 528-C3 CTM; 459-C9 WTM
Central Avenue Hgts 425-F8; 459-F5 WTM
Central Park DN-E2; 493-D2, H7 CTM
Century Oaks 389-J5 Z
Chadwick Sq 455-G8 B
Champion Acres 491-G9 WnT
Champion Vill 427-F4 LTM
Chapel Glen 491-A7 WnT
Chapel Hill 491-E7 WnT
Chapel Pines 491-A6 WnT
Chapel Ridge 491-A6 WnT
Char-Le-Sumac Ests 564-D2 FT
Charlamore Woods 497-G7 SCT
Charlemac Vill 564-C1 FT
Charleston Crossing 393-F8 F
Charlotte Pl 495-K5 WrT
Charter Oaks 455-B6 GT
Chas Etris 525-J8 DTM
Chatham Pointe 426-C10 WTM
Chatham Walk 495-G3 WrT
Chelsea Hgts 525-K1 WnT
Cherry Hill Farms 393-C8 F
Cherry Lake 462-G10 WrT
Cherry Tree Ests 562-D1 PeT
Cherry Tree Farms 359-A8 NT
Chesapeake 428-C7 LTM
Chester Pl 459-F8 WTM
Chesterfield 426-D10 WTM
Chesterton 426-A2 CTH
Chestnut Hill 394-G10 F
Chestnut Hills 423-G8 PTM
Cheswick 495-J1 WrT
Chimney Hgts 561-D5 PeT
Christian Park Hgts 494-F8 CTM
Christiana 492-H5 WnT
Churchhill Ranch 461-G7 L
Churchman 527-G7 BG
Churchman Ests 529-B8 FT
Cicero 325-F2 C
Circle Hgts 528-C6 BG; 393-H6 DTH
Clare 326-F5 NT
Clark Twp 563-F9; 564-D9; 597-F5; 598-C5 CTJ
Clarkston 389-K6 Z
Clarksville 361-E5 WyT
Classic View Ests 561-D9 PeT
Clay Twp 391-B6; 392-G4; 425-A2 CTH; 426-G2 WTM
Claypool Ross 525-K1; 526-A1 WnT
Clear View Farms 458-H2 WTM
Clearbrook Lakes 596-A6 G
Clearview 596-B4 G; 594-G7 WTJ
Clearview Ests 458-F2 WTM
Clearwater Cove 426-D5 WTM
Clemons Pl 458-H3 WTM
Clermont 456-J10; 490-H1 WnT
Clermont Hgts 456-F8 LTH
Cleveland Pl 494-A6 CTM
Clifden Pond 389-D10 Z
Clifford Pl 494-A5 CTM
Clifton on the River 459-A10 CTM
Clifton Pl 493-A1 CTM
Cloverdale 527-J10 PeT
Cloverleaf Farms 491-J9 WnT
Cloverleaf Vill 526-A9 DTM
Cobblefield Ests 496-K2 Cu
Cobblestone 457-B7 PTM
Cobblestone at Geist 428-J8 L
Cobblestone Springs 489-H8 A
Coil Park 459-G2 WTM
Cold Spring Ests 492-H2 WnT
Cold Spring Highlands 458-K7 WTM
Coldspring Hgts 458-H7 WTM
College Avenue Hgts 459-G4 WTM
College Crest 425-E3 WTM
College Meadows 425-G1 CTH
College Park 424-E4 PTM
College Park West 424-E4 PTM
College Way 425-G4 WTM
Collett Acres 592-H2 MTM
Collingswood Hillsborough 394-C10 F
Colonial Acres 558-K1 DTM
Colonial Ests 489-E6 WaT; 494-G3 WrT
Colonial Hgts 497-B4 BCT; 389-H6 Z
Colonial Manor 459-J5 WTM
Colonial Meadows 561-J10 G
Colonial Park Ests 458-G2 WTM
Colony Ests 426-E7 WTM
Colony Lake 523-J5 P
Colony Sq 389-E7 Z
Colony Woods 425-A8 WTM; 389-G6 Z
Colorado Hills 460-E7 WTM
Colorado Terr 494-E5 CTM
Columbia Pl 459-D8 WTM
Columbia Terr 494-H10 WrT
Community Arts Northeast 460-H1 WTM
Comptons Tr Pk 389-H9 Z
Concord Hgts 492-G5 WnT
Connatys DN-A3; 492-J8 CTM
Conner Creek 393-D8 F
Conner Knoll 393-G3 F
Connerwood 393-F2 DTH
Continental Ests 557-J7 GT
Cool Creek North 392-E3 Ca
Cooper Hgts 423-A1 ET
Cooper Pointe 458-G1 PTM
Copeland 561-J1 PeT
Copper Pointe 325-D6 N
Copperfield 427-F8 LTM
Copperleaf 594-H10 WTJ
Coppermill at the Park 457-E5 PTM
Cornerbrook Commons 425-K4 WTM
Cornerstone Vill 531-K4 SCT
Cornett Pl 494-B9 CTM
Coronado Ests 490-J8 WnT
Corydon 459-F9 CTM
Cottage Grove 493-J10 CTM
Cottage Home DN-F1; 493-J6 CTM
Cottage Park on the River 526-B10 DTM
Cottage Pl DN-F1; 493-J6 CTM
Cottingham Ests 393-J3 DTH
Cottingham North 393-J2 F
Country Air Ests 457-G5 PTM
Country Aire 596-G2 G
Country Charm 491-A5 WnT
Country Club Ests 491-A2 WnT
Country Club Hgts 457-A10 WnT
Country Club Pines 491-A2 WnT
Country Creek Ests 489-D5 WaT
Country Ests 562-B8 PeT
Country Farms 457-K3 PTM
Country Fields at Fishers 394-A2 F
Country Jct 491-A4 WnT
Country Lake Ests 324-H8 N
Country Lane Ests 395-C8 FCT
Country Meadow Ests 456-C9 LTH
Country Meadows 491-A4 WnT
Country Pl 561-B9 PeT
Country Pointe 491-A5 WnT
Country Side 425-H5 WTM
Country View 592-E7 BTM; 393-E8 F
Country Vill 491-B1 WnT
Country Walk 562-D8 PeT
Country Wood 326-G6 NT
Countrybrook 458-B2 PTM
Countrybrook North 425-A8 WTM
Countryside 531-D4 SCT; 525-A1 WnT
Courtyard Lakes 393-D8 F
Coventry Ridge 523-K5 WaT; 389-J5 Z
Coventry Woods 458-C5 PTM
Covington Ests 427-K1 F
Coxs 492-G6 WnT
Crafton Meadows 592-F2 M
Craig Highlands 326-C8 NT
Craigwood 561-F2 PeT
Craigwood Ests 561-D2 PeT
Cream Ridge 459-D6 WTM
Creek View Ests 460-E4 WTM
Creekbend 561-C2 PeT
Creekside Ests 523-K10 P
Creekside Sq 457-F3 PTM
Creekside Woods 496-D8 WrT
Creekview Acres 523-D1 WaT
Creekwood 427-G10 LTM; 426-B9 WTM
Creekwood Ests 455-G2 BTH
Creekwood Hills 496-G10 WrT
Cress 527-K2 CTM
Crest 459-E4 WTM
Creston 492-D8 WnT
Crestview 494-C8 CTM
Crestview Hgts 592-J7 MTM
Crestwood 496-A2 WrT
Crestwood Manor 530-G1 WrT
Critchfield 595-D4 WTJ
Crooked Creek Hgts 424-C5 PTM
Crooked Creek Ridge 458-G6 WTM
Crooked Creek Villages East 458-E1 PTM
Crooked Creek Villages West 424-F10 PTM
Crooked Stick 390-J8 CTH
Cross Creek 561-D2 PeT
Crossgate 562-B5 Spt
Crossing South 428-J5 L
Crosswind Commons 357-C8 WTH
Crosswinds at Windermere 428-D1 F
Crown Hill 459-E10 CTM
Crows Nest 459-C4 WTM
Crows Nest Ests 459-C2 WTM
Crows Nest South 459-A5 WTM
Crystal Bay 557-H2 P
Crystal Hgts 531-H4 SCT
Crystal Pointe 428-K5 L
Crystal Springs 523-D1 WaT
Cumberland 496-H7 SCT
Cumberland Cove 496-G4 WrT
Cumberland Crossing 394-C6 F
Cumberland Ests 496-G5 WrT
Cumberland Farms 496-G1 WrT
Cumberland Hgts 496-H6 Cu
Cumberland Manor 326-B7 NT
Cumberland Pl 394-B1 FCT
Cumberland Ridge 394-A10 F
Cumberland Vill 496-H5 Cu
Curzon Park 459-C10 WTM

D

Dahlia Gdns 561-E2 PeT
Dale-mar 395-J9 FCT
Damon Oaks 494-A1 CTM
Danbury Ests 392-A1 Ca
Dandy Trail Ests 561-D6 PeT
Dawnbury 459-K1; 460-A1 WTM
Dawson 459-G3 WTM
De Milt Gdns 529-J7 FT
Dean Meadows 426-E7 WTM
Dearburn Park 460-A10 CTM
Deauville Ests 460-C7 WTM
Debello Ests 491-A3 WnT
Debury Creft 460-F8 WTM
Decatur Commons 559-E1 DTM
Decatur Twp 525-D8; 526-C7; 559-E5; 560-A3 DTM
Deer Creek 458-A4 PTM
Deer Ridge 389-D8 ET; 428-C9 L
Deer Run 462-C4 L; 531-D3 SCT
Deerbrook 427-A1 F
Deerfield Tr Pk 524-A6 P
Deerwood 594-E6 WTJ
Delaware Common 426-D9 WTM
Delaware Hgts 527-F4 CTM; 459-E4 WTM
Delaware Oaks 425-A10 WTM
Delaware Pointe & Crossing 393-K9 F
Delaware Trails 425-A9 WTM
Delaware Trails North 425-B8 WTM
Delaware Trails West 425-A7 WTM
Delaware Twp 393-C3; 394-B3; 427-E1; 428-A2 DTH
Deming 324-E2 JT
Denton Trace 497-C8 SCT
Denwood 460-D8 WTM
Devon Ct 460-F7 WTM
Devon Hills 460-E6 WTM
Devon Lake 460-F7 WTM
Devon Lea 460-E7 WTM
Devon Ridge 460-E6 WTM
Devon Woods 460-D7 WTM
Devonshire 427-A9; 460-J1 LTM
Diamond Cove 557-F6 GT
Diamond Pl 424-J7 WTM
Diamond Pointe 428-G3 LTM
Diamondale West 489-A6 WaT
Dickson Pl DN-F2; 493-H7 CTM
Doe Creek Ests 531-A5, D1 SCT
Donnelly Hgts 455-F10 B
Dora 492-G5 WnT
Douglass Park 493-F2 CTM
Drake Hill 490-J3 WnT
Drexel 494-F5 CTM
Drexel Gdns 526-A2 WnT
Driftwood Hills 426-A3 WTM
Driskell Ct 528-F6 BG
Dukane Ct 491-G10 WnT
Dumont Est 527-D3 CTM
Durbin 361-E1 WyT
Durham Park 494-F5 CTM

E

Eagle Bay 457-D7 PTM
Eagle Cove 457-E8 PTM
Eagle Creek Ests 456-H1 BTH
Eagle Creek Meadows 456-J6 LTM
Eagle Creek Overlook 457-B4 PTM
Eagle Creek Woods 457-C5 PTM
Eagle Pines at Trittipo Farms 428-G7 L
Eagle Ridge 457-A6 PTM; 492-G10 WnT
Eagle Springs 457-C4 PTM
Eagle Trace 595-C5 WTJ
Eagle Twp 389-B7; 390-A6; 423-D2; 424-A1 ET
Eagle Vill 390-A7 ET; 456-G4 LTH
Eaglebrook Park 491-K4 S
Eagledale 458-B9; 492-A1 WnT
Eaglenest 427-G6 LTM
Eagles Crossing 457-C10 WnT
Eagles Knoll 457-G5 PTM
Eagles Landing 457-C8 PTM
Eagles Nest 422-F7 BTH
Eagles Way 457-F10 WnT
Eagleswatch 457-D6 PTM
Eagletown 356-K4 WTH
Eaglewood 491-K5 S
Eaglewood Ests 388-K8 ET
Earl Park 559-B8 DTM
Early Bluffs Wild Ridge 427-H9 LTM
East Blvd Hgts 459-K8 WTM
East Harbour 325-D7 N
East Highlands 495-K7 WrT
East Kessler 460-C2 WTM
East Lawn 494-E5 CTM
East Meridian Hgts 459-F5 WTM
East Monticello 459-H5 WTM
East Ridge 494-J5 WrT
Eastbrooke Meadows 462-B10 WrT
Easterbrooke 494-H9 WrT
Eastgate 495-C6 WrT
Eastland Terr 495-D5 WrT
Eastmoreland Pl 460-G9 WrT
Easton 495-J6 WrT
Eastowne 496-G6 Cu
Eastway Manor 495-G5 WrT
Eastwood 495-F3 WrT
Eastwood Park 490-J1 WnT
Eastworth 495-J4 WrT
Echo Crest 391-J8 CTH
Echo Pointe 428-D7 L
Eden Brook 392-C6 Ca
Eden Vill 458-B3 PTM
Edgehill 494-J6 WrT
Edgewater 493-H1 CTM
Edgewater Pl 425-H8 WTM
Edgewater Terr 428-B9 L
Edgewood 561-H1 PeT
Edgewood Acres 528-A10 PeT
Edgewood Pl 562-A2 PeT
Edmondsons 492-C9 WnT
El Beulah 427-D5 LTM
Eldorado 595-D6 WTJ
Ellen Ct 528-C4 BG
Ellen Park 528-E6 BG
Ellenberger Ct 494-H6 WrT
Ellenberger Plaza 494-J6 WrT
Eller Run 393-B10 F
Eller Trails 392-J10 F
Ellerslee 527-K10 PeT
Elmore 529-C1 WrT
Elmwood 494-A2 CTM; 459-H6 WTM
Emblegarde 425-F3 WTM
Emerald Green 457-F7 PTM
Emerald Lakes 596-H3 G
Emerson Crest 494-H2 WrT
Emerson Gdns 494-H3 WrT
Emerson Hgts 494-F6 CTM
Emerson Highlands 494-G5 CTM
Emerson Park 460-G6 WTM
Emerson Pl 528-G1 WrT
Emerson Woods 562-J3 FT
Emrichs 492-J4 WnT
Emsley W Johnsons Hgts 424-H7 WTM
Englewood 494-C8 CTM
English DN-F3; 493-J9 CTM
English Crossing 495-D9 WrT
English Hgts 494-E9 CTM
Enrights 458-G6 WTM
Evanston 526-A1 WnT
Evergreen Acres 525-J10; 559-J1 DTM
Executive Manor 427-J8 LTM
Exeter Park 425-J9 WTM

F

Factory Park 492-G6 WnT
Factory Pl 527-K2 CTM
Fair Meadows 491-E8 WnT
Fair Oaks 594-K2 WTJ
Fairfax 492-E6 WnT
Fairfield 494-C10 CTM
Fairfield Farms 326-A10 N
Fairfield Hgts 455-K9 B
Fairhaven Ests 562-F1 PeT
Fairhope 561-K2 PeT
Fairhurst College Corner 494-G8 CTM
Fairlawn 493-K1 CTM
Fairplains 528-B10 PeT
Fairview Hgts 459-D6 WTM
Fairview Park 459-C7, D5 WTM
Fairview Pl 459-B7 WTM
Fairway Ests 496-D1 WrT
Fairway Hills 489-A10 WaT
Fairway Vill 427-B5 LTM
Fairway Woods 458-E6 PTM
Fairwood Hills 427-F10 LTM
Falcon Creek 457-K7 PTM
Falcon Lakes 458-D2 PTM
Falcon Ridge 423-E5 PTM
Fall Creek DN-C1; 493-C5 CTM; 361-D10 FCT
Fall Creek Hgts 395-D7 FCT; 461-D4 L
Fall Creek Highlands 428-B7 L; 460-E4 WTM
Fall Creek Manor 460-F4 WTM
Fall Creek Pl 460-C6 WTM
Fall Creek Twp 395-D4; 429-E1 FCT
Fall Creek Vill 460-C7 WTM
Farhill Downs 528-H8 FT
Farhill Woods 562-J2 FT
Farley Meadows 491-K1 S
Farleys 491-E6; 526-D5 WnT
Farmbrook 489-A1 LTH
Farmington 462-C6 LTM
Fawn Lake Ests 422-H4 BTH; 422-H4 PTM
Fawnsbrook Hills 393-F5 F
Feather Bay 428-E6 LTM
Feather Cove 428-D6 LTM
Federal Hill 359-F3 N
Ferguson 561-E2 PeT
Ferndale 492-H5 WnT
Fernwood Sharps 525-F2 WnT
Ferrell Ests 425-C7 WTM
Fieldstone 458-A1 PTM
Firethorn Trace 427-D5 LTM
First Devington 460-J6 LTM
First State 460-D10 CTM
Fishback Hgts 422-J6 PTM
Fishback Hill 422-J9 PTM
Fishers 393-F7; 394-G8; 427-B1; 428-B2 F
Fishers Farm 394-A2 F
Fishers Pointe 393-G8 F
Fite 490-J9 WnT
Five Points 529-C4 FT; 593-A8 MTM; 529-C4 WrT
Flackville 492-E1 WnT
Flat Branch Ests 563-G5 FT
Fleming Garden Pl 492-C10 WnT
Floral Park 493-B3 CTM
Foothill Farms 561-D4 PeT
Forest Brook 565-E6 MTS; 460-E8 WTM
Forest Commons 489-H5 WaT
Forest Creek 530-C1 WrT
Forest Crest 425-C7 WTM
Forest Grove 460-C8 WTM
Forest Hgts 460-G2 LTM
Forest Hill Ests 359-F1 NT
Forest Hills 459-G3 WTM
Forest Home DN-E1; 493-G5 CTM
Forest Knoll 395-B8 FCT
Forest Lake Ests 456-G1 BTH
Forest Lake Park 528-E4 BG
Forest Manor Ests 460-E9 CTM
Forest Park 494-B8 CTM; 562-C10 G; 459-E3 WTM
Forest Ridge 393-K10 DTH; 557-G2 P; 459-D6 WTM
Forrest Acres 494-K1 WrT
Forrest Commons 561-E3 PeT
Forrests Edge 561-E3 PeT
Foster Ests 392-B1 Ca
Foster Hills 395-H1 FCT
Fountain Springs 428-B10 L
Fountain Vill 427-G4 LTM
Fox Cove 496-K9 SCT
Fox Glen 360-C7 NT
Fox Hill 593-E4 MTM
Fox Hill Acres 459-A2 WTM
Fox Hill Drive 458-J2 WTM
Fox Hill Ests 459-A2 WTM
Fox Hill Manor 458-K2 WTM
Fox Hill Terr 458-J2 WTM
Fox Hollow 423-E1 ET
Fox Hollow Ests 456-G2 BTH
Fox Orchard 457-D10 WnT
Fox Pointe 428-D9 L
Fox Ridge 561-C6 PeT; 491-D1 WnT
Fox Run 428-C1 F
Foxberry Trace 595-C4 WTJ
Foxchase 428-A6 LTM
Foxmoor 595-E1 G
Frances 595-D4 WTJ
Franklin Hgts 461-G9 WrT
Franklin Homeplace 529-G5 FT
Franklin Meadows 563-D6 FT
Franklin Park 563-G2 FT
Franklin Parke Ests 563-E4 FT
Franklin Pl 495-F6 WrT
Franklin Shire 563-J1 FT
Franklin Trails Ests 461-F4 L
Franklin Twp 529-E8; 530-C8; 563-D4; 564-C4 FT
Franklin Woods 528-J10 FT
Friendly Vill MHP 561-A9 WTJ
Friendswood 558-G7 GT
Friendswood Ests 558-G6 GT
Fultsville 457-K4 PTM

G

Galecrest 496-E6 Cu
Garden City 492-A8 WnT
Garden Ct Vill 494-G4 WrT
Garden Hgts 527-E7 PeT
Garden Park 526-J2 WnT
Garden Walk 460-E4 WTM
Garfield Hgts 527-G5 CTM
Garfield Park 527-J4 CTM
Garfield Plaza 527-F3 CTM
Garfield Terr 527-J3 CTM
Gateway 457-G8 PTM
Gateway West 457-H8 PTM
Gatewood 393-C9 F
Gay-La-Ridge 528-F2 CTM
Geist Bay Ests 395-F7 FCT
Geist Pointe Ests 428-J8 L
Geist Valley Ests 428-G8 L
Geist Woods 428-E2 FCT
Gem 497-G6 SCT
Georgetown Crossing 424-A10 PTM
Georgetown Vill 458-D10 WnT
Gerdenichs College Parkway 425-F10 WTM
Gerkings Home Pl 492-D10 WnT
German Church Woods 496-G4 WrT
German Park 493-A4 CTM
German Park Hgts 561-E8 PeT
Germania DN-A2; 492-H6 WnT
Glad Acres 531-H2 SCT
Gladden Farms 524-B7 P
Glastonbury Ct 427-D6 LTM
Glen Cove 428-G5 L
Glen Oaks 496-K4 Cu; 494-J6 WrT
Glen Oaks Vill 496-K6 Cu
Glenbrook 490-F7 WaT
Glencoe Pl 494-G4 CTM
Glencroft 460-C9 CTM
Glendale 460-B4 WTM
Glendale Hgts 426-B9 WTM
Glendale Meadows 426-B10 WTM
Glendale Tree 426-C9 WTM
Glenmora 426-G8 WTM
Glenn Abbey at Windermere 428-D1 F
Glennroy Vill 529-A4 WrT
Glenns Valley 560-H9 PeT
Glennview Park 560-J8 PeT
Glenridge 494-F4 CTM
Glenurban Ests 561-J7 PeT
Glenview Ests 426-F8 WTM
Glenwood 493-K6 CTM
Golden 527-J5 PeT
Golden Acres 527-G10 PeT
Golden Hill 459-A10 CTM
Golden Oaks 424-H3 WTM
Golf View Ests 456-H3 BTH
Golf View Manor 528-A4 CTM
Golfmoor 528-B4 CTM
Good Homes 528-A3 CTM
Goodlet 492-G5 WnT
Gordon Acres 423-G7 PTM
Gordon Hgts 455-G7 B
Governors Park 424-B4 PTM
Graceland Park 493-C2 CTM
Graham Avenue Hgts 494-J5 WrT
Grand View Ests 458-K1 WTM
Grandview 493-H1 CTM; 458-H1 WTM
Grandview Acres 561-J5 PeT
Grandview Ct 459-A1 WTM
Grandview Ests 592-F4 M
Grandview Meadows 424-K10 WTM
Grant Wood 427-E10 LTM
Grasmere 527-D1 WrT
Grassy Creek 496-E9 WrT
Grassy Creek Vill 462-C8 LTM
Gray Arbor 562-E2 PeT
Gray Manor 562-E3 PeT
Graylan Pl 359-D10 NT
Grays Manor 455-G6 B
Green Acres 461-E9 WrT
Green Braes Ests 456-K5 PTM
Green Hills 458-G9 WTM
Green Hills Ests 455-D6 LTH
Green Lawns 494-G3 WrT
Green Meadows 565-H10 MTS; 458-H8 WTM
Green Rock 528-H2 WrT
Green Street Vill 455-H1 B
Green Valley 326-A9 N; 595-G3 WTJ
Greenbriar 425-A6 WTM
Greenridge 425-F8 WTM
Greenslopes 527-B8 PeT
Greenway Ests 460-B1 WTM
Greenwood 561-E10; 562-B10; 595-H2; 596-A6 G
Greenwood Commons 595-J1 G
Greenwood Vill South 596-D5 G
Greer Dell Ests 459-A1 WTM
Greystone 562-K3 FT

Grinslade Parkside Hgts 527-G4 CTM
Grossmans 459-F1 WTM
Grove Pl 460-G10 CTM
Guilford Twp 523-B6; 524-D8; 557-D5; 558-D6 GT
Guion Creek Woods 458-C4 PTM
Guion Lakes 458-B3 PTM

H

Hadley Acres 557-J2 P
Haig Pt 394-D9 F
Halcyon Park 424-E7 PTM
Hall Pl 493-E4 CTM
Hamilton Hills 427-B2 F
Hammond Ests 460-B7 WTM
Hampton Ridge 459-C7 WTM
Hanna Hgts 526-B7 DTM
Hanover Grove 424-G4 PTM
Hansens 493-B4 CTM
Harbour Club 426-C7 WTM
Harbour Overlook 324-H5 N
Harbour Pines 428-A4 LTM
Harbour Pines North 428-A3 LTM
Harbour Vill 325-D6 N
Harbour Woods 324-H5 N
Hardins Ests 523-K9 P
Harrison Farms 429-A8 McC
Harrison Green 393-J2 F
Harrison Hgts 460-G9 WrT
Harrison Lakes 393-H2 F
Harrison Park 393-G3 F; 461-G5 L
Harrison Twp 593-K7 HT
Harrison Woods 393-H3 F
Hartford Park 455-D7 B
Harting Farms 531-F4 SCT
Hartman Farms 496-G5 WrT
Hartman Vill 496-H3 WrT
Harvard Park 393-A8 F
Harvest Glen 496-H5 Cu
Harvest Ridge 489-H6 A
Harvey 495-E8 WrT
Hasselman Pl 459-H9 CTM
Hastings Trace 456-G5 LTH
Hathaway 496-A5 WrT
Haughville 492-H5 WnT
Haughville Park 492-H5 WnT
Havenfair 496-B3 WrT
Haverstick Park 425-J7 WTM
Hawthorn Hills 394-D10 F
Hawthorn Manor 494-G4 WrT
Hawthorne 495-B9 WrT
Hawthorne Pl 494-G9 CTM
Hawthorne Ridge 557-K3 P
Hawthorne Yards 494-H10 WrT
Hawthornes at the Crossing 422-K3 PTM
Hearthstone Spinnaker Cove 427-C3 LTM
Heartland Crossing 559-C10 MTM
Heartland Ests 559-E10 MTM
Heather Hills 496-B3 WrT
Heather Pointe 394-J8 F
Heatherlea 496-D1 WrT
Heatherleigh 459-G7 WTM
Heatherwood Ests 491-F10 WnT
Heathery 491-A3 WnT
Heathwood 562-H8 FT
Heawich 458-J6 WTM
Helena Suburban 529-G6 FT
Helenworth 490-J1 WnT
Hendricks 595-F3 G
Hendricks Hgts 490-G5 WaT
Heritage Green 428-C1 F
Heritage Meadows 393-G9 F
Heritage Park 427-E9 LTM
Heritage Sq 562-D4 PeT
Herman Maple Hgts 460-J7 LTM
Heron Lake 460-B5 WTM
Heywood Park 493-F1 CTM
Hi-Acre Manor 526-C9 DTM
Hiawatha Gdns 461-D9 WrT
Hickory Road 530-B10 FT
Hickory Sq 457-D10 WnT
Hickory Woods 393-E8 F; 595-G2 G
Hidden Bay 457-F5 PTM
Hidden Creek at Geist 428-J8 L
Hidden Meadow Ests 496-B7 WrT
Hidden Valley 523-H4 WaT
High Acres 455-B8 LTH; 531-F1 SCT
High Gate 426-K9 LTM
High Knoll Ests 458-H5 WTM
High Ridge 425-C4 WTM
High School Vill 528-E3 BG
High Woods 459-A6 WTM
Highland 493-C1, K7 CTM
Highland Hgts 525-D1 WnT
Highland Kessler Ests 459-A3 WTM
Highland Manor 459-C4 WTM
Highland Park 595-B6 WTJ
Highland Pl 493-E3 CTM
Highland Springs 429-C2 FCT
Highlands Trail 457-F7 PTM
Highridge 459-E7 WTM
Highway Park 459-K8 WTM
Highwoods 458-G10 WTM
Hiland Manor 424-G8 PTM
Hill Pl DN-F3; 493-J8 CTM
Hill Valley Ests 561-B8 PeT
Hill-En-Dale 563-B4 FT
Hillcrest 527-K1 CTM; 523-H10 P
Hiller Hgts 495-C6 WrT
Hillside DN-F2; 493-J7 CTM
Hilly Acres 394-F6 FCT
Hilton 459-F8 WTM
Hilton Manor 528-E9 PeT
Hohlts Homeplace 526-G2 WnT
Holaday Hills and Dales 426-A1 CTH
Holcomb Ests 458-J7 WTM
Holiday 424-K9 WTM
Holiday Manor 495-H3 WrT
Holiday Park 455-H7 B
Hollaway Ridge 455-A2 B
Hollowbrook 523-K1 A
Hollowbrook West 523-J1 A
Holly Creek 425-K7 WTM
Holly Hgts 562-C6 PeT
Holly Hills 562-C4 PeT
Holly Meadows Southridge Vill 562-C5 PeT
Hollywood 492-F5 WnT
Hollywood Millerdale 494-G8 CTM
Holmes End West DN-A1; 492-H6 WnT
Home Lawn 494-F2 CTM; 456-J10 WnT
Home Pl 391-H10 CTH
Homecroft 561-J3 PeT
Homedell 527-G8 PeT
Homestead 492-G4 WnT
Homestead Lakes 424-J2 WTM
Homewood Park 461-F9 WrT
Homewood Park West 457-H9 WnT
Honey Manor 525-K10; 526-A10 DTM
Hoover Crest 425-B8 WTM
Hoover Park 425-A10 WTM
Horizon Ests 594-H7 WTJ
Hornaday Hgts 455-K7 B
Hortons 559-E6 DTM
Hortonville 323-E6 WTH
Hoss Acres 427-H7 LTM
Howard Pl 527-J10 PeT
Howards Dandy Trail 561-C6 PeT
Huckcreek Shades 598-K1 MTS
Huddleston Ests 561-D6 PeT
Hummel Park 557-H1 P
Hummingbird 491-F9 WnT
Hunt Club Vill 389-F9 Z
Hunters Cove 455-H9 B
Hunters Crossing 462-E8 WrT
Hunters Glen 427-H4 LTM
Hunters Green 457-F1 PTM
Hunters Knoll 391-H2 CTH
Hunters Pointe 595-B6 WTJ
Hunters Pt 389-F9 Z
Hunters Ridge 557-K2 GT
Hunters Run 561-A7 PeT
Hunters Woods 427-G5 LTM
Huntersfield 390-E10 CTH
Huntington Ests 423-D10 PTM
Huntington Hgts Plaza 496-B1 WrT
Huntington Park 525-H9 DTM
Huntington Pointe 423-F10 PTM
Huntington Ridge 423-F10 PTM; 527-G10 PeT
Huntington Woods 423-F1 ET
Hy View Meadows 461-C5 L
Hyde Park 493-D1 CTM

I

Illinois Hgts 459-D5 WTM
Illinois Kessler Terr 459-D3 WTM
Illinois Terr 459-D7 WTM
Imperial Gdns 461-D7 L
Imperial Hgts 495-A5 WrT
Imperial Hills 561-J9 G
Indian Creek 462-C6 LTM
Indian Creek Ests 564-F2 FT
Indian Lake 428-B8 L
Indian Pointe 428-C7 L
Indiana Park 491-K7 WnT
Indianapolis 525-F7; 526-H5; 559-B5 DTM; 530-B6; 563-D3; 564-C3 FT; 427-A4; 428-B6; 462-E7 LTM; 423-B4; 457-A8 PTM; 560-F5 PeT; 424-H5; 459-A4; 460-E5 WTM; 491-A8; 492-H4; 525-F7 WnT; 495-A4; 496-A8; 528-H3 WrT
Indianapolis Hgts 492-A10; 526-A1 WnT
Indianhead Lake 489-B5 WaT
Indigo Lake 394-A3 F
Innisbrooke 594-H2 WTJ
Inverness 491-B3 WnT
Inverness Ests 393-F1 DTH
Inwood Park Ests 426-F7 WTM
Irishman Run 423-C1 ET
Iron Springs 425-H6 WTM
Irongate 496-B9 WrT; 389-D9 Z
Ironwood Lake 455-K8 B
Irving Ridge 495-D5 WrT
Irvington 494-K7 WrT
Irvington Gdns 494-J6 WrT
Irvington Hgts 494-G6 WrT
Irvington Hill 494-F7 CTM
Irvington Hills 495-E6 WrT
Irvington Manor 494-K4 WrT
Irvington Pl 494-J7 WrT
Irvington Terr 495-A7 WrT
Island Park 425-K8 WTM
Islands East 457-C10 WnT
Ivanhoe 495-H8 WrT
Ivy Dale 530-K1 SCT
Ivy Hills 592-F5 BTM; 426-H7 WTM
Ivy Ridge 426-K8 LTM
Ivy Wood 524-A2 WaT

J

Jackson Park 493-J2 CTM
Jackson Twp 323-H2; 324-J2; 326-B3 JT
James Pl 359-J6 N
Jefferson Gdns 494-G10 CTM
Jelico Twins 561-F6 PeT
Jennings 460-C10 CTM
Jennings Field 389-F7 Z
Jessup Meadows 523-F6 WaT
Jolietville 356-D2 WTH
Jones Newlyn 525-K8 DTM
Joppa 557-B9 GT
Jordan Woods 392-A10 CTH
Julietta 530-G3 WrT
Justuscountry Club Est 496-D3 WrT

K

Karrington Ests 592-E2 M
Karrman Hgts 494-J1 WrT
Katherine Pl 528-E4 BG
Keeneland Crest 562-J8 FT
Keevers Rolling Acres 456-J5 LTM
Kenmore Hgts 495-A8 WrT
Kennedy 528-D4 BG
Kensington Ests 523-B8 P
Kensington Farms 462-C1 L
Kensington Park 596-A2 G
Kenwood 459-D10 CTM
Kenwood Forest 425-D5 WTM
Kenyons Highland Homeplace 525-J1 WnT
Kessler Commons 460-F3 WTM
Kessler Crest 459-B3 WTM
Kessler Ct 492-G2 WnT
Kessler Ests 460-D2, E3 WTM
Kessler Gdns 492-G2 WnT
Kessler Hgts 492-G3 WnT
Kessler Lane 460-E2 WTM
Kessler Pointe 460-E3 WTM
Kesslerwood 460-A2 WTM
Ketcham Pl 492-H7 WnT
Kevin Crest 460-C4 WTM
Keystone 494-A6 CTM
Keystone Hgts 425-K9 WTM
Keystone Manor 491-F8 WnT
Keystone Park 459-B10 CTM
Killarney Hgts 459-J4 WTM
Killarney Hill 560-J6 PeT
King Ests 425-C7 WTM
Kings Cove 425-A4 WTM
Kings Mill 390-G9 CTH
Kingston Ests 393-G1 DTH
Kingston Pl 528-E1 CTM
Kingswood 392-H9 CTH
Kirkwood Ests 525-E10 DTM
Kissel Hgts 495-E8 WrT
Knightsbridge 592-F1 M
Knollton Hgts 458-J6 WTM
Knollton Pl 458-J5 WTM
Knollwood 427-F9 LTM
Knollwood at the Creek 427-F10 LTM
Knollwood Valley 427-G9 LTM
Kopetsky Park 560-K1 PeT
Kramer 528-E5 BG

L

Lafayette 458-E10; 492-E1 WnT
Lafayette Hgts 526-B4 WnT
Lafayette Highlands 458-C10 WnT
Lafayette Villas 457-G4 PTM
Lago Vista 596-F3 G
Lagoon Park 425-J10 WTM
Lake Charlevoix 461-A2 LTM
Lake Clearwater 426-D7 WTM
Lake Clearwater Pointe 426-D6 WTM
Lake Forest 392-J7 Ca; 424-G3 PTM
Lake Kesslerwood East 460-G3 LTM
Lake Maxinhall Ests 460-C4 WTM
Lake of the Lantern Tr Pk 490-F3 WaT
Lake of the Pines 490-J4 WnT
Lake Park 495-D3 WrT
Lake Stonebridge 394-D7 F
Lakecrest 359-K5 N
Lakeland Manor 456-F3 LTH
Lakes at the Crossing 426-C5 WTM
Lakeside 423-D9 PTM; 460-C5 WTM
Lakeside Ests 324-K5 N
Lakeside Green 428-B2 F
Lakeside Woods 423-F9 PTM
Lakewood 392-C8 Ca
Lakewood Terr 490-D1 LTH
Lakewood Vill 426-K10 LTM
Lamong 322-H7 WTH
Lancastershire 561-F5 PeT
Landersdale 593-J1 MTM
Lantern Crossing 427-H2 F
Lantern Farms 393-H4 F
Lantern Forest 427-H8 LTM
Lantern Hills 427-J9 LTM
Lantern Park 457-H6 PTM
Lantern Pines 427-J1 F
Lantern Ridge 393-H5 F
Lantern Woods 497-H8 SCT
Lappinway 496-D2 WrT
Larry Stovall 461-C9 WrT
Larson Highlands 458-J7 WTM
Lasalle Park 494-C6 CTM
Lather Ests 493-C4 CTM
Latonia Park 494-G8 WrT
Laurel Hall 460-G5 LTM; 460-G5 WTM
Laurel Wood Ests 562-A8 PeT
Lawndale 561-K10; 595-K1 G
Lawrence 427-J10; 461-E6; 462-B5 L; 428-D5 LTM
Lawrence Manor 461-E6 L
Lawrence Park 461-E6 L
Lawrence Terr 461-D7 L
Lawrence Twp 428-D9 L; 427-D4; 460-H5; 462-E7 LTM
Lawton Pl 459-F4 WTM
Le Gore Crest 527-F5 PeT
Legendary Hills 423-H10 PTM
Legends at Geist 394-D8 F
Leland Hgts 562-A5 PeT
Leland Pl 458-H1 WTM
Lenore 528-K2 WrT
Lenox Pl 494-C1 CTM
Leo Wright 458-B9 WnT
Lewis Lake 455-D9 LTH
Lewis Woods 455-E9 LTH
Liberty Creek 457-H4 PTM
Liberty Creeknorth 457-J3 PTM
Liberty Gdns 495-D9 WrT
Liberty Oak 491-C3 WnT
Lighthouse Cove at Geist 428-D2 LTM
Lincoln Park 493-F2 CTM; 458-G2 WTM
Lincoln Pointe 455-K9 B
Lincoln Twp 455-B6; 456-C7; 489-D2; 490-C2 LTH
Lincolnwood 456-J9 LTM
Lindbergh Highlands 528-B9 PeT
Lindenwood 561-F5 PeT
Linwood 494-F5 CTM
Lions Creek 324-J5 N
Lionshead 425-D8 WTM
Little Big Run 529-F9 FT
Little Oak Lake 564-E4 FT
London 565-D10; 599-D1 MTS
London Hgts 565-D10 MTS
Londonderry Hgts 489-E4 WaT
Long Brook 390-A9 ET
Longacre 527-K9 PeT
Longwood 462-G8 WrT
Lookout Gdns 525-F1 WnT
Lookout Plaza 525-F1 WnT
Loveland 423-D3 PTM
Lowell Manor 528-B9 PeT
Lowell Park 529-B2 WrT
Lowell Pl 494-K7 WrT
Lucas Pl 561-J2 PeT
Lumley 526-F5 WnT
Luxhaven 395-H9 FCT
Lyndale 491-K9; 492-A9 WnT
Lynhurst 491-K9; 492-A9; 525-K1 WnT
Lynhurst Acres 492-A7 WnT
Lynhurst Hgts 526-A2 WnT
Lynwood Hills 393-F4 DTH

M

MacCarty 595-J3 G
Machlan Terr 528-G2 CTM
MacKinley Pl 494-A9 CTM
Madison Hgts 561-K1 PeT
Madison Terr 527-F4 CTM
Madison Twp 559-F10; 593-D5 MTM
Madora Sq 459-E8 WTM
Mallard Crossing 422-G10 BTH
Mallard Lake 460-D5 WTM
Malott Park 460-A4 WTM
Malvern 492-E7 WnT
Manderley 426-A4 WTM
Manhattan 525-J6 DTM
Mannandale 525-H10 DTM
Manneville Park 492-C7 WnT
Mansur Park 493-D2 CTM
Maple Brook 455-G7 B
Maple Creek Commons 496-E3 WrT
Maple Creek Ests 496-D3 WrT
Maple Crest 461-B6 LTM
Maple Ct 459-E8 WTM
Maple Downs 459-J7 WTM
Maple Glen 562-E1 PeT
Maple Grove 494-C6 CTM; 529-E5 FT; 596-G1 G; 524-B5 WaT; 492-E9 WnT
Maple Hgts 460-K8 LTM; 459-D8 WTM
Maple Hill 460-H8 LTM
Maple Hills 529-J8 FT
Maple Lawn 459-J3 WTM
Maple Lodge 459-C7 WTM
Maple Park 459-D8 WTM
Maple Pointe 455-J7 B
Maple Ridge 559-F2 DTM; 562-C5 PeT
Maple Ridge Ests 559-E2 DTM
Maple-Del 393-G8 F
Maplecrest 459-K9 CTM
Maplelawn Farm 559-A3 DTM
Maplewood 426-B10; 460-B1 WTM
Mar-Rae Acres 523-G3 WaT
Marcarla 528-H1 WrT
Marcy Vill 459-J6 WTM
Mardale 455-E6 B
Mares Meadows 557-K8 GT
Marion County 422-J9 PTM
Marion Highlands 460-C5 WTM
Marion Park 492-K3 CTM
Marion Twp 322-B6 MTB
Marlette Park 493-D3 CTM
Marleywoods 592-C1 M
Marott Park 459-E7 WTM
Marquis Manor 527-E6 PeT
Mars Hill 526-C4 WnT
Martin Burtons 527-J7 PeT
Maryknoll Park 562-B1 PeT
Masthead 394-G10; 428-G1 FCT; 428-D3 LTM
Matmore 460-C9 CTM
Mayfair 459-J5 WTM
Mayfair Lane 425-A2 WTM
Mayflower Meadows 426-G10 WTM
Mayflower Park 526-A9 DTM
Mayflower Vill 526-D7 DTM
Maynard 459-G5 WTM
Maywood 526-E4 WnT
Maywood Manor 526-E6 DTM
Maze Creek Ests 564-E8 FT
McClures 492-E9 WnT
McCords Crossing 428-K9 L
McCordsville 429-A4 McC
McFarland Farms 562-F5 PeT
McGlinchys 526-E1 WnT
McKean Pl 459-C8 WTM
McKinley Pl 493-K9 CTM
McLeser 526-J1 CTM
Meadland 493-H1 CTM
Meadlawn 494-D9 CTM
Meadow Brook Terr 492-E7 WnT
Meadow Crest 459-G2 WTM
Meadow Ests 490-B6 WaT
Meadow Lake Ests 497-J6 SCT
Meadow Park 528-A3 CTM
Meadow Vue Ct 561-E4 PeT
Meadowbrook 460-B8 WTM
Meadowbrooks 425-H5 WTM
Meadowood 491-H1 S
Meadows 326-B9 NT; 460-C5 WTM
Meadows Knoll 326-D9 N
Meadowview 460-J6 LTM
Meadowview Farms 462-E10 WrT
Meadowvue 496-A4 WrT
Mechanicsburg 456-J10 WnT
Medallion Meadows 524-F4 WaT
Mendenhall Meadows 559-D4 DTM
Mercator 596-D4 G
Meredith Meadows 564-A4 FT
Merhanna Pl 527-D7 PeT
Meridian 561-F8 PeT
Meridian Acres 527-F9 PeT
Meridian Hgts 459-F5 WTM
Meridian Hgts Pl 459-F6 WTM
Meridian Hills 425-D8 WTM
Meridian Hills Meadows 425-D8 WTM
Meridian Kessler Terr 459-E2 WTM
Meridian Knolls 459-F4 WTM
Meridian Meadows 561-E9 G; 561-E4 PeT
Meridian Park 459-F10; 493-F1 CTM; 561-D9 PeT; 459-E7 WTM
Meridian Park Ests 424-J10 WTM
Meridian Street 561-E1 PeT
Meridian Terr 459-E4 WTM
Meridian Vill 527-E8 PeT
Meridian Westfield 459-F3 WTM
Meridian Woods 425-B6 WTM
Meridian Woods Manor 561-B4 PeT
Meridian Woods Park 561-D4 PeT
Meridian Woods Vill 561-D2 PeT
Merrimac 357-C10 WTH
Merrit Pl DN-A2; 492-K6 CTM
Metz Forest 562-A2 PeT
Meyer Ests 529-C4 WrT
Michigan Ests 496-B6 WrT
Michigan Highlands 424-H10; 458-H1 WTM
Michigan Hills 528-J1 WrT
Michigan Road Gdns 424-G10 PTM
Michigan Terr 492-B7 WnT
Mickleyville 525-H2 WnT
Middle Twp 455-B2 MTH
Middleton Pl 394-A4 F
Mill Creek 359-A1 NT
Mill Pond 423-B7 PTM
Millena Ests 490-K7 WnT
Miller 593-F1 MTM
Millerdale 494-G8 CTM
Millersville 460-F4 WTM
Minerva Hgts 492-C10 WnT
Miniature Park DN-A2; 492-H7 WnT
Minnehaha 422-K5 PTM
Minnesota Hgts 528-C1 CTM
Minocqua Manor 528-C1 CTM
Mission Hills 596-H2 G
Misty Lake 424-K3 WTM
Mohawk Crossing 392-G4 Ca
Mohawk Hills 392-A6 Ca
Mohr Ests 531-H8 SCT
Monterey Vill 359-E1 N
Monticello 459-H5 WTM
Montrose 459-K6 WTM
Mooresville 557-G10; 558-A10; 592-A2, A8 M
Mootz 526-J1 WnT
Moral Twp 531-D9; 565-E5; 599-E1 MTS
Morgan Meadows 393-H8 F
Morgan Park 460-G10; 494-H1 WrT
Morningside 458-E5 PTM
Morris Park 526-E1 WnT
Morrow Wood 461-C5 L
Morse Overlook 325-E4 N
Morse Park Ests 325-D9 N
Morton Pl 493-F3 CTM
Moss Creek 562-G3 PeT
Mount Auburn 491-H5 WnT
Mount Comfort 463-D8 BCT
Mount Jackson 492-F8 WnT
Mount Pleasant 560-H10 WTJ
Muesing Creek Ests 496-G9 WrT
Muesing Farms 496-G10 WrT
Muir Woods 426-A5 WTM
Muirfield 563-B5 FT
Muirfield Vill 489-A8 WaT
Murphy Meadows 455-H5 B
Myers Manor 562-B3 PeT
Mystic Bay 425-K7; 426-A8 WTM

N

Nantucket Bay 426-C6 WTM
National Hgts 492-A10 WnT
Nesbit Hills 426-J6 WTM
New Augusta 424-C9 PTM
New Augusta Woods 424-C10 PTM
New Britton 393-J4 DTH
New Britton Woods 393-G4 F
New Fields 525-A1 WnT
New Heritage 525-F1 WnT
New Palestine 531-H6 NP
New Palestine Vill 531-E2 SCT
New Ralston Ests 493-K2 CTM
New Whiteland 596-C9 PTJ
Newark Vill 392-A6 Ca
Newlin Acres 557-J1 P
Newlin Ridge 557-F7 GT
Newlynn 526-A8 DTM
Newport Bay 426-B8 WTM
Noblesville 325-A7, H8; 326-C10; 358-G1, G8; 359-H4; 360-B6; 393-H1; 394-A1 N
Noblesville Twp 325-F7; 326-C6; 359-C9; 360-C4 NT
Noel Forest 423-C9 PTM
Nora 425-J5 WTM
Nora Woods 425-J3 WTM
Noraleigh 425-H5 WTM
Normandy Farms 423-D8 PTM
North Acre 527-K8 PeT
North Arsenal Park DN-F2; 493-J7 CTM
North Augusta 424-D1 CTH
North Brookside Park 494-C3 CTM
North Butler Terr 459-D4 WTM
North Central Manor 425-J6 WTM
North College Woods 425-G10 WTM
North Crows Nest 459-D2 WTM
North East Monticello 459-J5 WTM
North Eastern Park Hgts 460-B9 WTM
North Eastwood 461-G9 WrT
North Euclid Pl 494-G5 WrT
North Glen Eden 457-K5 PTM
North Hampton Vill 424-J7 WTM
North Harbour 325-B6 N
North Kessler Manor 460-A3 WTM
North Kessler Park 460-A3 WTM
North Lawrence Park 461-E5 L
North Meadow 457-J1 PTM
North Meridan 459-E7 WTM
North Meridian Highlands 425-E5 WTM
North Meridian Hills 425-F8 WTM
North Meridian Manor 425-E4 WTM
North Park 459-H10; 493-E1 CTM; 529-J7 FT; 592-A1 M
North Penncrest 425-F4 WTM
North Pl 459-F6 WTM
North Plaza 460-C10 CTM
North Pointe Bay 424-G2 PTM
North Port 525-F10 DTM
North Ridge Vill 425-F1 CTH
North Ripple 425-H10 WTM
North Sargent Hills 427-K4 LTM
North Side 459-J10 CTM
North Tuxedo 494-F6 CTM
North West Ests 455-B3 BTH
North Willow Farms 425-A4 WTM
North Willow Park 424-H3 PTM
North Willow Way 424-H4 PTM
North Willow Woods 424-H2 WTM
Northbrook 425-B7 WTM
Northcliffe 459-J2 WTM
Northcliffe Terr 459-J2 WTM
Northcroft 459-H6 WTM
Northdale 459-K3 WTM
Northdale Lake 459-K4 WTM
Northern Acres 455-J2 BTH
Northern Beach 392-J8 CTH
Northern Ests 458-E6 PTM; 458-E6 WTM
Northern Hgts 391-F8 CTH; 459-G8 WTM
Northern Hills 425-J6 WTM
Northern Meadows 389-H6 Z
Northern Park 562-E9 G
Northfield 558-K9 DTM
Northfield Ests 393-E10 F
Northfield Woods 523-G6 P
Northmead 459-C8 WTM
Northolm 458-J3 WTM
Northridge 455-F4 B; 359-J1 NT
Northup 459-F3 WTM
Northview 459-G3 WTM; 389-H5 Z
Northview Manor 425-J5 WTM
Northways 494-A4 CTM
Northwest Manor 423-F6 PTM
Northwestern Park 493-C1 CTM
Northwood 455-K2 BTH; 460-A8 WTM
Northwood Farms 392-J6 CTH
Northwood Hills 393-A7 CTH
Norwaldo 459-K2 WTM
Norwich 425-G10 WTM
Nottingham Park 458-H5 WTM
Nowland 494-C4 CTM
Noyes 459-D4 WTM

O

Oak Bend 489-E5 A

Oak Hgts 493-K3; 494-A3 CTM
Oak Hill 494-A3 CTM
Oak Lawn 492-B2 S
Oak Meadows 596-B3 G
Oak Meadows MHP 594-B8 WTJ
Oak Park 358-B7 WTH
Oak Park Vill 462-F1 L
Oak Ridge 557-A7 GT; 459-H3 WTM; 389-F4 Z
Oak Ridge Manor 459-B2 WTM
Oak Trace 559-H5 DTM
Oakbay 325-D5 N
Oakforge Lakes 458-B2 PTM
Oakforge Woods 458-C2 PTM
Oakhaven 428-A7 LTM
Oakland Hills at Geist 428-E8 L
Oakland Terr 460-B1 WTM
Oakland Vill 462-F1 L
Oakland Woods 428-H7 L
Oaklandon 428-J10; 462-J1 L
Oaklandon Meadows 428-J10 L
Oaklandon Northeast 428-H9 L
Oakley Hgts 527-G6 PeT
Oakmont 528-D4 BG; 359-D2 N; 425-C5 WTM
Oakpark 526-F1 WnT
Oaks 595-K3 G
Oaks Park 493-K3 CTM
Oakview 457-F1 PTM
Oakwood 496-J10 Cu
Oakwood Ests 491-G10 WnT
Old Colony 459-F7 WTM
Old Cricket Town Tree Vill 425-A4 WTM
Old Mill Park 559-K1 DTM
Olde Dominion 389-E9 Z
Olde Mill 425-D5 WTM
Olender Hgts 526-B7 DTM
Olio 395-C5 F; 395-C5 FCT
Olive Branch Ests 594-J5 WTJ
One West 425-E5 WTM
Orchard Acres 425-G6 WTM
Orchard Grove 494-E3 CTM; 494-K6; 528-K3 WrT
Orchard Hills 460-J2 LTM
Orchard Lawn 460-C4 WTM
Orchard Park 391-K10; 425-J1 CTH
Orme Park 594-G2 WTJ
Osborn Ridge 494-K6 WrT
Osman Acres 490-B4 WaT
Oxbow 459-H1 WTM
Oxford 494-B4 CTM
Oxford Park 494-B7; 526-J1 CTM; 393-A9 F
Oxford Pl 494-C7 CTM; 459-D7 WTM
Oxford Terr 494-B2 CTM
Oxford Vill 426-B10 WTM

P

Palmers Home Pl DN-A3; 492-K8 CTM
Parc Ests 491-G4 WnT
Parc Ests North 491-F3 WnT
Park at Buffalo Creek 561-G8 PeT
Park Avenue Hgts 425-F5 WTM
Park Crest 527-H4 CTM
Park Ests 489-F2 LTH
Park Forest 461-A6 LTM
Park Front DN-F1; 493-J5 CTM
Park Grove 528-D6 BG
Park Hgts 493-D1 CTM
Park Hoover Vill 425-A10; 459-A1 WTM
Park Lafayette 492-E3 WnT
Park Meadow 528-E6 PeT
Park Meadows 391-E4 Ca
Park of the Four Seasons 461-C6 L
Park Pl 489-H8 A; DN-F1; 493-E3, J5 CTM
Park Valley Ests 496-C4 WrT
Park View 559-H3 DTM
Parkshore 394-B2 F
Parkside 493-K8 CTM
Parkside Bus Park 394-A5 F
Parkview 493-A1 CTM; 459-H6 WTM
Parkview Ests 491-J2 S
Parkview Pl 491-J5 WnT
Parkway Gdns 527-A6 PeT
Parkwood Ct 460-H7 LTM
Parkwood Terr 495-K2 WrT
Parliament Park 462-A8 LTM
Pasadena Hgts 495-A2 WrT
Patios of Buffalo Creek 561-H8 PeT
Patterson Knoll 562-F2 PeT
Paul Sparks 456-H9 LTH
Peaceful Acres 524-G8 P
Peacemaker 358-K5 NT
Pebble Brook 358-J3 N
Pebble Hills 594-K1 WTJ
Pebble Run 594-H1 WTJ
Pendleton Hgts 460-H10 WrT
Penn Crest 459-E5 WTM
Penn Park 561-E3 PeT
Pennington Ests 594-J9 WTJ
Pennridge 425-F8 WTM
Pennsylvania Hgts 425-E5 WTM
Pennwood 425-F4 WTM
Pennwood North 425-E3 WTM
Perry Common 560-K5 PeT
Perry Lakes 561-K7 PeT
Perry Manor 562-C3 PeT
Perry Pines 562-E2 PeT
Perry Twp 388-A8; 422-B2 PTB; 527-A8; 528-C7; 561-D4; 562-E6 PeT
Perry Woods Ests 562-B2 PeT
Pheasant Run 559-J4 DTM
Pickwick 425-B4 WTM
Pickwick Vill 460-E2 WTM
Pike Twp 423-D7; 424-E9; 457-D5; 458-B4 PTM
Pin Oak Manor 455-G9 LTH
Pine Bluff Overlook 394-A9 F
Pine Crest 462-D9 WrT
Pine Hill Ests 462-G2 L
Pine Knoll 324-G7 N
Pine Ridge Ests 427-J3 LTM
Pine Way 422-F8 BTH
Pine Woods 424-B7 PTM
Pinecrest 456-K9 WnT
Pines 427-A2 F
Pines of Westfield 358-A5 WTH
Pinesprings 427-F7 LTM
Pioneer Country Ests 557-J10 BTM
Plainfield 523-D9; 524-C7; 557-F1; 558-B2 P
Plainfield Manor 523-C7 GT
Plantana 394-C2 F
Plantation Meadows 561-A5 PeT
Pleasant Acres 463-C3 BCT; 565-A4 MTS; 426-D8 WTM
Pleasant Hills 461-F10 WrT
Pleasant Lake Ests 562-C8 PeT
Pleasant Park 528-A1 CTM
Pleasant Ripple 494-E8 CTM
Pleasant Run 493-K10; 494-F7 CTM; 495-C6 WrT
Pleasant Run Plaza 495-A6 WrT
Pleasant Twp 561-H10 G; 563-A10; 595-J6; 596-F6 PTJ
Pleasant Valley 493-J10 CTM
Pleasant View 494-F7; 528-A2 CTM; 394-D4 F; 564-H4 MTS
Pleasant Vue Ests 455-C7 LTH
Pleasanton 494-G7 WrT
Pleasanton Hgts 494-H7 WrT
Pleasantview 524-J4 WnT
Plum Creek 392-K4 Ca
Polley Woods 427-G8 LTM
Polo Run 561-K10 G
Pomona Pl 459-D7 WTM
Ponds West 391-B1 CTH
Pope Pl 461-B6 L
Portalan Pleasant Plains 497-C2 BCT
Post Way Manor 495-H3 WrT
Potters Cove 456-K5 PTM
Potters Woods 325-J10 NT
Powers 561-E1 PeT
Powers Meridian Hgts 561-E8 PeT
Prairie Acres 495-D8 WrT
Prairie Manor 490-B7 WaT
Prairie View 393-B3 Ca
Prairie Vill 455-F7 B
Preston Ests 455-C1 BTH
Prestwick 489-A10 WaT
Prestwick Ests 523-B1 WaT
Primrose Vill 459-J4 WTM
Princeton Park 393-B9 F
Princeton Pl 493-F1 CTM
Prospect Hgts 494-D10 CTM
Provident 494-C1 CTM
Pyramid Pointe 424-E3 PTM

Q

Quail Creek 565-C1 MTS; 562-E2 PeT
Quail Ridge 423-H10; 457-H1 PTM; 357-F5 WTH
Quail Run 392-K3 Ca
Quaker Ridge 394-C9 F
Quillen Acres 558-K4 DTM

R

Radford Ct 461-C10 WrT
Raglands Urban 526-B1 WnT
Rahkewood 561-C1 PeT
Rainbow Highlands 428-C8 L
Rainbow Ridge 492-E4 WnT
Rainbow Valley 562-B7 PeT
Raintree Pl 389-K8 Z
Ralston Hgts 425-K8 WTM
Ravenswood 425-J8 WTM
Raymond Park 527-E3 CTM
Raymond Park Hgts 528-A3 CTM
Reagan Park 493-G2 CTM
Red Bud Ests 427-J6 LTM
Reds Corner 598-E4 CTJ
Reeds Acres 456-D10 LTH
Reel Creek 422-H9 BTH
Regency Circle Courts 457-G9 WnT
Reserve at Springmill 391-D10 CTH
Rhodius Park DN-A4; 492-J9 CTM
Richeys 526-K1 CTM
Richfield Ests 489-F6 WaT
Richwood Ests 489-E6 WaT
Riddle Manor 460-B2 WTM
Ridge Creek Pines 428-H8 L
Ridge Field East 462-C9 WrT
Ridge Hill Trails 560-K9 PeT
Ridge View 426-G8 WTM
Ridgecreek 558-J9 DTM
Ridgegate 424-C7 PTM
Ridgeline Ests 523-D6 P
Ridgewood 592-C4 M
Ridgewood Manor 527-G7 PeT
Ripple View 459-G4 WTM
Ritchling Acres 561-C3 PeT
Ritter Park 494-H3 WrT
River Glen 393-D6 F
River Hgts 425-J9 WTM
River Highlands 393-D6 F
River Oaks at Geist 428-F9 L
River Park 425-H8; 426-B7 WTM
River Ridge 393-B7 F
River Run 560-A3 DTM
River View 425-J8 WTM
Rivers Edge Ests 455-B1 BTH
Riverside 459-H10; 492-K1 CTM
Riverside Highlands 492-G1 WnT
Riverside II Tr Pk 489-D6 WaT
Riverside Lakeview 493-A1 CTM
Riverside Park 492-G4 WnT
Riverside Tr Pk 489-B6 WaT
Riverview 459-B5, F1 WTM
Riverwood 326-E4 NT; 460-C6 WTM
Roberson Vill 592-D1 M
Roberson Woods 592-E1 M
Roberts Creek 559-G4 DTM
Robertson Vill 458-E8 PTM
Robin Run Vill 458-A1 PTM
Robindale 492-B8 WnT
Robinwood 460-F10 CTM
Rocklane 597-J3 CTJ
Rocklyn 492-A8 WnT
Rockville Gdns 492-B7 WnT
Rockwood 531-A4 SCT
Rocky Ripple 459-B5 WTM
Roland Park 426-H6 WTM
Rolling Acres 455-C4 B
Rolling Fields 426-E8 WTM
Rolling Knolls 526-B8 DTM
Rolling Meadows 523-J9 P; 492-C2 WnT
Rolling R 455-F10 LTH
Rolling Ridge Pines 460-D3 WTM
Rooker Run 592-B5 M
Rosalia Pl 494-F4 CTM
Rose Hill 460-G8 WTM
Rose Manor 562-A8 PeT
Rosebay Commons 425-G5 WTM
Rosedale 494-C1 CTM
Rosedale Hills 528-A9 PeT
Rosedale Park 461-D7 L
Roselawn Park 525-J8 DTM
Rosemont 492-G9 WnT
Rosewood 394-B3 F
Rosslyn 460-B8 WTM
Round Stone 423-E1 ET
Round-Up 393-A9 DTH
Roundtree 425-D5 WTM
Roundtree Park 528-F1 CTM
Routon 559-A5 DTM
Roxbury 427-A2 F
Roxbury Arms 460-H4 LTM
Royal Parkview 493-A2 CTM
Royal Pine Ests 426-E8 WTM
Royal Troon 489-A10 WaT
Royalton 422-F2 ET
Rudgate 489-G4 WaT
Ruggles Trace 460-C3 WTM
Runnymeade Ests 394-C9 F
Rupp Park 494-B7 CTM
Russell Lake 389-B9 ET
Rybolts 492-C9 WnT

S

Saddle Ridge 422-J4 PTM
Saddlebrook 458-E3 PTM
Saddlebrook North 458-E3 PTM
Saddlebrook South 458-D6 PTM
Sail Pl 428-H1 FCT
Saint Andrews 460-F8 WTM
Saint Clair Pl 494-B6 CTM
Saint Francis Park 528-D4 BG
Saint Helena 528-D2 CTM
Salem Park 492-F8 WnT
Salem Sq 527-K8 PeT
San Rose Ests 425-D3 WTM
Sand Creek Woods 394-C7 F
Sandalwood Park 561-C5 PeT
Sandpiper Bay 424-E2 PTM
Sandstone Lakes 394-H6 F
Sandstone Meadows 394-K6 F
Sandstone Ridge 395-A8 F
Sandstone Vill 394-K8 F
Sandstone Woods 394-H7 F
Sandy Pt 426-C6 WTM
Saratoga 523-A7 P
Sargent Creek 427-J3 LTM
Sargent Woods 427-H6 LTM
Sarkine Park 489-F4 WaT
Sawgrass 394-E9 F
Sawyer 461-A10 WrT
Scarborough Farms 358-K10 NT
Scarborough Vill 427-G8 LTM
Schildmeier Vill 530-J4 SCT
Schildmeier Woods 530-K5 SCT
Secluded Acres 326-C5 NT
Secrest South 459-H5 WTM
Secrist Manor 525-J7 DTM
Seerley Creek 526-A6 DTM
Seifert Creek 531-J4 SCT
Selig 388-J6 ET
Settlers Mill 359-B1 N
Settles Landing 490-H1 WnT
Seven Oaks at Geist 428-G9 L
Seville 491-B1 WnT
Shadeland Acres 461-D6 L
Shadeland Manor 495-D4 WrT
Shadeland Park 461-C8 L
Shadeland Sta 427-C9 LTM
Shadeland Terr 461-D6 L
Shadeland Vill 461-C10 WrT
Shadow Hills 595-B2 WTJ
Shadow Pointe 458-D6 PTM
Shadow Ridge 427-F6 LTM
Shadow Wood 491-E10 WnT
Shadow Wood South 525-E1 WnT
Shadowlawn 393-C8 F
Shady Acres MHP 599-C2 MTS
Shady Creek 561-H10 G
Shady Hills 423-A7 PTM
Shady Knoll 425-B7 WTM
Shady Oaks 496-B1 WrT
Shadybrook 426-C1 Ca
Shamrock Hgts 495-G2 WrT
Shangri La 460-G10 WrT
Shannon Lakes 561-A6 PeT
Shannon Park 494-D6 CTM
Sheffield Park 489-G6 WaT
Sheffield Woods 496-C1 WrT
Shelby Gdns 527-H4 CTM
Shelton Hgts 492-D9 WnT
Shenandoah 525-F8 DTM
Shenandoah Valley Ests 561-G7 PeT
Sher Bella Vill 460-B7 WTM
Sheridan Hgts 461-A6, A8 LTM
Sherman Drive Park 528-C7 PeT
Sherman Hgts 494-D6 CTM
Sherman Manor 460-D7 WTM
Sherman Oaks 562-C7 PeT
Sherman Park 460-C9 CTM
Sherman Towne 528-D9 PeT
Sherwood Forest 425-J3 WTM
Sherwood Vill 425-G9 WTM
Shiloh Acres 490-G4 WaT
Shiloh Country Ests 490-F4 WaT
Shiloh Creek Ests 490-G7 WaT
Shiloh Crossing 490-E8 WaT
Shiloh Farms 490-E7 WaT
Shiloh Run 596-J4 G
Shoal Creek Ests 456-C3 BTH
Shore Acres 425-H10; 459-G1 WTM
Shorewalk 428-E6 LTM
Shrum Tr Pk 524-A7 P
Sielkens 526-H1 WnT
Silver Hills 528-J2 WrT
Silver Hills Ests 528-J2 WrT
Silver Springs 560-J9 WTJ
Silver Thorne 358-B10 WTH
Silverleaf Ests 425-C5 PTM
Simko Hgts 492-E5 WnT
Simpson Pl 528-D4 BG
Six Points 524-G4 WaT
Sleepy Hollow 427-H6 LTM
Smith Meadows 389-D4 Z
Smith Valley 594-K4 WTJ
Somerset 528-B5 PeT
Somerset Hills 425-C6 WTM
Son A Rose 562-E3 PeT
South Brookside 494-B4 CTM
South Butler Terr 459-C7 WTM
South Ct 561-J4 PeT
South Downs 561-J2 PeT
South Eastwood 528-G8 BG
South Grove 528-G7 BG
South Grove Woods 528-E8 BG
South Harbour 325-C9 N
South Haven Manor 561-D5 PeT
South Hill Ests 557-J2 P
South Indianapolis 527-K7 PeT
South Park 528-E6 BG
South Park Vill 528-G9 BG
Southcreek 561-D8 PeT
Southdale 527-D10 PeT
Southeast Manor 565-F10 MTS
Southeastern Hgts 494-D10 CTM
Southern 561-F9 PeT
Southern Hgts 528-E10 PeT; 528-J4 WrT
Southern Hills 561-E2 PeT
Southern Lakes Ests 563-A5 FT
Southern Oaks 561-B6 PeT
Southern Plateaux 563-A4 FT
Southern Springs 562-K7 FT
Southern Trails 563-A7 FT
Southern View 562-H1 FT
Southgate Farms 561-H5 PeT
Southport 562-A1 PeT; 561-J5; 562-A1 Spt
Southridge 455-C9 LTH
Southwest Hill 526-A6 DTM
Southwood Westwood MHP 596-C6 G
Sparrowood 428-J10 L
Speedway 491-H2; 492-A6 S
Speedway Cunningham Park 491-H4 S
Speedway Ests 492-A3 S
Speedway Manor 492-A3 S
Speedway Woods 491-H6 WnT
Speichers Highlands 525-E1 WnT
Spihers 492-E7 WnT
Spring Creek 457-J4 PTM
Spring Farms 391-C4 Ca
Spring Hill Pl 424-G6 PTM
Spring Hills 458-K7 WTM
Spring Hollow 425-C3 WTM
Spring Lake Ests 391-E6 CTH
Spring Lane 525-E9 DTM
Spring Meadow 425-C8 WTM
Spring Meadows 497-J8 SCT
Spring Mill 592-B4 M
Spring Mill Ct 425-D5 WTM
Spring Mill Ests 425-C10 WTM
Spring Mill Hgts 459-D1 WTM
Spring Mill Lakes 425-B3 WTM
Spring Mill Pl 391-D9 CTH
Spring Mill Ridge 425-D8 WTM
Spring Mill Woods 425-C4 WTM
Spring Oaks 563-A1 FT
Spring Valley 490-K10 WnT
Springbrook 561-B4 PeT
Springdale 494-A5 CTM; 393-K8 DTH
Springdale Farms 357-E8 WTH
Springmill Crossing 391-D3 CTH
Springmill Hills 425-D7 WTM
Springmill Villages 357-F8 WTH
Spyglass Hill 394-B8 F
Stable Chase Ests 496-E10 WrT
Stafford Pointe 524-A10 P
Stanley Cove 557-K7 GT
Stardust Vill 359-H1 NT
State Plaza 493-K7 CTM
State Sq 493-K9 CTM
Station Hill 489-C10 WaT
Steeplechase 427-B3 LTM
Steinmeier 426-H8 WTM
Steinmeier Farms 426-E9 WTM
Steinmeier Vill 426-G9 WTM
Sterling Green 394-A4 F
Sterling Hgts 525-D2 WnT
Stevens Pl DN-D3; 493-F9 CTM
Stevenson Mill 393-G3 F
Stiltz & Millers 494-F10 CTM
Stinemeyer Farm 494-J2 WrT
Stockdale Tr Pk 524-A7 P
Stone Mill 489-G10; 523-G1 A; 562-E1 PeT
Stonecrest 460-F7 WTM
Stonegate 561-E10 G; 427-F8 LTM
Stonehedge 391-J1 Ca
Stones Crossing 595-D8 WTJ
Stoneybrook 595-G2 G
Stony Brook 455-C4 B
Stonybrook 425-B10 WTM
Stouts 493-B4 CTM
Stovall Manor 461-G7 LTM
Stratford 494-D8 CTM
Stratford Glen 457-G2 PTM
Stratford of Avon 489-D7 WaT
Strathmore 460-A9 CTM
Strawtown 326-H1 WRT
Stuckys Homeplace 528-A10 PeT
Suburban Acres 596-A1 G; 495-G9 WrT
Suburban Ests Tr Pk 325-J6 NT
Suburban Hgts 523-G2 WaT
Suburban Hills 494-J2 WrT
Success 460-J10 WrT
Sugar Bush Farms 455-H9 B
Sugar Creek 565-E8 MTS
Sugar Creek Twp 497-E9; 531-C3 SCT; 599-D6 STS
Sugar Grove 459-G2 WTM
Sugarbush Hill 389-G10 Z
Sugarwood Ests 489-F5 WaT
Suger Grove 460-D10 CTM
Summer Ridge 425-A2 WTM
Summer Walk 562-B8 PeT
Summerfield 559-A10 MTM
Summerfield Pl 457-E10 WnT
Summerfield South 457-E10 WnT
Summerhill 529-H7 FT
Summerwood 427-J5 LTM
Summit River Crossing 426-D4 WTM
Sun Down 530-C4 WrT
Sun Lake 393-K5 F
Sun Meadow 458-G8 WTM
Sun Ridge Ests 530-K1 SCT
Sunblest 393-H6 F
Sunblest Apts 393-G7 F
Sunblest Farms 393-F6 F
Suncrest 529-E5 FT; 562-E9 G
Sunningdale Commons 490-J2 WnT
Sunny Breeze 562-F1 PeT
Sunny Knoll 455-D7 B
Sunny Meade 459-C5 WTM
Sunny Meadows 456-B5 LTH
Sunny Side 494-H8 WrT
Sunny Suburban Acres 489-F1 LTH
Sunny Sylvan Ests 426-D10 WTM
Sunnybrooke 428-D10 L
Sunnygrove 494-F4 CTM
Sunnyview 528-F1 CTM
Sunset Acres 525-K8 DTM
Sunset at Eagle Creek 457-F8 PTM
Sunset Cove 428-G7 L
Sunset Ests 523-E8 P
Sunset Hgts 425-D4 WTM
Sunset Lake 490-J9 WnT
Sunset Park 525-K1 WnT
Sunshine Gdns 526-G10 PeT
Superior Gdns 526-D8 DTM
Surar Tree 425-C4 WTM
Sutherland Avenue Hgts 459-J9 CTM
Swathmoor Hills 561-F4 PeT
Sweet Briar 394-C4 F
Sweet Creek Woods 531-B5 SCT
Sweet Springs Ests 393-G4 F
Sweetwater Ests 426-D8 WTM
Sycamore Bend 389-D7 ET
Sycamore Grove 425-A8 WTM
Sycamore Hills 531-J2 SCT
Sycamore Ridge 489-C8 WaT
Sycamore Springs 426-F6 WTM
Sycamore Terr 528-G2 WrT
Sylvan Ests 460-D1 WTM
Sylvan Meadows 426-C10 WTM
Sylvan Ridge Lakes 426-C8 WTM
Sylvan Woods 326-F6 NT

T

Tacoma Vill 460-A10; 494-B1 CTM
Tall Timbers 425-C2 WTM
Tamarack 425-B3 WTM
Tanglewood Ests 426-G10 WTM
Tansel Crossing 490-H3 WaT
Tansel Wood Ests 456-H8 PTM
Tansel Woods 456-J9 WnT
Tara 457-K10 WnT
Tatman Manor 460-G9 CTM
Tealpoint 496-D5 WrT
Tempo 495-G5 WrT
Tempo North 495-G4 WrT
Terra 426-C9 WTM
Terra Rose Ests 490-C5 WaT
Terra Vista 426-C10 WTM
Terra Vista East 426-C10 WTM
Terrace Beach 425-J8 WTM
Terry Lane 458-C9 WnT
The Anchorage 394-J10; 428-K1 FCT
The Arbors 461-F4 L
The Boulders 562-H2 FT
The Bronx 425-F8 WTM
The Colony 558-G9 GT
The Commons 593-A2 MTM
The Creek by the Woods 455-C7 LTH
The Depot 561-B8 PeT
The Forest of Rohan 422-K4 PTM
The Fountains 459-G4 WTM
The Freelands 527-K8 PeT
The Hamptons at Geist 428-A6 LTM
The Hawthorns 394-J9 F
The Hideaway 424-H6 PTM
The Highlands 557-J9 GT; 458-K4 WTM
The Highlands at Eagle Creek 457-E7 PTM
The Highlands at Geist 428-G6 L
The Homestead 523-B8 P
The Islands 457-C10 WnT
The Knoll 458-J8 WTM
The Landing 559-A10 MTM
The Links at Gray Eagle 395-B6 F
The Meadows 460-C8 WTM
The Mission 558-J10 MTM
The Moorings 428-C3 LTM
The North Woods at Geist 428-J6 L
The Oaks 495-E6 WrT
The Overlook 394-H10 F; 425-B5 WTM
The Paddock at Stable Chase 530-D1 WrT
The Park at Weston Pl 390-C9 CTH
The Pines 457-J1 PTM
The Pines of Avon 489-H10; 523-H1 A
The Pines of Fall Creek 427-E10 LTM
The Portage 394-K9 FCT
The Ridge 456-K6 PTM
The Sanctuary 593-B1 MTM
The Settlement 559-B9 DTM
The Shriner 460-J10 WrT
The Springs of Cambridge 395-B10; 429-A1 FCT
The Timbers 528-D8 PeT
The Traditions of Westmount 491-F7 WnT
The Trails 561-A9 PeT
The Trees 457-C4 PTM
The Trees II 457-C6 PTM
The Vill at Eagles Landing 457-D8 PTM
The Villas 559-A10 MTM
The Villas of Oakbrook 458-A2 PTM
The Vineyard of Fall Creek 428-A4 LTM
The Willows 457-G6 PTM
The Woodlands at Irishman Run Farm 423-D1 ET
The Woods at Gray Eagle 395-A7 F
Thistlewood 391-F3 CTH
Thomas Acres 563-A3 FT
Thompson Meadows 525-J10 DTM
Thornberry 459-F2 WTM
Thornberry Pl 526-H2 CTM
Thornburg 455-G10 B
Thornhill 389-C9 Z
Thornridge 489-D10 A
Thorny Ridge 394-G9 F
Thoroughbred Acres 423-C4 PTM
Thoroughbred Ests 423-E5 PTM
Thoroughbred Farms 422-H3 BTH; 422-H3 PTM
Thunderbird Hgts 528-E1 CTM
Thurston Pl 526-C3 WnT
Tilden Terr 455-A8 LTH
Timber Bend 523-D3 WaT
Timber Creek 561-F10 G
Timber Grove Manor 528-F6 BG
Timber Lane Ests 393-E8 F
Timber Mill 425-C8 WTM
Timber Ridge 455-E6 LTH
Timber Springs 393-E9 F
Timberbrook 489-A1 LTH
Timbercrest 427-G8 LTM
Timberidge 390-A9 ET
Timberlakes 563-F5 FT
Timberline 427-K7; 428-A7 LTM
Town & Country Ests 458-G3 WTM
Towne Park South 528-F2 CTM
Tracy Ridge 596-D10 NW
Traders Cove on the Lake 457-B6 PTM
Traders Hollow 423-B6 PTM
Traders Pt 422-F7 BTH; 423-C8 PTM
Traders Pt North 423-F7 PTM
Traders Pt West 422-J7 PTM
Traders Sta 422-G8 BTH
Traditions 462-C4 L
Trails End 392-K8 DTH
Traubs West DN-A3; 492-J8 CTM
Travis Hill 594-C8 WTJ
Trebla Acres 427-J5 LTM
Treeholm Park 494-D9 CTM

Treetop 425-B5 WTM
Tremont 394-B10 F; 595-D10 WTJ; 490-K8 WnT
Tremont Gdns 490-K7 WnT
Tri-Sab Manor 527-D5 PeT
Trilobi Hills 428-A9 L
Trinity Ests 495-J5 WrT
Trinity Ests & Paradise Pl 558-B10 M
Trinity Manor 495-J4 WrT
Trophy Club 457-C9 WnT
Troy Terr 527-F5 CTM
Tudor Park 462-A9 WrT
Tulip Terr 561-K4 PeT
Turfway Park 594-K4 WTJ
Turnberry 489-A9 WaT; 491-B3 WnT
Turne Grove 394-J9 F
Twin Brooks 562-B4 PeT
Twin Oaks 457-F10; 491-F1 WnT

U

Union Chapel 360-D8 NT
Union Park Pl 459-E9 CTM
Union Twp 322-A10; 356-A6; 389-A1; 390-A1 UT
University Hgts 527-H8 PeT
University Highlands 527-G8 PeT
University Pl 494-H8 WrT
Urbahns 426-J8 WTM

V

Valle Vista 596-G4 G
Valley Brook Ests 496-H4 Cu
Valley Brook Vill 496-J2 Cu
Valley Creek 496-G2 WrT
Valley Farms Ests 394-A9 F
Valley Mills 525-E9 DTM
Valley Mills Forest Manor 525-F9 DTM
Valley Park DN-B4; 493-A10 CTM
Valley Ridge 558-J9 DTM
Valley Ridge Farms 560-K7 PeT
Valley View 425-K10 WTM
Valley View Farms 560-J8 PeT
Valley View Park 425-K10 WTM
Valley Ville 525-J9 DTM
Valleybrook 392-F2 Ca
Van Arsdel 564-B2 FT
Verdant Acres 490-C1 LTH
Vernon Acres 461-B9 WrT
Vernon Park 494-C7 CTM
Vernon Ridge 427-E9 LTM
Vernon Twp 429-E5; 463-E1 VT
Victoria Ests 527-B10 PeT
Victory Terr 561-E4 PeT
Villa Park 528-A4 CTM
Village at Eagle Creek 457-D7 PTM
Village Gate 427-G4 LTM
Village Manor 427-E4 LTM
Village of Carmel 391-F1 CTH
Village of Orchard Park 561-D6 PeT
Village Walk 389-E8 Z
Village Woods 427-H3 LTM
Villages at Pebble Brook 358-F3 N
Villages of Longwood 425-H2 WTM
Villas 595-A1 WTJ
Vinings at Geist 428-F7 L
Vinton Woods 462-A8 LTM
Virginia Highlands 461-B7 LTM
Virginia Manor 460-F9 CTM

W

Wacema Pl 459-G9 CTM
Waddells 561-J1 PeT
Wagners Home Pl 495-A7 WrT
Wal Mack Hgts 495-B3 WrT
Waldemere 460-A8 WTM
Waldorf Hall 459-F4 WTM
Walkerhurst 492-G5 WnT
Wall Street Hgts 489-J5 WaT
Wallace Crossing 528-J2 WrT
Wallingford 461-E3 L
Walnut Creek 394-A9 F
Walnut Farms 561-G7 PeT
Walnut Hill 523-J8 P; 562-A4 Spt
Walnut Hills 459-A3 WTM; 492-F7 WnT
Walnut Ridge 529-K8 FT; 489-D1 LTH
Wanamaker 529-H7 FT
Wanamaker Ests 529-K8 FT
Wanamaker Vill 529-H8 FT
Wapahani 393-A7 DTH
Warfleigh 459-F1 WTM
Warren Hgts 494-G6 WrT
Warren Hills 496-B6 WrT
Warren Lakes 496-G4 WrT
Warren Park 495-B5 WrT
Warren Plaza 495-F6 WrT
Warren Terr 495-D4 WrT
Warren Twp 461-B10; 462-F9; 495-D7; 496-C7; 529-E3; 530-C3 WrT
Warren Woods 462-E9 WrT
Warrendale 494-G1 WrT
Warrington 459-G5 WTM
Washington Boulevard Terr 459-F2 WTM
Washington Hgts 459-G8 WTM
Washington Meadows 496-G5 Cu
Washington Park 459-F9; 460-C9 CTM; 459-E7 WTM
Washington Pl 495-H6 WrT
Washington Pl Hgts 495-G6 WrT
Washington Sq 459-E5 WTM
Washington Trail 496-D7 WrT
Washington Twp 322-H7; 324-C6; 357-B6; 358-C6; 390-H1 WTH; 425-E7; 426-D8; 459-B3; 460-B2 WTM; 489-D4; 490-C5; 523-D4; 524-C3 WaT
Washington Vill 460-C10 CTM
Waterbury 424-G3 PTM
Waterford 392-C7 Ca
Waterloo 594-J10 WTJ
Waterscape 325-D6 N
Waterside 423-E4 PTM
Waterside at Northlake 360-B1 N
Waterstone 457-E9 WnT
Waterwood at Eagle Creek 457-C9 WnT
Watson Farms 462-B1 L
Watson Park 459-H9 CTM
Waverly 459-H2 WTM
Wayco South West 525-K1 WnT
Wayne Park 492-F9 WnT
Wayne Twp DN-A4; 457-E9; 458-D10; 491-C5; 492-E2; 525-C3; 526-E3 WnT; 327-E7; 361-D6 WyT
Wayneaire 491-G10 WnT
Weaver Creek 393-H1 F
Weaver Woods 393-H2 F
Weaver Woods North 393-G1 F
Wedgewood 559-G2 DTM; 457-J7 PTM
Welch Lake 557-H9 GT
Wellington 459-G1 WTM
Wellington Commons 495-E3 WrT
Wellington Ests 359-G9 N; 459-E1 WTM
Wellington Green 495-E4 WrT
Wellington Hgts South 359-J10 NT
Wellington North 359-H8 N
Wellington Northeast 359-J7 N
Wellington Overlook 359-G8 N
Wellington Park DN-A4; 492-J10 CTM; 495-E4 WrT
Wellington Park Hgts 425-E10; 459-D1 WTM
Wellington Pl 427-J1 F
West Arlington 494-K2 WrT
West Crows Nest 459-C3 WTM
West Gimber Ct 527-D4 CTM
West Harbour 324-K8 N
West Kessler 458-F3 WTM; 492-G4 WnT
West Newton 559-D6 DTM
West Noblesville 359-G2 N
West Park DN-A3; 492-H7 WnT
West Parkview 491-D9 WnT
West Ridge 325-E8 N
West Side 492-F6 WnT
West Speedway 491-H5 S
West Troy 526-A4 WnT
West Wind Ests 523-J2 WaT
West Wood 491-D4 WnT
Westbrook 492-A10 WnT
Westbrook Vill 359-F5 N
Westchester Ests 424-G7 PTM
Westclay 390-J4 CTH
Westdale 492-A9 WnT
Westerleigh 492-G1 WnT
Westerleigh Park 492-F2 WnT
Westfield 323-H10; 324-A10; 357-G2; 358-A2 W
Westfield Hgts 425-H7 WTM
Westhaven 492-G4 WnT
Westlane Terr 425-B9 WTM
Westmont 359-D3 NT
Westmore Hgts 460-A1 WTM
Weston Ridge 390-D8 CTH
Westover 424-D7 PTM
Westridge 359-E4 N; 492-B9 WnT
Westridge Vill 491-E4 WnT
Westview Terr 490-B5 WaT
Westwood 490-H5 WnT
Westwood Park 490-G1 WnT
Westwood Tr Park 524-B6 P
Whispering Pines 561-B9 WTJ; 530-C2 WrT
Whispering Trails 561-E10 G
Whispering Winds 523-H1 A
Whitaker Farms 563-A6 FT
Whitcomb Lane 491-J8 WnT
Whitcomb Ridge 325-C10; 359-D1 N
White 461-F5 L
White Horse Rapids 392-K9 DTH
White Lick 523-D8 P
White Pine Cove 395-E8 FCT
White River Twp 327-D3 WRT; 560-E10; 594-E6 WTJ
Whitehall 458-C6 PTM
Whitehall Commons 458-C6 PTM
Whiteland 596-F10 Whl
Whitemire Glen 393-E8 F
Whitestown 388-F2 Wh
Whittington Ests 455-J2 B
Wilcox DN-A2; 492-J7 CTM
Wildwood 529-F6 FT; 424-B10 PTM
Wildwood Ests 393-A8 F
Wildwood Hills 563-C2 FT
Wildwood Park 493-F2 CTM
Willard Pl 493-J8 CTM
Williams Creek 425-F6 WTM
Williams Creek Est 425-F7 WTM
Williams Creek Ests Pl 425-E6 WTM
Williams Creek Hills 425-C6 WTM
Williams Creek Ridge 425-F7 WTM
Williams Lake in the Woods 489-B1 LTH
Williams West Highlands 525-E2 WnT
Williamsburg 523-H4 WaT; 491-F9 WnT
Williamshire 425-B4 WTM
Williston Green 425-B3 WTM
Willman Lake 558-D6 GT
Willow Brook 529-C2 WrT
Willow Creek 358-B3 WTH
Willow Crest 393-H1 DTH
Willow Grove 531-B2 SCT
Willow Lakes 595-B7 WTJ; 529-E1 WrT
Willow Lakes East 595-C8 WTJ
Willow Oaks 529-F2 WrT
Willow Pond 561-F4 PeT
Willow Springs 455-E8 B
Willow View 460-B6 WTM
Willowmere 495-B10 WrT
Willowood 425-D3 WTM
Willwood Manor 592-C6 BTM
Wilmet Park 495-J5 WrT
Wilmington Park 461-F6 L
Wilshire Glen West 456-H9 WnT
Winchester Vill 561-K7; 562-A7 PeT
Windcombe 425-G6 WTM
Windemere 390-H10 CTH
Windemere Hgts 460-E1 WTM
Windermere Pointe 394-F10 F
Windermere Villas 394-E10 F
Windham Lake 457-B9 WnT
Winding Creek 455-G1 BTH; 393-F5 F
Winding Ridge 462-E5 L
Winding Way MHP 359-E10 NT
Windjammer 428-E1 FCT
Windmill Pointe 523-J3 WaT
Windpointe 392-G6 Ca
Windridge 455-E1 BTH; 460-G4 LTM; 460-G4 WTM
Windsong 428-G5 LTM
Windsong Ests 595-A3 WTJ
Windsor Pl 493-K5 CTM
Windsor Vill 495-A2 WrT
Windstar 462-F8 LTM
Windwood At Morse 325-E9 N
Winmar Pl 494-E7 CTM
Winston Island Woods 425-J10 WTM
Wintercove in the Woods 393-D9 F
Winthrop Ct 459-G8 WTM
Wiser 593-D2 MTM
Wolfington 458-E8 PTM
Wolfla Ests 428-A4 LTM
Wolverine 528-G1 CTM
Wood Creek Farms 489-G3 WaT
Wood Dale 497-F8 SCT
Wood Haven 390-C8 CTH
Wood-Lyn 526-B4 WnT
Woodacre 391-H3 Ca; 456-J4 LTM
Woodbrook 426-K4 LTM
Woodbury 429-H5 VT
Woodcliffe Manor 491-C1 WnT
Woodcreek 392-H8 Ca
Woodcreek Terr 561-B10 WTJ
Woodcroft 459-G7 WTM
Wooden Ests 425-C7 WTM
Woodfield 392-H1 Ca; 460-D8 WTM
Woodfox Ests 461-A7 LTM
Woodgate 392-E1 Ca
Woodland Country Club 392-A8 CTH
Woodland Ests 455-A5 LTH; 523-H9 P; 495-K9 WrT
Woodland Gdns 527-H6 PeT
Woodland Greens 392-F8 Ca
Woodland Hgts 426-A2 WTM
Woodland Lane Terr 425-J7 WTM
Woodland Park 494-H8 WrT
Woodland Pl 494-D7 CTM; 457-J7 PTM
Woodland Streams 595-B10 WTJ
Woodlands 428-A1 F
Woodlawn DN-F4; 493-J9 CTM
Woodpointe 490-J6 WnT
Woodpointe Vill 490-K5 WnT
Woodridge 595-B1 WTJ; 489-E6 WaT
Woodridge Longacre 527-H9 PeT
Woodruff Pl 493-K6 CTM
Woods Edge 428-A1, B1 F; 427-J7 LTM
Woods N Meadows 562-G1 PeT
Woods of Britton 393-J2 F
Woods of North Kessler 458-G8 WTM
Woodside 494-A8 CTM; 460-B1 WTM; 495-D6 WrT
Woodstock 459-A8 WTM
Worth Twp 388-E4 WTB
Worthington at West 86th 423-F4 PTM
Wrighthurst 494-F3 CTM
Wyndemere Ct 428-B4 LTM
Wynfield 462-D3 L
Wynnedale 458-H7 WTM
Wynnedale Ests 458-H6 WTM
Wynnedale Hgts 458-G7 WTM
Wynstone 392-G6 Ca
Wynterway Ests 427-A9 LTM

Y

Yorkshire 427-F5 LTM
Yorktown 595-J3 G
Young 592-F3 BTM

Z

Zion Hill 390-A6 ET
Zionsville 389-G6; 390-A7; 423-H1 Z

AIRPORTS

Eagle Cr 457-C8 PTM
Greenwood Mun 562-G9 G
Indianapolis Brookside Airpark 429-C5 McC
Indianapolis Intl 525-B4 DTM; 525-B4 WnT
Indianapolis Metropolitan 393-C10; 427-D1 F
Mount Comfort 463-G5 BCT
Noblesville 360-F10 NT
Post Aire 495-H10; 529-J1 WrT
Speedway 490-D2 LTH
Westfield 357-E2 WTH

BRIDGES

Eagle Cr Dam 457-A8 PTM; 457-A8 WnT
Eller Br 392-K7 CTH; 392-K7 DTH
Haunted Br 489-D9 A; 489-D9 WaT
Potters Covered Br 325-K9 NT

BUSINESS PARKS

Airport Technology Ctr 491-B8; 525-C1 WnT
Airwest Bus Pk 524-C10; 558-D1 GT; 524-C10; 558-D1 P
Allison Engine Manufacturing Fac 526-F3 WnT
Allison Pointe Office Pk 426-G5 WTM
Andico Ind Pk 523-H6 P
Andrade Ind Pk 390-A9 ET
Avon Bus Ctr 489-H9 A
Avon Commercial Pk 489-J9 A
Bauer Commercial Pk 426-D2 Ca
Beech Grove Ind Pk 528-K6 BG
Belmont Warehousing Complex DN-A3; 492-H9 CTM; DN-A3; 492-H9 WnT
Brookville Bus Pk 495-C10 WrT
Brownsburg Bus Pk 455-J4 B
Cambridge Sq Bus Pk 558-A3 P
Carmel Ind Pk 391-J7 Ca
Carmel Science & Technology Pk 391-G6 Ca
Castle Creek Office Pk 426-K4 WTM
Castleton Ind Pk 427-D4 LTM
Corporate Ctr North Ind Pk 423-G10; 457-H1 PTM
Country Club Ind Pk 491-A5 WnT
Crosspoint Bus Pk 393-G9 F; 427-E2 LTM
Daimler Chrysler Foundry 492-E10 WnT
Delaware Bus Pk 393-G10; 427-H1 F
Dow Chemicals Facility 423-H3 PTM
Eagle Bus Pk 389-G9 ET; 529-J5 FT; 389-G9 Z
Eastwood Ind Pk 495-A1 WrT
Exit Five Bus Pk 394-A7 DTH; 393-K7, K9 F
Fairlane Ctr Bus Pk 393-J4 F
Ford Automotive Plant 495-B8 WrT
Franklin Road Ind Pk 495-G7 WrT
General Motors Metal Ctr DN-B3 CTM
Greenwood Bus Ctr 596-J1 G; 596-J1 PTJ
Greenwood Ind Airpark 562-F10; 596-E1 G
Greenwood Ind Pk 596-E7 G
Hawthorne Yards 494-H10 WrT
Heartland Crossing Bus Pk 558-G8 DTM; 558-G8 GT
Heritage Bus Pk 455-G2 B; 455-G2 BTH
Hunter Creek Bus Ctr 461-K10 WrT
Indianapolis Power & Light DN-C3 CTM
Jackson Ind Pk 461-G10 LTM; 495-G1 WrT
Keystone at the Crossings Office Pk 426-C3 WTM
Library Pk Office Pk 595-F4 G
Lilly Corp Ctr DN-D4; 493-F10 CTM
Lilly Ind Ctr 493-A10; 527-A2 CTM
Loma Ind Pk 393-E10; 427-E1 DTH
Meridian Technology Ctr 391-F7 Ca
Midwest Ind Pk 491-B4 WnT
Navistar Intl Fac 494-J9 WrT
Near North Ind Pk DN-D1; 493-D5 CTM
New Britton Commercial Pk 393-J3 F
North By Northeast Bus Pk 427-G1 F
North By Northwest Bus Pk 424-A5 PTM
Northeast Business Ctr 427-E3 LTM
Northeast Commerce Pk 393-J6 F
Northwest Bus Pk 423-H4 PTM
Olin Brass Fac 526-E2 WnT
Park 100 Ind Pk 423-H6; 424-A7 PTM
Park 32 West Ind Pk 359-B4 NT
Park 65 North Ind Pk 458-D8 PTM
Park 70 East Ind Pk 495-E2 WrT
Park 800 Bus Pk 596-E6 G
Park Fletcher Ind Pk 525-J3 DTM; 525-J3 WnT
Park Plaza Ind Pk 426-H10 WTM
Park West Office Comm 457-E8 PTM
Parkeast Ind Pk 462-A9 WrT
Parkside Bus Pk 393-K4 F
Plainfield Bus Pk 558-B2 P
Reilly Industries 526-E2 WnT
Reynolds Ind Pk 393-K5 F
Robbins Ind Pk 423-K4; 424-A5 PTM
Rock Island Refinery (Marathon Oil) 423-K3; 424-A4 PTM
Schmoll Ind Pk 426-G10; 460-G1 WTM
Shadeland Commerce Ctr 495-B1 WrT
Sherman Pk Ind Pk 494-D6 CTM
Shiloh Bus Pk 490-E8 WaT
Signature Pk Northeast Bus Pk 393-H9 F
South Park Bus Pk 596-G1 G
Speedway Ind Pk 492-B5 S; 492-B5 WnT
Stony Creek Ind Pk 359-J8 N
Sugar Bush Commercial Ctr 455-F9 B
Sunblest Commercial Pk 393-D7 F
The Mote Prof Mall 455-H4 B
Tobey Drive Ind Pk 495-G1 WrT
Western Select Ind Pk 495-D1 WrT
Westridge Bus Pk 489-F9 A
Whittington Commercial Pk 455-H2 B

CAMPSITES

Beechwood Day Camp 393-A7 DTH
Boys Club 324-G5 WTH
Camp Dellwood (Girl Scouts of America) 491-E3 WnT
Camp Nothingmuchere 356-K9 WTH
Goldman Union Camp Institute 423-E3 PTM
Indian Lake Retreat 428-B7 L
Indiana St Fairgrounds 459-K7 WTM
Indianapolis KOA 463-E10 BCT
Nazarene Ch Camp 558-H4 GT
River Bend 326-F3 WRT
Walnut Grove 599-C7 STS
White River Pk 326-E1 WRT

CEMETERIES

Anderson 495-A6 WrT
Arnett 463-G8 BCT; 395-H8 FCT
Barlow 489-C5 WaT
Bell 560-K1 PeT
Bethel 457-K5 PTM
Bethel Fellowship Bapt 361-A5 WyT
Bethlehem 395-D3 F
Bills 428-K3 LTM
Boggstown 599-C9 STS
Brooks 395-C10 FCT
Buck Creek Chr 530-E6 FT
Burris 497-D2 BCT
Calvary 527-D6 PeT
Chester 323-K9 WTH
Clarkstown 389-K5 ET
Colonial Hills Bapt 426-B6 WTM
Concordia 527-E4 CTM
Cotton 423-F3 PTM
Cox 389-J3 ET
Crown Hill 459-B9 CTM; 459-B9 WTM
Crown Pt 423-A8 PTM
Crownland 359-K2 N
Cunningham 531-G9 MTS
Dake 565-B10 MTS
Dobel 565-C6 MTS
Dunn 463-J7 BCT
Eagle Cr 356-D9 WTH
Eastes 463-F9 BCT
Emery 428-B7 L
Ervin 361-A10 WyT
Fall Creek 460-B7 WTM
Farley 392-C10 CTH
First General Bapt 526-C6 DTM
Fish 496-J5 Cu
Floral Pk 490-J4; 492-D8 WnT
Forest Lawn 595-F6 WTJ
Francis 599-B6 STS
Freeman 530-G3 WrT
Friends 559-F6 DTM
Gallagher 599-C9 STS
Glade 597-D7 CTJ
Glen Haven Mem Pk 458-G3 WTM
Gossett 523-G1 WaT
Gray Friends 358-F10 NT
Greenwood 596-A2 G
Hair 327-G10 WyT
Hamilton Mem Gdns 358-D3 WTH
Heady 393-E6 F
Hebrew 527-D3 CTM
Helm 395-H6 FCT
Highland 394-F8 F
Hinkle Creek Friends 324-F4 JT
Honey Creek United Meth 595-H8 WTJ
Hopewell 423-E7 PTM
Hoss 462-D3 L
Hough 599-C8 STS
House 599-B1 MTS
Huntington 496-F7 WrT
Hurlock 360-B6 NT
Johnson 599-G10 STS
Jones 388-E6 ET
Jones Chapel 456-K4 PTM
Kinnaman 395-G5 FCT
Kitley 496-F9 WrT
Klepfer 428-D6 LTM
Langenberger 497-C9 SCT
Lincoln Memory Gdns 388-D10 ET
Lowe 594-E7 WTJ
Lowery 394-E3 FCT
Luebking 496-D9 WrT
Macedonia 422-F7 BTH
Maple Hill 523-G9 P
McCord 428-J9 L; 388-G3 WTB
McDaniels 455-E5 LTH
McKay 429-D1 FCT
Memorial Pk 495-K6 WrT
Merritt 489-F10 A
Messersmith 595-B3 WTJ
Mock 462-F2 L
Mohr 565-E2 MTS
Mount Auburn 595-E7 WTJ
Mount Comfort United Meth 463-D8 BCT
Mount Jackson 492-F7 WnT
Mount Olive 593-G3 MTM
Mount Pleasant 463-F3 BCT; 559-K3 DTM; 560-J10 WTJ
Mount Zion 395-E10 FCT
Muesing 496-G10; 530-G1 WrT
Murnan 565-E2 MTS
New Crown 528-B2 CTM
New Palestine 531-H7 SCT
Nolan 597-G1 CTJ
North Lawn 489-E8 A
Northwest Assembly of God 425-C2 WTM
Oaklandon 428-G9 L
Oaklawn Mem Gdns 426-K1 F
Old Sugar Creek 565-J2 MTS
Old Union 491-E3 WnT
Pitzer 388-J6 ET
Pleasant Hill 423-D6 PTM
Pleasant View 530-D2 WrT
Poplar Ridge 391-B3 CTH
Prairie Bapt 327-F6 WyT
Richmond 497-D10 SCT
Riverview 359-G3 N
Round Hill 527-E10; 561-E1 PeT
Saint Johns 529-E4 WrT
Saint Joseph & Holy Cross 527-D3 CTM
Salem 428-A6 LTM; 458-D2 PTM; 594-F10 WTJ
Schildmeier 531-A3 SCT
Schramm 497-D9 SCT
Scotten 497-B1 BCT
Sheets 423-F1 ET
Shiloh Crossomg United Meth 490-G7 WaT
Silon 558-J10 MTM
Snider 496-K1 BCT
Sparks 455-B1 BTH
Steele 463-J6 BCT
Stony Cr 360-K4 WyT
Sugar Grove 557-F2 GT; 356-C8 WTH
Summit Lawn 357-K6; 358-A6 WTH
Sutherland 460-A7 WTM
Todd 428-D7 L
Union Grove 322-H4 AT
Washington Pk 496-D6 WrT
Washington Pk Cem North 458-G4 WTM
Weaver 393-G1 DTH; 359-C8 NT
Wesley Chapel 462-E6 LTM
Wesley United Meth 492-E1 WnT
West Grove 324-B2 JT
Westfield Friends Meeting 357-K4 W
White Chapel 392-G8 Ca
Williams 597-G10 CTJ
Witte 496-C9 WrT
Zimmer 326-C6 NT
Zion 529-J4 WrT
Zion Luth 531-C2 SCT

COLLEGES & UNIVERSITIES

American Coll of Sports Medicine DN-D2 CTM
Butler Univ 459-B6 WTM
Cavanaugh Hall DN-C2 CTM
Christian Theological Seminary 459-B7 WTM
Heritage Bapt Univ 561-H9 G
Herron, John Sch of Art 493-E4 CTM
Indiana Univ Natatorium DN-C2 CTM
Indiana Univ Purdue Univ Indianapolis (IUPUI) DN-B2; 493-A7 CTM
Indiana Votech Coll 525-F3 WnT

Indianapolis Colts Training Ctr 457-E4 PTM
IUPUI (38th Street Campus) 459-H9 CTM
IUPUI Track & Field Stadium DN-B2 CTM
Ivy Tech St Coll 493-E2 CTM
John Herron Sch of Art 493-E4 CTM
Lockyear Coll 427-B8 LTM
Marion Coll 458-H10; 492-H1 WnT
Martin Univ 494-D3 CTM
Saint Maur Theological Ctr 459-A7 WTM
Union Bible Coll & Academy 357-K4 W
University of Indianapolis 527-H7 PeT

COMMUNITY & RECREATION CENTERS

Cool Cr Nature Ctr 357-K9 WTH
Craig Pk 596-D3 G
Forest Pk 359-H1 N
Hornet Pk 528-G7 BG
Jewish 425-C10 WTM
Mooresville Senior Ctr 592-E5 BTM
Smith Valley 594-H5 WTJ
Thatcher 492-B7 WnT
Water Sports Ctr 457-C3 PTM
YMCA 561-H6 PeT

FIRE COMPANIES

Avon 489-G8 A
Beech Grove Sta 1 528-H6 BG
Beech Grove Sta 2 528-E5 BG
Brown Twp 592-B2 M
Brownsburg Sta 1 455-G6 B
Buck Creek Twp 463-D8 BCT
Carmel 391-K6 Ca
Carmel-Clay Sta 2 390-G8 CTH
Carmel-Clay Sta 3 392-B10 Ca
Carmel-Clay Sta 4 392-H4 Ca
Carmel-Clay Sta 5 391-G10 CTH
Fishers Sta 1 393-G7 F
Fishers Sta 2 394-J7 FCT
Fishers Sta 3 393-B10 F
Greenwood Sta 1 596-D2 G
Greenwood Sta 2 561-H10 G
Greenwood Sta 3 596-B6 G
Indianapolis 494-C2 CTM; 562-B7 PeT
Indianapolis Sta 1 492-K6 CTM
Indianapolis Sta 2 462-B7 LTM
Indianapolis Sta 3 DN-F4; 493-H10 CTM
Indianapolis Sta 5 493-D4 CTM
Indianapolis Sta 7 DN-E2; 493-F6 CTM
Indianapolis Sta 10 460-D10 CTM
Indianapolis Sta 11 DN-F3; 493-K8 CTM
Indianapolis Sta 13 DN-C2; 493-D7 CTM
Indianapolis Sta 14 493-E1 CTM
Indianapolis Sta 15 494-C10 CTM
Indianapolis Sta 16 459-E4 WTM
Indianapolis Sta 18 492-G8 WnT
Indianapolis Sta 19 DN-C4; 493-B10 CTM
Indianapolis Sta 20 494-G4 CTM
Indianapolis Sta 22 493-J1 CTM
Indianapolis Sta 23 493-B3 CTM
Indianapolis Sta 24 460-H8 LTM
Indianapolis Sta 25 495-A7 WrT
Indianapolis Sta 26 527-H7 PeT
Indianapolis Sta 27 494-B6 CTM
Indianapolis Sta 29 527-G3 CTM
Indianapolis Sta 30 492-F2 WnT
Indianapolis Sta 31 459-G7 WTM
Indianapolis Sta 32 459-H1 WTM
Indianapolis Sta 33 457-J10 PTM
Indianapolis Sta 34 461-F10 WrT
Lawrence Sta 1 461-F6 L
Lawrence Sta 2 461-E6 L
Lawrence Twp Sta 1 427-A4 LTM
Lawrence Twp Sta 2 427-D8 LTM
Lawrence Twp Sta 3 428-G10 L; 428-B5 LTM
Lawrence Twp Sta 4 428-G7 L
Madison Twp Sta 1 592-K9 MTM
Madison Twp Sta 2 593-C2 MTM
McCordsville 429-C8 McC
Noblesville Sta 1 359-H3 N
Noblesville Sta 3 359-K6 N
Perry Twp Sta 1 527-H9 PeT
Perry Twp Sta 2 561-E5 PeT
Perry Twp Sta 4 527-A10 PeT
Pike Twp Sta 1 424-B9 PTM
Pike Twp Sta 2 423-B8 PTM
Pike Twp Sta 3 424-D5 PTM
Pike Twp Sta 4 457-J5 PTM
Pike Twp Sta 5 457-D7 PTM
Plainfield Hdq 524-A8 P
Plainfield Sta 1 524-A8 P
Plainfield Sta 3 558-A5 GT
Speedway Sta 1 491-K5 S
Speedway Sta 2 491-J2 S
Sta 2 325-C10 N; 523-F8 P
Sta 4 325-E6 N
Sugar Creek Twp Sta 1 531-G5 NP
Warren Twp Sta 1 496-D5 WrT
Warren Twp Sta 2 495-F10 WrT
Warren Twp Sta 3 495-E5 WrT
Warren Twp Sta 4 495-D1 WrT
Warren Twp Sta 5 496-D1 WrT
Washington Twp Sta 1 426-A9 WTM
Washington Twp Sta 2 458-H4 WTM
Washington Twp Sta 3 425-J5 WTM
Washington Twp Sta 4 425-A5 WTM
Washington Twp Sta 5 460-D4 WTM
Wayne Twp 361-E2 WyT
Westfield 357-F4 WTH
Westfield Sta 2 358-A9 WTH
Westfield Sta 3 357-K4 W
White River Twp Sta 1 594-K5 WTJ
White River Twp Sta 2 595-E1 G
Whitestown 388-E1 Wh
Zionsville 389-F8 Z

GOLF COURSES

Bear Slide GC 325-C1 JT
Bluff Cr GC 594-A8 WTJ
Brickyard Crossing GC 492-C3, D3 S
Britton GC 393-K3; 394-A4 F
Broadmoor CC 458-H4 WTM
Brookshire GC 392-E7 Ca
Carl Smock GC 562-E8 PeT
Clermont GC 456-F7 LTH
Coffin GC 492-H3 WnT
Country Club of Indianapolis 491-B2 WnT
Crooked Cr GC 424-C8 PTM
Crooked Stick GC 390-K9 CTH
Douglass GC 493-J1 CTM
Eagle Cr GC 456-J3 PTM
Forest Pk GC 359-H2 N
Fox Prairie GC 325-G10; 359-F1 N
Friendswood GC 558-F7 GT
Gleneagles GC 422-D6 BTH
Golf Club of Indiana 388-B10; 422-B1 PTB
Grassy Cr GC 496-E1 WrT
Hanging Tree GC 356-K8 WTH
Harbour Trees GC 325-B6 N
Hawthorns GC 394-H9 F
Heartland Crossing GC 559-B10; 593-A1 MTM
Highland CC 459-A4 WTM
Hillcrest CC 427-A10; 461-A1 LTM
Indian Lake CC 428-D8 L
Ironwood at Windermere GC 394-D10; 428-F1 F
Ironwood GC 394-D9 F
Maple Cr CC 496-D4 WrT
Meridian Hills CC 425-D10 WTM
Mohawk GC 392-A5 Ca
Morningstar GC 496-C8 WrT
Old Oakland GC 428-G8 L
Orchard GC 595-E1 G
Pebble Bk GC 358-G2 N
Pleasant Run GC 495-A6 WrT
Plum Cr CC 393-A5 Ca
Prairie View CC 393-D4 CTH
Prestwick GC 489-A10; 523-A1 WaT
Riverglen GC 393-C6 F
Riverside GC 458-J10 CTM; 492-J1 WnT
Royal Oak CC 595-D7 WTJ
Saddlebrook GC 458-D5 PTM
Sarah Shank GC 528-B4 CTM
South Grove GC 492-J3 CTM
Stony Cr GC 360-F5 NT
Sunrise GC 425-K1 CTH
Thatcher GC 492-B7 WnT
The Fort Golf Resort 461-J2 L
The Links GC 531-C9 MTS
Twin Lakes GC 424-F1 CTH
Valle Vista GC 596-F3 G
Walnut Ridge GC 594-J6 WTJ
West Chase GC 455-A2 B
Whispering Hills GC 530-D3 WrT
William S Sahm GC 427-B4 LTM
Winding Ridge GC 462-F4 L
Winding River GC 559-K8 DTM; 560-A8 PeT
Woodland CC 392-B8 CTH
Woodstock G & CC 459-A9 CTM
Zionsville GC 389-H7 Z

HOSPITALS

Columbia Womens 424-J6 WTM
Community East 494-H5 WrT
Community North 427-C6 LTM
Community South 561-J8 PeT
Fairbanks 427-C10 LTM
James Whitcomb Riley Childrens DN-B1; 493-A6 CTM
Kendrick Mem 592-C3 M
Larue Carter DN-B1; 493-A6 CTM
Long DN-B2; 493-B6 CTM
Methodist 493-D4 CTM
Richard L Roudebush Vet Affairs Med Ctr DN-B1; 493-A6 CTM
Riverview 359-G3 N
Saint Francis 528-D5 BG
Saint Vincent 424-J5 WTM
Saint Vincent Carmel 391-G3 CTH
University DN-C2; 493-B6 CTM
Westview Osteopathic Med 458-E9 WnT
Winona 459-D10 CTM
Wishard Mem DN-C1; 493-B6 CTM

INFORMATION CENTERS

Carmel C of C 391-K4 Ca
Chamber of Commerce 493-E7 CTM
City Ctr DN-D3; 493-E8 CTM
Eagle Cr Pk Office 457-C4 PTM
Fishers Chamber of Commerce 393-H7 F
Greenwood Chamber of Commerce 596-B3 G
Hamilton Co Vis Ctr 393-H7 F
Indiana Univ Purdue Univ Indianapolis DN-C2 CTM
Indianapolis Chamber of Commerce DN-D2; 493-F7 CTM
Noblesville Chamber of Commerce 359-H3 N
Pumphouse Vis Ctr DN-C3; 493-C8 CTM
Westfield Chamber of Commerce 357-K3 W
Zionsville Chamber of Commerce 389-J8 Z

LAKES & STREAMS

Abner Cr 523-A2 WaT
Allison Run 426-F5 WTM
Alverna Cr 425-A3 WTM
Amity Br 497-A4 BCT; 497-A4 Cu
Ams Run 391-C7 CTH
Army Br 524-A3 WaT
Auburn Br 595-C6 WTJ
Augusta Br 424-D9; 458-F1 PTM
Avon Cr 490-J9 WnT
Bailey Cr 425-K10; 426-B9 WTM
Bean Cr 527-G3; 528-A4 CTM; 528-G1 WrT
Bear Cr 390-C1 CTH; 390-C1 WTH
Bear Slide Cr 325-B1 JT
Bee Camp Cr 429-B1 FCT
Beech Cr 528-G7 BG
Behner Bk 427-B3 LTM
Bells Cr 461-J6 L; 462-A7 LTM
Big Eagle Cr 526-H1 CTM; 389-F1 ET; 491-E2; 492-C7 S; 457-A10; 491-E2; 492-C7; 526-H1 WnT; 389-F1 Z
Big Run Cr 529-D7, H8; 530-B8 FT
Billings Cr 462-C4 L
Bills Br 429-A2 McC
Bird Br 457-J1; 458-A1 PTM
Black Cr 558-E5 GT
Blue Cr 427-B10; 461-B2 LTM
Blue Lake 526-G1 WnT
Blue Woods Cr 392-H10; 426-G1 CTH
Bluff Cr 593-K10 HT; 524-G6 P; 593-K10; 594-A10 WTJ; 524-G6 WaT
Boone Cr 390-B5 CTH; 389-K6 ET
Breier Arm 497-B6 SCT
Breier Cr 496-K10 SCT
Brian Ditch 462-E8 WrT
Bridge Cr 524-F3 WaT
Brier Cr 530-F3 WrT
Britton Br 393-K4 DTH; 393-K4; 394-A3 F
Brock Ditch 392-K2 CTH
Brookside Cr 494-D4 CTM; 494-D4 WrT
Brown Ditch 456-E10; 490-E2 LTH
Buck Cr 463-E10, H3; 496-J6; 497-B2 BCT; 564-G7 CTJ; 496-J6 Cu; 530-F5, F9; 564-G2, G7 FT; 564-G7; 598-J1 MTS; 496-J6 SCT; 429-K10 VT; 496-F10; 530-F1 WrT
Buckley Bk 563-A2 FT
Budd Run 426-J2 LTM; 426-J2 WTM
Buffalo Cr 561-G8, J7 PeT; 561-B9 WRT; 561-B9 WTJ
Bullard Cr 456-D9 LTH
Bunker Cr 563-B4 FT
Bushs Run 423-H8 PTM
Camby Cr 558-H4 DTM; 558-H4 GT
Camp Cr 461-J1 L
Campbell Ditch 597-H5; 598-A6 CTJ
Carmel Cr 391-J7; 392-A10 CTH; 391-J7; 392-A10 Ca; 426-E4 WTM
Carson Cr 528-F9 BG; 528-F9 PeT
Castle Cr 426-J4 LTM; 426-J4 WTM
Cemetery Cr 389-H10; 390-A10 ET
Center Bk 594-J8 WTJ
Center Cr 390-J7 CTH; 524-H9 DTM; 524-H9 GT
Chapel Run 530-E6 FT
Charlemac Run 530-F10 FT
Cheeney Cr 392-K10 DTH; 392-K10 F
Churchman Cr 528-J7 BG
Churchman Ditch 561-A5 PeT
Cicero Cr 325-D9; 359-D2 N; 325-D9; 359-D2 NT
Clair Br 389-C2 ET
Clarks Cr 490-C10; 524-C2 A; 523-K10; 557-J5, K1; 558-A2 GT; 523-K10; 524-A8; 557-J5 P; 524-C2 WaT
Clay Cr 390-K7 CTH
Clermont Cr 456-J10 PTM
Clifden Pond 389-E10 Z
Colbertson Ditch 459-J1 WTM
Comb Run 490-D7 WaT
Cool Cr 392-E7 CTH; 392-A3, E7 Ca; 357-K7; 358-B4, B9 WTH
Coon Run 530-A3 WrT
Cotton Cr 423-H4 PTM
Cox Cr 389-J4 ET; 389-J4 Z
Cox Ditch 490-D5, G6 WaT
Crest Br 456-J1 PTM
Crooked Cr 424-D1 CTH; 458-H9 CTM; 424-F8; 458-H5 WTM; 458-H9 WnT
Cross Bk 389-H7 Z
Cutsinger Ditch 597-K9; 598-A9 CTJ
Dandy Cr 456-J4 PTM
Davis Cr 525-H6 DTM
Dead Run 524-G2 WaT; 524-G2 WnT
Del Wood Br 491-F1 WnT
Delaware Cr 424-H5 CT; 424-H5 PTM
Delaware Lake 461-H1 L
Delight Cr 393-A8 DTH; 393-A8 F
DeLong Cr 456-J4 PTM
Derbyshire Cr 562-A4 PeT
Devon Cr 460-F6 LTM
Dodrill Cr 528-B10 PeT
Doe Cr 530-G6 FT; 497-D10; 530-G6; 531-A4 SCT
Dollar Hide Cr 525-H9; 559-J1; 560-A3 DTM
Drexel Run 525-H3 WnT
Dry Br 428-G7 L; 429-D6 McC; 429-D6 VT
Dry Fork 565-H8; 599-E3 MTS; 599-E3, F8 STS
Dry Run 457-G7 PTM; 491-J1; 492-A2, B2 S; 491-J1 WnT
Duck Pond 461-K1 L
Dunn Ditch 463-A7 BCT
Eagle Cr 389-H10; 423-F2 ET; 322-A1 MTB; 423-D7 PTM; 389-H10 Z
Eagle Cr Res 423-B10; 457-A5 PTM
Eagle Crest Cr 456-G1 BTH; 456-G1 PTM
Eagle Lake 390-A1 ET
East Fork 490-D1 LTH
East Fork Indian Br 324-G8 NT
East Fork White Lick Cr 592-B6 BTM; 524-G10 DTM; 524-G10; 558-D9, F4 GT; 592-B6 M; 524-G10 P; 491-A10; 524-J3 WnT
Eli Cr 456-H3 PTM
Eller Run 427-B1 DTH; 427-B1 F
Elliot Cr 391-A4 CTH
Etter Ditch 388-A7, A8, A10; 422-A1 PTB
Fair Bk 595-E2 G
Fair Cr 558-G5 DTM; 558-G5 GT
Fairview Cr 595-C2 G; 595-C2 WTJ
Falcon Cr 457-H5; 458-A8 PTM; 458-A8; 492-C1 WnT
Fall Cr DN-B1; 459-H10; 493-B4, E3 CTM; 395-G9 FCT; 427-J10; 461-D2 L; 427-J10; 428-B7 LTM; 459-H10; 460-A7 WTM
Farley Cr 491-E6 WnT
Fawn Run 561-H2 PeT
Feather Run 563-A4 FT
Feeney Ditch 490-B5 WaT
Ferris Ditch 565-A4 MTS
Ficher Ditch 529-H5; 530-A3 FT; 530-A5 WrT
Field Cr 461-H8; 462-A7 LTM
Finley Cr 322-G5 AT; 356-A2 UT; 322-D9, G5 WTH
Fishback Cr 422-G2 BTH; 388-J7; 422-G2 ET; 422-J8 PTM; 388-C4 WTB
Fisher Br 529-F7 FT
Fisher Cr 495-D9; 529-E1 WrT
Flat Br 564-C9; 598-D7, F1 CTJ; 563-J7; 564-C9 FT
Flatfork Cr 395-J9 FCT
Flynn Cr 558-K3 DTM; 558-G4 GT
Forest Lake 456-G1 BTH; 489-E10 WaT
Fort Br 461-J1 L
Fountain Cr 561-J8 G; 561-J8; 562-A8 PeT
Frances Cr 595-B3 WTJ
Friends Cr 558-G7 DTM; 558-G7 GT
Gander Cr 559-F10 MTM
Garden Run 461-C1 L; 461-C1 LTM
Geist Res 395-A9; 428-F2 FCT; 428-F2 LTM
Gem Cr 389-G3 ET
George Booth Drain 358-F2 N; 358-F2 NT; 358-F2 WTH
George Cr 524-A9; 558-A1 GT; 524-A9 P
Glen Cr 457-G1 PTM
Goose Cr 559-D3, G7 DTM; 559-G7; 593-J5 MTM
Grassy Br 357-G3; 358-A4 W; 357-G3 WTH
Grassy Cr 596-D8 G; 596-D8, H10 PTJ; 596-H10 Whl; 496-C8, D3; 530-D2 WrT
Green Ditch 388-B10 PTB
Grove Cr 595-A8 WTJ
Grubbs Ditch 563-C9 CTJ; 563-C9 PTJ
Guilford Bk 558-E2 GT
Guion Cr 458-C5, E2 PTM
Gwinn Ditch 327-G5 WyT
Hack Ditch 531-E3 SCT
Hare Ditch 560-E2 PeT
Harness Ditch 560-D8 PeT; 560-D8 WTJ
Harting Ditch 528-J10; 562-J2 FT
Hartman Ditch 495-J9; 496-A9 WrT
Hatchery Cr 458-F9 WnT
Haueisen Ditch 526-J9; 527-B10 PeT
Haverstick Cr 425-G2; 426-A5 WTM
Hay Run 496-D4 WrT
Heinrich Ditch 462-J9 BCT
Hendricks Cr 558-D6 GT
Hendricks Ditch 562-G5 FT; 562-G5 PeT
Henley Cr 391-B3 CTH
Henry Knock Ditch 529-E1 WrT
Heron Lake 460-B5 WTM
Highland Cr 527-C6 PeT
Hill Cr 456-J1 PTM
Hinkle Cr 324-D1, G4 JT; 324-G4 NT
Hiway Run 391-J1 Ca
Holiday Cr 389-C3 ET
Holiday Lake 389-F3 ET
Holly Cr 425-G6 WTM
Honey Cr 595-G9 PTJ; 594-D2, K8; 595-G9 WTJ
Hook Cr 422-G7 BTH; 422-G7 PTM
Hopewell Cr 423-E7 PTM
Horn Cr 529-D10; 563-C1 FT
Hoss Cr 462-F3 L
Howard Johnson Ditch 424-K10 WTM
Howe Cr 426-D8 WTM
Howland Ditch 427-A5 LTM; 425-J10; 426-F8 WTM
Hunter Ditch 529-J10; 530-A10; 564-A1 FT
Hunter Mitthoefer Ditch 462-B8 LTM
Hurricane Cr 597-D3, F9 CTJ
Ice Skating Pond 457-D2 PTM
India Br Trittipo Ditch 428-G9 L
Indian Br East Fork 324-G8 NT
Indian Br West Fork 324-F9 NT
Indian Cr 428-A9, E9; 462-D7, E3 L; 462-D7 LTM
Indian Lake 428-B9 L
Indianapolis Water Company Canal DN-D1; 493-C3 CTM; 459-A8 WTM
Indianhead Lake 489-B5 WaT
Ingerman Ditch 325-J5; 326-A7 NT
Irishman Run 389-D10; 423-D1 ET
Jackson Run 389-D1 ET; 388-G1 WTB
Jay Ditch 323-C3 AT; 462-J6; 463-B5 BCT
Jeto Lake 489-C4 WaT
John Heath Ditch 427-B2 DTH; 392-J10; 427-B2 F
Jolly Br 562-B10 G
Jones Ditch 324-C5 JT; 463-K1 VT; 323-J7; 324-C5 WTH
Julia Cr 491-C10; 525-A2 WnT
Kirkendall Cr 358-J8 N; 358-E7, J8 NT; 358-E7 WTH
Kirkhoff Ditch 497-K2 BCT
Klondike Cr 524-F5 P
Klondike Pond 524-E4 P
Kollman Br 525-F9 DTM
Kreager Ditch 322-A6 AT; 322-A6 MTB; 322-A6 WTH
Kuhn Ditch 495-J6, K4 WrT
Lake Br 559-D7 DTM
Lake Clearwater 426-D6 WTM
Lake Kessler 460-G3 LTM
Lake Maxinhall 460-B4 WTM
Lake Run 595-A7 WTJ
Lake Sullivan 458-J9 CTM
Lake View 489-E8 A
Lake Woodland 392-D9 Ca
Lambert Lake 558-J10 MTM
Lantern Run 427-G6 LTM
Lawrence Cr 461-F4 L
Le-An-Wa Lake 560-C5 PeT
Lead Cr 496-H2 BCT; 496-H2 Cu
Leather Run 563-J8; 564-A9 CTJ; 563-J8 FT
Leather Run Cr 598-C5 CTJ
Leatherwood Cr 563-E8; 597-J1; 598-A2 CTJ; 563-E8 FT
Leg Cr 558-D7 GT
Leona Lake 593-B2 MTM
Lewis Lake 455-E8 LTH
Liberty Br 457-G3 PTM
Lick Cr 528-C8 BG; 528-F3 CTM; 526-J7 DTM; 526-J7; 527-C8, H9; 528-C8 PeT; 495-B10, G6; 528-F3; 529-A1 WrT
Light Br 393-D7 F
Lilly Cr 456-H2 PTM
Lilly Lake 457-C2 PTM
Lincoln Cr 456-H8 PTM
Lindley Ditch 323-J5; 324-A5 WTH
Little Buck Cr 529-E10; 563-A3 FT; 560-D3; 561-A4, H4; 562-C4 PeT
Little Cool Cr 391-G2 CTH; 391-G2 Ca
Little Dollar Hide Cr 525-G8 DTM
Little Eagle Cr 389-K7; 390-A4 ET; 424-A6; 457-K4; 458-A2, B7 PTM; 492-D5 S; 356-C9, G5 WTH; 458-B7; 492-D5, D6 WnT; 389-K7 Z
Little Mann Cr 559-H2 DTM
Little Sugar Cr 598-D9 CTJ; 531-J10; 565-G2 MTS
Little White Lick Cr 456-A8 LTH
Log Run 456-H8 LTH; 456-H8 PTM
Long Br 390-B8 CTH; 389-K9; 390-B8 ET
Lowe Cr 594-E7 WTJ
Lowell Br 529-A1 WrT
Lowman Cr 528-A9 PeT
Luck Cr 558-H2 DTM; 558-H2 GT
Lynn Cr 491-G8; 492-B9 WnT
Maibucker Ditch 459-K10 CTM
Mallard Lake 460-D5 WTM
Mallery Granger Ditch 325-F8 NT
Mann Cr 559-J5; 560-A4 DTM
Manor Lake 456-H3 LTH
March Cr 524-B2 WaT
Mario Cr 490-J2; 491-B2 WnT
Marithon Cr 558-H6 DTM; 558-H6 GT
Mars Ditch 526-A5 DTM; 525-J5; 526-A5 WnT
Maze Cr 564-E8 FT
McCord Cr 388-G5 ET; 388-G5 WTB
McCracken Cr 557-B10 BTM
McCurdy Cr 423-A7 PTM
McFarland Cr 528-D9 BG
Mcfarland Cr 528-D9 PeT
Meadows Bk 460-B7 WTM
Merlau Ditch 531-F3 SCT
Merry Bk 562-F8 G; 562-F8 PeT
Meski Lake 557-H7 GT
Messersmith Cr 594-G3 WTJ
Meyers Ditch 458-A9; 492-A1 WnT
Mickley Run 492-A10 WnT
Middle Cr 524-F10 GT; 524-F10 P
Middle Fork 428-J6 L
Milhouse Cr 559-E3 DTM
Mill Run 491-J7; 492-A7 WnT
Miller McGaughey Ditch 529-G6; 530-A5 FT
Mitchener Ditch 392-G2, K7 CTH; 392-G2 Ca
Mock Cr 462-F2 L
Moon Cr 460-K5 LTM
Moore Cr 558-C8 GT
Morris Ditch 496-A7 WrT
Morse Res 325-D4 C; 325-D4 JT; 325-C8 N
Mount Zion Bk 395-D9 FCT
Mud Cr 393-K10; 427-K2 DTH; 393-K10; 394-B9; 395-A6 F; 395-F2 FCT; 461-F1 L; 427-G9 LTM; 361-H10 WyT
Mud Run 457-G8 PTM
Muesing Cr 496-H10; 530-F1 WrT
Mulliner Ditch 565-H2 MTS
National Cr 524-G3 WaT; 524-G3 WnT
Neeld Ditch 491-J10; 492-A10 WnT
Newton Br 559-D5 DTM
North Bluff Cr 593-K9 HT; 594-B7 WTJ
North Br 461-E10; 495-D1 WrT
North Cr 525-A10; 558-J1 DTM
North Fork 428-J5 L; 428-J5 LTM; 429-D4 McC; 429-D4 VT
O'Brian Ditch 462-D9 WrT
Oil Cr 424-B4 PTM
Opo Run 529-J2; 530-A2 WrT
Opossum Run 496-A9; 530-B1 WrT
Orme Ditch 560-H7; 561-A5 PeT
Osborn Ditch 462-D2 L
Overdorff Br 359-G8 N; 359-G8 NT
Paddock Run 558-J9 DTM; 558-J9 MTM
Palestine Br 531-E5 NP; 531-E5 SCT
Parker Eastes Ditch 463-G8 BCT
Payne Br 424-E6 PTM
Pee Wee Cr 389-E5 Z
Penn Lake 456-F6 LTH
Penns Run 558-E9 GT
Peyton Lake 560-A4 DTM
Pleasant Cr 562-E10; 596-E1 G; 562-E10; 596-E1 PTJ
Pleasant Run 494-B10; 527-C4, H2 CTM; 562-F8; 563-A7 FT; 561-G10; 562-B10; 595-C1, J1; 596-A2 G; 560-E10; 562-B10, F8 PeT; 560-E10, K9; 594-D1; 595-C1 WTJ; 495-A6, D3 WrT
Pogues Run DN-F2; 493-J6; 494-B4, F2 CTM; 461-A8 LTM; 494-F2 WrT
Pollard & Todd Ditch 489-G3 WaT
Pond Br 561-G7 PeT
Poplar Grove Lake 592-G7 MTM
Poss Br 529-K1; 530-A1 WrT
Prospect Br 559-D10; 593-F1 MTM
Pullman Cr 528-F4 BG
Pump Run 422-A5 BTH
Quack Br 559-F9 DTM; 559-F9 MTM
Quill Cr 559-E7 DTM
Quinn Ditch 456-A6 B

Rail Cr 528-H3 WrT
Rail Run 558-F7 GT
Ransdell Ditch 597-H6; 598-A7 CTJ
Rayburn Ditch 563-H3; 564-A4 FT
Ream Cr 425-J1 CTH; 426-A3 WTM
Reel Cr 422-G8 BTH; 422-G8 PTM
Ristow Br 492-B7 WnT
Robin Run 423-K10; 458-A1 PTM
Rock Cr 558-E4 GT
Rocklane Cr 597-H3 CTJ
Rogers Cr 524-B10; 558-A2 GT; 524-B10; 558-A2 P
Rothe Ditch 496-E1 WrT
Rouark Ditch 496-D2 WrT
Royal Run 388-F10 ET
Russell Lake 389-C9 ET
Salem Bk 594-D10 WTJ
Salem Cr 490-F10 A; 524-H1 WaT; 524-H1 WnT
Sand Cr 394-B8 F; 394-B8, G3 FCT; 361-B9 WyT
Sawmill Run 422-G5 BTH; 422-G5 PTM
Schoen Cr 461-G2 L
School Br 422-C10 BTH; 456-F5 LTH; 456-F5 PTM
School Cr 525-G10 DTM
Schooler Cr 388-E5 WTB
Scout Br 461-D2 L
Seerley Cr 525-J7; 526-A6 DTM
Shamrock Bk 423-C2 ET; 423-C2 PTM
Shannon Lake 560-D7 PeT
Sheets Cr 423-B2 ET; 423-B2 PTM
Shiloh Cr 490-H8 WnT
Shoemaker Br 393-E5 F
Shop Cr 528-H3 WrT
Short Run 596-A7 PTJ
Silon Cr 558-E10 BTM; 558-E10 MTM
Sinking Cr 593-E6 MTM
Sloan Ditch 529-A6 FT
Sly Run 324-K10; 359-B1 N; 359-B1 NT
Small Br 531-D10 MTS; 531-D10 SCT
Smith Run 594-J5 WTJ
Smock Cr 393-C6 F
Snail Cr 599-H8 BTS; 599-C9, H8 STS
Snider Bk 496-K2 BCT; 496-K2 Cu
South Br 558-J1 DTM; 495-E1 WrT
South Cr 495-A6 WrT
Sparrow Hollow 457-H1 PTM
Spring Mill Cr 390-J9 CTH
Spring Mill Run 425-A1 CTH
Springer Ditch 530-B7 FT
Squaw Run 462-F4 L
Stanbrough Cr 357-H9 WTH
Stansbury Ditch 463-C2 BCT; 429-D10 VT
Starkey Bk 389-G9 ET; 389-G9 Z
State Ditch 526-C6, C10; 560-C1 DTM; 526-C10; 560-C1 PeT; 526-C6 WnT
Steele Ditch 462-J5 BCT; 462-E7 LTM
Stonebridge Lake 394-D8 F
Stony Cr 359-J6; 360-A6 N; 359-J6; 360-A6 NT; 327-E9; 360-K3 WyT
Strange Cr 426-F10; 460-C1, D1 WTM
Straw Br 496-A3 WrT
Sugar Cr 531-G10; 565-B10, E3; 599-A2 MTS; 531-G10 NP; 531-J3 SCT; 599-B9 STS
Sum Bk 495-J10; 530-A1 WrT
Sum Br 529-K1 WrT
Swamp Cr 559-J6; 560-A8 DTM
Sweet Cr 531-C10; 565-B1 MTS; 531-C4 SCT
Sylvian Br 460-E1 WTM
Tansel Br 490-J3 WnT
Thompson Ditch 525-A2 WnT
Thor Run 395-F9 FCT
Thorpe Cr 395-F7, J4 FCT
Tincher Run 559-H2 DTM
Topp Cr 491-E5 WnT
Tracy Ditch 596-C8 G; 596-C8 PTJ
Traders Hollow 423-B7 PTM
Traders Point Lake 423-E9 PTM
Travis Cr 594-C8 WTJ
Trittipo Ditch 463-A1 VT
Trittipo Ditch India Br 428-G9 L
Trotter Cr 558-J9 DTM
Turkey Pen Cr 594-K5 WTJ
Vestal Ditch 393-A3 CTH; 393-A3 Ca; 359-A9 N; 359-A9 NT
Victory Run 528-G8 BG
Warren Cr 495-C4 WrT
Water Loo Run 595-A10 WTJ
Web Run 559-G10 MTM
Webb Ditch 592-D9 BTM
Well Run 390-F9 CTH
West Fork 557-B5, E8; 558-C6 GT
West Fork Indian Br 324-F9 NT
West Fork White Lick Cr 455-A3 B; 455-B5 LTH; 455-A3 MTH
West Lake 491-H7, J6 WnT
West Little Sugar Cr 531-C10; 564-K9; 565-B3 MTS; 531-C10 SCT
Westwood Br 490-F5 WaT
Wetnight Ditch 528-E10; 562-B2 PeT
White Lick Cr 455-F6 B; 455-F6 BTH; 557-H9; 592-A5 BTM; 557-G1, H9 GT; 455-D9 LTH; 523-E7; 557-G1 P; 489-C6; 490-G3; 523-C4 WaT
White Lick Cr West Fork 455-A3 B; 455-B5 LTH; 455-A3 MTH
White River 393-A7, D2; 426-G4 CTH; DN-B2; 458-K10; 492-J4; 493-C10; 527-B4 CTM; 393-A7, D2 DTH; 526-E9; 560-C9, D3 DTM; 393-A7; 426-G4 F; 593-J10 HT; 359-G4 N; 325-H10; 326-B8; 359-G9 NT; 526-E9; 560-C9, D3 PeT; 326-E2, K1 WRT; 560-C9; 593-J10; 594-A3 WTJ; 425-F10, J9; 426-A8, G4; 458-K10; 459-D4, H1 WTM; 492-J4 WnT
Wildcat Bk 563-J2; 564-D3 FT
Wildcat Cr 564-D4 FT
Wildcat Run 563-H5; 564-A5, D5 FT
Wildwood Lake 593-C5 MTM
Will Cr 391-A6 CTH
William Lehr Ditch 360-H10 WyT
William Lock Ditch 327-G5 WRT; 327-B9, G5 WyT
Williams Cr 391-C6, D2; 425-C1 CTH; 391-D2 Ca; 425-F7 WTM
Windsor Br 495-B4 WrT
Wood Br 456-H5 LTH
Wood Haven Cr 490-J4 WnT
Woodruff Br 356-D5 WTH
Woolen Run 461-C2 L
Young Ditch 496-E8 Cu; 496-E8 WrT
Zion Cr 529-J4; 530-A4 WrT

LIBRARIES

Avon 489-F7 A
Beech Grove 528-E5 BG
Brightwood 494-D2 CTM
Broad Ripple 459-J1 WTM
Broadway 459-G7 WTM
Brown 494-J7 WrT
Brownsburg 455-G7 B
Carmel-Clay 392-A4 Ca
Decatur 525-F10 DTM
Eagle 458-B10 WnT
East Washington 494-B8 CTM
Emerson 460-G9 CTM
Fishers 393-H7 F
Fountain Sq DN-F4; 493-H10 CTM
Franklin 563-G1 FT
Greenwood 596-C3 G
Haughville 492-D7 WnT
Hussey-Mayfield Mem 389-G8 Z
Indiana Univ Perdue Univ Indianapolis 493-C7 CTM
Indiana Univ Purdue Univ Indianapolis DN-C2 CTM
Indianapolis Marion Co DN-D1; 493-E6 CTM
Lawrence 427-E7 LTM
Medical Research DN-C2 CTM
New Palestine 531-G5 NP
Noblesville Southeastern 360-A3 N
Nora 425-H4 WTM
Pike 423-J10 PTM
Shelby 527-H4 CTM
Southport 562-B6 PeT
Spades Pk 493-K5 CTM
State DN-D2; 493-D7 CTM
Wanamaker 529-H8 FT
Warren 496-A3 WrT
Wayne 491-D9 WnT
West Indianapolis 492-J10 CTM
Westfield 357-K3 W
White River 595-F3 G

MARINAS & RAMPS

Indianapolis Sailing Club 428-H1 FCT
Indianapolis Yacht Club 429-A2 FCT
Morse Lake 325-E5 N

MILITARY & FEDERAL FEATURES

Federal Courthouse DN-D2; 493-E7 CTM
Federal Office Bldg DN-D2; 493-F7 CTM
Fort Harrison Reuse Authority 461-H3 L
Indiana Natl Guard (Stout Field Fac) 526-D2 WnT
Indiana Natl Guard Armory 526-D1 WnT
Major General Emmet J Bean Finance Ctr (US Army) 461-H4 L
National Guard Armory 359-K1 N
US Army Reserve 492-G2 WnT

PARK & RIDE

Greenwood Pk Mall 562-A10 G
Lafayette Sq Mall 458-B8 PTM
Washington Sq Mall 496-B6 WrT

PARKS & RECREATION

30th & German Church Pk 462-D10; 496-C1 WrT
61st & Broadway Pk 459-G2 WTM
AJAA Baseball Pk 523-D1 WaT
American Legion Mall DN-D2; 493-E6 CTM
Arbuckle Acres Pk 455-F5 B
Arsenal Pk 459-J6 WTM
Avon Pk 489-C9 A
Avon Soccer Fields 489-C7 WaT
Avon Softball Pk 489-D9 WaT
Azionaqua Swim Club 389-J5 Z
Beckwith Pk 460-A10; 494-A1 CTM
Bellamy Pk 462-A9 WrT
Belmont Pk 492-J5 CTM
Bertha Ross Pk 459-A9 CTM
Bethel Pk 528-B1 CTM
Bloch Cancer Survivors Pk DN-C1 CTM
Bluff Pk 527-C7 PeT
Boggstown Pk 599-C10 STS
Bowman Pk 458-A9 WnT
Broad Ripple Pk 459-K1 WTM
Brookside Pk 494-C4 CTM
Carey Grove Pk 392-C2 Ca
Carmel Ice Skadium 391-J6 Ca
Carmel-Clay Parks & Rec Dept 391-J6 Ca
Carmelot Pk 392-G10 Ca
Carson Pk 559-H1 DTM
Centennial & Groff Pk 492-F3 WnT
Chapel Hill Pk 491-D6 WnT
Charney Pk 461-H5 L
Cherry Tree Picnic Area 461-G1 L
Christian Pk 494-E9 CTM
Clayton & LaSalle Pk 494-C9 CTM
Cool Cr Pk 357-K8; 358-A8 WTH
Cottingham Pk 393-J3 DTH
Craig Pk 596-D3 G
Cumberland Pk 496-J5 Cu; 394-A10 DTH; 393-K10; 427-K1 F
Dads Club Pk 392-H4 Ca
Delaware Lake Picnic Area 461-G1 L
Denver Pk 492-G5 WnT
Douglass Pk 493-J2 CTM
Dubarry Pk 461-H9 WrT
Eagle Cr Pk 422-K10; 456-H2, J7; 457-C7, D2, G3 PTM; 457-C7 WnT
Ellenberger Pk 494-H6 WrT
Explorer Pk 461-E5 L
Fall Cr & 16th Pk DN-C1; 493-B5 CTM
Fall Cr Greenway 459-H10; 493-D3, G1 CTM; 460-C6 LTM
Fishers Comm Pk 393-G6 F
Flowing Well Pk 392-F7 Ca
Forest Manor Pk 494-D3 CTM
Forest Pk 359-G1 N
Fort Harrison St Pk 427-J10; 428-A8; 461-E2 L
Fort Harrison St Pk Offices 461-G3 L
Fort Harrison St Pk Wildlife Refuge 427-G10 L
Fox Hill Manor Pk 458-K3 WTM
Franklin Pk 563-J2 FT; 523-E7 P
Friendship Garden Pk 523-F9 P
Gardener Pk 461-C6 LTM
Garfield Pk 527-G3 CTM
George Washington Pk 460-B10; 494-B1 CTM
German Pk 561-E8 PeT
Greene Pk 495-F4 WrT
Greenwood Pool Pk 596-B3 G
Gustafson Pk 491-J1 WnT
Hamilton Co 4-H Fairgrounds 359-K5; 360-A4 N
Hamilton Co Parks & Rec Dept 357-K8 WTH
Hartman Pk 528-E7 BG
Haughville Pk DN-A2; 492-H6 WnT
Hawthorne Pk DN-A3; 492-H8 WnT
Highland Pk DN-F2; 493-H7 CTM
Hill Pk 493-J4 CTM
Holliday Pk 459-E1 WTM
Hornet Pk 528-G7 BG
Indiana St Fairgrounds 459-J7 WTM
Indianapolis Motor Speedway 492-B2 S
Indianapolis Motor Speedway Admin Offices 492-B4 S
Indianapolis Raceway Pk 456-E10; 490-E1 LTH
Indianapolis Soccer & Sports Ctr 492-K4 CTM
Indianapolis Zoo DN-B3; 493-B8 CTM
Jennings Pk 389-F7 Z
Juan Soloman Pk 459-A2 WTM
Krannert Pk 491-H9 WnT
Lawrence Comm Pk 461-G5 L
Lawrence Soccer Pk 461-E7 L
Lentz Pk DN-A1; 492-J6 CTM
Leonard Pk 491-K5 S
Lions Pk 389-J8 Z
Major Taylor Velodrome 458-H9 WnT
Marion Co Fair Grounds 529-D4 WrT
Marott Pk 425-G8 WTM
Martin Luther King Pk 493-G3 CTM
Max Bahr Pk 492-G7 WnT
Meadowlark Pk 391-J3 Ca
Meadowood Pk 491-H2 S
Military Pk DN-C2; 493-C7 CTM
Mongans Rec Pk 523-B10; 557-C1 GT
Monon Greenway Tr 391-J2, J8 CTH; 391-J2, J8 Ca
Monon Greenway Trail 459-H7 WTM
Moreland Pk 492-F1 WnT
Morse Pk 325-C9 N
National Road Pk 496-F6 Cu
Noblesville Parks & Rec Dept 359-G2 N
Noblesville Soccer Fields 325-H9 N
Northeast Pk 562-D10; 596-D1 G
Northwest Pk 561-H10 G
Northwestway Pk 457-K2; 458-A2 PTM
Old Town Pk 592-B3 M
Olin Pk 492-D6 WnT
Oxford Terr Pk 494-B1 CTM
Paul Ruster Pk 496-F9 WrT
Pepsi Coliseum 459-J8 WTM
Perry Pk 561-F6 PeT
Pleasant Grove Pk 391-F9 CTH
Pleasant Run Greenway 494-B10, E8; 527-E4, H2; 528-A1 CTM; 494-K6 WrT
Pogues Run Greenway Pk DN-F1; 493-K4 CTM
Post Road Pk 495-J10; 496-A10 WrT
Potters Bridge Pk 325-K9; 326-A9 NT
Raymond Pk 529-G2 WrT
RCA Dome 493-D8 CTM
Rhodius Pk DN-A4; 492-J10 CTM
Ridenour Pk 492-E8 WnT
Riley Pk DN-C4; 493-B10 CTM
Ritchey Woods Nature Preserve 393-D10 F
River Heritage Pk 393-A7 CTH
Riverside Pk 458-J9; 492-J2 CTM; 458-J9; 492-J2 WnT
Roark Stadium 455-H7 B
Roselawn Pk 460-F8 WTM
Rosey Pk 490-K2 WnT
Sarah Bolton Pk 528-D6 BG
Sarkine Picnic Pk 489-E4 WaT
Seminary Pk 359-J4 N
Skiles Test Pk 427-B10; 461-B1 LTM
South Grove Pk 528-G7 BG
Southeastway Pk 530-G10; 564-G1 FT
Southside Pk 359-G4 N; 527-K7; 528-A7 PeT
Southwestway Pk 559-K6; 560-A6 DTM
Starkey Pk 389-G10 ET; 389-G10; 423-G1 Z
Stringtown Pk DN-B3; 492-K7 CTM
Swinford Pk 523-H10 P
Tarkington Pk 459-E8 WTM
Thompson Pk 393-H3 F
Tibbs & 21st St Pk 492-F3 WnT
University Pk DN-D2; 493-E7 CTM
Veterans Mem Pk 462-H1 L
Veterans Mem Plaza DN-D2; 493-E7 CTM
Vic Overman Sportsfield Pk 455-J8 B
Victory Field DN-C3; 493-C8 CTM
Watkins Pk 493-C2 CTM
Wes Montgomery Pk 460-H9 WrT
West Pk 390-G7 CTH
Westside Pk 595-K2; 596-A2 G
White River Pk 326-E1 WRT
White River St Pk DN-B3; 493-B8 CTM
Whitestown Pk 388-D2 WTB
Willard Pk 493-K8 CTM
Williams Pk 455-D8 B
Windsor Vill Family Pk 495-A2 WrT
YMCA 561-H6 PeT

PLACES OF WORSHIP

66th Street Bapt 425-G10 WTM
Abiding Faith Lighthouse 490-J10 WnT
Abundant Faith Missionary Bapt 494-A3 CTM
Abundant Life Mem 427-D6 LTM
Abyssinian Bapt 494-E1 CTM
Acton Bapt 564-E6 FT
Acton United Meth 564-D1 FT
Agape Apostolic 494-C2 CTM
Agape Chr 462-C4 L
Aldersgate 495-J3 WrT
Aldersgate Free Meth 490-J3 WnT
All Saints Cath 492-H7 WnT
All Souls 460-K4 LTM
Allen Chapel AME DN-E1; 493-H5 CTM
Allisonville Chr 426-G8 WTM
Ambassador Bapt 493-J3 CTM
American Bapt DN-D1; 493-F5 CTM
Amity United Meth 497-D3 BCT
Antioch 427-E9 LTM
Antioch Apostolic 497-A6 Cu
Antioch Bapt 459-G10 CTM
Apostolic Bible 492-C9 WnT
Apostolic Chr 427-D9 LTM; 527-J6 PeT
Apostolic Lighthouse Tabernacle 526-G10 PeT
Arlington Avenue Bapt 562-K3 FT
Arlington Hgts Chr 494-J3 WrT
Asbury United Meth 461-H7 LTM
Assumption Cath DN-B4; 492-K10 CTM
Augusta Chr 424-F9 PTM
Avon Chr 523-G1 A
Avon Comm Ch of the Nazarene 489-E8 WaT
Avon United Meth 489-F8 A
Baha'i Faith-Indianapolis Assembly 460-E9 CTM
Baptist Academy 528-A3 CTM
Beech Grove Ch of the Nazarene 528-G6 BG
Beech Grove Wesleyan 493-F6 CTM
Belery 360-D8 NT
Believers in Christ 494-A1 CTM
Bellaire United Meth 459-K5 WTM
Bells Chapel 462-B7 LTM
Ben Davis Chr 491-H10 WnT
Berean Bible Bapt 494-A4 CTM
Bethany 460-J4 LTM
Bethany Ch of God 493-H4 CTM
Bethany Chr 528-D9 PeT
Bethany Luth 460-J6 LTM
Bethany Missionary Bapt 494-C10 CTM
Bethany Moravian 562-K4 FT
Bethany Presb 460-J3 LTM
Bethany Temple Apostolic Faith 527-J1 CTM
Bethany Wesleyan 527-H4 CTM
Bethel 528-G1 CTM
Bethel AME DN-C2; 493-D7 CTM
Bethel Bapt 489-G6 WaT
Bethel Chapel 527-E1 CTM
Bethel Faith Temple Pent Ch of God 491-G9 WnT
Bethel Fellowship Bapt 361-A5 WyT
Bethel Luth 326-A6 NT
Bethel Mem 562-B4 Spt
Bethel Missionary Bapt 561-F1 PeT
Bethel Tabernacle 494-F3 CTM
Bethel United Meth 457-K5 PTM
Bethesda Temple Pent 492-J3 CTM
Bethlehem 395-D3 F
Bethlehem Bapt 493-H5 CTM
Bethlehem Luth 459-G5 WTM
Bethlehem Missionary Bapt 460-A7 WTM
Bethlehem Temple 460-H10 WrT
Bethul Tabernacle 526-D8 DTM
Bible United Pent 494-D9 CTM
Biltmore Gdns Ch of Christ 491-J10 WnT
Binding Force Chr Ctr 427-C5 LTM
Blessed Holy Light Bapt 524-J2 WnT
Blessed Hope Bapt 492-K3 CTM
Bluff Avenue Bapt 527-A6 PeT
Breeding Tabernacle 460-G9 WrT
Bridgeport Central Bapt 524-J4 WnT
Bridgeport Nazarene 524-K4 WnT
Bridgeport United Meth 524-J1 WnT
Brookside United Meth 494-C5 CTM
Brookville Road Comm 530-K3 SCT
Brownsburg Chr 455-F5 B
Buck Creek Chr 530-E6 FT
Burge Terr Bapt 529-K2 WrT
Calvary Bapt 462-E10 WrT
Calvary Luth 561-H2 PeT
Calvary Mission Temple 528-G9 FT
Calvary Tabernacle DN-E4; 493-H9 CTM
Calvary Temple Assembly of God 495-J1 WrT
Calvary United Meth 455-G7 B; DN-F4; 493-K9 CTM
Calvary Wesleyan 461-B7 LTM
Camby Comm 558-K5 DTM
Campbell Chapel 492-E7 WnT
Canaan Bapt 492-G6 WnT
Capital City Bapt 561-B2 PeT
Capitol City Seventh Day Adventist 459-K6 WTM
Carmel Apostolic 391-G4 CTH
Carmel Chr 392-A4 Ca
Carmel Friends 391-J4 Ca
Carmel Luth 392-F4 Ca
Carmel United Meth 391-K5 Ca
Carmelite Monastery 492-H2 WnT
Carters Mem Bapt 425-G5 WTM
Castleton Ch of the Nazarene 426-G7 WTM
Castleton Chr 427-D9 LTM
Castleton United Meth 427-C9 LTM
Cathedral of Praise Bibleway Ch Worldwide 460-A1 WTM
Cathedral of Serenity Missionary Bapt 493-H3 CTM
Centenary Chr 494-B5 CTM
Center 524-G9 GT
Center Grove Presb 595-E8 WTJ
Center United Meth 561-C1 PeT
Central Avenue United Meth DN-E1; 493-G5 CTM
Central Bapt 459-F2 WTM
Central Chr DN-D2; 493-F6 CTM
Chapel Glen Ch of Christ 490-J6 WnT
Chapel Hill United Meth 491-D6 WnT
Chapel of Prayer 494-G8 WrT
Chapel Rock Chr 491-D4 WnT
Chapelwood Bapt 491-D8 WnT
Chapters of Light Ministries 460-A5 WTM
Charity Bapt 456-H10 WnT
Charity Chapel General Bapt 494-E6 CTM
Charity Chr Ctr 494-K2 WrT
Charity Missionary Bapt 460-F10 CTM
Charity Tabernacle 526-F4 WnT
Chinese Comm 562-J1 FT
Christ Ch Apostolic 459-C1 WTM
Christ Ch Cathedral DN-D2; 493-E7 CTM
Christ Ch Lawrence 461-E4 L
Christ Comm 392-F4 Ca
Christ Cumberland Presb 561-E2 PeT
Christ Emmanuel Missionary Bapt 460-H10 WrT
Christ Evangelical Luth 455-J7 B
Christ Fellowship 594-F10 WTJ
Christ Luth 360-B1 NT
Christ Luth Irvington 495-A7 WrT
Christ Missionary Bapt 493-B1 CTM
Christ Presb 460-G8 WTM
Christ Temple 493-D3 CTM
Christ the King 459-J3 WTM
Christ the Saviour Brotherhood 493-F4 CTM
Christ United Meth 461-H8 LTM
Christian 592-A1 M
Christian Israelite 494-B5 CTM
Christian Life Ctr DN-E4; 493-H9 CTM; 489-K7 WaT
Christian Pk Reformed 494-E8 CTM
Christian Tabernacle 495-F9 WrT
Christian Valley Missionary Bapt 493-G2 CTM
Christion Comm 459-G9 CTM
Christs Open Door Bapt 527-K1 CTM
Christway Missionary Bapt 492-H4 WnT
Church at the Crossing 426-B3 WTM
Church of Acts 528-A6 PeT
Church of Christ 596-B2 G; 461-G6 L; 523-H5 P; 491-G1 WnT
Church of Christ at Eagle Valley 491-A1 WnT
Church of Christ Barrington 528-B2 CTM
Church of Christ Castleton 427-E5 LTM
Church of Christ Eastside 496-B2 WrT
Church of Christ Emerson Avenue 460-G8 LTM
Church of Christ Fountain Sq DN-F4; 493-J10 CTM
Church of Christ Garfield Hgts 527-G4 CTM
Church of Christ North Coll Avenue 459-F8 WTM
Church of Christ Northeast 494-J1 WrT
Church of Christ of East Street 525-J2 WnT
Church of Christ Scientist 424-C5 PTM; 424-K8 WTM; 494-H7 WrT
Church of Christ Scientist Second 460-B3 WTM
Church of Christ Shelbyville Road 528-F10 PeT
Church of Christ South Keystone 528-A7 PeT
Church of Christ Southport 561-J4 Spt
Church of Christ Westlake 491-F7 WnT
Church of God 455-G6 B
Church of God in Christ 493-K3 CTM
Church of God of Prophecy 525-F10 DTM
Church of God United Assembly 527-A5 PeT
Church of Jesus 494-D2 CTM
Church of Jesus Christ Apostolic Faith DN-E4; 493-G9 CTM
Church of the Apostolic Faith 494-D2 CTM; 459-H6 WTM
Church of the First Born DN-E4; 493-H10 CTM
Church of the Gospel 593-E3 MTM
Church of the Holy Cross DN-F3; 493-J8 CTM
Church of the Holy Spirit 495-D5 WrT
Church of the Living God 459-G10; 460-A9, E10 CTM; 460-F6 LTM; 492-H6 WnT

Church of the Master American Bapt 491-E5 WnT
Church of the Nativity 427-H9 LTM
Church of the Savior United Meth 460-H1 WTM
Citadel of Faith 494-A2 CTM
Clarksville Chr 361-D6 WyT
Clearview Comm 592-K8 MTM
Clermont Ch of the Nazarene 456-H10 WnT
Clermont Chr 456-J10 WnT
Cloverleaf Bapt 491-J9 WnT
College Pk Bapt 424-H2 PTM
Colonial Hills Bapt 426-B6 WTM
Community Ch of Greenwood 595-G3 WTJ
Community Ch Southport 562-H4 FT
Community Chr 531-G2 SCT; 460-A8 WTM
Community Missionary Bapt 425-B2 WTM
Compassion Temple Ch of God in Christ 459-J6 WTM
Concordia Luth 596-A1 G
Congregation B'Nai Torah 459-C1 WTM
Congregation Beth-El Zedeck 425-C9 WTM
Congregation of the Covenants 530-A9 FT
Congregation Simhat Yeshua 424-E3 PTM
Coppin Chapel AME 459-E10 CTM
Cornerstone Assembly 494-K8 WrT
Cornerstone Bapt 462-D4 L
Covenant 495-B2 WrT
Covenant Bapt 492-C1 WnT
Crestview 425-A4 WTM
Crestview Chr 425-A5 WTM
Cross And Crown Luth 426-H7 WTM
Crossroad Temple 494-J10 WrT
Crossroads Bapt 494-K10 WrT
Cumberland Ch of God Cleveland Assemblies 496-B9 WrT
Cumberland Chr 496-H6 Cu
Cumberland Road Ch of Christ 394-B5 F
Cumberland United Meth 496-H6 Cu
Cyntheanne 395-K4 FCT
Dayspring Assembly 425-K9 WTM
Devington 460-J6 LTM
Divine Savior Luth 427-D8 LTM
Eagle Alliance 423-H9 PTM
Eagle Cr Grace Brethren 457-E6 PTM
Eagle Creek Assembly of God 459-B3 WTM
Eagledale Bapt 458-B10 WnT
Eagledale Ch of the Nazarene 458-B9 WnT
Eagledale Wesleyan 458-B10 WnT
East 91st Street Chr 426-K4 WTM
East Park United Meth 494-A7 CTM
East Side Trinity 530-A2 WrT
East Sixteenth Chr 494-E4 CTM
East Tenth Street Ch of God 495-F5 WrT
East Tenth Street United Meth 494-A6 CTM
Eastgate Chr 495-G4 WrT
Eastlawn Wesleyan 461-H10 WrT
Eastminster Presb 495-C6 WrT
Eastside Ch of the Nazarene 494-E4 CTM
Eastside Seventh Day Adventist 460-D10 CTM
Eastside Trinity Gospel Tabernacle 494-F10 CTM
Eastview Vineyard Fellowship 497-D1 BCT
Ebenezer Ch & World Ministries 494-B6 CTM
Edgewood United Meth 561-K1 PeT
Edwin Ray United Meth DN-F4; 493-J10 CTM
El-Bethel Bapt 495-D4 WrT
Ellenberger United Ch of Christ 494-J6 WrT
Emmanuel 493-A3 CTM
Emmanuel Bapt DN-F4; 493-J10; 494-G1 CTM; 595-F8 WTJ
Emmanuel Ch of God in Christ DN-E1; 493-G5 CTM
Emmanuel Free Will Bapt 493-B2 CTM
Emmanuel Luth 461-A6 LTM
Emmanuel Temple 461-A9 WrT
Emmanuel United Meth 360-A7 NT; 460-K10 WrT
Emmaus Luth DN-F4; 493-J10 CTM
Englewood Neighborhood Chr Ministries 494-B7 CTM
Epworth United Meth 426-F10 WTM
Eternal Life Bapt 558-A9 GT
Etz Chaim Sephardic Congregation 459-C1 WTM
Evangelical Orth 526-K1 CTM
Evanston Wesleyan 425-K10 WTM
Fairfax Chr 425-D3 WTM
Fairfield 558-F5 GT
Fairview Hgts Presb 459-E6 WTM
Faith 427-E6 LTM
Faith Assembly of God 528-C4 BG
Faith Bapt 489-G8 A
Faith Evangelistic Ctr 527-F4 CTM
Faith Foursquare 528-G10 PeT
Faith in Action Ministry 461-F9 WrT
Faith Luth 491-H10 WnT
Faith Missionary 425-G3 WTM
Faith Missionary Bapt 461-A9 WrT
Faith Tabernacle 494-H6 WrT
Faith Temple Pent 527-H3 CTM
Faith United Ch of Christ 528-D9 PeT
Faith United Meth 495-J4 WrT
Faith United Meth Northwest 458-G2 WMT
Faithway Bapt 461-E8 LTM
Fall Creek Bapt 427-J10 LTM
Fall Creek Ch of Christ 493-F2 CTM
Fall Creek Ch of The Nazarene 460-F5 WTM
Far Eastside Bapt 459-C7 WTM
Fellowship Bapt 494-D7 CTM
Fellowship Ch of the Nazarene DN-A2 WnT
Fellowship Missionary Bapt 492-H10 WnT
Fifth Ch of Christ Scientist 459-G2 WTM
First Assembly of God 491-K7 WnT
First Bapt 526-J1 CTM; 392-C5 Ca; 524-K3 WnT
First Bapt Beech Grove 528-J6 BG
First Bapt of Cumberland 496-G6 Cu
First Bapt of Indianapolis 425-G4 WTM
First Bible 494-H2 WrT
First Born Saints 494-B2 CTM
First Ch of God 359-K1 NT
First Ch of Religious Science 425-E3 WTM
First Ch of the Open Bible 494-F3 CTM
First Chr Ch of Beech Grove 528-F5 BG
First Chr Missionary Bapt 461-A8 LTM
First Cong 425-F9 WTM
First Free Will Bapt 493-A2 CTM
First Friends Meeting 460-C3 WTM
First Friendship 527-E3 CTM
First General Bapt 526-C6 DTM
First Inspirational Missionary Bapt 460-C10 CTM
First Korean United Meth 496-C3 WrT
First Luth DN-D2; 493-F6 CTM
First Mennonite 458-J3 WMT
First Presb Ch of Southport 561-H4 PeT
First Separate Bapt in Christ 527-E9 PeT
First Trinity Luth 460-G7 LTM
First United Evangelical 526-F5 WnT
Fishers United Meth 393-K8 F
Flanner House 493-C2 CTM
Fleming Garden Chr 492-F9 WnT
Forest Manor United Meth 460-D9 CTM
Fountain Sq Chr 527-J4 CTM
Fountain Sq Pilgrim Holiness DN-E4; 493-H10 CTM
Franklin Central Chr 529-G7 FT
Franklin Road Bapt 495-F7 WrT
Franklin Road Ch of Christ 495-F6 WrT
Free Meth 558-A10 M
Free Meth of North America World Hdq 491-F6 WnT
Free Presb Ch of Indianapolis 529-G1 WrT
Free Spirit Bapt 492-D10 WnT
Freedom Missionary Bapt 492-A7 WnT
Friedens 561-E7 PeT
Friendly Ch of the Nazarene 492-H10 WnT
Friendship Bapt DN-A1 WnT
Full Gospel Apostolic 460-A6 WTM
Full Gospel Missionary DN-A4; 492-J10 CTM
Garden Bapt 493-K4 CTM
Garden City Chr 492-A8 WnT
Garfield Chr 527-J3 CTM
Garfield Pk Bapt 527-H4 CTM
Garfield Pk Ch of God 527-F4 CTM
Garfield Pk United Ch of Christ 527-G2 CTM
Gateway Bapt 495-B3 WrT
Geist Chr 428-A5 LTM
Geist Comm Bapt 462-F1 L
Gershom 459-J6 WTM
Gethsemane General Bapt 526-C5 WnT
Gethsemane Luth 495-C6 WrT
Glad Tidings Assembly of God 455-G9 LTH
Glendale Chr 425-K9 WTM
Glendale Seventh Day Adventist 460-A2 WTM
Glory Missionary Bapt 493-G1 CTM
Gold Bell Bapt 493-H2 CTM
Golden Gate Bible 495-E10 WrT
Good News Mission 494-B8 CTM
Good Shepard Cath 527-H3, J4 CTM
Good Shepherd Chr Ctr 460-B9 WTM
Good Shepherd Luth 460-C3 WTM
Good Shepherd United Meth 528-K2 WrT
Goodwill Bapt DN-F1; 493-J5 CTM
Gospel Assembly 561-B1 PeT
Gospel Chapel 492-C9 WnT
Gospel Lighthouse DN-E4; 493-G9 CTM
Grace Apostolic 493-G3 CTM
Grace Assembly of God 596-D8 G
Grace Bapt 493-K10 CTM; 561-G9 G
Grace Bapt of Sterling Hgts 525-E1 WnT
Grace Bible 462-C2 L
Grace Brethren 427-G3 LTM
Grace Comm DN-B4; 493-A10 CTM
Grace Evangelical Luth 491-K8 WnT
Grace Mem Bapt 494-C1 CTM
Grace Missionary 592-D1 M
Grace Missionary Bapt 493-B3 CTM
Grace Presb Ch in America 426-G7 WTM
Grace United Meth 494-D7 CTM
Gray Friends 358-F10 NT
Gray Road Chr 528-D10 PeT
Greater Antioch Missionary Bapt 493-G2 CTM
Greater Canaan Bapt 493-J3 CTM
Greater Galilee Missionary Bapt 460-K7 LTM
Greater Gethsemane Missionary Bapt 494-F6 CTM
Greater King Solomon Bapt DN-A2 CTM
Greater Love Missionary Bapt 494-A2 CTM
Greater Love Temple 493-B4 CTM
Greater Morning Star Missionary Bapt 493-F2 CTM
Greater Northeast Bapt 462-A7 LTM
Greater Northwest Bapt 458-E2 PTM
Greater Progressive Bapt 494-C5 CTM
Greater Saint James Bapt DN-D1; 493-D6 CTM
Greater Saint Mark Bapt 460-H9 WrT
Greater Shepard Missionary Bapt 494-A4 CTM
Greater Southern Bapt 425-C5 WTM
Greater Triedstone Missionary Bapt 425-B3 WTM
Greater Whitestone Bapt 492-F6 WnT
Greek Orth Ch of the Holy Trinity 459-F8 WTM
Greenwood Chr DN-D4 CTM; 596-C3 G
Greenwood First Bapt 596-C2 G
Greenwood First Presb 596-C2 G
Greenwood United Meth 596-B1 G
Hansing Pk Chr 528-B6 PeT
Harding Street Ch of God 493-A2 CTM
Harmony Bapt 460-H9 WrT
Harvest Foursquare 492-E5 WnT
Harvestime Chr 529-J2 WrT
Haverford Moravian 459-H4 WTM
Hawthorne Bapt Chapel 492-H9 WnT
Heather Hills Bapt 496-E5 WrT
Heavenly Life 492-B1 WnT
Hinkle Creek Friends 324-F4 JT
Hispanic Ministries United Meth 495-H6 WrT
Holy Angels Cath 493-B2 CTM
Holy Cross Luth 428-G6 L
Holy Family Epis Word Alive Fellowship 563-J6 FT
Holy Family Shelter 527-E1 CTM
Holy Name of Jesus Cath 528-D5 BG
Holy Rosary Cath DN-E4; 493-G9 CTM
Holy Spirit 495-D6 WrT
Holy Spirit Ch at Geist 427-F4 LTM
Holy Temple 493-F3 CTM
Holy Trinity Cath 494-A6 CTM
Honey Creek United Meth 595-H8 WTJ
Hope 562-C7 PeT
Hope Bapt 491-D6 WnT
Hope Chapel 527-K5 PeT
Hope Evangelical Covenant 425-D4 WTM
Hope Evangelical Luth 460-J10 WrT
Hortonville Friends 323-F7 WTH
Hortonville United Meth 323-D7 WTH
House of Prayer 495-G9 WrT
House of Prayer Tabernacle 528-F10 PeT
Hunter Road Bible 529-C3 WrT
Iglesia Apostolica Hispana 494-F7 CTM
Immaculate Heart of Mary Parish 459-G4 WTM
Immanuel Evangelical Bapt 424-B9 PTM
Immanuel Presb 460-D8 WTM
Immanuel United Ch of Christ DN-E4 CTM
Immanuel United Meth 461-A8 LTM
Indian Creek Chr 563-H2 FT
Indiana Bapt 460-B8 WTM
Indianapolis Bapt Bible Fellowship 495-F2 WrT
Indianapolis Bapt Tabernacle 528-J4 WrT
Indianapolis Bapt Temple 494-A2 CTM
Indianapolis Chr Fellowship 527-J8 PeT
Indianapolis Chr Reformed 491-C4 WnT
Indianapolis Comm Alliance DN-F1 CTM
Indianapolis First Ch of the Nazarene 495-D6 WrT
Indianapolis Foursquare Gospel 527-J2 CTM
Indianapolis Grace 562-H3 FT
Indianapolis Hebrew Congregation 425-F10 WTM
Indianapolis Nazarene Chapel 494-H4 WrT
Inner City Bapt 424-G9 PTM
Inner City Chapel DN-E2; 493-G7 CTM
Irvington Bapt Chapel 494-E10 CTM
Irvington First Bapt 495-H7 WrT
Irvington Friends Meeting 495-C6 WrT
Irvington Presb 494-J8 WrT
Irvington United Meth 494-J7 WrT
Islamic Ctr 557-J4 GT
Jehovahs Witnesses 460-J5 LTM
Jehovahs Witnesses Airport 526-B1 WnT
Jehovahs Witnesses Chr Pk 494-F10 CTM
Jehovahs Witnesses Craigwood 561-E4 PeT
Jehovahs Witnesses Downtown 425-F6 WTM
Jehovahs Witnesses Eagle Cr 457-K5 PTM
Jehovahs Witnesses East Lawrence 461-D6 L
Jehovahs Witnesses Forest Manor 460-D10 CTM
Jehovahs Witnesses Glendale 460-A4 WTM
Jehovahs Witnesses Heather Hills 495-C3 WrT
Jehovahs Witnesses Kessler 458-K4 WTM
Jehovahs Witnesses Pleasant Run 528-C3 CTM
Jehovahs Witnesses Raymond Pk 529-H2 WrT
Jehovahs Witnesses Southeast 562-G1 FT
Jehovahs Witnesses-Assembly Hall DN-D1; 493-F5 CTM
Jester Mem Ch of the Nazarene 460-B9 CTM
Jesus Christ Gospel 494-A1 CTM
Jesus is Lord Fellowship 458-H1 WMT
Jesus is the Word 492-F5 WnT
Jesus Saves Lighthouse 462-B8 LTM
Jesus The Way 492-F2 WnT
John Knox United Presb 491-G1 S
John Wesley Free Meth 457-H6 PTM
Jones Tabernacle AME Zion 460-A10 CTM
Jordan River Bapt 458-F5 WTM
Joy Bapt 424-C7 PTM
Kessler Krest Bapt 458-F4 WTM
Keystone 460-A1 WTM
Keystone Chr 460-A4 WTM
King of Glory Luth 392-B10 CTH
Kingdom Hall 593-B8 MTM; 531-C4 SCT
Kingsway Chr 489-J6 WaT
Korean Bapt of Indianapolis 496-A1 WrT
Korean Cath Comm 461-D6 L
Korean Seventh Day Adventist 462-A8 LTM
Lakeview Chr Ctr 491-D8 WnT
Landmark Bapt 528-C2 CTM
Lativian Evangelical Luth 494-F6 CTM
Lawrence Bapt 461-H7 L
Lawrence Ch of God 461-J7 LTM
Lawrence Ch of the Nazarene 462-A6 L
Lawrence Missionary 461-H6 L
Lawrence United Meth 461-C5 L
LDS Crossroads 494-C9 CTM
LDS Cumberland 496-F1 WrT
LDS Indianapolis First & Third Ward 561-H4 PeT
LDS Reorganized 494-E6 CTM
LDS-Fall Creek 460-A6 WTM
LDS-White River DN-D2; 493-E7 CTM
Lee Temple Ch of God in Christ 492-G7 WnT
Life Unlimited 493-K9 CTM
Lifegate Bapt 528-G6 BG
Light of Life Free Meth 523-K1 WaT
Light of the World Chr 460-J9 WrT
Light of the World Missionary Bapt 459-C8 WTM
Lighthouse Bapt 529-C2 WrT
Lighthouse Comm 494-B8 CTM
Lighthouse Tabernacle 426-C2 CTH
Lighthouses Ministries DN-E3; 493-G8 CTM
Linwood Chr 494-E6 CTM
Little Bethel Bapt 459-J10 CTM
Little Eagle Cr 356-D8 WTH
Little Egypt Bapt 494-A1 CTM
Little Flock DN-A1 CTM
Little People Missionary Bapt 494-C2 CTM
Little Stone Bapt 493-J1 CTM
Living Hope Chr Fellowship 524-J3 WnT
Lockerbie Sq United Meth 492-E8 WnT
Lord of Life 461-K8 LTM
Love Chr Fellowship 460-A6 WTM
Loving Bapt Missionary 425-G5 WTM
Loving Kindness Ch of God in Chr DN-A2 WnT
Loving Kindness Ch of God in Christ 492-J7 WnT
Lynhurst Bapt 525-K1 WnT
Macedonia 422-F7 BTH
Madison Avenue Bapt 562-A6 PeT
Maple Grove Bapt 461-A6 LTM
Maple Hill 529-H8 FT
Maplehill United Meth 461-E6 L
Maranatha 491-C8 WnT
Mars Hill Bapt Bible 526-B4 WnT
Mars Hill Free Meth 526-D5 WnT
Mars Hill General Bapt 526-E4 WnT
Mars View Chr 526-E6 DTM
Marwood 526-B7 DTM
Masjid Al-Fajr 492-H1 WnT
McClendon Tabernacle 494-E2 CTM
McCordsville United Meth 429-B7 McC
Meadlawn Chr 494-E9 CTM
Meadowbrook Ch of the Nazarene 525-J7 DTM
Meadowdale United Meth 457-J10 WnT
Memorial Bapt 455-F10 LTH; 492-G4 WnT
Meridian Ch of God 561-E6 PeT
Meridian Hgts Presb 459-G6 WTM
Meridian Street Ch of the Nazarene 527-D2 CTM
Meridian Street United Meth 459-E4 WTM
Meridian Woods Bapt 561-D3 PeT
Messiah Luth 455-F8 B
Messiah Luth LCMS 457-G8 PTM
Messiah Missionary Bapt 493-C2 CTM
Metropolitan Bapt 493-G1 CTM
Metropolitan Comm 496-A6 WrT
Missionary Bible Bapt 527-J6 PeT
Missionary Free Chr 461-G7 LTM
Mooresville Ch of God 592-A2 M
Morris Street United Meth 493-F10 CTM
Mount Auburn United Meth 595-D8 WTJ
Mount Calvary Apostolic 461-B7 LTM
Mount Calvary Bapt 460-A3 WTM
Mount Calvary Evangelistic Ctr 528-F2 CTM
Mount Calvary Freewill Bapt 494-C2 CTM
Mount Calvary Full Gospel 527-G5 CTM
Mount Calvary Missionary Bapt 564-F6 FT
Mount Carmel Bapt 460-H9 WrT
Mount Carmel Freewill Bapt 494-H2 WrT
Mount Comfort United Meth 463-D8 BCT
Mount Gerizim Bapt 462-A7 LTM
Mount Gilead 592-K6 MTM
Mount Helm Missionary Bapt 493-G4 CTM
Mount Lebanon Bapt 459-K6 WTM
Mount Nebo Bapt 493-K3 CTM
Mount Olive Missionary Bapt 493-B4 CTM
Mount Olive United Meth 525-G1 WnT
Mount Paran Bapt 459-D10 CTM
Mount Pilgram Bapt 527-H2 CTM
Mount Pisgah Bapt 494-B3 CTM
Mount Pleasant 560-A3 DTM
Mount Pleasant Bapt 458-A2 PTM
Mount Tabor 494-A6 CTM
Mount Vernon Missionary Bapt DN-A2 CTM
Mount Zion 395-E10 FCT
Mount Zion Bapt 459-D9 CTM
Mount Zion General Bapt 528-A6 PeT
Native American 496-A4 WrT
Nativity Cath 529-D5 FT
Nazarene 592-A1 M
Nazarene Chapel 527-J3 CTM
Nazarene Missionary Bapt 460-C9 CTM
New Bapt 425-A6 WTM
New Bethany Bapt 531-J6 NP
New Bethel Bapt 494-E5 CTM
New Commandment Bapt 460-K10 WrT
New Covenant Missionary Bapt 459-G8 WTM
New Day Pent 425-B5 WTM
New Deliverence Temple 493-E5 CTM
New Fellowship Missionary Bapt 459-K9 CTM
New Garfield Bapt 528-B1 CTM
New Genesis Missionary Bapt 457-C9 WnT
New Greater Zion MB DN-A1 WnT
New Harmony General Bapt 527-J6 PeT
New Haven Bapt 459-K9 CTM
New Hope United Bapt 494-F1 CTM
New Horizons of Eagle Creek United Meth 423-E9 PTM
New Jerusalem Missionary Bapt 460-H10 WrT
New Liberty Spiritual 460-D9 CTM
New Life DN-A4 CTM
New Life Assembly of God 525-K7 DTM
New Light Bapt 425-B6 WTM
New Mission Bapt 493-K2 CTM
New Palestine United Meth 531-G3 SCT
New Salem Missionary Bapt 493-H1 CTM
New Testament Ch of God 495-F6 WrT
New Testament Missionary Bapt 524-G5 P
New Vision Bapt 493-C2 CTM
New Zion Tabernacle 494-B2 CTM
North Bapt 459-K5 WTM
North Central 425-K4 WTM
North Liberty Chr 457-H5 PTM
North Madison Bapt 593-E1 MTM
North Meadow Circle of Friends 493-F4 CTM
North Suburban Bapt 425-A5 WTM
North United Meth 459-E9 CTM
Northeast United Ch of Christ 461-F9 WrT
Northeastwood Chr 496-A1 WrT
Northminster Presb Ch of Indianapolis 459-J2 WTM
Northside Bapt 426-B9 WTM
Northside Ch of the Nazarene 424-G10 PTM
Northside New Era Bapt 493-C1 CTM
Northside Wesleyan 459-J6 WTM
Northview Ch of the Brethren 460-J6 LTM
Northwest Assembly of God 425-C2 WTM
Northwest Bapt 457-G10 WnT
Oak Pk Bapt 526-F1 WnT
Oaklandon Bapt 428-J10 L
Oaklandon Chr 428-G10 L
Oaklandon Unitn Universalist 428-H10 L
Old Bethel United Meth 495-F3 WrT
Olivet Missionary Bapt DN-E4; 493-H10 CTM
One Way Apostolic 494-K4 WrT
Open Door Bapt 492-H1 WnT
Open Door First Meth 326-D6 NT
Original Ch of God 493-E3 CTM
Otterbein United Meth 494-G3 CTM
Our Lady of Grace Cath 326-B10 N
Our Lady of Lourdes 494-G7 WrT
Our Lady of the Greenwood 596-D3 G
Our Redeemer Luth 494-C10 CTM
Our Savior Missionary Bapt 526-K1 CTM
Our Shepherd Luth 490-H6 WnT
Parc-Way Assembly of God 528-C10 PeT
Park Avenue Ch of Christ DN-E1 CTM
Park Hgts 460-B10 CTM
Peace Free Will Bapt 528-G9 FT
Peace Luth for the Deaf 461-A6 LTM
Penick Chapel AME Zion 494-B10 CTM
Pentecostal Assemblies of the World 460-C8 WTM
Pentecostal Ch of Promises DN-F4; 493-J9 CTM
Pentecostal Liberty Tabernacle 424-C6 PTM
Pentecostal Workers Assembly DN-D4; 493-E9 CTM

Peter Rock Bapt DN-A1; 492-K6 CTM
Philadelphia Apostolic 460-G8 LTM
Phillips Temple 459-F9 CTM
Pilgrim 425-E1 Ca
Pilgrim Bapt 493-A1 CTM
Pilgrim Chapel DN-B2 CTM
Pilgrim Chapel Missionary Bapt 494-B3 CTM
Pilgrim Holiness 359-C4 NT
Pillar of Truth Ministries 461-F5 L
Pioneer Missionary Bapt 493-J4 CTM
Plainfield Chr 523-J5 P
Pleasant Grove 391-F9 CTH
Pleasant Hgts Bapt 525-K6 DTM
Pleasant Run United Ch of Christ 527-E3 CTM
Pleasant Union Bapt 493-A1 CTM
Pleasant Valley United Ch of Christ 564-E9; 598-D1 CTJ
Pleasant View Luth 425-C9 WTM
Post Road Chr 495-J5 WrT
Power House Ch of God in Christ 494-D1 CTM
Prairie Bapt 327-F6 WyT
Praise and Worship Evangelistic Ctr 424-E3 PTM
Prentice 460-F8 WTM
Primera Inglesia Bautista Hispana DN-B4; 493-A9 CTM
Prince of Peace 458-C9 WnT
Prince of Peace United Ch of Christ 595-E10 WTJ
Progressive Missionary Bapt 460-K9 WrT
Prove All Things Ch of Christ 461-A9 WrT
Providence AME 493-B2 CTM
Psalms Missionary 460-C10 CTM
Psychic Science Spiritualist DN-E1; 493-G5 CTM
Puritan Bapt 493-C2 CTM
Raceway Road Bapt 492-A8 WnT
Rainbow Acres Ch of God 490-G8 WaT
Ravenbrook Widow Missionary Bapt 459-G5 WTM
Rawles Avenue Presb 495-G9 WrT
Reformed Presb 561-E4 PeT
Refuge Chr 326-G9 NT
Refuge Mem Apostolic 527-J1 CTM
Religious Science 425-J10 WTM
Religious Science Ctr 527-H10 PeT
Rescue Free Will Bapt 494-G1 CTM
Resurrection 561-G6 PeT
Resurrection Luth 561-F4 PeT
Revival Temple DN-A2 CTM
Ritter Avenue Ch of the Nazarene 494-F2 CTM
Ritter Avenue Free Meth 494-J4 WrT
Ritter Avenue General Bapt 494-J7 WrT
River Avenue Bapt DN-B4; 493-B10 CTM
River Oaks Comm 391-G4 Ca
Roberts Pk United Meth DN-D2; 493-F7 CTM
Robinson Comm 459-G6 WTM
Rocklane Chr 597-H2 CTJ
Rosedale Hills United Meth 528-A9 PeT
Sacred Heart 527-E1 CTM
Saint Albans Epis 460-G6 LTM
Saint Alphonsus Cath 389-E8 Z
Saint Andrew Presb 460-A9 CTM
Saint Andrew the Apostle 460-D8 WTM
Saint Andrew United Meth 528-A4 CTM
Saint Andrews Luth 491-J3 S
Saint Ann 526-E5 WnT
Saint Anthony Cath 492-G7 WnT
Saint Athanasius Byzantine Cath 496-B2 WrT
Saint Barnabas Cath 491-A8 WnT
Saint Bernadettes Cath 494-F9 CTM
Saint Bridgets Cath 494-C6 CTM
Saint Catherine Chapel 527-G3 CTM
Saint Christophers Epis 391-F4 CTH
Saint Constantine & Elena 492-G4 WnT
Saint Edward the Confessor 460-A1 WTM
Saint Gabriel Cath 457-H10 WnT
Saint George Orth Chr 460-D8 WTM
Saint James 493-D1 CTM
Saint James Chapel 527-J5 PeT
Saint Joan of Arc 459-G7 WTM
Saint John AME 493-J4 CTM
Saint John Cath DN-D3; 493-E8 CTM
Saint John Evangelical Luth 561-G3 PeT; 529-B4 WrT
Saint John United Ch of Christ 496-E6 Cu
Saint Johns Epis 491-J1 S
Saint Johns Missionary Bapt 528-E1 CTM
Saint Johns United Ch of Christ 427-C9 LTM
Saint Joseph & Holy Cross 527-D3 CTM
Saint Joseph Spiritual 494-C1 CTM
Saint Josephs Cath 525-J1 WnT
Saint Jude 460-H10 WrT
Saint Lawrence 461-C6 L
Saint Luke Cath 425-E8 WTM
Saint Luke Missionary Bapt 493-J1 CTM
Saint Lukes Chapel 494-E7 CTM
Saint Lukes United Ch of Christ 491-K4 S
Saint Lukes United Meth 425-D4 WTM
Saint Malachy 455-F5 B
Saint Maria Goretti 357-D5 WTH
Saint Mark AME Zion 527-H2 CTM
Saint Mark Cath 561-F2 PeT
Saint Mark Ch of God in Christ 493-H3 CTM
Saint Marks Luth 493-J10 CTM; 388-E1 Wh
Saint Marys Cath Hispanic Apostolate DN-E2; 493-F7 CTM
Saint Matthew Bapt 493-J1 CTM
Saint Matthew Luth 494-B7 CTM
Saint Matthews Epis 495-G5 WrT
Saint Maur Monastery Hospitality Ctr 494-F6 CTM
Saint Maur Theological Ctr 459-A7 WTM
Saint Michael 492-G1 WnT
Saint Michael Cath 492-F1 WnT
Saint Mission Bapt 527-K4 CTM
Saint Monica Cath 459-H2 WTM; 461-A9 WrT
Saint Nicholas Serbian Orth 492-E4 WnT
Saint Paul AME 493-K2 CTM
Saint Paul United Meth 494-D2 CTM
Saint Pauls Epis 459-E2 WTM
Saint Pauls Luth DN-E4; 493-F9 CTM
Saint Peters Evangelical Luth 494-A5 CTM
Saint Peters United Ch of Christ 392-B6 Ca
Saint Philip Neri 494-A6 CTM
Saint Philips Epis DN-C1; 493-C5 CTM
Saint Pius X Cath 426-B9 WTM
Saint Rita JTV 493-H4 CTM
Saint Roch Cath 527-E6 PeT
Saint Susanna Cath 523-J7 P
Saint Therese Little Flower Cath 494-E5 CTM
Saint Thomas Aquinas 459-E6 WTM
Saint Timothys Epis 528-B10 PeT
Saint Timothys Tabernacle 493-J2 CTM
Saints Francis & Clare Cath 594-F6 WTJ
Saints Peter & Paul Cathedral DN-D1; 493-E5 CTM
Salem 388-J10 ET
Salem Luth 424-B9 PTM
Salt of the Earth Bapt 458-B10 WTM
Sanders Temple Ch of God in Christ 460-C8 WTM
Scott United Meth 494-C3 CTM
Second Bapt DN-A3 WnT
Second Fall Creek 395-C5 FCT
Second Moravian 459-J10 CTM
Second Presb 425-E7 WTM
Second Reformed Presb 494-F7 CTM
Second Saint James 460-G10 WrT
Second Saint Paul Bapt 460-E10 CTM
Seerley Creek Chr 525-K6 DTM
Servants of Christ Luth 428-H7 L
Seven Stars Bapt 493-G1 CTM
Seventh & Eighth United Chr 492-G1 WnT
Seventh Day Adventist Irvington 529-F2 WrT
Seventh Day Adventist Southside 528-F10 PeT
Shadeland Bapt 461-E10 WrT
Shalom Mennonite 495-K2 WrT
Shelby Street Pent 561-J6 PeT
Shepherd Comm Ch of the Nazarene DN-F3; 493-K8 CTM
Shiloh Crossomg United Meth 490-G7 WaT
Shiloh Missionary Bapt 460-E8 WTM
Shiloh United Meth DN-E4; 493-H9 CTM
Shout the Victory Chr Ctr DN-B4; 493-B9 CTM
Smith Valley Bapt 594-K3 WTJ
Smith Valley United Meth 594-H4 WTJ
Solomons Temple Ch of God in Christ 460-D10 CTM
Sonshine Inn Coffeehouse DN-F3 CTM
South Calvary Bapt DN-D4; 493-E10 CTM
South Emerson Ch of God 528-G7 BG
South Irvington Ch of the Nazarene 528-H9 FT; 494-H9 WrT
South Sherman Drive Ch of God 528-D6 PeT
Southeastern Ch of Christ 561-G3 PeT
Southern Bapt 495-J2 WrT
Southern Pointe Comm 528-F9 BG
Southminster Presb 428-A4 LTM
Southport Bapt 562-B3 PeT
Southport Ch of the Nazarene 561-H4 PeT
Southport Chr 561-F1 PeT
Southport Hgts Chr 424-K9 WTM
Southport Presb Chr 562-C6 PeT
Southport United Meth 561-K4 Spt
Southside Ch of the Nazarene 528-A10 PeT
Southside Missionary Bapt 527-K6 PeT
Southview Wesleyan 528-F10 PeT
Southwest Ch of God 559-D2 DTM
Southwest Ch of the Nazarene 525-K10 DTM
Southwood Assembly of God 561-E8 PeT
Speedway Bapt 491-K1 WnT
Speedway Ch of Christ 492-B6 S
Speedway Ch of the Nazarene 492-A4 S
Speedway Chr 492-A5 S
Speedway United Meth 492-A5 S
Spirit of Life 491-E1 WnT
State Convention of Bapt 491-G6 WnT
Stewart Mem 528-C1 CTM
Suburban Bapt 561-H9 PeT
Sugar Creek 565-K2 MTS
Sugar Grove 557-F2 GT
Sunnyside Road Bapt 462-E1 L
Sunnyside Road Ch of God 462-D1 L
Sunrise at Geist United Meth 428-G8 L
Sunrise Bapt 493-G4 CTM
Sunshine Gdns Wesleyan 560-G1 PeT
Sunshine Inn Coffeehouse 493-J8 CTM
Tabernacle Bapt 494-B1 CTM
Tabernacle Presb 459-F9 CTM
Tallwood Chapel 561-H1 PeT
TCM Intl 491-G1 S
Temple 561-B2 PeT
Temple of Israel 459-K7 WTM
Tenth Street Bapt 494-C6 CTM
The Bapt 527-G1 CTM
The Bible Way Temple 493-A1 CTM
The Ch Within 459-G5 WTM
The Chr Ctr 529-F1 WrT
The Chr Ctr Spiritual 494-C1 CTM
The Eastside Bapt 493-K1 CTM
The Open Door Missionary Bapt 528-A2 CTM
The Spiritual Israel Ch and Its Army 460-G9 WrT
The Wesleyan 426-K6 WTM
Thesalonian Missionary Bapt 459-E10 CTM
Third Chr 460-H3 LTM
This Rock Apostolic DN-A2 WnT
Thompson Road Bapt 527-K10 PeT
Traders Pt Ch of Christ 423-A6 PTM
Traders Pt Chr 423-B7 PTM
Travelers Rest Bapt 459-D9 CTM
Trinity 494-F3 CTM; 425-F5 WTM
Trinity Bapt 459-K10 CTM; 323-K10 WTH
Trinity Chr 459-F10 CTM
Trinity Epis 459-E10 CTM
Trinity Fellowship Ch of God 494-A9 CTM
Trinity General Bapt 561-J1 PeT
Trinity Presb 425-G4 WTM
Trinity Southern Bapt 561-F4 PeT
Trinity Wesleyan 426-K2 F
True Belief Missionary Bapt 460-F8 WTM
True Tried Missionary Bapt 493-D2 CTM
True Vine Missionary Bapt 460-A8 WTM
Trueword Bapt 527-K4 CTM
Tuxedo Pk Bapt 494-E7 CTM
Unification 459-F8 CTM
Union Bapt 526-J1 CTM
Union Chapel United Meth 426-B4 WTM
Union United Meth 327-A10 WyT
Unitarian Ch All Souls 460-K4 LTM
Unitarian Universalist 459-D7 WTM
United Orth Hebrew Cong 459-G3 WTM
Unity Fellowship Missionary Bapt 494-D1 CTM
Unity of Indianapolis DN-D1 CTM
Universal Ch of Truth 459-K10 CTM
Universal Free Apostolic DN-F4; 493-J10 CTM
University Hgts Bapt 526-H2 WnT
University Hgts Ch of the Nazarene 527-J6 PeT
University Hgts Chr 527-H8 PeT
University Hgts United Meth 527-J7 PeT
University United Meth 458-K2 WTM
Valley Mills Chr 559-F1 DTM
Valley Mills Friends 525-E10 DTM
Vickery Bapt 325-H9 NT
Victory Bapt 460-H1 WTM
Victory Chapel Comm 327-B4 WRT
Victory Independent Bapt 497-K6 SCT
Victory Tabernacle of the Apostolic Faith 459-K10 CTM
Villa Bapt 528-A4 CTM
Villa Hgts Ch of God 595-F2 G
Vineyard Chr Fellowship 460-A2 WTM
Vineyard Chr Fellowship Southside 561-E2 PeT
Voice of Pentecost DN-D4; 493-E10 CTM
Wallace Street United Presb 494-F6 CTM
Walnut Grove Chapel 426-J3 WTM
Warren Bapt 495-K3 WrT
Warren Hills Chr 496-B6 WrT
Warren Pk Wesleyan 495-A5 WrT
Washington Street Presb DN-A3 CTM
Washington Street United Meth 492-H8 WnT
Wesley United Meth 492-E1 WnT
Wesleyan Bible 494-D6 CTM
West Minster United Presb DN-F2; 493-K7 CTM
West Morris Street Free Meth 492-H10 WnT
West Newton Ch of Christ 559-E6 DTM
West Newton Friends 559-G4 DTM
West Newton Full Gospel 559-C7 DTM
West Newton United Meth 559-E4 DTM
West Park Chr 492-H8 WnT
West Parkview Missionary Bapt 491-C9 WnT
Westbrook Ch of the Nazarene 492-B10 WnT
Westbrook New Testament Bapt 492-B9 WnT
Westfield Friends Meeting 357-K4 W
Westlake Comm Ch of God 491-F8 WnT
Westlane Chr 424-K9 WTM
Westside Assembly of God 526-J1 WnT
Westside Ch of Christ 526-G4 WnT
Westside Ch of God 493-B1 CTM
Westside Ch of the Nazarene 490-J6 WnT
Westside Chr 490-K6 WnT
Westside Missionary Bapt DN-A1 CTM
Westview Chr 457-H10 WnT
Westview Chr Life 492-G6 WnT
Westwood Missionary Bapt 490-H4 WnT
White Chapel 392-G8 Ca
White Harvest United Meth 425-A7 WTM
White Lick Presb 489-C2 LTH
White River Chr 325-J10 NT
Whitestown Bapt 388-E1 Wh
Whitestown United Meth 388-D1 Wh
Williams Creek 425-B2 WTM
Womack Mem 459-H7 WTM
Woodland 527-F5 PeT
Woodland Bapt 462-B10 WrT
Woodland Springs Chr 392-A8 CTH
Woodruff Pl Bapt DN-F2; 493-K7 CTM
Woodside United Meth 494-A9 CTM
Word of Life 460-J7 LTM
Word of the Lord Bapt 527-H5 PeT
World Wide Ch of God DN-C1; 493-C5 CTM
Zion 529-J4 WrT
Zion Bapt 494-D2 CTM
Zion Hope Bapt 460-K6 LTM
Zion Luth 531-C2 SCT
Zion Tabernacle Apostolic Faith 460-D8 WTM
Zionsville Chr 389-G8 Z
Zionsville Meth 389-F8 Z
Zionsville Presb 390-B8 ET

POINTS OF INTEREST

300 North Meridian DN-D2 CTM
Air Traffic Control Ctr 525-E5 WnT
American Legion Natl Hdq DN-D1 CTM
American United Life Tower DN-D2 CTM
Artsgarden DN-D2 CTM
Athenaeum DN-E2 CTM
Bank One Circle Bldg DN-D2 CTM
Bank One Indiana Ctr DN-D2 CTM
Canal Walk DN-D2 CTM
Chamber of Commerce 489-G9 A
Childrens Mus 493-E1 CTM
Conference Ctr DN-C2 CTM
Conner Prairie Settlement Mus 393-F3 F
Cool Cr Music Pavilion 358-A9 WTH
Crown Hill Cem Mausoleum 459-C8 WTM
Deer Cr Music Ctr 361-A10 WyT
Downtown Heliport DN-E3 CTM
Eagle Cr Pk Amphitheatre 457-C3 PTM
Eagle Cr Pk Nature Ctr 457-C1 PTM
Eagle Cr Pk Ranger Sta 457-C3 PTM
Eiteljorg Mus of American Indians & Western Art DN-C3 CTM
First Indiana Plaza DN-D2 CTM
Governors Mansion 459-E6 WTM
Grave of President Benjamin Harrison 459-B10 CTM
Greyhound Bus Terminal DN-D3 CTM
Hamilton Co Humane Soc 360-A2 N
Hilbert Circle Theatre DN-D3 CTM
Historic Hanna House 527-H7 PeT
Historic Landmarks Foundation DN-D2 CTM
Hooks Hist Drug Store 459-H8 WTM
IMAX 3-D Theatre DN-C2 CTM
Indiana Convention Ctr DN-D3 CTM
Indiana Hist Soc DN-C2 CTM
Indiana HS Athletic Association 425-E2 WTM
Indiana Repertory Theater DN-D3 CTM
Indiana St Fairgrounds 459-J7 WTM
Indiana St Mus DN-E2 CTM
Indiana Transportation Mus 359-G1 N
Indiana Womens Prison 493-K7 CTM
Indiana World War Mem DN-D2 CTM
Indianapolis Board of Realtors 493-D4 CTM
Indianapolis Motor Speedway 492-B2 S
Indianapolis Motor Speedway Admin Offices 492-B4 S
Indianapolis Motor Speedway Hall of Fame Mus 492-C4 S
Indianapolis Mus of Art 459-A8 WTM
Indianapolis Power & Light 493-C9 CTM
Indianapolis Zoo DN-B3 CTM
James Whitcomb Riley Home DN-E2 CTM
James Whitcomb Riley Mon 459-B9 CTM
Little Eagle Cr Music Festival 356-F6 WTH
Little League Central Region Hdq 462-A6 LTM
Madame Walker Theatre Ctr DN-C2 CTM
Major Taylor Velodrome 458-H9 PTM
Market Sq Arena DN-E3 CTM
Market Tower DN-D2 CTM
Morris-Butler House Mus DN-E1 CTM
Munce Art Ctr 389-J9 Z
Murat Shrine Ctr Theatre DN-E2 CTM
Murat Shrine Temple DN-E2; 493-F7 CTM
Museum of Miniature Houses 391-K4 Ca
National Art Mus of Sport DN-C2 CTM
National Institute for Fitness & Sport DN-C3 CTM
National Track & Field Hall of Fame DN-D3 CTM
National Weather Bureau 525-E7 DTM
NCAA Natl Hdq & Hall of Champions DN-C2 CTM
Odyssey Map Store DN-D1 CTM
One Indiana Sq DN-D2 CTM
Passenger Terminal 525-G4 WnT
Patrick Henry Sullivan Mus 389-H9 Z
Peace Garden DN-D2 CTM
Pepsi Coliseum 459-J8 WTM
Phoenix Theatre DN-E1 CTM
Power Plant DN-C3 CTM
President Benjamin Harrison Home DN-D1 CTM
RCA Dome DN-D3; 493-D8 CTM
Riviera Club 459-E4 WTM
Roark Stadium 455-H7 B
Scottish Rite Cathedral DN-D2; 493-E6 CTM
Soldiers & Sailors Mon DN-D3 CTM
Stony Cr Farm 360-F4 NT
The Red Mills 599-C8 STS
Theatre on The Sq DN-E2 CTM
USS Indianapolis Mem DN-D1 CTM
Victory Field DN-C3; 493-C8 CTM

POLICE STATIONS

Avon 489-G9 A
Beech Grove 528-H6 BG
Brownsburg 455-G6 B
Carmel 391-K6 Ca
Cumberland 496-G7 Cu
Downtown Dist 493-F6 CTM
Fishers 393-H7 F
Greenwood 596-D3 G
Hamilton Co Sheriff 360-A2 N
Indianapolis 457-C2 PTM
Indianapolis Downtown Dist DN-E1 CTM
Indianapolis East Dist 494-C1 CTM
Indianapolis North Dist 459-H7 WTM
Indianapolis South Dist DN-F4 CTM
Indianapolis West Dist 492-H6 WnT
Marion Co Jail DN-D3 CTM
McCordsville 429-D7 McC
New Whiteland 596-D10 NW
South Dist 493-H10 CTM
State Hdq 526-D3 WnT
State Post 52 495-H3 WrT
Westfield 357-F4 WTH
Zionsville 389-H9 Z

POST OFFICES

Acton 564-E6 FT
Airport Mail Ctr 525-G4 WnT
Bacon 460-A4 WTM
Beech Grove 528-G5 BG
Boggstown 599-E10 STS
Bridgeport 524-K3 WnT
Brightwood 494-D1 CTM
Broad Ripple 459-G1 WTM
Brownsburg 455-H3 B
Carmel 392-A7 Ca
Castleton 427-C4 LTM
Circle City DN-D2; 493-E7 CTM
Clermont 490-J1 WnT
Cumberland 496-G6 Cu
Eagle Cr 457-G8 PTM
Eastgate 495-C6 WrT
Fishers 393-H7 F
Garfield 527-K2 CTM
Greenwood 596-C2 G
Indiana Univ Purdue Univ Indianapolis DN-B2 CTM
Indianapolis DN-D3; 493-E9; 494-B7 CTM
Lawrence 461-F6 L
Linwood 494-E6 CTM
Mapleton 459-D8 WTM
McCordsville 429-C7 McC
New Augusta 424-B10 PTM
Noblesville 359-K4 N
Nora 425-H4 WTM
Oaklandon 428-H10 L
Park Fletcher 525-K3 WnT
Rainbow 492-F4 WnT
Southport 561-K2 PeT
Speedway 491-H2, K4 S
Wanamaker 529-H8 FT
West Indianapolis 492-J10 WnT
Westfield 357-F4 WTH
Whitestown 388-E1 Wh
Zionsville 389-E9 Z

RAILROAD STATIONS

AMTRAK DN-D3 CTM
Union Sta DN-D3; 493-E9 CTM

SCHOOLS

Abraham Lincoln ES 527-D10 PeT
Acton ES 564-E6 FT
Adams, Mary ES 563-E6 FT
Allison, James A ES 492-A3 S
Allisonville ES 426-F7 WTM
Amy Beverland ES 428-G6 LTM
Anna Brochhausen ES #88 494-J4 WrT
Aquinas, Saint Thomas 459-E6 WTM
Arlington ES 562-K1 FT
Arlington HS 460-K5 LTM
Arlington Woods MS 494-J1 WrT
Arsenal Tech HS DN-F2; 493-J6 CTM
Arthur C Newby ES 491-J4 S
Attucks, Crispus MS DN-C1; 493-C5 CTM
Avon Comm Sch Admin 489-H8 A
Avon HS 489-G9 A; 523-H2 WaT
Avon MS 489-F9 A
Baptist Academy 527-K4 CTM
Beech Grove MS 528-E4 BG
Beech Grove SHS 528-H7 BG
Bell, William A ES #60 459-F10 CTM
Bellamy, Francis ES #102 461-K9 WrT
Belzer MS 461-E4 L
Ben Davis HS 491-D5 WnT
Ben Davis JHS 491-H10 WnT
Beverland, Amy ES 428-G6 LTM
Bingham, Joseph J ES #84 459-F3 WTM

Bishop Chatard HS 459-K3 WTM
Blaker, Aliza A ES #55 459-J4 WTM
Booth Tarkington ES #92 461-A7 LTM
Brandes, Raymond F ES #65 527-K7; 528-A8 PeT
Brebeuf Preparatory 424-G5 PTM
Brentwood ES 523-J8 P
Broad Ripple HS 459-H2 WTM
Brochhausen, Anna ES #88 494-J4 WrT
Brook Pk ES 461-C4 L
Brookside ES #54 494-C5 CTM
Brookview ES 496-B5 WrT
Brown ES 455-H7 B
Brown, Otis E ES #20 527-J1 CTM
Browning 494-E1 CTM
Brownsburg Comm Sch Admin 455-G6 B
Brownsburg HS 455-H8 B
Brownsburg JHS 455-J9 B
Bryan, Mary ES 562-E7 PeT
Buck, George MS 495-G1 WrT
Bunker Hill ES 563-B4 FT
Burkhart, Henry William ES 561-F1 PeT
Calvary Chr DN-E4 CTM
Calvary Luth 561-H2 PeT
Cardinal Ritter HS 458-F10; 492-F1 WnT
Carey Ridge ES 358-D9 WTH
Carl G Fisher ES 492-A5 S
Carl Wilde ES #79 458-A9 WnT
Carmel ES 392-A4 Ca
Carmel HS 392-A3 Ca
Carmel JHS 391-H4 Ca
Carver, George W ES #87 493-C2 CTM
Cathedral HS 460-G4 LTM
Center Grove Comm Sch Admin 594-J9 WTJ
Center Grove ES 594-J7 WTJ
Center Grove HS 594-J8 WTJ
Center Grove MS 594-J8 WTJ
Central ES 523-G8 P
Central ES/Beech Grove 528-E5 BG
Central ES/Pike Twp 423-J10 PTM
Central Nine Career Ctr 596-E6 G
Central Wesleyan Parsonage 493-J10 CTM
Chapel Chr 491-D6 WnT
Chapel Glen ES 490-K6 WnT
Chapelwood ES 491-D5 WnT
Charity Dye ES #27 493-G4 CTM
Charles W Fairbanks ES #105 461-H8 LTM
Cherry Tree ES 392-J2 Ca
Childrens Home 494-J8 WrT
Christ the King 459-J3 WTM
Christian Pk ES #82 494-E9 CTM
Clarence L Farrington MS 492-C1 WnT
Clark ES 598-A7 CTJ
Clavery Chr 493-H9 CTM
Clay JHS 392-G5 Ca
Clinton Young ES 562-B1 PeT
Cold Spring ES 458-H9 WnT
Coleman, Julian D MS 493-J1 CTM
Coleman, Julion D MS 459-K10 CTM
College Pk ES 424-G4 PTM
College Wood ES 391-G5 Ca
Colonial Chr 426-A6 WTM
Convent Chr HS 491-D4 WnT
Craig MS 428-E10; 462-E1 L
Creston MS 496-E10 WrT
Crestview ES 427-E9 LTM
Crispus Attucks MS DN-C1; 493-C5 CTM
Crooked Creek ES 458-J3 WTM
Cumberland Road ES 394-A3 F
Daniel Webster ES #46 526-K1 CTM
Decatur Central HS 525-F10; 559-F1 DTM
Decatur MS 525-G10; 559-G1 DTM
Decatur, Stephen ES 526-D6 DTM
Deer Run ES 457-G4 PTM
Diggs, Elder W ES #42 493-B2 CTM
Divine Savior Evangelical Luth 427-C8 LTM
Doe Creek MS 497-D10 SCT
Donnan, Emma MS 527-J5 CTM
Douglas MacArthur ES 561-F6 PeT
Douglass, Frederick MS 527-K2 CTM
Durbin ES 361-E2 WyT
Dye, Charity ES #27 493-G4 CTM
Eagle Cr ES 457-E7 PTM
Eagle ES 455-H8 B; 389-G8 Z
Eagle-Union Comm Schools Admin 389-G8 Z
Eagledale Chr 458-A10 WnT
Eastbrook ES 424-C7 PTM
Eastlawn Chr Academy 461-J9 WrT
Eastridge ES 496-D5 WrT
Eastwood MS 460-F2 WTM
Edgar H Evans ES #11 460-C7 WTM
Edison, Thomas A 493-B9 CTM
Edison, Thomas A MS DN-C4 CTM
Elder W Diggs ES #42 493-B2 CTM
Eleanor Skillen ES #34 527-J3 CTM
Eliza A Blaker ES #55 459-J4 WTM
Emerson, Ralph Waldo ES #58 494-F7 CTM
Emma Donnan MS 527-J5 CTM
Emmaus Luth 493-J10 CTM
Emmerich Manual HS 527-F3 CTM
Ernie Pyle ES #90 492-F4 WnT
Evans, Edgar H ES #11 460-C7 WTM
Fairbanks, Charles W ES #105 461-H8 LTM
Fall Creek ES 395-C6 F
Fall Creek IS 395-D6 F
Fall Creek Valley MS 462-A1 L
Farrington, Clarence L MS 492-C1 WnT
Fay, Florence ES #21 494-A9 CTM
Fisher, Carl G ES 492-A5 S
Fisher, George H ES #93 461-C9 WrT
Fishers ES 393-H8 F
Fishers JHS 394-A3 F
Florence Fay ES #21 494-A9 CTM
Floro Torrence ES #83 460-F7 WTM
Forest Dale ES 392-C10 Ca
Forest Glen ES 462-A1 L
Forest Hill ES 359-G2 N
Forest Manor MS 460-F10; 494-F1 CTM
Foster, Stephen Collins ES #67 492-E6 WnT
Fox Hill ES 459-C2 WTM
Frances W Parker ES #56 493-H2 CTM
Francis Bellamy ES #102 461-K9; 462-A9 WrT
Francis Scott Key ES #103 462-A7 LTM
Frank H Wheeler ES 491-H1 S
Franklin Central HS 563-H2 FT
Franklin Twp MS 563-H2 FT
Frederick Douglass MS 527-K2 CTM
Frost, Robert Lee ES #106 460-J5 LTM
Fulton JHS 491-D6 WnT
Gage Inst 459-G2 WTM
Garden City ES 492-B8 WnT
Garfield, James A ES #31 527-F1 CTM
George Buck MS 495-G1 WrT
George H Fisher ES #93 461-C9 WrT
George W Carver ES #87 493-C2 CTM
George W Julian ES #57 494-H7 WrT
Glenns Valley ES 560-J7 PeT
Grassy Creek ES 496-C9 WrT
Greenbriar ES 425-A6 WTM
Greenwood Comm Schools Admin 596-B4 G
Greenwood HS 596-A4 G
Greenwood MS 596-C3 G
Gregg, Thomas D ES #15 494-A7 CTM
Guion Creek ES 458-C5 PTM
Guion Creek MS 458-C5 PTM
H L Harshman MS DN-F1; 493-J6 CTM
Hamilton Southeastern HS 395-D6 F
Hamilton Southeastern JHS 395-C6 F
Hamilton Southeastern Sch Admin 394-A3 F
Harcourt ES 424-K8 WTM
Harriet Beecher Stowe ES #64 528-A1 CTM
Harris ES 455-G7 B
Harrison Hill ES 461-E4 L
Harrison Pkwy ES 393-J1 F
Harshman, H L MS DN-F1; 493-J6 CTM
Hartmann, Minnie ES #78 494-D7 CTM
Hasten Hebrew Academy of Indianapolis 425-B10 WTM
Hawthorne ES 495-G9 WrT
Hazel Dell ES 358-H4 NT
Hazel Hart Hendricks ES #37 494-A2 CTM
Heather Hills ES 496-C3 WrT
Hendricks, Hazel Hart ES #37 494-A2 CTM
Henry W Longfellow MS DN-F4; 493-J9 CTM
Heritage Chr 427-A8 LTM
Herron, John Sch of Art 493-E4 CTM
Hinkle Creek ES 325-B10 N
Holy Angels Cath 493-B2 CTM
Holy Cross Central DN-F2; 493-J7 CTM
Holy Name of Jesus Cath 528-D5 BG
Holy Spirit 495-D6 WrT
Homecroft ES 561-J4 PeT
Howe HS 494-G8 CTM
Immaculate Heart 459-F3 WTM
Indian Creek ES 462-D4 L
Indiana Girls Sch Correctional Inst 491-C2 WnT
Indiana Sch for the Blind 425-G7 WTM
Indiana Sch for the Deaf 459-J7 WTM
Indianapolis Junior Academy 460-B1 WTM
International Sch of Indiana 459-C7 WTM
IPS #11 460-C7 WTM
IPS #14 DN-F3; 493-J8 CTM
IPS #15 494-A7 CTM
IPS #20 527-J1 CTM
IPS #21 494-A9 CTM
IPS #27 493-G4 CTM
IPS #31 527-F1 CTM
IPS #34 527-J3 CTM
IPS #37 494-A2 CTM
IPS #39 DN-F4; 493-K9 CTM
IPS #42 493-B2 CTM
IPS #43 459-D8 WTM
IPS #46 526-K1 CTM
IPS #48 459-F9 CTM
IPS #49 DN-A4; 492-K10 CTM
IPS #54 494-C5 CTM
IPS #55 459-J4 WTM
IPS #56 493-H2 CTM
IPS #57 494-H7 WrT
IPS #58 494-F7 CTM
IPS #60 459-F10 CTM
IPS #64 528-A1 CTM
IPS #65 527-K7; 528-A8 PeT
IPS #67 492-E6 WnT
IPS #68 494-F3 CTM
IPS #69 460-A9 CTM
IPS #70 459-G6 WTM
IPS #74 DN-F1; 493-J6 CTM
IPS #78 494-D7 CTM
IPS #79 458-A9 WnT
IPS #81 494-C4 CTM
IPS #82 494-E9 CTM
IPS #83 460-F7 WTM
IPS #84 459-F3 WTM
IPS #87 493-C2 CTM
IPS #88 494-J4 WrT
IPS #90 492-F4 WnT
IPS #91 459-K5 WTM
IPS #92 461-A7 LTM
IPS #93 461-C9 WrT
IPS #98 461-H9 WrT
IPS #102 461-K9 WrT
IPS #105 461-H8 LTM
IPS #106 460-J5 LTM
IPS #114 528-F3 CTM
Irving, Washington ES #14 DN-F3; 493-J8 CTM
Isom, V O ES 596-C2 G
James A Allison ES 491-K3; 492-A3 S
James A Garfield ES #31 527-F1 CTM
James Whitcomb Riley ES #43 459-D8 WTM
John Herron Sch of Art 493-E4 CTM
John Marshall MS 462-B9 WrT
John Strange ES 460-C1 WTM
Joseph J Bingham ES #84 459-F3 WTM
Joyce Kilmer ES #69 460-A9 CTM
Julian D Coleman MS 493-J1 CTM
Julian, George W ES #57 494-H7 WrT
Julion D Coleman MS 459-K10 CTM
Kendall 494-F6 CTM
Kilmer, Joyce ES #69 460-A9 CTM
Kingsway Chr 489-J6 WaT
Lakeside ES 496-A3 WrT
Lantern Road ES 393-H10 F
Lawrence Central HS 461-D4 L
Lawrence North HS 427-E7 LTM
Lawrence Pk ES 461-G6 L
Leach, Susan Roll ES #68 494-F3 CTM
Lew Wallace ES #107 457-H10 WnT
Lincoln ES 455-H6 B
Lincoln MS 423-J10 PTM
Lincoln, Abraham ES 527-D10 PeT
Longfellow, Henry W MS DN-F4; 493-J9 CTM
Loom 494-K8 WrT
Louis B Russell Jr ES #48 459-F9 CTM
Lowell 494-C2 CTM
Lowell ES 529-B2 WrT
Lutheran HS 528-K10; 563-A1 FT
Lynwood ES 526-A6 DTM
MacArthur, Douglas ES 561-F6 PeT
Manual, Emmerich HS 527-F3 CTM
Maple ES 489-H9 A
Maple Grove ES 594-J8 WTJ
Maplewood ES 526-B2 WnT
Margaret McFarland MS 528-C3 CTM
Mary Adams ES 563-E6 FT
Mary Bryan ES 562-E7 PeT
Mary E Nicholson ES #70 459-G6 WTM
Mary Evelyn Castle ES 427-H5 LTM
McClellan, Rousseau ES #91 459-K5 WTM
McClelland ES 491-F10 WnT
McFarland, Margaret MS 528-C3 CTM
McKinley, William ES #39 DN-F4; 493-K9 CTM
Meredith Nicholson ES #96 457-J9 WnT
Merle Sidener MS 460-A2 WTM
Metropolitan Sch Dist Lawrence Admin 461-E4 L
Miller, Paul I ES #114 528-F3 CTM
Minnie Hartmann ES #78 494-D7 CTM
Mohawk Trails ES 392-D5 Ca
Moorhead ES 495-H5 WrT
Mott 494-B7 CTM
Mount Comfort ES 463-E8 BCT
Neil Armstrong ES 592-C4 M
Neri, Saint Philip 494-A6 CTM
New Augusta Public Academy 424-D10; 458-E1 PTM
New Britton ES 393-H4 F
New Palestine HS 531-H5 NP
Nicholson, Mary E ES #70 459-G6 WTM
Noblesville HS 360-A2 N
Noblesville IS 359-K1 N
Noblesville MS 359-K3; 360-A3 N
Noblesville Schools Admin 359-J1 N
Nora ES 425-G3 WTM
North Central HS 425-K5 WTM
North Central HS & Northview MS 426-A5 WTM
North ES 359-J2 N
North Grove ES 595-D1 WTJ
North Madison ES 593-D2 MTM
North Wayne ES 457-E10 WnT
Northeast ES 562-E10 G
Northview MS 425-J5 WTM
Northwest HS 457-J10; 491-J1 WnT
Oaklandon ES 428-G10 L
One Way Chr 494-K4 WrT
Orchard Pk ES 391-J10 CTH
Otis E Brown ES #20 527-J1 CTM
Our Lady of Lourdes 494-G7 WrT
Our Lady of Mount Carmel 391-G1 CTH
Our Lady of the Greenwood 596-D3 G
Our Shepherd 490-J6 WnT
Park Tudor 425-G9 WTM
Parker, Frances W ES #56 493-H2 CTM
Parkview ES #81 494-C4 CTM
Paul I Miller ES #114 528-F3 CTM
Penn, William ES #49 DN-A4; 492-K10 CTM
Perry Meridian HS 561-D7 PeT
Perry Meridian MS 561-E6 PeT
Pike HS 423-K10; 457-K1 PTM
Pine Tree ES 489-J10; 523-J1 A
Plainfield Chr 523-G8 P
Plainfield Comm MS 523-K8; 524-A8 P
Plainfield HS 523-G9 P
Plainfield JHS 523-G9 P
Pleasant Grove ES 594-J2 WTJ
Pleasant Run ES 495-F4 WrT
Pleasant View ES 389-E5 Z
Potter, Theodore ES 493-J6 CTM
Potter, Theodore ES #74 DN-F1 CTM
Pyle, Ernie ES #90 492-F4 WnT
Ralph Waldo Emerson ES #58 494-F7 CTM
Raymond F Brandes ES #65 527-K7; 528-A8 PeT
Raymond Pk MS 529-H2 WrT
Rhoades ES 492-A9 WnT
Riley, James Whitcomb ES #43 459-D8 WTM
Riverside ES #44 493-A3 CTM
Robert Lee Frost ES #106 460-J5 LTM
Robey ES 490-K1 WnT
Roncalli HS 528-C10 PeT
Rousseau McClellan ES #91 459-K5 WTM
Russell, Louis B Jr ES #48 459-F9 CTM
Saint Andrew the Apostle 460-D8 WTM
Saint Barnabas 561-C7 PeT
Saint Bernadettes Cath 494-F9 CTM
Saint Christopher 491-J5 S
Saint Christophers Epis 391-F4 CTH
Saint Gabriel 457-H10 WnT
Saint John Evangelical Luth 529-B4 WrT
Saint Jude ES 528-C10 PeT
Saint Lawrence 461-C6 L
Saint Luke 425-E8 WTM
Saint Malachy 455-G5 B
Saint Maria Goretti 357-D5 WTH
Saint Matthew 460-E3 WTM
Saint Michael 492-G1 WnT
Saint Monica 458-H2 WTM
Saint Philip Neri 494-A6 CTM
Saint Pius X 426-B9 WTM
Saint Richards 459-F10 CTM
Saint Roch Cath 527-E6 PeT
Saint Simon The Apostle 495-G2 WrT
Saint Therese Little Flower Cath 494-E5 CTM
Saint Thomas Aquinas 459-E6 WTM
Sand Creek MS 394-F4 FCT
Sanders Spec Ed 526-A4 WnT
Scecina Mem 494-F5 CTM
Shamrock Springs ES 357-C7 WTH
Shortridge MS 459-E9 CTM
Sidener, Merle MS 460-A2 WTM
Skiles Test ES 427-B9 LTM
Skillen, Eleanor ES #34 527-J3 CTM
Smokey Row ES 391-C3 CTH
South Grove ES 528-F7 BG
South Wayne JHS 526-A4 WnT
Southport ES 562-B5 Spt
Southport HS 561-H3 PeT
Southport MS 561-J3 PeT
Southport Presb Chr 562-C6 PeT
Southwest ES 596-A4 G
Speedway JHS 491-K5; 492-A5 S
Speedway SHS 491-K2 S
Spring Mill ES 425-D6 WTM
Steele, T C ES #98 461-H9 WrT
Stephen Collins Foster ES #67 492-E6 WnT
Stephen Decatur ES 526-D6 DTM
Stony Creek ES 359-J5 N
Stonybrook MS 496-F1 WrT
Stout Field ES 526-D3 WnT
Stowe, Harriet Beecher ES #64 528-A1 CTM
Strange, John ES 460-C1 WTM
Suburban Bapt 561-H9 PeT
Sugar Grove ES 595-A4 WTJ
Sunny Hgts ES 496-E1 WrT
Susan Roll Leach ES #68 494-F3 CTM
Sycamore 458-K1 WTM
Sycamore ES 489-J6 WaT
T C Steele ES #98 461-H9 WrT
Tabernacle Chr Academy 426-B2 CTH
Tarkington, Booth ES #92 461-A7 LTM
The Orchard 459-C1 WTM
The Renaissance HS 495-J1 WrT
Theodore Potter ES #74 DN-F1; 493-J6 CTM
Thomas A Edison MS DN-C4; 493-B9 CTM
Thomas D Gregg ES #15 494-A7 CTM
Torrence, Floro ES #83 460-F7 WTM
Traders Pt Chr Academy 423-A7 PTM
Trinity Luth 495-H4 WrT
Union Bible Coll & Academy 357-K4 W
V O Isom ES 596-C2 G
Valley Mills ES 525-H10 DTM
Van Buren ES 523-G8 P
Walker 494-K2 WrT
Wanamaker ES 529-J7 FT
Warren Central HS 495-K4; 496-A4 WrT
Washington ES 357-J3 W
Washington Irving ES #14 DN-F3; 493-J8 CTM
Webster, Daniel ES #46 526-K1 CTM
West Grove ES 594-F3 WTJ
West Newton ES 559-F6 DTM
Westfield HS 357-K2 W
Westfield IS 357-J3 W
Westfield MS 357-K3 W
Westfield-Washington Comm Schools Admin 357-H4 W
Westlake ES 491-F7 WnT
Westlane MS 425-A9 WTM
Westwood ES 595-J4 G
White Lick ES 455-H9 B
White Oak ES 489-G9 A
White River ES 326-B10; 360-B1 N
Wilde, Carl ES #79 458-A9 WnT
Willard J Gambold MS 457-H9 WnT
William A Bell ES #60 459-F10 CTM
William Henry Burkhart ES 561-F1 PeT
William McKinley ES #39 DN-F4 CTM
William Penn ES #49 DN-A4; 492-K10 CTM
Winchester Vill ES 561-K7 PeT
Woodbrook ES 392-E8 Ca
Young, Clinton ES 562-B1 PeT
Zion Luth 531-C2 SCT
Zionsville Comm HS 389-G7 Z
Zionsville Lower MS 389-E5 Z
Zionsville Upper MS 389-G7 Z

SHOPPING CENTERS

38th Street Plaza 457-G8 PTM
96 Sta 426-K2 LTM
500 Speedway 492-C5 S
56th & Georgetown Sq 458-A4 PTM
8900 Plaza 461-H6 L
Allison Run 426-H6 WTM
Allisonville Ctr 426-H6 WTM
Allisonville Plaza 426-H5 WTM
Augusta Plaza 424-G9 PTM
Avon 489-F8 A
Avon Crossing 489-J8 A
Avon Sta 489-K8 A
Avon Vill 490-C8 WaT
Beech Crest Sq 528-D3 CTM
Boone Vill 389-F8 Z
Braeburn Vill 495-G3 WrT
Brookshire 392-F5 Ca
Brownsburg Shoppette 455-K6 B
Brownsburg Sq 455-H4 B
Carmel 391-G4 Ca
Carmel Gate Ctr 391-K5 Ca
Carmel Plaza 391-K5 Ca
Carson Sq 528-C10 PeT
Castle Creek Plaza 426-J4 WTM
Castleton Corner 426-J5 WTM
Castleton Plaza 426-J5 WTM
Castleton Run 427-A5 LTM
Castleton Sq Mall 426-K5 LTM
Castleton Vill 427-A5 LTM
Centre at Smith Valley 595-E4 WTJ
Centre North 427-G2 F
Chapel Hill 491-D6 WnT
Cherry Tree 496-A7 WrT
Churchman Hill Plaza 528-G6 BG
Circle Centre Mall DN-D3 CTM
City Market DN-D3 CTM
Clearwater Crossing 426-D5 WTM
College Pk 424-E5 PTM
College Pk Pl 424-D4 PTM
County Line Mall 561-K8; 562-A8 PeT
Creston Vill Sq 562-A7 PeT
Crooked Creek Centre 424-F7 PTM
Cross Cr Centre 458-B4 PTM
Devington Plaza 461-A6 LTM
Eagledale Plaza 492-E2 WnT
East Washington Plaza 495-F7 WrT
Eastgate Consumer Mall 495-D6 WrT
Emerson Plaza 528-G10 FT
Esquire Plaza 461-G6 L
Fishers Crossing 393-C7 F
Fishers Landing 393-C8 F
Fishers Sta 393-D7 F
Ford Centre 389-E8 Z
Franklin Gables 461-F8 WrT
Geist Centre 428-G6 L
Georgetown Sq 492-B1 WnT
Glendale 460-A2 WTM
Glenlake Plaza 426-A10; 460-A1 WTM
Green Street Sq 455-H2 B
Greenbriar 425-A5 WTM
Greenbrook Shoppes 561-J7 PeT
Greendale 562-A10; 596-B1 G
Greenwood Corner 561-K8 PeT
Greenwood Pk Mall 561-K9; 562-A9 G
Greenwood Pl 561-J6 PeT
Greenwood Pt 561-H7 PeT
Greenwood Shoppes 561-K9; 562-A10 G
Harbor Town Shops 324-K6 N
Hawthorn Plaza 460-F2 WTM
Heather Hills 496-B3 WrT
Highland Shoppes 457-E8 PTM
Honey Cr 457-J9 WnT
Honeycreek 457-K8 PTM
Hunters Quest 391-K6; 392-A6 Ca
Irvington Plaza 495-B7 WrT
K-Mart Plaza 461-D8 LTM; 495-G7 WrT
Key Hanna Plaza 528-A7 PeT
Keystone at the Crossings Mall 426-C4 WTM
Keystone Crossing Shoppes 426-C5 WTM
Keystone Plaza 459-K5; 460-A4 WTM
Lafayette Pl 458-D9 WnT
Lafayette Plaza 458-A8 PTM
Lafayette Sq Mall 458-C8 WnT
Lakewood Vill Shoppes 426-J9 LTM
Linwood 494-E6 CTM
Lockerbie Marketplace DN-E2 CTM
Madison Pl 562-A6 PeT
Madison Sq 561-K4 Spt
Market Plaza 596-C3 G
Market Sq Ctr DN-D2 CTM
Maywood Plaza 526-C6 DTM
Meadowood Ctr 491-H1 S
Meadows 460-B8 WTM
Merchants Sq Mall 392-B7 Ca
Meridian Pk 391-E6 CTH; 391-E6 Ca; 595-E2 G
Meridian Plaza 527-E7 PeT
Meridian Vill Plaza 391-H3 CTH
Metroplex 427-B6 LTM
Mohawk Landing 391-K5 Ca
Mohawk Plaza 391-K5 Ca
National City Plaza DN-D3 CTM
Noble Creek Shoppes 360-A4 N
Noblesville Commons 360-B3 N
Noblesville Plaza 360-A3 N
Noblesville Sq 359-F3 N
Nora Corner 425-J4 WTM
Nora Plaza 425-H4 WTM
Norgate 426-A9 WTM
North By Northeast 427-H2 F
North Eastwood 461-H8 WrT
North Willow Mall 424-H4 WTM
North Willows Commons 425-A4 WTM
Northbrook 425-A5 WTM
Northview Mall 425-J4 WTM
Old Town Shops 425-A4 WTM
Pendleton Shoppes 461-F7 L
Plainfield Commons 524-C6 P
Plainfield Shoppes 524-C6 P
Post 67 461-K5 L
Post Plaza 495-J3 WrT
Prestwick Ctr 489-A9 WaT
Prestwick Pointe 489-A9 WaT
Raceway Plaza 490-G8 WaT
Red Carpet 562-A9 PeT
Riverplace 359-G3 N
Rockville Plaza 491-D8 WnT
Shadeland Plaza 495-C3 WrT
Shadeland Sta 427-C8 LTM
Sherman Commons 494-D8 CTM
Shoppes of Avon 489-J9 A
South 31 Plaza 527-F6 PeT
South Meridian Shoppes 561-E6 PeT
South Vill Plaza 561-E9 PeT
Southern Plaza 527-F8 PeT
Southgate Plaza 527-G7 PeT
Southgreen Plaza 527-H10 PeT
Southport Centre 561-H5 PeT
Speedway Plaza 491-G3 S
Speedway Super 491-H3 S
Sugar Grove Shoppes 594-J3 WTJ

Sunblest Pl 393-D8 F
Target East 461-B8 LTM
Target East Washington 495-G7 WrT
Target Northwest 424-G9 PTM
Target Plaza 524-D6 P
Target West 492-G2 WnT
Target West Washington 525-G1 WnT
Tenth & Arlington 494-J5 WrT
The Centre 391-K7 Ca
The Corner 391-K8 Ca
The Vill at Eagle Cr 457-E9 WnT
Town & Country 360-A5 N; 460-A7 WTM
Triangle 493-K9 CTM
Twin-Aire 494-B9 CTM
Village Pk Plaza 357-K10; 358-A10 WTH

Village Sq at Main Street 393-D8 F
Vista Vill 596-G2 G
Wal-Mart Plaza 524-B6 P
Wards 592-A4 M
Washington Centre East 496-E6 WrT
Washington Corner 496-A6 WrT
Washington Market 496-D7 WrT
Washington Pl 496-C7 WrT
Washington Pt Centre 496-C6 WrT
Washington Shoppes 496-B7 WrT
Washington Sq Mall 496-C6 WrT
Washington Vill Shoppes 495-K7 WrT
Western Plaza 359-F3 N
Westlane 424-G9 PTM

Westpoint Commons 491-B8 WnT
Willow Lake 424-G4 PTM
Windridge Shops 460-G4 WTM
Windsor Vill 494-K3 WrT
Woodfield Ctr 426-A5 WTM
Woodland Shoppes 391-K7; 392-A7 Ca

STATE, COUNTY & MUNICIPAL FEATURES

Avon Town Hall 489-G9 A
Beech Grove City Hall 528-F5 BG

Brownsburg Comm Sch Admin 455-G6 B
Brownsburg Town Hall 455-G6 B
Capitol Ctr North DN-D2 CTM
Capitol Ctr South DN-D2 CTM
Carmel City Hall 391-K6 Ca
Clay Twp Govt Ctr 391-G10 CTH
Cumberland Town Hall 496-F6 Cu
Eagle-Union Comm Schools Admin 389-G8 Z
Fishers Town Hall 393-G7 F
Greenwood Municipal Bldg 596-C2 G
Hamilton Co Courthouse 359-G3 N
Hamilton Co Govt Ctr 359-G3 N
Hamilton Co Jail 360-A2 N

Hamilton Co Parks & Rec Dept 357-K8 WTH
Indiana Girls Sch Correctional Inst 491-C2 WnT
Indiana Law Enforcement Academy 557-E1 P
Indiana State Capitol DN-D3; 493-D7 CTM
Indiana State Dept of Health DN-B2 CTM
Indiana State Govt Ctr North DN-D2 CTM
Indiana State Govt Ctr South DN-C3; 493-D8 CTM
Indiana Womens Prison 493-K7 CTM
Indianapolis City Bldg DN-D3; 493-F8 CTM
Indianapolis City Hall 491-K5 S

Indianapolis Disposal Plant (Belmont) 526-J3 CTM
Indianapolis Disposal Plant (Southport) 560-E4 PeT
Marion Co Bldg DN-D3; 493-F8 CTM
Marion Co Health Care Ctr 530-H2 WrT
Marion Co Jail DN-D3 CTM
Marion Co Juvenile Ctr 494-A2 CTM
McCordsville Town Hall 429-D7 McC
Metropolitan Sch Dist-Lawrence Admin 461-E4 L
New Palestine Town Hall 531-H5 NP
Noblesville City Hall 359-J3 N

Noblesville Parks & Rec Dept 359-G2 N
Noblesville Schools Admin 359-J1 N
Plainfield Correctional Facility 523-D10; 557-D1 P
Plainfield Juvenile Correctional Facility 523-E9; 557-E1 P
Plainfield Town Hall 523-F8 P
Southport City Hall 562-A4 Spt
Warren Twp Govt Ctr 495-K5 WrT
Westfield Town Hall 357-K3 W
Westfield-Washington Comm Schools Admin 357-H4 W
Whitestown Town Hall 388-E1 Wh
Zionsville Town Hall 389-H9 Z

NOTES

NOTES

NOTES